Language in Canada

Language in Canada provides an up-to-date account of the linguistic and cultural situation in Canada, primarily from a sociolinguistic perspective. The strong central theme connecting language with group and identity will offer insights into the current linguistic and cultural tension in Canada. The book provides comprehensive accounts of the original 'charter' languages, French and English, as well as the aboriginal and immigrant varieties which now contribute to the overall picture. It explains how they came into contact – and sometimes into conflict – and looks at the many ways in which they weave themselves through and around the Canadian social fabric. The public policy issues, particularly official bilingualism and educational policy and language, are also given extensive coverage. Non-specialists as well as linguists will find in this volume, a companion to *Language in Australia, Language in the USA* and *Language in the British Isles*, an indispensable guide and reference to the linguistic heritage of Canada.

Language in Canada

Edited by John Edwards

St Francis Xavier University, Nova Scotia

CAMBRIDGE
UNIVERSITY PRESS

Published by the Press Syndicate of the University of Cambridge
The Pitt Building, Trumpington Street, Cambridge CB2 1RP, United Kingdom

Cambridge University Press
The Edinburgh Building, Cambridge CB2 2RU, UK
40 West 20th Street, New York, NY 10011–4211, USA
10 Stamford Road, Oakleigh, Melbourne 3166, Australia

First published 1998
Transferred to digital printing 2001

Printed in Great Britain by Biddles Short Run Books, King's Lynn

Typeset in Berthold Concorde Condensed 10/13.5pt using QuarkXPress [GC]

A catalogue record for this book is available from the British Library

ISBN 0 521 56328 3 hardback

Contents

Contents

Figures

Maps

Tables

Contributors

Réal Allard is Professor of Education and Director of the Centre de recherche et de développement en éducation at the Université de Moncton. Co-developer of a model of factors determining bilingualism, his research focuses on the cognitive–affective development of linguistic group members. He is particularly interested in subjective ethnolinguistic vitality, beliefs and attitudes in various language-group settings.

Philippe Barbaud is Professor of Linguistics at the Université du Québec à Montréal. His interests include French syntax, semantics and morphology, as well as the historical sociology of the language. He is the editor of the *Revue québécoise de linguistique*, and his books include *Le choc des patois en nouvelle-France* (1984) and *Le français sans façon* (1987).

John Berry is Professor of Psychology at Queen's University in Kingston. He has been a Fellow of the Netherlands Institute for Advanced Study and a Visiting Professor at the Université de Nice and the Université de Genève. He is a past Secretary-General, past President and Honorary Fellow of the International Association for Cross-Cultural Psychology, has been an associate editor of the *Journal of Cross-Cultural Psychology*, and is senior editor of the *Handbook of Cross-Cultural Psychology*. Berry is the author or editor of more than twenty books in cross-cultural, social and cognitive psychology, and his research interests include acculturation, multiculturalism, immigration, health and education.

Gary Caldwell, formerly of Bishop's University (Lennoxville, Québec) and the Institut québécois de recherche sur la culture, is now an independent researcher and writer. His major interests are social change in post-war Québec, English Québec and the role of cultural and intellectual élites in contemporary society. He recently published *La question du Québec anglais* (1994) and 'Differing levels of low fertility', in *Convergence or Divergence* (1995).

Charles Castonguay is Associate Professor of Mathematics and Statistics at the University of Ottawa. His main research interest is language shift in Canada. His books include *Exogamie et anglicisation dans les régions de Montréal, Hull, Ottawa et Sudbury* (1981) and *L'assimilation linguistique: mesure et évolution 1971–1986* (1994).

J. K. Chambers is Professor of Linguistics at the University of Toronto. He edited *Canadian English: Origins and Structures* (1975), the first book about Canadian English. Chambers also co-authored *Dialectology* (1980) and co-edited *Dialects of English: Studies in Grammatical Variation* (1991), both with Peter Trudgill. His most recent book is *Sociolinguistic Theory: Linguistic Variation and its Social Significance* (1995).

Sandra Clarke is Professor of Linguistics at Memorial University of Newfoundland. Her research focuses upon sociolinguistics, particularly with respect to Newfoundland and Canadian English, language and gender, and Algonquian. Her publications include the edited volume *Focus on Canada* (1993) and a grammar of Labrador Innu (Montagnais).

Richard Clément is Professor of Psychology at the University of Ottawa. His research interests concern the processes and consequences of intercultural commun-ication. Clément's books include *Contact inter-ethnique et communication: processus et conséquences* (1994) and *The Effect of Context on the Composition and Role of Orientations in Second Language Acquisition* (1986). He has recently edited a special issue of the *Journal of Language and Social Psychology* on intergroup communication (1996).

Eung-Do Cook is Professor of Linguistics at the University of Calgary. His recent publications include *A Sarcee Grammar* (1984), 'Linguistic divergence in Fort Chipewyan' (in *Language in Society*, 1991), 'Against moraic licensing in Bella Coola' (in *Linguistic Inquiry*, 1994) and 'Third-person plural subject prefix in Northern Athapaskan' (in *International Journal of American Linguistics*, 1996).

Ronald Cosper is Professor of Sociology at Saint Mary's University (Halifax), and a facul-ty member in the Linguistics Program. He has published 'Ethnicity in Atlantic Canada: a survey' (1989). Cosper is currently conducting field research on the lin-guistics and sociolinguistics of northern Nigeria, and is preparing a dictionary and grammar of Polci.

Jim Cummins is Professor in the Department of Teaching, Learning and Curriculum in the Ontario Institute for Studies in Education, University of Toronto. His research has focused on second-language acquisition and bilingualism, with particular emphasis upon the social and educational barriers that limit academic success for culturally diverse students.

Wilfrid Denis is Professor of Sociology at St Thomas More College, University of Saskatchewan. He has published in the areas of prairie agriculture, and Canadian minority relations.

Lynn Drapeau is Professor of Linguistics at the Université du Québec à Montréal. Her main research interests are the description of Montagnais and language contact studies, as well as language planning and bilingual education for indigenous groups. Her books include a Montagnais–French dictionary (1991) and a *Practical Guide to Montagnais Orthography* (1989). Drapeau has also written reports on 'Aboriginal language conservation and revitalization in Canada' (1995) and 'Language and education for native populations in Québec' (1995).

Leo Driedger is Professor of Sociology at the University of Manitoba (Winnipeg). His books include *The Ethnic Canadian Mosaic* (1978), *Aging and Ethnicity* (with Chappell, 1987), *The Ethnic Factor* (1989), *Ethnic Demography* (with Halli and Trovato, 1990), *The Urban Factor* (1991) and *Multi-Ethnic Canada* (1996).

John Edwards is Professor of Psychology at St Francis Xavier University in Nova Scotia. His books include *The Irish Language* (1983), *Linguistic Minorities, Policies and Pluralism* (1984), *Language, Society and Identity* (1985) and *Multilingualism* (1994). He is the editor of the *Journal of Multilingual and Multicultural Development*.

James Frideres is Professor and Head of the Sociology Department at the University of Calgary. His recent books include *Freedom Within the Margins: The Politics of Exclusion* (with Pizanias, 1995) and *Canada's Native People* (1994). Frideres is coeditor of *Canadian Ethnic Studies* and a board member of the Prairie Centre of Excellence for Research on Immigration and Integration.

Fred Genesee is in the Division of Education, University of California (Davis). He has conducted research on second-language acquisition in school-age and pre-school children, and his books include *Learning Through Two Languages* (1987), *Educating Second Language Children* (1994) and *Classroom-Based Evaluation in Second Language Education* (1996).

Josiane Hamers is Professor in the Department of Languages and Linguistics at Université Laval (Quebec). Her main research interests are in bilingual development and the social psychology of second-language acquisition. Among her numerous books and articles is *Bilinguality and Bilingualism* (1989), written with Michel Blanc.

Betty Harnum has just completed a four-year term as the first Languages Commissioner for the Northwest Territories. Before that, she was Chair of the Northwest Territories' Interpreter/Translator Society Examinations Committee for several years. She has been intensively involved in many aspects of interpretation and translation, and has conducted research on northern languages for twenty years.

Kirsten Hummel is Professor in the Department of Languages and Linguistics at Université Laval (Quebec). Her research interests include psycholinguistic aspects of bilingualism, second-language acquisition and language planning and policy.

Ruth King is Associate Professor of Linguistics at York University (Toronto). She is interested in quantitative sociolinguistics, language and gender, microparametric variation in syntax, and language contact. She is the first author of *Talking Gender* (1991) and has published articles on (socio)linguistic variation and change.

Rodrigue Landry is Professor of Education and Dean of the Faculté des sciences de l'éducation at the Université de Moncton. Co-developer of a macroscopic model of the factors determining bilingual development, Landry's research focuses on minority education and the cognitive and affective dimensions of bilingualism. His most recent work analyses the subtractive and additive effects of ethnolinguistic vitality among minority and majority group members.

Robert Leavitt is Chair of the Department of Curriculum and Instruction, and Director of the Micmac–Maliseet Institute, at the University of New Brunswick (Fredericton). He is the author of Maliseet and Micmac: First Nations of the Maritimes, and his current projects include the editing and translation of historical Maliseet–Passamaquoddy texts and the development of a dictionary.

William Mackey is a Fellow of the Royal Society of Canada and of the Royal Academy of Belgium. He is currently Research Professor at the Centre international de recherche en aménagement linguistique (and founding director of the research centre for bilingualism, from which CIRAL developed) at Université Laval (Quebec). Mackey is the author of more than 200 articles and two dozen books on language contact, language policy and language education; these include *Bilinguisme et contact des langues* (1976), *Le bilinguisme canadien* (1978), *Sociolinguistic Studies in Language Contact* (1979) and *Education and Bilingualism* (1987).

Kenneth McRae is Professor Emeritus of Political Science at Carleton University (Ottawa). His work is on political thought and comparative politics, and his publications include *Conflict and Compromise in Multilingual Societies* (volume 1, on Switzerland, 1983; volume 2, Belgium, 1986; volume 3, Finland, to appear in 1997), *The Federal Capital: Government Institutions* (1969) and *Consociational Democracy* (1974).

Raymond Mougeon is Professor of French Linguistics at York University (Toronto). His books include *Linguistic Consequences of Language Contact and Restriction* (1991), *Le français canadien parle hors Québec* (1989) and *Les origines du français québécois* (1994).

Kimberly Noels is Assistant Professor in the Department of Psychology, University of Saskatchewan. Her interests lie in the affective and motivational aspects of second-language learning, and the role of language in acculturation. She has published articles in the *Canadian Journal of Behavioural Science*, the *Canadian Modern Language Review*, and elsewhere.

Robert Papen is Professor of Linguistics at the Université du Québec à Montréal. His main research interests are in North American French dialects, and second-language acquisition. He has recently written articles on Michif (with Bakker; to appear in Thomason's *Contact Languages: A Wider Perspective*) and Cajun French (with Rottet; to appear in Valdman's *French and Creole in Louisiana*). Papen is editor of the *Journal of the Canadian Association of Applied Linguistics*.

T. K. Pratt is Professor of English at the University of Prince Edward Island (Charlottetown), and a consultant in lexicography. He has edited the *Dictionary of Prince Edward Island English* (1988) and *Prince Edward Island Sayings: A Thematic Dictionary* (with Burke; forthcoming).

Gunter Schaarschmidt is Professor in the Department of Slavonic Studies at the University of Victoria. He is interested in minority languages (particularly Sorbian in Germany) and language for specific purposes (especially Russian for science and business). He has written *The Historical Phonology of the Upper and Lower Sorbian Languages* (forthcoming).

Map 1 Canada

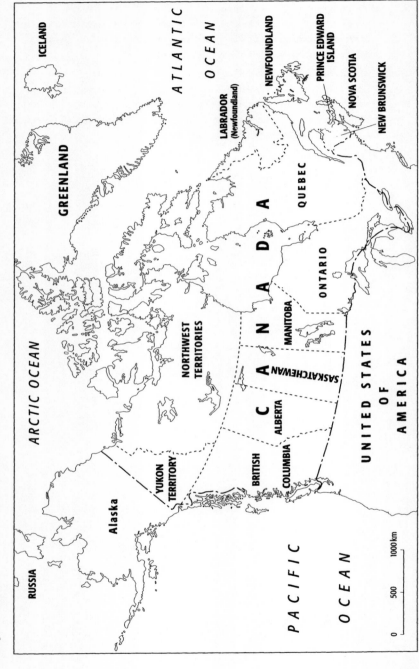

Introduction

John Edwards

Most readers will know that issues of language and culture are central to current Canadian social and political life. Recent constitutional crises have, one regrets to say, made the country – and Quebec in particular – excellent contexts in which to observe languages in contact, minority-group and ethnolinguistic dynamics, the relationship between language and nationalism, and the strains under which officially sponsored policies of 'social engineering' (bilingualism and multiculturalism) must now operate. In some settings, disputes over language and culture are largely symbolic; deeper problems between groups lie elsewhere, usually in political or economic domains, and language, or religion, or tradition act mainly as team jerseys. To discuss symbolism, of course, is not to discuss something inconsequential. The power attaching to what people believe best represents their culture can be considerable. Indeed, the intangible strength of 'blood and belonging' has made itself all too evident historically. In Canada, it is quite clear that this sort of powerful symbolic marking is at work but, in addition, the force of nationalism is itself central to much of the debate. It is not economic deprivation or lack of effective political representation which most accurately characterizes the Quebec sovereignty movement, for example. It is, rather, what John Stuart Mill referred to more than a century ago:

> If ... unreconciled nationalities are geographically separate, and especially if their local position is such that there is no natural fitness or convenience in their being under the same government ... there is not only an obvious propriety, but, if either freedom or concord is cared for, a necessity, for breaking the connection altogether. (1964 [1861], pp. 361–366)

In this sense, the struggle of Quebec nationalists is entirely understandable and has many historic parallels: it is the struggle of those who believe that nationalistic feelings dictate, at the most profound level, that the only possible government is self-government. If this sense is deep enough, then its very intangibility proves to be its greatest strength.

We are living now in the aftermath of an extremely close referendum on sovereignty, held in Quebec on 30 October 1995. The question put to the voters was this:

> Do you agree that Québec should become sovereign, after having made a formal offer to Canada for a new economic and political partnership, within the scope of the Bill respecting the future of Québec and of the agreement signed on June 12, 1995?

Among a very large turn-out, 48.5 per cent said yes, 49.7 per cent no. The difference between 'yes' and 'no' amounted to only 53,498 votes out of a total of 4.7 million (the number of spoiled or rejected ballots was considerably greater than this difference).

It is not my purpose here to go into any detail about the convoluted events leading up to the October referendum (see, however, Edwards, 1994, 1995, in press), but it is obvious from the referendum results alone that the story is not completed. It is a story which has concentrated minds wonderfully – but it is insufficiently appreciated how the debate over the place of Quebec within (or without) the Canadian federation has drawn in *all* groups, including aboriginal and allophone populations, and has occasioned intense scrutiny of *all* matters dealing with language, culture and inter-group accommodation.

The major players in the drama continue to act out their accustomed roles: most Quebec francophones clearly want substantial changes in federal-provincial arrangements, and many are committed to outright independence; anglophones and allophones debate about how much change (if any) ought to be made and, as well, argue for a reworking of their own positions in the mosaic; aboriginal groups are adamant that if any 'distinct' status (such as Quebec has historically argued for within Canada) were to be on offer, they should surely be the first and most obvious recipients. They also argue that their members in Quebec cannot be taken out of Canada, against their will, by the secessionists – thus raising interesting and vexing questions about where democratic rights of secession end. (It is clear, by the way, that Quebec nationalists who argue that they have a right to secede – following a successful referendum – would generally deny that same course of action to the James Bay Cree. *Quod licet Jovi non licet bovi*, after all, could be the motto of many nationalist groups who have to deal with internal divisions.)

These, as I say, are (and have been) the main players, and it is important to realize that the francophone–anglophone debate has in fact acted as a catalyst for broader discussions, among virtually all constituencies, about the shape of the country. It is not unfair to suggest that all group affiliations and all identities

– as well as all official and non-official manifestations of, and support for, them – are now in a state of flux.

A consideration of language in Canada is intrinsically interesting, no matter what the state of political play. Like Australia or the United States, Canada is a new-world 'receiving' country, made up of many different indigenous and immigrant groups, cultures and languages. And, like these other states, it has recently been struggling with the multicultural and multilingual realities to which a modern, diverse, liberal society must – by its deepest principles – be sensitive. The question, as always, is how best to act (or, indeed, to refrain from acting) on this sensitivity. It is a considerable pleasure to be able to say that Canadian writers and intellectuals have, themselves, been in the recent forefront of this discussion (see, for example, Kymlicka, 1995a, 1995b; Taylor, 1992, 1994).

If, however, a consideration of language – an enduringly important aspect of the Canadian social fabric – is of abiding intrinsic interest, how much greater is that interest now, given the contemporary stresses briefly alluded to above? The contributors to this volume would all agree, I am sure, that this is a particularly useful time at which to take stock, to assess the central linguistic and cultural strands in the Canadian pattern, and to present an up-to-date overview.

Language in Canada is the fourth such volume to be produced by Cambridge. In 1981, *Language in the USA* appeared, edited by Charles Ferguson and Shirley Brice Heath. Its chapters dealt with the history and the current status of the language situation in the United States, as well as with likely or possible changes thereto. In his foreword, Dell Hymes observed that it was a much-needed book, 'a resource to citizens, a spur to scholars, a challenge to those who shape policy and public life' (p. ix). The book contained five chapters on English in America, four on 'languages before English' (aboriginal varieties and Spanish), and seven on languages after English. This last section was something of a mixed bag, touching upon Italian, Spanish, French, German and other languages; it also included one state 'profile' – for Montana.

Peter Trudgill's *Language in the British Isles* was published in 1984. In his preface, the editor (like Hymes, above) argued for the utility of the book for a wide audience:

> It is also hoped that much of the information contained in this work will percolate into spheres outside those inhabited by academic linguists. Many educationists, journalists, broadcasters, lawyers, social scientists and politicians have begun to realize, and many more will surely do so, that they need more information about languages and language situations to aid them in decision-making and policy-forming of various sorts. (p. ix)

This broader appeal was particularly aimed at in the book's final section, on sociolinguistics. Here, nine chapters discuss the 'social, cultural, demographic and political situations' (p. 406) of indigenous and immigrant minority languages. The other three sections of the book are more explicitly *linguistic* in emphasis (as Trudgill points out): fourteen chapters are devoted to varieties of English, six to Celtic languages, and four to 'other languages' (including Romani, Norn and Shelta).

The third previous volume in this Cambridge 'series' is that edited by Suzanne Romaine in 1991, *Language in Australia*. The editor introduces the collection as a 'companion and complement' to Ferguson and Heath, and Trudgill, and one which stresses sociolinguistic perspectives. The book has five sections. The first (comprising eight chapters) treats aboriginal varieties, the second has five contributions on Australian pidgin and creole languages, the third devotes six chapters to 'transplanted languages other than English' (Greek, Dutch, German, etc.), the fourth presents three chapters on varieties of Australian English, and the final section is on 'public policy and social issues' – another mixed bag, in that its three chapters discuss national language policy and planning, social-class lexical variation, and the Plain English movement.

I profited greatly from a detailed analysis of these preceding volumes, and found each to be an extremely useful compendium. All three contain generally clear writing and are successful in their aim of broad audience accessibility. In planning *Language in Canada*, I too had in mind style and content that would attract a wide readership. I hoped that the contributing authors would – in line with the material and guidelines supplied when the project was introduced to them – achieve a jargon-free clarity appealing to both a scholarly and a non-academic audience, to both a specialist and a non-specialist readership. Two further guidelines emerged from the preceding volumes. The first was that the present book ought to be more sociolinguistic, or sociology-of-language, in nature and should, wherever possible, avoid more technical linguistic treatments. That is, the overall desire here was to provide a comprehensive review of the social contexts in which languages in Canada have existed, now exist, and are likely to exist in the future. (At some points, of course, more purely linguistic details *are* called for, and it would have been inappropriate not to have included them.)

The second guideline was suggested by the chapter on Montana (by Anthony Beltramo), in the Ferguson and Heath collection. As a general profile, this works well, but one is left wondering about the *particular* rationale for discussing Montana; after all, other states (one imagines) might have served as well, or better, as sociolinguistic exemplars. If, on the other hand, a regional coverage for its own sake is important, then one such chapter is obviously insufficient.

Given that regional coverage can indeed be both important and interesting, the idea then arose – for this volume – of combining both thematic and regional coverage under one roof. That is, the goal became a book of two main sections: the first would round up the usual (for Canada, at any rate) thematic suspects, while the second would provide brief overviews of regions. The dozen provinces and territories naturally suggested themselves here as the obvious, and not too unwieldy, subjects. The reader interested in heritage-language education in general will find a thematic chapter devoted to that subject, one which touches upon the matter from a national perspective; the reader more particularly concerned with the teaching of Spanish in Ontario – or, indeed, with the general state of language affairs in that province – will find a more regionally focused discussion.

It became necessary, then, to ensure that not too much overlap occurred between the 'thematic' and the 'geographic' chapters. Authors were given the overall outline, of course, and the general aims of the volume were explained to them. Beyond that, however, contributors were encouraged to consult among themselves, as appropriate, so as to coordinate and unite forces. Some slight overlap has, inevitably, crept in. Authors can be requested to follow certain guidelines, but it is both difficult and inappropriate to constrain them unduly. Besides, a little redundancy is not a bad thing in a volume of this size, and it is unlikely, in any event, that reading two authors on the same matter will amount to straightforward repetition. Cross-referencing notes, by the way, are largely absent here. This is because, in most cases, it is perfectly clear to the reader which other chapters are likely to contain complementary information; and because there are detailed indexes provided.

Language in Canada is thus in two sections: the first, of fifteen chapters, deals with the most important current language and language-related matters in a thematic way; the second contains eleven 'regional' chapters, covering the ten provinces and (in one contribution) the two northern territories.

In chapter 1, William Mackey introduces the collection with a comprehensive historical overview. He provides a picture of Canada before the arrival of European fishermen, traders and settlers, noting that – a generation before Cartier's historic voyages – some aboriginal people had been brought to France in the hope that they would learn French. Later attempts to learn each other's languages included rather dubious undertakings, as Mackey points out. As well, linguistic 'conceptual frameworks' alien to the French contributed to the drive to acculturate the aboriginal peoples to a new society. Mackey then turns to the expansion of

5

French throughout the country, the fall of New France to Britain, and the consequent spread of English. He then adds to the picture the arrival of the so-called 'heritage' languages – which, in the Canadian context, are all languages other than French, English and aboriginal. Brief comments on the emerging *varieties* of French and English precede Mackey's important remarks on the political and linguistic clash between Canadian francophones and anglophones. Throughout his chapter, Mackey interweaves the story of language with the broader history and, were the reader to progress no farther than this opening contribution, he or she would still obtain a good general summary.

For chapter 2, Charles Castonguay was asked to clarify the sometimes confusing official data bearing upon language numbers, concentrations, distributions, and so on. Although Canada is now a country of many languages, Castonguay observes that 'society still remains essentially [linguistically] dual' – about 92 per cent of the Canadian population speaks either French or English at home, and the assimilation of allophone varieties – especially by English – continues apace. Castonguay also points out that French and English are, by and large, geographically separate, and their territorialization is increasing; thus, 'official mother-tongue minorities – English in Quebec and French outside Quebec – are both steadily declining in relative importance'. He notes the asymmetry of language abilities existing between the francophone and anglophone populations: census data reveal both a *quantitative* asymmetry (there are more francophones with competence in English than there are anglophones with French abilities) and a *qualitative* one (many more francophones than anglophones have advanced skills in the second language). At the end of a chapter packed full of information, Castonguay suggests that the traditional Canadian linguistic duality is waning, and an increasingly ethnically diverse – but generally English-speaking – society is evolving.

Kenneth McRae presents a satisfying description of official Canadian bilingualism in chapter 3. The foundation, deliberations and recommendations of the Royal Commission on Bilingualism and Biculturalism (established in 1963) are considered in some detail, as are the federal government's policy responses. The Official Languages Act (1969), recognizing English and French as co-official varieties was indeed a 'landmark statute'. The chapter is particularly strong in its treatment of the reconfiguration of the federal public service following the 1969 Act, and there is an intriguing section dealing with the idea – never acted upon – of the formal establishment of bilingual districts, and the arguments over the 'territorial' and 'personality' principles applicable to bilingual policy. McRae's chapter concludes with a careful five-point summary.

In chapter 4, John Berry describes the other relevant Canadian policy of social engineering – official multiculturalism. He outlines the policy itself and reactions to it, and notes how an understanding of multiculturalism must necessarily accompany any consideration of language matters. On the latter point, it is instructive to recall that, from its inception in 1971, the Canadian multicultural policy was to exist 'within a bilingual framework' – while one can understand why the government would wish to present the policy in this way, one can also realize that potential stresses were likely to result. Berry discusses this, as well as the criticisms of official multiculturalism, chief among which are the views that the policy perpetuates ethnic separateness and is, in any event, an act of political opportunism. In charting public attitudes towards multiculturalism, Berry draws upon his own previous research, notably his fourfold model of acculturation. In his concluding pages, the author discusses multiculturalism – and the general public endorsement of diversity – in the context of the falling away of 'heritage' languages.

Chapter 5, by Kimberly Noels and Richard Clément, is the first of three contributions emphasizing educational matters (see also chapters 14 and 15). Here, the authors attend principally to the learning of French and English as second languages. They present first an overview of language education policies, particularly since the establishment of official bilingualism and multiculturalism. They then move to a consideration of the all-important *contexts* in which language learning is to occur, providing a useful review of the relevant literature. Noels and Clément also discuss some of the important effects second-language learning can have upon personal and group identity and adjustment. Throughout their detailed chapter, they emphasize that language learning is not only a pedagogical matter, but also a social one – in the Canadian context this is a particularly relevant observation.

Chapters 6 and 7 (by Eung-Do Cook and Lynn Drapeau, respectively) deal with the history and current status of aboriginal languages in Canada. Beginning with some notes on language origins and classifications, Cook provides an excellent summary of the aboriginal varieties found in Canada, paying particular attention to distributions and inter-relationships. The author then turns to the often difficult matters of estimating speaker numbers and assessing language vitality. If we compare some of Cook's numbers with those cited by Drapeau, we observe some quite striking differences: consider their estimates for speakers of Chipewyan or Tsimshian, for example. Some of the variation here is due to authors' restriction (or not) to mother-tongue speakers, but this is not the whole story. Difficulties here arise for many other reasons – some of which are touched upon in the two chapters – and are of intrinsic interest themselves. Readers may like to know that Cook and Drapeau were in touch with one another during the preparation stages. Drapeau's chapter complements the previous one, and begins with a consideration of aboriginal definition and demolinguistics. She then outlines aboriginal language rights pertaining to education (from both historical and contemporary perspectives). More broadly, Drapeau assesses the state of legal protection for aboriginal varieties and the demands currently being made by aboriginal groups in defense of their languages and cultures.

In the next four chapters (8, 9, 10 and 11), we turn from aboriginal languages to French. In chapter 8, Robert Papen provides an overview of Canadian varieties of French. While providing some historical detail concerning the spread of French in the country, the author emphasizes phonological variation. Papen's contribution is the most 'linguistic' in the book, but non-specialist readers ought not to be put off by the symbols his presentation requires: he provides an excellent introduction to his subject, with a host of examples. Quebec French, Ontario French, Acadian and Métis varieties, the French of western Canada – all are dealt with here, and Papen also inserts, where appropriate, notes about influence from English. The following three chapters then give more sociolinguistic detail about French in Canada, in its most obviously important settings: first, in Quebec, where it is strongest; second, in New Brunswick, the only officially bilingual province, where francophones comprise about one-third of the population; third, in the rest of the country, where French has a much more troubled existence.

Philippe Barbaud (chapter 9) presents a picture in which French in Québec is numerically dominant but still insecure. It is threatened by English, but also (particularly in Montreal, of course) by the 'weak attraction' it exerts upon allophone immigrant groups. Barbaud discusses the various official efforts to intervene on behalf of French – the Office de la langue française, the French Language Charter (Bill 101), and so on – as well as the many unofficial pressures which assail it. To say that this is a timely discussion is an understatement of some magnitude. In June 1996, for example, the Quebec government tabled *Bill 40*, a series of amendments to the French Language Charter which has been in effect for almost twenty years. If enacted, this new bill provides for (among other things) the resurrection of the Commission de protection de la langue française – the so-called 'language police' (sometimes, even more pejoratively, termed 'tongue troopers') who would oversee the status of French in designated contexts. This possibility seems to have galvanized the anglophone minority in Quebec, who have become more vociferous in resisting what it sees as infringements on basic language rights. Equally – and, indeed, reinforced by anglophone protest – many Quebec francophones are becoming more intransigent on language matters.

In chapter 10, Réal Allard and Rodrigue Landry document the status of French in New Brunswick, Canada's only officially bilingual province. They do this largely from the social psychological perspective of *language vitality*, an approach with which they are thoroughly familiar. This model, particularly appropriate where two or more languages are in contact, considers both sociological and psychological factors – including the group's demographic, economic and cultural 'capital', as well as group members' language competencies, attitudes and networks. Allard and Landry thus provide us with a succinct and up-to-date analysis of French in the province, one which reveals the intertwining of language with other relevant facets of social life. As in other minority-language discussions, the reader will observe that – running through this chapter – there is a central thread of group identity. To complete this group of chapters, Raymond Mougeon (in chapter 11) describes French outside the provinces of New Brunswick and Quebec. He begins with an historical overview, followed by a thorough review of current status. Relating his assessment to previous work, Mougeon emphasizes the most important domains of language transmission and continuity – home, neighbourhood, school, work and religion.

With chapter 12 and chapter 13 (by Jack Chambers and Gary Caldwell, respectively), attention switches from French to English. The reader may think that English has been somewhat slighted here – having only two chapters directly devoted to it, compared to the four given to French – but the position of English in the country, outside Quebec, does not call for the attention demanded by French (for obvious reasons). Chambers's chapter is in some ways analogous to Papen's (chapter 8), but it is more discursive and less linguistically technical. There is also a strong emphasis here upon the historical background to present-day varieties of Canadian English. Caldwell, too (in his chapter 13), provides the necessary background to an understanding of the status of anglophones and their language in Quebec. 'English Quebec', as Caldwell defines it, is in serious decline, and (as my notes to Barbaud's chapter 9 suggest) recent political developments have aggravated the relationship between anglophones and francophones in the province. When Caldwell describes English Quebec as a 'culture under siege', he reflects well the feelings of many within anglophone society – despite the fact that the Parti Québécois government would no doubt claim that this is a considerable exaggeration. It *is* true that Quebec's English speakers have historically been able to live their lives more or less completely in their own language – a state of affairs foreign to most minorities – and, indeed, this is still possible. However, what some have characterized as the 'whining posture' now adopted by the community derives, in part, from the self-perception that, in *Canada*, they are *not* a minority, that the province remains a part of the whole and that, therefore, their linguistic and cultural rights are somehow being unfairly abrogated. Such is the outcome of a clash of identities, of disputed conceptions of what is or is not a minority group, of debates surrounding individual versus collective rights, and so on.

From analyses of francophone and anglophone dynamics, we turn (in Jim Cummins's chapter 14) to the allophone population and, more specifically, to the teaching of languages other than English, French or aboriginal varieties. These allophone varieties, once styled 'heritage languages', are now officially designated as 'international languages'. There are, certainly, points of interest concerning these languages other than educationally-related ones, but their school status is, arguably, the single most important dimension. (In the 'regional' chapters, 16 to 26, more particular treatments are given, where appropriate, to allophone vari- eties.) Apart from outlining the educational status of international languages in various jurisdictions, Cummins describes some of the more important research evaluating their teaching and learning. Of particular import here are those findings which probe beyond language competencies and teaching methods to illuminate the broader social and cognitive correlates of international-language education.

In chapter 15, Fred Genesee assesses French immersion education – perhaps the best-known Canadian innovation in language teaching. He places his discussion in the context of French-English relations, language attitudes and practices. A thorough description of the current status of immersion follows, with due regard given to the various types of programmes. While (naturally) treating the direct pedagogical outcomes of immersion education, Genesee also considers the broader social impact – students' attitudes and actual use of French competence. This is particularly important since, for many, immersion has been seen not only as a superior language-acquisition technique, but also as the best educational bridge between the two classic Canadian 'solitudes'.

The final eleven contributions (chapters 16 to 26) deal with the linguistic landscape in Canada's ten provinces and two territories. There is, reasonably enough, some degree of variation in their contents – authors have emphasized what they considered to be the most salient aspects, as well as indulging (to some extent, at least) in topics of more particular interest to them. I did, however, make an effort to enlist the services of contributors who could be relied upon to provide broad overviews, and I provided them all with some general guidelines. Without wishing to impose too much on authors' freedom of movement (which is, as I have noted above, an unwise and unfruitful editorial move in any event), I asked that, where at all appropriate, the following sorts of information should be provided: the position and status of the most important regional varieties, the interpenetration of linguistic and cultural issues with wider social and political currents, and the relationship between Canada's multicultural and multilingual 'mosaic' and group identity (both for specific cultural entities, and for the much-debated overall Canadian self-depiction – something often viewed as still in an emergent form). While the reader will find some of these 'regional' treatments more detailed than others, and while some may prove more immediately useful than others for specific purposes, I believe that, collectively, they provide a valuable insight; their value is enhanced, as well, by fairly extensive referencing to the relevant literature (this applies to the 'thematic' chapters too, of course).

Overall, *Language in Canada* aims to be of use to both specialists and non-specialists, to those wishing an outline of the major linguistic currents which is reasonably complete in itself, as well as to those seeking a well-referenced introduction to further study. The breadth of material presented here should attract and inform both Canadian and non-Canadian readers. Of course, some readers may find topics of specific interest less than completely dealt with here and, in some cases, outright omissions may be detected. I am sure, however, that such readers will appreciate that no one volume can hope to do more than lightly score the surface of what is, after all, a complex and multifaceted subject.

Language in Canada, like the three companion volumes which have preceded it, is intended – above all – to describe something of the past, present and future status of the many languages existing under a single state roof. As already noted, the present is a particularly trying time for Canada, and this implies an obvious timeliness for the book. When better to try to describe and assess than when the relevant matters have been pushed to the forefront of social and political life? Equally, however, it is desirable to avoid a decontextualized or disembodied snapshot which presents events and issues solely in their immediacy, and which lacks background. This is one of the most common complaints made of social scientific investigation but it is not, I hope, warranted here. If an adequate job has been done in outlining past and present matters of interest, then it follows that a base has been established from which further developments can be considered. Indeed, most authors in this collection have, explicitly or implicitly, had an eye to the future.

My final point is that the Canadian scene – precisely because of its linguistic and cultural complexity, now under an intense sociopolitical microscope – can illuminate many issues of importance in other settings. Canada is a 'receiving' country, in which multilingualism and multiculturalism are deeply embedded in the social fabric. This suggests that events, issues and policies here may be of interest in other contexts where many immigrants mingle, and confront a 'mainstream'. Equally, however, Canadian social life involves confrontations and accommodations among more established populations – some more indigenous than others, some commentators would wish to argue – and this suggests another range of insights. Most important of all, perhaps, is that the Canadian experience demonstrates the dynamic nature of the 'mainstream' itself. Viewed against the larger backdrop of transition in almost every corner of the world – the more violent manifestations of which Canadians have been spared – the powerful and sometimes painful lesson that the *status quo* can (and likely will) alter is of the greatest significance.

References

Edwards, J. (1994). Ethnolinguistic pluralism and its discontents: a Canadian study, and some general observations. *International Journal of the Sociology of Language, 110*, 5–85.

Edwards, J. (1995). Monolingualism, bilingualism, multiculturalism and identity: lessons and insights from recent Canadian experience. *Current Issues in Language and Society, 2*, 5–57.

Edwards, J. (in press). French and English in Canada: before and after the Québec referendum of October 1995. In P. Weber (ed.), *Recent Studies in Contact Linguistics.* Bonn: Dümmler.

Ferguson, C. and Heath, S. (eds.) (1981). *Language in the USA.* Cambridge: Cambridge University Press.

Kymlicka, W. (1995a). *Multicultural Citizenship.* Oxford: Clarendon Press.

Kymlicka, W. (ed.) (1995b). *The Rights of Minority Cultures.* Oxford: Oxford University Press.

Mill, J. S. (1861 [1964]). *Considerations on Representative Government.* London: Dent.

Romaine, S. (ed.) (1991). *Language in Australia.* Cambridge: Cambridge University Press.

Taylor, C. (1992). *Multiculturalism and 'The Politics of Recognition'.* Princeton: Princeton University Press.

Taylor, C. (1994). *Multiculturalism: Examining the Politics of Recognition.* Princeton: Princeton University Press.

Trudgill, P. (ed.) (1984). *Language in the British Isles.* Cambridge: Cambridge University Press.

1 The foundations

William F. Mackey

INTRODUCTION

To contemplate a map of Canada while thinking of its languages is
to induce an optical illusion. For the language boundaries do not coincide with
the lines on the map – and they never have. The straight lines that separate the
provinces have never been language boundaries – nor has the 3,000-mile international boundary that separates Canada from the United States. Of the many
languages spoken in Canada, none is exclusively Canadian with the exception
of certain Amerindian languages. These, however, belong to language families
which extend into the United States; their territory in some cases straddles the
international boundary line. So do the language boundaries of French and
English. All the languages of Canadian immigrants can also be heard south of
the border. While Canada's national and intra-national political boundaries are
artificial and often arbitrary, having been created by the hazards of war or the
accommodations of peace, the language boundaries of Canada have been
fashioned by the movement of people, settling into a vast and sparsely
populated continent.

The history of language in Canada is that of three different geolinguistic
types – the native languages, the colonial languages and the immigrant languages. The development of each has long been intertwined with that of the
others, since the settlement of the continent has inevitably brought one group
into contact – and often into conflict – with the others: the English with the
French and the Indians with both colonial settlers. The fate of each has been
fashioned, not only by trade, industry and birth rate, but also by war, disease
and famine.

THE FIRST LANGUAGES

Before the arrival of the European colonists in the early sixteenth century,
at a time when the population of Europe itself was in the order of 100 million,
there were already about 15 million people living in America. These people

spoke languages unrelated to any in Europe – and often unrelated to one another. In the northern third of the North American continent, which is now Canada, there were some sixty distinct languages belonging to a dozen different families. These language families could be as different one from the other as are the languages of Europe and those of Asia – as different as English is from Japanese, for example. Within each of these families, however, the different languages could be as genetically related as French is to Italian, or English to German. Within the Algonquian family, for example, Cree and Ojibwa are distinct languages, each with a number of regional sublanguages with names like Ottawa, Mississauga, and Saulteaux spread over vast areas, extending from Quebec in the east to the foothills of the Canadian Rockies in the west (Campbell and Mithun, 1979).

The greatest number of different language families, however, is still located around the earliest Amerindian settlement along Canada's west coast. Some have been there for more than a millennium. They include such important language groups as Salishan, Haida, Tlingit, Tsimshian and Wakashan and, on the other side of the Rockies, in the plateau region of southeastern British Columbia straddling the American border, the isolated Kutenai family. Most of the rest of what is now Canada was divided into four language families: in the west, the Athabaskan family of more than a dozen languages extending from Northern Alaska to the southern shore of Hudson Bay, westward to the Rockies and down through the United States, all the way into Mexico. Second was the Eskimo-Aleut family beginning in Continental Asia across the Bering Strait and encompassing all the Arctic lands from Alaska in the west to Greenland in the east. Thirdly, the rest of the country – including what is now the southern half of Alberta, Saskatchewan and Manitoba, Ontario, Quebec and the Maritimes – was the area dominated by ten of the Algonquian languages, notably Cree, Ojibwa, Montagnais and Micmac. All of this was Algonquian territory, with the exception of an area extending from the Great Lakes to the mouth of the St Lawrence River, land occupied by peoples speaking Iroquoian varieties. It was with the eastern languages of the Algonquian and Iroquoian families that the first European settlers came into contact.

The earliest contact between the native peoples of Canada and the French is generally associated with the early voyages (1534–35) of Jacques Cartier. This Breton navigator had been commissioned by the French king, Francis I, to duplicate the colonial exploits of his great rival Spain, the dominant power in Europe at the time. In addition to finding a route to the Orient, Cartier was to 'discover certain islands and lands where it is said a great quantity of gold and other precious things are to be found' (quoted in Mackey, 1996).

Yet a generation before Cartier, there had already been contacts between French sailors and Amerindians, whenever European fishing fleets had to go ashore from time to time to build the scaffolding on which they could cure and dry their catches of cod. One of the navigators, Thomas Hubert of Dieppe, who made contact in 1504, brought to France some Indian youths in the hope that they would learn his language. His experiment resulted in failure, while his economic experience proved to be a success, for contact with the Amerindians resulted in a profitable exchange of European hardware for animal pelts which, on the home market, netted the fishermen more than did the fish. On successive voyages, then, they began bringing home more furs and less fish.

This explains the context of Cartier's first contact with Amerindians, who approached him offering pelts for trade. But Cartier's immediate preoccupation was to sail on in search of a route to the Indies (he now believed that he might be within sailing distance of Japan). To do so, he needed reliable information about what lay ahead, information he could obtain only from the inhabitants, in a language neither he nor his crew understood. It was evident that either some of his men would have to learn the new language or his potential guides would have to learn French.

Both approaches were tried. Cartier began by painfully learning some six words of badly transcribed Micmac. However, these proved of no use at all when, two weeks later, he met the Iroquois at Stadacona and heard a language belonging to an entirely different family. Cartier then tried the second approach, that of having the natives learn French. To do so, he resorted to kidnapping two sons of the chief Donacona and brought them back to France – partly as trophies, partly as potential future interpreters. This act set the stage for the long-lasting mistrust between the Iroquois and the French.

Among the different languages which the French explorers encountered, the most important for them was Huron; they expended a great deal of effort in making glossaries of this language. Why did they favour the speech of such a small tribe? It was because Huron had become the lingua franca of travel and trade along the waterways leading to the interior of the continent, as witnessed by the place names it left behind. With a smattering of this important language, Cartier and his crew were able to explore the St Lawrence up to what is now Quebec City, to a village called *Ganada* /ganá:da/ ('settlement' in Huron), transcribed in French as Canada. The name of this village was consequently applied to an ever-expanding territory which now spans a continent.

When Cartier returned in 1541, he found that the Iroquois (some 60,000 people), having been replaced by semi-nomadic bands speaking languages of the Algonquian family, had disappeared from the St Lawrence Valley. The languages of the Huron, the Neuters and the Petun (Tobacco People) had vanished. The Iroquois languages found today in Canada (Mohawk, Seneca, Cayuga, Oneida, Onondaga and Tuscarora) are those of immigrants who, in 1784, fled north with the United Empire Loyalists after the American Revolution.

Although some French explorers continued to learn the native languages of America, France's expanding imperial policy was at the time one of ethnic assimilation. The explorers were reported to have said to the native onlookers : 'Our sons will marry your daughters and we will become one people.' However, this is not what happened. Some 130 years later, Jean-Baptiste Colbert, France's most powerful minister and Secretary of State to Louis XIV, would complain to Jean Talon, the first *intendant* of New France, that the native populations had not yet been forced to learn French, but that those Frenchmen who wanted to trade with them had to learn their language.

Colbert had expected the two races to merge into one – '*un mesme peuple et un mesme sang*'. Those closest to the native peoples knew that this was unlikely to happen and for many reasons – demographic, cultural, linguistic and economic. As the founder of the Ursuline convent in Quebec City was to explain in 1639, it was much easier for Frenchmen to go native than for natives to become French. French youths were only too happy to free themselves of the many social constraints of the European society of the period. On the pretext of preparing to become interpreters for the state, they went to live among the native peoples, adopted their languages and customs and prospered as go-betweens and free agents. A good example is found in the career of Etienne Brulé. In 1610, after wintering on the Ile des Allumettes, he returned briefly in the spring to the French settlement with a new language, a new suit ('*habillé à la sauvage*') and an eagerness to get back as soon as possible. There he lived out his short life as a full-time go-between. Such agents could become independent, rich and powerful. Anyone with connections and with a sufficient knowledge of the languages to assure delivery of animal pelts from the Great Lakes to the spring fur fair in Hochelaga (Montreal) could command a substantial fee.

Men such as Brulé knew that their language skills had made them indispensable; they could remain independent of both church and state. The Jesuit and Recollet missionaries who needed their language skills in order to evangelize the population could not count on them to help as teachers or even as interpreters, for they kept their unique skills almost as trade secrets. Some of the missionaries therefore decided to follow in the footsteps of these daring and enterprising young men: they tried to learn the languages of the native peoples by living among them. A few, like the unfortunate Etienne Brulé, were killed and cannibalized for their efforts.

Nor did those missionaries who tried to teach the natives French have an easier time of it. The Jesuit Gabriel Biard wondered why the same mouths that could so easily masticate his samples of French food could not mouth French syllables. He tells of his experience with a young Huron who, even after some 300 attempts, could not pronounce '*Père Gabriel*'. He pronounced what he heard in terms of his own phonological system; through this audiophonological filter, he heard and repeated '*tère aviel*'. Like other languages of the Iroquoian family, Huron operated with only fifteen phonemes as against some thirty for French; these languages could get by quite well without labials like /p/ and /b/ for example. Similar reactions were recorded for the Amerindian experience with French grammar.

The remarkable differences in grammatical and phonological structures are surpassed only by the profound gaps between European and Amerindian conceptual universes. It is understandable that the well-meaning missionaries – whose thought processes had been fashioned for them by the only languages they knew (all Indo-European), coupled with the conceptual artifacts of their Graeco-Roman philosophy and Judeo-Christian beliefs – should fail to grasp the existence of conceptual frameworks so remote from their own. Sagard, who in 1632 published the first dictionary of Huron, the most complete work at the time on any Amerindian language, wrote about the lack of words for the vocabulary of religion and such concepts as 'faith', 'virtue', 'vice', 'belief' and 'soul'. The dichotomies of western thought were also foreign to the Amerindians, who conceived their world not in the straight lines and closed squares of European conceptual categories, but rather in the circles and spirals of natural processes coded in languages fit for talking about the ever-changing face of nature – clouds, snow and water. That is why their languages had to be rich in prefixes, suffixes and infixes of the -ish and -like category. Sugar was something sweet and sand-like. Thunder and lightning were not nouns but events. 'It' cannot snow or rain in these languages, as it can in languages whose verbs require subjects, albeit fictitious ones.

It was in ignorance of these conceptual differences that the long-lasting acculturation of the Amerindian peoples took place. The recorded history of their country became that of those who had conquered it; for in the politics of knowledge, the past belongs to those who have the power to appropriate it. Defeated by European arms, decimated by European diseases, the outnumbered Amerindian peoples became a scattered population of isolated bands. After having been exploited by European traders, their cultures and languages were systematically eradicated in the name of Christianity and civilization. Amerindians were settled on reserves, and children were separated from their families, placed in far-away residential schools, taught in a colonial tongue, and punished for using their home language.

By the middle of the twentieth century, several Amerindian languages had hardly any speakers under the age of twenty. Many of them (such as Tsetsaut, Nicola, Songish and Puntlatch) had become extinct, and the moments of their demise have remained unrecorded – with the possible exception of Beothuk in Newfoundland, whose last speaker died in 1829. The most moribund languages were in the areas of the earliest European settlements; language death became the price of socio-economic equality. By the 1950s, very few languages could count more than 1,000 speakers, and only three (Inuktitut, Ojibwa, and Cree), those most often used in the home, numbered more than 10,000.

Very few Amerindian communities had flourished through intermarriage with Europeans. Yet, from the early eighteenth century onward, some such communities did exist as far away as the Great Lakes, as informal biracial outposts. They were known by Indian names such as Chicago and Milwaukee, or by French names such as Detroit and Sault-Ste-Marie. A century later, there were biracial (Métis) colonies in the centre of the continent – notably in the Red River Valley at Fort Garry, which was to become the nucleus of the province of Manitoba.

Apart from the Métis, France's initial policy of creating a new biracial people remained unfulfilled. Unable, after a century, to assimilate a mobile and numerically superior population, and also unable to control the form of the intermarriages '*à la façon du pays*' – much less their offspring – France formally abandoned the policy of exogamy. During the eighteenth century it changed its policy of promoting biracial marriages and saw to it that a sufficient number of French women emigrated to the colony through various schemes, including such enterprises as '*les filles du Roy*'.

THE EXPANSION OF FRENCH

The expansion of the French language in Canada was not the result of successive waves of massive immigration from France. It was a gradual process initiated by explorers, fur traders and settlers seeking opportunities in farming, mining and forestry, mostly by successive generations of colonists from New France and Acadia.

From the beginning of the settlement along the St Lawrence River, French fur traders continually extended their domains southward and westward. By the 1670s, they had reached beyond the Great Lakes. In 1701, a French colony was founded near Detroit in Fort Pontchartrain (now in Ontario); by 1760, it had some 2,500 inhabitants. By the 1740s, there were French trading posts west of the Mississippi and it was during this period that the French explorer La Vérendrye was pushing westward to the Canadian Rockies.

In the intervening time, France had ceded many of its American possessions to Britain, in exchange for trading concessions in India, according to the provisions of the Treaty of Utrecht of 1713. One of these possessions was the French colony of Acadia. Unlike the explorers and fur traders of New France, the self-sufficient Acadians were content to remain in the idyllic homeland they had built in what is now Nova Scotia. Wishing only peace and neutrality, they yet became unwilling pawns in the colonial wars between England and France.

The period 1760–1860

Unable to take sides, most of the Acadians were deported and dispersed. Between 1760 and 1769, they were resettled all along the eastern seaboard of America from Maine to Georgia, and along the Gulf Coast from the Florida panhandle to the mouth of the Mississippi. Some ended up in the Antilles. In the final decades of the century, hundreds of Acadians returned to the Canadian Maritimes, not to their former homelands – which were now occupied by refugees from the American Revolution – but to coastal and less fertile areas of the new British provinces of Nova Scotia, New Brunswick and St John's Island (now Prince Edward Island). There, they began to re-establish their culture and language in a continent which was no longer under French rule (Wright, 1955).

Although the fall of New France in 1763 had put a complete halt to any possible immigration from France, it did not put an end to the continued expansion of French. While the French military governmental and administrative bureaucracy had returned to France, those who remained, mostly native-born *Canadiens*, had no intention of abandoning their land, their language or their religion. They formed a coherent majority population of some 65,000 people, speaking a language whose prestige at the time surpassed that of English, and which was then the international language of Europe. Their remaining elite – mostly clergy – had not abandoned their vision of French America. Some began to regard the lands discovered by the French explorers as their rightful heritage lands to be colonized, Christianized, and civilized.

Various economic attractions motivated the continental expansion of the French language. Apart from the forced displacement of the Acadians, there was the constant lure of making a better living elsewhere – either in the lucrative fur trade, in the lumber industry, in mining or in farming – the motives varying over time from one part of the continent to the other.

The fur trade, whether French or British, had a growing need for the services of *coureurs de bois*, men born and bred among the Indians, skilled in the ways of the land. Serving as transporters (*voyageurs*), brokers, traders and intermediaries between the merchants of the east and the hunters of the west, from the Assiniboine Valley to the central plains, they ignored all political boundaries. From their intimate relations and intermarriages with the native peoples sprang independent biracial settlements.

The period 1860–1930

By the 1870s, many of the French Canadians settling the American midwest were coming from the Canadian west, where the number of French speakers already accounted for more than half of the non-Indian population. The French Canadian population was now sufficient to support its own institutions; French-speaking communities developed in Detroit, which in 1808 founded its own parish, as did Grand Rapids in 1820. Parishes were established in Missouri in 1828, in rural Illinois in 1832, in Kansas in 1860; some of these were placed under the new diocese created in Chicago in 1863 (Louder and Waddell, 1993).

These parishes were replicas of those in Quebec. Even the conflicts within the Quebec hierarchy extended into the parishes of the midwest. The fate of the temperance crusader, Father Charles Chiniquy, is a case in point. Chiniquy arrived in Bourbonnais, Illinois in 1852 with a second wave of immigrants from Quebec. After his independent views had split the community, he became involved in a land dispute which ended up in court. At his trial, he was defended by prairie lawyer (and future president) Abraham Lincoln. In 1856, having been excommunicated for his views, Chiniquy became a minister of the Presbyterian church and took his French-speaking supporters with him to his new parish in Ste. Anne, Illinois (Trudel, 1955).

French-Canadian colleges were founded in Illinois (Bourbonnais 1865), in Manitoba (St Boniface 1903), in Alberta (Edmonton 1913), in Saskatchewan (Gravelbourg 1917). French-speaking populations in these new towns increased sufficiently to support local newspapers: in Saskatchewan (*Le Patriote de l'Ouest* 1910-1941), in Manitoba (*La Liberté* 1913-1981) and in Alberta (*La Survivance* 1928–). These large settlements had not all originated as fur-trading or agricultural communities. On the west coast, skilled French-Canadian forestry workers were brought in from the Ottawa Valley to work the saw mills near Vancouver.

A priest was invited in 1908 to found a parish in a community to be named after him – the French-speaking town of Maillardville, British Columbia.

Some of these French-speaking communities formed the core of agricultural settlements attracting immigrants from Quebec. It is true that many successive waves of immigrants were actively recruited by the local elite – mostly clerics – with the motive of maintaining a favourable balance of population in the face of the rising tide of English-speaking settlers. For about half a century, between 1870 and 1930, French Canadians were recruited in eastern Canada and New England, with offers of free land and services to all those willing to go west. Agents were hired to attract immigrants from French-speaking areas in Europe. The peak period for French European immigration was from 1890 to 1914, when the influx was averaging about 30,000 immigrants a year; they came from Belgium, Switzerland, Brittany, and Alsace-Lorraine – but proportionately less from France, when it became illegal to encourage French citizens to emigrate. By the end of this period, there were some 150,000 French speakers in the three prairie provinces.

Credit for this ethnolinguistic success must go to the French-Canadian clergy and its remarkable, all-encompassing sociolinguistic parochial and diocesan organizations, forming the heart of all the religious, social and cultural life of the settlers, responding to all their needs and providing them with both security and a sense of identity (Wade, 1968). These parishes had the same role as they had in New France when the clergy had to fill much of the void left by the departure of the French military and governing elite, after the colony fell under British rule. As an example, if we look at the typical French-Canadian parish of St Paul in Quebec, we find that parishioners had access to more than fifty parochial and diocesan organizations or associations – cultural, political and recreational – some of a purely devotional nature, others concerned with providing material and social welfare (Falardeau, 1969).

By encompassing the most pivotal institutions of family and school, the French Canadian parish represented a coherent culture, based on a common ethnicity, a common religion, a common language, and a high birth-rate which could double the population every generation (Henripin, 1954).

THE EXPANSION OF ENGLISH

When New France fell under British rule, French long remained as the majority language. It is true that as French military and civilian administrations (and some merchants) returned to France, they were replaced by their British counterparts, but the English (or Scottish) military governors had little interest in complicating their task by promoting an influx of British immigrants. However, when British civil government was installed after the Treaty of Paris of 1763, entrepreneurs often used their political influence in London to overrule the governor.

The cities, soon controlled by a British merchant class, became progressively English-speaking. Within less than a century, Montreal became an English-speaking area, while in Quebec City half the population spoke English. Outside the cities, French continued to dominate, but not everywhere. What initially modified the demographic dominance of French were the consequences of the American Revolution and its political refugees. Almost 100,000 of these rural conservative anti-revolutionaries (later called the Loyalists) – some of them born in Britain – fled the new republic. Most of them settled in different parts of eastern Canada. Arriving overland or by boat, they settled along the coast of Nova Scotia in the St John's River Valley, the Gaspé Coast, the mouth of the Richelieu River, the Niagara Peninsula and in what are now the cities of Toronto, Kingston, Cornwall and Brockville – providing these regions with their first sizeable populations. They achieved this with some aid from the imperial authorities who had to create for them new political entities, notably the provinces of New Brunswick and Cape Breton in 1784 and the province of Upper Canada (now Ontario) in 1791 (Wright, 1955). Loyal to the crown and to the empire, they remained contemptuous of the Americans with their 4th-of-July 'rebel picnic', and forever wary of possible contamination of British North America by American republicanism. They and their descendants would make a long-lasting imprint on Anglo-Canadian identity (Brown, 1969).

Not only were the English-speaking settlers in Canada of the same origin as those in New England, but it was from among these American colonists that came the masses that were to form the first demographic basis of English Canada. At the time of the American Revolution – when the English population of Canada was less than 9,000 (as against 65,000 French) – the number of American anti-revolutionaries fleeing the revolution numbered upward of 100,000, the majority of whom settled in Canada, many in what is now Ontario; by 1812, the population of York (Toronto) was over 50,000. These Loyalists had brought with them not only their speech but also their ideals and their institutions. And they soon dominated not only linguistically, but also socially, economically and – eventually – politically. It is true that some had been recent immigrants from Britain, especially Ireland and Scotland. Of the forty-seven members in the 1825 legislative assembly of Upper Canada, fifteen were born in the United States, thirteen in Canada, twelve in Ireland or Scotland, and only seven in England.

The economic development of Canada, with its vast land mass and rich material resources, required the importation of thousands of workers for its agricultural and extractive sectors and for the construction of roads, railways and canals for bringing the resulting products to market. As a British colony, Canada favoured immigration from England – both officially and privately. The policy was one of British preference, with support for all sorts of privately funded English immigration schemes. One of the most original of these was that of an English physician, Dr Barnardo, who had established a charitable foundation to house and feed homeless English children, of whom there were so many in the London of Charles Dickens. Under the slogan 'Save a child and help the Empire', thousands of these children were placed in Canadian homes between 1905 and 1931, to serve as farm hands or domestic help. They and their descendants contributed to the making of an English working class. So did the recruitment policies of Canada's largest companies. For example, the Canadian Pacific Railway called upon the British union of metal workers to supply English labour for its workshops, and retail companies recruited directly from London the employees of their stores and factories.

Many of the employers were mistrustful of foreigners. Even the Irish were not accepted; although most of them did speak English, they were often treated as foreign papist intruders whose loyalty to the Crown was suspect. Signs read: 'Help wanted (No Irish need apply)'. Yet, tens of thousands arrived during the famines of 1840–50, contributing to the labour force of the big cities.

In sum, most of the settlers coming to Canada after the British conquest were English-speaking (some also spoke Irish, Welsh or Scottish Gaelic). By the 1860s, they outnumbered French speakers two to one. By the 1870s, when the population of Canada was just over three and a half million, two million were speakers of English and one million speakers of French. During the following century, almost ten million people immigrated to Canada, most of them English-speaking. In spite of later efforts to recruit settlers from French-speaking Europe, the proportion of French speakers to English speakers had fallen from a half to a quarter. But this increase in the number of English speakers was due not only to English immigration. It was also due in some part to the assimilation of French-speaking minorities. When French speakers are part of a community where English is the dominant speech, they inevitably have to work in that language; their children become bilingual, intermarry, and produce offspring who speak the dominant language. By 1980, for example, only 55 per cent of the population of French origin in the provinces of Saskatchewan and Alberta could still claim French as their mother tongue. For other minorities – Ukrainian, German,

Italian – the proportion was even less. Most grandchildren of the first settlers from Germany, Italy, the Ukraine and other countries did not preserve their ethnic tongue as their home language.

THE HERITAGE LANGUAGES

It eventually proved impossible to attract a sufficient number of skilled workers from England, France or the United States to man the rapidly expanding extractive, agricultural and manufacturing economies. Even as early as the 1700s, German immigrants were brought in to bolster the Scottish population in Nova Scotia.

German settlers created colonies in Ontario at the end of the nineteenth century. German-speaking religious sects like the Mennonites and Hutterites set up successful self-sufficient agricultural communes in the West. Some (like Steinbach in Manitoba) published German textbooks on their own printing presses. By the 1870s the population of German settlers, now numbering about 250,000, comprised the largest group of immigrants after the English and the French. In 1914, however, with the outbreak of war with Germany, all German immigration came to a halt. War hysteria and anti-German sentiment discouraged the use of the language. Some of the best-established German settlements were forced to change their names. In Ontario, the town of Berlin was renamed after Lord Kitchener of the British high command. At that time, the policy on foreigners was that they belonged in foreign armies, and they were encouraged to return to their country of origin. After the war, the frantic search for immigrants obliged the government to broaden its 'preferred' category to include newcomers from most northern European countries. Meanwhile, other religious sects had formed self-sufficient communes on the prairies and as far away as the west Coast. Most notorious of these were the Russian-speaking Doukhobors, whose settlements had been financed by Leo Tolstoy. In the centre of the continent, along the shores of Lake Winnipeg (at Gimli), Icelanders established communities, Finns settled on the shores of Lake Superior, Ukrainians and Dutch on the prairies. There were large concentrations of Italian, Polish, Jewish, and Greek immigrants in the cities. Each group published its own newspaper; by the outbreak of the Second World War, Canada's ethnic press included over 100 newspapers in more than thirty languages.

After the Second World War, a different flood of immigrants entered Canada from Europe – displaced persons, people eager to get away from their ravaged homelands and to start a new life in the New World. Many of these immigrants were highly educated and, once they were settled, soon left the unskilled labour market for professional jobs, some of which had been previously reserved for immigrants from Britain, Germany, the Netherlands, and other preferred countries. At the same time, immigrants from the low-wage countries of southern Europe and the West Indies were admitted to do the sort of jobs in construction and the service industries that Canadians would not accept. All this transformed each of Canada's large cities into a veritable multiethnic metropolis. It is true that most of these 'ethnic' immigrants had been admitted to Canada as agricultural workers; but many, unhappy with rural isolation, had gravitated to the big cities. Others had intended to stay in Canada only long enough to amass sufficient capital to pay their debts and buy land at home. But many of these, by choice or by necessity, did not return. Most immigrants were now located in Canadian cities where, having become conspicuous by their number, their presence awakened old ethnic anxieties and prejudices previously reserved mostly for the Irish. Canada's population policy had evolved from one of the most restrictive to one of the most liberal.

In the early 1960s, Canada began gradually to develop a universal and non-discriminatory immigration policy, which culminated in the Immigration Act of 1978. This included obligations in relation to refugees and the financing of various voluntary agencies and immigrant support groups. Refugees from leftist Hungary, Czechoslovakia and Poland were as welcome as those from rightist Chile, Uganda and Southeast Asia. Canada had become a major magnet for immigrants from all over the world.

The immigrants eventually realized that the country in which they had settled was really a cohabitation of two equally ethnocentric societies. Deciding to integrate into 'Canadian society', especially in areas with French-speaking populations, became an either/or proposition – becoming Anglo-Canadian or French Canadian. In either case, the children – whether European, Asian or African – were taught to identify with the colonial ancestors of only one of 'the founding peoples', whose history dominated the curriculum. As a prerequisite to integration, they and their parents were expected to become competent in either English or French. In 1947, competence in one of the official languages became one of the requirements for Canadian citizenship. Before 1947, Canadians were legally British subjects. The Canadian Citizenship Act created a distinct non-British Canadian citizenship. The provisions of the Act were to be implemented by the Canadian Citizenship Branch in conjunction with the federal judiciary, since only a judge had the power to decide whether the conditions for citizenship had been met. Immigrants who were not competent in one of the official languages could follow special courses funded by the Branch, in cooperation with the provinces. But since education was constitutionally under provincial jurisdiction, some provinces – particularly Quebec – refused to cooperate.

The cumulative effect of massive immigration from countries which were neither English-speaking nor French-speaking was to profoundly alter the ethnic character of the country. In more and more areas, the population of English ethnic stock was becoming a minority. Outside Quebec and French-speaking Acadia, French Canadians were no longer demographically dominant. And even within French-speaking Quebec, the ethnic vote was becoming a decisive political force. Politicians could no longer afford to ignore this population. As it was for native groups comprising the 'first nations', so it was difficult for an increasingly multicultural population to accept the very premise on which Canadian official-language policy had been based – the proposition that Canada belonged to the 'two founding peoples'. As a result, the Canadian government, in 1971, had to develop some sort of policy of multiculturalism based on the premise of the survival of different cultures and of what came to be known as the 'heritage' languages.

THE GENESIS OF CANADIAN LANGUAGE VARIETIES

The sources of Canadian language varieties may be traced to the speech of the colonists who settled America during the seventeenth and early eighteenth centuries. Independent of the evolution of their languages, which later produced the urban standards of Paris and London, these early colonists set the stage for the development of American standards in patterns to be followed by later settlers and their descendants. Although their speech did not echo the language of the court, but rather that of the provinces, the first colonists of New France and New England did not settle the land according to the dialect divisions of their homeland. On the contrary, the mixture of their dialects gradually resulted in a common language, less dialectal than those of Europe. This levelling process of American speech – both English and French – persisted well into the twentieth century.

Patterns of Canadian English were set by the first great wave of immigration from New England during the period of the American Revolution. Upon this substratum of eighteenth-century English, more locally directed contingents of immigrants from Ireland, Scotland, Yorkshire, Devon and continental Europe did later impart some degree of regional flavour to the sounds and words of certain rural areas. In the Ottawa Valley twang, for example, and the brogue of the Newfoundland outports, one can still detect traces of Irish speech. In Canadian French, the throaty aspiration of the consonants of words like *George* by rural elders in the Beauce Country reflects the regional speech of their ancestors. Likewise, the lasting isogloss of the R-phoneme separating the Montreal and Quebec areas could be used to demark different accents.

Persistent differences in vocabulary have also been minor. They are to be found mostly in the occupational speech of isolated rural areas in regions devoted to fishing, mining, forestry and agriculture – especially among the older inhabitants. Yet by mid-century they were still sufficient in number to justify the publication of studies of Canadian English (Scargill, 1977) and Canadian French (Dulong and Bergeron, 1980).

If one had to divide Canada into dialect areas, one could identify, for English: British Columbia, the Prairies, western Ontario, the eastern Townships (Quebec and eastern Ontario), the Maritimes and Newfoundland. Urban speech – that of the people who established Canada's first English-speaking cities – has remained fairly uniform. In the case of French, two regions developed distinct accents, according to the different origins of the settlers of the first two French colonies in America – Acadia and New France. Most of the Acadian settlers came from the western provinces of France south of the Loire River – Poitou, Aunis and Saintonge; less than 10 per cent came from areas north of the Loire. Conversely, in New France, most came from areas north of the Loire valley (Normandy, Brittany, Maine, Picardy, Ile-de-France, and adjacent regions) and less than a third originated from areas to the south. It is to these two different types of regional admixtures that can be attributed many of the differences heard today between Acadian and French Canadian speech.

When settlers break direct ties with their homeland, they and their descendants cease to be affected by changes in their home language. Thus, for example, the Canadian pronunciations of words like *clerk* and *aunt* are still those of eighteenth-century England. Sounds of eighteenth-century France can still be heard in Canada, but rarely if ever in France, for after Canada had fallen under British rule, France underwent profound sociolinguistic changes – brought on by the French Revolution and the replacement of the power of regional aristocracies by that of a metropolitan proletariat and its spokesmen, who saw to it that henceforth the French language would be identified, not with the speech of the aristocracy, but with the dialect of the common people of Paris. This urban basilect was thus raised to the status of a national acrolect. Even the lawyers who launched the revolution in the name of the people insisted on talking like them: '*Il faut parler peuple*'.

But these changes did not affect French North America since, a generation earlier, all immigration from France had ceased. At that time, much of the dialectal variation of the seventeenth century had blended into a common speech, while the speech of France was still fragmented into dozens of local *patois*. It is significant that before the French Revolution most visitors from France extolled the quality of Canadian French; after the Revolution, they denigrated its pronunciation. Before the Revolution, one noted remarks like those of Charlevoix in 1744: '*Nul part ailleur on parle plus purement notre langue*', or Bacqueville de la Potherie in 1753: '*On parle ici au Canada parfaitement bien, sans mauvais accent*', and even Montcalm in 1758: '*Les paysans canadiens parlent très bien le français*' (Dulong, 1966). After the Revolution, this same language sounded to the ears of Volney in 1803, Pavie in 1850, and other French visitors like: '*un français passable*' or '*un vieux français peu élégant*' (Dulong, 1966).

At the same time, the English held similar views of the colonial accents of Canadian English. Even in the twentieth century, the great Canadian humorist Stephen Leacock felt compelled to preface his lectures in England with the remark: 'I don't like this accent any more than you, but it's the best I can do'. For, to English ears, his accent was American. Just as the French Revolution had provincialized Canadian French, the American Revolution had provincialized Canadian English.

If the basis of Canadian speech can be found in the accents of its first French and English colonists, its special vocabulary comes from the people with whom they came into contact. From the native peoples came such words as *caribou, chipmunk, wigwam*. And, from French to Canadian English came *portage, rapids, lacrosse;* from English to French came *boom, chum, cute*, and many more.

The history of the development of the languages *written* in Canada is quite different from that of their spoken varieties. While the speech forms remained those of the times of first settlements and places of origin, the written languages followed the development of national standards in England and France which still supplied most of the reading material. From the outset, both in Canada and the United States, great pains were taken not to deviate too much from the written standards of the mother country.

LANGUAGE CONFLICT AND POLITICAL ACCOMMODATION

It was perhaps inevitable that two peoples so different in language and culture should clash in the political arena. So long as the French Canadians remained isolated in self-contained rural communities, with their own laws and institutions, contact with the English conquerors remained at quasi-diplomatic levels. It was in the interest of the British Empire that it remain so, for the spectre of the French-Canadian majority joining the increasingly rebellious New England colonies in their fight against the English aroused fears that the rising tide of American republicanism might engulf the whole continent. This anxiety undoubtedly motivated the accommodations of the Quebec Act of 1774, which guaranteed the maintenance of French civil law and customs as well as freedom of religion and education.

In the aftermath of the American Revolution, however, the tens of thousands of political English-speaking refugees changed the demographic patterns of settlement in Canada to such an extent that new territorial and administrative entities had to be created (see above). The British parliament, through the Constitutional Act of 1791, divided the country into Upper Canada (now in Ontario) and Lower Canada (now in Quebec). But the amount of self-government permitted in these new entities remained unchanged, as did the amount of British control of local affairs which the colonists perceived as too demanding and often unjust. The Loyalists and their descendants in Upper Canada began to think and act as had their American forebears in their revolution against the imperial dominance of Britain. They demanded that the people who governed the colony be responsible to those they governed. In 1837, they took up arms to defend the principle and were soon joined by their French-speaking compatriots in Lower Canada. But the rebels were no match for the British army, which soon crushed the rebellion. The British government then instituted an investigation to be directed by Lord Durham.

The Durham Report was tabled in the British House of Commons in 1839. It was implemented the following year in the Act of Union. While satisfying the demands of English-speaking Upper Canada for greater autonomy, the Act was designed on the premise that the French-Canadian population of 658,000 would eventually become assimilated by an English-speaking population, still in the minority. And although the population of English speakers numbered only 450,800, English was to be the only official language of the new Province of Canada.

The fate reserved for the Canadian French-speaking population in this policy of ethnic assimilation was perceived not only as a threat to the French language but – what was more important at the time – a menace to the role of the Catholic church. Religion was tightly bonded with language and culture in the daily lives of the French-speaking population, since their main intellectual elite was the clergy. The French language being the only means of communication between the clergy and the people, it was perceived as a *sine qua non* for the preservation of the faith: '*La langue, gardienne de la foi*'. The responsibility for the maintenance of French-Canadian identity fell naturally upon the leadership of the

Church. For almost a century thereafter, the French-Canadian hierarchy would play an increasingly important role in the maintenance and expansion of French in America.

From the outset, Lord Durham's policy and its consequences in the Act of Union were perceived as fundamentally unjust. But it was not until years later that any of its provisions were repealed. In 1848, the use of French was admitted in Parliament; its official status was confirmed later in an act of the British parliament, the British North America Act of 1867, which created the Dominion of Canada as a confederation of four provinces. The following year, after the new dominion had bought Rupert's Land and the Northwest Territories from the Hudson's Bay Company, the way was paved for the addition of four more provinces to the west.

When the Dominion expanded its control to the west of the continent, it was decided, after negotiations between the Métis and their leader Louis Riel, to encompass the Métis population into the new province of Manitoba. Out of some 11,000 Manitoba inhabitants, the Métis could count almost 10,000. Of these, more than half used French as a home language. The rest of the population spoke Amerindian languages or English. Ignoring the former, the constitution of the new province, created in 1870 by the Manitoba Act, declared French and English as the official languages.

After the Dominion had decided to populate and develop its new territories, new settlers were brought in, mostly from English-speaking Ontario or directly from Britain. Many settled on lands further west which the Métis and native peoples had always considered their own. In 1884, under Riel, these lands had been grouped into a separate Métis political entity. To the Dominion government, this initiative constituted an act of rebellion; it therefore sent in the army to crush the new state. Its leader, Riel, was convicted of high treason in 1885 and hanged.

As with the political uprising of a half-century earlier, the anti-Riel backlash resulted in another setback to the status of the French language in Canada. In 1890, French was banned from both the judiciary and the legislature of Manitoba. Henceforth, all laws were passed in English only – until almost a century later, when the Supreme Court of Canada declared invalid all Manitoba laws dated after 1890, since they had been enacted only in English. French was banned, not only in Manitoba, but also in Ontario in 1912, at a time when a fifth of the population of that province was French-speaking. It was also banned in Saskatchewan where, in 1916, French was no longer to be taught in public schools.

Meanwhile, these losses in the legal status of French had not brought to a halt the continental expansion of French settlements. Faced with the massive influx of English-speaking settlers after 1870, it became evident to the French-Canadian hierarchy in the west that only an aggressive immigration from French-speaking countries could preserve the bilingual balance. French-speaking Catholic settlers were recruited from Quebec, New England, Belgium, Switzerland and from certain parts of France (see above). It was a new vision of French America. This vision was most eloquently stated by such clerical leaders as Henri-Raymond Casgrain and Louis-Alphonse Pâquet who, in 1902, proclaimed: '*Notre race semble avoir été choisie pour enseigner au monde moderne le culte du beau ... Dès lors ne s'impose-t-il pas que notre mission à nous, Canadiens Français, est de faire pour l'Amérique ce que la mère patrie a fait pour l'Europe*' (Pâquet, 1915, p. 187).

Private and public colonizing associations under Church leadership, coordinated by a permanent secretariat in Quebec, continued to flourish for another half-century, until a chain of circumstances after the Great Depression of the 1930s brought to a halt the continental expansion of French in America.

The years 1930–1950, the period between the Great Depression and the Quiet Revolution (see below), were ones of decline in traditional French-Canadian society, rooted in the golden age of pre-revolutionary France with its symbiosis of Church and State. After the fall of New France, the essentials of this traditional society had been guaranteed by the Articles of Capitulation and re-affirmed by the Quebec Act in the protection they provided to the rights of the French-Canadian population to their language, customs, laws and religion, meaning that the sociopolitical function remained intact. Taken for granted was a monopoly on education, culture, social policy, welfare and civil status based on ethical principles accepted by a population under clerical leadership. In areas where this population had achieved political power, as in Quebec before 1960, any civil legislation by the party in power was first checked with the hierarchy.

The decline of the old order began during the Great Depression with its rural impoverishment, urban unemployment and population mobility. It accelerated during the Second World War as rural men and women migrated to urban war factories. Between 1930 and 1960, an ever increasing number of young French Canadians left the farms to work in the cities. Even by the end of the 1930s, more than half were living in cities; by the end of the 1960s, city-dwellers accounted for more than 80 per cent of the French-speaking population (Levine, 1990). What followed was the rise of a French-Canadian urban proletariat, a non-clerical intelligentsia and a politicized middle class – the beginnings of the so-called Quiet Revolution.

In cities where half the population had been English-speaking, the resulting mixture of urban, rural and Americanized speech varieties merged into the French urban sociolect which came to be known as *joual.* It remained a transitional spoken basilect until about 1965, when it gave rise to a militant literature. But it became progressively marginalized, as an educated, urban French-speaking middle class began to dominate the media. Socially, thiͻ new middle class began to fill the gaps created by a massive decline in the nurnber of clergy. Before and during the 1930s, the number of clergy ordained in Quebec continued at the rate of some 2,000 a year; at the end of the 1960s, that number had fallen to less than 100. At the same time as churches were closing, many of the most successful social organizations maintained by the clergy began to fold. In 1957, the body coordinating the work of all French parishes in America, the Conseil de la Vie française en Amérique, closed its doors after the death of its last director, Monsignor Primeau of Chicago (Louder and Waddell, 1993).

The decline in the number of clergy, however, can partly be attributed to the decline in the French-Canadian birth rate from the highest to the lowest in Canada. By the early 1970s, that birth rate had fallen by almost half of what it had been a decade earlier – 28.3 per 1,000 in 1959 to 14.8 per 1,000 in 1971 (Henripin *et al.,* 1974). As Quebec society became more secular, the social and educational functions of the clergy diminished – as had indeed their pastoral role. By the late 1960s, attendance at Sunday mass was only half of what it had been a decade earlier. In the age group 15–35, only 12 per cent attended.

The long association of the Church with the dominant political party (the Union nationale) did little to ingratiate it with a political opposition dominated by a rising urban middle class. In the 1960s, this opposition came to power under the banner of a militant liberal party, and the political and social prerogatives of the Church began to disappear. This new non-clerical class faced three obstacles in its quest for real power: the social power of the Church, with its monopoly on education, civil status and social services; the progressively centralized power of the federal government; and the economic power of the English elite. All through this period, the Church had fought against the laicization of its institutions, indeed, against anything that resembled Republican France. It had preferred corporatism on the model of Franco's Spain, Mussolini's Italy and Salazar's Portugal. It had fought against the Americanized materialism of the English-speaking population and against urban civilization, which it associated with capitalism, public education, feminism, divorce and birth control. All this frustrated the efforts of the rising professional and intellectual middle class seeking a role in the development of Quebec's society. For them, the policies of the Church represented conservative immobilism, dogmatism, authoritarianism and xenophobia (Trudeau, 1956).

In less than two decades, the multiple barriers maintained by a militant and omnipresent Church had crumbled. Every pore of Quebec society was now open to outside influences. These influences upon its traditional values transformed Quebec into a consumer society: secular, materialistic and Americanized. No longer dominated by religion, its identity depended to a greater extent on language. For all these reasons, the maintenance of the French language in Quebec now became more important than ever before.

In 1964, the Department of Public Instruction, controlled by the Council of Bishops, was abolished and a secular Ministry of Education was created in its place. The government likewise took control of social services. This was not without a price; the cost of education and social services which accounted for 43 per cent of Quebec's total budget in the early 1960s had risen by the early 1970s to 83 per cent. The education and integration of immigrants became especially important. Since the French-speaking population was barely reproducing itself, maintenance of its demographic strength depended more and more on immigration. Because immigrants had traditionally sent their children to English schools, measures had to be taken to reverse this trend. In 1974, the new Liberal government in Quebec passed a law (Bill 22) making French the official language and obliging immigrant children to attend French schools.

On the economic front, Quebec developed a policy to nationalize basic utilities, particularly electricity (1962), and to promote the development of a French-speaking business and entrepreneurial class. On the political front the action was not limited to federal-provincial relations. Different popular movements for supporting Quebec's independence began staging public demonstrations. By 1968, they had coalesced into a full-fledged political party (Le Parti Québécois) which was elected to power in 1976, and re-elected in 1981.

This development of Quebec's growing desire for greater mastery of its own affairs, as heard in its political slogan '*Maître chez nous*' – masters in our own house – had aroused the fears of the central government as far back as the beginning of the Quiet Revolution. The federal government had long functioned mostly, or only, in English, ignoring 'the French fact' in Canada. Now in Quebec, where language, no longer religion, had become the main indicator of identity, this indifference became intolerable. In 1963, under intense political pressure, a top- priority and lavishly financed commission of inquiry was established to investigate the condition of Canada's French-speaking population in relation to its English-speaking one, and the relationship between themselves and with other ethnic populations. Named the Royal Commission on Bilingualism and Biculturalism, it produced voluminous research reports and recommendations which inspired the authors of the federal Official Languages Act of 1969. Since this law could only cover areas under federal jurisdiction, it was hoped that the other provinces would also protect the use of French in areas under their control. But the only province to follow suit was New Brunswick which, the same year, declared itself an officially bilingual province.

The Act enshrined French/English bilingualism in all federal laws and documents and guaranteed services for francophones and anglophones in the language of their choice. It also provided for a parliament-appointed Commissioner of Official Languages to see that the language laws and regulations were respected. These provisions were later enshrined in the new Canadian constitution when it was repatriated in 1982, and also in a new Canadian Charter of Rights and Freedoms. Since this constitution did not give it the right to a veto, Quebec refused to sign it.

Meanwhile, the Quebec government had created its own commission (the Gendron Commission) of investigation into the situation of French within its borders. Tabled in 1972, its recommendations inspired the creation of a Charter of the French Language (Bill 101) which declared French the only official language in Quebec. This was one of the most comprehensive language laws ever enacted – but it did not remain uncontested. One of its main clauses, which states that only the French version of any Quebec law is official, was judged unconstitutional by the Supreme Court of Canada in 1979.

The rise of Quebec nationalism had a profound effect on the traditional French-Canadian identity. For the corollary of change from religion-oriented identity, with a universal church bent on a continental mission and imbued with religious mystique, to a politically oriented ideology and a nationalist mystique – no longer French America but French Quebec – was the need for a territorial identity. French institutions were soon transformed into Quebec institutions; *Le mouvement laïque de langue française* became *Le mouvement laïque québécois*, for example. The territorialization of the French language in Quebec led all other French minorities to seek their own territorial identity: *Fransaskois, Franco-Manitobain, Franco-Ontarien, Franco-terreneuvien*, etc. These now turned to the federal government for support and protection. They also turned inward to themselves and created in 1975 the Fédération des francophones hors Québec to lobby for their interests. In 1978, they published an influential volume of documents comparing the demographic and legal position of French-speaking minorities throughout Canada. It was entitled *The Heirs of Lord Durham: Manifesto of a Vanishing People.*

Meanwhile, speakers of Amerindian languages were beginning to find themselves equally provincialized. In the 1970s, this widespread population banded together to form the Assembly of First Nations to lobby for the protection of their land claims and their cultures. They sometimes made common cause with three other nation-wide federations: those of the Inuit organizations, the Métis groups and the associations of non-status Indians. The post-colonial myth of 'two founding peoples' was no longer politically tenable, not among the Canadian Indian population, nor among immigrant groups, less and less among the Canadian English and the new generation of *Québécois.* As the twentieth century draws to a close a new concept of Canada is in the making.

References

Brown, W. (1969). *The Good Americans.* New York: Morrow.

Campbell, L. and Mithun, M. (eds.) (1979). *The Languages of Native America: Historical and Comparative Assessment.* Austin: University of Texas Press.

Dulong, G. (1966). *Bibliographie linguistique du Canada français.* Paris: Klincksieck.

Dulong, G. and Bergeron, G. (1980). *Le parler populaire du Québec et de ses régions voisines: un atlas linguistique de l'Est du Canada* (10 vols). Quebec: Ministère des Communications.

Falardeau, J.-C. (1969). The parish as an institutional type. In *Canadian Society: Sociological Perspectives* (3rd edn) (pp. 530–535). Toronto: University of Toronto Press.

Henripin, J. (1954). *La population canadienne au début du 18e siècle.* Paris: INED (Cahier 22).

Henripin, J., Lapierre-Adamcyk, E. and Festy, P. (1974). *La fin de la revanche des berceaux.* Montreal: Presses de l'Université de Montréal.

Levine, M. V. (1990). *The Reconquest of Montreal.* Philadelphia: Temple University Press.

Louder, D. and Waddell, E. (eds.) (1993). *French America.* Baton Rouge: Louisiana State University Press.

Mackey, W. (1996). Preface. In J. Maurais (ed.), *Quebec's Aboriginal Languages: History, Planning and Development.* Clevedon, Avon: Multilingual Matters.

Pâquet, L. A. (1915). *Discours et allocutions.* Quebec: Imprimerie franciscaine.

Scargill, M. H. (1977). *A Short History of Canadian English.* Victoria: Sononis Press.

Trudeau, P. E. (ed.) (1956). *La grève de l'amiante : une étape de la révolution industrielle au Québec.* Montreal: Éditions du Jour.

Trudel, M. (1955). *Chiniguy.* Trois-Rivières: Éditions du Bien Public.

Wade, M. (1968). *The French Canadians* (2 vols.). Toronto: Macmillan.

Wright, E. C. (1955). *The Loyalists of New Brunswick.* Wolfville, N.S.: E. C. Wright.

2 The fading Canadian duality

Charles Castonguay

Census data are by far the best source of statistical information on language in Canada. Surveys have occasionally investigated language behaviour in greater depth, but their results inevitably suffer from limited sample size and lack of comparability. Though the earliest censuses recorded only the ethnic origins of Canadians, reasonably consistent data on mother tongue and ability to speak English or French were also collected by 1931. A question on current home language has been included since 1971, following the dissatisfaction of the Royal Commission on Bilingualism and Biculturalism at having to deal with mother-tongue data alone: 'the mother tongue of the individual does not tell us which language he commonly uses. The information is a generation behind the facts' (RCBB, 1967, p. 18). Finally, the 1991 census added a question on ability to speak languages other than English or French. Thus, census data not only allow us to follow trends, but also provide a fair overview of Canada's present linguistic make-up.

ORIGIN TRENDS

Canada has been the scene of demographic competition between English and French since conquest by the British in 1759–1760. Though Canadians of British origin soon outnumbered those of French origin, high French-Canadian fertility subsequently offset the effect of international immigration and, from the mid nineteenth century up until the mid twentieth, succeeded in maintaining the French portion of the total population at about 30 per cent. Following the Second World War, however, French fertility dropped rapidly and, by the early 1970s, fell below the replacement level of 2.1 children per woman – where it has remained ever since. As a result, after close to a century of relative stability since Confederation, the French-origin share of the population is once again on the decline.

Table 2.1 Population by ethnic origin, Canada, 1871–1991

Census	Total	British		French		Other	
		Number	%	Number	%	Number	%
1871[1]	3,485,761	2,110,502	60.5	1,082,940	31.1	292,319	8.4
1901[2]	5,371,315	3,063,195	57.0	1,649,371	30.7	658,749	12.3
1931[2]	10,376,786	5,381,071	51.9	2,927,990	28.2	2,067,725	19.9
1961	18,238,247	7,996,669	43.8	5,540,346	30.4	4,701,232	25.8
1991[3]	26,994,040	9,793,193	36.3	7,168,703	26.6	10,032,145	37.2

[1] Nova Scotia, New Brunswick, Quebec and Ontario only.
[2] Not including Newfoundland.
[3] Claims of mixed origins have been divided equally among the origins reported.
Sources: Lachapelle and Henripin, 1982, table B.1, and Statistics Canada, 1993b, table 1.

Table 2.1 makes it equally clear that the essentially dual British and French origin of the population is also a thing of the past. Following massive international immigration of Other origins, British origin lost its status as an absolute majority after 1931, and has continued to decrease in relative importance due to inadequate fertility and continued immigration of Other origins. One must none the less bear in mind that today's Other-origin category is extremely fragmented, with components ranging from aboriginal populations, through descendants of earlier immigration from northern, eastern and southern Europe, to contemporary immigrants from Asia, Africa and Latin America. The British-origin stock still remains, therefore, the largest linguistically homogeneous ingredient of the Canadian population. As such, it continues to weigh decisively on language use.

Consequently, ethnic origin is a poor indicator of language behaviour in Canadian society. Though the latest census shows that 37.2 per cent of Canadians claimed to be of neither British nor French origin, only half as many – more exactly, 18.5 per cent – claimed ability to speak a language other than English or French, whether as a first or as a more occasional language (Statistics Canada, 1993c, table 5). Individual language shift to English also leads naturally to under-reporting of origins other than English among subsequent generations, especially after the 1971 census introduced data collection by self-enumeration (Castonguay, 1994). Reporting of Other origins fluctuates importantly, too, with the political and military world context. The census origin question itself has changed considerably over time. Finally, extensive intermarriage renders the simplification of mixed origins into distinct categories an increasingly artificial exercise: fully 28.9 per cent of Canadians claimed two or more ethnic origins in 1991. For all these reasons, we shall not further elaborate on origin data in this chapter.

ENGLISH-FRENCH DUALITY

Notwithstanding the growing diversity of its ethnic origins, Canadian society still remains essentially dual from the standpoint of language. This is clearly borne out by the mother-tongue data in table 2.2. Discussion of them is simplified by using *anglophone, francophone* and *allophone* to designate the English, French and Other mother-tongue populations respectively. To further simplify comparison of data from different censuses – in this table, as well as in those to follow – reports of two or more languages in 1991 have been apportioned in equal parts to the languages claimed.

The anglophone portion of the Canadian population has steadily preserved its majority status. By contrast, the francophone share of the population has been decreasing since the Second World War. The fact that, as census follows census, French mother-tongue counts in table 2.2 fall lower and lower than corresponding counts for French ethnic origin in table 2.1, indicates the cumulative effect of net anglicization of parents or ancestors of French origin. Similarly, due to extensive anglicization and, to a much lesser extent, some francization, the allophone population is progressively smaller than that of Other ethnic origin: Canadians of Other mother tongues barely rise above 15 per cent, even after periods of intensive international immigration.

Again, as for the origin statistics, the Other mother-tongue fraction of the population is very diversified. Its three largest components in 1991 – Chinese, Italian and German – each number about half a million, which is less than 2 per

Table 2.2 Population by mother tongue, Canada, 1931–1991

Census	Total	English		French		Other	
		Number	%	Number	%	Number	%
1931[1]	10,376,786	5,914,402	57.0	2,832,298	27.3	1,630,086	15.7
1941[1]	11,506,655	6,488,190	56.4	3,354,753	29.2	1,663,712	14.5
1951	14,009,429	8,280,809	59.1	4,068,850	29.0	1,859,770	11.8
1961	18,238,247	10,660,534	58.5	5,123,151	28.1	2,454,562	13.5
1971	21,568,310	12,973,810	60.2	5,793,650	26.9	2,800,850	13.0
1981	24,083,505	14,784,810	61.4	6,177,795	25.7	3,120,900	13.0
1991	26,994,040	16,311,210	60.4	6,562,065	24.3	4,120,770	15.3

[1] Data prior to 1951 do not include Newfoundland.
Sources: Lachapelle and Henripin, 1982, table B.2, and Statistics Canada, 1994, table A.1.

Table 2.3 Population by current home language, Canada, 1971–1991

Census	Total	English		French		Other	
		Number	%	Number	%	Number	%
1971	21,568,310	14,446,235	67.0	5,546,025	25.7	1,576,050	7.3
1981	24,083,505	16,375,315	68.0	5,919,855	24.6	1,788,325	7.4
1991	26,994,040	18,440,540	68.3	6,288,430	23.3	2,265,075	8.4

Source: Statistics Canada, 1994, table A.2.

cent of the total population (Statistics Canada, 1992b, table 2). Only 1.2 per cent of Canadians claimed two or more mother tongues, almost always including English (Statistics Canada, 1993a, table 5). Multiple responses to the mother-tongue question are thus much less frequent than for ethnic origin and essentially bear witness, as an intermediary stage, to intergenerational language shift to English.

The fundamental English–French linguistic duality is brought to light even more clearly by the data on current home language, that is, the language most often spoken at home by each Canadian at the time the census is taken. As noted, a question about current home language has been asked since 1971; it takes into account the effect of individual language shift. Table 2.3 shows that more than two-thirds of Canadians commonly speak English at home. The remainder use French or, to a much lesser degree, Other home languages.

Once more, the French home-language counts are somewhat below those for French mother tongue, which indicates continuing net anglicization of francophones, and the French home-language portion of the population is declining over time. Similarly, the fact that at the latest census only 8.4 per cent of the population claimed to mainly speak a language other than English or French at home reflects the heavy ongoing anglicization of allophone Canadians. Of course, the home-language data concern the language spoken *most often* by the respondent at home, and do not exclude less frequent use of another language. In 1991, only 1.8 per cent of Canadians claimed two or more home languages, which included English more than nine times out of ten (Statistics Canada, 1993a, table 1).

The Other home-language population is again extremely mixed, though with a difference: the 409,663 Canadians speaking Chinese as the main home language in 1991 stand out as a single major component, accounting alone for close to one-fifth of the Other home-language total. In comparison, older immigrant languages fade in importance. Due to heavy individual anglicization,

Italian and German are each spoken as a home language by less than 1 per cent of the population (Statistics Canada, 1993a, table 2).

Unfortunately, the series of census data on language can present comparability problems too, though to a lesser degree than with ethnic origin. For instance, the new 1991 census questionnaire has caused an artificial increase in language shift relative to earlier censuses (Castonguay, 1996). This must be taken into account when evaluating language-shift trends.

It is equally important to keep in mind that the data on language shift slightly underestimate individual anglicization rates, because of an inappropriate notion of mother tongue – which has, in fact, plagued Canadian census data since 1931. The census concept is not a permanent characteristic: one's 'mother tongue' can change, as a result of the deepest form of language shift, namely, language loss. In particular, the 1991 mother-tongue question read as follows: 'What is the language that this person **first learned** at home **in childhood** and **still understands**? *If this person no longer understands the first language learned, indicate the second language learned*'. More explicitly than in any previous census, this precludes observation of language loss: francophones who have become so deeply anglicized that they no longer understand French are actually considered for census purposes to be of English mother tongue. A similar *caveat* applies to mother-tongue data and anglicization rates for allophones, which systematically underestimate both the Other mother-tongue population, and individual language shift from Other languages to English, by an amount equal to language loss, notably among older adults.

While close to 92 per cent of Canadians speak either English or French at home, there is obviously a difference in kind between the situations of the two components of Canada's linguistic duality. The strength of English resides in its power of assimilation, whereas that of French lies basically in its far greater resistance to anglicization compared to Other languages. While both major language groups now suffer from inadequate fertility, anglicization has thus far compensated efficiently for insufficient anglophone birth rates and allophone immigration. In contrast, the decline in French origin, mother-tongue and home-language fractions of the Canadian population over the last decades shows that similar compensation through assimilation does not exist for French. It is mainly the concentration of francophones within the province of Quebec which has ensured the relatively successful survival of French in Canada.

The Canadian Official Languages Act of 1969, which gave equal status to English and French; a similar measure adopted the same year by the province of New Brunswick, followed in 1981 by a bill recognizing equality of status of its

English- and French-speaking *communities*; and Bills 22 and 101 favouring the use of French at school and at work, adopted by the province of Quebec in 1974 and 1977 respectively – all these measures can be construed as attempts to bolster the French-speaking minority's resistance to anglicization at the Canadian level, and, within Quebec, to give French a new power of assimilation among allophone immigrants – ultimately, to compensate at least partially for inadequate francophone fertility in Quebec by means of francization, just as the anglophone majority succeeds in doing via anglicization at the Canadian level.

To some extent, the survival of Canada itself hinges on the success of such recent legislation in stabilizing the French-speaking portion of the population in Quebec, if not in Canada as a whole. Examination of the language situation in this light requires investigation of basic language data for Quebec and for the rest of Canada.

GROWING TERRITORIALIZATION

French in Quebec and English in the remainder of Canada have to a remarkable degree maintained their demographic ascendancy – Quebec being, of course, the only province with a French-speaking majority. Despite decreasing fertility since the Second World War, French mother tongue has hovered above 80 per cent of the Quebec population, while in the rest of Canada, English mother tongue has been regularly nudging the 80 per cent mark from below.

Table 2.4 shows a further point of symmetry: the official mother-tongue minorities – English in Quebec and French outside Quebec – are both steadily declining in relative importance. In terms of absolute numbers, the anglophone minority in Quebec has decreased markedly since 1971, while the francophone population outside Quebec has ceased to grow significantly. Finally, the allophone population shows a regular increase in both absolute number and relative weight in Quebec, and in number if not in weight in the rest of Canada.

On the whole, the current home-language data in table 2.5 indicate similar trends, but with some differences due in the main to language shift to English. While the French home-language counts in Quebec remain very close to those for French mother tongue, the home-language data give English in the rest of Canada an even more absolute majority status – over 87 per cent of the total population – than that enjoyed by French in its Quebec stronghold. Table 2.5 also shows a somewhat milder decrease of English as home language than as mother tongue in Quebec, and a drop in absolute numbers of the French home-language minority in the rest of Canada.

Table 2.4 Population by mother tongue, Quebec and rest of Canada, 1951–1991

Census	Total	English		French		Other	
		Number	%	Number	%	Number	%
Quebec							
1951	4,055,681	558,256	13.8	3,347,030	82.5	150,395	3.7
1961	5,259,211	697,402	13.3	4,269,689	81.2	292,120	5.6
1971	6,027,765	789,185	13.1	4,867,250	80.7	371,330	6.2
1981	6,369,055	693,600	10.9	5,254,195	82.5	421,265	6.6
1991	6,810,305	626,200	9.2	5,585,650	82.0	598,455	8.8
Rest of Canada							
1951	9,953,748	7,722,553	77.6	721,820	7.3	1,509,375	15.2
1961	12,979,036	9,963,132	76.8	853,462	6.6	2,162,442	16.7
1971	15,540,545	12,184,625	78.4	926,400	6.0	2,429,520	15.6
1981	17,714,450	14,091,215	79.5	923,605	5.2	2,699,635	15.2
1991	20,183,735	15,685,005	77.7	976,415	4.8	3,522,315	17.5

Source: Statistics Canada, 1994, table A.1.

Table 2.5 Population by current home language, Quebec and rest of Canada, 1971–1991

Census	Total	English		French		Other	
		Number	%	Number	%	Number	%
Quebec							
1971	6,027,765	887,875	14.7	4,870,100	80.8	269,790	4.5
1981	6,369,075	806,785	12.7	5,253,070	82.5	309,220	4.9
1991	6,810,300	761,815	11.2	5,651,795	83.0	396,695	5.8
Rest of Canada							
1971	15,540,545	13,558,360	87.2	675,925	4.3	1,306,260	8.4
1981	17,714,420	15,568,530	87.9	666,785	3.8	1,479,105	8.3
1991	20,183,745	17,678,730	87.6	636,640	3.2	1,868,380	9.3

Source: Statistics Canada, 1994, table A.2.

Upon closer examination, comparison of tables 2.4 and 2.5 reveals that the latter trends have been accentuated in 1991 by a marked increase in language-shift gains for English in Quebec, and in the anglicization of francophones in the rest of Canada, relative to previous census results. Similarly, French suddenly shows net gains through language shift of 66,145 in Quebec in 1991, a figure equivalent to a full 1 per cent of the province's population, whereas the difference between French mother-tongue and French home-language counts at previous censuses was not even statistically significant. These anomalies in language-shift trends basically reflect the inflationary impact of the new 1991 census questionnaire on language shift among minorities of all kinds (Castonguay, 1996).

The decrease in size of the official-language minorities since 1971, coupled with continued growth of the corresponding official-language majorities, all visible in table 2.5, leads to greater concentration of Canada's French-speaking population within the province of Quebec, and of its English-speaking population in the rest of the country. By 1991, 90 per cent of Canada's French home-language population was to be found in Quebec, while 96 per cent of the English home-language population was enumerated in the rest of Canada.

Distinct processes underlie this growing territorialization of Canada's linguistic duality. On the one hand, Quebec's English-speaking population has been prone to migrate to Ontario and more westerly provinces, since at least Confederation (Beaujot and McQuillan, 1982; Caldwell, 1974; Joy, 1967). On the other, the anglicization of francophones in the rest of Canada was extensively documented decades ago (Joy, 1967; Lieberson, 1970; RCBB, 1967). In order to adequately assess the more recent impact of these two processes, they must be examined in the overall demographic context of Canada's two major language regions.

THE PREDOMINANCE OF FRENCH IN QUEBEC

Beginning in 1971, the census has included a question on place of residence five years earlier. The resulting statistics have borne out the forecast that, after Quebec's Quiet Revolution, a considerable fraction of its English-speaking minority would choose to leave the province, being either unable or unwilling to adjust to the growing importance of French, notably as language of work (Joy, 1967). Table 2.6 confirms high anglophone out-migration throughout the

Table 2.6 Interprovincial migration by mother tongue, Quebec, 1966–1991 (in thousands)

Period	English			French			Other		
	In	Out	Net	In	Out	Net	In	Out	Net
1966–1971	47	99	−52	33	47	−14	5	14	−9
1971–1976	42	94	−52	37	41	−4	5	10	−5
1976–1981	25	132	−106	32	50	−18	4	21	−17
1981–1986	29	71	−42	33	46	−13	5	14	−9
1986–1991	32	54	−22	43	38	5	7	16	−9

Source: Statistics Canada, 1994, table 5.3.

Table 2.7 Total fertility rate by mother tongue, Quebec, 1956–1991

Period	English	French	Other
1956–1961	3.26	4.22	2.79
1961–1966	3.04	3.54	2.93
1966–1971	2.09	2.27	2.58
1971–1976	1.62	1.81	2.26
1976–1981	1.46	1.71	2.04
1981–1986	1.46	1.47	1.79
1986–1991	1.54	1.49	1.78

Source: Statistics Canada, 1994, table 5.1.

twenty-year period from 1966 to 1986. The trend reached a maximum shortly after the 1976 election of a sovereignist provincial government, but anglophone out-migration already totalled 193,000 between 1966 and 1976, which is only slightly less than the 232,000 who left during the next ten years. In light of this, one cannot attribute the recent demographic decrease of English in Quebec exclusively to out-migration after 1976.

Table 2.7 reveals as well that, since 1971, Quebec's anglophone minority has experienced two full decades of extremely low fertility. Together with the migratory trend to go west, this has worked powerfully to offset English gains through language shift – whence the decrease in absolute numbers of Quebec's English-speaking minority since 1971.

Though table 2.6 also shows some out-migration of francophones from Quebec, this is mostly compensated by in-migration of francophones from the rest of Canada. Francophone migration to Ontario and more westerly provinces has thus just about dried up. Table 2.7 indicates that the main demographic drain on Quebec's French-speaking majority has become, instead, inadequate fertility.

The drop in francophone fertility was phenomenally rapid during the 1960s. With an average of 1.48 children per woman over the last decade, the francophone total fertility rate seems to have stabilized at only 70 per cent of the intergenerational replacement level of 2.1 children per woman. Over twenty years of insufficient fertility spells a coming decline in absolute numbers for the francophone population in Quebec – *a fortiori* in Canada as a whole – beginning early in the next century (Termote, 1994, 1996). Table 2.8 illustrates the steadily shrinking base of the francophone age pyramid in Quebec, following the maximum attained among those aged 30 to 39, who were born in the 1950s.

After some four centuries of continued francophone expansion in North America, this demographic about-turn is of major consequence, particularly

Table 2.8 Age distribution of English, French, and Other mother-tongue populations, Quebec, 1991

Age group	English		French		Other	
	Number	%	Number	%	Number	%
70+	52,522	8.4	337,197	6.0	40,476	6.8
60–69	59,154	9.4	463,643	8.3	60,518	10.1
50–59	58,218	9.3	548,153	9.8	71,284	11.9
40–49	83,908	13.4	822,971	14.7	84,711	14.2
30–39	100,592	16.1	1,025,077	18.4	104,736	17.5
20–29	102,358	16.3	861,863	15.4	103,239	17.3
10–19	82,994	13.3	781,964	14.0	71,012	11.9
0–9	86,452	13.8	744,754	13.3	62,189	10.4
Total	626,200	100.0	5,585,650	100.0	598,455	100.0

Source: Statistics Canada, 1992a, table 4.

in the domain of language policy. More recently, Quebec's linguistic majority has attempted to supplement its numbers through increased allophone immigration, as witnessed in table 2.4, but so far this has essentially amounted to the replacement of migrating anglophones by an equivalent number of allophones. Even if we consider the results of the 1991 questionnaire to be directly comparable to those of 1981, the apparent net gain of 66,145 made by French through individual language shift during the 1980s, and the resulting intergenerational language shift to French, remain far short of compensating for the fertility deficit of approximately 300,000 francophone children over the same decade, estimated from table 2.8 by comparing the number of young adults aged 30 to 39 to the number of children aged 0 to 9.

The inadequacy of this compensation can be more directly brought out by linguistic reproduction rates, which gauge quite simply the combined effect of fertility and language shift. The francophone reproduction rate, for example, equals the number of francophone children aged 0 to 9 divided by the number of young francophone adults aged 25 to 34. Approximately a generation separates the two ten-year age groups. The result depends on francophone fertility, but also on intergenerational language shift, that is, on the language transmitted as mother tongue by parents to their children. The latter is largely determined by individual language shift among young adults: the children's mother tongue is usually the language commonly spoken at home by their parents.

In essence, a language group's reproduction rate is simply a statistical summary of the lower portion of its age pyramid. A reproduction rate greater than unity means the base of the pyramid is widening, and the group is on the increase; a rate smaller than 1.00 indicates a shrinking base, and generally heralds a future decrease.

Reproduction rates for Quebec's mother-tongue populations in 1991 were as follows: English, 0.81; French, 0.73; and Other, 0.56 (Statistics Canada, 1992a, table 4). The francophone reproduction rate of 0.73, or 73 per cent, is slightly greater than the ratio of 70 per cent between its recent overall total fertility rate of 1.48 and the replacement level of 2.1 children per woman. This marginal improvement reflects the proportionally small net language shift in favour of French in Quebec noted above for 1991. While anglophone fertility was practic-ally as low as for francophones throughout the 1980s (table 2.7), the anglophone reproduction rate of 0.81 is substantially greater than that for francophones, because of proportionally much greater language shift to English: tables 2.4 and 2.5 show a net gain of 135,615 more Quebecers of English home language than of English mother tongue. Conversely, even though allophone fertility is the highest, the allophone reproduction rate is the lowest, due to high individual and intergenerational language shift to either English or French. Nevertheless, Quebec's Other mother-tongue population continues to grow through inter-national immigration, basically made up of allophones.

It thus appears, overall, that the French language group has more recently maintained its predominance in Quebec not so much through its own vitality, as by default, thanks to anglophone over-representation in the province's migratory deficit with the rest of Canada.

ENGLISH CANADA

Like the English-speaking minority in Quebec, the anglophone majority in the rest of Canada suffers from inadequate fertility. Indeed, insufficient birth rates are widespread among language groups throughout Canada, though not quite to the same degree as in Quebec. The 1986–1991 total fertility rates out-side Quebec were 1.68 children per woman among anglophones, 1.56 among francophones, and 1.79 among allophones (Statistics Canada, 1994, table 2.5), all of which are somewhat higher than their Quebec counterparts in table 2.7. Furthermore, heavy anglicization of the relatively more important allophone population, as well as of the francophone minorities, almost entirely makes up for low anglophone fertility.

Linguistic reproduction rates handily sum up once again the combined impact of fertility and language shift in 1991 on the different mother-tongue populations outside Quebec, as follows: English, 0.89; French, 0.52; and Other,

0.48 (Statistics Canada, 1992a, table 4). At 0.89, anglophone reproduction is almost adequate. Anglophone in-migration from Quebec and from other countries, along with continuing anglicization of steadily arriving allophone immigrants, suffice to keep numbers growing. As a result, decrease in the anglophone majority is nowhere in the offing, and discussion of demographic issues in English Canada is commonly limited to the ageing of the Canadian population and its consequences.

In contrast, the francophone reproduction rate of 0.52 outside Quebec is practically equal to that of allophones, at 0.48. Unlike the allophone shortfall, the francophone intergenerational deficit of close to 50 per cent is not compensated for by international immigration. We have also seen that francophone migration from Quebec to English Canada has practically dried up: table 2.6 even shows a slight net gain for Quebec's francophone population through interprovincial migration over the latest five-year period. A decrease in francophone numbers outside Quebec therefore appears inevitable, and is already visible in terms of French home language (table 2.5).

Finally, though allophone fertility rates during the 1980s have been somewhat lower in Quebec than in the rest of Canada (table 2.7), the reverse is true of allophone reproduction rates, at 0.56 in Quebec compared to 0.48 elsewhere. This reflects higher rates of allophone language shift in English Canada than in Quebec, which can also be directly verified by comparing tables 2.4 and 2.5. It appears that ambiguity over which of English or French is the dominant language in Quebec – French is certainly the provincial majority language, but English is the language of the Canadian majority – encourages language maintenance among Quebec allophones. Outside Quebec, anglo-conformity is unchallenged, and leads to more rapid linguistic assimilation.

Francophone reproduction rates outside Quebec vary considerably by province. The highest is 0.71 in New Brunswick, followed by 0.52 in Ontario and 0.51 in Manitoba, then dropping to 0.37 or less in the remaining provinces, with a bottom value of 0.25 in British Columbia. Allophone reproduction rates are actually higher than francophone rates in all of the provinces outside Quebec, except in New Brunswick and Ontario.

At approximately 30 per cent, the intergenerational shortfall of the francophone minority in New Brunswick is of the same order as that of Quebec's francophone majority. This means that the age 'pyramid' for both populations is, in reality, pear-shaped. However, the causes underlying the shrinking bases of the two populations are different. Insufficient fertility is the whole of the problem in Quebec, and is even slightly alleviated by some allophone francization. In New

Brunswick, a low birth rate explains about two-thirds of the shortfall but, as we shall see below, net anglicization also contributes appreciably to reducing the francophone reproduction rate.

In Ontario, insufficient fertility and anglicization account just about equally for the demographic collapse of the francophone minority, resulting in a diamond-shaped age structure, in lieu of a pyramid. The similar collapse of each of the remaining francophone minorities is principally due to anglicization, and only secondarily to insufficient birth rates. Their age 'pyramids' are decidedly top-heavy, and resemble inverted pears.

A minority-language population can be said to undergo *collective assimilation* when it both suffers net losses through language shift and no longer sustains a fertility rate high enough to make up for such losses (Lieberson, 1965, uses the term *aggregate* assimilation). When this occurs, the intergenerational shortfall can be used to measure the minority's collective assimilation rate. Thus the collective assimilation rate of the francophone minority is 30 per cent in New Brunswick, 48 per cent in Ontario, and 75 per cent in British Columbia.

Without substantial and sustained migratory support from exterior sources, collective assimilation leads to more or less rapid numerical decrease. In such a context, a reproduction rate of 0.50, or 50 per cent, literally means that each generation is half as numerous as the preceding one. The age 'pyramid' of Ontario's francophone population or, for that matter, that of the French mother-tongue minority in the whole of English Canada, is today essentially identical to that of the Ukrainian mother-tongue population at the 1961 census: diamond-shaped, with a reproduction rate of around 50 per cent (RCBB, 1969, figure 1.3). The Ukrainian mother-tongue count at the 1961 census was 361,500, second in importance only to German among Canadians of Other mother tongues (Kralt, 1976, table 2). Thirty years – approximately one generation – later, immigration from the Ukraine having been negligible, the 1991 census enumerated 181,500 Canadians of Ukrainian mother tongue, almost exactly half as many as in 1961 (Statistics Canada, 1992b, table 2). The demographic implications of collective assimilation can hardly be more clear.

To sum up, several factors underlie the growing territorialization of Canada's linguistic duality. The decline in Quebec's English-speaking minority is not only the result of out-migration, but also of inadequate anglophone fertility. That of the French-speaking population in the rest of Canada is caused not only by anglicization, but also by insufficient fertility and the drying up of francophone out-migration from Quebec.

CANADA'S BILINGUAL BELT

A further feature of Canada's linguistic duality is the contact area between English and French, which extends along the border between Quebec, on the one hand, and the provinces of Ontario and New Brunswick as well as the northeastern United States, on the other. The Bilingual Belt, as it has been conveniently called (Joy, 1967), inspired the Royal Commission on Bilingualism and Biculturalism to recommend the creation of bilingual districts in those border areas of Quebec, New Brunswick, and Ontario which comprise sizeable English- or French-speaking minorities. In some portions of the Belt the official-language minority actually forms the majority of the local population. Patterned on Finland's territorial bilingualism policy *vis-à-vis* its Swedish-speaking minority, the bilingual districts were to form the 'cornerstone' of Canada's official language policy (RCBB, 1967). Though the concept of bilingual districts was eventually abandoned, the official-language minorities in the Bilingual Belt, as well as in more isolated 'language islands', have since been the object of extensive research (Cartwright, 1976, 1980; Castonguay, 1994; Kralt, 1976; Lachapelle and Henripin, 1982; Termote and Gauvreau, 1988).

More than three-quarters of the 976,415 francophones enumerated outside Quebec in 1991 were to be found in Ontario and New Brunswick. The 503,345 francophones in Ontario represent only 5.0 per cent of the provincial population, whereas in New Brunswick, the 243,690 francophones account for 34.0 per cent.

Moreover, almost two-thirds of Ontario's francophones were concentrated in two portions of the Bilingual Belt along the Quebec border, with 192,663 francophones enumerated in a group of five southeastern counties including the city of Ottawa, and 133,674 in four contiguous northeastern counties including the city of Sudbury (Statistics Canada, 1991 census special tabulation). No less than 128,186 – which represents two-thirds of francophones in the southeastern segment, and over one-quarter of Ontario's total francophone population – were found in the census metropolitan area of Ottawa. The Canadian capital region alone thus contains, by far, the single most important concentration of francophones outside Quebec and New Brunswick. In the rural counties of Prescott and Russell, midway between the cities of Ottawa and Montreal, francophones were in the majority, with 71 per cent of the local population.

Similarly, in New Brunswick, 227,000 francophones – over 93 per cent of the francophone minority – were concentrated in the northeastern half of the province. This part of the Bilingual Belt is made up of a block of seven counties below the Quebec border. In four of these, French is the majority language, and in three, francophones comprised over 80 per cent of the population. Obviously, such strong concentration favours minority-language maintenance.

The major part of the Bilingual Belt inside the province of Quebec is comprised of a group of four counties in the Outaouais region to the north of the city of Ottawa, the metropolitan region of Montreal, and the seven counties known as the Eastern Townships just north of Quebec's border with the United States. Over 85 per cent of Quebec's 626,200 anglophones lived in these segments of the Bilingual Belt, and fully three-quarters were concentrated in the densely populated Montreal region alone. Anglophones formed the majority in several municipalities in the western part of the island of Montreal, commonly known as Montreal's 'West Island', as well as in the westernmost county of Pontiac in the Outaouais region.

Certain components of the allophone population – such as those of German, Cree or Inuktitut mother tongue – form local majorities in some of Canada's non-urban areas, while others – for example, of Italian or Chinese mother tongue – are strongly concentrated in certain neighbourhoods within major metropolitan regions. But, as a substantial extension of Canada's language duality beyond the basic Quebec/rest of Canada dichotomy, the Bilingual Belt is an integral part of the most important aspect of language in Canada.

LANGUAGE-SHIFT TRENDS IN QUEBEC

By means of the series of census data on mother tongue and home language which now extends over the twenty-year period from 1971 to 1991, we can monitor the impact on language shift of the various federal and provincial language policies aimed at strengthening the position of French in Quebec and in the rest of Canada. This will require investigating language shift by province, as well as in the major components of the Bilingual Belt. We shall limit our observations to trends regarding French; similar analyses can be carried out with respect to any other Canadian minority language. Most of the data discussed below are based on special tabulations purchased from Statistics Canada, and the trends reported have withstood basic tests of comparability (Castonguay, 1996).

In Quebec, English continues to enjoy a tangible advantage over French in direct shift between the two official languages. In particular, in the western part of the island of Montreal as well as in the western half of the Outaouais region, where English and French are most nearly on an equal numerical footing, French suffers net language-shift losses to English which are of the same order in 1991 as in 1971. More exactly, *net individual anglicization* of francophones, that is, the shortfall of French home language with respect to French mother tongue, represented, at both censuses, 7 per cent of the francophone population of Montreal's West Island, and 4 per cent of the francophone population in the Outaouais region's Pontiac and Gatineau counties (Castonguay, 1996). Language legislation adopted by the provincial government in the mid-70s does not appear, therefore, to have modified English's edge over French in direct shift between the two principal language groups in Quebec.

However, the share of French in language shift from Quebec's allophone population – which we shall call its *relative francization rate* – has increased significantly from 30 per cent in 1971 to 39 per cent in 1991. Interestingly, this evolution towards greater Francization is the result of diverging trends. While the share of French in language shift among Canadian-born allophones decreased notably from 32 per cent in 1971 to only 24 per cent in 1991, relative francization among allophone immigrants increased more importantly still, from 27 to 48 per cent. The latter trend reflects an important difference in language-shift preferences between immigrants who arrived before Quebec's Quiet Revolution, and more recent newcomers.

According to the 1991 data, relative francization among allophones who had immigrated to Quebec prior to 1966 was only 25 per cent, compared to 42 per cent among those who arrived between 1966 and 1971, and 55 per cent among the 1971–1976 cohort. A profound change in the linguistic composition of allophone immigration to Quebec explains this first and very striking progression: immigration of newcomers more easily drawn to French, such as those of Spanish or Portuguese mother tongue, or hailing from former French colonies or protectorates such as Haiti, Vietnam, Lebanon or Morocco, made up only 7 per cent of allophone immigration before 1966, but quickly rose to over half of allophone immigration by the early 70s, where it has remained since (Castonguay, 1994).

Adopted by the Quebec National Assembly in 1974 and 1977 respectively, Bills 22 and 101 gave a second notable boost to francization, by making public education in French schools compulsory for children of future immigrants to Quebec. This measure can be shown to explain the further increase of relative francization, to 69 per cent among allophones who immigrated to Quebec between 1976 and 1991. In contrast, efforts to make French the common language of work, especially in the Montreal region, do not seem to have had any perceptible impact on allophone language shift (Castonguay, 1994).

If allophone immigration were to be neutral, that is, to have no effect on the balance between English and French in Quebec, four-fifths of those allophones who do adopt a new home language would choose French, leaving one-fifth to English. At 39 per cent in 1991, relative francization in Quebec remains very far from this equilibrium point. Even the relative francization rate of 69 per cent among allophones who arrived since the mid-70s is not quite sufficient to this end. Furthermore, relative francization no longer seems to be increasing: it has remained constant at around 69 per cent for each of the 1976–1981, 1981–1986, and 1986–1991 cohorts of allophone immigrants.

It must also be borne in mind that nine out of ten allophone immigrants choose to reside in the Montreal region, and that three out of four settle in the island of Montreal. Together with highly inadequate francophone fertility in the metropolitan area and francophone migration to surrounding suburbs, this will soon cause the francophone share of the total population on the island of Montreal to fall below 50 per cent (Termote, 1996): francophone children already account for less than 54 per cent of the younger segment of the island's population, and allophone children form the majority in a growing number of the island's French public schools. In such a context, English is used more and more as *lingua franca* between members of different segments of the allophone population. It is therefore a moot point whether French will sustain, in the future, its recent advantage over English among allophone newcomers to Quebec.

In fact, the new power of assimilation of French among recent immigrants remains itself subject to confirmation, as it is based on a rather limited number of cases of language shift. Language maintenance was still the norm in 1991 for close to three-quarters of the 193,300 allophone residents of Quebec who had immigrated between 1976 and 1991. Of the 53,100 who claimed in 1991 to have adopted English or French as a new home language, 16,500 reported shift to English as against 36,600 for French – whence the relative francization rate of 69 per cent. The numbers are small, and, aside from having little demographic bearing on the French majority's reproduction problem, may present a different picture as further shifting takes place. There is some evidence that the power of assimilation of English relative to French increases with length of stay in Quebec (Castonguay, 1994).

ANGLICIZATION TRENDS IN THE REST OF CANADA

Outside Quebec, language-shift trends are easier to follow. Practically all shifting is from French or Other languages to English. On the basis of the data in tables 2.4 and 2.5, the net individual anglicization rate of the overall francophone population in English Canada rose from 27.0 per cent in 1971 to 34.8 per cent in 1991.

Table 2.9 Net anglicization rate of francophones, total population and 35–44 age group, provinces outside Quebec, 1971 and 1991 (percentage)

Province	All ages		Age 35–44	
	1971	1991	1971	1991
Newfoundland	37	53	35	65
Prince Edward Island	40	47	50	55
Nova Scotia	31	41	42	51
New Brunswick	8	8	12	11
Ontario	27	37	38	43
Manitoba	35	51	45	63
Saskatchewan	50	67	60	79
Alberta	51	64	64	74
British Columbia	70	72	77	76

Source: Statistics Canada, 1974, table 11, and 1993a, tables 4 and 5.

A minor part of this increase can be attributed to inflation of minority-language shift caused by the new 1991 questionnaire. A further minor portion can be explained by the ageing of the francophone population. Language shift is indeed an age-specific phenomenon, and usually does not occur among children. As a consequence, a decrease in the relative weight of children in the total population, following a drop in fertility, automatically causes overall language-shift rates to rise. Because of this, it is imperative to compare language-shift rates for specific age groups – and, in order to gauge relevantly the full effect of the phenomenon, to consider adults mature enough to be no longer subject to substantial shifting, yet young enough to bear witness to the intensity of shift in the one or two decades immediately preceding the census. To this end, our comparisons include anglicization rates of francophones aged 35 to 44.

Table 2.9 shows that the net anglicization rate of the overall francophone population has increased in each province outside Quebec, except New Brunswick. Age-specific anglicization among the 35–44 age group also shows a general, though often somewhat lesser, increase, and even a slight decrease in New Brunswick. It can be shown that only a minor part of the latter general increase in age-specific anglicization rates remains due to the inflationary effect of the 1991 questionnaire (Castonguay, 1996).

We may therefore conclude that anglicization of francophones in each province has indeed increased everywhere since 1971, save in New Brunswick. Since Statistics Canada (1992a) considers the language data collected using the new 1991 questionnaire to be of better quality than that of previous censuses, we may also conclude from the last column of table 2.9 that, during the crucial period of transition between childhood and mature adulthood, anglicization has now become the norm among all francophone minorities except in New Brunswick and, for the moment, Ontario.

Closer examination shows that in Ontario's southeastern segment of the Bilingual Belt, net anglicization of francophones aged 35–44 increased from 19 per cent in 1971 to 25 per cent in 1991; among Ontario-born adult francophones in the Ottawa metropolitan area alone, anglicization rose from 25 to 35 per cent. In the northeastern segment, anglicization among mature francophone adults increased from 21 to 32 per cent. Finally, in the remainder of Ontario, similar age-specific anglicization rates rose from 62 to 67 per cent.

On the whole, a wide variety of contemporary trends has favoured increased contact between francophone minorities and the English-speaking majority: urbanization, greater religious tolerance, decline of the primary sector of the economy, higher education and professional mobility, the mass media explosion, information technology, the omnipresence of the Anglo-American continental culture, adoption of North American consumer society values, and the waning sense of French-Canadian nationhood – all have no doubt led together to generally higher anglicization of francophones outside Quebec. Many of these factors were already fully operative decades ago (Joy, 1967).

The New Brunswick exception – at least as regards individual, if not collective, assimilation – confirms the rule. Gradual acquisition over the last three decades of a complete and self-administered French school system has contributed to maintaining a certain minimal distance between New Brunswick francophones and the English-speaking majority. Perhaps constitutional recognition of a distinct French-speaking *community* in New Brunswick, if not of an Acadian nation *per se*, has also played some role in this.

In comparison, the Canadian government has failed to adequately implement French as the language of work for its francophone employees in Canada's capital. More than a quarter of a century after the Royal Commission on Bilingualism and Biculturalism exposed the domination of English as the language of work among francophone federal civil servants in Ottawa, a 1993 survey has confirmed that three out of four French-speaking federal employees in the Ottawa area still use, mainly or exclusively, English in key work situations (Commissioner of Official Languages, 1995). Little wonder, then, that anglicization of francophones has continued apace in the Canadian capital region and, *a fortiori*, in southeastern Ontario.

Collective assimilation rates throw further light on the situation in Ontario. Since fertility is usually lower in large urban centres, the francophone reproduction rate in the Ottawa metropolitan area is only 0.53. As a result, the collective assimilation rate of the francophone population in Ontario's northeast, at 32 per cent, is lower than in the southeast, at 38 per cent. Collective assimilation of francophones is 47 per cent in the Ottawa area alone, and 67 per cent in the rest of the province. Thus, though individual anglicization of francophones in the northeastern portion of the Bilingual Belt is somewhat higher than in the southeast, collective assimilation in the northeast is lower. Nevertheless, the francophone population in the northeast is decreasing through out-migration, due to decline of the mining and forestry sectors of the economy, while that of the southeast has been steadily growing, notably through the hiring of francophones by the federal government. Similar processes have been recorded among francophone minorities in other provinces (Cartwright, 1976).

Comparatively speaking, however, anglicization rates remain relatively low in the two major components of the Bilingual Belt in Ontario and, of course, in New Brunswick. Outside these three regions, the 1991 census shows that 50 per cent or more of francophones have adopted English as the main home language by the time they reach mature adulthood, and collective assimilation rates are generally of a similar order. Excess fertility and francophone out-migration from Quebec are no longer slowing the process which had already been correctly anticipated at the time of the Royal Commission on Bilingualism and Biculturalism: 'Outside Quebec, French will continue to be spoken in the border counties of Ontario and New Brunswick but will virtually disappear from Southern Ontario, the Atlantic Region and the Western Provinces' (Joy, 1967, p. 135).

That the francophone 'language islands' were slated to disappear became even more obvious once information on current language shift was available, following the 1971 census: 'Language shift from French to English ... will probably ultimately result in the virtual disappearance of French in Canada outside Quebec and the border counties' (Kralt, 1976, p. 71); 'We fail to see how these scattered francophones could keep on using French for more than a couple of generations, at least a French language that would have any sort of social significance, without a very large influx of francophones from other areas' (Lachapelle and Henripin, 1982, p. 18).

Though decline also appears inevitable now in the Bilingual Belt outside Quebec and even, because of inadequate fertility, in Quebec itself, the size of the francophone populations involved ensures that French will remain widely spoken as a first language in these areas for the foreseeable future.

OFFICIAL LANGUAGE ASYMMETRY

Census data on ability to speak Canada's official languages are primitive at best. The question is rather vague: 'Can you speak English or French well enough to conduct a conversation?' The answers are entirely subjective and only of the yes/no type.

In 1988, Statistics Canada tested a more precise question, asking whether the respondent could speak English or French well enough to conduct a 'fairly long' conversation 'on different topics'. Compared to the usual formulation, the results showed that the more precise question would considerably reduce self-reported *official bilingualism*, that is, the number of Canadians claiming to be able to speak both English and French. In particular, the number of Quebec francophones reporting ability to speak English would be reduced by one-sixth, while the number of anglophones outside Quebec claiming ability to speak French would be practically halved (Statistics Canada, 1988a). Though it was decided not to use the more precise question in the following census, this information should be borne in mind when interpreting the census data on official bilingualism. The detailed module on language ability and use contained in the 1986 General Social Survey shed a similar light on official bilingualism. The results showed that while 55 per cent of francophones in Canada who claimed to be able to speak English well rated their ability as better than just 'good', only 24 per cent of anglophone Canadians who claimed to speak French well similarly rated their ability as better than 'good' (Statistics Canada, 1988b).

This qualitative asymmetry naturally reflects a better-known quantitative asymmetry in self-reported official bilingualism among anglophones and francophones. Inadequate as they are, the census data showed that, in 1991, 39 per cent of the francophone minority in Canada claimed ability to 'conduct a conversation' in English, compared to only 8 per cent of the anglophone majority who claimed similar ability to speak French. In Quebec, 31 per cent of the francophone majority reported ability to speak English, while 59 per cent of the anglophone minority claimed to speak French. In the rest of Canada, 81 per cent of the francophone minority claimed to speak English, and only 6 per cent of the anglophone majority reported ability to speak French (Statistics Canada, 1993c, table 3). It is worth noting that in Quebec, out-migration of unilingual anglophones has considerably raised reported ability to speak French among those anglophones who have remained.

Quantitative asymmetry is also striking among allophones. In Quebec, 68 per cent claimed to speak English, and 69 per cent French; outside Quebec, 91 per cent claimed to speak English, and only 7 per cent French.

The age structure of official bilingualism suggests an explanation for differences between anglophones and francophones in reported ability to speak the 'other' official language. Among Canadian anglophones in 1991, reported ability to speak French quickly peaks at 17 per cent among the 15–19 age group, then drops away rapidly to 12 per cent at 20–24 and 8 per cent or less for older age groups (Statistics Canada, 1994, table 4.5). A similar structure was visible in earlier census data, and clearly points to school-learning of French, followed by little use of French in the work world. This receives some confirmation from longitudinal comparison of official bilingualism rates for corresponding anglophone birth-cohorts in 1981 and 1991: claims to speak French drop from 10 per cent among anglophones aged 15–24 in 1981, to 8 per cent among the same cohort aged 25–34 in 1991.

The opposite holds among francophones: reported ability to speak English increases regularly, reaching a maximum of 49.5 per cent in the 20–24 age group, and remains above 47 per cent thereafter, only dropping to 43 per cent by the ages of 55–64. This hints at constant usage of English by adult francophones in the work world and, perhaps, growing official bilingualism through higher education. Longitudinal comparison of birth-cohorts shows a continuing increase in the reported ability to speak English beyond adolescence and early adulthood.

Survey results confirm the substantial use of English by francophones in the work world. In the Montreal metropolitan area, 36 per cent of francophones working in the private sector in 1989 claimed to use English frequently at work (*Conseil de la langue française*, 1995). We have seen already that English has remained the usual language of work for most francophone federal civil servants in the Ottawa area. Overall, the 1986 General Social Survey estimated that, outside Quebec, 63 per cent of francophones use mainly or exclusively English at work (Statistics Canada, 1994).

The latter survey found in addition that most francophones outside Quebec use mainly or exclusively English with friends, in medical consultations and for leisure activities. Conversely, anglophones in Quebec generally use English in all of the situations investigated. A staggering linguistic asymmetry persists, furthermore, in federal government services to the public, even after a quarter-century of official bilingualism in Canada. A 1994 survey showed that satisfactory service in French was not available in 35 per cent of offices – such as postal outlets or employment centres – designated to supply federal services in French outside Quebec, whereas satisfactory service in English was available in practically all similar offices designated to offer services in English in Quebec (Bragg, 1995).

Data on language ability from different censuses are not easily compared. Self-reported ability to speak English in Canada has increased regularly from 79 per cent in 1951 to 82 per cent in 1991, while ability to speak French has remained constant at 32 per cent. Underlying these trends, claims to speak only English have remained constant at 67 per cent, while reported ability to speak only French has decreased from 20 to 15 per cent, and claims to speak both English and French have increased from 12 to 16 per cent (Statistics Canada, 1994, table A.3). Part of the apparent increase in official bilingualism is due to the ageing of the Canadian population, since adults are more likely to be bilingual than young children, especially among francophones. An even more important share of the increase may be caused by an enhanced popularity of English–French bilingualism attributable to the Canadian official-languages policy. Self-reporting of an ability is, no doubt, particularly sensitive to social and political context.

BEYOND DUALITY

Tables 2.2 and 2.3 show that although the Canadian allophone population has been rapidly increasing, its overall individual anglicization – and very marginally francization – rate in 1991 was 45 per cent. Age-specific rates among adults are higher still. From the very first census data on individual language shift, it was clear that insofar as the immigrant-language component of the allophone population is concerned 'we can safely say that most of them are doomed: they or their children will be using English at home within the next few decades ... This group has no specifically Canadian existence: it can only maintain itself by migratory inflow from other countries' (Lachapelle and Henripin, 1982, pp. 20 and 174).

Indeed, collective assimilation rates for immigrant-language populations appear decisive: 79 per cent among the highly urban Italian mother-tongue population, 64 per cent for the more often rural German-speaking minority, and even 44 per cent among the more recently arrived Chinese mother-tongue population (Statistics Canada, 1992a, table 4). Only certain Aboriginal-language populations appear firmly rooted, in that they are not undergoing collective assimilation. The intergenerational reproduction rate in 1991 was 1.15 for the Cree-speaking population, and 1.67 for the Inuktitut mother-tongue minority.

Language statistics show, therefore, that in all likelihood, language duality in Canada will continue to wane, making way for an ethnically more diversified, yet more broadly English-speaking population. This is having a profound impact on Canadian identity, including at the political level.

References

Beaujot, R. and McQuillan, K. (1982). *Growth and Dualism: The Demographic Development of Canadian Society*. Toronto: Gage.

Bragg, M. (1995). *Service to the Public: A Study of Federal Offices Designated to Respond to the Public in Both English and French*. Ottawa: Office of the Commissioner of Official Languages.

Caldwell, G. (1974). *A Demographic Profile of English-speaking Quebec 1921–1971*. Quebec: International Centre for Research on Bilingualism.

Cartwright, D. G. (1976). *Language Zones in Canada: A Reference Supplement to the Report of the Second Bilingual Districts Advisory Board*. Ottawa: Information Canada.

(1980). *Official Language Populations in Canada: Patterns and Contacts*. Montreal: Institute for Research on Public Policy.

Castonguay, C. (1994). *L'Assimilation linguistique: mesure et évolution 1971–1986*. Quebec: Conseil de la langue française.

(1996). Assimilation trends among official-language minorities, 1971–1991. In *Towards the XXIst Century: Emerging Socio-Demographic Trends and Political Issues in Canada* (pp. 201–205). Ottawa: Federation of Canadian Demographers.

Commissioner of Official Languages. (1995). *Annual Report 1994*. Ottawa.

Conseil de la langue française. (1995). *Indicateurs de la langue de travail au Québec*. Quebec.

Joy, R. J. (1967). *Languages in Conflict: The Canadian Experience*. Ottawa: published by the author. Reprinted in 1972 by McClelland and Stewart, Toronto.

Kralt, J. (1976). *Language in Canada*. Ottawa: Statistics Canada.

Lachapelle, R. and Henripin, J. (1982). *The Demolinguistic Situation in Canada: Past Trends and Future Prospects*. Montreal: Institute for Research on Public Policy.

Lieberson, S. (1965). Bilingualism in Montreal: A demographic analysis. *American Journal of Sociology, 71*, 10–25.

(1970). *Language and Ethnic Relations in Canada*. New York: Wiley.

Royal Commission on Bilingualism and Biculturalism. (1967). *Report, Book I: The Official Languages*. Ottawa: The Queen's Printer.

(1969). *Report, Book IV: The Cultural Contribution of the Other Ethnic Groups*. Ottawa: The Queen's Printer.

Statistics Canada. (1974). *Language by Age Groups*. Ottawa.

(1988a). *National Census Test*. Ottawa.

(1988b). *The 1986 General Social Survey: Language Module Preliminary Data*. Ottawa.

(1992a). *Mother Tongue: 20% Sample Data*. Ottawa.

(1992b). *Mother Tongue*. Ottawa.

(1993a). *Home Language and Mother Tongue.* Ottawa.

(1993b). *Ethnic Origin.* Ottawa.

(1993c). *Knowledge of Languages.* Ottawa.

(1994). *Languages in Canada.* Scarborough: Prentice-Hall.

Termote, M. (1994). *L'Avenir démolinguistique du Québec et de ses régions.* Quebec: Conseil de la langue française.

(1996). Tendances démolinguistiques au Canada et implications politiques. In *Towards the XXIst Century: Emerging Socio-Demographic Trends and Political Issues in Canada* (pp. 161–172). Ottawa: Federation of Canadian Demographers.

Termote, M. and Gauvreau, D. (1988). *La situation démolinguistique au Québec.* Quebec: Conseil de la langue française.

3 Official bilingualism: from the 1960s to the 1990s

Kenneth McRae

While Canada's federal system could lay claim to some elements of a language policy before the 1960s, the content of this policy was quite narrow. It consisted mainly in guarantees of rights to use English and French in the federal Parliament, federal courts, the Quebec legislature and Quebec courts. The vast bulk of citizen contacts with federal authorities was untouched by law or regulation. In the 1960s, this situation would change. A primary reason was the 'Quiet Revolution' in Quebec, which not only transformed and modernized society, but also led to fundamental questioning of the position of Quebec in Canada and of the language situation in both these jurisdictions. In a wider sense, the decade of the 1960s was a period of rapidly expanding contacts between citizens and governments throughout Canada because of an expanding welfare state.

THE ROYAL COMMISSION ON BILINGUALISM AND BICULTURALISM

When the Liberals returned to power after the federal general election of 1963, one of the first acts of the Pearson government was to establish a Royal Commission on Bilingualism and Biculturalism to study these growing linguistic and political strains in some depth. Also known as the Laurendeau–Dunton Commission, it was one of a series of large-scale public policy investigations that have marked the Canadian political landscape (beginning with the landmark Rowell–Sirois Royal Commission on Dominion–Provincial Relations of 1937). Unlike its predecessors, however, the Laurendeau–Dunton Commission was a meticulously balanced group of five predominantly French-speaking and five predominantly English-speaking members. Further, in recognition of other language groups in Canada, one of the five francophones was of Polish origin and one of the five anglophones was of Ukrainian origin.

The terms of reference of the inquiry were specified by the government. In general, the commission was asked to inquire into and report upon the existing state of bilingualism and biculturalism in Canada and to recommend what steps should be taken to develop the Canadian Confederation on the basis of an equal partnership between the two founding races, taking into account the contribution made by the other ethnic groups to the cultural enrichment of Canada and the measures that should be taken to safeguard that contribution.

More particularly, it was asked to report and make recommendations: (a) on 'the situation and practice of bilingualism' within all federal agencies, and how 'to ensure the bilingual and basically bicultural character of the federal administration'; (b) on the role of 'public and private organizations', including the mass media, in promoting bilingualism and better intercultural understanding; (c) on opportunities to learn English and French and 'what could be done to enable Canadians to become bilingual'. In recognition of the provinces' constitutional jurisdiction over education, this third topic was to be pursued through discussion with the provincial governments (RCBB, 1967–70, 1, pp. 173–74).

As the commission was soon to discover, these terms of reference contained a number of snares and pitfalls. The unfortunate reference to 'the two founding races' could only be construed as a linguistic anachronism – or possibly a mistranslation of the more innocuous phrase in the French version, *les deux peuples qui l'ont fondée* – but much of the animosity that it generated was directed towards the commission itself. More than any other single factor, the implication of two charter groups, somehow differentiated from other citizens, led to a massive mobilization of briefs and presentations, by associations and individuals from other ethnic groups, contesting any such view of Canadian society. Encouraging and promoting individual bilingualism, almost equally contentious, was soon perceived to be not central to the problem of developing bilingual public institutions. Discussions with provincial governments opened up further areas of disagreement and divergent policy priorities. As the commission's work proceeded, it focused increasingly on the key phrase of 'equal partnership' between the two main speech communities and the ways in which such a partnership could be understood and implemented.

The Laurendeau–Dunton Commission went through the normal stages of a major royal commission, receiving more than 400 formal briefs, holding public hearings across the country, commissioning some 165 research studies, and meeting with provincial governments to discuss educational policy. Its final report appeared in six volumes between 1967 and 1970. Early in 1964, however, it had held a series of twenty-three informal meetings across the country to explain its purpose and to assess the concerns of the public. This led in 1965 to the publication of a *Preliminary Report* which drew attention to sharply divergent public perceptions and warned – a full three decades before the close 1995 Quebec referendum on sovereignty – that Canada was 'passing through the greatest crisis in its history' (RCBB, 1965, p. 13).

The first volume of the final *Report*, published in 1967, centred upon the two official languages and their legal recognition and protection. The most important of its fourteen recommendations called for their official recognition, not only in Parliament and the federal courts, as previously, but throughout the federal government and administration. Similar recognition was urged upon the governments of New Brunswick and Ontario, the two provinces with the largest francophone minorities. A regime of full linguistic equality was proposed for all levels of government in the federal capital area, which straddles the border between Ontario and Quebec. To provide appropriate bilingual services else-where, the commission recommended a system of bilingual districts similar to those existing in Finland, to be established in areas or regions where the official-language minorities attained 10 per cent or more of the population. As in Finland, these districts would be reviewed after each decennial census, in order to adjust their boundaries to demolinguistic changes. Finally, it suggested that these provisions be adopted and secured by a federal law on official languages, constitutional guarantees for language rights in bilingual districts, and the cre-ation of a post of Commissioner of Official Languages as a sort of ombudsman for language policy and its application (RCBB, 1967–70, 1, pp. 147–49).

Although Book 1 of the final *Report* treats equality between the two official languages in a general and symbolic way, the more specialized language issues were elaborated in Books 2, 3, 4 and 5. Book 2, devoted to education, developed detailed recommendations on minority-language schooling and on second-language learning. The commission emphasized the importance of mother-tongue education, and recommended that it be made generally available for the official-language minorities in the newly proposed bilingual districts and in major metropolitan centres. In recognition of provincial jurisdiction over schooling, it recommended partial federal financial assistance to the provinces for minority-language education, but only enough to cover the additional costs of providing an educational stream in the other official language. Further recommendations in this volume called for obligatory study of the second official language as a subject, for all pupils, with a gradual expansion of programmes from the early primary grades to the end of the secondary cycle.

Book 3 was a detailed inquiry into the working world, divided into two volumes that addressed the public and private sectors separately. For the federal public service and the armed forces, the commission's research found a public sector that had been functioning almost exclusively in English, and according to English-Canadian norms, except for services delivered in Quebec. The problem, as visualized by the commission, was to develop a federal public sector that would be as accessible to unilingual francophones as it was to unilingual anglophones in terms of entry and career development. To this end it proposed the establishment of some operating units in which the normal language of work would be French, though it explicitly rejected the notion of full-scale parallel structures, as exemplified in Belgium. Such a change required comprehensive translation of internal forms, manuals and documents, and also appropriate development of personal bilingualism in senior ranks and in positions involving public contact in both languages. Since the starting point for many anglophones was effectively unilingualism, this implied a need for massive language training to meet these objectives. This first volume of Book 3 contains a detailed prescription for the public service and the armed forces to orient them towards these objectives (RCBB, 1967–70, 3A).

For the private sector, the major problem was seen to be a Quebec industrial structure that had been operating largely in English at senior management levels, and that posed serious entry and promotion barriers for francophone graduates of the rapidly modernizing Quebec educational system. The highlight of Book 3B was Recommendation 42, which called for French to become the 'principal language of work at all levels' of the Quebec industrial system, especially in major enterprises, though the same section noted also that smaller firms should be able to operate in English in Quebec or in French elsewhere in Canada. The vehicle for developing and implementing such policies, the commission suggested, should be provincial task forces in Quebec, Ontario and New Brunswick. Enterprises outside Quebec, said another recommendation, should develop appropriate bilingual marketing capacity within that province (RCBB, 1967–70, 3B).

Book 4 focused on other ethnic groups and on languages other than English or French. Some of its recommendations were not directly on language. The provinces were encouraged to make greater efforts to remove ethnic and religious discrimination in employment and housing. Certain federal agencies were asked to project a more visible, positive image of Canada's growing population of non-British and non-French origins. On the language side, the commission asked for wider teaching of languages other than English and French in schools where sufficient demand existed. It also recommended that existing restrictions on the use of languages other than English or French in both public and private broadcasting should be eased (RCBB, 1967–70, 4).

Two further books of the report were published in 1970 in a single volume. Book 5 recommended that the federal capital area should be developed on the basis of strict equality between the two official languages and a more balanced distribution of federal resources and buildings between the Ontario and Quebec sectors of the capital region. Book 6 dealt with voluntary associations, avoiding direct recommendations to these bodies but describing alternative patterns of cooperation and integration and the role of these bodies in enhancing communication across Canadian society.

The original plan for the commission's final *Report*, as outlined in the Preface to Book 1, had envisaged four additional books, which would focus on federal institutions (Parliament, the Cabinet, the Supreme Court), on arts and letters, on the mass media and, finally, a general conclusion that would 'offer a synthesis of our views' and 'approach important constitutional questions concerning the relations and future of the two societies' (RCBB, 1967–70, 1, pp. xvii–xviii). These four books were never completed. By 1970 the commissioners were feeling the strain of seven years of intensive effort, many senior staff members had dispersed, and financial stringency had become a problem, with the Trudeau government pressing for early termination of the work. More important, when the commissioners met early in 1970 to consider a final statement, it became clear that no consensus existed on the political and constitutional issues. These four books, had they been completed, would doubtless have added some further recommendations on institutional bilingualism, but they would probably have given more emphasis to the implications of biculturalism and to political and constitutional aspects of equal partnership. As it happened, the initiative in these topics left unfinished by the Laurendeau–Dunton Commission was next entrusted to the Pepin–Roberts Task Force on Canadian Unity in 1977, by which date Quebec electors had chosen a government committed to sovereignty and a looser form of association with Canada.

IMPLEMENTING A MORE COMPREHENSIVE LANGUAGE POLICY

Meanwhile, attention focused on implementation of the proposals of the Laurendeau–Dunton Commission. The commission had recommended a broad range of language-related reforms, and their implementation can be traced in five major directions: (a) more extensive formal recognition of English and French as official languages of Canada; (b) restructuring of the public service and other federal institutions to adjust to this recognition of official bilingualism; (c) reforms to provincial education systems to aid official-language minority schools and to encourage study of the other official language; (d) promotion of French as the main language of work in the Quebec private sector; (e) elaboration of a cultural policy consonant with the growing cultural diversity of Canada. Of these five topics, changes in education and the working world have been implemented primarily at the provincial level and will be dealt with in later chapters. The development of federal cultural policy, which since 1971 has diverged significantly from the commission's own views, will be examined in the next chapter. The present chapter will therefore emphasize the first two of these directions: the legal recognition of official bilingualism and its consequences for the federal public service.

Statutory recognition and entrenchment of language rights

Even before the appearance of Book 3 of the commission's *Report*, the federal government introduced legislation to implement several recommendations from Book 1. The Official Languages Act of 1969 was a landmark statute that recognized English and French as official languages on the basis of legal equality for all purposes of the federal government (and not, as hitherto, for legislative and judicial purposes only). It required that a comprehensive range of external and internal documents, notices, decisions, and forms be published in both languages, and within deadlines specified according to the type of document. It established obligations for federal departments and agencies to provide services in both languages in the Ottawa–Hull area (the National Capital Region) and in a series of bilingual districts to be proclaimed later. Outside these officially bilingual areas, services to the public were to be available in the predominant language of the region, English or French. The bilingual districts were a key feature of the *Report* and were soon to prove a source of difficulties, for several reasons that will be explored more fully below. Finally, the 1969 Act established a Commissioner of Official Languages as a linguistic auditor and ombudsman, to oversee application of the act by federal agencies, to receive and investigate complaints, to initiate independent studies of problem areas, and to report annually on these matters to Parliament.

The 1969 Act was an ordinary statute, and its language provisions were not constitutionally entrenched. The opportunity for entrenchment of language rights arose during the repatriation from Britain of the original federal constitution, the 1867 British North America Act. This process, completed in 1982 after prolonged negotiations, was the occasion for development and adoption of a general Canadian Charter of Rights and Freedoms. In addition to more conventional human rights, this incorporated separate constitutional guarantees for language equality and minority-language education. Sections 16 to 20 of the Charter guarantee the equal status of English and French as official languages in the Parliament and government of Canada, and in federal courts. Members of the public are given the right to use either official language in communications with the head office of any federal department or agency, and with any other office where 'there is significant demand' or even where 'it is reasonable' due to the 'nature of the office'. The same sections include corresponding guarantees concerning the legislature, government, and court system of New Brunswick, guarantees incorporated into the Charter by provincial request.

While the sections of the Charter on language equality confer rights very broadly, the rights to minority-language education in English or French in Section 23 are curiously circumscribed. They are open only to Canadian citizens, and only to those whose mother tongue, or whose language of elementary education – if received *in Canada* – is that of the minority language in question. It is the *children* of such citizens, and also siblings of children already in the system or qualified for it, who may receive primary and secondary minority-language schooling, but this entitlement applies only in areas where their numbers are sufficient to warrant provision of public funds for minority-language instruction. The entire text of Section 23 is a contradictory tangle of privileges and exclusions that resonate more of narrow intergovernmental bargaining than of general human rights.[1] It is also a reminder that reliance on the principle of personality – rather than territoriality – in the allocation of rights can lead not to freedom of choice, as is sometimes assumed (Goreham, 1994), but to invidious discrimination between groups that qualify and others that do not.

Restructuring the federal public service

The second area of federal response to official bilingualism lay in adapting the public service to the needs of a new language regime. Here we encounter a complex pattern of experimentation and change that characterizes the years following adoption of the Official Languages Act of 1969. To trace these years in evolutionary detail would go well beyond the scope of this chapter. Indeed, a thorough knowledge of these developments appears to be a narrow preserve of the managers and control agencies that have guided them. There is a striking lack of informed research and evaluation by outside researchers. One can, however, identify three major components of policy in this period: external service to the public in both official languages; balanced participation of anglophones and francophones in the public service; and freedom of choice in the language of work. These three areas can be linked in turn to various supporting programmes, such as second-language training and testing, translation, and payment of a bonus for bilingualism.

As early as April 1966, some three years before the Laurendeau–Dunton Commission published its volumes on the working world, Prime Minister Pearson announced the government's objectives concerning language policy in the public service. This statement emphasized expanded personal bilingualism at both senior and lower levels, service to the public in the client's own language, the right of public servants to work in either official language, and recognition of the 'linguistic and cultural values' of both language groups in civil service recruitment and training. In order to develop the 'bicultural character of the civil service in the national capital', the statement also promised early establishment of French-language secondary education in the Ottawa area (reprinted in RCBB, 1967–70, 3A, pp. 353–355). By implication at least, this statement touched on the three primary elements of later public service policy: service to the public, balanced participation, and the right to work in either official language. The question for the Royal Commission therefore became how to achieve these objectives, and its detailed recommendations for the public service and the armed forces in Book 3A were developed with these aims in view.

The goal most easily understood, and considered most urgent, was that of serving the public in either official language at the option of the client. The 1969 Official Languages Act, by giving the public a general right to use either English or French in communications with the federal government, created corresponding obligations for the public service to respond and serve in either language. Bilingual services, however, were not offered everywhere. At first it was recommended and planned to offer them at the headquarters of federal agencies, departments and in the bilingual districts proposed for areas where the official-language minority reached 10 per cent or more. When the concept of these bilingual districts was delayed and later abandoned, federal authorities proceeded by internal administrative regulation to develop their own criteria for provision of bilingual services to the public, beginning with the head offices of all federal agencies, whether inside or outside the capital region. In place of bilingual districts, the 1982 Charter of Rights listed more subjective criteria of 'significant demand' and 'the nature of the office' as benchmarks for providing service in both official languages.

Around these general concepts grew up a highly complex web of administrative regulation to specify *where* and *what* offices or functions would be required to offer bilingual services. Under 'significant demand' a range of conditions is spelled out for all kinds of localities, ranging from major metropolitan areas to villages with official-language minorities of 200 persons or fewer. Variable criteria in several combinations determine the number of local offices and the types of service that must be offered in each locality. Other specific rules apply to federal transportation carriers, air terminals, railway stations, significant border crossings, and ancillary private concessionaires in terminals or carriers. Bilingual services required on grounds of 'the nature of the office' are specified for embassies abroad, national parks, some federal offices in the Yukon and Northwest Territories, major border crossings, and a range of activities linked to the health, safety and security of the public (*Official Languages Regulations*, 1994). Taken together, this dense network of regulations savours more of bureaucratic complexity than of basic principles to appeal to the general public.

The second policy component, balanced participation, was studied extensively by the Laurendeau–Dunton Commission. It reported that under examination procedures and cultural norms inspired primarily by anglophone educational practices, the participation of francophones in the federal public service had declined from an estimated 22 per cent in 1918 to 13 per cent in 1946 (RCBB, 1967–70, 3A). A major concern of the commission, and of continuing federal policy since then, was to bring about a reasonable balance between official languages in the public-sector work force. In this effort the central focus has been less on lower level positions, which are mainly recruited locally and thus reflect the local population base, than on managerial and scientific posts. For the public service as a whole, the proportion of employees having French as their first official language rose from 23 per cent in 1974 to 28 per cent in 1984 and then remained constant into the mid-1990s. In attaining these levels the departmental public service increased by 25 per cent, from 183,000 in 1974 to 228,000 in 1984, representing an increase of 17 per cent for anglophones and 50 per cent for francophones. By 1995 the total had been downsized back to 207,000. For the entire federal work force of 439,000 in 1994–95 (including Crown corporations and armed forces), the proportion of francophones was 27 per cent (Treasury Board, 1994–95).

These levels of participation have been achieved without recourse to formal quotas, which have been repeatedly repudiated as incompatible with the merit system. A closer study of participation data does indeed show somewhat larger anomalies than in the countrywide averages at the level of regions, occupational categories, and individual departments or agencies. But, conversely, recent participation levels are not merely fortuitous. To all appearances they are a result of planned, deliberate 'staffing strategy' aimed at a reasonably proportionate participation of anglophone and francophone employees (in terms of their preferred working language) in each broad occupational category, in each department or agency, and in each of the major regions (Treasury Board, 1991–92).[2]

A major instrument for managing and shaping official bilingualism in the public service has been the designation of all positions in four categories: bilingual, English-essential, French-essential, and either English- or French-essential. Bilingual designation predates the Laurendeau–Dunton Commission, and payment of a bonus of $50 per year for bilingual capability can be traced as early as 1888. The Royal Commission found 9 per cent of federal positions designated as bilingual in 1966. Of these 15,800 bilingual positions, 44 per cent were in the Ottawa–Hull capital area and a further 49 per cent were in Quebec outside the capital region. As a result of subsequent development of the system, the overall proportion of bilingual positions rose to 21 per cent in 1974 and 29 per cent in 1995, while the proportion of job incumbents who met the linguistic requirements of their posts rose from 70 per cent in 1978 to 91 per cent in 1995 (RCBB, 1967–70, 3A; Treasury Board, 1994–95). The system of linguistic designation has been further developed and refined by grading for levels of proficiency – minimum (A), intermediate (B), or superior (C) – and also by language function, so that each bilingual position may be given a sextuple profile by department officials (e.g., CBB/CBB for reading, writing, and oral interaction skills in English and French respectively). This process, like many others, is not immune to the usual manipulations of organizational politics.

The third policy component, the right to work in the official language of one's choice, is at once the most nebulous and difficult to implement. The issue of language choice was explicitly recognized as early as 1966 in the Pearson statement to Parliament, where it was founded on an assumption that passive bilingualism – that is, an ability to read and understand the other official language – would become 'normal practice' in the public service. To make this ideal workable, the Laurendeau–Dunton Commission recommended the creation of a series of French-language units with a variety of functions in all departments and agencies, units that would be large and viable enough to introduce French as a working language into a milieu that had hitherto operated overwhelmingly in English. Such units were established beginning in 1970 and at their peak involved some 28,000 public servants, but they proved shortlived. They were soon abandoned, amid mixed perceptions that they had provided a sufficient impetus to introduce French as a language of work but constituted a possible obstacle to career advancement from the standpoint of those working in them (Beaty, 1988; Robichaud, 1983).

In spite of ongoing difficulties of implementation, the right of employees to work in either official language was spelled out in the revised Official Languages Act of 1988. But there are important limitations. The right to choose one's language of work exists only in the National Capital Region and in designated bilingual regions. These were first established administratively in 1973, after plans for statutory census-based bilingual districts were delayed. After later adjustments, bilingual regions currently include: parts of northern and eastern Ontario and western Quebec; the Montreal area; the Eastern Townships and Gaspé; and the province of New Brunswick. All regions not so designated are unilingual – in English or French – for purposes of internal communication, though federal offices may still be obliged to provide services to the public in some localities in both official languages. In a case of conflict, the right of the public to choose the language of service prevails over the right of public servants to choose their language of work, and even other public servants have statutory rights to receive certain departmental services, work instruments, data systems, and supervisory contacts in their own language.

Beyond these formal rights and restrictions, however, some exploratory research has been undertaken for the Commissioner of Official Languages on small focus groups of public servants from Ottawa and Montreal. The results suggest that subtle differences in psychological and psycholinguistic climate and in the working milieu have combined to maintain English in Ottawa and French in Montreal as the normal, preferred, expected, and thus dominant language of work in these two cities, and to make innovative use of the minority language in either city abnormal and professionally risky for the individuals involved. Discussions in these groups suggested a considerable gap between the formal policy of free choice and a more complex social reality of everyday language contacts (Hay Management Consultants, 1993; Heller, 1993).

As noted earlier, the policy of official bilingualism in the public service has been aided and complemented by key support services: language training and testing, a pay bonus for bilingualism, expanded translation and interpretation. The first language training courses were established by the Public Service Commission as early as 1964, but after the 1969 Official Languages Act such training became a minor growth industry and a major agent of change. Although training programmes were at first expected to be temporary, experience through the 1980s and policy revisions in November 1988 appear to confirm their permanence. The quantity of training provided, either through the government directly or by approved private suppliers, was 1.5 million hours in 1994–95, down slightly from an average of 1.9 million for the three years preceding (Treasury Board, 1988–89, 1994–95; Tsai, 1989). Figures for individual recipients are difficult to establish, because these programmes are developed by individual departments according to their own priorities. They have expanded to cover not only basic second-language learning up to the levels prescribed for testing but also a variety of shorter courses and workshops for special situations. These include training to improve employee skills in oral or written situations in either their first or second official language, as needed. Employees in designated bilingual positions who meet the requisite language levels receive a bilingual bonus of $800 per year, an amount unchanged since the bonus principle was reinstituted in 1977.

The translation of parliamentary and public documents predates the Confederation of 1867, but only in 1934 were the parliamentary and departmental translators grouped and organized in a Translation Bureau under the Secretary of State. At that date fewer than 100 translators were responsible for House of Commons debates, departmental annual reports, and other documents. Prior to this rationalization, about a third of government publications were translated into French, some with delays of two years or more after the appearance of the English version. In 1958, the Diefenbaker government introduced simultaneous interpretation of debates in the House of Commons. The 1969 Official Languages Act signalled more important changes, including a vastly increased volume of work and heightened concern for the strong predominance of English-to-French translation. The staff of the Translation Bureau rose from 74 in 1934 to 320 by 1964, and to 1,900 by 1978. Its budget rose from $2 million in 1964 to $82 million by 1984, and the volume of translation from 1984 to 1995 averaged about 238 million words per year. Beyond its more routine work, the Bureau has developed a massive English–French terminology bank and has experimented with computer assisted translation (Delisle, 1985; Treasury Board, 1994–95).

It is these major support programmes – translation, language training, and the bilingual bonus – that account for the largest part of the direct cost of official bilingualism at the federal level. Official figures for the 1994–95 fiscal year show $128 million for translation by the Bureau and other departments or agencies, $72 million for language training, and $87 million for the bilingual bonus – or about 90 per cent of the total direct cost of $319 million (Treasury Board, 1994–95).

BILINGUAL DISTRICTS: AN IDEA ADOPTED AND ABANDONED

The Laurendeau-Dunton Commission, having studied the notion of flexible bilingual districts as they had developed under Finland's Language Law of 1922, recommended their adoption in similar form in Canada. They were described as 'the cornerstone of our proposed system ... a just, flexible, and realistic system which does not impose rigid rules and unjustified obligations on anyone' (RCBB, 1967–70, 1, p. 116). As noted earlier, they were adopted formally in the 1969 Official Languages Act, apparently with little or no further research on the dynamics of their history in Finland itself. As in Finland, the Canadian legislation called for decennial boundary reviews based on demolinguistic changes, and these were to be carried out by an *ad hoc* Bilingual Districts Advisory Board after each complete census. The first such board was appointed in 1970 but it reported just three months prior to the 1971 census. Its report was contentious in Quebec, and the government elected to wait. The report of the second board, delayed until late 1975, was even more contentious, and again the government vacillated until 1977, when it announced that it would not proceed with bilingual districts as recognized by the Official Languages Act. These developments deserve closer scrutiny for what they reveal about federal language policy.

The Laurendeau–Dunton Commission was explicit in explaining its choice of Finland as a model. In a chapter devoted to the theoretical options facing them, the commissioners explained and rejected the principle of linguistic territoriality, as practised in Belgium or the Swiss cantons, arguing that territoriality 'would run counter to deep historical and social realities in our country' and was more appropriate for European countries with ancient linguistic frontiers. They also rejected, though more reluctantly, the alternative principle of personality as then practised in South Africa, on the practical grounds that (a) Canada's two major language groups were more separated geographically, and (b) that Canada fell far short of South Africa's high levels of personal bilingualism that made the personality system possible. The commissioners clearly felt that Finland, with its adjustable combination of personality and territoriality, represented more closely the appropriate middle way for Canada. Such a regime was consonant with the Commission's general outlook: '*We take as a guiding principle the recognition of both official languages, in law and in practice, wherever the minority is numerous enough to be viable as a group*' (RCBB, 1967–70, 1, pp. 84–86; italics in original text).

The underlying thought or assumption behind this choice, though never stated explicitly, appears to have been that the official-language minorities constituted a force for integration in the Canadian federal system and, indeed, the results of commission surveys showed that both anglophone respondents in Quebec and francophones outside Quebec were more strongly oriented towards federal politics than were their counterpart majority groups. Further, commission research had highlighted below-average mobility of francophone *Québécois* to other provinces as a major obstacle to francophone business careers, but there was some hope and expectation that interprovincial mobility would increase under a more liberal language regime. Finally, one may note that five of the ten commissioners, two francophones and three anglophones, were connected with the official-language minorities by their background or professional affiliation or both.

In transplanting the concept of bilingual districts to a new setting, Canadian lawmakers ran into several special problems. While Finland's entire territory was divided into municipalities or communes, Canada had vast unorganized areas, and no countrywide unit of local government. The result was that Bilingual Districts Advisory Boards had a vast discretion in selecting boundaries, a freedom that increased the level of politicization of their task. A second problem, which can only be described as a legislative error, was to make bilingual services from federal regional offices compulsory only when *the office itself* was in a bilingual district – whereas in Finland the requirement is that the resident population of a bilingual district must be served in either language regardless of the location of the office providing service.

A third and more fundamental problem lay in adapting bilingual districts to federalism, an issue for which the case of Finland offered no guidance. Here the commission recommended – and the 1969 legislation in turn required – a process of consultation designed to achieve federal-provincial agreement on bilingual-district boundaries. The aims were to establish a symmetrical country-wide system and, at the same time, to reinforce the minorities' linguistic and cultural security. On this point the federal side seriously misjudged the political dynamics of the situation. The outcome from the advisory board reports was a patchwork of proposed dissimilar districts that represented the triumph of certain provincial priorities over federal ones.

The first Bilingual Districts Advisory Board, appointed in February 1970, used census data of 1961 that were nine years old. It reported quickly, briefly, and unanimously in March 1971, just prior to the 1971 census. By stretching the criteria a little for outlying small minorities in British Columbia and Newfoundland, it was able to recommend thirty-seven bilingual districts located in all ten provinces. It also recommended that the entire provinces of New Brunswick and Quebec become bilingual districts, even though a normal reading of the 1969 statute and the census data would have suggested extensive unilingual areas in both cases. To explain its departure from normal practice in New Brunswick, the board cited the relative size of that province's linguistic minority and the importance of the southern cities (Fredericton and Saint John) as centres for providing federal services and absorbing labour from other parts of the province. For Quebec, it praised the province's historic tolerance and generosity in language matters and 'considered that there was nothing to be gained' by restricting that tradition to a smaller territory. The board acknowledged its use of variable standards for different provinces, fending off future critics by noting that 'the legislative text is sufficiently flexible to make it possible to obey the spirit rather than the letter of the law'. This observation was correct, but it did not augur well for the future (BDAB, 1971; McRae, 1978, pp. 340–41).

The second Bilingual Districts Advisory Board, appointed in May 1972, encountered serious problems and did not report until October 1975. In some respects, it followed in the footsteps of the first board. It retained bilingual status for the whole of New Brunswick, as had been urged by the provincial government, and it recommended bilingual districts approximately as before for seven of the eight other predominantly anglophone provinces, British Columbia excepted. It also proposed innovative solutions for official-language minorities of 5,000 or more in cities, and for all provincial capitals regardless of minority size, because of their role in providing provincial and federal services. However, this board encountered rock-hard opposition from the Quebec government, which contested the very principle of federal language legislation as an infringement of provincial jurisdiction. In responding to this challenge, the board itself become seriously divided over a fundamental issue: whether the same or different standards should be applied to Quebec and to predominantly anglophone provinces. In the board's own language,

> Some members … were convinced that … all areas that had a statutory right to be recommended as bilingual districts should be treated in similar fashion, regardless of other considerations.
>
> After lengthy and intensive discussions in the Board, a majority of the members concluded that while they supported in general the principles of legal right and parity, there were occasions in which, when bilingual districts were being considered, greater attention should be paid to factors other than legal entitlement and parity. These factors included the different position of the French and English minorities … the question of the actual need for a bilingual district to ensure bilingual services, the possibility of there being an alternative means to provide such services, and the existence of particular local conditions. (BDAB, 1975, pp. 33–34)

What stands out at many points in this second report is a shift in fundamental emphasis, from a primary concern for individual speakers of the official languages to a concern for the position of the languages themselves, not only in the federal government but in Canadian society generally. Because of past and continuing language disparity, the board saw its role as 'redressing the existing imbalance in the provision of services in the French language'. The strategy for rectifying the disparity, in the majority view, was to create bilingual districts more generously for francophone minorities outside Quebec and more sparingly for anglophone minorities within Quebec, where the majority language was under greater pressure. To this end the board majority recommended five bilingual districts for anglophone minorities in outlying areas of Quebec – districts similar to those for rural francophone minorities outside Quebec – but decided not to recommend such a district for the 595,000 anglophones of metropolitan Montreal, or for several other Quebec towns and cities with anglophone minorities that met the census criterion, suggesting that their service needs could be met in other, less obtrusive ways. The pressures on French in North America were indeed well documented from many sources, but there was nothing in the 1969 statute to justify such a radical departure from symmetry of treatment. This point was emphasized forcefully by three of the four dissenting board members (BDAB, 1975; McRae, 1978).

The linguistic activism of the board's majority led to an insoluble political stalemate. By a strange irony, the minister who introduced the report at its tabling in Parliament on 21 November 1975, was the member for Westmount, the most solidly anglophone constituency of metropolitan Montreal. In his first remarks, he announced the government's rejection of the board's double standard and promised a review of all Quebec areas 'using the same approach and principles' as for bilingual districts elsewhere in Canada. However, the government's freedom of action on this issue was sharply reduced by the election in November 1976 of a separatist provincial government committed to the independence of Quebec. In 1977 the federal government announced its intention of abandoning the concept of bilingual districts, which meant that after publication of the 1981 census results, the Trudeau government was directly contravening its own 1969 legislation by not appointing another board.

THE OFFICIAL LANGUAGES ACT OF 1988

The difficulties and eventual abandonment of the bilingual district idea were not the only problem of federal language policy in the 1980s. The 1969 act had brought various legal cases before the courts and some of these had been decided in ways that limited the force of the legislation. Key decisions had held that the statute was essentially declaratory of the status of official languages and that it lacked executory force. The adoption of the Charter of Rights in 1982 changed the orientation from institutional obligations to individual rights, and after 1982 the government established a general review of earlier federal laws to assess their conformity with the Charter. In addition, the management of official bilingualism within the public service had evolved a long way since 1969. In 1985 the government therefore decided on a general process of policy analysis, consultation, legislative drafting, and parliamentary committee hearings to arrive at a completely revised Official Languages Act, which became law in 1988 (Low, 1989).

The 1988 Act differs substantially from its predecessor. In the first place, it is longer and more comprehensive, requiring thirty-five pages of double-column bilingual text, compared to twenty-one for the 1969 Act. The text has a noticeably different quality, clearly rooted in management experience, segmented into well-defined sections according to established policy objectives. Unlike the 1969 Act, which contained no introduction or preamble, the 1988 Act begins with a two-page preamble that refers to constitutional requirements, philosophical principles of equality, and policy goals. At first glance, the 1969 languages Act could be likened to an architect's design for a future project, the 1988 law to an engineer's operations manual for an ongoing system. A closer inspection, however, will show that some sections of the 1988 Act look beyond day-to-day operations.

After the preamble, a brief statement of purpose, and a section on key definitions, the 1988 Act goes on to deal with substantive areas of policy. Several of these sections follow the topics already examined in previous sections as emerging policies, including: language use in Parliament (part I); legislative instruments, including executive instruments under powers delegated by Parliament, tabled documents, treaties, federal-provincial agreements, regulations, notices, and other documents intended for the public (part II); the administration of justice in federal courts (part III); communications between federal agencies and the public (part IV); the language of work within federal institutions (part V); and equitable linguistic participation in the public service (part VI). Two later parts of the Act define the respective responsibilities of Treasury Board (part VIII) and the Commissioner of Official Languages (part IX). The latter's functions had been outlined in some detail in the 1969 Act, but the role of Treasury Board as central manager and coordinator of the official languages program emerged only after 1972.

The most obvious general thrust of the 1988 law is to develop more powerful language legislation (Beaty, 1987; Fortier, 1987). One of the statute's key features is a provision in section 82 that its main operative sections, parts I to V, will override 'any other act of Parliament or regulation thereunder' in the event of inconsistency, with the sole exception of the Canadian Human Rights Act. As the Commissioner of Official Languages explained, these five parts 'have a quasi-constitutional nature' (Fortier, 1988, p. 5). This feature appears to carry Canadian legal thinking back to older medieval and early modern notions of fundamental laws, laws that take precedence over other existing or future statutes.[3] A further strengthening feature of the 1988 Act is a provision that any person who brings a complaint before the Commissioner of Official Languages under the major operative sections of the Act will have a guarantee of legal remedy before the Federal Court. The Commissioner also may initiate such proceedings, or appear as a party in them (part X).

During its passage through Parliament, the 1988 Act underwent a lengthy debate at the committee stage, between those who considered the bill too strong and others who would have made it even stronger (Acker, 1988). In the end, sections were added to require that regulations made under the act be tabled in Parliament for thirty sitting days prior to publication in the *Canada Gazette*, with a further thirty-day period allowed for 'interested persons to make representations' before any regulation can take effect. Changes to bilingual regions (for language-of-work purposes) are made subject to parliamentary challenge, and the entire act, as well as regulations made under it and all reports on its management, are made subject to permanent review by a designated parliamentary committee (Sections 85–88). In the last major substantive section, however, the balance tilts again, with a sweeping provision that the government may make regulations 'prescribing anything that the Governor in Council considers necessary to effect compliance with this Act' in all federal institutions other than those of Parliament itself (Section 93).

If the 1988 Act was primarily concerned with coordinating and managing official bilingualism in federal institutions, in one respect it reaches far beyond. Part VII of the Act confers on the Secretary of State of Canada a general mandate for the 'advancement' (in French, *promotion*) of English and French in Canadian society, requiring that the minister 'shall take such measures as he considers appropriate to advance the equality of status and use of English and French in Canadian society'. A more specific goal is to 'enhance the vitality [*favoriser l'épanouissement*] of the English and French linguistic minority communities in Canada and support and assist their development'.[4] Other listed goals include measures to 'encourage and support the learning of French and English in Canada' and to 'foster an acceptance and appreciation of both English and French by members of the public'. Part VII also calls for the Secretary of State to develop a coordinated approach in pursuit of these objectives, in collaboration with other federal institutions, provincial governments, and also economic organizations and voluntary associations in the private sector. The same goals may also be pursued through negotiated federal–provincial agreements, or through international agreements that 'recognize and advance the bilingual character of Canada'.

More than any other part of the 1988 Act, part VII illustrates the expansion of the federal government's general mandate to coordinate and manage language policy outside and beyond the operations of federal institutions. Some elements of this development are not new. In particular, federal grants in support of minority-language education and second-language learning were recommended by the Laurendeau–Dunton Commission and initiated as early as 1970. Other support for official-language minorities began as early as 1969 and over the years became a series of programs that focused on community development and led to the establishment of the Fédération des francophones hors Québec in 1975 and *Alliance Quebec* in 1982. These programs lacked a statutory base but were developed through use of the federal spending power. The 1988 Official Languages Act provided the missing statutory base and facilitated programme consolidation. As the departmental annual report notes, what distinguishes the 1988 Act from the 1969 Act is its second main purpose: 'to guide government policy and pursue efforts to promote the official languages in Canadian society as a whole' (Secretary of State, 1988–89, p. 26).[5]

As the preceding analysis has indicated, the federal policy of promoting language equality has been marked by a particular emphasis on the official-language minorities, that is, on francophones outside Quebec and anglophones in Quebec. Such an emphasis has a lineage as far back as the Laurendeau–Dunton Commission, but it grew visibly stronger with the 1988 Act. While minority status of any kind is doubtless not one to be envied, the official-language minorities have nevertheless been accorded a privileged status in the development of Canada's federal language policy.[6]

In one further respect the 1988 Act reached out beyond the boundaries of federal institutions. Part XII amended the federal Criminal Code to give accused persons the right to trial in the official language of their choice. In Canada, however, while the criminal law is federal, criminal trials are held in courts organized and run by the provinces. From 1990, therefore, the anglophone provinces have been required to offer criminal trials in the official language of the accused, before a judge and prosecutor who can speak the accused's language, and even the trial judgement and its reasons must be made available to the accused in that language. For Quebec, this was not a major change, because official bilingualism had been a requirement in all Quebec courts by virtue of the British North America Act of 1867.

Kenneth McRae

CONCLUSION

The time is not yet at hand for a serious evaluation of Canada's policy of official bilingualism. For one thing, such an evaluation should be founded on sustained academic research on policy outcomes, on success in attaining declared objectives, and on the worth of the objectives themselves. Up to the mid-1990s, such studies have been conspicuously lacking. In the quarter century since 1969, federal policy has reached a certain coherence and maturity at the level of planning or design, but its implementation has been selective and sporadic.[7] What is possible at this stage is to note some of the general directions and characteristics of this policy, as a first step towards more rigorous analysis and evaluation. For present purposes, one may emphasize five main points:

1. Official bilingualism has evolved mainly as an internal matter inside the public service, with a minimum of input from the general public or the political process. This has led to low levels of public awareness, and to a tendency for misinformation to take root and evoke negative reactions. Unlike such issues as minority-language schools, which attract public debate and wide press coverage, public service language policy and especially its more recent development have remained almost unknown to the public at large.

2. Even though independent research is lacking, internal documentation indicates that major changes have indeed occurred in public service language behaviour. Of the three major declared objectives, it seems likely that studies in depth would show greater success in service to the public and in balanced linguistic participation, but perhaps less in offering public servants an effective choice of language of work. The expansion of bilingual services to the public and more balanced participation of francophone and anglophone personnel have undoubtedly helped to remove, or at least diminish, a longstanding grievance of francophone Canadians against the federal government.

3. In the evolution of official bilingualism, the federal government and its public servants acquired a radically enlarged mandate. From a 1969 statute concerned primarily with language management in federal institutions, the expansion of federal spending programmes led by stages to the stronger and more comprehensive statute of 1988, which encompassed not only language management as before but a new and wider mission 'to advance the equality of status and use of English and French in Canadian society'. This wider vision, spelled out in part VII of the 1988

80

Act, remains largely unknown to the public, and even – as one survey showed – to a sample of senior managers in federal institutions themselves (COL, 1994, pp. 48 – 49).

4. The appearance in the 1988 Act of these wider objectives for Canadian society as a whole opens up the possibility of a sizeable gap between the federal vision and the everyday language situation of Canadian society. The design itself is both elegant and symmetrical, but how far it is realistic or attainable in the current or future Canadian language context remains largely undiscussed and unexplored. It is also far from clear that measures to support and strengthen the official-language minorities – the major strategy cited for advancing equality of the two official languages – would contribute to improving relations between the two majority groups, that is francophones in Quebec and anglophones outside Quebec. As early as 1965, the Laurendeau–Dunton Commission had identified Canada's central problem in intergroup relations as one of divergences 'more particularly between French Quebec and English-speaking Canada' (RCBB, 1965, p. 109).

5. By a policy of active support and developmental assistance for the English and French linguistic minority communities, the federal government opted for a policy that set it at variance with provincial language policies in all provinces except New Brunswick. For the other provinces with anglophone majorities, these differences were not crucial. They set a proactive federal authority against provincial regimes that were mainly reactive or passive in language matters. But in Quebec they ranged a federal authority proactive in favour of anglophones against Quebec governments even more strongly proactive in defending what they saw as vital interests of their linguistically besieged francophone majority. In this way divergent language policies became one more item in a growing dossier of Quebec's dissatisfaction with Canadian federalism.

Notes

This chapter is based in part on a larger four-country project under the title 'Conflict and Compromise in Multilingual Societies'. Its previous stages, on Switzerland, Belgium and Finland, have been supported by the Social Sciences and Humanities Research Council of Canada and the Killam Program of the Canada Council.

1 One source has argued that the narrow precision of Section 23 arose because it intervened in the provincial field of education and 'directly overruled a provincial law already in existence', Quebec's Bill 101 (Mandel, 1989, p. 104).

2 Thus in Quebec, where anglophones comprise 13 per cent of the population but only 5 per cent of federal public servants, there have been continuing federal efforts to correct this imbalance (Treasury Board, 1988–89, 1991–92, 1994–95).

3 Such thinking is not new or unprecedented. It surfaced in Prime Minister Diefenbaker's Bill of Rights of 1960, and is usually treated by orthodox jurists as a rule of statutory interpretation. This in turn has further implications of fundamental law.

4 The official-language minorities are given legal recognition in a later section, which requires a cabinet minister to consult them on any proposed regulations to be made under the statute. While the English text requires the minister to seek the 'views of members' of these minorities, the French text treats these minorities as collectivities (Section 84).

5 This statutory base is important. The 1982 Charter of Rights guarantees the power of Parliament or a legislature to 'advance the equality of status or use (*favoriser la progression vers l'égalité de statut ou d'usage*) of English and French', but only legislative actions are protected in this way against other Charter rights.

6 One reason for this emphasis in 1988 is that the existence of the official-language minorities was becoming constitutionally recognized and entrenched as a 'fundamental characteristic of Canada' in the ill-fated Meech Lake Accord, which had been approved by a conference of first ministers in 1987 but which failed to obtain the necessary unanimous ratification by provincial legislatures within the three-year time limit ending in June 1990.

7 In the absence of in-depth studies, provisional evaluations diverge widely. While a former Commissioner of Official Languages has categorized official bilingualism policies positively as 'a quiet revolution' that progressed far beyond expectations 'in less than one generation' (Fortier, 1994, p. 95), a leading anglophone expert on Quebec politics has criticized them as founded on 'illusions and delusions', bearing 'only a loose relationship to the reality of language use in Canada' (McRoberts, 1989, p. 163).

References

Acker, S. (1988). The 1988 Official Languages Act and the Legislative Committee. *Language and Society, 25,* 7–8.

BDAB (Bilingual Districts Advisory Board). (1971). *Recommendations.* Ottawa: Information Canada.

(Bilingual Districts Advisory Board). (1975). *Report.* Ottawa: Information Canada.

Beaty, S. (1987). Acts of faith. *Language and Society, 20,* 7–10.

(1988). From the B and B Commission to C-72: degrees of choice. *Language and Society, 24,* 13–14.

COL (Commissioner of Official Languages). (Various years). *Annual Report.* Ottawa: Minister of Supply and Services.

Delisle, J. (1985). Serving official bilingualism for half a century. *Language and Society, 15,* 4–9.

Fortier, D. (1987). The quest for linguistic equality. *Language and Society, 20,* 6–7.

(1988). Doing more, doing better. *Language and Society, 25*, 4–6.

(1994). Official languages policies in Canada: a quiet revolution. *International Journal of the Sociology of Language, 105/106*, 69–97.

Goreham, R. (1994). The principles of individual choice and territoriality in the implementation of language rights. Ottawa: Commissioner of Official Languages. (Multilithed).

Hay Management Consultants. (1993). Negotiating language choice in the federal civil service. Toronto: Hay Management Consultants. (Multilithed).

Heller, M. (1993). Language choice project: report on focus groups. (A working paper).

Low, D. M. (1989). The roots of change: legal sources of the 1988 Official Languages Act. *Language and Society* (Special Report), R25–R26.

McRae, K. D. (1978). Bilingual language districts in Finland and Canada: adventures in the transplanting of an institution. *Canadian Public Policy, 4*, 331–51.

McRoberts, K. (1989). Making Canada bilingual: illusions and delusions of federal language policy. In D. P. Shugarman and R. Whitaker (eds.), *Federalism and Political Community* (pp. 141–171). Peterborough: Broadview Press.

Mandel, M. (1989). *The Charter of Rights and the Legalization of Politics in Canada.* Toronto: Wall and Thompson.

Official Languages Act: A Guide for Canadians. (1993). Ottawa: Minister of Supply and Services.

Official Languages Act: Annotated version. (1992). Ottawa: Minister of Supply and Services.

Official Languages Regulations on Service to the Public – Synoptic Table. (1994). Ottawa: Treasury Board.

RCBB (Royal Commission on Bilingualism and Biculturalism). (1965). *Preliminary Report.* Ottawa: Queen's Printer.

(1967–70). *Report.* (6 vols). Ottawa: Queen's Printer.

Robichaud, J. (1983). Le bilinguisme dans l'administration fédérale du Canada (1969–1982). *Les Cahiers de droit, 24*, 115–30.

Secretary of State. (Various years). *Annual Report: Official Languages.* Ottawa: Minister of Supply and Services.

Treasury Board. (Various years). *Official Languages in Federal Institutions: Annual Report.* Ottawa: Minister of Supply and Services.

Tsai, G. (1989). L'aménagement linguistique dans les institutions fédérales canadiennes. Paper presented at the Journée de conférences sur les langues nationales dans l'administration fédérale suisse, Bern.

4 Official multiculturalism

John Berry

INTRODUCTION

In this chapter I briefly outline the history and current status of multicultural policy in Canada, then turn to a description of public attitudes towards the policy, and end with a consideration of how multicultural and language issues relate to each other.

While numerous attempts were made historically to assimilate Canada's diverse population to British cultural norms (Palmer, 1975), by 1956 the federal government's view was that assimilation had not worked anywhere in the contemporary world, and that it was impracticable as a general policy. In 1971, the Prime Minister announced a policy of multiculturalism. The key sections were:

> A policy of *multiculturalism within a bilingual framework* [emphasis added] commends itself to the Government as the most suitable means of assuring the cultural freedom of Canadians. Such a policy should help to break down discriminatory attitudes and cultural jealousies. National unity, if it is to mean anything in the deeply personal sense, must be founded on confidence in one's own individual identity; out of this can grow respect for that of others and a willingness to share ideas, attitudes and assumptions. A vigorous policy of multiculturalism will help create this initial confidence. It can form the base of a society which is based on fair play for all.
>
> The Government will support and encourage the various cultures and ethnic groups that give structure and vitality to our society. They will be encouraged to share their cultural expression and values with other Canadians and so contribute to a richer life for all. (Government of Canada, 1971)

To assist our understanding of the policy, we may identify four elements of it, and place them in a framework (see figure 4.1) (Berry, 1984). First, it is clear that the policy wishes to avoid assimilation by encouraging ethnic groups to maintain and develop themselves as distinctive groups within Canadian society; this element we may term 'own group maintenance and development'. Secondly, a fundamental purpose of the policy is to increase intergroup harmony and the

Figure 4.1 Four components of Canadian multiculturalism policy

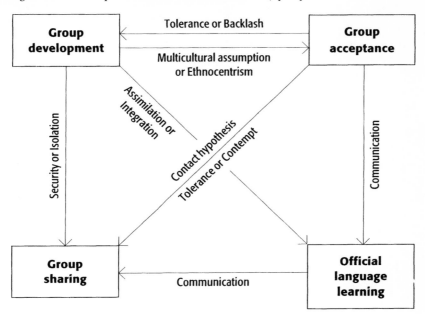

mutual acceptance of all groups which maintain and develop themselves; this we term 'other group acceptance and tolerance'. Thirdly, the policy argues that group development by itself is not sufficient to lead to group acceptance; 'inter-group contact and sharing' is also required. Fourthly, full participation by cultural groups cannot be achieved if some common language is not learned; thus the 'learning of official languages' (English and French) is also encouraged by the policy. In addition to identifying these four elements, figure 4.1 also displays some inter-relationships (connecting lines between elements). A few of these are explicit in the policy, others are implicit, and still others may be derived from the social-psychological literature on ethnic relations.

A central question is whether the policy intends to encourage the main-tenance of numerous and full-scale cultural systems (as implied in the term multi-*culturalism*), or whether it is designed to be supportive of some lesser phenomenon (such as various aspects of ethnicity which are derived from a full cultural system). Burnet (1978) has argued that 'ethnicity' rather than 'culture' is the actual and realistic focus of such a policy: most groups lack their own separ-ate social and political institutions, many lack their own (ancestral) language and numbers are not always large. Thus the maintenance of shared features which are *derived* from a heritage culture (i.e., ethnic phenomena) are more likely to be possible than is the maintenance of full-scale cultures ('museum cultures', in Burnet's terms).

An important criticism of multiculturalism has been levelled by John Porter (1972, 1975), who argued that maintaining interest in ethnicity merely perpetuates ethnic stratification in Canadian society: multiculturalism may serve only to keep particular groups in their place in the 'vertical mosaic'. It may also provide a basis for discrimination. While undoubtedly there has been important stratification according to ethnic-group membership in the past, and perhaps at the present time for some groups (Shamai, 1992), some evidence (e.g., Boyd *et al.*, 1981; Breton *et al.*, 1990) suggests that ethnicity is no longer related to status in Canada. Indeed, the educational and occupational aspirations and attainments of some newer immigrant groups now exceed those of groups at the top of Porter's original hierarchy (Richmond, 1986; Samuda *et al.*, 1989).

A second criticism of multiculturalism policy is that, when set 'within a bilingual framework' there is an inherent contradiction: how can there be multiculturalism without multilingualism, since language is such an essential component of culture? This issue was first raised by Rocher (1973), and will be addressed in detail in a later section.

A third difficulty is that multiculturalism is widely viewed as a policy only for the non-British and non-French portions of the Canadian population. From this perspective, it is seen by some as a crude attempt to attract the 'ethnic vote' (Bissoondath, 1994), or as being a divisive force (Bibby, 1990). While having its roots in concerns about the place of 'the other ethnic groups', the initial policy statement in 1971, as well as more recent statements (see Multiculturalism and Citizenship Canada, *Annual Reports*), emphasize that the policy is for all Canadians, whether they are members of a dominant or nondominant, majority or minority, ethnic group.

After a decade and a half of activity based upon the 1971 statement, multiculturalism was formally achieved by the enactment (1988) of a Multiculturalism Act. This is explicitly linked to a number of current features of Canadian policy: the constitutional recognition of the importance of preserving and enhancing the multicultural heritage of Canadians, of the rights of the aboriginal peoples of Canada, and of two official languages in Canada; the equality of all Canadians, whether so by birth or by choice; the equality of opportunity, regardless of race, national or ethnic origin or colour; freedom from discrimination based on culture, religion or language; and the recognition of the diversity of Canadians as a fundamental characteristic of Canadian society.

Canada has been a culturally plural society from the beginning (1871 Census: 60 per cent British; 31 per cent French; 9 per cent others, including native peoples). However, a considerable impetus was given to multiculturalism by the increasingly diverse sources of immigration over the past century. Initially from eastern Europe, then from southern Europe, and now increasingly from places other than Europe, immigration can be said to have given rise to multiculturalism (Hawkins, 1972; Palmer, 1975).

At the present time (1991 Census), British and French origins still account for the majority of the national population but this varies widely by region. Other than British and French provenance, German, Italian, Ukrainian, Dutch and aboriginal origins are the most frequent. While still relatively small in total number in Canada, visible minorities represent substantial elements of regional and urban populations, and their immigration continues at a relatively high proportion. For example, in 1994, over 60 per cent of immigrants came from Asia. Despite these numerous changes and trends, the proportion of foreign-born has tended to remain a fairly constant proportion (between 15 and 20 per cent) of the total population.

MULTICULTURAL ATTITUDES

As with any policy, official intentions are likely to succeed only when there is widespread support in the general population. It is clear that multicultural policy is intended to 'manage' intercultural relations in Canada's plural society, with the ultimate goal of achieving mutual intergroup acceptance (as illustrated in the upper right of figure 4.1). The policy proposes to approach this goal by a kind of 'balancing act' between the promotion of cultural maintenance and of social interaction (on the left of figure 4.1), while also promoting official language learning. What do we know about public perceptions and acceptance of this approach?

Acculturation attitudes

Drawing on some concepts developed in acculturation research (Berry, 1990), a framework for understanding people's orientations to multiculturalism is shown in figure 4.2. Perhaps the most useful way to identify the various orientations towards acculturation is to note that two issues predominate in the daily life of most acculturating individuals. One pertains to the maintenance and development of one's ethnic distinctiveness in society, deciding whether or not one's own cultural identity and customs are of value and to be retained. The other issue involves the desirability of inter-ethnic contact, deciding whether

Figure 4.2 Four acculturation strategies, based upon orientation to two issues

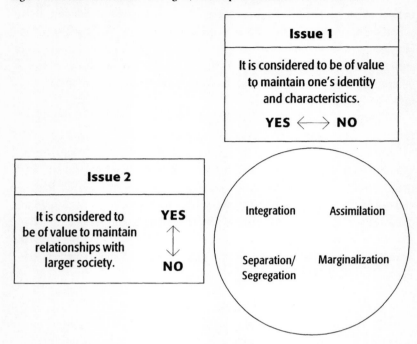

relations with other groups in the larger society are of value and to be sought. These two questions are obviously similar to two key elements of multicultural-ism policy: heritage cultural maintenance, and social participation and sharing. The two issues are essentially questions of values, and may be responded to on a continuous scale, from positive to negative. For conceptual purposes, however, they can be treated as dichotomous ('yes' and 'no') preferences, thus generating a four-fold model (see figure 4.2). Each cell in this fourfold classification is consid-ered to be an acculturation strategy or option available to individuals and to groups in plural societies, towards which individuals may hold attitudes; these strategies are *assimilation, integration, separation,* and *marginalization.*

When the first question is answered 'no', and the second is answered 'yes' the assimilation strategy is defined, namely, relinquishing one's cultural identity and moving into the larger society. This can take place by way of absorption of a nondominant group by an established dominant group; or, it can be by way of the merging of many groups to form a new society, as in the 'melting pot' concept.

The *integration* strategy implies the maintenance of the cultural integrity of the group, as well as the movement by the group to become an integral part of a larger societal framework. In this case there is a large number of distinguishable ethnic groups, all cooperating within a larger social system. Such an arrangement may occur where there is some degree of structural assimilation but little cultural and behavioural assimilation, resulting in the 'mosaic' that is promoted in Canada.

When there are no relations with the larger society, and this is accompanied by a maintenance of ethnic identity and traditions, another strategy is defined. Depending upon which group (the dominant or nondominant) controls the situation, this strategy may take the form of either *segregation* or *separation*. When the pattern is imposed by the dominant group, classic segregation to keep people in 'their place' appears. On the other hand, the maintenance of a traditional way of life outside full participation in the larger society may derive from a group's desire to lead an independent existence, as in the case of separatist movements. In these terms, segregation and separation differ primarily with respect to which group or groups have the power to determine the outcome.

Finally, there is an option that is difficult to define precisely, possibly because it is accompanied by a good deal of collective and individual confusion and anxiety. It is characterized by striking out against the larger society and by feelings of alienation, loss of identity and acculturative stress. This option is *marginalization*, in which groups lose cultural and psychological contact with both their traditional culture and the larger society. When imposed by the larger society, it is tantamount to ethnocide. When stabilized in a nondominant group, it constitutes the classical situation of marginality (Stonequist, 1937).

A number of points should be made with respect to the model in figure 4.2. First, these strategies pertain to both individuals and groups in plural societies. One individual may follow a course toward assimilation, whereas another may not; one ethnic group may, through its formal organizations, opt for separation, whereas another may seek integration. It should be obvious, however, that choices among the options are not entirely independent. If all of one's group pursues assimilation, one is left without a membership group, rendering the other options meaningless; and, if group assimilation is widespread, the culturally plural character of the larger society is eliminated, again voiding the other options.

Second, the various strategies may be pursued by politically dominant or non-dominant groups. For example, if assimilation is sought by a particular ethnic group, it is an example of the 'melting pot', whereas if it is enforced as national policy, we may characterize it as a 'pressure cooker'. Similarly, as already noted, separation occurs when a group wishes to set up shop on its own, whereas the classic forms of segregation exist when such 'apartness' is forced on it by the dominant groups.

Third, there can be flux and inconsistency with respect to which strategies are pursued within a society. Flux occurs over time as an individual or a group experiments with differing options; for example, French Canadians, long in fear of assimilation, may be viewed as currently exploring the relative merits of the integration and separation options (federalism versus independence). Inconsistency occurs when, at a single point in time, for example, an individual may accept linguistic and economic assimilation, but wish to avoid it in all other areas of daily life.

From a social psychological point of view, what conditions need to be met in order to successfully manage a multicultural society? A recent answer is that:

> First, there needs to be general support for multiculturalism, including acceptance of various aspects and consequences of the policy, and of cultural diversity as a valuable resource for a society. Second, there should be overall low levels of intolerance or prejudice in the population. Third, there should be generally positive mutual attitudes among the various ethnocultural groups that constitute the society. And fourth, there needs to be a degree of attachment to the larger Canadian society, but without derogation of its constituent ethnocultural groups. (Berry and Kalin, 1995, p. 302)

A number of these conditions have been examined in two national surveys (1974 and 1991) and a few community and small-group studies. What follows here is based primarily on results of the 1991 national survey (N = 3325). Since the study addressed some fairly fundamental psychological characteristics, it is likely that, while almost five years old, the basic picture remains valid. Three broad sorts of information are considered. First are some *general indicators of acceptance of cultural diversity*: do Canadians like living in a heterogeneous society, do they enjoy intercultural differences and encounters? Second, there are some *specific intergroup attitudes*, based on a single measure of how comfortable people are in the company of those of various specific ethnic backgrounds. And finally, we examine how people *identify themselves* (in civic or ethnic terms), and how much they identify with the Canadian state. In most cases, the information will be presented aggregated by ethnic origin of respondent (British, French, or other) and region of residence (inside or outside Quebec).

General orientations

Two scales are of interest: *Multicultural Ideology* and *Tolerance–Prejudice*. In the national population as a whole, both the acceptance of multiculturalism, and the level of tolerance (essentially the opposite to prejudice) are moderately high, and the long-term trends have been for both to increase over the past fifteen years. On the 7-point response scale used, the means were 4.59 and 5.37 respectively. When analysed by ethnic origin and region, figures 4.3 and 4.4 show the resulting pattern (Berry and Kalin, 1995).

While there are some similarities in the distribution of these two general orientations (e.g., there is no effect of ethnic origin in either case), there are some important differences. Most evident is the presence of a regional effect for tolerance-prejudice, but an interaction effect for multicultural ideology; this indicates that different explanations are needed to account for scores on the two scales. For tolerance–prejudice, it may be that where intergroup relations are contentious (such as in Quebec) all groups are relatively less tolerant. For multicultural ideology, a kind of 'self-interest' seems to account for the distribution: where people are advantaged by policies and programmes supporting multiculturalism (e.g., British and Others inside Quebec; French outside Quebec) support is high; but where people may be threatened by pluralist policies (e.g., French in Quebec) support for diversity is lower.

Figure 4.3 Distribution of mean scores on multicultural ideology by ethnic origin and region of residence of respondents

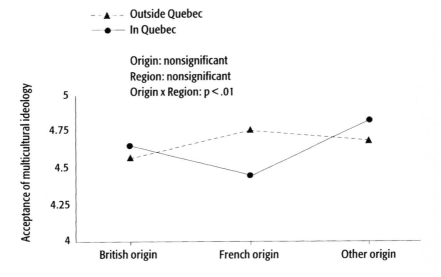

Figure 4.4 Distribution of mean scores on tolerance–prejudice by ethnic origin and region of residence of respondents

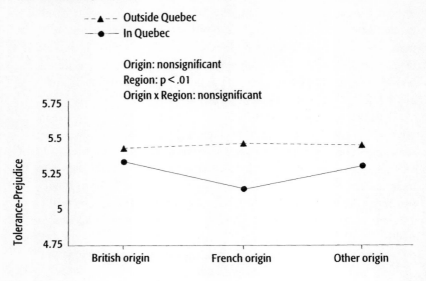

Specific ethnic attitudes

Respondents indicated their degree of comfort being around persons of selected ethnic backgrounds. Figure 4.5 shows these 'comfort levels' according to ethnic origin of the respondent (in the total sample). There are three important aspects. First, while comfort levels were generally high, not all groups received the same ratings. There is a hierarchy of acceptance in which British through to Native Canadians are evaluated more positively than other groups. Secondly, while there are no differences between the attitudes held by British- and Other-origin raters, those given by French-origin respondents are noticeably less positive. A third observation is that those groups that are generally less positively rated tend to receive even less positive ratings by French-origin respondents (i.e., there is an interaction between the first two observations).

There is thus a clear hierarchy of acceptance, but its interpretation is not entirely clear. One possibility is that prejudice (in particular, racism) accounts for these ratings. This possibility will be examined below, but it can be noted here that Chinese Canadians and Native Canadians are as generally highly rated as those of European background; thus, a simple *racism* interpretation is not generally valid. Other explanations include: *familiarity* with various groups, with

Figure 4.5 Mean comfort levels by ethnic origin of respondents in the national sample

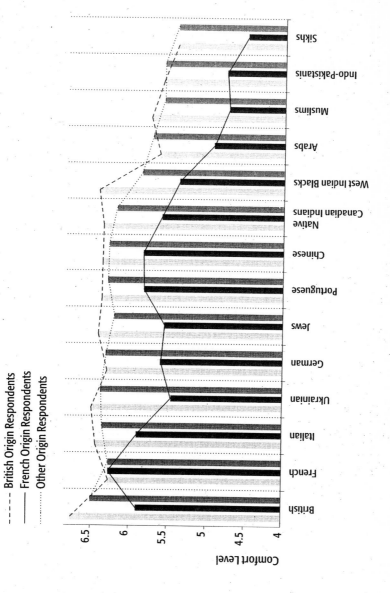

Figure 4.6 Positive or negative group preference in total sample as a function of tolerance–prejudice

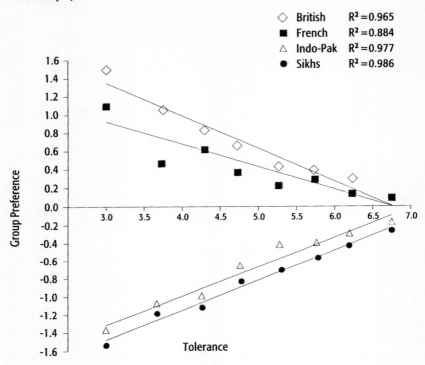

those groups who are less numerous and not as long-established in Canada being rated less positively; and *similarity*, with those whose cultural origins are less similar to the dominant (European-based) population being rated less positively.

Since there may have been extraneous factors (e.g., response style) affecting the use of the comfort level scale, these scores were standardized (with zero being the average rating given by a respondent to all fourteen groups; attitudes are then expressed as positive or negative deviation from this mean of zero). These standard ethnic attitude scores can be related to scores on the Tolerance–Prejudice scale. Figure 4.6 shows these relationships in the total sample, using attitudes towards British, French, IndoPakistani and Sikh Canadians. Note that while the most tolerant respondents make very little distinction between any groups, the least tolerant make the greatest distinction between their attitudes towards the two 'charter' groups and the two South Asian groups. Importantly (but not shown in this figure), even the least tolerant British- and French-origin respondents maintain a positive attitude towards the other 'charter' group; that is, they seem to serve as *positive reference groups* for each other.

Ethnic and civic identity

The third area of interest is how people identify themselves. The 1991 survey had three questions: an ethnic *origin* question (similar to the 1991 Census question); an *identity* question (how respondents usually thought of themselves), with various ethnic options provided, based on answers to the first question, along with regional and national options (e.g., 'Québécois', 'Canadian'); and a *strength* of identification question (on a 7-point scale) analysed for three identities ('Canadian'/'Canadien'; provincial; ethnic). Related to these identity questions was a scale of *Canadianism*, attempting to assess one's sense of attachment and commitment to Canada.

Responses to the identity questions are presented in table 4.1 according to respondents' ethnic origin for both the 1974 and 1991 surveys, and in table 4.2 for strength of identification by region, for 1991 only (Kalin and Berry, 1995). In both the 1974 and 1991 surveys (table 4.1) the most frequent identity was 'Canadian'/'Canadien'; however, this was more the case among British- and Other-origin than among French-origin respondents. Among the latter, the most frequent identity in 1974 was 'Canadien-Français', but this mostly shifted to a provincial (largely 'Québécois') identity in 1991, and somewhat less to a 'Canadien' identity. 'Other Ethnic' identities were the third most frequent, but declined from 1974 to 1991. There appears to be no important variation (in table 4.2) in

Table 4.1 Self-identity (in percentage) of respondents in two national surveys, by ethnic origin

	1974 SURVEY				1991 SURVEY			
	Ethnic origin				Ethnic origin			
Self identity	Total	British	French	OEthnic	Total	British	French	OEthnic
Canadian/Canadien	59	80	26	59	64	80	32	65
British Canadian	7	13	3	3	2	6	0	0
French-Canadian	15	3	47	3	4	1	16	0
Provincial	7	1	22	1	19	9	47	9
Other Ethnic-Canadian	8	0	0	28	7	1	1	20
Other national	3	2	2	5	4	3	4	5
Overall number	1,810	708	376	541	3,276	1,392	746	1,027

Source: from Kalin and Berry, 1995

Table 4.2 Mean strength of identification with three identities by region of residence in 1991 survey

	Region					
Identity	Total	Atlantic	Quebec	Ontario	Prairies	British Columbia
Canadian/Canadien	6.3	6.7	5.2	6.6	6.6	6.7
Provincial	5.3	5.8	6.0	4.4	5.5	5.5
'Ethnic' origin	4.1	3.5	4.6	3.9	4.1	4.0
Overall number	3,320	300	863	1,191	584	383

Note: Mean scores are on a 7-point scale, with higher scores indicating stronger identification
Source: from Kalin and Berry, 1995

strength of identification as 'Canadian'/'Canadien'. However, respondents in Quebec had a lower strength rating for this identity, combined with a slightly higher strength rating for a 'provincial' (i.e., 'Québécois') identity.

When these identities are related to the two general orientations within the three ethnic-origin categories, some variations do appear (Kalin and Berry, 1995). For British-origin respondents, those with a 'provincial' identity were lower than those with other identities on tolerance (but not on multicultural ideology). The reverse was true for French-origin respondents: those with a 'provincial' identity were lower than those with other identities on multicultural ideology (but not on tolerance). As one might expect, among Other-origin Canadians, those with an 'Ethnic' identity were most supportive of a multicultural ideology, while those with a 'provincial' identity were least tolerant. Most importantly, there is no evidence that those who identify as 'Canadian' are less supportive of diversity.

Findings for the Canadianism scale are shown in figure 4.7, according to ethnic origin and region of residence. Unlike the two other scale distributions (see figures 4.3 and 4.4), scores on Canadianism vary significantly by ethnic origin, and region, and in their interaction. All three features are evidently due to the lower score on the scale among French-origin respondents living in Quebec. When these scale scores are related to the three identity categories, a common and significant pattern appears in all three ethnic-origin groups: those with a 'provincial' identity score low on Canadianism, and (not surprisingly) those with a 'Canadian' identity score higher. And for British- and Other-origin groups, those with an 'ethnic' identity do not score lower on the Canadianism scale, indicating that the much-maligned 'hyphenated identity' is no threat to one's attachment to Canada.

Figure 4.7 Distribution of mean scores on Canadianism by ethnic origin and region of residence of respondents

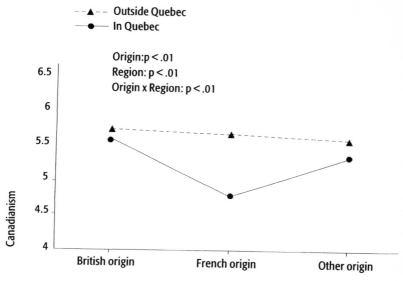

These findings may be summarized as follows: First, there is broad general acceptance of diversity. Secondly, ethnic attitudes are generally positive. And thirdly, identity as 'Canadian' and attachment to Canada are generally widespread and strong.

Obviously this general pattern is affected by ethnic origin, region of residence, and the object of the attitude (i.e., which group, which issue). More specifically, compared to other respondents, Quebecers (sometimes only francophone Quebecers) show a slightly lesser acceptance of diversity (multicultural ideology, tolerance), lesser attachment to Canada (Canadianism), less positive ethnic attitudes (comfort levels), lower frequency of identity as 'Canadien' (more frequently as 'Québécois'), and a less strong identity as 'Canadien' (more strongly as 'Québécois'). This pattern has been observed over the past few decades (Bourhis, 1994a; Kalin and Berry, 1982).

MULTICULTURALISM AND LANGUAGE

Early in the period of official multiculturalism in Canada, a major study was carried out on the knowledge and use of 'non-official' languages (O'Bryan, Reitz and Kuplowska, 1976). This study set out to discover the degree of retention of 'non-official' languages (i.e., not English and French, but those other languages now called 'heritage languages') among ten ethnic groups in five cities. It was commissioned (along with a companion study by Berry, Kalin and Taylor, 1977) by the federal Ministry of Multiculturalism to provide baseline data for the assessment and further development of multicultural programmes in Canada. It can also provide evidence about the role (and possible necessity) of heritage languages in achieving multiculturalism. As noted earlier, there has been a continuing debate about the relationship between language retention and cultural retention (Cummins, 1991; Lalande, 1992; Rocher, 1973), and about the effect of heritage-language promotion on official bilingualism (Blais, 1990; Bourhis 1994b).

The main conclusions of the study (O'Bryan *et al.*, 1976, p. 167) were that heritage languages 'are in active and viable usage in Canadian cities', but that language use 'falls off in the second and third generations, even more rapidly than does language knowledge'. Furthermore, 'language use falls off rapidly as one moves away from the informal and relatively intimate context of family and friends' towards more formal and public arenas.

Curiously, Rocher's (1973) criticisms were not mentioned in their study, despite its obvious relevance to the issue. However, when their conclusions are juxtaposed with those of Berry *et al.* (1977) and Berry and Kalin (1995), it is possible to assert that multiculturalism is alive and well in Canada, despite the 'dropping off' of heritage-language retention beyond the first generation, and outside the family (see also Reitz, 1985). In other words, support for and practice of cultural diversity does not appear to depend on heritage-language knowledge and use. The promotion of 'multiculturalism within a bilingual framework' seems not to be a contradiction, as was claimed by Rocher (1973) and others (e.g., Foster and Seitz, 1989).

Further evidence to support this conclusion comes from research on ethnic identity (Edwards and Chisholm, 1987; Kalin and Berry, 1995). In the first study, respondents maintained an attachment to a particular ethnic group, despite not knowing that group's language. In the second study, identification with an ethnic group was associated with acceptance of multiculturalism, but again in the absence of heritage-language retention.

This is not to say that the retention of heritage languages plays no role in cultural maintenance. In a number of studies (e.g., Driedger and Hengstenberg, 1986; Feuerverger, 1991) language knowledge and use are intimately associated with other aspects of a group's culture, particularly with religious practice. Moreover, evidence (Cummins, 1991; Danesi, 1991) shows that there are multiple advantages (social, intellectual and international) to non-official bilingualism and multilingualism. These advantages are likely to remain, independently of any link to multiculturalism.

CONCLUSIONS

Multiculturalism is both a social fact and a social policy in Canada. Fortunately, despite various criticisms of fact and policy, there is general support in the national population for maintaining and promoting cultural diversity. Although introduced as 'multiculturalism within a bilingual framework', considerable effort and resources have been directed towards supporting 'non-official' or 'heritage' languages as one component of the numerous cultures that thrive in Canada. While there are some clear advantages to multilingualism (to match and contribute to the extant multiculturalism), widespread heritage-language knowledge and use appear not to be necessary conditions for either the acceptance or practice of multiculturalism.

References

Berry, J. W. (1984). Multicultural policy in Canada: a social psychological analysis. *Canadian Journal of Behavioural Science, 16*, 353–370.

(1990). Psychology of acculturation. In R. Brislin (ed.), *Applied Cross-Cultural Psychology* (pp. 232–253). London: Sage.

Berry, J. W. and Kalin R. (1995). Multicultural and ethnic attitudes in Canada: an overview of the 1991 national survey. *Canadian Journal of Behavioural Science, 27*, 301–320.

Berry, J. W., Kalin, R. and Taylor, D. (1977). *Multiculturalism and Ethnic Attitudes in Canada.* Ottawa: Supply and Services.

Bibby, R. W. (1990). *Mosaic Madness.* Toronto: Stoddart.

Bissoondath, N. (1994). *Selling Illusions: The Cult of Multiculturalism in Canada.* Toronto: Penguin.

Blais, A. (1990). Le clivage linguistique au Canada. In K. Jürgensen and H.-J. Niederehe (eds.), *Zeitschrift der Gesellschaft für Kanada-Studien* (pp. 71–81). Neumünster: Karl Wachholst Verlag.

Bourhis, R. (1994a). Ethnic and language attitudes in Quebec. In J. W. Berry and J. A. Laponce (eds.), *Ethnicity and Culture in Canada: The Research Landscape* (pp. 322–360). Toronto: University of Toronto Press.

(1994b). Introduction and overview of language events in Canada. *International Journal of the Sociology of Language, 105/106*, 5–36.

Boyd, M., Goyder, J., Jones, F., McRoberts, H., Pineo, P. and Porter, J. (1981). Status attainment in Canada: findings of the Canadian mobility study. *Canadian Review of Sociology and Anthropology, 18*, 657–673.

Breton, R., Isajiw, W., Kalbach, W. and Reitz, J. (1990). *Ethnic Identity and Equality.* Toronto: University of Toronto Press.

Burnet, J. (1978). The policy of multiculturalism within a bilingual framework: a stock-taking. *Canadian Ethnic Studies, 10,* 107–113.

Cummins, J. (1991). Introduction. *Canadian Modern Language Review, 47,* 601–605.

Danesi, M. (1991). Revisiting the research funding on heritage language learning: three interpretive frames. *Canadian Modern Language Review, 47,* 650–659.

Driedger, L. and Hengstenberg, P. (1986). Non-official multiculturalism: factors affecting German language competence, use and maintenance in Canada. *Canadian Ethnic Studies, 18,* 90–109.

Edwards, J. and Chisholm, J. (1987). Language, multiculturalism and identity. *Journal of Multilingual and Multicultural Development, 8,* 391–408.

Feuerverger, G. (1991). University students' perception of heritage language learning, and ethnic identity maintenance. *Canadian Modern Language Review, 47,* 660–677.

Foster, L. and Seitz, A. (1989). The politicization of language issues in multicultural societies. *Canadian Ethnic Studies, 21,* 55–73.

Government of Canada. (1971). Statement to the House by the Prime Minister, 8 October 1971, in response to the recommendations of the Royal Commission on Bilingualism and Biculturalism, Book IV, *The Cultural Contribution of the Other Ethnic Groups.*

Hawkins, F. (1972). *Canada and Immigration: Public Policy and Public Concerns.* Montreal: McGill-Queen's Press.

Kalin, R. and Berry, J. W. (1982). Canadian ethnic attitudes and identity in the context of national unity. *Journal of Canadian Studies, 17,* 103–110.

(1995). Ethnic and civic self-identity in Canada: analyses of the 1974 and 1991 National Surveys. *Canadian Ethnic Studies, 28,* 1–16.

Lalande, G. (1992). A skeptical view of multiculturalism. In S. Hryniuk (ed.), *Twenty Years of Multiculturalism* (pp. 73–75). Winnipeg: St John's College Press.

O'Bryan, K., Reitz, J. and Kuplowska, O. (1976). *Non-official Languages: A study in Canadian Multiculturalism.* Ottawa: Supply and Services.

Palmer, H. (1975). *Immigration and the Rise of Multiculturalism.* Toronto: Copp Clark.

Porter, J. (1972). Dilemmas and contradictions of a multiethnic society. *Transactions of the Royal Society of Canada, 10,* 193–205.

(1975). Ethnic pluralism in Canadian perspective. In N. Glazer and D. Moynihan (eds.), *Ethnicity: Theory and Experience* (pp. 267–304). Cambridge, MA: Harvard University Press.

Reitz, J. (1985). Language and ethnic community survival. In R. Bienvenue and J. Goldstein (eds.), *Ethnicity and Ethnic relations in Canada* (pp. 105–123). Toronto: Butterworths.

Richmond, A. (1986). Ethnogenerational variation in educational achievement. *Canadian Ethnic Studies, 18,* 75–89.

Rocher, G. (1973). *Le Québec en mutation.* Montreal: Hurtubise.

Samuda, R., Chodzinski, R., Berry, J. W. and Lewis, J. (1989). *Educational and Occupational Aspirations of Secondary School Students in Relation to Ethnic Group Membership.* Report submitted to Ministry of Multiculturalism.

Shamai, S. (1992). Ethnicity and educational achievement in Canada (1941–1981). *Canadian Ethnic Studies, 24,* 43–57.

Stonequist, E. V. (1937). *The Marginal Man.* New York: Scribner.

5 Language in education: bridging educational policy and social psychological research

Kimberly A. Noels and Richard Clément

A brief reflection on ethnic relations in Canada reveals considerable discontent (see Bissoondath, 1994; Edwards, 1994): after several decades, interaction between French and English Canada still reflects 'two solitudes', the First Nations continue in their demands for redress for past and present transgressions, and other non-official ethnolinguistic groups press for increased representation in government and education. There has been a variety of attempts by the Canadian federal government to overcome these difficulties. Important here have been language education programmes promoting the harmonious and efficient interaction between citizens from diverse cultural backgrounds. The purpose of this chapter is, therefore, to examine how the socio-political climate influences language learning, directly and indirectly, through language education programmes and policies. By considering socio-educational policy and social psychological research in tandem, we hope to illustrate that not only does policy affect language programmes, language learning and related outcomes, but also that the research on the social psychology of language learning can inform policy and programmes.

Following this goal, the structure of this chapter is two-fold. The first part considers the ramifications of a policy of 'multiculturalism in a bilingual framework' for language education in Canada. It is argued that in addition to the traditional pedagogical concerns of developing language competence, this ideology supports an educational orientation relevant to intergroup relations (Diffey, 1995). In particular, the government's interest in cultural diversity supports language programmes that are designed to encourage cultural retention, particularly identity maintenance, and social integration, involving equitable and respectful interactions among cultural groups and their members (Berry, 1992; Labelle, 1989). Although these two goals may receive varying emphasis across language programmes, Canadian policies on cultural diversity are explicit in the social psychological implications that language programmes are expected to have.

102

The second part of this chapter considers, through a selective review of research conducted primarily by Canadian researchers, several social psychological influences on, and implications of, learning official and non-official languages. Very little of this research was designed to evaluate specific language programmes in light of the goals of the government policies. None the less, the findings indicate that social psychological phenomena, such as intergroup power dynamics and cultural identity issues, play an important role in language learning and are important outcomes of the language learning process. Of necessity, the discussion herein will focus primarily on the learning of French and English as second languages (L2) and, to a lesser extent, on the learning of non-official, heritage languages. Coverage of French immersion, and a more elaborate treatment of heritage and aboriginal languages, may be found elsewhere in this book.

AN OVERVIEW OF LANGUAGE AND LANGUAGE EDUCATION POLICIES IN CANADA

The current concerns with language-group relations are part of a discussion that has been going on for well over thirty years. Originally centred on the two founding nations, this discussion has been extended to consider the role of non-official language groups in Canadian society. In this section, the sociopolitical development of the federal government's policy of 'multiculturalism in a bilingual framework' is first briefly described (more detailed accounts can be found in Bourhis, 1994; Edwards, 1994; Fortier, 1994). The implications of this policy for language education programmes are then discussed. Secondly, the reactions of several ethnic groups to this policy are considered, particularly as they affect the manifestation of the federal government's perspective on cultural diversity in language programmes.

'Multiculturalism in a bilingual framework': the federal government and language education

The federal government's position on the importance of language education for maintaining a harmonious, culturally diverse society can be extracted from the Official Languages (1969; 1988) and Multiculturalism Acts (1971; 1988). The Royal Commission on Bilingualism and Biculturalism, mandated in 1963 in response to heated French–English relations, had as its principal objective the creation of an official languages charter. Although recognizing each group's cultural distinctiveness, this Charter emphasized the equal contributions of the French and English groups to Canadian society (Fortier, 1994). The Charter, and the later Official Languages Act (1988), mandated the federal government to promote the official languages throughout Canada and to support the official language minorities.

The federal government elaborated a number of policy guidelines directed specifically towards official language education (Fortier, 1994). For example, under section 23 of the Charter, anglophone and francophone students are guaranteed public education in the minority official language, depending upon the demographic representation of that minority group in the region. Because education is provincially regulated, the exact figure is determined by each province independently. Additionally, the federal government provides funding to the provinces to assist in the provision of language education. According to Fortier (1994), over the last twenty years, more than \$2.5 billion was provided to the provincial governments to promote second-language and minority-language education.

The idea of multiculturalism within a bilingual framework was developed in response to Book IV of the Report of the Royal Commission on Bilingualism and Biculturalism (1970; see Burnet, 1989), and formally stated in the Multiculturalism Act (1971; see Breton, 1986; Labelle, 1989 for overviews of this Act). Its objectives, and those of the later Multiculturalism Act (1988), can be classified into at least two interrelated issues (Labelle, 1989). The first pertains to the development of retention of cultural knowledge and identity, including a sense of self-esteem with regard to one's cultural background. The second relates to issues of sociocultural integration – by focusing on the elimination of racism and discrimination, the policy would reduce barriers to active involvement in Canadian society. At least initially, the first goal of ethnic identity maintenance was viewed as fundamental to the objectives of multiculturalism (Berry, 1992; Gamlin, Berndorff, Mitsopulos and Demetriou, 1994). The government's belief in the importance of language in fulfilling these objectives is illustrated by its commitment to 'preserve and enhance the use of languages other than English and French, while strengthening the status and use of the official languages of Canada' (Multiculturalism Act, 1988, p. 6). Currently, most provincial governments, in conjunction with the specific non-official language community, support heritage-language programmes, although classes usually take place outside regularly scheduled classroom hours (Cummins, 1994; Cummins and Danesi, 1990).

In summary, the policy of the federal government with regard to cultural diversity can be broadly described as supporting both cultural maintenance and integration into the broader Canadian society. Language is viewed as integral to these goals and, accordingly, the government is committed to language education.

The response to the policies and their manifestation in language education

Reactions to the implementation of the language and culture framework have been mixed. According to Bibby (1989; cited in Fortier, 1994), about 58 per cent of the Canadians polled endorse a dual official-language policy. Elsewhere, a poll by Angus Reid (1992; cited in Fortier, 1994) indicated that 65 per cent of those polled were at least moderately supportive of such a policy. Examination of the public reaction to the Multiculturalism Act (1971) also suggests a relatively positive picture: depending upon the question asked, about two-thirds of Canadians supported the idea that immigrants should retain their cultural and linguistic traditions, although some accommodation to the mainstream society should also take place (Berry, Kalin and Taylor, 1977; Kalin and Berry, 1994). A non-official languages study (O'Bryan, Reitz and Kuplowska, 1976) examined attitudes towards heritage-language teaching in the public school system and found that, for many, language loss was a major problem and that language maintenance programmes were sought. Users of heritage-language programmes do see them as helpful in preventing this loss. For instance, Keyser and Brown (1981, cited in Cummins, 1994) report that heritage-language programmes promote better communication between the student and his or her family members.

Despite this apparent acceptance of bilingualism and multiculturalism, criticism of government policies comes from several quarters (see Friesen, 1993, for an overview). A first critique is that the fundamental assumption – that inter-group relations are enhanced by promoting distinctive ethnic identities – is flawed. Rather, the promotion of group differences is seen to maintain distance and conflict between groups (e.g., Bissoondath, 1994). To develop a unified nation, then, a perspective which emphasises the communalities shared by all Canadians is necessary. One educational implication of this perspective might be that common school systems, in which all children learn to deal with others from other cultural backgrounds, are preferable to separate schools (see Singh, 1995, for discussion).

Among those who would support the maintenance of cultural and linguistic distinctiveness, there is also discontent with the government's approach to cultural diversity, both in terms of policy and practice. Some members of non-official minority groups reacted against the Official Languages Act's promotion of linguistic duality, claiming that it is, in fact, assimilationist, and relegates the role of 'other' ethnic groups to a less prominent position (Breton, 1986). It is felt that by legislating English and French as official languages, these cultures hence define mainstream Canadian society. Reactions to the Multiculturalism Act have been no less negative – some suggest that the strategies adopted by proponents of multiculturalism reflect only a superficial support of artistic and folkloric aspects of culture, and are less concerned about maintaining and validating ways of life and reducing status differentials between groups (Cummins, 1994). Cultural diversity, as promoted by the Canadian government, effectively maintains power divisions between groups, such that anglophones maintain a higher status relative to other ethnic groups.

Some francophones are threatened by both bilingualism and multiculturalism policies. In the first case, bilingualism may be taken as a subtle form of assimilation because the equal promotion of English does little to counteract the considerable pressures to assimilate to anglophone culture. In the latter case, the premise that all groups with distinctive languages and cultures merit federal support is upsetting. According to Burnet (1989), francophones may thus view multiculturalism as threatening to their position as a 'founding nation', with a special status relative to other ethnic minority groups. Given that French itself was losing vitality in Canadian society, especially in minority French contexts (Castonguay, 1987; de Vries, 1994), the promotion of diversity is seen as doing little to augment *la francophonie* in Canadian society (Hébert, 1992).

The importance of these varied reactions to the policies on cultural diversity lies in the possibility that these perspectives affect how the policies will be interpreted and enacted across regions. For example, provincial interpretations and enactment of the policies vary (Fortier, 1994). According to Gérin-Lajoie (1995; see also Gérin-Lajoie, Gauthier and Heller, 1991; McAndrew, 1991), in addition to endorsing the development and understanding of heritage cultures, the Quebec government's policy of *interculturalisme* emphasizes dialogue and interaction between ethnolinguistic groups, with a focus on the adaptation of newcomer and host societies to each other. It is felt that in this way a French-speaking society can be forged in which all will be equal participants. Thus, the provincial government's promotion of cultural diversity centres on equitable interaction, and coexists with efforts to safeguard the French language.

In English Canada, the promotion of multiculturalism has often been translated into language education programmes that teach cultural awareness and/or heritage culture and language programmes. For example, language programmes for minority francophones outside Quebec have the explicit purpose of maintaining the original language and culture (Gérin-Lajoie, 1995) and, unlike Quebec, have been less focused on integration issues. Indeed, in her study of Albertan francophone teachers of minority French classes, Tardif (1993) found that these teachers saw their primary role as that of promoter of the French language and culture. Other variants are also evident. For instance, legislation in Ontario has reoriented the educational perspective in that province to attend more to issues of anti-racism and ethnocultural equity (Gérin-Lajoie, 1995). Until recently, then, the emphasis in Ontario figured more on the development of awareness of both one's own and others' ethnicities.

In summary, whether the federal government's attempt to promote 'multiculturalism in a bilingual framework' is seen to go too far or as not going far enough, there is indeed an 'intrusion' of the government into language education (Diffey, 1995; Sackney, 1990). Not only are linguistic and communicative objectives specified, but also the kinds of social psychological and socio-political ends that ought to come about. This attempt to manage intergroup relations has received varied interpretations. Policies and reactions, then, mediate the effect of the socio-political context on language programmes and, by extension, language learning. We turn now to consider how this intergroup situation is directly related to the language learning process and its outcomes.

BILINGUALISM AND SECOND LANGUAGE ACQUISITION

The implicit and explicit policies promoting ethnolinguistic diversity, combined with the climate of polarization and ambivalence regarding the value of this diversity, have substantial implications for the language learning process. In addition to influencing curriculum development, the socio-political context influences language learning as well as the eventual outcomes of language learning in a variety of ways. The next sections are devoted, first, to the intergroup, interpersonal and individual contexts impinging on language acquisition and, second, to the non-linguistic outcomes associated with language learning.

Contexts of language learning

The intergroup context

As has been implied in the preceding discussion of language policies, anglophones, as a dominant majority group, face consequences of L2 acquisition which are different from those for francophones who occupy a relatively less dominant position, or for non-official, heritage-language learners. Following Gardner and Clément (1990), the relative contextual preeminence of languages can be defined along two complementary dimensions, concerned with the structural characteristics of the community and their perceptual correlates.

Structural characteristics. Language groups vary in terms of their 'ethnolinguistic vitality'. Coined by Giles, Bourhis and Taylor (1977; see also Prujiner

107

et al., 1984), this term refers to the relative demographic representation of the two communities, their relative socio-economic power, the extent to which they are represented in institutions such as the government and the church, and their level of legislative protection. It would be expected that the language of a group with high ethnolinguistic vitality would retain greater prestige, attract more speakers and, generally, be used more frequently in daily exchanges. It would also be the L2 of choice in educational programmes designed for minority-group members.

Perceptual characteristics. The structural characteristics discussed above refer to objective states of affairs, which may be evaluated from the perspective of an external observer through demographic, sociological or political analysis, for example. The available evidence suggests that the social context of inter-ethnic contact does indeed have an effect on a number of L2 outcomes. A complete understanding of that relationship, however, requires an explanation of how events, external to the individual, come to influence the process of L2 acquisition.

A first step in that direction has been the formulation of a subjective version of the concept of ethnolinguistic vitality. Clément (1980, 1984) proposed that subjective vitality was related to affective processes of the type described above and, ultimately, to motivation and L2 proficiency. Results of empirical observations using the *Subjective Vitality Questionnaire* (Bourhis, Giles and Rosenthal, 1981) provided mixed results (Clément, 1986; Gardner, Lalonde, Nero and Young, 1988; Labrie and Clément, 1986). Subsequent psychometric work has resulted in more refined measures that suggest a closer link between L2 subjective vitality and L2 education outcomes and correlates (see also Landry and Allard, 1992).

The influence of L2 vitality cannot, however, be considered independently from that of the first language. In fact, L1 and L2 vitality interact according to a process best identified as a social version of the linguistic interdependence hypothesis. Cummins (1979) proposed that, from a cognitive standpoint, the level of competence in the L2 is a function of the level of competence in the first language. By extension, social psychological and cultural benefits accruing from L2 education would be related to the extent to which the first language and culture are well established and valued (Clément, 1980; Landry and Allard, 1990). For majority-group members such as Canadian anglophones, second-language learning does not represent a problem. For minority-group members, however – such as francophones living outside of Quebec, and any other ethnic minority whose first language is not English – a harmonious integration in an English world might require the 'shielding' of the first language and culture from the erosive effects of contact, at least for the time that it takes to firmly establish them. Thus, apprehensions formulated by minority-group members regarding the assimilationist effects of language policies find an echo in research on language education and learning.

The interpersonal context

The effects of ethnolinguistic vitality may not, however, be felt directly and entirely by language learners. Conditions prevailing in society at large may be mediated or buffered by the proximal linguistic environment in which the individual evolves. In fact, it is conceivable that, in a secluded or sheltered linguistic milieu, minority-group members would show little of the linguistic pressure born outside that milieu. The concept encapsulating such a possibility is that of personal communication networks (e.g., Milroy, 1980; Rogers and Kincaid, 1981). A communication network refers to the group of individuals with whom we communicate on a regular basis. That group can be characterized according to the relative importance of the L1 and L2 (and any subsequent language) subnetworks, the extent to which they are closely knit, and their redundancy. It would be expected that a minority ethnolinguistic situation could be adequately compensated by an important first-language subnetwork acting as an enclave against the majority L2 pressure (Clément, 1984; Prujiner *et al.*, 1984). Conversely, an important L2 network could promote its usage even for members of a majority group where L2 is a minority language.

Whether members of a high or a low vitality group, language learners are faced with individuals in their immediate interpersonal contexts who can influence both the language learning process and language learning outcomes. Thus, even unilingual settings provide for a language context, or at least for its simulation in the classroom. As shown by the work of Gardner and Smythe (1975), high levels of proficiency may be attained in unilingual settings. Furthermore, such proficiency is also correlated with attitudes towards the L2-speaking group, even in its relative absence. Students participating in immersion programmes (Genesee, 1987; Swain and Lapkin, 1982) in settings in which the L2 group is absent may also develop high levels of proficiency, at least with respect to aspects of communicative competence. The importance of the classroom as a L2 context, and of the L2 teacher as a representative of the L2 group, is suggested by the recurrent relation between the evaluation of these aspects by the students and attitudes towards the L2 group and desire for contact (e.g., Gardner, 1983, 1985). As illustrated by Hume, Lepicq and Bourhis (1993), cues as subtle as the accent of the teacher's speech may provoke more or less positive evaluations from the learner. Indeed, the role assumed by the L2 teacher may, in unilingual communities, be an important vector of attitude formation and change.

Parents also provide a familial context in which L2 education may be moderated or enhanced. Gardner (1988) has suggested that parents may play an active role by encouraging efforts and monitoring their child's language-learning progress. They may also play a passive role by modelling personal interest in the language and the corresponding group and, generally, by displaying positive inter-ethnic attitudes and values. Few studies have concerned themselves with these issues but what information is available (e.g., Colletta, Clément and Edwards, 1983; Clément, 1978) corroborates the roles and functions hypothesized by Gardner (1988).

Parents and teachers remain important in contexts where inter-ethnic contact is possible, but their influence must be understood in conjunction with the outcome and correlates of intergroup contact. Genesee, Rogers and Holobow (1983) report that an important correlate of immersion students' French usage outside the classroom was the extent to which they felt supported by their francophone interlocutors. What this and other studies (e.g., Cleghorn and Genesee, 1984) show is that the outcome of language education reflects wider societal conditions and tensions. This finding is not only germane to Canada. In their world-wide review of bilingualism programmes, Hamers and Blanc (1989) conclude that affective, linguistic and cognitive outcomes of these programmes are intimately linked to wider social conditions – most importantly, the relative valorization of the L1 and L2, an assumption of the Canadian policy described above.

The intra-individual context

In addition to the societal and interpersonal context, characteristics of the individual – particularly the attitudes and beliefs about other ethnic groups and their ability to communicate in the L2 – have an influence on language learning. Central to the concerns of researchers investigating social psychological aspects of individual differences is the role of motivation. Motivation to learn a L2 has been shown not only to be related to proficiency but also to a family of interrelated phenomena, including the use and maintenance of L2 (Gardner, Moorcroft and Metford, 1989), persistence in taking courses when they are optional (Clément, Smythe and Gardner, 1978; Lewis and Shapson, 1989) and activity in the classroom (Frohlich, Stern and Todesco, 1978; Gliksman, Gardner and Smythe, 1982).

In a seminal study, Gardner and Lambert (1959) showed that motivation to acquire an L2 was related to a positive attitude towards the L2 group and a desire to become similar to valued members of the L2 community. With the accumulation of empirical evidence, the attitudinal aspects sustaining motivation came to be associated with a variety of concomitant affective predispositions. Thus, evidence stemming from numerous factor analytic studies supported the relation between positive intergroup attitudes, positive attitudes towards foreign languages, the L2 course and teacher and interethnic contact (Clément, Dörnyei and Noels, 1994; Gardner, 1985; Gardner and Clément, 1990, for a review). The tendency suggested by this recurrent cluster of variables has been identified as corresponding to an integrative motive or, more simply, integrativeness (Gardner and Smythe, 1975).

If the link between motivation and integrativeness has been repeatedly shown, it is also evident that other individual characteristics may influence and/or moderate language-learning outcomes. At least three lines of research illustrate this. First, an implication of the attitude–motivation relationship is that more positive attitudes will lead to greater effort and desire to learn the L2. One way of making attitudes more positive might be to promote interethnic contact. The few studies which have looked at the effects of contact in the context of L2-learning programmes, however, report mixed results. From their study of bilingual exchange programmes specifically aimed at this issue, Hanna and Smith (1979) conclude that attitudes towards the other group are not of great significance to the participants. Clément, Gardner and Smythe (1977) report, however, that interethnic contact programmes meant to stimulate L2 learning motivation may work only for those participants who actively avail themselves of communication opportunities once in the contact situation. Adverse effects could be expected for those who do not achieve some measure of exchange once in the contact situation (see also Desrochers and Gardner, 1981). Clearly, the matter of the relationship between attitude change and motivation change is not a simple one. Mediating and moderating factors are operating here and further studies are warranted.

The singularity of the relationship between attitude and motivation is also challenged by results pertaining to the influence of fear of assimilation on L2 learning. As long as the target language is that of a minority group, as with the acquisition of French by anglophones in most of the Canadian context, there is little reason to believe that fearing the loss of the first language and culture would have any impact on motivation. The matter may be quite different from the perspective of the minority-group student learning a majority-group language. Research by Clément and his colleagues (e.g., Clément, 1984, 1986; Clément and Kruidenier, 1985) has shown that, at least with minority group members, the potential loss of membership in the native ethnolinguistic community is related to poorer quality and frequency of contact with the L2 community, and to lower motivation to learn the L2.

Integrativeness and fear of assimilation may be seen as opposing forces within an individual affective process (Clément, 1980, 1984). To the extent that one is more salient than the other, interethnic contact and L2 communication may be either facilitated or disrupted. The influence of this affective process on the motivation to learn an L2 and eventual proficiency is, however, mediated through a further construct, L2 self-confidence.

L2 self-confidence refers to the relationship between the speaker and the L2. It corresponds to the belief in being able to communicate in the L2 in an adaptive and efficient manner. It has two components. The first cognitive component corresponds to the self-evaluation of L2 skills, a judgement made by the speaker about the degree of mastery achieved in the L2. The second affective component corresponds to L2 anxiety. This refers specifically to the discomfort experienced when using a L2, and has been the object of much research, mostly from the classroom perspective (Clément, Gardner and Smythe, 1977, 1980; MacIntyre and Gardner, 1991). The results reported by Clément and his colleagues (1994) support the relationship between language anxiety and self-evaluation and demonstrate the value of combining the two variables into a single, self-confidence construct. Furthermore, L2 confidence has been shown to be related to aspects of intergroup contact (Clément and Kruidenier, 1985), to actual competence in the L2 (Clément, 1986) and, as will be discussed below, to several non-linguistic outcomes such as identity and psychological adjustment (e.g., Noels, Pon and Clément, 1996).

Taken together, the results concerning the effects of attitude change, fear of assimilation and L2 self-confidence suggest the existence of social psychological processes which reinforce and extend the original attitude-based formulation of L2 motivation. Specifically, they point to the importance of the social context as a moderator of the effects of individual differences on L2 learning outcomes. Thus, as much as it influences language learning indirectly through the implementation of cultural diversity policies, the social context is reflected in the impact of variations which have been considered as highly individualized.

Non-linguistic outcomes

As noted earlier, the socio-political context, as indexed by the vitality of the ethnolinguistic group to which one belongs (relative to that of other groups), may have implications for social outcomes of language learning.

112

Much of the discussion on this topic hearkens back to the distinction made by Lambert (1975) between 'additive' and 'subtractive' bilingualism. That is, in the process of acquiring an L2, one also potentially acquires a second cultural referent group. The implications of L2 acquisition for the L1 and L1-group belonging depend upon the sociostructural status of the group to which the individual belongs. For minority-group members, the acquisition of the L2 implies a lessening of L1 abilities and identity, but for majority-group members there is no necessary effect on the L1 or identity, and possibly an enhancement of these aspects (Clément, 1980, 1986; Landry and Allard, 1984, 1990, 1992). The discussion, then, turns to consider two interrelated factors: identity and adaptation.

Identity

Results of some research concerning the relation between ethnolinguistic identity and language learning suggest that there is a positive relation between various L2 indices of competence and indices of identification with the L2 group. Correspondingly, correlations between L2 competence and identification with the original language group are often negative (Landry and Allard, 1992; Noels *et al.*, 1996). This pattern of subtractive bilingualism does not necessarily imply that ethnic identity is completely lost once the original group language is lost. Edwards (1977, 1985, 1992) suggests that the maintenance of language for communicative purposes is not essential for the maintenance of feelings of own-group ethnic identification. Indeed, while several studies do suggest that language is an important dimension of ethnic identity (e.g., Driedger, 1975; Taylor, Bassili and Aboud, 1973), others indicate that it is not necessarily a defining feature of ethnic-group membership. For example, Edwards and his colleagues (e.g., Edwards and Chisholm, 1987; Edwards and Doucette, 1987) found that several subjects in their studies used a hyphenated ethnolinguistic label for self-description, although they could not speak the language of both groups. Thus, other cultural features besides language, including physical characteristics and/or religious affiliation, can support a sense of ethnic identity.

At the same time, for those groups who define themselves primarily along linguistic lines, variations in language use may be linked to variations in ethnic identity. Clément, Gauthier and Noels (1993; see also Cameron and Lalonde, 1994) examined Franco-Ontarian adolescents who spoke primarily French or primarily English. Francophones who spoke primarily English identified less strongly with the francophone group than did francophones who spoke primarily French. Shifts in communicative behaviour, then, may be indicative of changes in identity.

The link between identification and language may be complicated by a consideration of the situation in which language use takes place. Just as L2 use may depend upon the specific situation (Landry and Allard, 1994), variations in feelings of identity may depend upon the situation. Clément and Noels (1992; Noels and Clément, 1996) suggest that identity is negotiated through language choices in different situations, such that the degree of identification with each group depends upon with whom one interacts and the normative expectations of that situation. Their research on anglophone and francophone students at a bilingual university showed that, for anglophones, identity is more likely to be stronger in a situation that includes the possibility of interethnic contact, and perhaps L2 use, than in more private situations where contact with the L2-group is restricted (see Edwards, 1985). This pattern, however, was not found for francophones. At the same time, all groups of students had equivalent levels of identification with the L2-group in the university context, suggesting that contexts can be created that shelter the minority-group members from the acculturative effects of intergroup contact found in other settings. Moreover, these special contexts may also promote L2-group identification in majority-group members.

In summary, several issues concerning the language-identity link require resolution. An examination of the research on this topic suggests that where language is an important characteristic of identity, L2 use is related to lessened identity, at least for minority-group members. Specific situations, such as the school environment, may shelter the language and temper identity loss. This would support the premise of language education policy, that state intervention in language issues is both warranted and an effective way of achieving cultural policy goals.

Adjustment

Several researchers maintain that developing proficiency in a L2 can also affect emotional adjustment for better or for worse (e.g., Gardner, 1977; Lambert, 1975). In line with other discussions of acculturation stress (e.g., Berry and Kim, 1988; Phinney, 1991), adjustment corresponds to mental health status, and may include physical, psychological and social aspects (Berry, Kim, Minde and Mok, 1987). Lambert (1975) suggests that, on the one hand, bilingualism may have a negative effect on well-being as a result of identity conflicts. On the other hand, knowledge of the L2 and access to a second culture may give the individual additional resources to meet the demands of daily life.

Some evidence supports the second hypothesis. Several researchers suggest that acquiring competence in a L2 may have positive implications for the individual who is in contact with the L2 culture (Church, 1982; Deutsch and Won,

1963; Nicassio, 1985; Nishida, 1985; Redmond and Bunyi, 1993; Wong-Rieger, 1984). According to Kim (1988), it is through communication that we learn to relate to the environment and are able to fulfil various human needs. The better able we are to communicate, the more harmonious our adaptation will be. If we are unable to communicate, adaptation is unlikely, and symptoms of distress will arise. In multicultural settings, it becomes necessary to acquire the skills and knowledge necessary to operate effectively and appropriately with members of the other culture (Rogler, Cortes and Malgady, 1991; Tran, 1990).

Indeed, L2 variables, including a preference for, knowledge of and self-confidence in the L2, have been shown to be linked to lower levels of stress (Chataway and Berry, 1989; Noels *et al.*, 1996) and higher levels of satisfaction with the self and society and/or a higher sense of personal control (Dion, Dion and Pak, 1990; Noels *et al.*, 1996; Pak, Dion and Dion, 1985) in a variety of ethnic groups. Pesner and Auld (1980), for example, found that bilingual high-school students have higher self-esteem than unilingual students, at least in some situations.

In their examination of Inuit, White and mixed-heritage children registered in Inuttitut, French and English programmes in Northern Quebec, Wright and Taylor (1995) evaluated the impact of heritage-language programmes on both personal (i.e., pertaining to the self as an individual) and collective (i.e., pertaining to the self as a member of a particular ethnic group) esteem. Generally, Inuit children had lower personal self-esteem than mixed-heritage and other children, but all children increased in personal self-esteem over time. An analysis of Inuit children enrolled in Inuttitut (i.e., heritage-language) classes showed that these children, but not Inuit children enrolled in French or English (i.e., L2) classes, experienced significant increases in personal self-esteem over the course of the school year. There was less evidence that the language programmes influenced collective self-esteem. Thus, at least with regard to personal self-esteem, heritage-language education can promote a positive self-image.

The link between language learning and self-esteem is central to the arguments of many proponents of bilingual education. Some research evidence suggests that L2 competence and self-confidence may mediate the influence of intergroup contact on emotional adjustment, and the educational context may have a critical role to play in this regard. At the same time, the limited amount of published research available on this topic precludes any clear conclusions about the validity of this link. As emphasized by Alexander and Baker (1992), without such support the promotion of esteem as a benefit of bilingualism and bilingual education remains tenuous.

115

The preceding discussion of additive and subtractive bilingualism has suggested that developing competence in the L2 is part of an acculturation process which has certain social psychological costs and benefits. Sheltered contexts can help to attenuate this process but, at the same time, the dynamics within the classroom may be influenced by external circumstances (Heller, 1984). Moreover, it is not clear whether the effects of the school ambience extend to identity in other areas of life. As Edwards (1993) suggests, the prevailing societal and economic forces could well override the influences of a heritage-language programme. It should also be recognized that not all individuals desire to maintain ethnic identity and language – many wish to join the larger society without such maintenance. Indeed, this relinquishment of identity may have positive correlates in some cases: although greater L2 competence may be related to lessened L1-group identity, it may also be related to better psychological well-being (Noels *et al.*, 1996). Such a pattern of findings suggests that non-linguistic correlates of L2 learning may not show parallel patterns of acculturation, pointing to the need for multidimensional assessments of 'additive' and 'subtractive' bilingualism (Landry and Allard, 1990; Noels *et al.*, 1996).

CONCLUSION

Since the early work on bilingualism and bilingual education (e.g., Gardner and Lambert, 1972; see Gardner, 1985, for a review), considerable emphasis has been placed on the contention that language learning is not solely a pedagogical issue, but also a social one. This review demonstrates the common influence of the socio-political context and values on both educational policy and expectations, and language-acquisition processes and outcomes. The political debate and language research results mirror respective concerns and, to some extent, answer reciprocal questions. How does language relate to the maintenance of cultural identity and self-esteem? What are the implications of language learning for the development of respect and equality between groups? Can learning a second language contribute to the reduction of prejudice? Ultimately, one might wonder if language education, by itself, can realize these ideals.

It would seem that any language programme that strives to achieve societal goals would have to go beyond traditional emphases on developing linguistic and communicative competence, and incorporate elements from other social science perspectives. One promising venture in this direction is the curriculum developed in the National Core French Study (see LeBlanc, 1990; see also Stern, 1982), which includes cultural and language awareness syllabi. Such a curriculum might also be informed by theory and research on intercultural communication training, which emphasizes the development of strategies for the negotiation of meaning between different cultural groups (Wiseman, 1995), as well as the importance of improving attitudes towards members of the other group (Cargile and Giles, 1996).

Whatever programme is adopted to reflect policies on pluralism, we maintain that a systematic evaluation of the effects of that programme is essential. As this review has indicated, some of the more socially relevant issues raised in governmental policies have received limited empirical attention. Although the objectives of many language education programmes include the goal of engendering the societal ideals of cultural diversity as outlined in the Official Languages and Multiculturalism Acts, there has been little evaluation of how well these goals are achieved in specific programmes (but see Gardner, MacIntyre and Lysynchuk, 1990). From our perspective, social psychologists interested in language learning bring considerable experience to bear on many of these issues, and an expertise which could be profitably applied to the evaluation of these policies.

Over the last twenty years, Canada has evolved into a multicultural and multilingual society. The question now is what emphasis pluralist policies and programmes will receive. How can we encourage children to have pride in their heritage and respect for that of others? How can we, at the same time, best recognize ethnic group identity and develop a common Canadian identity? Expecting language teachers to respond to all these issues would not be realistic or fair – not without a restructuring of language education, and not without the integration of social approaches into the curriculum. Given the centrality of language issues for inter-ethnic relations, however, educators may be obliged to do so.

Note

Completion of this chapter was facilitated by a post-doctoral fellowship from the Social Sciences and Humanities Research Council of Canada to the first author and a research grant from the same agency to the second author. The authors would like to thank Howard Giles for his helpful comments on an earlier draft of this paper.

References

Alexander, S. and Baker, K. (1992). Some ethical issues in applied social psychology. The case of bilingual education and self-esteem. *Journal of Applied Social Psychology, 22,* 1741–1757.

Berry, J. W. (1992). Costs and benefits of multiculturalism: a social psychological analysis. In S. Hryniuk (ed.), *Twenty Years of Multiculturalism: Successes and Failures* (pp. 183–199). Winnipeg: St John's College Press.

Berry, J. W., Kalin, R. and Taylor, D. M. (1977). *Multiculturalism and Ethnic Attitudes in Canada.* Ottawa: Supply and Services Canada.

Berry, J. W. and Kim, U. (1988). Acculturation and mental health. In P. Dasen, J. W. Berry and N. Sartorius (eds.), *Health and Cross-Cultural Psychology* (pp. 207–236). London: Sage.

Berry, J. W., Kim, U., Minde, T. and Mok, D. (1987). Comparative studies of acculturative stress. *International Migration Review, 21,* 491–511.

Bissoondath, N. (1994). *Selling Illusions: The Cult of Multiculturalism in Canada.* Toronto: Penguin.

Bourhis, R. Y. (1994). Introduction and overview of language events in Canada. *International Journal of the Sociology of Language, 102,* 5–36.

Bourhis, R. Y., Giles, H. and Rosenthal, D. (1981). Notes on the construction of a 'Subjective Vitality Questionnaire' for ethnolinguistic groups. *Journal of Multilingual and Multicultural Development, 2,* 145–155.

Breton, R. (1986). Multiculturalism and Canadian nation-building. In A. Cairns and C. Williams (eds.), *The Politics of Gender, Ethnicity, and Language in Canada* (pp. 27–66). Toronto: University of Toronto Press.

Burnet, J. (1989). Taking into account: the other ethnic groups and the Royal Commission on Bilingualism and Biculturalism. In J. S. Frideres (ed.), *Multiculturalism and Intergroup Relations* (pp. 9–17). Westport, CT: Greenwood.

Cameron, J. E. and Lalonde, R. N. (1994). Self-ethnicity, and social group memberships in two generations of Italian Canadians. *Journal of Personality and Social Psychology, 20,* 514–520.

Cargile, A. C. and Giles, H. (1996). Intercultural communication training: review critique, and a new theoretical framework. In B. R. Burleson (ed.), *Communication Yearbook* (pp. 385–423). Thousand Oaks, CA: Sage.

Castonguay, C. (1987). The anglicization of Canada, 1971–1981. *Language Problems and Language Planning, 11,* 22–34.

Chataway, C. J. and Berry, J. W. (1989). Acculturation experiences, appraisal, coping and adaptation: a comparison of Hong Kong Chinese, French, and English students in Canada. *Canadian Journal of Behavioural Science, 21,* 295–309.

Church, A. T. (1982). Sojourner adjustment. *Psychological Bulletin, 91,* 540–572.

Cleghorn, A. and Genesee, F. (1984). Languages in contact: an ethnographic study of interaction in an immersion school. *TESOL Quarterly, 18,* 595–625.

Clément, R. (1978). *Motivational Characteristics of Francophones Learning English.* Quebec City: International Centre for Research on Bilingualism, Laval University.

    (1980). Ethnicity, contact and communicative competence in a second language. In H. Giles, W. P. Robinson and P. Smith (eds.), *Language: Social Psychological Perspectives* (pp. 147–154). Oxford: Pergamon Press.

(1984). Aspects socio-psychologiques de la communication inter-ethnique et de l'identité sociale. *Recherches Sociologiques, 15,* 293–312.

(1986). Second language proficiency and acculturation: an investigation of the effects of language status and individual characteristics. *Journal of Language and Social Psychology, 5,* 271–290.

Clément, R., Dörnyei, Z. and Noels, K. A. (1994). Motivation, self-confidence and group cohesion in the foreign language classroom. *Language Learning, 44,* 417–448.

Clément, R., Gardner, R. C. and Smythe, P. C. (1977). Motivational variables in second language acquisition: a study of francophones learning English. *Canadian Journal of Behavioural Science, 9,* 123–133.

(1980). Social and individual factors in second language acquisition. *Canadian Journal of Behavioural Science, 12,* 293–302.

Clément, R., Gauthier, R. and Noels, K. A. (1993). Choix langagiers en milieu minoritaire: attitudes et identité concomitantes. *Canadian Journal of Behavioural Science, 25,* 149–164.

Clément, R. and Kruidenier, B. G. (1985). Aptitude, attitude and motivation in second language proficiency: a test of Clément's model. *Journal of Language and Social Psychology, 4,* 21–37.

Clément, R. and Noels, K. A. (1992). Towards a situated approach to ethnolinguistic identity: the effects of status on individuals and groups. *Journal of Language and Social Psychology, 11,* 203–232.

Clément, R., Smythe, P. C. and Gardner, R. C. (1978). Persistence in second language study: motivational considerations. *Canadian Modern Language Review, 34,* 688–694.

Colletta, S., Clément, R. and Edwards, H. P. (1983). *Community and Parental Influence: Effects on Student Motivation and French Second Language Proficiency.* Quebec City: International Center for Research on Bilingualism, Laval University.

Cummins, J. (1979). Linguistic interdependence and the educational development of bilingual children. *Review of Educational Research, 49,* 222–251.

(1994). Heritage language learning and teaching. In J. W. Berry and J. A. Laponce (eds.), *Ethnicity and Culture in Canada* (pp. 435–456). Toronto: University of Toronto Press.

Cummins, J. and Danesi, M. (1990). *Heritage Languages: The Development and Denial of Canada's Linguistic Resources.* Toronto: Garamond/Our Schools-Ourselves Education Foundation.

Desrochers, A. and Gardner, R. C. (1981). *Second Language Acquisition: An Investigation of a Bicultural Excursion Experience.* Quebec City: International Centre for Research on Bilingualism, Laval University.

Deutsch, S. E. and Won, G. Y. M. (1963). Some social factors in the adjustment of foreign nationals in the United States. *Journal of Social Issues, 19,* 115–122.

de Vries, J. (1994). Canada's official language communities: an overview of the current demolinguistic situation. *International Journal of the Sociology of Language, 106,* 37–68.

Diffey, N. (1995). Second-language curriculum models and program design: recent trends in North America. *Canadian Journal of Education, 17,* 208–219.

Dion, K. K., Dion, K. L. and Pak, A. W. (1990). The role of self-reported language proficiencies in the cultural and psychosocial adaptation among members of Toronto, Canada's Chinese community. *Journal of Asian Pacific Communication, 1,* 173–189.

Driedger, L. (1975). In search of cultural identity factors: a comparison of ethnic students. *Canadian Review of Sociology and Anthropology, 12,* 150–162.

Edwards, J. (1977). Ethnic identity and bilingual education. In H. Giles (ed.), *Language, Ethnicity and Intergroup Relations* (pp. 253–282). London: Academic Press.

(1985). *Language, Society and Identity.* Oxford: Basil Blackwell.

(1992). Language in group and individual identity. In G. M. Breakwell (ed.), *Social Psychology of Identity and the Self Concept* (pp. 129–146). San Diego: Academic Press.

(1993). Identity and language in the Canadian educational context. In M. Danesi, K. McLeod and S. Morris (eds.), *Heritage Languages and Education: The Canadian Experience* (pp. 123–135). Oakville, ON: Mosaic.

(1994). Ethnolinguistic pluralism and its discontents: a Canadian study, and some general observations. *International Journal of the Sociology of Language, 110,* 5–85.

Edwards, J. and Chisholm, J. (1987). Language, multiculturalism and identity: a Canadian study. *Journal of Multilingual and Multicultural Development, 8,* 391–408.

Edwards, J. and Doucette L. (1987). Ethnic salience, identity and symbolic ethnicity. *Canadian Ethnic Studies, 19,* 52–62.

Fortier, D. (1994). Official language policies in Canada: a quiet revolution. *International Journal of the Sociology of Language, 105/106,* 69–97.

Friesen, J. W. (1993). *When Cultures Clash* (2nd edn). Calgary: Detselig.

Frohlich, M., Stern, H. H. and Todesco, A. (1978). *The Good Language Learner.* Toronto: Ontario Institute for Studies in Education.

Gamlin, P. J., Berndorff, D., Mitsopulos, A. and Demetriou, K. (1994). Multicultural education in Canada from a global perspective. In J. W. Berry and J. A. Laponce (eds.), *Ethnicity and Culture in Canada: The Research Landscape* (pp. 457–482). Toronto: University of Toronto Press.

Gardner, R. C. (1977). Social factors in second language acquisition and binguality. In W. H. Coons, D. M. Taylor and M. Tremblay (eds.), *The Individual, Language and Society in Canada* (pp. 105–148). Ottawa: The Canada Council.

Gardner, R. C. (1983). Learning another language: a true social psychological experiment. *Journal of Language and Social Psychology, 2,* 219–239.

Gardner, R. C. (1985). *Social Psychology and Second Language Learning: The Role of Attitudes and Motivation.* London: Arnold.

(1988). The socio-educational model of second language learning: assumptions, findings and issues. *Language Learning, 38,* 101–126.

Gardner, R. C. and Clément, R. (1990). Social psychological perspectives on second language acquisition. In H. Giles and W. P. Robinson (eds.), *The Handbook of Language and Social Psychology* (pp. 495–517). Chichester: Wiley.

Gardner, R. C., Lalonde, R. N., Nero, A. M. and Young, M. Y. (1988). Ethnic stereotypes: implications of measurement strategy. *Social Cognition, 6*, 40–60.

Gardner, R. C. and Lambert, W. E. (1959). Motivational variables in second language acquisition. *Canadian Journal of Psychology, 13*, 266–272.

Gardner, R. C. and Lambert, W. E. (1972). *Attitudes and Motivation in Second Language Learning.* Rowley, MA: Newbury House.

Gardner, R. C., MacIntyre, P. D. and Lysynchuk, L. M. (1990). Affection dimension in second language programme evaluation. *Language, Culture and Curriculum, 2*, 39–64.

Gardner, R. C., Moorcroft, R. and Metford, J. (1989). Second language learning in an immersion programme: factors influencing acquisition and retention. *Journal of Language and Social Psychology, 8*, 287–305.

Gardner, R. C. and Smythe, P. C. (1975). Second language acquisition: a social psychological approach. *Research Bulletin No. 33.* London, Ontario: University of Western Ontario, Department of Psychology.

Genesee, F. (1987). *Learning Through Two Languages.* Cambridge, MA: Newbury House.

Genesee, F., Rogers, P. and Holobow, N. (1983). The social psychology of second language learning: another point of view. *Language Learning, 33*, 209–224.

Gérin-Lajoie, D. (1995). La politique d'antiracisme et d'équité ethnoculturelle dans les écoles de langage française de l'Ontario. *Éducation et francophonie, 23*, 20–24.

Gérin-Lajoie, D., Gauthier, L. and Heller, M. (1991). *Les politiques en matière d'éducation multiculturelle/interculturelle dans les écoles de langue française au Canada.* Ottawa: Comité Canadien Francophone pour l'Education Interculturelle.

Giles, H., Bourhis, R. Y. and Taylor, D. M. (1977). Towards a theory of language in ethnic group-relations. In H. Giles (ed.), *Language, Ethnicity and Intergroup Relations* (pp. 307–348). New York: Academic Press.

Gliksman, L., Gardner, R. C. and Smythe, P. C. (1982). The role of the integrative motive on students' participation in the French classroom. *Canadian Modern Language Review, 38*, 625–647.

Hamers, J. F. and Blanc, M. H. A. (1989). *Bilinguality and Bilingualism.* Cambridge: Cambridge University Press.

Hanna, G. and Smith, A. H. (1979). Evaluating summer bilingual exchanges: a progress report. *Working Papers on Bilingualism, 19*, 29–58.

Hébert, R. (1992). Francophone perspectives on multiculturalism. In S. Hryniuk (ed.), *Twenty Years of Multiculturalism: Successes and Failures* (pp. 59–72). Winnipeg: St John's College Press.

Heller, M. (1984). Language and ethnic identity in a Toronto French-language school. *Canadian Ethnic Studies, 16*, 1–13.

Hume, E., Lepicq, D. and Bourhis, R. (1993). Attitudes des étudiants canadiens anglais face aux accents des professeurs de français en Ontario. *Canadian Modern Language Review, 49,* 209–235.

Kalin, R. and Berry, J. W. (1994). Ethnic and multicultural attitudes. In J. W. Berry and J. A. Laponce (eds.), *Ethnicity and Culture in Canada* (pp. 293–321). Toronto: University of Toronto Press.

Kim, Y. Y. (1988). *Communication and Cross-Cultural Adaptation: An Integrative Theory.* Clevedon, Avon: Multilingual Matters.

Krause, N., Bennett, J. and Tran, T. V. (1989). Age differences in the acculturation process. *Psychology and Aging, 4,* 321–332.

Labelle, H. (1989). Multiculturalism and government. In J. S. Frideres (ed.), *Multiculturalism and Intergroup Relations* (pp. 1–7). Westport, CT: Greenwood.

Labrie, N. and Clément, R. (1986). Ethnolinguistic vitality, self-confidence and second language proficiency: an investigation. *Journal of Multilingual and Multicultural Development, 7,* 269–282.

Lambert, W. E. (1975). Culture and language as factors in learning and education. In A. Wolfgang (ed.), *Education of Immigrant Students* (pp. 55–83). Toronto: Ontario Institute for Studies in Education.

Landry, R. and Allard, R. (1984). Bilinguisme additif, bilinguisme soustractif et identité ethnolinguistique. *Recherches Sociologiques, 15,* 337–358.

(1990). Contact des langues et développement bilingue: un modèle macroscopique. *Canadian Modern Language Review, 46,* 527–553.

(1992). Ethnolinguistic vitality and the bilingual development of minority and majority group students. In W. Fase, K. Jaspaert and S. Kroon (eds.), *Maintenance and Loss of Minority Languages* (pp. 223–251). Amsterdam: John Benjamins.

(1994). Diglossia, ethnolinguistic vitality, and language behavior. *International Journal of the Sociology of Language, 108,* 15–42.

LeBlanc, R. (1990). *Étude nationale sur le français de base – Rapport synthèse.* (Association Canadienne des Professeurs de Langues Secondes). Quebec: Presses des Ateliers graphiques Marc Veilleux à Cap-Saint Ignace.

Lewis, C. and Shapson, S. M. (1989). Secondary French immersion: a study of students who leave the program. *Canadian Modern Language Journal, 45,* 539–578.

McAndrew, M. (1991). L'enseignement des langues d'origine à l'école publique en Ontario et au Québec: politiques et enjeu. *Canadian Modern Language Review, 47,* 617–634.

MacIntyre, P. D. and Gardner, R. C. (1991). Methods and results in the study of anxiety and language learning: a review of the literature. *Language Learning, 41,* 85–117.

Milroy, L. (1980). *Language and Social Networks.* Oxford: Blackwell.

Nicassio, P. M. (1985). The psychosocial adjustment of the Southeast Asian refugee: an overview of empirical findings and theoretical models. *Journal of Cross-Cultural Psychology, 16,* 153–173.

Nishida, H. (1985). Japanese intercultural communication competence and cross-cultural adjustment. *International Journal of Intercultural Relations, 9,* 247-269.

Noels, K. A. and Clément, R. (1996). Communicating across cultures. *Canadian Journal of Behavioural Science, 28,* 214-228.

Noels, K. A., Pon, G. and Clément, R. (1996). Attitudes, identity, language and stress: the acculturation experience of Chinese university students in Ottawa. *Journal of Language and Social Psychology, 15,* 246-264.

O'Bryan, K. G., Reitz, J. G. and Kuplowska, O. (1976). *Non-Official Languages: A Study of Canadian Multiculturalism.* Ottawa: Supply and Services Canada.

Pak, A. W., Dion, K. L. and Dion, K. K. (1985). Correlates of self-confidence with English among Chinese students in Toronto. *Canadian Journal of Behavioural Sciences, 17,* 369-378.

Pesner, J. W. and Auld, F. (1980). The relationship between bilingual proficiency and self-esteem. *International Journal of Intercultural Relations, 4,* 339-351.

Phinney, J. S. (1991). Ethnic identity and self-esteem: a review and integration. *Hispanic Journal of Behavioral Sciences, 13,* 193-208.

Prujiner, A., Deshaies, D., Hamers, J. M., Blanc, M., Clément, R. and Landry, R. (1984). *Variation du comportement langagier lorsque deux langues sont en contact* (Série G, no. 5.). Quebec: International Centre for Research on Bilingualism.

Redmond, M. V. and Bunyi, J. M. (1993). The relationship of intercultural communication competence with stress and the handling of stress as reported by international students. *International Journal of Intercultural Relations, 17,* 235-254.

Rogers, E. M. and Kincaid, D. L. (1981). *Communication Networks.* New York: Free Press.

Rogler, L. H., Cortes, D. E. and Malgady, R. G. (1991). Acculturation and mental health status among Hispanics: convergence and new directions for research. *American Psychologist, 46,* 585-597.

Sackney, L. E. (1990). Federal intrusions into education through immersion and second language programs. In J. Y. L. Yam (ed.), *Canadian Public Education System* (pp. 123-141). Calgary: Detselig.

Singh, B. R. (1995). Shared values, particular values and education for a multicultural society. *Educational Review, 47,* 11-24.

Stern, H. H. (1982). French Core Programs across Canada: how can we improve them? *Canadian Modern Language Review, 39,* 34-47.

Swain, M. and Lapkin, S. (1982). *Evaluating Bilingual Education: A Canadian Case Study.* Clevedon, Avon: Multilingual Matters.

Tardif, C. (1993). L'identité culturelle dans les écoles francophones minoritaires: perceptions et croyances des enseignants. *Canadian Modern Language Review, 49,* 787-798.

Taylor, D. M., Bassili, J. N. and Aboud, F. E. (1973). Dimensions of ethnic identity: an example from Québec. *Journal of Social Psychology, 89,* 185-192.

Tran, T. V. (1990). Language acculturation among older Vietnamese refugee adults. *Gerontologist, 30,* 94-99.

Wiseman, R. L. (ed.) (1995). *Intercultural Communication Theory.* Thousand Oaks, CA: Sage.

Wong-Rieger, D. (1984). Testing a model of emotional and coping responses to problems in adaptation: foreign students at a Canadian university. *International Journal of Intercultural Relations, 8,* 153–184.

Wright, S. C. and Taylor, D. M. (1995). Identity and the language of the classroom: investigating the impact of heritage versus second language instruction on personal and collective self-esteem. *Educational Psychology, 87,* 241–252.

6 **Aboriginal languages: history**

Eung-Do Cook

INTRODUCTION

According to Bright (1994), as many as 300 aboriginal languages may
have been spoken in North America, although the number has been significantly reduced since the first contact with Europeans, and many are on the verge
of extinction. Canada's fifty-three aboriginal languages are classified into eleven
families and isolates (Foster, 1982). Despite the genetic and typological diversity
of aboriginal languages that have existed since prehistoric times, their intricate
grammars and enriched vocabularies have not been recognized and appreciated
for what they are by the general public. Although the situation has been changing, one often encounters people who believe that there are only two aboriginal
languages, 'Eskimo' and 'Indian' and that these languages are 'primitive' – without an elaborate grammar or vocabulary. Needless to say, that is far from true,
and such a myth is largely attributable to the lack of accessible information and
inadequate documentation, even in the professional literature. This chapter,
therefore, addresses an audience which is little informed of the basic facts about
aboriginal languages from a historical perspective. Specifically, this chapter deals
with such questions as: (a) are the indigenous languages related to those of the
Old World; (b) how are they classified genetically; (c) how are they distributed;
(d) how viable are they in the multilingual Canadian society?

THE ORIGIN OF THE NEW WORLD LANGUAGES

Greenberg's (1987) *Language in the Americas* triggered vigorous
debates, mostly rejecting his claims and criticizing his cavalier method and
data handling. The main thesis of the book is that all aboriginal languages of the
Americas, except those grouped under two superstocks,[1] Na-Dene and Eskimo-
Aleut (see below), fall under one large superstock that Greenberg calls 'Amerind'
– i.e., all aboriginal languages of the Americas are descendants of the three protolanguages, Amerind, Na-Dene and Eskimo-Aleut. Greenberg links these three

ancestral languages to three waves of migration from the Old World through Beringia (what is now the Bering Strait). It is believed that those who entered North America 12,000 years ago spoke Amerind. These people are referred to as Paleo-Indians of the Clovis culture. The second wave of migrants included the speakers of Na-Dene who were associated with the Paleo-Arctic or Beringian Culture of 7,000–10,000 years ago. These earlier migrants were displaced and dispersed to the south and southeast as the speakers of Eskimo-Aleut, who were associated with the Anangula Culture of the eastern Aleutian islands (8,500–10,000 years old), entered the New World after Na-Dene.

Although Greenberg's proposal for Amerind and his comparative method have been soundly rejected by specialists (see Campbell, 1988 and Matisoff, 1990, among others), there are certain aspects of his work that are consistent with the 'received academic view on the colonization of the New World' (Nichols, 1990, p. 476). These aspects include: (a) Eurasian origins of the Native Americans; (b) northwest passages through Beringia and subsequent dispersion to the south and east; (c) the latest entry by Eskimo-Aleut preceded by Na-Dene and others who first entered the New World 12,000–20,000 years ago. The last point requires further comment, not only because there is emerging archaeological evidence that suggests pre-Clovis cultures (see Rogers, 1994), but also because of linguistic arguments that challenge the suggested chronology.

Sapir (1916), in commenting on the correlation between time depth and the degree of linguistic differentiation, implied that even 20,000 years is not long enough for a single language to have diversified into the many languages observed in North America (see especially his note 45). This view is consistent with the conclusion drawn by Nichols (1990, p. 475) in her study: '[t]he unmistakable testimony of the linguistic evidence is that the New World has been inhabited nearly as long as Australia or New Guinea, perhaps some 35,000 years. Genetic unity for "Amerind" is incompatible with the chronology demanded by the linguistic facts.' It is simply impossible to prove, with the current comparative method, any possible genetic unity over that stretch of time. How could such an extensive linguistic diversity in aboriginal America have arisen? This question has been and will continue to be an important topic of research.

CLASSIFICATION

Of the three approaches to the classification of the aboriginal languages (genetic, typological, and areal), genetic classification has been considered to be the ultimate goal where it is assumed, implicitly or explicitly, that all aboriginal languages have developed from a handful of protolanguages and, further, that these protolanguages may be related to languages in the Old World. It is also assumed by some who are engaged in remote genetic classification that the comparative method, based on systematic sound correspondences, will ultimately distinguish those varieties that are genetically related from those that are not. While the validity of the method has been well established, and the principle of systematic sound correspondences has been successfully employed in classifying both written and unwritten languages, it has not been demonstrated that such a method is effective in 'megalocomparison' (Matisoff, 1990) – i.e., in proving distant genetic affinity. Languages separated by 10,000 years or more are not likely to retain enough cognates for comparison. And even if a certain number of cognates are retained after such a long period of time, would there still be traces of systematic correspondences after a few cycles of sound change? There are also problems of convergence, as pointed out by Boas as early as 1911 in the celebrated 'Introduction' to the *Handbook of American Indian Languages*, repeated in 1917 in the 'Introduction' to the inaugural issue of the *International Journal of American Linguistics*, and again reiterated three years later (Boas, 1920). When two or more languages are mixed through intimate contact to such an extent as in a pidgin and creole, it would be impossible to determine the genetic affinity of the mixed variety with a particular language. As Boas (1920, pp. 374–375) put it, 'the whole theory of "Ursprache" for every group of modern languages must be held in abeyance until we can prove that they have not originated, to a large extent, by the process of acculturation'. Métif [mítᴄif], spoken by Métis, is a good Canadian example, which is based on Cree verb structure and French nominal lexicon (see Bakker, 1989). It is speculated that Tlingit also originated from a mixture of two languages (see below). There is no evidence, however, that Boas' remark has been taken seriously by Sapir and his followers, who attempted to establish remote genetic unities in terms of superstocks in a family tree model.

In order to provide background information on Canada's aboriginal languages, it is worth commenting on the classifications by Powell (1891), Sapir (1929), and Campbell and Mithun (1979), among others. 'All modern genetic classifications of North American Indian languages harken back to Major John Wesley Powell's classification, first presented in 1891' (Campbell and Mithun, 1979, p. 4). Powell accomplished the first comprehensive and accurate classification of all aboriginal languages north of Mexico (into fifty-eight families), which Sapir (1917, p. 79) hailed as 'the cornerstone of the linguistic edifice in aboriginal North America'. What followed Powell's achievement were attempts

Figure 6.1 Sapir's Na-Dene phylum

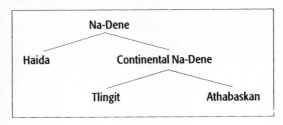

to reduce the genetic unities by establishing internal hierarchical relationships among the 58 families, in terms of stocks and superstocks (phyla). This reductionist trend culminated in Sapir's (1929) proposal for just six superstocks – Eskimo-Aleut, Algonkin-Wakashan, Na-Dene, Penutian, Hokan-Siouan and Aztec-Tanoan. Each of these superstocks is split into two or more stocks, and each stock in turn into two or more families. In order to illustrate the genealogical hierarchy of the superstocks, Sapir's Nadene (more commonly spelled 'Na-Dene' and 'Na-Dené') is converted into a tree diagram in figure 6.1.

As Sapir himself stated, his proposal was only suggestive, with no demonstrable evidence. Despite the tentative nature, this scheme has had a profound impact, both negative and positive. Negative, because '[i]t was assumed to have been established by valid linguistic method and froze into accepted doctrine' (Campbell and Mithun, 1979, p. 29), but also positive, because it has stimulated more careful scholars to scrutinize the scheme, the results of which have been to confirm, negate, or rearrange various groups and subgroups. If Powell's fifty-eight families instigated 'lumping', Sapir's superstocks instigated 'splitting'.

Campbell and Mithun's classification consists of sixty-two (actually sixty-three; see note 2) genetic groups, many of which are either families or isolates, but some are more like stocks than families (see below). This classification is 'conservative and not very controversial, but rather represents something of an encapsulation of current received opinion' (Campbell and Mithun, 1979, p. 39). Of these genetic groups, only eleven (excluding Beothuk, now extinct) are represented in Canada.

CANADIAN ABORIGINAL LANGUAGES

In discussing Canadian aboriginal languages, references are made to the following groups in Campbell and Mithun's (C&M) classification: Eskimo-Aleut, Na-Dene (Athabaskan and Tlingit), Algonquian-Ritwan, Siouan family, Iroquoian family, Tsimshian isolate, Beothuk isolate, Kutenai isolate, Salish family, Wakashan family and Haida.[2] These groups are discussed in the order of distribution, from the northwest to the southeast, with comments on population figures cited from various sources, including Foster (1982), Chafe (1962), the Canadian census and Bright's (1992) *International Encyclopedia of Linguistics*, among others (see also below). While no groups other than the eleven mentioned above are known to have been spoken in Canada, none of these is spoken exclusively within Canada.

Eskimo-Aleut

This group consists of Eskimo and Aleutian, and Eskimo in turn is divided into two groups: Yupik in southern Alaska and Siberia, and Inuit-Inupiaq, which extends from east of Norton Sound across Arctic Alaska and Canada to the coasts of Labrador and Greenland (Woodbury, 1984). In Canada, Inuit-Inupiaq is commonly referred to as Inuktitut, which has four western and six eastern dialects. These dialects, stretching over a huge landmass from northern Alaska to Greenland, were intelligible to Rasmussen while travelling from Greenland to Alaska (Driver, 1961) – which indicates a relatively shallow time depth involved since the Inuit ancestors' movement across the Yukon River took place. Woodbury's estimate (20,000) and the census figure (22,210) suggest that the speaker population is rapidly increasing (see below).

The possibility of a remote genetic relationship between Eskimo-Aleut and the Chukotko-Kamchatkan languages of Siberia is contemplated as a link between the languages of the Old and the New World (see Swadesh, 1962).

Na-Dene

Na-Dene in C&M classification is the same as that of Sapir (1929) except for the exclusion of Haida and the inclusion of Eyak. Sapir included Haida and Tlingit in Na-Dene mainly because of morphological similarities between these and Athabaskan (also spelled 'Athapaskan'); and Eyak was not known to him. While there is no demonstrable evidence that Haida is related to Na-Dene, more positive evidence for Tlingit's affiliation with Athabaskan and Eyak has been put forward (Krauss and Leer, 1981). However, it is not yet clear whether Tlingit is a sister of Proto-Eyak-Athabaskan or a hybrid between Proto-Eyak-Athabaskan and another unrelated language (see Krauss and Golla, 1981). With Eyak's closest affinity being Athabaskan (Krauss, 1964), Na-Dene is revised as shown in figure 6.2, where the broken line indicates that Tlingit's status in Na-Dene is not clear.

Figure 6.2 Na-Dene revised

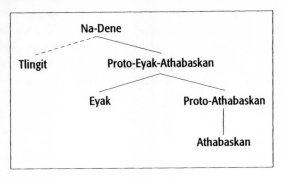

Haida isolate

Haida has two dialects (Skidegate and Masset), and is spoken primarily on the Queen Charlotte Islands. Chafe's (1962) estimate of 700 speakers (Canada and Alaska combined) can be compared with Foster's (1982) estimate of 225 (which happens to correspond to the 1986 census data) and with 295 (in Bright, 1992). The latter two estimates do not include another 100 speakers in Alaska. The number of speakers has been reduced by one half within one generation.

Tlingit isolate

Krauss (1979) estimated that no more than 2,000 out of 10,000 Tlingits spoke the language. While most Tlingits live in southeastern Alaska, about 500 are centred around Atlin in northernmost British Columbia and Teslin in the Yukon Territory. Krauss' estimate of 200 Tlingit speakers in Canada appears more realistic than Foster's estimate of 500, considering the census figure of 155.

Athabaskan family

Athabaskan is the most widespread of all indigenous North American languages, from Alaska to the American midwest. This family consists of three groups: Northern, Pacific-Coast, and Apachean (see Cook, 1992). The greatest linguistic diversity is found in the Northern group, with twenty-three languages. The Pacific-Coast languages, most of which are now extinct, include those once spoken in Washington and Oregon, as well as in California. By contrast, Navajo of the Apachean group is thriving with more than 100,000 speakers. Among the Canadian Athabaskan languages, Chipewyan is most widespread – from Fort Resolution, in the Northwest Territories, to Fond du Lac, Saskatchewan, and to Churchill, Manitoba. It has the largest speaker population among the Northern

Table 6.1 Distribution of Northern Athabaskan languages

Alaska: Koyukon, Holikachuk, Ingalik, Tanaina, Ahtna, Kolchan, Lower Tanana, Tanacross,
Upper Tanana, Han
Yukon: Gwich'in (Kutchin), Han, Northern Tutchone, Southern Tutchone, Kaska, Tagish,
Upper Tanana (see chapter 26)
British Columbia: Tagish, Kaska, Tahltan, Slavey, Sekani, Beaver, Babine, Carrier, Chilcotin
Northwest Territories, Alberta, Saskatchewan and Manitoba: Slavey, Dogrib, Chipewyan,
Beaver, Sarcee

Athabaskan languages, estimated at 12,000 (see Cook, 1991) in no less than
twenty different communities in the three prairie provinces and the Northwest
Territories. More significantly, Chipewyan is being acquired by children in at
least four communities in Saskatchewan where the population is growing.[3]

Krauss has maintained that the Northern Athabaskan languages cannot be
classified into historically meaningful subgroups because 'intergroup communication has ordinarily been constant, and no Northern Athapaskan language or
dialect was ever completely isolated from the others for long' (Krauss and Golla,
1981, p. 68). The Northern Athabaskan languages are listed according to their
distribution (the order roughly indicating northwestern to southeastern) as
shown in table 6.1. Some languages are listed twice as they are spoken on both
sides of a boundary. The list of Northern Athabaskan languages shown in table 6.1
is somewhat different from that of Krauss and Golla (1981). It does not include
Tsetsaut and Nicola, which have been extinct for nearly a century. Also, Krauss
and Golla list Tahltan-Kaska-Tagish as a single language whereas table 6.1
shows three separate languages.[4] Krauss and Golla also recognize four dialects
for Slavey-Hare, but it is customary in the Northwest Territories to group the
dialects into Southern Slavey and Northern Slavey.

Krauss and Golla indicate that all Alaskan languages are 'moribund', some
ten languages in Canada are 'viable', and others 'precarious'. They report thirty
speakers for Han (in Alaska and the Yukon). Gwich'in (also called Kutchin or
Loucheux) is the only language considered *not* moribund in the Yukon and
Alaska. Gwich'in speakers are estimated at 1,200 (Krauss and Golla, 1981),
including 500 in the Yukon and the Northwest Territories (Foster, 1982). This
language is exceptionally well maintained in that region, probably because of
an orthography and religious literature promoted by the Anglican Archdeacon
Robert McDonald (1829–1913). Tagish still has several speakers, and other languages in the Yukon and northwestern British Columbia (Tahltan, Kaska,
Sekani) are all moribund with only a few hundred speakers each. Chipewyan,

Slavey and Dogrib are the most viable, not only because they have the largest number of speakers (Chipewyan 12,000, Slavey 6,000, Dogrib 2,000), but also because they are acquired by children. Babine, Carrier and Chilcotin are also categorized as 'viable' with some 2,000 speakers each. According to a well informed source, Beaver is moribund with less than 200 speakers (not viable with 900, as Krauss and Golla maintained). Sarcee (now called Tsúut'ína) is the southernmost Northern Athabaskan language in the Plains culture area. It is moribund with about 50 speakers.

Tsimshian

Tsimshian is listed as an isolate in C&M classification, but it is a family of three languages, Nass-Gitksan, Coast Tsimshian and Southern Tsimshian, of which the last is virtually extinct. The Tsimshian communities are located along the coast of north-central British Columbia and along the Nass and Skeena rivers. Foster's (1982) estimate for all Tsimshian speakers is 3,500, which appears to be out of date considering the 1989 census figure of 1,185.

Wakashan family

Wakashan is a family of six languages divided into two branches; thus, Kwakiutlan (Northern Wakashan) comprises Haisla, Heiltsuk and Kwakiutl, while Nootkan (Southern Wakashan) includes Nootka, Nitinat and Makah (Jacobsen, 1979). Of the Nootkan branch, Nootka has the largest number of speakers (600; Kinkade, 1991), and is located along the west coast of Vancouver Island. Nitinat is restricted to a smaller area just south of Nootka, and Makah is spoken at Cape Flattery, Washington. Of the three Northern Wakashan languages, Kwakiutl (now called Kwak'wala) is spoken in the northern part of Vancouver Island and its neighbouring mainland coastal area. It may have had a large number of speakers, estimated at 1,000 (Bright, 1992; Chafe, 1962; Foster, 1982), which has been reduced to 250 (Kinkade, 1991). Heiltsuk and Haisla have 200–300 speakers each, and are northern neighbours of Kwak'wala along the central coast.

Salish family

Salish is a large family of twenty-three languages distributed over British Columbia and the neighbouring states of Washington, Idaho, Montana and Oregon. Kinkade (1992) organizes the Salish languages into five branches (see table 6.2). His classification is somewhat different from that of Thompson (1979), whose more elaborate classification sets Bella Coola apart from the rest, which

Table 6.2 Salish family: branches and languages

Bella Coola[1]
Central Salish:
    Comox[1]/Sliammon, Clallam, Halkomelem[1], Lushootseed, Nooksack, Pentlatch[1], Sechelt[1],
    Squamish[1], Straits Salish[1], Twana
Interior Salish:
    Lillooet[1], Okanagan/Colville[1], Shuswap[1], Thompson[1], Coeur d'Alene, Columbian,
    Kalispel/Flathead/Spokane
Tillamook
Tsamosan:
    Lower Chehalis, Upper Chehalis, Cowlitz, Quinault

[1] languages found in British Columbia

implies that Bella Coola of the west coast is the earliest offshoot. The languages in British Columbia include Bella Coola and those that belong to Central and Interior Salish. Those grouped under Tsamosan are all located in western Washington, along the Pacific coast, while Tillamook is found along the northern Pacific coast of Oregon. The eleven languages found in British Columbia are identified in table 6.2. Of these, Pentlatch (Vancouver Island) has been extinct for several decades. The languages with the most speakers (Chafe, 1962; Foster, 1982) belong to Interior Salish – i.e., Shuswap 1,000–2,000, Thom-pson 1,000, and Lillooet 1,000. These numbers are now down by one half or more, according to recent estimates by Kinkade (1991), which more or less agree with the figures in Bright (1992): Shuswap? 500, Thompson fewer than 500 (in Kinkade, but fewer than 50 in Bright), and Lillooet 300–400. The languages in the Central Salish branch are likely to reach extinction first (50 or fewer for each), except for Halkomelem (500). Bella Coola speakers are reduced to fewer than 50 (Bright, 1992), from 200 (Chafe, 1962; Foster, 1982).

Following Sapir's (1929) proposal, a distant genetic relationship of Salish to Wakashan, Kutenai and Chimakuan has been considered, but no convincing evidence has been produced (see Thompson, 1979).

Kutenai isolate

Kutenai (Kootenay) of British Columbia (and adjacent Idaho and Montana) is a single language with two dialects (Thompson, 1973). Foster's (1982) estimate of Kutenai speakers is 200, which compares well with the census figure of 180. Sapir (1929) placed Kutenai in his Algonkin-Wakashan super-stock, but there is no demonstrable evidence for its relation to any language.

Algonquian-Ritwan

This stock consists of two distantly related families. The relationship of Ritwan (Yurok and Wiyot of California) to Algonquian was proposed by Sapir (1913), which triggered rigorous debates, to be confirmed finally by Haas (1958). At a more distant level, Beothuk (known to have been spoken in Newfoundland) may be linked to Algonquian, but no demonstrable evidence is available (Goddard, 1979). The Algonquian languages are spread from the Canadian Rockies to the Atlantic coast. More than twenty-five languages (including several extinct ones) are divided into three geographical groups: Eastern, Central and Plains (Goddard, 1992). Canada's Algonquian languages are classified into four genetic groups: Blackfoot; Cree complex (Cree, Montagnais-Naskapi); Ojibwa complex (Ojibwa, Odawa [Ottawa], Algonquin [Algonkin], Saulteaux); Eastern (Delaware, Abenaki, Micmac, Malecite [Maleseet]) (after Kaye, 1979b).

Blackfoot is structurally most distinct from the rest of the Canadian Algonquian languages, and one of the earliest to be separated (Sapir, 1916). It has a few thousand speakers in three reserves in southern Alberta and the Blackfeet (*sic*) Reservation in Montana. A chain of Cree and Montagnais-Naskapi dialects, extending from northern Quebec and Labrador to the Rocky Mountains, has the largest speaker population, estimated at 60,000, and has well-established orthographies. Ojibwa has the second largest number of speakers, estimated at 40,000, and its population is concentrated around the Great Lakes. The western dialect (Saulteaux) extends to Manitoba and Saskatchewan, and a band of Saulteaux speakers has settled in the Peace River area, British Columbia. Of the Eastern group, Micmac has the largest number of speakers, 3,000–5,000 (Foster, 1982; Kaye, 1979a – not the 8,100 reported in Bright, 1992), and is distributed in Quebec, Nova Scotia, New Brunswick and Newfoundland. Kaye (1979b) reports over 1,000 Malecite speakers in New Brunswick, along the St John River. Abenaki must be extinct by now, and a few Delaware speakers may survive in the United States.

Siouan family

This family consists of about twenty languages spoken widely in central North America, from the Canadian plains to the southern Mississippi Valley. They are subclassified into four groups: Southeastern, Mississippi Valley, Mandan and Missouri River (Rood, 1992). The Southeastern group is extinct, and Mandan is almost extinct. The Missouri River group consists of Hidatsa (North Dakota) and Crow (Montana), with about 1,000 and 5,000 speakers respectively (Bright, 1992). The Mississippi Valley group is the largest, with four branches: Dhegiha, Chiwere, Winnebago and Dakotan.

Figure 6.3 Dakota branch of Siouan

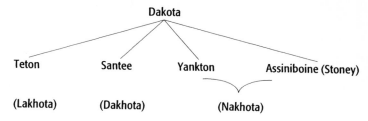

The Siouan languages in Canada belong to the Dakotan branch (Sioux proper), with a speaker population estimated at 19,000–20,000 (Bright, 1992; Chafe, 1973). This branch consists of the five languages shown in figure 6.3 (after Chafe, 1973). An earlier map of aboriginal tribes shows only Assiniboine in southern Manitoba and Saskatchewan (Driver, 1961). However, all Dakota languages are now spoken in Canada: Teton in southern Saskatchewan (and the midwestern States), Santee in southern Manitoba, Yankton in northern Saskatchewan (and the midwestern States), and Assiniboine (Stoney) in Alberta (and Montana). Two small bands in central Alberta (Paul and Alexis) have made the most north-westerly migration. The Stoney dialect in Morley and its vicinities in southern Alberta is well maintained among 3,600 residents, as it is acquired by children in about three-quarters of households. So, Foster's (1982) estimate (5,000 speakers) for Dakota languages in Canada is likely near the mark, but Bright's (1992) figure of 150–200 for 'Assiniboin' is not.

For a distant genetic connection, Chafe (1973) seriously considered a hypothesis for Macro-Siouan which links Siouan with Caddoan and Iroquoian.

Iroquoian family

At the time of the first European settlers, Iroquoian languages were spread from Quebec north to Georgia in the south, and from the coasts of Virginia and the Carolinas to Ontario, Pennsylvania and Ohio. It is probably the first North American language to be recorded (Mithun, 1979). According to Foster (1982), the name *Canada* derives from the St Lawrence Iroquoian word [ganá:da] 'settlement', which referred to what is now Quebec City. Iroquoian is subclassified into two groups: Northern (comprising Tuscarora-Nottaway, Laurentian, Huron-Wyandot, Five Nations [Seneca, Cayuga, Onondaga, Oneida, Mohawk]) and Southern (Cherokee) (after Mithun, 1979).

All Canada's Iroquoian languages belong to the Northern branch spoken in Ontario and Quebec. Foster (1982) includes six Iroquoian languages (Five Nations plus Tuscarora) in Canada. Of these, Mohawk has the largest number of speakers, but the total number of all Iroquoian speakers (including those in the United States) is less than 3,000 according to Foster. Cayuga is the second largest, with 360–380 speakers (Bright, 1992; Foster, 1982). Laurentian and Huron are extinct, while Tuscarora is probably near extinction. The rest of the Five Nations languages are spoken by a small number of adults, mostly elders. By contrast, Cherokee in North Carolina and Oklahoma is healthy with 12,100 speakers (in 1986, according to Bright, 1992).

Summary

As noted in the introduction, Canada's indigenous languages are classified into eight families and three isolates. Such largely diversified families as Algonquian and Siouan have been settled in North America for much longer than the Eskimo languages and dialects, which can be grouped into only two languages. The hypothesis of the movement of aboriginal peoples from north-west to southeast is also well supported by linguistic evidence, and Sapir's (1936) etymological study proving Navajo's northern origin is particularly worthy of note. However, any genetic affinity of aboriginal languages (except Eskimo-Aleut) with Eurasian languages is yet to be proven, and the extensive diversification of them, both genetic and typological, has not been explained satisfactorily.

With respect to viability, Foster (1982) grouped Canada's indigenous languages into six categories, ranging from 'verging on extinction' (with fewer than ten speakers) to 'excellent chances of survival' (with more than 5,000 speakers). The first category includes eight languages: Abenaki and Delaware of Algonquian, Tagish, Han and Sarcee of Athabaskan, Tuscarora of Iroquoian, Sechelt of Salish, and Southern Tsimshian. These languages are probably extinct now, with the exception of Sarcee, Han and Sechelt, whose speaker populations were probably not correctly reported (see next section for an explanation). Only three languages are included in Foster's latter category, Cree and Ojibwa of Algonquian, and Inuktitut. Chipewyan is excluded from this category because of an incorrect estimate of speakers (5,000 in Foster); however, with a growing speaker population of 12,000, Chipewyan is one of the healthiest languages. While the number of speakers is used as the primary indicator for viability by Foster and others (Kinkade, 1991; Krauss and Golla, 1981), there are other criteria that must be considered, some details of which are discussed in the next section.

VIABILITY AND LANGUAGE SHIFT

In determining viability, the number of speakers is taken as the most reliable indicator – but then comes the question of how reliable speaker

Table 6.3 Comparison of three estimates of speaker populations

Language	Chafe (1962)	Foster (1982)	Kinkade (1991)
Shuswap	1,000–2,000	1,000–2,000	500?
Thompson	1,000–2,000	1,000	fewer than 500
Lillooet	1,000–2,000	1,000	300–400
Bella Coola	200–400	200	fewer than 200
Halkomelem	1,000–2,000	500	500
Haisla	100–1,000	100–1,000	fewer than 200
Heiltsuk	100–1,000	300	300?
Kwakw'ala	1,000	1,000	fewer than 250 good speakers
Nootka	1,000–2,000	1,000–2,000	fewer than 600 good speakers

population estimates are. The sources of estimates cited in the preceding section include Chafe (1962), Kinkade (1991), Bright (1992) and the Canadian census, among others. These sources, based on different methods of collecting information, have different degrees of reliability and limitations, so that the figures must be taken with care and discretion. Zepeda and Hill (1991, p. 136) consider that Chafe's estimates 'remain the best source of information on indigenous languages and their speakers'. It may have been quite accurate in the sixties, but is now more than three decades old. In table 6.3, for example, we can compare Chafe's and Foster's figures with those of Kinkade (1991), who must have more accurate information, particularly on Salish and Wakashan. Interestingly, Kinkade's figures are more or less identical to those given in Bright (1992), with the exception of Bella Coola, for which Bright's figure is 'fewer than 50' reported in 1990. Putting aside the accuracy of estimates, it is clear that the speaker population has been dramatically reduced over one generation. One might expect the Canadian census data to provide more accurate figures, but this source has its own problems. For example, in a table prepared by Multiculturalism and Citizenship Canada from the 1989 census, Beaver, Babine, Sekani and Sarcee are not included in Athabaskan, whereas Yellowknife, which no longer exists, is included (with five speakers).[5] To cite another example, under 'Salish languages' a total of 1,870 speakers is cited with no identification of individual languages. As well, some differences in the estimates may be attributable to changing attitudes. Two decades ago, few young people were eager to be counted in an estimate; an aboriginal language was not considered an asset or something to be proud of. Now the young people's attitude has changed, and even those whose competence in an aboriginal language is marginal are eager to be counted. This change in outlook is largely due to policies to promote multiculturalism, as well as to aboriginal peoples' aspirations to preserve their own language and culture.

A remarkable change in government policies occurred in 1984 when the Northwest Territories Legislative Assembly passed its first Official Languages Act, declaring seven aboriginal languages as 'official aboriginal languages'. In 1990, this Act was amended to give equal official status to the following eight languages: English, French, Chipewyan, Cree, Dogrib, Gwich'in , Inuktitut and Slavey. By the amendment of the Act, the Office of Languages Commissioner was also created. Along with legislative changes and funding provided by the federal government, the Territorial government has been able to initiate a number of programmes promoting aboriginal languages, training interpreters, offering courses related to aboriginal languages through Arctic College, and so forth. Educational and research programmes on aboriginal languages have also been established elsewhere in the country at many colleges and universities during the last two decades – e.g., Yukon Native Language Centre, Saskatchewan Indian Languages Institute, and Department of Native Studies at the University of Manitoba, to name only three. What effect these programmes will have on aboriginal languages remains to be seen, but there are some interesting statistics released by the Languages Commissioner of the Northwest Territories.

The most interesting statistics concern the rate of language shift, which is measured by comparing the number of people who have retained a mother tongue at home with the number of those who have switched to another language. Consider tables 6.4 and 6.5, which are excerpted from tables V and VI, respectively, in the Languages Commissioner's report (1993). These analyses are based on the 1986 and 1991 Canadian censuses. Each language is listed in column 1, with the number of people who reported the language as a mother tongue in column 2, the number of people who have retained it as a home language in column 3, and the rate of shift from the mother tongue in the last column. Both tables show that the rate of shift is smallest for Inuktitut with 16 per

Table 6.4 Rate of language shift in the Northwest Territories 1986

Languages	Mother tongue	Home language	% of shift
Inuktitut	14,535	12,155	16
Dogrib	1,885	1,515	20
Slavey	2,285	1,305	43
Chipewyan	480	270	44
French	1,290	570	56
Gwich'in	165	45	73
Cree	155	30	81
Total	20,795	15,890	

Table 6.5 Rate of language shift in the Northwest Territories 1991

Languages	Mother tongue	Home language	% of shift
Inuktitut	16,565	13,585	18
Dogrib	2,110	1,625	23
Slavey	2,310	1,300	44
French	1,385	610	56
Chipewyan	555	225	59
Cree	195	20	90
Gwich'in	310	25	92
Total	23,430	17,390	

cent (1986) and 18 per cent (1991), whereas the rates are largest for Gwich'in
and Cree with 73 per cent and 81 per cent respectively in 1986, and 92 per cent
and 90 per cent in 1991. These figures reflect the fact that Inuktitut and Dogrib
are acquired by children, but Cree and Gwich'in are not. When the two tables are
compared an interesting correlation can be seen between the figure in the home
language column and that for rate of shift. Where the rate of shift is less than 25
per cent the actual number of those who have retained their mother tongue as a
home language increases between the two census years. By contrast, where the
rate of shift is greater than 40 per cent the actual number of those who have retained their mother tongue has dramatically dropped in five years. The mother
tongue figures for Chipewyan, Gwich'in and Cree in table 6.5 appear anomalous
when they are compared with the corresponding figures in table 6.4. It is not
likely that those acquiring an aboriginal language as their mother tongue actually
increased in 1991; rather, it is likely that more people reported an aboriginal
language as one of their mother tongues (probably due to those changes in
attitude alluded to earlier). In any case, the two tables also reveal an interesting
trend. The change in the rate of shift between the two census years is smallest
(3 per cent or less) for Inuktitut, Dogrib and Slavey, but the change for the other
aboriginal languages is remarkably large (between 15 per cent and 19 per cent),
where the rate remains intact for French. Again, this difference reflects the fact
that Chipewyan, Gwich'in and Cree are not acquired by children. However,
while Chipewyan in the Northwest Territories is facing extinction, it is one of the
most thriving languages elsewhere. In at least four communities in Saskatchewan, the population of which ranges from 1,000 to 3,000, Chipewyan is spoken
in virtually every household and children acquire it as their first language.
Stoney in Morley, Alberta should also be noted in this regard – about 75 per cent
out of 200 Grade 1 children speak Stoney as their first language. Here too, the

actual number of children learning Stoney may have increased with the growing population, although the ratio of home-language shift to English may also have been increasing. In any case, Stoney has a better chance of survival with children acquiring it than do other languages which have a larger speaker population, but which are not being learned by children.

In determining viability, an indicator which may be more important than the number of speakers is whether or not the language is used at home. One's proficiency in a language will have no effect on its transmission unless it is used at home. As shown in tables 6.4 and 6.5, the number of Inuktitut and Dogrib speakers who have retained their mother tongue as a home language has increased between the two census years by about 10 per cent and 7 per cent, respectively, while the rate of shift has also increased by 2 per cent and 3 per cent, respectively. While there is no comprehensive acquisition study, or studies on mother-tongue shift in other regions, at least Chipewyan and Dogrib of Athabaskan should be included among those languages that have excellent chances of survival. Perhaps Slavey and Stoney (Siouan) should also be counted, in addition to the three that Foster mentioned in 1982 (i.e., Cree and Ojibwa of Algonquian, and Inuktitut).

It should be obvious by now that the existing estimates of speakers are not all that reliable or complete. Particularly lacking are data on bilingualism. In many native communities, an aboriginal language is used along with English or French, and the two languages maintain a functional relationship, analogous to diglossia. Betsiamites Montagnais (Algonquian) in Quebec is a good example. Although low in prestige, Betsiamites is spoken in every household and is taught at elementary schools, where French is a dominant language (see Cyr, 1995). Betsiamites will probably continue to coexist with French, while heavily converging with the dominant language. I suspect that the number of similar bilingual communities, in which an aboriginal language is acquired and maintained as a second language, is growing. If so, the future of aboriginal languages is not so bleak as might have been suggested by the assessors of declining speaker populations.

Notes

I wish to thank Betty Harnum and Leah Bortolin, who assisted me with the preparation of this chapter.

1 For the convenience of exposition, languages are classified as 'families', 'stocks', and 'superstocks' (or 'phyla') with the understanding that no genetic relationship is proven for those grouped under a superstock, but that a remote genetic relationship is proven for those grouped under a stock as well as a family.

2 Haida is excluded from Na-Dene by Campbell and Mithun, for lack of evidence, but it is not listed in their classification as an isolate – apparently inadvertently. With Haida as an isolate, the number of language families and isolates in Campbell and Mithun's classification amounts to sixty-three.

3 Smith's (1981) figures for 'Chipewyan population by bands, 1970' are out of date. For example, Fond du Lac has nearly 1,000 residents instead of 552, and La Loche has nearly 2,300 instead of 249. Fond du Lac, La Loche, Wollaston Lake, Black Lake and Patuanak (all in Saskatchewan) are the largest Chipewyan communities, not Fort Chipewyan, Cold Lake, Fort Resolution, etc. in Alberta and the Northwest Territories as reported in Krauss and Golla (1981).

4 The dialect spoken in Lower Post, British Columbia that Cook (1972) reported on is Tahltan, not a Kaska dialect as suggested by Krauss and Golla (1981). Speakers of both Tahltan and Kaska live in the vicinity of Lower Post, and there is a large degree of mutual intelligibility between the two languages.

5 Yellowknife is believed to be a variety of Chipewyan, but there is no linguistic documentation on the dialect.

References

Bakker, P. (1989). Relexification in Canada: the case of Métif (French-Cree). *Canadian Journal of Linguistics, 34,* 339–350.

Boas, F. (1911). Introduction. In F. Boas (ed.), *Handbook of American Indian Languages, Part 1* (pp. 1–83). Washington: Bureau of American Ethnology, Bulletin 40.

(1917). Introduction. *International Journal of American Linguistics, 1,* 1–8.

(1920). The classification of American languages. *American Anthropologist, 22,* 367–376.

Bright, W. (1994). Native North American languages. In D. Champagne (ed.), *The Native North American Almanac: A Reference Work on Native North Americans in the United States and Canada* (pp. 427–447). Detroit: Gale Research.

Bright, W. (ed.) (1992). *International Encyclopedia of Linguistics* (4 volumes). Oxford: Oxford University Press.

Campbell, L. (1988). Review of *Language in the Americas* (J. H. Greenberg). *Language, 64,* 591–615.

Campbell, L. and Mithun, M. (1979). Introduction: North American Indian historical linguistics in current perspective. In L. Campbell and M. Mithun (eds.), *The Language of Native America* (pp. 3–69). Austin: University of Texas Press.

Chafe, W. L. (1962). Estimates regarding the present speakers of North American Indian languages. *International Journal of American Linguistics, 28,* 162–171.

(1973). Siouan, Iroquoian, and Caddoan. In T. A. Sebeok (ed.), *Current Trends in Linguistics, Vol. 10: Linguistics in North America* (pp. 1164–1209). The Hague: Mouton.

Cook, E.-D. (1972). Stress and related rules in Tahltan. *International Journal of American Linguistics, 38,* 231–234.

(1991). Linguistic divergence in Fort Chipewyan. *Language in Society, 20,* 423–440.

(1992). Athabaskan languages. In W. Bright (ed.), *International Encyclopedia of Linguistics, Vol. 1* (pp. 122–126). Oxford: Oxford University Press.

Cyr, D. (1995). Review of *Dictionnaire montagnais-français* (L. Drapeau). *International Journal of American Linguistics, 61,* 431–434.

Driver, H. E. (1961). *Indians of North America* (2nd edn, revised). Chicago: University of Chicago Press.

Foster, M. K. (1982). Canada's indigenous languages: present and future. *Language and Society, 7,* 7–16.

Goddard, I. (1979). Comparative Algonquian. In L. Campbell and M. Mithun (eds.), *The Languages of Native America* (pp. 70–132). Austin: University of Texas Press.

(1992). Algonkian languages. In W. Bright (ed.), *International Encyclopedia of Linguistics, Vol. 1* (pp. 44–46). Oxford: Oxford University Press.

Greenberg, J. H. (1987). *Language in the Americas.* Stanford: Stanford University Press.

Haas, M. R. (1958). Algonkian-Ritwan: the end of a controversy. *International Journal of American Linguistics, 24,* 159–173.

Jacobsen, W. H. (1979). Wakashan comparative studies. In L. Campbell and M. Mithun (eds.), *The Languages of Native America* (pp. 766–791). Austin: University of Texas Press.

Kaye, J. D. (1979a). The Indian languages of Canada. In J. K. Chambers (ed.), *The Languages of Canada* (pp. 15–19). Montreal: Didier.

(1979b). The Algonquian languages. In J. K. Chambers (ed.), *The Languages of Canada* (pp. 20–53). Montreal: Didier.

Kinkade, M. D. (1991). The decline of Native languages in Canada. In R. H. Robins and E. M. Uhlenbeck (eds.), *Endangered Languages* (pp. 157–176). Oxford/New York: Berg.

(1992). Salishan languages. In W. Bright (ed.), *International Encyclopedia of Linguistics, Vol. 3* (pp. 359–362). Oxford: Oxford University Press.

Krauss, M. E. (1964). Proto-Athapaskan-Eyak and the problem of Na-Dene I: the phonology. *International Journal of American Linguistics, 30,* 118–131.

(1973). Na-Dene. In T. A. Sebeok (ed.), *Current Trends in Linguistics, Vol. 10: Linguistics in North America* (pp. 903–978). The Hague: Mouton.

(1979). Na-Dene and Eskimo-Aleut. In L. Campbell and M. Mithun (eds.), *The Languages of Native America* (pp. 803–901). Austin: University of Texas Press.

Krauss, M. E. and Golla, V. K. (1981). Northern Athapaskan languages. In W. C. Sturtevant (ed.), *Handbook of North American Indians, Vol. 6: Subarctic* (June Helm, volume editor) (pp. 67–85). Washington: Smithsonian Institution.

Krauss, M. E. and Leer, J. A. (1981). *Athabaskan, Eyak, and Tlingit Sonorants.* Fairbanks, Alaska: Alaska Native Language Center Research Paper No. 5.

Languages Commissioner of the Northwest Territories (1993). *Eight Official Languages: Meeting the Challenges* (First Annual Report of the Languages Commissioner of the Northwest Territories for the year 1992–1993). Yellowknife: Office of the Languages Commissioner of the N.W.T.

Matisoff, J. A. (1990). On megalocomparison. *Language, 66*, 106–120.

Mithun, M. (1979). Iroquoian. In L. Campbell and M. Mithun (eds.), *The Languages of Native America* (pp. 133–212). Austin: University of Texas Press.

Multiculturalism and Citizenship Canada (1989). *Mother Tongue: 1986 Census of Canada.* Ottawa: Department of Multiculturalism & Citizenship.

Nichols, J. (1990). Linguistic diversity and the first settlement of the New World. *Language, 66*, 475–521.

Powell, J. W. (1891). Indian linguistic families of America north of Mexico. Washington: Bureau of American Ethnology, Seventh Annual Report.

Rogers, D. (1994). Chronology of Native North American history before 1500. In D. Champagne (ed.), *The Native North American Almanac: A Reference Work on Native North Americans in the United States and Canada* (pp. 1–17). Detroit: Gale Research.

Rood, D. (1992). Siouan languages. In W. Bright (ed.), *International Encyclopedia of Linguistics, Vol. 3* (pp. 449–451). Oxford: Oxford University Press.

Sapir, E. (1913). Wiyot and Yurok, Algonkin languages of California. *American Anthropologist, 15*, 617–646.

(1916). Time perspective in aboriginal American culture: a study in method. (Memoir 90, Anthropological Series, No. 13). Ottawa: Department of Mines, Geological Survey.

(1917). Linguistic publications of the Bureau of American Ethnology, a general review. *International Journal of American Linguistics, 1*, 76–81.

(1929). Central and North American languages. *Encyclopedia Britannica* (14th edn), *5*, 138–141.

(1936). Internal linguistic evidence suggestive of the northern origin of the Navaho. *American Anthropologist, 38*, 224–235.

Smith, J. G. E. (1981). Chipewyan. In W. C. Sturtevant (ed), *Handbook of North American Indians, Vol. 6: Subarctic* (June Helm, volume editor) (pp. 271–284). Washington: Smithsonian Institution.

Swadesh, M. (1962). Linguistic relations across Bering Strait. *American Anthropologist, 64*, 1262–1291.

Thompson, L. C. (1973). The Northwest. In T. A. Sebeok (ed.), *Current Trends in Linguistics, Vol. 10: Linguistics in North America* (pp. 979–1045). The Hague: Mouton.

(1979). Salishan and the Northwest. In L. Campbell and M. Mithun (eds.), *The Languages of Native America* (pp. 692–765). Austin: University of Texas Press.

Woodbury, A. C. (1984). Eskimo and Aleut languages. In W. C. Sturtevant (ed.), *Handbook of North American Indians, Vol. 5: Arctic* (David Adams, volume editor) (pp. 49–63). Washington: Smithsonian Institution.

Zepeda, O. and Hill, J. H. (1991). The condition of Native American languages in the United States. In R. H. Robins and E. M. Uhlenbeck (eds.), *Endangered Languages* (pp. 135–155). Oxford/New York: Berg.

7 Aboriginal languages: current status

Lynn Drapeau

There is general agreement that Canada's aboriginal languages may be grouped into eleven distinct families and isolates. Cook (this volume) provides a list of over fifty aboriginal languages and indicates in which areas they are spoken; none of the families is uniquely contained within the Canadian borders. The Eskimo-Aleut family is represented by Inuktitut, a dialect continuum stretching across the Canadian Arctic (and into Alaska), also referred to as Eskimo. Languages belonging to the Iroquoian family are located in the provinces of Quebec and Ontario. The Algonquian family is represented by a wide array of languages spoken in a domain stretching from Alberta to the Maritimes. The remaining eight language families are to be found only in western Canada. Siouan and Athapaskan languages are spoken in the prairies, but the latter group of languages is mostly found in the Northwest Territories, the Yukon and British Columbia. Six language groups (three isolates, Haida, Tlingit and Kutenai, as well as the Salishan, Tsimshian and Wakashan families) are to be found only in British Columbia, an area of great linguistic complexity.

WHO ARE THE CANADIAN ABORIGINAL PEOPLE?

According to the 1991 Canadian census, slightly over one million (1,016,335) people declared aboriginal origins, roughly 3.8 per cent of the Canadian population (Statistics Canada, 1995). Following the census, a large-scale assessment, the *Aboriginal Peoples Survey* (henceforth APS), was conducted on a sample of persons who had reported aboriginal origins or who had reported being registered under the Indian Act. Approximately 180,000 were thus sampled.[1] The results of the APS indicated that, of the million persons above, 625,710 stated that they actually considered themselves as Canadian Aboriginals (Statistics Canada, 1993).

These aboriginal people of Canada may be of various origins: North American Indian, Métis or Inuit. North American Indians may be Registered

144

or non-Registered under the Indian Act of Canada. A separate group known as
the Métis grew, in the western provinces, out of the inter-marriage of French
Canadian traders with Indian women. Many of them never acquired official
Indian status. Nevertheless, they have not integrated into Euro-Canadian culture
but have maintained a separate identity. The Inuit are racially and culturally distinct from Indians. Legally speaking, they do not fall under the jurisdiction of
the Indian Act.

The 1991 APS has shown that the total population of those who *identify as
aboriginal and/or are registered Indians* is distributed as follows: 73.6 per cent
identify as North American Indians, 21.62 per cent as Métis and 5.79 per cent
as Inuit (including multiple responses). A little over 1 per cent identified with
two such origins. Aboriginal peoples are scattered across Canada; some live in
segregated communities (Indian reserves or establishments, Inuit villages), while
others have migrated into cities. Close to half (48 per cent) of registered Indians
live in a reserve environment, but 81 per cent of those who claim aboriginal
ancestry live off Indian reserves.

In the remainder of this chapter I will use aboriginal and native interchangeably and will refer among them to Amerindian (or Indian), Métis and Inuit (or
Eskimo) peoples.

ABORIGINAL DEMOLINGUISTICS

The state of aboriginal-language conservation and use in Canada has
been a subject of concern both for scholars and for the aboriginal groups themselves who, understandably, wish to monitor the situation as closely as possible.
For an analysis of the 1981 census returns, see Burnaby (1986) and Burnaby
and Beaujot (1987). Kinkade (1991) provides an appraisal of the situation in
every linguistic group, but see also Bauman (1980), Price (1981), Foster (1982),
Robinson (1985), Grimes (1988) and, more recently, Norton and Fettes (1994).

The returns of the 1991 census and of the APS provide useful information
on overall aboriginal-language competence and use across Canada. The general
Canadian census reveals that, of the total population with aboriginal origins,
17 per cent claimed an aboriginal mother tongue, roughly 0.6 per cent of the
Canadian population. Moreover, about 11 per cent of those who reported
aboriginal ancestry also reported using an aboriginal language at home
(Statistics Canada, 1995).

Considering now the population of those *who identify as Canadian
Aboriginals*, the picture seems somewhat less dismal. Drapeau (1995b) reports
that, of respondents five years of age and over who identified as aboriginal,

145

Lynn Drapeau

Table 7.1 Percentage of speakers of an aboriginal language by age group and by aboriginal group, Canada 1991

Age	Total aboriginal	Registered	Non-registered	Métis	Inuit
5–14 years	21.9	28.6	5.2	5.1	67
15–24 years	27.4	33.7	8.6	8.2	71.2
25–54 years	36.7	47.6	9.7	18.1	74.5
55+ years	63.1	74.7	24.5	43.5	90.6
Overall % of speakers 5+	32.7	41.8	9	14.4	72.5

Source: this table and the following ones were compiled using the custom tabulations prepared by the Research Directorate of the Royal Commission on Aboriginal Peoples. These were based on the Aboriginal Peoples Survey of Statistics Canada (Statistics Canada, Cat. No. 93-317, 93-333).

50 per cent do not understand any aboriginal language, 17.3 per cent understand one but cannot speak it, and 32.7 per cent can speak such a language (see table 7.1). The percentage of those who do not speak and/or do not understand an aboriginal language is especially high among non-registered Indians (79.8 per cent) and Métis (68.6 per cent). Among the Inuit sample, table 7.1 shows that 72.5 per cent speak the language, but among registered Indians this percentage only reaches 41.8. The Métis (14.4 per cent) and the non-registered Indians (9 per cent) have the lowest overall percentage of aboriginal-language speakers.

When the figures are broken down into age groups the decreasing competence becomes more apparent, as shown in table 7.1. Among the Inuit, there is a 23.6 per cent decline between the 55+ group and the 5–14 group. Similar declines are seen among non-registered Indians (19.3 per cent), the Métis (38.4 per cent) and registered Indians (46.1 per cent). Across the present generations, the registered Indians seem to have suffered the sharpest reduction in aboriginal-language transmission. Upon examination of the proportion of speakers in the 5–14 group, it appears that aboriginal languages are in critical condition among the Métis and non-registered Indians, and in very poor condition among registered Indians, as only 28.6 per cent of that age group can speak an aboriginal language.

The reserve environment would seem to favour aboriginal-language retention. Indeed, 66.6 per cent of the total aboriginal sample (15+) living on reserves declared some ability to speak an aboriginal language, as compared to 24.2 per cent of those living off reserve.

Table 7.2 shows that a total of 190,165 people claimed to have an aboriginal mother tongue (this figure includes multiple responses). The figures provided in table 7.2 have been broken down for every language family, excluding

146

Table 7.2 Population by aboriginal mother tongue and aboriginal home language, Canada 1991

Major linguistic group	Mother tongue	Home language	Ratio of home language to mother tongue (%)
Algonquian	131,330	96,230	73
Athapaskan	19,140	13,750	72
Haida (isolate)	165	45	27
Iroquoian	–	–	–
Kutenai (isolate)	175	40	23
Salish	2,835	835	30
Dakota (Siouan)	4,105	2,965	72
Tlingit (isolate)	105	10	10
Tsimshian	395	65	17
Wakashan	3,445	1,090	32
Amerindian	2,925	1,065	36
Inuktitut	24,995	21,905	88
Total	189,615	138,105	73

Note: Mother tongue and *home language* include single and multiple responses. The *Amerindian* label groups all reports on languages that for some reason could not be subsumed under the other language groups. Iroquoian language data are of little value, given that Mohawk reserves refused to participate in the 1991 Census. I have therefore chosen to omit the partial data provided for this language group in tables 7.2 and 7.3.

Iroquoian speakers from the tabulations as the data on them are notoriously unreliable. On the basis of the remaining data, table 7.3 shows what proportion each family group represents of the total number of aboriginal mother-tongue speakers. Reported Algonquian mother tongue amounts to 69 per cent of all aboriginal mother-tongue reports, Inuktitut accounts for 13 per cent and Athapaskan for 10 per cent. Thus, 92.5 per cent of all aboriginal mother-tongue reports originate from three linguistic groups.

Looking at tables 7.2, 7.4 and 7.5, the absolute population figures for some language families are astonishingly low and many languages appear to be in a very critical condition. The linguistic isolates have very few mother-tongue speakers left: Haida has only 165, Kutenai has 175 and Tlingit 105. Tsimshian has less than 400. Wakashan can be broken down into six distinct languages, with a total of less than 3500 mother-tongue speakers. The fact that some of the languages are also spoken in the United States does not help as the situation there is as desolate – if not worse – as it is in Canada. There are at least a dozen Salishan languages and yet they total only a little over 2,800 mother-tongue speakers.

Table 7.3 Ratio of mother tongue (by linguistic group) to total native-language mother tongue, Canada 1991

Linguistic group	Mother tongue	Ratio (%)
Algonquian	131,330	69.26
Athapaskan	19,140	10.09
Haida	165	0.09
Kutenai	175	0.09
Salish	2,835	1.50
Dakota (Siouan)	4,105	2.16
Tlingit	105	0.06
Tsimshian	395	0.21
Wakashan	3,445	1.82
Amerindian	2,925	1.54
Inuktitut	24,995	13.18
Total	189,615	100.00

Table 7.4 Population by Algonquian mother tongue and Algonquian home language, Canada 1991

Language	Mother tongue	Home language	Ratio of home language to mother tongue (%)
Blackfoot	4,005	2,520	63
Cree	82,070	60,885	74
Malecite	255	70	28
Micmac	6,255	4,740	76
Montagnais	7,580	7,380	97
Ojibwa	25,255	15,675	62
Other	5,915	4,990	84
Total	131,335	96,260	73

Table 7.4 gives the figures for each separate Algonquian language and table 7.5 for the Athapaskan languages. Among the former, Cree has the greatest number of mother-tongue speakers (82,070). Indeed, 43 per cent of *all* aboriginal mother-tongue speakers in Canada are Cree. One must be wary of taking comfort in these figures though, since the label *Cree* covers several dialects that are not necessarily mutually intelligible from one pole of the dialect continuum to the other.

Ojibwa also has a sizeable number of mother-tongue speakers (25,255), who account for 13 per cent of all aboriginal mother-tongue speakers. But the same caveat as for Cree may apply. In the Algonquian group, Malecite has very few

Table 7.5 Population by Athapaskan mother tongue and Athapaskan home language, Canada 1991

Language	Mother tongue	Home language	Ratio of home language to mother tongue (%)
Carrier	1,995	1,070	54
Chilcotin	945	715	76
Chipewyan	2,620	1,480	57
Dogrib	2,255	1,955	87
Kutchin-Gwich'in	470	70	15
North Slavey	35	15	43
South Slavey	3,520	2,425	69
Other	7,315	6,025	82
Total	19,155	13,755	72

speakers, 255 in all in Canada. The absolute number of mother-tongue speakers for all the languages in the Athapaskan family is very low, as shown in table 7.5.

Unfortunately, the 1991 census does not provide figures for each individual language, so we must rely on information provided by other surveys, at the regional level, for more detailed information on some languages.[2]

One of the major indicators of the level of linguistic vitality is the relationship between census reports on mother tongue and those on actual language use in the home. It can be seen in table 7.2 that the linguistic group with the greatest vitality is Inuktitut, which has a ratio of home-language use to mother tongue of 88 per cent, followed by Algonquian, Athapaskan and Siouan, which have ratios around 73 per cent. Many groups are currently witnessing a very sharp decline. Roughly speaking, only one out of three mother-tongue speakers of Salish (30 per cent) and Wakashan (32 per cent) report that they use it at home. The proportion is roughly one out of four for Haida (27 per cent) and Kutenai (23 per cent), less than one out of five for Tsimshian (17 per cent) and only one out of ten for Tlingit (10 per cent).

The ratios of actual home use to the number of mother-tongue speakers, combined with the absolute number of mother-tongue speakers, are testimony that several languages are in extremely critical condition. Languages spoken by only a few thousand speakers may be judged endangered by any account. Conversely, languages boasting larger numbers of speakers *and* a high overall ratio of transmission at home may be judged as still viable. Cree, Montagnais, Ojibwa and Inuktitut would appear to fall into this group.

The 1991 census data on Iroquoian languages are unreliable but, on the basis of the information provided by Norton and Fettes (1994), all of the Iroquoian languages spoken in Canada are in critical condition – with the exception perhaps of Mohawk. We know, however, that the latter is also declining rapidly (Maurais, 1992).

The clash between cultures often brings about the demise of minority languages. In shifting to the majority language, a community may however stop short of acquiring full native-like command of that language, and may settle for a form of it that is more or less heavily influenced by features of the ancestral variety (Thomason and Kaufman, 1988). Reservation English exemplifies this phenomenon among aboriginal groups in North America (Bartelt, Jasper and Hoffer, 1982; Fleischer, 1982; Mulder, 1982; Rigsby, 1987).

Moreover, intense contact with the majority language and widespread bilingualism in the community may also bring about a gradual erosion of competence in the aboriginal language among the younger generations – even in communities where normal intergenerational transmission of the ancestral language is perpetuated (Drapeau, 1993, 1995a). Changes may be triggered, the most easily detectable being heavy borrowing and code-mixing and, possibly, the crystallization of a mixed language. The development of Michif in the prairie provinces, a mixed language of Cree origin with strong French admixtures, is a bewildering example (Bakker, 1992; Crawford, 1985).

LANGUAGE RIGHTS AND STATUS

Historical perspective on language rights in education

Canadian Indians and their lands fell under the jurisdiction of the federal government with the British North America Act of 1867. They then became wards of the federal government, ultimately of the Indian Affairs Department.

Through three Indian Acts between 1876 and 1886, the federal government essentially abolished all political autonomy for Indians and assumed jurisdiction over matters such as economic and social life, as well as education. This was a radical departure from the legislative framework operating for non-Indians as the 1867 act gave the control of education to the provinces. It was thought that Indian affairs (lands, education, finance, social services) should be managed on their behalf until they became sufficiently emancipated and civilized as to shed the reserve system and integrate into the majority society. From 1871, the Canadian government, through a series of treaties, progressively accelerated the implementation of the reserve system which, at the time, was seen as a transient order leading progressively to full emancipation. Indian education policy was also elaborated (see Barman, Hébert and McCaskill, 1986b; Frideres, 1988; Richstone, 1989; Savard and Proulx, 1982; Trudel, 1992) and vast areas of Indian lands were traded off against modest compensation and a promise to guarantee a school on each reserve.

Funds were given to religious congregations for the maintenance of existing day-schools on the reserves of Quebec, Ontario and the Maritimes. They were also to build residential schools in the vicinity of Indian reserves in the west and wherever day-schools were not available. The policy aimed at complete assimilation to the majority culture and language (English or French). The implementation of residential schooling is analyzed from various perspectives in Barman, Hébert and McCaskill (1986a). The policy was revised at the turn of this century and enforced until its middle years. As Barman *et al.* note, 'the revised education policy announced in 1910 had as its goal to fit the Indian for civilized life in his own environment' (p. 9). The curriculum was simplified and geared towards practical skills, and the use of Indian languages was restricted to catechism and religious services.

Despite the advent of compulsory education for all Canadians in 1920, nearly half of native school-age children were still without formal education in 1951. One-third of the remaining half went as far as Grade 3, and only one out of ten went to Grade 6. Recognition of the extremely low standards in federal native schools eventually led to the revocation of the segregation policy. A 1946 Joint Committee of the Senate and House of Commons advocated immediate Indian integration by schooling Indian children together with non-Indians.

The contemporary period: self-determination

In June 1969, following the publication of the Hawthorne Report on the situation of Canadian Indians, the new federal government led by Prime Minister Pierre Trudeau issued a White Paper on the elimination of all legislative and constitutional bases for racial discrimination. It proposed the abolition of the Indian Act and all discriminatory status, and the elimination of the reserve system. However, Indian reaction to the White Paper was so overwhelmingly negative that the federal government had to withdraw it. The Indian political organizations were calling for increased self-determination. In educational and language matters, the National Indian Brotherhood (established in 1968) issued a policy paper (1972) demanding Indian control of Indian education at the band level. An agreement was reached with the federal government in 1973; jurisdiction was gradually to be transferred to the Indian bands on demand. They were to assume decisions over educational content and operate their own schools. Remaining federal residential schools were closed down. The policy paper also advocated formal instruction through the medium of native languages, at least in kindergarten and primary-school classes, and the teaching of Native-as-a-second-language among groups who had shifted to English or French.

The Department of Indian Affairs and Northern Development (henceforth, DIAND) provides funding for aboriginal languages to band-operated schools, as well as to federal schools on reserves. Some form of support for language programmes may also be included in transfer payments to provincial education authorities. 'More recent DIAND figures show a gradual increase in native language instruction in most parts of the country: some 60 per cent of children on reserve now receive some aboriginal-language instruction. There are still dramatic differences between regions' (Norton and Fettes, 1994, p. 21).

Similarly, the Assembly of First Nations reports:

> Although there are many excellent aboriginal-language programs currently offered in various parts of the country, overall existing language programs do not promote fluency or language retention. Of the 267 language programs operating at the time of the survey 177 or 66 per cent were at the preschool and elementary levels. Classes in aboriginal languages were generally available only to grade three. Almost 70% of bands did not have language instruction for the secondary level and over 80% did not offer adult classes. Aboriginal language class is primarily taught as a core subject [*sic*] it is therefore restricted to approximately two hours of instruction per week. (Assembly of First Nations, 1990, p. ii)

This somewhat pessimistic outlook is also reflected in the conclusions of a recent comprehensive national survey performed by the Canadian Education Association (Kirkness and Bowman, 1992, p. 43): very few schools in their sample 'indicated that an aboriginal language was used as the language of instruction at any grade level, in any province'. With respect to bilingual programmes, 'the majority of the elementary programs indicated do not include all grades, but are generally limited to grades 1 to 3 only'.[3]

Cultural/educational centres have burgeoned across Canada, funded by DIAND, to foster the study of aboriginal history, culture and language. They develop curriculum materials in native languages and support special archives and museums. Meanwhile, a number of Canadian universities and junior colleges have established Native Studies programmes. The Secretary of State also administers the Native Social and Cultural Development Program, largely aimed at supporting aboriginal-language retention. The budget has been sharply curtailed in the past years and now stands at about $1 million annually.

Legal protection for aboriginal languages[4]

Canadian laws offer very little explicit protection for aboriginal languages. The Constitution of 1982 includes the Canadian Charter of Rights and Freedoms and an important section on native rights: 'When combined with section 27, section 15 is likely to offer the best guarantee with respect to aboriginal languages. Section 27 compels the courts to interpret the Charter "with the aim of promoting the maintenance and value of the multicultural heritage of Canadians", and clearly ... aboriginal languages are part of the multicultural heritage of this country' (Richstone, 1989, p. 262). Richstone mentions that Sections 15 and 27 cannot, however, be interpreted as compelling governments to allocate money to the promotion of any aspect of this multicultural heritage.

Section 35(1) of the Constitution guarantees that existing inherent or treaty rights will be acknowledged and ratified. The definition of 'inherent aboriginal rights' may be seen as including linguistic rights, but 'it would be difficult to argue that an aboriginal linguistic right, as noted in section 35, includes more than the right to use and promote aboriginal languages and cultures *within* the communities involved ... we are hard put to see in section 35 a right-of-claim allowing aboriginal peoples to demand public grants for the transmission and development of their languages' (Richstone, 1989, p. 268; emphasis added). The Assembly of First Nations, however, argues that 'section 35 of the Constitutional Act appears to provide the basis for a generous definition of aboriginal-language rights' (Norton and Fettes, 1994, p. iii).

Four constitutional conferences were held in Canada between 1983 and 1987, with the aim of defining the aboriginal rights that were to be enshrined within the Constitution. Aboriginal self-government became the central theme of these conferences and has since remained central in the agenda of aboriginal peoples. Self-government is, however, negotiated locally on a band basis or, at best, on a group basis – and not on a provincial, let alone national one. It is not clear what will become of language rights, services and programmes in this context.

The land claims agreement signed by Canada, Quebec, and the Cree and Inuit of Quebec in 1975 (known as the James Bay Agreement) includes provisions for aboriginal self-government and for native services in Cree and Inuktitut. The Agreement provides for court interpreters and translations of acts and other court proceedings. It also creates the Cree Regional School Board and the Inuit Kativik School Board, which are responsible for providing educational services and have the right to use such means as are judged necessary to promote and perpetuate their languages and cultures. The language of instruction may be the aboriginal variety, with the proviso that French be taught as a second language (so that education can be furthered elsewhere in Quebec). Further to the James Bay Agreement, the Canadian (federal) government passed a bill known as the *Law on the Cree and Naskapi of Quebec*, which acknowledges the right to use their language in band council meetings and proceedings.

Few provincial legislatures have ruled on aboriginal languages. The Quebec Charter of the French Language is an important exception (Gouvernement du Québec, 1989). The Charter, in its preamble, acknowledges the right to preserve and develop the languages and cultures of Quebec Amerindian and Inuit peoples. Sections of it explicitly state that Indian reserves are not subject to its stipulations and are thus free to choose the language of education (see Richstone, 1989; Trudel, 1992).

Earlier, in 1983, the Quebec National Assembly had adopted fifteen principles governing future relations with the aboriginal peoples, three of which bear on language. Aboriginal peoples are recognized as distinct nations, entitled to their own languages, who have the right to the promotion of their distinct identity. The declaration also entitles them to control their institutions and to receive public funding to further their own aims. In 1989, the Quebec *Secrétariat aux affaires autochtones* issued a policy for 'safeguarding and promoting Quebec aboriginal languages'. It states that aboriginal nations are primarily responsible for their own languages and deems their languages worthy of support (see Drapeau and Corbeil, forthcoming, for an appraisal of this policy).

The majority of people in the Northwest Territories are aboriginal and the government there adopted an Official Languages Act in 1984. Part I identifies seven 'official aboriginal languages': Chipewyan, Cree, Dogrib, Kutchin, North and South Slavey, and Inuktitut. A revision of the Act in 1988 gave these languages equal status with English and French, and created the Office of the Language Commissioner. Official language status includes: (a) the right to use the language in debates and proceedings of the Legislative Assembly, with interpretation available on request; (b) the right to court proceedings in the language, and simultaneous translation as required; (c) provision of court decisions of public interest in the language, upon request; (d) provision of government services in the language, if 'a significant demand exists'. In a 1995 Agreement, the federal government allocated $11.2 million 'for the revitalization, maintenance and enhancement of aboriginal languages in the Northwest Territories', as well as for 'the provision of services in aboriginal languages so as to assist in their implementation as official languages in the Northwest Territories'.

Yukon adopted a language act in 1988 that: (a) recognizes the significance of its aboriginal languages; (b) resolves to act to preserve, develop and enhance

154

them; (c) acknowledges the right to use them in debates and proceedings of the Legislative Assembly; (d) empowers the government or the Legislative Assembly to provide aboriginal language services. The Yukon Education Act, adopted in 1990, also grants strong support for aboriginal languages. Besides these Acts, an aboriginal Language Services Branch was established, an extensive survey of the primary aboriginal languages was carried out, eight fluent aboriginal language speakers were hired as interpreters, an aboriginal languages conference was held in 1991 and a Community Initiatives Funding Program was launched (See Norton and Fettes, 1994).

In May 1993, the Canadian government signed an agreement with 18,000 Inuit, creating Nunavut – a territory covering 350,000 square kilometres in the Northwest Territories. It is planned that, by 1999, Nunavut will have its own territorial government, as is the case in the Yukon and Northwest Territories. This agreement should have a profound impact on the future of Inuktitut.

There is no explicit policy or legislation with respect to aboriginal languages in Newfoundland, Prince Edward Island, Nova Scotia and Ontario. New Brunswick adopted a policy on Malecite and Micmac education in 1991. It includes a commitment to provide aboriginal-language programmes when the number of pupils warrants, and upon the availability of a qualified teacher.

Aboriginal demands

The Assembly of First Nations (AFN) demands official status for aboriginal languages, constitutional recognition and effective legislative protection. The AFN interprets the Constitution as entitling language development and maintenance and it has been preparing for an Aboriginal Languages Act. Instruction in aboriginal languages is seen as a fundamental human right (Assembly of First Nations, 1990). Therefore, the federal government is requested to provide sufficient funding for the provision of aboriginal languages from kindergarten to the end of secondary school. It is understood that 'an entirely new approach is needed, based on a comprehensive system of aboriginal self-government' and 'a single federal program for aboriginal languages should be established within the Department of Canadian Heritage, and piecemeal federal funding of individual projects should be ended in favor of provincial and territorial funding agreements' (Norton and Fettes, 1994, pp. iv-v). Meanwhile, provincial policy should include stable, multi-year funding.

The sheer complexity of aboriginal languages in Canada precludes the possibility of setting up all-inclusive, one-size-fits-all language policy. There is, therefore, a tendency to fall back on the community level for language planning and development – thus unfortunately losing leverage. The AFN has developed a community-based policy for language maintenance and revitalization in which language programmes are to involve all aspects of community life and are not to be restricted to the school alone (Fettes, 1992; Norton and Fettes, 1994).

The proposal for the creation of a National Institute of Aboriginal Languages, first advocated in 1988 by the Secretary of State, has so far remained unfulfilled. Kirkness (1989) recommended the federal establishment of an aboriginal Languages Foundation, a proposal later taken up by the AFN, who also request the establishment of a national clearinghouse, under aboriginal control, to act as a public information, research and resource centre. At the provincial and territorial levels, several aboriginal organizations are also very active in developing coherent language policy. The Inuit are represented by Inuit Tapirisat and the Métis by the Métis National Council. An Official First Nations Act of the Federation of Saskatchewan Indian Nations establishes five aboriginal languages as official 'First Nations languages'. The Royal Commission on Aboriginal Peoples, created in 1992, is due to publish its final report in 1996. It will no doubt contain recommendations for the preservation and development of Canadian aboriginal languages.

CONCLUSION

Minority languages are universally at risk and aboriginal varieties are thus not the only ones lying in the shadow of extinction. The consensus among researchers today is that the phenomenon has reached acute and unprecedented proportions (Diamond, 1993; Grimes, 1988; Robins and Uhlenbeck, 1991). Some linguists feel that only a few hundred of the world's languages actually face no danger on a long-term basis.

Aboriginal languages are especially endangered. Native-language groups form linguistic enclaves, scattered over an immense territory and encapsulated within white society. Geographic isolation no longer protects them and lack of concentrated geolinguistic strongholds is a powerful drawback. Likewise, the dearth of written corpora in most aboriginal languages has a profound impact on their survival, and on the type of efforts that can effectively be attempted to strengthen their position. The maintenance, let alone the revival, of Canada's aboriginal languages is therefore a major challenge facing their speakers, and Canadian society in general. Language being a powerful component of identity, the relationship between aboriginal and majority languages is now at the forefront of native claims and concerns.

Even with increasing control and self-government, aboriginal people never-theless make up a small minority with only minimal power. It remains to be seen if they can, within the context of majority society, summon the political will and attract the necessary funding to effectively devise and successfully enact plans to revive, protect and maintain their ancestral languages.

Notes

1 A sizeable number of Indian reserves either did not participate in the census or were incompletely enumerated. They represent 38,000 persons on 78 reserves or settlements. Furthermore, an additional 20,000 persons did not participate in the APS despite having participated in the general 1991 census. The non-participation by the Mohawks in Quebec (3 communities) and approximately half the reserves in New Brunswick has an impact on the figures pertaining to the Mohawk and the Micmac languages.

2 See Maurais (1992) for Quebec languages; Saskatchewan Indigenous Languages Committee (1991); Sioux Lookout District First Nations (1993) for Dakota (mentioned by Ahenakew, Blair and Fredeen 1994); Government of the Northwest Territories (1993); Yukon Executive Council Office (1991). Norton and Fettes (1994) have also compiled statistics from various sources on individual languages. Assembly of First Nations (1990) provides the results of a detailed language survey among 150 bands. Additional communities were surveyed in 1991 (Assembly of First Nations, 1992).

3 For further discussion of native language policy and education, see Burnaby (1989).

4 Much of the information reported in this section is drawn from Richstone (1989).

References

Ahenakew, F., Blair, H. and Fredeen, S. (1994). *Aboriginal Language Policy and Planning in Canada.* Draft paper. Ottawa: Royal Commission on Aboriginal Peoples.

Assembly of First Nations. (1990). *Towards Linguistic Justice for First Nations.* Ottawa: Assembly of First Nations.

(1992). *Towards Rebirth of First Nations Languages.* Ottawa: Assembly of First Nations.

Bakker, P. (1992). A language of our own. The genesis of Michif, the mixed Cree-French language of the Canadian Metis. Ph.D. dissertation, University of Amsterdam.

Barman, J, Hébert, Y and McCaskill, D. (1986a). *Indian Education in Canada. Volume 1: The Legacy.* Vancouver: University of British Columbia Press.

(1986b). The legacy of the past: an overview. In J. Barman, Y. Hébert and D. McCaskill (eds.), *Indian Education in Canada. Volume 1: The Legacy* (pp. 1–22). Vancouver: University of British Columbia Press.

Bartelt, H. G., Jasper, S. P. and Hoffer, B. L. (1982). *Essays in Native American English.* San Antonio, Texas: Trinity University.

Bauman, J. (1980). *A Guide to Issues in Indian Language Retention.* Washington, DC: Center for Applied Linguistics.

Burnaby, B. (1986). Speakers of Canadian aboriginal languages. In W. Cowan (ed.), *Papers of the Seventeenth Algonquian Conference* (pp. 47–64). Ottawa: Carleton University Press.

(1989). Language policy and the education of Native peoples: identifying the issues. In P. Pupier and J. Werhling (eds.), *Langue et droit* (pp. 279–289). Montreal: Wilson et Lafleur.

Burnaby, B. and Beaujot, R. (1987). *The Use of Aboriginal Languages in Canada: An Analysis of the 1981 Census Data.* Ottawa: Department of the Secretary of State.

Crawford, J. C. (1985). What is Michif: language in the Métis tradition. In J. Peterson and J. S. H. Brown (eds.), *The New People: Being and Becoming a Métis in North America* (pp. 231–241). Winnipeg: The University of Manitoba Press.

Diamond, J. (1993). Speaking with a single tongue. *Discover, 14,* 78–85.

Drapeau, L. (1993). Language birth: an alternative to language death. In A. Crochetière, J.-C. Boulanger and C. Ouellon (eds.). *Proceedings of the XVth International Congress of Linguistics* (pp. 141–144). Quebec: Presses de l'Université Laval.

(1995a). Code-switching in caretaker speech and bilingual competence in a native village of northern Quebec. *International Journal of the Sociology of Language, 113,* 157–164.

(1995b). *Perspectives on Aboriginal Language Conservation and Revitalization in Canada.* Draft Paper. Ottawa: Royal Commission on Aboriginal Peoples.

Drapeau, L. and Corbeil, J.-C. (forthcoming). Language planning for indigenous languages. In J. Maurais (ed.), *The Indigenous Languages of Quebec.* Clevedon: Multilingual Matters.

Fettes, M. (1992). *A Guide to Language Strategies for First Nations Communities.* Ottawa: Assembly of First Nations.

Fleischer, M. (1982). The educational implications of American Indian English. In R. S. Clair and W. Leap (eds.), *Language Renewal among American Indian Tribes* (pp. 141–148). Rosslyn, VA: National Clearinghouse for Bilingual Education.

Foster, M. K. (1982). Canada's first languages. *Langue et société, 7,* 7–16.

Frideres, J. S. (1988). *Native Peoples in Canada. Contemporary Conflicts.* Scarborough, Ont.: Prentice-Hall Canada.

Gouvernement du Québec. (1989). *Charte de la langue francaise.* L.R.Q., chapitre C-11, à jour au ler août 1989. Quebec: Editeur official du Québec.

Government of the Northwest Territories. (1993). *Eight Official Languages: First Annual Report of the Languages Commissioner of the NWT for the Year 1992–1993.* Yellowknife.

Grimes, B. F. (1988). *Ethnologue: Languages of the World.* Dallas: Summer Institute of Linguistics.

Kinkade, D. (1991). The decline of native languages in Canada. In R. H. Robins and E. M. Uhlenbeck (eds.), *Endangered Languages* (pp. 157–176). Oxford: Berg.

Kirkness, V. (1989). Aboriginal Language Foundation: a mechanism for language renewal. *Canadian Journal of Native Education, 16,* 25–41.

Kirkness, V. and Bowman, S. (1992). *First Nations and Schools: Triumphs and Struggles.* Toronto: Canadian Education Association/ Association canadienne d'éducation.

Maurais, J. (1992). *Les langues autochtones du Québec.* Quebec: Publications du Québec.

Mulder, J. (1982). The Tshimshian English dialect: the result of language interference. In H. G. Bartelt, S. P. Jasper and B. L. Hoffer (eds.), *Essays in Native American English* (pp. 95–111). San Antonio, Texas: Trinity University.

National Indian Brotherhood. (1972). *Indian Control of Indian Education.* Ottawa.

Norton, R. and Fettes, M. (1994). *Taking Back the Talk.* Draft paper. Ottawa: Royal Commission on Aboriginal Peoples.

Price, J. A. (1981). The viability of Indian languages in Canada. *Canadian Journal of Native Studies, 1,* 339–346.

Richstone, J. (1989). La protection juridique des langues autochtones au Canada. In P. Pupier and J. Werhling (eds.), *Langue et droit* (pp. 259–278). Montreal: Wilson et Lafleur.

Rigsby, B. (1987). Indigenous language shift and maintenance in Fourth World settings. *Multilingua, 6,* 359–378.

Robins, R. H., and Uhlenbeck, E. M. (1991). *Endangered Languages.* Oxford: Berg.

Robinson, P. (1985). Language retention among Canadian Indians: a simultaneous equations model with dichotomous endogenous variables. *American Sociological Review, 50,* 515–528.

Saskatchewan Indigenous Languages Committee. (1991). *Sociolinguistic Survey of Indigenous Languages in Saskatchewan: On the Critical List.* Saskatoon.

Savard, R. and Proulx, J. R. (1982). *Canada: derrière l'épopée, les autochtones.* Montreal: L' Hexagone.

Secrétariat aux affaires autochtones. (1989). *Maintien et développement des langues autochtones au Québec.* Quebec.

Statistics Canada. (1993). *Language, Tradition, Health, Lifestyle and Social Issues. 1991 Aboriginal Peoples Survey.* Ottawa: Industry, Science and Technology. Cat. No. 89-533.

    (1995). *Profile of Canada's Aboriginal Population. 1991 Census of Canada.* Ottawa: Industry, Science and Technology Canada. Cat. No. 94-325.

Thomason, S. G. and Kaufman, T. (1988). *Language Contact, Creolization, and Genetic Linguistics.* Berkeley: University of California Press.

Trudel, F. (1992). La politique des gouvernements du Québec et du Canada en matière de langue autochtone. In J. Maurais (ed.), *Les langues autochtones du Québec* (pp. 151–182). Quebec: Publications du Québec.

Yukon Executive Council Office. (1991). *A Profile of Aboriginal Languages in the Yukon.* Yukon: Aboriginal Language Services.

8 French: Canadian varieties

Robert A. Papen

INTRODUCTION

The first French-speaking colony in North America was established by Champlain in 1604 at Port-Royal (present-day Annapolis Royal, Nova Scotia) on the Bay of Fundy, which came to be called 'l'Acadie' (Acadia). Four years later, Champlain founded a colony at Quebec, on the St Lawrence River, which was to become the centre of New France. These two establishments were to have separate and independent development and were to give rise to the two principal French dialect areas in Canada: Acadian French (AF) and Quebec French (QF). From the very beginning, AF and QF were relatively distinct since the great majority of the early settlers in Acadia came from the Poitou, Aunis and Saintonge area of western France and were mainly agricultural workers; the Laurentian colonists (Trois-Rivières was founded in 1634 and Montreal in 1642) came from a great number of areas of central, western and northern France, but particularly from Normandy (some 19 per cent), Île-de-France (18 per cent) as well as from Poitou-Aunis (22 per cent); settlers from the latter did not arrive until after 1640 (Charbonneau and Guillemette, 1994).

In this brief chapter, my purpose is not to review the history of the French-speaking populations of Canada but rather to describe some of the linguistic features that characterize Canadian French (CF) varieties. AF is spoken in all three Maritime provinces as well as in Newfoundland, the Magdalen Islands of Quebec and, historically at least, on the Gaspé Peninsula and in a number of small towns throughout Quebec ('les petites Cadies') to which Acadians had emigrated during the 'Grand dérangement' (1755–1768). QF is of course spoken throughout Quebec, where it is the mother tongue of approximately 85 per cent of the population.

French-speaking traders and trappers had begun quite early in the history of New France to travel the waterways west to the Great Lakes, where they established communities such as Detroit (1701), Michilimackinac (1716) – now

160

Mackinaw City Michigan, where the first 'Métis' society was born – Sault Ste Marie, etc. Later, throughout the nineteenth and twentieth centuries, successive waves of French-speaking immigrants from Quebec, as well as from Europe, settled in southern, eastern, central and northeastern Ontario. The percentage of francophones in the general population varies from as high as 85 per cent in Hawkesbury and 70 per cent in Hearst, to 40 per cent in Sudbury and 35 per cent in Cornwall, and as low as 17 per cent in North Bay and 8 per cent in Pembroke. Mougeon and Beniak (1991) calculate that no less than 84 per cent of the French mother-tongue population of Ontario are active bilinguals, as compared to only 29 per cent of French mother-tongue speakers in Quebec. It thus seems that bilingualism is the key characteristic which differentiates Franco-Ontarians from Franco-Quebecers.

The French-speaking population of the 'Prairie' provinces (Manitoba, Saskatchewan and Alberta) originates from three distinct sources, which makes the sociolinguistic situation rather unique since, elsewhere outside Quebec, speakers originate mostly from a single source: Quebec for Franco-Ontarians and Acadia for the Maritime provinces.

The first speakers of French to establish themselves on a permanent basis west of the Great Lakes were (again) fur traders and trappers who, as early as the beginning of the nineteenth century, travelled the waterways of western Ontario into the vast western plains. Some of these adventurous *coureurs de bois* decided to live with the local Indian population and were soon married *à la façon du pays*, the result being the creation of what was to become not only a new culture, halfway between the Euro-American way of life and the traditional native one, but also a new French-speaking ethnic group: the Red River Métis. From their rather humble beginnings until the creation of the province of Manitoba in 1870, for which they are largely responsible, the Red River Métis represented the majority of French speakers west of Ontario. However, subsequent and continuous immigration of francophones from Quebec, sometimes by way of the New England states or from Ontario, until well into the twentieth century, has meant that, today, the majority of French speakers in the three prairie provinces have roots in Quebec. Today, French-speaking Métis can be found in a number of villages and towns in the three western provinces, although the town of Saint-Laurent in Manitoba is the only one where they are in the majority.

What makes the francophone population of two of the three provinces particularly interesting is the important influx of European French-speaking immigrants from the 1890s until the beginning of World War I. These Europeans established a number of villages, in both Manitoba and Saskatchewan, and their descendants have succeeded in maintaining a number of linguistic traits which set them apart from both CF speakers and, of course, Métis French speakers (Frémont, 1959; Jackson, 1974).

The only established French-speaking community of some size in British Columbia was in Maillardville, a suburb of New Westminster on the Fraser River. It was founded by some seventy-five families from Quebec in 1909 who came to work in the lumber mills. According to Frémont (1959) the French-speaking population in 1959 numbered over 1,000 but assimilation to English has been rapid and extensive and, today, it is doubtful that there are any native speakers of French under the age of fifty. The only study of Maillardville French is that of Ellis (1965), which shows that, phonologically at least, it is identical to other western Canadian varieties. Of course, a great many Franco-Quebecers have established themselves in British Columbia in recent years, as have numerous French-speaking Europeans, but they do not constitute a speech community *per se.*

During the past twenty years much has been published on CF varieties, particularly on all aspects of QF; there is also a growing literature on AF and Ontario French (OF). Unfortunately, little has been published on western Canadian varieties and what little exists is mainly limited to phonological characteristics (the exception being Papen (1984) for Métis French). My purpose here is not to survey the phonological, morphological, syntactic and lexical features of CF; rather I will limit my comments to phonological features. I shall also provide a brief discussion of the influence of English on each variety. In the following sections, I describe Quebec French, Ontario French, western Canadian French – including Métis French and western Canadian European French – and Acadian French.

QUEBEC FRENCH

As in any language, French in Quebec, and in Canada in general, varies according to characteristics of the speaker (age, sex, social status, place of residence, etc.) and the nature of the communicative situation (degree of formality, subject matter, tone of the conversation, etc.).

In Quebec, a particular distinction must be made between two language varieties: the 'standard' variety, which is used in all spoken and written official, formal or institutional situations and the 'familiar', 'informal', or even 'popular' spoken variety used in all other situations. A number of authors have argued that Standard Quebec French (SQF) is a myth, and that it is simply Standard European French (SEF), also called International French (Nemni, 1993). Other linguists have taken a more balanced view and submit that, orally at least, the standard or normative variety that has developed in Quebec is different from both the more archaic rural QF and the typical 'Parisian' pronunciation, which Quebecers find too 'foreign'. This variety has often been called the 'Radio-Canada model'. However, Quebecers have always adopted SEF written norms; in other words, they wish to speak *à la québécoise* but to write *à la française*! Martel and Cajolet-Laganière (1995) do note some small differences between SQF and SEF, but they are for the most part limited to spelling. Léard (1995) also identifies a number of syntactic usages which clearly differentiate SQF from SEF: *Avoir voulu, j'aurais pu finir plus vite.* ('Had I wanted to, I could have finished faster'), for example, is impossible in SEF. On the whole, the principal source of difference between SEF and SQF is the lexicon. Although the vast majority of lexical items of SEF and SQF are common to both, an important portion of the SQF lexicon consists of: (a) innovations (new words, new meanings for established words, new referents, new collocations, etc.) - for example, *traversier* 'ferry', *poudrerie* 'blowing snow', *dépanneur* 'convenience store', *carte-soleil* 'medical insurance card', *baccalauréat* 'bachelor's degree', *caisse populaire* 'credit union'; (b) calques - *balle molle* 'soft ball', *papier de toilette* 'toilet paper', *(auto) compacte* 'compact car'; (c) semantic loans (loan shifts) - *banc de neige* 'snow bank', *graduation* 'graduation'; (d) infrequent items borrowed from a variety of native Indian languages - *atoca/ataca* 'cranberry', *mocassin* 'soft leather shoe', *ouaouaron* 'bull frog', etc. SQF also contains a very large number of idiomatic expressions which are unknown in SEF: *donner l'heure juste* 'set someone straight', *ne pas être la tête à Papineau* 'not to be overly bright', *avoir le bec sucré* 'to have a sweet tooth', *avoir les yeux pleins d'eau* 'to be teary-eyed'. Of course, 'popular' QF also contains a great number of archaisms and dialectisms, as well as assimilated and unassimilated loans from English.

I shall adopt Léard's (1995) distinction between Common Quebec French (CQF), the variety spontaneously used and understood by most Quebecers, and Standard Quebec French (which Léard calls 'Official Quebec French'). The former variety has two registers, 'popular' and 'familiar', while SQF is used in more or less formal situations by relatively well-educated speakers; it is the variety largely used on radio and television (but not necessarily in the popular 'soaps' or on open-line radio talk-shows), in schools, universities, etc. SQF is therefore to be considered the 'norm'.

The term *joual* (from *cheval* 'horse') was used in the 1960s and 1970s to refer to popular or familiar CQF, as well as to popular Montreal French in particular. It was regularly depreciated and denigrated, many considering it to be a non-language, a hodge-podge of bad French and English with faulty and unde-cipherable pronunciations, and so on. Today, the term has more or less fallen out of use since attempts to define it in a rigorous way have proved to be difficult, if not impossible, and more neutral terms, such as *français populaire* have become preferred.

In reality, SQF and CQF form the opposite ends of a continuum, and it is difficult to determine where one ceases to speak CQF and begins to use SQF since the continuum exists at all linguistics levels.

The QF phonological system

Taken as a whole, the phonological system of QF is similar to that of SEF. The differences lie specifically in the phonetic realizations of each phoneme. However, the prosodic system is sufficiently different from SEF to give QF its unique 'accent'. For example, the penultimate syllable is often slightly longer and more strongly stressed than the final syllable, which is usually shorter than in SEF.

The phonological system of QF is different from SEF in that it has main-tained all four nasal vowels (/ɛ̃/, /ɑ̃/, /ɔ̃/ and /œ̃/) (SEF /ɛ̃/ has replaced /œ̃/); it has also maintained the historic length distinctions between /ɛ/ and /ɛː/ (thus, *renne* [Rɛn] 'reindeer' vs *reine* [Rɛːn] 'queen') and between /a/ and /ɑː/ (e.g., *patte* [pat] 'paw' vs *pâte* [pɑːt] 'dough'). Most SEF speakers no longer maintain these length distinctions, although they still exist in regional French varieties or among very conservative SEF speakers.

There is a number of phonetic realizations typical of QF. For example, the high vowels /i/, /y/ and /u/ are obligatorily laxed to [ɪ], [ʏ], [ʊ] in stressed sylla-bles checked by a 'non-lengthening' consonant (e.g., all consonants other than /z/, /ʒ/, /v/, /R/ and the cluster /vR/) – thus, *vite* [vɪt], *rude* [Rʏd], *pouce* [pʊs], etc. High vowel laxing is one of the most noticeable and general pronunciation traits of QF since it occurs in all regional varieties and social registers, though more rarely in the speech of radio and television broadcasters. In the Saguenay-Lac St Jean and the Beauce area, high vowels can be laxed even before the 'lengthen-ing' consonants, other than /R/ (for example, *église* [eglɪz], *rouge* [Rʊʒ], *écluse* [eklʏz]) (Boulanger, 1986). The high vowel laxing rule applies optionally in unstressed syllables – *équilibre* [ekilɪb] or [ekɪlɪb]. High vowels can devoice in unstressed syllables if preceded or followed by at least one unvoiced consonant (*municipalité* [mynɪsɪpalite]) and can even delete completely (*université* [ynivɛRste], *député* [depte]).

The closed mid-vowels /ø/ and /o/, as well as the nasal vowels, are systematically lengthened in any stressed checked syllable – *jeûne* [ʒøːn] but *jeu* [ʒø], *paume* [poːm] but *peau* [po], *dinde* [dẽːd] but *daim* [dẽ], *tante* [tãːt] but *tant* [tã]. Besides these historically long vowels, any vowel can be lengthened by the 'lengthening' consonants in a stressed syllable (e.g., *pour* [puːʀ], *cuve* [kyːv], *îvre* [iːv]).

In CQF, phonemically and phonetically long vowels have a tendency to be unstable, resulting in a variety of diphthongs, particularly in stressed syllables – e.g., *rêve* [ʀaᶜv], *pâte* [pɑᵘt], *peur* [pœʸʀ], *corps* [kaᵘʀ], *sainte* [sɛ̃ⁱt], *pendre* [pãᵘd], *songe* [sɔ̃ᵘʒ], *défunte* [defœ̃ʸt], etc. Speakers in the Mauricie area (seventy-five kilometres north of Trois-Rivières) systematically diphthongize vowels as above but do so also in free stressed or unstressed syllables – *brûlé* [bʀʏʸle], *graissé* [gʀɛⁱseⁱ], *fourneau* [fuᵘʀnoᵘ], *parfum* [paʀfœ̃ʸ], etc. (Demharter, 1990).

/ɛ̃/ is phonetically realized as [ẽ] rather than [ɛ̃], as in SEF; /ã/ is phonetically [ã], or even [æ̃] ~ [ɛ̃] in popular Montreal French and /ɔ̃/ is realized as [ɔ̃] rather than [õ] as in SEF.

/a/ has three variants in free word-final position: [ɔ] or [ɒ] are the most typical variants in CQF (*Canada* [kanadɔ] ~ [kanadɒ]); [ɑ] is the SQF variant. The [a] variant, the most common in SEF, is much rarer in QF. The pronunciation of *oi* is extremely variable in QF and is lexically, structurally and socially determined. In SQF, the variants are [wa] and [wɑ]; the former is heard in words such as *moi, toi, roi, foi, toit*, etc., the latter in words such as *trois, mois, noix* and *bois* (noun). A third SQF variant is [wɑː], which is used in checked syllables such as *boîte, poivre, soir*, etc. In CQF, the following can be distinguished: in words such as *moi, toi, roi,* [we] is the traditional variant but it is now somewhat stigmatized and is often replaced by [wɛ]; [wɔ] is the variant used in words such as *mois, bois, trois*. In stressed checked syllables, the diphthong [wɑᵘ] or [waᵉ] is used – e.g., *soir* [swaᵉʀ]. The words *froid* and *droit* are regularly pronounced [fʀɛt] and [dʀɛt], and *oignon* and *poigner* are [ɔɲɔ̃] and [pɔɲe].

/ɛ/ in absolute word-final position can be pronounced as [æ] – *lait* [læ] (but *laitier* [lɛᵗsje]). It can also be realized as either [a] or [æ] in any syllable checked by /ʀ/ + any consonant (*couverte* [kuvæʀt], *perdu* [paʀdᶻy]). Today, such pronunciations are typical of relatively uneducated or rural speakers.

The consonant phonemic inventory of QF is identical to SEF and differs from it only in phonetic details. The most common trait of QF is the assibilation of the dental plosives /t/ and /d/ before high front vowels and glides – *type* [tsɪp], *dire* [dᶻiːʀ], *turc* [tsyʀk], *dure* [dᶻyːʀ], *tiens* [tsjɛ̃], *diable* [dᶻjaːb], *tuile* [tsɥɪl], etc.

Assibilation is obligatory within the word but it can optionally occur even across word boundaries: *Saint-Isidore* is [sɛ̃tɪzɪdɔːʁ] or [sɛ̃tˢɪzɪdɔːʁ] (Dumas, 1987).

Dental consonants can optionally palatalize before /j/ or even delete – *tiens* [tˢjɛ̃] ~ [kʲɛ̃], *diable* [dᶻjɑːb] ~ [gʲɑːb] ~ [jɑːb], *canadien* [kanadᶻjɛ̃] ~ [kanajɛ̃]. Optionally, the velar stops /k/ and /g/ can also palatalize before front vowels (*quille* [kʲɪj], *guêpe* [gʲɛːp] ~ [gʲaᵉp]). Whereas palatalization of /k/ and /g/ is considered archaic and substandard, assibilation is now so categorical that it is unnoticed by the general population.

In some areas such as Joliette and Lac St Jean, /ʒ/ is velarized or glottalized – *jamais* [xamæ] or [ɦamæ], *Joliette* [xɔljɛt] or [ɦɔljɛt].

The pronunciation of /ʁ/ has had a long and complex history in French. It is well known that, originally, French favoured an apico-dental (or alveolar) trill [r] or flap [ɾ]. It was eventually replaced by a more 'urban' uvular trill [ʁ] and, more recently, a velar or uvular fricative [ʁ] – though [r]/[ɾ] survives in rural areas of France, particularly in the Midi. It is generally agreed that from an early date in the colony, eastern Quebec (centred around the city of Quebec) tended to favour uvular 'r', while western and southern Quebec (centred on the Montreal area) maintained the more archaic dental 'r'. However, the uvular variant has been gaining ground throughout the province for the past fifty years. Today, in the Montreal area, younger speakers categorically use [ʁ] (or even the velar fricative [ʁ]) in all positions, while older speakers still vary between [ʁ] and [r]/[ɾ], depending on the nature of contiguous segments, its position in the syllable (in syllable initial position, [r] is favoured; in syllable final position, [ʁ] is preferred), the formality of the speech style, etc. A fourth variant of 'r' is sometimes heard in English loanwords such as *gear* [giːɹ], (*Chicago*) *Bears* [beːɪz], etc. A fifth variant is possible in word-final position where, when preceded by a long diphthongized vowel, it simply deletes; thus *porc* [paᵘ], *faire* [fæⁱ]. Finally, 'r' also regularly deletes in absolute word final position when preceded by another consonant, much as in popular French: *sucre* [syk], *cadre* [kɑːd], etc. (Ostiguy and Toussignant, 1993).

As in popular French, final consonant clusters are regularly simplified in CQF. Word final liquids (/ʁ/ and /l/) delete after obstruents (*table* [tab]); stops delete after obtruents (*correct* [kɔʁɛk]), but obstruents remain after sonorants – e.g., *sourde* [suʁd], *halte* [alt].

In rapid CQF, initial /l/ of definite articles and pronoun clitics *la, les, lui*, as well as final /l/ of *il, elle* and final /ʁ/ of the preposition *sur* typically delete. This gives rise to various vowel sequences (hiatus), which French tends to avoid. The QF solution is to fuse the vowel sequences into long vowels: *sur la table* [syʁlatabl] becomes [sɥatab] which becomes [saːtab]; *sur les planches* [syʀleplãːʃ] becomes [sɥeplãːʃ] which in turn becomes [seːplãːʃ]; *elle a mangé* [alamãʒe] becomes [aːmãʒe]. L-deletion seems to be another Canadian innovation, since it has not been attested in any other French speech variety (Bougaïeff & Cardinal, 1980). In CQF, a 'liaison' /l/ is often inserted between the clitic pronouns *ça* or *on* and a following vowel initial verb: *Ça l'arrive souvent* 'It often happens', *Ça l'a pas de bon sens* 'It doesn't make any sense', *On l'avait un téléphone* 'We had a telephone'. Intrusive /l/ can also be found in a number of compound constructions containing the preposition *à*: *lampe à l'huile* 'oil lamp', *pompe à l'eau* 'water pump', etc.

English influence on QF

The general and often naive opinion concerning the influence of English on QF is that it is both massive and pervasive; witness the large number of dictionaries or 'lists' that have been published in the twentieth century, whose specific purpose is to identify and help eradicate such forms (Bélisle, 1971; Colpron, 1982; etc.). However, Mougeon (1994) contends that more recent socio-linguistic studies have shown that such views were based on superficial or erroneous analyses. In fact, most lexical studies bearing on rates of borrowing from English have shown them to be statistically insignificant. For example, Poirier (1980) states that research on current QF usage tends to demonstrate that the percentage of anglicisms rarely reaches 1 per cent for a given corpus, even in regions where contact between the two languages has been the longest.

Of course, no one would deny that English has had a great influence on certain French-speaking communities in North America. Thus, French Canadians outside Quebec, living in an essentially anglophone milieu, have undoubtedly adopted a great number of anglicisms which are only marginally known in Quebec. The same can be said for the phenomenon of code-switching, which is certainly much more prevalent outside Quebec than within, with the possible exception of the speech of fluently bilingual Montrealers. Thus Poirier (1994) correctly considers that influence from English is one of the principal factors which differentiates French varieties in North America.

Although QF has been borrowing words from English since 1763, data allowing phonological analyses of borrowed forms go back only to the beginning of this century. It seems that from early on, borrowed English forms were totally integrated in the French phonological system. For example, dental stops were assibilated: *team* was pronounced [tˢɪm]; diphthongs were regularly pronounced as monophthongs (*crate* was [kʀeːt], *goal* [goːl], *crowd* [kʀɑːd]). On the other hand, there has always been a great deal of variation in the treatment of English high tense vowels, for example *bean(s)* was either [biːn] or [bɪn]; for some words the long vowel was categorical (*seal* is always [siːl], *cheap* is always [tʃiːp]); for other terms, the lax vowel was preferred (*loose* [lʊs], *team* [tˢɪm]). Recent borrowings contain only the long tense vowel and assibilation is rare: *beat* [biːt], *cool* [kuːl], *team teaching* [tiːmtiːtˢɪŋ] (Patry, 1986).

ONTARIO FRENCH

I agree with Haden (1973), who states that the French spoken in the QF diaspora (Ontario and the western Canadian provinces) is quite similar, if not identical, to CQF. The slight differences are often lexical, or are due to greater influence from English. Often, French spoken in these areas, particularly by elderly speakers, tends to be somewhat more archaic or conservative and thus reflects the speech of older, rural QF speakers.

OF phonology

By and large, the OF phonological system is identical to that of CQF. As Thomas (1989) states, one is particularly struck by the extreme variability of the phonetic realizations in OF, pointing to a phonological system in transition, which seems to have begun adopting SQF or even SEF characteristics without having totally abandoned its traditional (i.e., CQF) features. For example, in a limited number of words beginning with the so-called *h aspiré*, the /h/ is still pronounced as [x] or [ɦ]: *hache* [ɦaʃ], *haut* [xo], *dehors* [dəɦɔːr]. As well, the digraph *oi* is still pronounced as it is in CQF (see preceding section). However, certain phonetic traits, such as the decrease in the use of [e] in *père, mère*, etc., the loss of the distinction between /ɛ/ and /ɛː/, the tendency towards non-diph-thongization of long vowels, the decrease in high vowel laxing, the tendency to realize final /a/ as [a] rather than [ɔ], the decreased use of the anterior variant [æ̃] of the nasal vowel /ɑ̃/ (SEF [ɑ̃] is now the urban working-class norm while the anterior variant is favoured by rural residents and urban middle-class speakers) and the increased use of uvular /ʀ/ by younger speakers lead to the conclusion that the younger generation is adopting a more 'standardized' pronunciation (*à la* 'Radio-Canada').

All sociophonetic studies of OF conclude that English influence has been minimal; for example, Thomas (1986) observes only a 3 per cent use of English /ɹ/ by speakers in Sudbury, and St-Yves (quoted in Léon and Cichocki, 1989) estimates a 6 per cent use of /ɹ/ for speakers in Welland. Léon and Cichocki (1989) suggest, however, that English-dominant bilinguals are beginning to aspirate initial voiceless plosive consonants, as in English, and that intonation patterns are increasingly typical of English. Thomas' (1986) study of Sudbury speakers reveals that younger English-dominant speakers tend to avoid stigmatized conservative (rural) phonetic traits since their principal contact with French is through schooling, where a more careful style is used. For non-stigmatized forms, such as high vowel laxing, English-dominant bilinguals pronounce much the same as their French-dominant peers.

OF lexical borrowing

Poplack (1989) shows that the majority (57 per cent) of borrowed lexical items in her Ottawa-Hull corpus are 'established' loans, well attested in Canadian or European dictionaries. Borrowed nouns, verbs and adjectives are morphologically and syntactically fully integrated into the French system, but the degree of phonological integration depends on how long ago the borrowing occurred and on how widely the loan is diffused in the community; 'spontaneous' (nonce) loans are more likely to have an English pronunciation.

Poplack shows that the degree of competence in English is a powerful predictor of rate and type of borrowing; more fluently bilingual speakers borrow more heavily and use spontaneous loans more often. However, the status of French in the community in which a given speaker lives is equally important. There are systematic differences between the francophone areas of Ottawa and those of Hull; Ottawa residents, being more exposed to English, borrow more heavily. Social class has a negative effect on borrowing: middle-class speakers, under pressure to speak 'correctly', tend to avoid borrowing. However, other social factors such as age, sex and level of education seem to have little effect.

It is interesting to note that local norms bear more importantly than the degree of bilingualism on rate or amount of borrowing; no matter how fluently bilingual a speaker is, he or she will tend to obey local borrowing norms: in Ottawa, where borrowing is common and accepted, a fluent bilingual will borrow more heavily than an equally bilingual speaker from Hull, where borrowing is not as easily accepted socially. Thus, speaker behaviour in the matter of borrowing seems to be acquired rather than linked to lexical need. The influence of local norms may not be so important for semantic loans, however, since these often pass unnoticed even by monolingual speakers.

It should be pointed out that the highest rate of borrowing by informants in the Ottawa-Hull studies is 4.7 per cent and that, even though Ottawa speakers borrow more heavily than Hull speakers do, the average rate of borrowing in Ottawa is 1.2 per cent and between 0.51 per cent and 0.72 per cent in Hull.

CANADIAN FRENCH VARIETIES WEST OF ONTARIO

Very little research has been done on western varieties of CF and the few that have been published are limited to questions of phonology (Thogmartin, 1974, for Manitoba French; Jackson, 1968, 1974, for Saskatchewan French; Rochet, 1994, for Alberta French; Ellis, 1965, for British Columbia French). These studies show that the varieties of French spoken in western Canada are very similar to those of OF, thus to CQF in general, although the range of variation is perhaps somewhat less extreme. For example, /R/ is still generally pronounced as the apical trill [r] or flap [ɾ], although younger speakers who have learned most of their French at school now tend to adopt the QF uvular variant, much as in OF. /h/ is still pronounced as [ɦ] or [x] in words such as *haut, hache, dehors, haine*, but other words which have aspirate-h in SEF and disallow *liaison* are treated as if they were mute-h words by Alberta French speakers: *l'hibou* [libu], *les hiboux* [lezibu] (Rochet 1994). Rochet also notes that borrowed English words do not assibilate as they do – or, at least, did – in QF: *teepee* is pronounced [ti:pi] and not *[tˢi:pi].

European French varieties

As discussed in the introduction, during the latter part of the nineteenth and the beginning of the twentieth century, a large number of European French speakers established several communities in the prairie provinces, particularly in Manitoba and Saskatchewan. The descendants of these early pioneers have for the most part intermarried with either francophones or anglophones. The latter have usually adopted the language of the dominant group, and for all practical purposes have been completely assimilated to English. The former have often adopted CF speech norms and can now be considered as average CF speakers. However, a number of them have managed to maintain several SEF traits which distinguish them from all other CF speakers: they regularly realize /R/ as [ʀ] or [ʁ], never [r]; they do not assibilate /t/ or /d/; they do not diphthongize long vowels; they realize *oi* as [wa] rather than [we] or [wɛ]; they produce word-final /a/ as [a] or [ɑ] rather than [ɔ] and they do not realize /ɛ/ as [a] before /R/ + consonant clusters (Jackson, 1974; Thogmartin, 1974).

Métis French

Métis French represents a rather special variety of CF in that it exhibits both very conservative CF norms and unique innovations, some undoubtedly due to contact with a variety of local Indian languages – generally Saulteux, a dialect of Ojibwa, or Cree, closely related Algonquian languages (Métis French has been described by Douaud, 1985; Papen, 1984, 1993).

Older Métis French speakers tend to realize /t/ and /d/ before high front vowels and glides as pre-palatal affricates [tʲ] and [dᶾ], rather than as alveolar affricates [tˢ], [dᶻ] as in QF. Poirier (1994) suggests that the process of assibilation occurs in stages, the first being simple palatalization ([tʲ], [dʲ]), followed by a first type of affrication [tʲ], [dᶾ] and finally the alveolar variant [tˢ], [dᶻ], typical of modern QF; Métis French would thus be somewhat more conservative than QF in that respect.

Close mid vowels /e/, /ø/ and /o/ tend to be phonetically realized as high vowels [i], [y] and [u] – thus, *été* 'summer' is pronounced [iti], *poteau* 'post' [putu], *heureux* 'happy' [yry], etc. Raising /ø/ to [y] and /o/ to [u] (and more rarely /e/ to [i]) are well-attested archaic QF features (Juneau, 1972). This tendency may have been reinforced by the extreme variability in the phonetic realizations of high and mid vowels in Cree.

Métis French tends to maintain a close variant of /ɛ/ before /r/ as in conservative QF: *mère* [mer], *père* [per] etc. Also, as opposed to most French dialects, vowels are not usually lengthened before /r/ and as such never diphthongize, as in CQF.

Voiced plosives following nasal vowels tend to be assimilated: *tombe* 'tomb' [tɔ̃m], *prendre* 'to take' [prãn], *longue* 'long' [lɔ̃ŋ]. This feature is not attested in any variety of CF but it is quite common in the 'Cajun' French spoken in Louisiana, as well as in many French-based Creoles.

ACADIAN FRENCH

AF varieties have been quite extensively described, particularly since the 1970s. The first major lexical study of AF was Massignon's (1962) extensive dialect survey of all AF varieties; this remains the fundamental work to be consulted for traditional lexical and phonetic information. The most recent studies have been more sociolinguistically oriented (Flikeid, 1984, 1989a, 1989b; King, 1989, 1994; King & Ryan, 1989; Péronnet, 1989a, 1989b; etc.). We are therefore beginning to get a fairly good idea of the various specific features of AF, as well as better information on its regional, social and situational varieties. Although I shall be describing Acadian French in general, there exists a great deal of regional variation, as the studies just cited have amply shown. Descriptive work has been done on several New Brunswick varieties (northeast and southeast), on several Nova Scotia varieties (Baie-Ste-Marie, Cheticamp, Pomquet, Pubnico, Ile-Madame), on Newfoundland French and on Prince Edward Island French.

Acadian French phonology

The underlying AF vocalic system differs from QF in that AF has only the three nasal vowels /ɛ̃/, /ɑ̃/ and /ɔ̃/, as in SEF. However, there are important differences in the phonetic output of the phonological rules. These differences are either generalized for all AF varieties or are geographically, socially or situationally determined within AF. As in QF, high vowels are laxed in both stressed checked syllables or in pretonic (unstressed) syllables, due to vowel harmony. Vowels are lengthened before 'lengthening' consonants as in QF, and inherently long vowels are always long in checked stressed syllables. The vowels /e/ and /ɛ/ contrast in word final position: *dé - dais, pré - près*, etc. The vowel /ɛ/ in word final position is always realized as [ɛ] in New Brunswick French, never as [æ] or [a] as in conservative QF, but the low anterior variant [a] is quite widespread in Nova Scotia French. In stressed checked syllables, [ɛ] or [ɛː] is typical, but before /r/, the open mid vowels /ɛ/, /œ/ and /ɔ/ are variably closed to [e], [ø] and [o] – thus, *mer* 'sea' [meːr], *beurre* 'butter' [bøːr] and *port* 'port' [poːr]. This is also typical of conservative QF. Before a /r/ + consonant cluster, /ɛ/ is variably realized as [æ] or [a], particularly by older, less-educated rural speakers: *couverte* 'blanket' [kuvart], *verge* 'yard' [værʒ]. This is again a well-attested conservative QF feature. Both /ɛ/ – /ɛː/ and /a/ – /ɑ/ distinctions are maintained, as in QF. Also, word-final /a/ is phonetically [ɑ] (*estomac* 'chest' [ɛstumɑ]) and word-final /ɑ/ is phonetically [ɔ]: *cas* 'case' [kɔ].

AF phonetic forms differ from QF in the following important ways. First, /o/ is often closed to [u] or [ʊ] in a number of lexically restricted words – *ôte* 'take away' [ʊt], *beaucoup* 'a lot' [buku], *grosse* 'big, fat' [grʊs], *chose* 'thing' [ʃʊz]. Before a nasal consonant, /ɔ/ is variably pronounced [ʊ], [o] or [œ] (and [ɔ] in careful speech): *comment* [kʊmɑ̃] ~ [komɑ̃] ~ [kɔmɑ̃]; *personne* [parsʊn] ~ [parsœn] ~ [pɛrsɔn], etc.

Long oral vowels are never diphthongized in checked stressed syllables as in QF but, in word final free syllables, vowels in some varieties of Nova Scotia French (Pubnico and Baie-Ste-Marie) can be realized as diphthongs: *beau* [bɔ^u], *deux* [dœ^ɥ].

The digraph *oi* is pronounced somewhat differently than in QF: in final free syllables such as in *moi, quoi*, the most common pronunciation is [wɛ]; words such as *bois, mois*, are pronounced [wɑ] and *oi* in final checked syllables is typically (but still variably) pronounced [wɛː] or [weː]: *boire* [bwɛːr] ~ [bweːr].

Many descriptions of AF state that the nasal vowel /ɔ̃/ in absolute word final position is most often heard as [ɑ̃], which implies a neutralization of the distinction between words such as *temps* 'time' and *ton* 'tone', both pronounced [tɑ̃]. In fact, the situation is somewhat more complex, particularly if regional varieties are considered. In New Brunswick French, /ã/ is [ã], /ɔ̃/ is variably [ã] or [ɔ̃] and /ɛ̃/ is variably [ɛ̃], or more open [æ̃]. In Îles-de-la-Madeleine (Magdalen Islands) French, /ã/ is [ã], /ɔ̃/ is [ɔ̃] but /ɛ̃/ is also regularly [ã]. In Prince Edward Island French, /ã/ is variably [ã] or [æ̃], /ɔ̃/ is variably [ɔ̃] ~ [ã] ~ [æ̃] and /ɛ̃/ is [ɛ̃]. Nova Scotia French also shows extreme variability since, in Pubnico and Baie-Ste-Marie, /ã/ is [æ̃], /ɔ̃/ is also [æ̃] and /ɛ̃/ is [ɔ̃], while in Île-Madame, /ã/ is [ã] or [æ̃], /ɔ̃/ is [ɔ̃] or [æ̃] and /ɛ̃/ is [ã]!! There has therefore been a complete and unprecedented restructuring of the nasal vowel phonemes, with a very clear tendency towards lower (anterior or posterior) vowel variants. This restructuring occurs only in absolute word final position and nasal vowels retain their 'original' values in other word positions.

The AF consonant inventory is equally quite similar to its QF counterpart, but with the addition of a lexically determined /h/ (pronounced [ɦ]): *haut, homard, dehors,* etc.

/t/ and /d/ before a yod (/j/) are palatalized or even pronounced as pre-palatal affricates (and the yod is erased): *tiens* [tjɛ̃] ~ [tʲɛ̃], *diable* [djɑːb] ~ [dʲɑːb]. The consonants /t/ and /d/ do not assibilate before high front vowels and glides as in QF; this is one of the most typical phonetic features distinguishing AF from QF. Surprisingly, King and Ryan (1989) note that most Prince Edward Island French speakers in Evangeline parish produce [tˢ] and [dᶻ] before high front vowels and glides, just as in QF, even though these speakers have had no contacts with QF speakers. This remains to be explained.

The phonemes /k/ and /g/ palatalize or even become pre-palatal affricates before front vowels (older speakers in informal speech): *quai* 'dock' is pronounced [k̟e] ~ [kʲe] ~ [tʲe], *guêpe* 'wasp' is [ɡɛːp] ~ [dʒɛːp]. However, palatalization does not occur before the verb suffixes *-er* or *-é*: *guetter* 'to watch' is [ɡete], never *[dʒete].

As in some varieties of QF, /ʃ/ and /ʒ/ are sometimes produced as a velar or glottal fricative, particularly before back vowels: *char* 'car' [xɑːr], *jamais* 'never' [ɦamɛ].

The phoneme /ʀ/ has the following phonetic variants: [r] (or [ɾ]) everywhere except in word final position, where it can either be devoiced ([r̥]) or deleted completely. However, Flikeid's (1984) study of northeastern New Brunswick French shows that both apico-dental and dorso-uvular variants are used. Generally, older speakers tend to use [r]/[ɾ] systematically, younger speakers have both [r]/[ɾ] and [ʀ]; the choice of the variant is then uniquely determined by its syllabic position, much as in QF.

Influences from English

As might be expected, AF is more heavily influenced by English than is QF, although recent research has shown that this influence is not as important as popular belief would have it. At the level of the lexicon, Péronnet's (1989b) study of southeastern New Brunswick French shows that the percentage of borrowed forms varies from 0.3 per cent to 0.7 per cent and that the proportion of occurrences varies from 0.4 per cent to 1.4 per cent. These figures are very similar to those obtained by Poplack for the Ottawa-Hull region.

Flikeid's (1989b) study of five French-speaking regions of Nova Scotia, in both formal and informal speech situations, demonstrates that speakers systematically reduce their borrowing from English when in a formal speech situation (i.e., when speaking to a stranger) and that there is an increase in borrowing by younger speakers, although the highest rate of borrowing is 17 per cent (the general opinion is that it is closer to 50 per cent!). Her study reveals that Cheticamp speakers borrow at about the same rate (1.8 per cent) as do the Ottawa-Hull speakers (between 0.05 per cent and 1.2 per cent), but that Pubnico informants' average rate is 5 per cent, rising to an average rate of 8 per cent for younger speakers. Slightly more than 50 per cent of the borrowed forms are spontaneous loans, occurring only once in the corpus, and 69 per cent are produced by a single speaker. These loans are generally not phonologically integrated. Even if verbs are usually morphologically and syntactically well integrated, their English roots tend to maintain English phonology: *ça m'a really hurté* 'It really hurt me'; *faut que tu stand pour tes rights de français!* 'You have to stand for your French rights!' (Flikeid, 1989b, pp. 219–222).

References

Bélisle, L.-A. (1971). *Dictionnaire général de la langue française au Canada.* 2nd edn. Quebec: Bélisle Éditeur.

Bougaïeff, A. and Cardinal, P. (1980). La chute du /l/ dans le français populaire du Québec. *La linguistique, 16*, 91–102.

Boulanger, A. (1986). Les parlers en [ɪz]. *Revue québécoise de linguistique théorique et appliquée, 5(4),* 9–143.

Charbonneau, H. & Guillemette, A. (1994). Provinces et habitats d'origine des pionniers de la vallée laurentienne. In C. Poirier *et al.* (eds.), *Langue, espace, société. Les variétés du français en Amérique du Nord* (pp. 157–183). Ste-Foy: Les Presses de l'Université Laval.

Colpron, G. (1982). *Dictionnaire des anglicismes.* 2nd edn. Montreal: Beauchemin.

Demharter, C. (1990). Les diphthongues du français canadien de la Mauricie. *French Review, 53(6),* 848–862.

Douaud, P. (1985). *Ethnolinguistic Profile of the Canadian Métis.* Ottawa: National Museum of Man, Mercury Series 99.

Dumas, D. (1987). *Nos façons de parler. Les prononciations en français québécois.* Sillery, Quebec: Les Presses de l'Université du Québéc.

Ellis, P. M. (1965). Les phonèmes du français maillardvillois. *Canadian Journal of Linguistics, 11(1),* 30.

Flikeid, K. (1984). *La variabilité phonétique dans le parlé acadien du nord-est du Nouveau-Brunswick: Étude sociolinguistique.* New York: Peter Lang.

(1989a). Recherches sociolinguistiques sur les parlers acadiens du Nouveau-Brunswick et de la Nouvelle-Écosse. In R. Mougeon and É. Beniak (eds.), *Le français parlé hors Québec* (pp. 183–199). Quebec: Les Presses de l'Université Laval.

(1989b). Moitié anglais, moitié français? Emprunts et alternance de langues dans les communautés acadiennes de la Nouvelle-Écosse. *Revue québécoise de linguistique théorique et appliquée, 8(2),* 177–228.

Frémont, D. (1959). *Les Français dans l'Ouest canadien.* Winnipeg: Les Éditions de la Liberté.

Haden, E. (1973). French dialect geography in North America. In T. Sebeok (ed.), *Current Trends in Linguistics.* Vol. 10. *Linguistics in North America* (pp. 422–439). The Hague: Mouton.

Jackson, M. (1968). Étude du sytème vocalique du parler de Gravelbourg, (Saskatchewan). In P. Léon (ed.), *Recherches sur la structure phonique du français canadien* (pp. 61–78). Montreal: Didier (Collection Studia Phonetica).

(1974). Aperçu des tendances phonétiques du parler français en Saskatchewan. *Canadian Journal of Linguistics, 19(2),* 121–133.

Juneau, M. (1972). *Contribution à l'histoire de la prononciation française du Québec.* Quebec: Les Presses de l'Université Laval.

King, R. (1989). Le français terre-neuvien: aperçu général. In R. Mougeon and É. Beniak (eds.), *Le français parlé hors Québec* (pp. 227–244). Quebec: Les Presses de l'Université Laval.

(1994). Subject–verb agreement in Newfoundland French. *Language Variation and Change, 6,* 239–253.

King R. and Ryan, R. (1989). La phonologie des parlers acadiens de l'Île-du-Prince-Édouard. In R. Mougeon and É. Beniak (eds.), *Le français parlé hors Québec.* (pp. 245–259). Quebec: Les Presses de l'Université Laval.

Léard, J.-M. (1995). *Grammaire québécoise d'aujourd'hui: comprendre les québécismes.* Montreal: Guérin Universitaire.

Léon, P. and Cichocki, W. (1989). Bilan et problématique des études sociophonétiques franco-ontariennes. In R. Mougeon and É. Beniak (eds.), *Le français parlé hors Québec* (pp. 37–52). Quebec: Les Presses de l'Université Laval.

Martel, P. and Cajolet-Laganière, H. (1995). Oui . . . au français québécois standard. *Interface, 16(5),* 14–25.

Robert A. Papen

Massignon, G. (1962). *Les parlers français d'Acadie.* 2 vols. Paris: Klincksieck.

Mougeon, R. (1994). La question de l'interférence de l'anglais à la lumière de la socio-linguistique. In C. Poirier *et al.* (eds.), *Langue, espace, société. Les variétés du français en Amérique du Nord* (pp. 25–40). Ste-Foy: Les Presses de l'Université Laval.

Mougeon, R. and Beniak, É. (1991). *Linguistic Consequences of Language Contact and Restriction.* Oxford: Clarendon.

Nemni, M. (1993). Le dictionnaire québécois d'aujourd'hui ou la description de deux chimères. *Cité libre,* April–May, 33–34.

Ostiguy, L. and Toussignant, C. (1993). *Le français québécois: normes et usages.* Montreal: Guérin Universitaire.

Papen, R. A. (1984). Quelques remarques sur un parler français méconnu de l'Ouest canadien: le métis. *Revue québécoise de linguistique, 14(1),* 113–139.

(1993). La variation dialectale dans le parler français des Métis de l'Ouest canadien. *Francophonies des Amériques, 3,* 25–38.

Patry, R. (1986). Le traitement de la durée vocalique dans l'évolution des emprunts à l'anglais en français québécois historique. *Revue québécoise de linguistique théorique et appliquée, 5(4),* 145–177.

Péronnet, L. (1989a). *Le parler acadien du sud-est du Nouveau-Brunswick: éléments grammaticaux et lexicaux.* New York: Peter Lang.

(1989b). Analyse des emprunts dans un corpus acadien. *Revue québécoise de linguistique théorique et appliquée, 8(2),* 229–251.

Poirier, C. (1980). Le lexique québécois: son évolution, ses composantes. *Stanford French Review, 19,* 43–80.

(1994). Les causes de la variation géolinguistique du français en Amérique du Nord: l'éclairage de l'approche comparative. In C. Poirier *et al.* (eds.), *Langue, espace, société. Les variétés du français en Amérique du Nord* (pp. 69–95). Ste-Foy: Les Presses de l'Université Laval.

Poplack, S. (1989). Statut de langue et accommodation langagière le long d'une frontière linguistique. In R. Mougeon and É. Béniak (eds.), *Le français parlé hors Québec* (pp. 127–151). Quebec: Les Presses de l'Université Laval.

Rochet, B. (1994). Le français à l'ouest de l'Ontario: tendances phonétiques du français parlé en Alberta. In C. Poirier *et al.* (eds.), *Langue, espace, société. Les variétés du français en Amérique du Nord* (pp. 433–455). Ste-Foy: Les Presses de l'Université Laval.

Thogmartin, C. (1974). The phonology of three varieties of French in Manitoba. *Orbis, 23(2),* 335–345.

Thomas, A. (1986). *La variation phonétique: cas du franco-ontarien.* Ville La Salle (Quebec): Didier.

(1989). Le franco-ontarien: portrait linguistique. In R. Mougeon and É. Beniak (eds.), *Le français parlé hors Québec* (pp. 19–35). Ste-Foy: Les Presses de l'Université Laval.

9 French in Quebec

Philippe Barbaud

HISTORICAL BACKGROUND

In 1774, fifteen years after the surrender of Quebec to the troops of General Wolfe, King George III signed the Quebec Act to restore the *coutume de Paris* (the ancestor of the present civil code) in the new province. He implicitly recognized, at the same time, the legality of the French language in this part of North America. It was a decision fraught with consequences, as we know, but was done to avoid a possible uprising among the French Canadians and their Amerindian allies.[1] In fact, the French Canadians were living with the obsessive fear of being deported (as were their French fellows in Acadia between 1755 and 1763, an 'ethnic purification' that affected more than 90 per cent of the 12,000 Acadians settled in this other colony of France). The threat of an uprising was combined, too, with that of an invasion of the former French possessions by the rebel troops of the United States, whose independence would be unilaterally proclaimed in 1776. These concerns also pushed George III to sign the Constitutional Act in 1791, granting a parliament to Lower Canada. This was another decision fraught with consequences because, to ensure the allegiance of his French subjects – needed to maintain his commercial hold north of the 45th parallel – the king provided them with a form of statehood. What came to be called the 'French fact' in North America thus became, at the same time, a territorial enclave in which the French language would lie fallow for a long time.

Language and power

These introductory remarks show that the French language was associated, from the time of the Conquest, with the exercise of a political power collectively assumed by a society already greatly conscious of its distinctness.[2] It is from this convergence of language and power that one should describe the linguistic situation of Quebec, in order to deal with the universal phenomenon of 'languages in contact' from the most suitable angle for this particular, indeed exclusive, enclave in North America (an enclave where 83 per cent of the population have French as the home language, but which forms less than 2 per cent of the whole continent's population).

The particularity of Quebec goes beyond simple contact between common languages or dialects in the general context of movements of populations, cross-border linguistic exchanges or historical cohabitation. It illustrates a *choc des langues* (Bouthillier and Meynaud, 1972), indeed, a *guerre des langues* (Calvet, 1987; Leclerc, 1989). From the very institution of English government, the French language has been perceived by the French Canadians as the spearhead of a ceaseless fight, an instrument of political claims for social justice and material equality. But except for some insurgent confrontations, such as the '*Révolte des Patriotes*' in 1837, the battle over conscription in 1942, the riots in Saint-Léonard in 1969 and the terrorism of the Front de Libération du Québec (FLQ) in the 1970s, the growing antagonism that marks the relations between French and English people in Canada is 'characterized by a remarkable degree of non-violence' (Lemco, 1992, p. 426).

It was only from the beginning of the 1960s, a period of accelerated modernization (the so-called 'Quiet Revolution'), that the French Canadians of Quebec learned to articulate their claims in a context of coherent political action – notably by defining themselves collectively in relation to the federal ideology of bilingualism and multiculturalism. This ideology began in 1963 with the creation of the Royal Commission on Bilingualism and Biculturalism (the Laurendeau–Dunton Commission), whose works revealed to Canadian public opinion the real importance of the age-old inferiority felt by francophones in their own country.[3] The government of Quebec also took an initiative in 1968, with the Commission d'enquête sur la situation linguistique de la langue française et sur les droits linguistiques au Québec (the Gendron Commission). Besides the important linguistic laws that resulted from the recommendations of these two commissions, several facts were widely publicized by the media during the 1960s and 1970s.

Demographic loss of power

Canadians of all origins began to be affected by the tyranny of statistics – on linguistic demography, provincial economy, state education, immigration, birthrates and so on – which helped to define a new social consciousness. From the interpretation of the statistics came a new vocabulary that would mould ideas and attitudes. French Canadians became 'Quebecers', easily confused with 'francophones'. The French 'people' of Canada mentioned in the British North

America Act became a minority speaking one of the two official languages, ending up one 'community' among others in a multiethnic and multicultural Canada. But, above all, French Canadians noted not only the declining influence of their ethnic group but also the possible loss of political power at the federal level, in terms of their parliamentary representation in the House of Commons and, especially, in the Supreme Court. In 1867, with 33 per cent of the Canadian population, Quebec's representation in the Commons was 65 elected members (of 181, a proportion of 36 per cent). In 1962, with 28.8 per cent of the Canadian population, Quebec's representation was 75 out of 259 (also about 29 per cent – 80 per cent of which was francophone). Today, the French-speaking population of Quebec is only 21 per cent of the Canadian total, but its House of Commons standing is the same as it was in 1962. Quite obviously, there is now a political over-representation, and the economist Matthews (1994, p. 156) has noted that '[b]y the time francophones in Quebec represent less than 20% of the Canadian population ... claims will probably be made for a revision of the bilingualism policy in the federal public and parapublic service'. In other words, the notion of the equality of languages, represented by official bilingualism, is doomed to disappear, which will inevitably lead to a fundamental redefinition of Canada as a country.

The French language and prosperity in the 1960s

Francophone Quebecers also learned of a negative relation between their language and economic prosperity. Their economic strength, as noted in the report of the Laurendeau–Dunton Commission, has been deteriorating since 1930, with the best jobs held by anglophones. It is in Montreal, and in Quebec in general, that the gap between anglophones and francophones is the most striking: anglophones are favoured on the national level, more in Quebec, more again in Montreal.

The incomes of the two speech communities naturally reflect this job disparity. The Laurendeau–Dunton Commission found that the average income of a French Canadian was 20 per cent below the national average. In Quebec, the average income of a francophone was 35 per cent less than that of anglophones. In fact, francophones learned that, in 1961, they were ranked next of last on the salary scale – just before Italians, who ranked ninth. Ten years later, in 1970, they had regressed to the last rung (Vaillancourt, 1985). For comparative purposes, it is interesting to note the following distribution of average Quebec incomes in 1961 (Wardhaugh, 1983, p. 79): unilingual anglophones of British origin, $6,049; bilingual anglophones, $5,929; unilingual anglophones of French origin, $5,775;

bilingual francophones, $4,523; unilingual francophones of French origin, $3,107; unilingual francophones of British origin, $2,783. As Corbeil (1980, p. 44) writes, Quebec thus appears 'as a privileged place for anglophones; we then understand one of the deep reasons for their hostility to linguistic laws in Quebec'.

The French language and immigration in the 1960s

The third most striking aspect of the linguistic situation in the 1960s was unquestionably the matter of immigration. For the first time, Quebecers were confronted with specific knowledge of linguistic assimilation, of theirs and others' – particularly that of the 'allophones'. The important difference between the usually-spoken home language and the census-declared mother tongue was also revealed, as was the importance of primary and secondary education in the process of linguistic minorization.

According to an influential report published in January 1967, titled *Quand la majorité n'assimile pas*, stemming from the Comité interministériel sur l'enseignement des langues aux Néo-Canadiens (see Bouthillier and Meynaud, 1972), there were more than 500,000 immigrants from other countries who entered Quebec between 1945 and 1965, an annual average of 25,000. French-speaking immigration was only 60,000 to 65,000 individuals (12 per cent to 13 per cent) whereas immigrants of British and American origin represented 32 per cent to 35 per cent, and the others about 55 per cent. These proportions must be seen relative to other factors – for instance, interprovincial migration. In a more detailed study, Termote (1980) estimated 30,000 average annual entries to Quebec since 1951 but, considering the weak retention rate of the province, an annual *net* average of about 21,000 international immigrants (at least for the period 1951 to 1977). He also estimated an average annual outgoing of 57,000 during the same period; most of these were English-speaking individuals, one assumes.

The situation verged on tragedy with the question of immigrants' academic options. The same report showed that more than 90 per cent of all new Canadian children attended English school in the Montreal area. Between 1931 and 1937, the distribution of new Canadian pupils was almost equal in each linguistic sector (52.3 per cent went to the French educational sector and 47.7 per cent to the English). Since then, however, the French sector has lost ground, falling to 33.5 per cent in 1947–48 and to 25.3 per cent in 1962–63.

It was towards the end of the 1950s that the Italian immigrant community, the most numerous non-anglophone group, began to change its linguistic attitude. In 1961, there were still 61,488 Italians speaking French in Montreal and only 49,449 speaking English; 12,409 of them stated that French was their mother tongue, against 5,650 for English. But while in 1951–52 they were sending almost half of their children (49 per cent) to the French schools of the Commission des écoles catholiques de Montréal, this proportion fell to 12 per cent in 1967–68.

It is true that the indifference of the population and the negligence of those in power in Quebec were greatly responsible for the weak attraction that the French-Canadian milieu had for the allophones of Montreal. We cannot cite Catholicism, either, to explain the decline of the French school network, in comparison with certain other traditionally Catholic ethnic communities (Polish, Ukrainian, Hungarian, etc.). Nevertheless, international immigration was perceived as a worrying threat for the survival of the French language, especially in Montreal where it was massively concentrated.

A mutilated metropolis

It was also during the 1960s that a popular consciousness of the quality of spoken and written French developed in Quebec. The fight against anglicisms led by a handful of educated people in the century that followed confederation occurred on virgin ground: labelling of consumer goods, commercial display, advertising and toponymy. Montreal, which prided itself on being the second French city in the world, suddenly revealed itself as ugly and depreciated from the outside. Its commercial streets had lost their 'French face'. The Quebec metropolis was 55 per cent anglophone in 1851 and the domination of English in the business environment continued into the 1970s, in spite of the steady growth of its French population. In the census of 1971, Montreal was 67 per cent francophone, but its demographic decline began with the increasing migration of its anglophones to other provinces, and the exodus of its francophones to the suburbs.

An alienated speech

Overall, we can say that Canadian public opinion became considerably alerted to the problem of national unity, as a consequence of an economic cleavage in a modern society superposed on an old linguistic dispute. In Quebec, however, opinion leaders were more preoccupied by the problem of equality than by that of unity. 'Equality or sovereignty' was the slogan of the election campaign led by Daniel Johnson, elected premier in 1967. Prompted by a double stigma – colonization by the British and abandonment by France, the shameful motherland – a certain newly educated elite undertook its task of popular education through searching for a distinctive Quebec identity.

The vernacular Quebec French known as *joual* became the linguistic symbol of this new identity. It gained the adherence of a new generation of writers and educated people, and was propelled in the forums of schools, colleges and universities.[4] That is why, nowadays, the vernacular speech of the working class still maintains its respectability in the linguistic consciousness of a vast majority of francophone Quebecers. The chief merit of the discussion of *joual* was to bring to light the essential difference between the oral and the cultivated written code within a language (to discuss, that is, *diglossia*: see Chantefort, 1976; Daoust and Maurais, 1987; Ferguson, 1959; Saint-Pierre, 1976).

In the 1970s, however, the *joual* 'movement' retreated before a speech much more homogeneous and less socially marked. The advent of the Quebec speech of today (discussed further below) is largely the result of the sudden growth of the public service between 1965 and 1980, and the setting up of social infrastructures: education networks, hospitals, courts of justice, state-owned companies, etc. As soon as he came to power in 1970, Premier Bourassa issued a directive to state employees on the use of French. From 25,000 in 1959, the number of permanent state employees grew to 53,800 in 1969, and to 62,500 in 1979 (Ambroise, 1986). Becoming more than 95 per cent francophone, the Quebec state service acted as a linguistic regulator, according to Corbeil (1980), by diffusing the speech of fairly educated people and by constantly promulgating a standard of public written French.

STATE INTERVENTIONISM

What is the situation of the French language in Quebec today? To answer this question one must first assess the legal context in which linguistic evolution took place (see Bourhis, 1994; Daoust, 1982; Maurais, 1987; Plourde, 1988), for it is in the law that the convergence of power and language finds its clearest expression. Further, the present vitality of French in Quebec can not only be attributed to the will of francophones in this province; it results from the combined forces of both exterior sources, Anglo-Canadian or foreign, and interior ones. It is in the name of the overall unity that the federal government makes its initiatives, while it is on the basis of the equality of the two founder nations that the government of Quebec acts. These two sorts of state initiative lead to interventionist measures from the two levels of government, which can produce a mix of federal and provincial laws (influenced by the decisions of the Supreme Court of Canada).

The Office de la langue française du Québec

The first law joining politics and linguistics was that of Quebec – it created the *Office de la langue française* in 1961. As an expression of a political will to protect and standardize a language in jeopardy, this organization dedicated itself to the 'enrichment' and the 'correction' of spoken and written French. It favoured a 'voluntarist' and non-interventionist approach to language 'quality', particularly during the debate on *joual* (Maurais, 1987). For the first time in its history, Quebec acknowledged its social responsibility in the matter of French, but the question of linguistic norms remained unsolved. The following decades were marked by an internal linguistic instability engendered by a more or less permanent diglossia (Chantefort, 1976; Saint-Pierre, 1976).

The Official Languages Act

The next initiative came from Prime Minister Trudeau's federal government which, in July 1969, passed the Official Languages Act of Canada. Besides instituting the position of Commissioner of Official Languages, entrusted with ensuring the proper representation of French and English in the state machinery, this law acted as a powerful lever for the promotion of French, especially in Quebec. More importantly, it signalled Canada as an officially bilingual country on the international scene; thus, the second article of the Act stipulated that 'the status, rights and privileges of English and French are equal'. Often trapped by the ideal of linguistic equality conveyed by the Act, Canada has sometimes had difficulty in following its logic – in diplomacy and other fields of international negotiation (World Bank, World Health Organization, General Agreement on Tariffs and Trade, etc.).

Linguistic legislation driven by crisis: Act 63

The impasse reached by the school board of Saint-Léonard, an eastern Montreal suburb with a strong Italian concentration, illustrates the deterioration of the linguistic balance of power that had occurred there between 1960 and 1967. A regulation previously passed, to create bilingual primary schools for the allophone population, was rejected by a small majority of commissioners anxious to institute French unilingualism at this level. In fact, the primary-level bilingual classes were an avenue to assimilation to English, because almost 70 per cent of immigrant children were registered in English classes.

The virulence of the confrontations between francophones and italophones surprised everybody; the freedom of choice for the language of education was at the heart of the debate. Premier Bertrand's government attempted to resolve the conflict by passing Act 63, the Loi pour promouvoir la langue française au Québec. This law confirmed general registration in French schools but allowed access to English ones on request. This, of course, was viewed negatively by francophones, inasmuch as it gave the green light to the massive anglicization of immigrants (and also to francophones anxious to see their children become perfect bilinguals). In 1971–72, about 27,600 francophone pupils studied in English – while 18,200 anglophones studied in French (St-Germain, 1980). This represents about 2 per cent of all primary and secondary pupils (1,378,300), a proportion which increase to 2.5 per cent in 1974–75.

Advent of a double market: commercial bilingualism

The importance for French of the 1974 passage of the federal Consumer Packaging and Labelling Act has been generally underestimated (Barbaud, 1993). English–French bilingualism became an economic reality to be reckoned with; the francophone consumer's rights were now to be respected. In fact, the Commissioner of Official Languages has had a hard job in fully applying this law. There are, for example, potential difficulties insofar as international jurisprudence tends to consider linguistic laws as economic obstacles to the free movement of goods (Woehrling, 1993). The famous 'cultural exception' won in a hard-fought struggle during both the negotiations of the North American Free Trade Agreement and the General Agreement on Tariffs and Trade (Uruguay Round) shows how difficult it is to reconcile language protection and commercial practice (Barbaud, 1994).

Act 22 (Loi sur la langue officielle)

Act 22, passed in Quebec in 1974 following recommendations of the Gendron Commission, had greater scope than anything previous, because of increasing linguistic tensions. French became the official language of the province and its use was prescribed in public services, companies and professions, the working and business world generally, and education. But this last sector proved to be its Achilles' heel because of the many dispensations the law granted – notably by means of a clause citing 'sufficient knowledge' of English as established by ministerial tests. Thus, the educational thrust became unenforceable in practice, and it also displeased the majority of francophones who wished to see immigrant children register predominantly in French schools. However, a great leap had been taken forward, especially in the matter of the language of work. One of the merits of Act 22 was to reinforce public opinion that it was legitimate and possible, in this part of North America, to conduct business and earn one's living in French. However, the challenge remained to alter the attitudes and habits acquired in a sphere largely assimilated to English for 200 years.

The French Language Charter (Bill 101)

The coming to power of René Lévesque's sovereigntist party in November 1976 had a dramatic effect. Building on the structure of Act 22, Bill 101 (the French Language Charter) was passed in August 1977 and rapidly became the emblem – and even a sacred text in some people's eyes (Grey, 1995) – of the nationalist movement. This law, a real piece of linguistic planning, is characterized by its comprehensive measures, often seen as coercive.[5] It spells the end of free choice in education, for example. Only children whose father or mother received most of their primary education in English, in Quebec, have access to English schools (a 'Quebec clause' later to be overturned by the 'Canada clause': see below). Bilingual public communication, for towns whose population is at least 50 per cent anglophone, was allowed for in the new Bill.

It is in the matter of language of work that Bill 101 is the most significant. Its impact is felt in all companies of fifty employees or more, thanks to a series of measures aimed at a broad process of francization. These affect both internal communications between management and staff and hiring operations. Everything hitherto in English – instructions, service manuals, identification of machine parts, etc. – must have now its clearly visible French equivalent. The *Office de la langue française* is given the responsibility of looking after the application and enforcement of Bill 101, backed up by a *Commission de surveillance* (which in 1983, became the *Commission de protection de la langue française*) endowed with the power of inquiry, and by francization committees in every company. The commission is not only given the task of granting companies a francization certificate, but also of adjusting French terminology. A *Commission d'appel* receives complaints from companies that are in litigation with the *Office de la langue française*. A *Commission de toponymie* is in charge of planning place names. Finally, Bill 101 renewed the mandate of the *Conseil de la langue française*, a consultative organization for studying the linguistic situation and providing advice to the government.

Bill 101 has been blamed for provoking a so-called exodus of anglophone Quebecers. Maurais (1987) reports that 131,530 anglophones (61 per cent unilinguals) left Quebec between 1976 and 1981 (25,000 came to Quebec from other provinces). Nevertheless, between 1971 and 1976 – before Bill 101 was passed – 94,000 anglophones had done the same (Baillargeon, 1983). Indeed, Statistics

Canada notes that over the twenty-five years previous to the 1991 census, about 450,000 anglophones left Quebec for other provinces. The migration of anglophones is not a new phenomenon (see Joy, 1967, who anticipated, however, that this movement will accelerate if French increases its power and prestige).

The Constitutional Act of 1982: The Canada Clause

The 1980 Quebec referendum ended in bitter failure for the supporters of independence but, since Prime Minister Trudeau had committed himself to renewing the Canadian Constitution, Quebecers re-elected the *indépendantiste* government of René Lévesque in 1981 with a significant majority. At the close of constitutional negotiations involving all the provincial governments, as well as native representatives, the federal government passed the Constitutional Act (1982) – regardless of the opposition of Quebec and the natives. This was considered a betrayal by a majority of francophone Quebecers.

The important linguistic dimension arises because the Constitutional Act was accompanied by the Canadian Charter of Rights and Freedoms. Its Articles 16 to 22 reiterate the declaration that French and English are the two official languages in Canada. Article 23 expressly stipulates that all Canadian citizens whose mother tongue is French or English, or who received their primary education in one of these two languages, have the right to have all their children educated, at the primary and secondary levels, in the same language (the 'Canada Clause', see above).[6] On this subject, Plourde (1988, p. 102; corroborated by Maurais, 1987), a former president of the Office de la langue française, gave the following opinion:

> The judges of the Supreme Court recognized that Article 23 of the Constitutional Act of 1982 had been expressly composed by the federal legislator in order to counter the arrangements of Quebec's Bill 101 relating to the language of education. At the same time, they recognized that Quebec, by legislating in the matter of language, exercised its legitimate right. This was therefore asserting clearly that this article of the Canadian Constitution, to which Quebec had not adhered, was specifically planned to invalidate after the fact a chapter of Bill 101 which, for seven years, had been legal and legitimate. Thus the legal aspect prevailed over the legitimate aspect.

The new constitution considerably modified the impact of Bill 101, as shown in several court decisions. First came Quebec's Bill 57 (1983) which restored institutional bilingualism in public and parapublic organizations. Then Bill 142 was passed in 1986; it ensured to the anglophone minority social and health services in English. In 1988, Bill 178 – because of an escape or 'notwithstanding' override clause applicable for a renewable period of five years – stipulated that bilingual signs would be allowed *inside* commercial stores with fewer than fifty employees but permitted only French on *outside* commercial signs (Bourhis, 1994), in response to a judgement of the Supreme Court which held that language display was covered by the individual right of free expression assured by the Canadian Constitution. Finally, Bill 86 (1993) relaxed the preceding one, and put an end to five years of exceptional arrangements by allowing bilingualism in commercial display, provided that French is predominant.

THE VITALITY OF FRENCH IN QUEBEC

The vitality of a language depends on the number of people who actually speak it and on its real use in society. History shows that French-speaking Quebecers have not hesitated to swap their language for more prosperity, in English. Between 1840 and 1930 – the year the United States decided to close its frontiers – more than 1.2 million francophones emigrated to escape from poverty (Lavoie, 1973), mainly to the manufacturing towns of New England; this represents an annual average of 5 to 10 per cent of the total population of Quebec. At the dawn of the third millennium, could economic laws decimate the French population of Quebec anew?

Assimilation and linguistic transfers

Francophone emigration might be the next threat hovering over the future of French in Quebec considering the recent mediocre economic situation. Nevertheless, at the present time, assimilation is more to be feared than is emigration. We know that the best measure of assimilation is provided by the rate of linguistic transfer. From the point of view of French, linguistic assimilation is anglicization. This happens when the French home-language level is lower than the French mother-tongue level. Francization occurs when the French home-language level increases through linguistic losses among other populations.

Generally speaking, the census of 1991 shows that, over the last forty years, the population of French mother tongue remained stable (82 per cent) in Quebec, while the French home-language level constantly increased since 1971, reaching 83 per cent in 1991 (see table 9.1). That year, the French home-language level surpassed by some 66,000 people that of mother tongue. Considering this slight difference of 1 per cent, can we then maintain that the future of French in Quebec is safe?

What seems to be progress in absolute figures must be investigated. A closer examination of the 1991 census data provided by Statistics Canada reveals two major causes of this presumed progress: first, the decrease of the mainly

Table 9.1 French mother-tongue and home-language levels in Quebec (percentages show the numbers as proportions of the total province population: 6,810,300 in 1991)

	1951	1961	1971	1981	1991
Mother tongue	3,347,000	4,270,000	4,867,000	5,254,000	5,586,000
	(82.5%)	*(81.2%)*	*(80.7%)*	*(82.5%)*	*(82.0%)*
Home language	–	–	4,870,000	5,253,000	5,652,000
			(80.8%)	*(82.5%)*	*(83.0%)*

Source: Statistics Canada, 1994.

unilingual anglophone population; second, gains realized by endogenous transfers, which compensate for the losses recorded among francophones themselves
(exogenous transfers). In other words, even in Quebec, fewer people of French
mother tongue use their language at home (see Castonguay, 1994c on this matter). This is especially true for what Joy (1967) has called the 'bilingual belt'
which, in Quebec, corresponds roughly to the 'West Quebec' studied by
Castonguay (1994b).

According to the 1991 census data, there are, in Quebec, 5,573,300 people
of French mother tongue – a figure which includes French/third language bilinguals but excludes French/English bilinguals (we are assuming here that a third
language does not compete with French, and that French–English bilinguals
form a population on their own, insofar as their definitive linguistic option is
deferred). Now, the number of people who claimed to speak French at home –
either exclusively or with a third language – amounts to 5,473,000; this excludes
all transfers from English or a third language, or non-francophone bilinguals.
Thus, the exogenous transfer amounts to 100,300 francophones – including
85,500 who moved to English (anglicization) – which shows a drop of 1.8 per cent
in the use of French by 'core' francophones. Fortunately, we can also observe
163,000 endogenous transfers (francization) – including 91,000 from ethnic communities – that compensate for this loss. These transfers appear in table 9.2.

Although the 1991 census data must be used with caution – because of
changes in asking language questions – they nevertheless indicate that French
does not gain by allophone linguistic changes. Though my computation differs
slightly from that of Statistics Canada, table 9.2 reveals that among the 236,000
allophone transfers, 38.5 per cent opt for French (37 per cent according to Statistics Canada) and 61.4 per cent for English (63 per cent, Statistics Canada). There
is a clear improvement for French in comparison to the rate in 1981 (28 per cent)
and in 1986 (29 per cent), according to the federal source. However, we have to
bear in mind that the number of francophones who anglicized (93,000) is greater

Table 9.2 Linguistic transfers in Quebec, for four census periods

	From French to English	From English to French	From a third language to French	From a third language to English
1971	73,515	49,060	34,580	84,440
1981	74,995	40,950	32,545	84,745
1986	73,375	35,965	29,355	73,265
1991	93,000[a]	72,000[b]	91,000[c]	145,000[d]

Sources: Statistics Canada for the 1991 year and the *Conseil de la langue française* (Quebec) for other years.

Notes:

[a] Mother-tongue and home-language unilinguals, French–English mother-tongue bilinguals who become unilinguals, and French mother-tongue unilinguals who become French–English bilinguals at home. French or English unilinguals can also speak other languages than official ones.

[b] Mother-tongue and home-language unilinguals, and French–English mother-tongue bilinguals who become unilinguals.

[c] Excludes allophones who become French–English bilinguals.

[d] Includes allophones who become French–English bilinguals.

Table 9.3 Net gains for French, English and other languages (calculated from table 9.2)

	French	English	Other
1971	10,125	108,895	−119,020
1981	−1,500	118,790	−117,290
1986	−8,055	110,675	−102,620
1991	70,000	166,000	−236,000

than that of allophones who francized (91,000). Furthermore, I estimate that the number of anglophones who completely francized (a gain of 72,000 individuals, against the 54,000 according to Statistics Canada) is countered by the number of francophones who completely anglicized (a loss of 93,000 individuals, against Statistics Canada's estimate of 55,000). In calculating the net balance of all endogenous (gains) and exogenous (losses) transfers of each official language, we see that the gains of French are less than half those of English (see table 9.3).

Although somewhat encouraging, the current situation remains fragile and not very convincing. First, if 756,200 English speakers can assimilate 166,000 non-English speakers, a rate of assimilation results of nearly 22 per cent. On the other hand, with a majority population of 5.6 million speakers which assimilates 70,000 non-French speakers, French shows a rate of assimilation of 1.25 per cent.

With this balance of power in favour of English, can we reasonably say that French has won the game in North America?

Second, there is the progress of bilingualism. For French, unilingualism is at the heart of resistance to assimilation (Lieberson, 1970), while bilingualism constitutes potential assimilation. In Quebec, the number of unilingual francophones (those who use French exclusively) amounts to 3,860,000, which represents 57 per cent of the total population of the province and 69 per cent of its francophone population. At first glance, this is reassuring. But, according to Castonguay (1994a), the number of bilinguals among the francophone population grew to 1,765,000 people (32 per cent) in 1991, while it was 29 per cent in 1981 and 26 per cent in 1971. One encouraging sign is that, among those declaring themselves of bilingual mother tongue, 17,200 have French as home language, twice as many as English (7,500).

The weight of Montreal

With its 3,091,115 inhabitants, Greater Montreal has more than 45 per cent of the Quebec population, but less than 38 per cent of its francophone population. Some 68 per cent in Montreal have a francophone origin; the same percentage reports French as the home language. Everywhere else in the province this proportion is 94 per cent. Unilingual francophones in Montreal comprise less than 21 per cent of the provincial francophone population. The safety of French in the major metropolis seems insecure, and the future of the language in North America may well be decided in Montreal – because it is there that francophone Quebecers lose a great part of their strength.

The francophone population of Montreal island was 64 per cent in 1951 (Bonin, 1990). It dropped to 60 per cent in 1986, and to 56.6 per cent in 1991, while the proportion of allophones rose from 18.7 per cent to 24 per cent (Levine, 1993). On the other hand, the rate of French-English bilingualism is 48 per cent in metropolitan Montreal, a percentage naturally much higher than the provincial rate. Among the francophones of Montreal, bilingualism is at 45.5 per cent, which is both remarkable and worrying. The number of exogenous transfers (anglicization) affecting only this population amounts to 60,000 – i.e., 64 per cent of all transfers affecting Quebec francophones. As we would expect, almost all of these transfers occur among the bilingual francophone population: 57,900 transfers among Montreal bilinguals as against 1,800 among unilingual francophones. Thus, bilingualism (defined here as the knowledge and not the use of both official languages) can clearly be a middle step towards changing linguistic allegiance.

Montreal is the site of 89 per cent of all gains in favour of French (some 62,400 additional speakers). It is also in Montreal that English makes almost all of *its* gains (98 per cent). Nevertheless, it is not in the Montreal area that anglophones are most likely to francize themselves. It is elsewhere in the province. In fact, only 49 per cent (35,500 of 72,200) of all cases of francization of anglophones occur in Montreal, where almost 80 per cent of the English home-language population lives (625,400 among 801,900 for the whole province).

The western part of Montreal island, home to most of the anglophones of Quebec, reveals growing anglicization since 1971. Castonguay (1994b) notes that the net rate of anglicization among francophones and allophones was higher in 1991 than it was in 1971 – despite the decreased number of anglophones (mother-tongue) in this region – which allows the latter population to hold steady at about the same level. In West Island French schools, linguistic transfers to English among allophones exceeded those to French in 1989–90 (11.9 per cent versus 8.3 per cent) (Levine, 1993).

The birth-rate decrease and linguistic persistence

A decreasing Quebec birth rate represents another threat to French. While the fertility rate is 1.86 for Canada as a whole, that of Quebec is only 1.63 (since 1970), which is below the replacement threshold of 2.1 children per woman (Duchesne, 1993). Matthews (1994) anticipated that Montreal would start its depopulation trend in 1994, a decade before that of (overall) Quebec (which is generally foreseen for 2006). Moreover, in a study that takes into account several international immigration scenarios, Termote (1993) forecasts 'defrancization', not only in the metropolitan region (Montreal and Laval) but also on a provincial scale. He makes the following assumption: 'Should immigration stabilize to an average level (the one observed in 1986–1991) and present fertility (that of 1986–1991) hold steady ... barely 50 per cent of the inhabitants [of this region] would speak French in 2046, which means that, on the *island* of Montreal, more than half the inhabitants would not speak French' (Termote, 1993, p. 70). Developments are proving him right.

The decrease of the birth rate has direct repercussions on the linguistic balance in Montreal, and combines not only with the decline of francophones there, but also with a higher birth rate among allophone women (2.1). According to the analyses of Levine (1993) and Paillé (1996), urban spread has attracted low-income francophone families to suburban areas, leading to a depopulation of the metropolis' downtown area – to the extent that the francophone population has fallen below 50 per cent among those aged eighteen and under. As well, the veiled resistance to integration from several ethnic communities has led to the formation of completely defrancized urban zones on Montreal island. Not only do they understandably prefer to gather rather than to disperse among franco-phones, but their languages persist as home languages; Kralt and Pendakur (1991) have noted that it is in Quebec that the rates of conservation of third languages are the highest. More than 45 per cent of Quebec children whose mother had a non-official language as mother tongue share this same language while, outside of Quebec, only 32 per cent of children speak their mother's mother tongue. The authors add that 'the degree to which children move to the French language is quite low; it goes from 6% for the Greeks to 38% for Arabs' (Kralt and Pendakur, 1991, pp. 13–14).

The linguistic tolerance that characterizes the province of Quebec, and espe-cially Montreal, is real but it is the result, in the end, of the French language's helplessness to assert itself as *the* language of Quebec identity – or, at least, of belonging to French society among the new citizens, who rather have a tendency to consider themselves as *Canadians* residing in Quebec. The advantage for an immigrant of being linguistically less constrained in this part of Canada is con-sistent with the fact that Montreal has a retention rate of immigration much higher than that of Toronto: 88 per cent against 63 per cent (Bonin, 1990).

French at school

People attach great importance to the fact that immigrant children settled in Quebec have registered in French schools since Bill 101 was passed. The change is unquestionably remarkable. During the years it was in force, the 'Quebec Clause' reversed the historical trend; we have yet to ascertain the real impact of the 'Canada Clause', imposed by the Supreme Court in 1984. The pro-portion of allophone students who studied in French at the primary and second-ary levels went from 38.7 per cent in 1980–81 to 75.8 per cent in 1990–91. Over the same period, the proportion of anglophone students who did the same went from 16 per cent to 19.5 per cent. But, being a student in a French school does not necessarily lead to becoming a French home-language speaker. A 1995 report to the School Council of Montreal Island shows that only 13 per cent of allophone students in the French network adopt French as home-language, a rate slightly below that noted by Levine (1993) for the period between 1983–84 and 1989–90. Moreover, of 76,000 allophone students in Greater Montreal in 1990–91, only 10.6 per cent chose to speak French at home (14.2 per cent chose to speak English). Therefore, progress seems to have reached a ceiling since then.

The same report also notes that the concentration of francophone students required to exercise some attractive force on their allophone fellows is decreasing on the island of Montreal. Francophones now represent only 47.5 per cent of the students in the 454 public primary and secondary schools. In 1977, the year Bill 101 was promulgated, this proportion was 59 per cent. Almost one school in five now has an allophone majority.

As well, the progress of French is not very strong at the college (CEGEP) level. The French sector increased registrations among allophones from 14 per cent to 45 per cent between 1980 and 1990. However, the 'rate of perseverance' in French education from secondary to collegial levels declined between 1986 (81.2 per cent) and 1990 (72.6 per cent). The twelve francophone universities recruit a minority of allophones (43 per cent in 1990), while the three anglophone universities attract 57 per cent of them. Finally, since bilingualism is more 'instrumental', and less likely to lead to language shift among educated populations (Castonguay, 1994c), it is indeed worrying that only 7.7 per cent of francophones hold a university diploma, in comparison with 12 per cent of allophones and 14.7 per cent of anglophones.

French and economic promotion

The objective of economic equity between French and English enshrined in Bills 22 and 101 had two main thrusts. First, the use of French was to become general in all employment sectors and at all rungs of the salary scale. Second, companies with more than 100 (and later 50) employees were to become francized. These two thrusts formed the theme of 'French, language of work'. However, federal and 'Crown' employees are not subject to the French Language Charter, and small and medium enterprises with less than fifty employees proliferate in Quebec. Gaston Cholette, a former president of the Office de la langue française, estimated that one million workers (among 2.8 million) were not subject to the measures of the Charter (Maurais, 1987). The most obvious effects of the legislative measures are felt at the level of the linguistic environment: corporate names, roadsigns, commercial display, documentation and advertising. But the deepest effects are those touching upon the economic promotion of francophones in their own province. Whether by taking advantage of Bills 22 and 101, or through coercive measures, the changes among both francophones and anglophones have been dramatic.

To legislate French as the 'normal and usual' language of work – in the only Canadian province where it is the sole official language – appears today as a legitimate initiative of 'positive discrimination', one which 'delivered the goods'.

In fact, the legislative action only stimulated a movement initiated much earlier – from the beginning of the Quiet Revolution. The Conseil de la langue française has recently noted that the proportion of francophones in the labour market went from 77 per cent in 1971 to 82 per cent in 1991 (from 63 per cent to 70 per cent in Montreal).

Progress is not attributable only to the numerical factor. It is also qualitative. Consider first the success of the francization programme operating under the aegis of the Office de la langue française. In 1994, 68 per cent of the 1,866 large companies registered with the Office had obtained their francization certificate (it was 33 per cent in 1984). Of the 2,368 small and medium enterprises (with fifty to ninety-nine employees) registered, 84 per cent had their certificate, as against 41 per cent. The qualitative nature of the advance of French is also revealed by looking at certain sectors. For instance, in the Greater Montreal area, finance, company-service and high-tech industries have historically been the most anglicized. In 1971, francophones held 57 per cent, 56 per cent and 54 per cent of the positions in these sectors, respectively. In 1981, their presence climbed to 71 per cent, 68 per cent and 65 per cent, proportions that correspond closely to the real weight of francophones in the metropolitan region.

In any case, French has become the language of work of the labour force in all Quebec regions except that of Montreal, growing from 84 per cent in 1971 to 88 per cent in 1989. In the metropolitan region, the increase has been from 42 per cent to 56 per cent (*Rapport du comité interministériel sur la situation de la langue française*, 1996). The unemployment rate now affects francophones, anglophones and allophones more or less equally, while in 1971 language was a significant variable – because francophones had the highest unemployment rate, 10.6 per cent, against 9.3 per cent for anglophones and 8.2 per cent for allophones. Nevertheless, with regard to income, the historical tendency has been reversed. Now, bilingual francophones in Greater Montreal earn 7 per cent more than unilingual francophones and 4 per cent more than bilingual and unilingual anglophones (*Rapport du comité interministériel sur la situation de la langue française*, 1996). Naturally, the economic progress of francophones coincides with their professional advancement in highly qualified positions (administrators, professionals and technicians). From 1971 to 1991, in the metropolitan region, the proportion of francophone administrators in the labour market went from 2 per cent to 6 per cent (6 per cent to 8 per cent for anglophones) and that of francophone professionals went from 6 per cent to 11 per cent (a steady 14 per cent for anglophones over the same period), whereas that of francophone technicians remained the same, at 4 per cent (14 per cent for anglophones). Over the same period, the proportion of francophones in administrative positions went from 41 per cent to 67 per cent, from 45 per cent to 67 per cent among professionals and from 53 per cent to 69 per cent among technicians (*Rapport du comité interministériel sur la situation de la langue française*, 1996). These increases, though substantial, still do not reflect general demographic patterns.

There is still a lot to do before the French language is fully established in the working world of Quebec. Consider, for instance, the linguistic pressure exercised by the computer environment on regular mouse users. Indeed, almost four companies in ten (37 per cent) use only English software, while a quarter of them use French software. Half of the high-tech manufacturing companies have logistic support written in English only; only a third have French documentation. In brief, new technologies create additional difficulties for all non-anglophone workers.

A language-planning law like Bill 101 is not a magic potion, and gains made are always the result of a catching up, where the starting point was one of discrimination. Gains are often obtained only with a fight and, in this respect, the conflict over bilingualism in air traffic control illustrates well the humiliating nature of certain gains (see Borins, 1983). It took six years of aggravated quarrels between 1973 and 1979 to obtain what is considered perfectly normal everywhere else in the world. Two trade unions, the Canadian Air Traffic Controllers' Association and the Canadian Air Line Pilots' Association, led an all-out assault on AGAQ (Association des Gens de l'Air du Québec) to prevent the institution of bilingualism in the Quebec sky by the Canadian Ministry of Transport. The action was based only on the argument that the use of two languages would reduce air safety.

In 1974, the federal government set up a group to study bilingualism in air communications. Several of its recommendations supported the institution of partial bilingualism in Quebec air space. The two anglophone unions launched a strike against bilingualism, supported by favourable public opinion in English Canada, and by a powerful publicity campaign. During the summer of 1976, the federal government instituted a commission of investigation. AGAQ won a case which allowed French in the cockpit, and provided for translation of flight manuals into French, and the conclusions of the commission of inquiry's preliminary report added to these legal victories – the use of two languages in air communications was found not to affect air safety. Studies demonstrate that bilingualism in air communications is as safe as English unilingualism, that it works perfectly well in many airports worldwide (e.g., Geneva and Mexico City), and that it can be established at a fair cost. In brief, French does not make planes crash.

Philippe Barbaud

The 'French look' of Quebec

As far as the quality of life is concerned, Quebec has again become French in its external aspect; there is a 'French look' in 'la belle province'. With roadsigns, commercial display or exterior advertising, things seem satisfactory, especially in Montreal. For instance, a study by the Conseil de la langue française evaluated the degree of French unilingualism on display in certain sectors in Montreal in 1986 at between 65 per cent and 78 per cent – depending on whether or not one includes posters that cannot be linguistically classified (because of proper nouns or brand names). English is not always excluded: in August 1983, the Commission de protection de la langue française noted the names of 3,603 Montreal commercial establishments and determined that 21 per cent of them could preserve English words without contravening the French Language Charter (Maurais, 1987). Between 1978 and 1992, Quebec's toponymy reached a francization level of 78 per cent. Over the same period, English place names had doubled (to 11 per cent).

Given North American cultural uniformity and the popularity of American culture, it is not surprising that 'French suffered a decline between 1978 and 1991 in young people's cultural activities' (Rocher, 1993, p. 174). Some areas resist better than others. For instance, French-language publishing manages rather well, even if 23 per cent of francophones do not read books (14 per cent and 17 per cent for anglophones and allophones, respectively). There are about ten French-language daily newspapers in Quebec and some 165 different weeklies; in fact, the proportion of French weeklies went from 52 per cent in 1960 to 86 per cent in 1991. This progress is artificial, however, because it is due to the decline of the English press, which owes its survival to the allophone readership. Francophone readership of French-language newspapers has varied between 84 per cent and 92 per cent since 1990 (*Rapport du comité interministériel sur la situation de la langue française*, 1996). The year 1980 represented a peak for book publishing, with 91 per cent French-language production and, since then, the trend is down, probably due to economic restrictions. In 1990, 84 per cent of titles were in French, and it is probable that this proportion is now what it was in 1972, less than 82 per cent.

The American monopoly of cinema and video does not leave much space for French-language cinema in Quebec: in 1994, American movies captured 85 per cent of the total audience. In 1987, cinema critic Luc Perreault denounced the fact that in a generally francophone area of Montreal, he counted only eleven theatres (of seventy-two) whose programming was intended for the francophone public – and, in an adjacent area, only one theatre in twenty-five. The percentage of movies in French in Quebec went from 72 per cent in 1976 to 54 per cent in 1987, rising again to 61 per cent in 1990. Quicker availability of versions dubbed in French is helping here. The proportion of rented French videos went from 56 per cent in 1986 to 70 per cent in 1990, to fall again to 67 per cent in 1991. Moreover, 92 per cent of video games in Quebec are in English.

In 1991, there were some 130 radio stations in Quebec, of which 57 AM and 56 FM broadcast in French. In 1970, there were 68. In Montreal, francophone radio stations get only 64 per cent of the listening hours, against 35 per cent for the anglophone stations; elsewhere in the province, the francophone percentage is 92. It would be useful to know the real impact of government measures imposing French broadcast quotas on the listening habits of various segments of the Quebec population.

Finally, in 1983, francophone Montrealers watched 28 per cent English-Canadian or American television programmes. This was a high, however, and since then there has been a constant decline; during the autumn of 1991, the rate fell to 12 per cent. Elsewhere in Quebec, francophones watch television in English only 6 per cent of the time.

The future of the vernacular

We must return to the dialectal reality of Quebec French. Obviously, the French language has considerably strengthened its position in its Quebec enclave, not only on the objective or quantitative plane but also on the qualitative level (see Cajolet-Laganière and Martel, 1995). But isn't the concept of *French* language at odds with that of *home* language? Even with 'standard Quebec French' as a model, the Quebec mass continues to obey its own linguistic laws, so that the protection of the French language may one day become the protection of a ghost.

However, an established model of standard Quebec French will always be linked to the written code of the standard French language, while the vernacular pursues a divergent trajectory at all points: lexical, morphological, syntactic, semantic and stylistic (Barbaud, in press). In fact, it does so all the more securely, since its link to the written code no longer rests upon a mass instruction particularly focused on the mastery of standard French.

The utilitarian conception of French programmes, born of the communicative approach, combined with the linguistic egalitarianism born of the cult of tolerance at any price, encourages the unbridled use of an approximative language. The result is alarming. Bibeau (1990, p. 230) estimated 'that there is at least a good 50 per cent [of our students] who finish their secondary education without knowing how to write or even read French properly'. In its 1995 report submitted to the Commission des États généraux sur l'éducation, the Conseil de la langue française stated that, in the national exams of the last 14 years, 'barely 40 per cent [of young Quebecers] succeed criteria (sic) relating to grammar and syntax at secondary level, while in college the average mark obtained in 1992 and 1993 is about 50 per cent' – i.e., there is one grammatical, syntactic or spelling mistake every ten or twelve words. Similar results are observable in the written French tests that universities are forced to administer to their students. The *Conseil* stresses, in its recommendations, the necessity for young Quebecers to master standard French, both oral and written, and a re-emphasis on the way language works – notably grammar and, particularly at primary level, sentence analysis and parsing, seen as 'an exercise of logic and familiarization with the complexity and the subtlety of the mind'.

CONCLUDING STATEMENT

If the French-Canadians of Quebec have had success in leading their language to the gates of the twenty-first century in North America, it is because they were always able to make the most of available political power. That is the explanation of a unique example (Wardhaugh, 1987) in the annals of languages in contact. The search for increased political power, incarnate in the aspiration for the sovereignty of Quebec among francophone nationalists, follows a logic firmly fixed in modern times. The new world situation, with its unprecedented challenges, requires new means to accomplish old historical tasks.

Notes

1 On the alliance of French people and Amerindians, see the recent work of Vaugeois (1995). The population of the former French colony was 69,335 in 1765 (Berthet, 1995).

2 In 1831, in his famous work, *De la démocratie en Amérique*, Alexis de Tocqueville wrote: 'Lower Canada (Quebec) . . . forms a state on its own. The French population in Lower Canada is ten times the size of the English. It is dense. It has its own government and parliament. It really forms a distinct nation. In the parliament, composed of 84 members, there are 64 French and 20 English' (quoted in Bouthillier and Meynaud, 1972).

3 The Canadian government had earlier adopted some symbolic bilingual measures – e.g., postage stamps in 1927; banknotes in 1936; family allowances cheques in 1945, in Quebec only; simultaneous translation in 1959.

4 '*Joual*' – a phonetic alteration of '*cheval*' (horse) – can be defined as a sociologically inferior speech linked to the oral tradition, organized from a highly anglicized

instrumental vocabulary and characterized by a hybrid morphology, a rudimentary syntax, an approximative semantics and a vast repertoire of swearwords. For more details, see Cajolet-Laganière and Martel (1995).

5 An English-version summary of this law can be found in Crawford (1992, pp. 435–445).

6 The original text of these constitutional clauses can be found in Crawford (1992, pp. 433–435).

References

Ambroise, A. (1986). Modernisation politique et administrative au Québec (1960–1985). In R. Pelletier and J. Zylberberg (eds.), *État et société au Canada* (pp. 133–167). Quebec: Université Laval.

Baillargeon, M. (1983). Évolution et caractéristiques linguistiques des échanges migratoires interprovinciaux et internationaux du Québec depuis 1981. In *L'état de la langue française au Québec: Bilan et prospectives, IV: La situation démographique* (pp. 127–200). Quebec: Conseil de la langue française.

Barbaud, P. (1993). La loi de la langue. *Le Devoir* (27 October).

(1994). Protection de la langue et économie. *Québec français, 93*, 69–74.

(in press). Tendances lourdes du français québécois. In *Actes du colloque d'Avignon sur 'Les français d'Amérique du Nord en situation minoritaire'*.

Berthet, T. (1992). *Seigneurs et colons de Nouvelle-France*. Cachan: Éditions de l'École nationale supérieure de Cachan.

Bibeau, G. (1990). L'enseignement du français. In F. Dumont and Y. Martin (eds.), *L'éducation 25 ans plus tard! Et après?* (pp. 227–240). Quebec: Institut québécois de recherche sur la culture.

Bonin, D. (1990). L'immigration au Québec en 1990: à l'heure des choix. In R. L. Watts and D. M. Brown (eds.), *Canada: The State of the Federation 1990* (pp. 137–176). Kingston: Queen's University, Institute of Intergovernmental Relations.

Borins, S. F. (1983). *The Language of the Skies: The Bilingual Air Traffic Control Conflict in Canada*. Montreal/Kingston: McGill-Queen's University Press.

Bourhis, R. Y. (1994). Introduction and overview of language evens in Canada. *International Journal of the Sociology of Language, 105/106*, 5–36.

Bouthillier, G. and Meynaud, J. (1972). *Le choc des langues au Québec 1760–1970*. Montreal: Presses de l'Université du Québec.

Cajolet-Laganière, H. and Martel, P. (1995). *La qualité de la langue au Québec*. Quebec: Institut Québécois de recherche sur la culture.

Calvet, J.-L. (1987). *La guerre des langues et les politiques linguistiques*. Paris: Payot.

Castonguay, C. (1994a). La langue en question. *Le Devoir* (11 January).

(1994b). Dominance de l'anglais. *Le Devoir* (23 November).

(1994c). *L'assimilation linguistique: mesure et évolution 1971–1986*. Ste-Foy: Les Publications au Québec: Conseil de la langue française.

Chantefort, P. (1976). Diglossie au Québec: limites et tendances actuelles. *Cahiers de linguistique de l'université du Québec, 6*, 23–54.

Corbeil, J.-C. (1980). *L'aménagement linguistique du Québec.* Montreal: Guérin.

Crawford, J. (ed.). (1992). *Language Loyalties.* Chicago/London: Chicago University Press.

Daoust, D. (1982). La planification linguistique au Québec: un aperçu des lois sur la langue. *Revue québécoise de linguistique, 12*(1), 9–76.

Daoust, D. and Maurais, J. (1987). L'aménagement linguistique. In J. Maurais (ed.), *Politique et aménagement linguistique* (pp. 5–46). Montreal/Paris: Conseil de la langue française/Le Robert.

Duchesne, L. (1993). *La situation démographique au Québec.* Quebec: Les Publications du Québec.

Ferguson, C. (1959). Diglossia. *Word, 15,* 325–340.

Grey, J. (1995). Des 'vérités' à démolir. *Le Devoir* (5 December).

Kralt, J. and Pendakur, R. (1991). *Ethnicité, immigration et transfert linguistique.* Ottawa: Secretary of State.

Joy, R. (1967). *Languages in Conflict: The Canadian Experience.* Toronto: McClelland and Stewart.

Lavoie, Y. (1973). Les mouvements migratoires des Canadiens entre leur pays et les États-Unis au XIXe et au XXe siècle: étude quantitative. In H. Charbonneau (ed.), *La population du Québec, études rétrospectives* (pp. 73–88). Montreal: Boréal Express.

Leclerc, J. (1987). *La guerre des langues dans l'affichage. Essai.* Montreal: VLB.

Lemco, J. (1992). Quebec's 'distinctive character' and the question of minority rights. In J. Crawford (ed.), *Language Loyalties* (pp. 423–445). Chicago: Chicago University Press.

Levine, M. V. (1993). Au-delà des lois linguistiques; la politique gouvernementale et le caractère linguistique de Montréal dans les années 1990. In *Contextes de la politique linguistique québécoise* (pp. 1–40). Quebec: Les Publications du Québec/Conseil de la langue française.

Lieberson, S. (1970). *Language and Ethnic Relations in Canada.* New York: Wiley.

Matthews, G. (1984). *Le choc démographique.* Montreal: Boréal Express.

Maurais, J. (1987). L'expérience québécoise d'aménagement linguistique. In J. Maurais (ed.), *Politique et aménagement linguistique* (pp. 361–416). Montreal/Paris: Conseil de la langue française/Le Robert.

Paillé, M. (1996). Pour en finir avec les 'pures laines'. *Le Devoir* (5 January).

Perreault, L. (1987). La situation dans le domaine du cinéma. In *L'avenir du français au Québec* (pp. 165–174). Montreal: Québec-Amérique.

Plourde, M. (1988). *La politique linguistique du Québec 1977–1978.* Quebec: Institut québécois de recherche sur la culture.

Rapport du comité interministériel sur la situation de la langue française (1996). *Le français langue commune.* Quebec.

Rocher, U. (1993). La force d'attraction du français et les attitudes et les comportements des jeunes. In *Contextes de la politique linguistique québécoise* (pp. 157–181). Quebec: Les Publications du Québec/Conseil de la langue française.

St-Germain, C. (1980). *La situation linguistique dans les écoles primaires et secondaires 1971–72 à 1978–79.* Quebec: Conseil de la langue française.

Saint-Pierre, M. (1976). Bilinguisme et diglossie dans la région montréalaise. *Cahiers de linguistique de l'université du Québec, 6,* 179–198.

Termote, M. (1980). Le bilan migratoire du Québec, 1951–1977 – L'évolution récente située dans une perspective de long terme. In M. Amyot (ed.), *La situation démolinguistique au Québec et la Charte de la langue française* (pp. 13–40). Quebec: Conseil de la langue française.

——— (1993). L'incidence du facteur démographique sur l'usage du français au Québec. In *Contexte de la politique linguistique québécoise* (pp. 41–78). Quebec: Les Publications du Québec.

Vaillancourt, F. (1985). Un aperçu de la situation économique des anglophones et francophones du Québec, de 1961 à 1971, et de l'impact possible sur cette situation du projet de loi 1. In F. Vaillancourt (ed.), *Économie et langue* (pp. 117–156). Quebec: Conseil de la langue française.

Vaugeois, D. (1995). *La fin des alliances franco-indiennes.* Montreal; Boréal.

Wardhaugh, R. (1983). *Language and Nationhood: The Canadian Experience.* Vancouver: New Star Books.

——— (1987). *Languages in Competition.* Oxford/New York: Basil Blackwell.

Woehrling, J. (1993). Politique linguistique et libre-échange: l'incidence de l'Accord de libre-échange entre le Canada et les États-Unis sur la législation linguistique du Québec (à la lumière de l'expérience de la Communauté économique européenne). In *Contextes de la politique linguistique québécoise* (pp. 79–124). Quebec: Les Publications du Québec/Conseil de la langue française.

10 French in New Brunswick

Réal Allard and Rodrigue Landry

INTRODUCTION

New Brunswick is the only officially bilingual province in Canada.
Its French-speaking minority is the second largest, in absolute numbers, in a
Canadian province (250,175 compared to 547,300 in Ontario), but it is by far
the most important in terms of its proportion of the provincial population (34.6
per cent compared to 5.4 per cent for the Franco-Ontarians).[1] As a group, New
Brunswick francophones[2] meet the four basic criteria identified by Allardt
(1984) for the existence of a language minority: self-ascription or categorization
by others as members of the group exists, an important majority of the group
members are bound to the group by descent or ancestry, the language minority
has some distinctive attributes (linguistic, cultural or historical traits) related to
language and, finally, there is a structure of social interaction which allows the
persistence of cultural differences.

Francophones have been present on the territory known from 1604 to 1710
as *Acadie*, then as Nova Scotia (1713 to 1783), and on which we now find the
provinces of New Brunswick, Nova Scotia and Prince Edward Island, since the
beginning of the seventeeth century (shortly after the establishment of the first
French colony in North America on the *Île Sainte-Croix* in 1604 and of the first
permanent French settlement at *Port Royal* in 1605). In 1783, twenty-eight years
after the beginning of the deportation of two-thirds of the 13,400 Acadians from
Nova Scotia (the name given to *Acadie* after the British conquest), the territory
which was to become New Brunswick in 1784 had approximately 3,000 English,
2,000 French and 2,000 Indian inhabitants (McLaughlin, 1986).[3] Its French
inhabitants were mostly Acadians who had fled north to escape the deportation
and Acadians who, after having been deported, attempted to return some years
later – only to find that their lands and properties had been handed over to

British settlers. The French have therefore been a language minority in New Brunswick since its creation.

The main purpose of the present chapter is to provide an assessment, from a social psychological perspective, of the present vitality of the French-speaking Acadian community and of the French language in New Brunswick. Our conceptual model concerning the factors determining additive and subtractive bilingual development in francophone communities in the ten Canadian provinces, and in the states of Louisiana and Maine in the United States (Landry and Allard, 1990; Landry and Allard, 1991), will serve as the chapter's framework. Since we have provided detailed descriptions of this model elsewhere, we present only a brief summary here.

The model proposes that the vitality of a language, or extent to which a language is used in a context where two or more languages are in contact, depends on a multitude of sociological (macrosocial), sociopsychological (microsocial), and psychological factors. Each of these groups of factors represents a different level of analysis. The *macrosocial factors* (first level of analysis) reflect a community's ethnolinguistic vitality (EV) – i.e., the probability that it will survive and develop as a distinct and active collectivity in its relationships with other ethnolinguistic and cultural communities (Giles, Bourhis and Taylor, 1977) – which depends on its demographic, cultural, political and economic capital, relative to the majority with which it is in contact (Prujiner *et al.*, 1984).

A linguistic minority's *demographic capital* is reflected in the absolute number of its members, in their number relative to the linguistic majority, and in their relative concentration on a given territory. The group's birth and fertility rates, rates of endogamy and exogamy, and rates of immigration and emigration influence these factors (Giles *et al.*, 1977). The minority's *political capital* is reflected in the degree to which it is represented by some of its members within the government and in the decision- and policy-making apparatus, in the degree to which its language is used in public services at the federal, provincial and municipal levels, the linguistic rights conferred on the group and their translation into administrative regulations and policy, and the degree to which groups and movements acting on the group's behalf can influence decision-makers. Its *economic capital* is reflected by its status, relative to that of the majority, on indices such as the socioeconomic level and the language of work of its members, its control of commercial and financial institutions, the presence of its language on commercial and public signs, the degree to which its members participate in the workforce, and average income. Finally, the minority's *cultural capital* is reflected in the resources and institutions it has at its disposal to transmit its culture and language to its members, and for intragroup communication. These resources and institutions pertain to education, the arts, religion, the mass media, and sports and recreation.

The *microsocial factors* (second level of analysis) reflect the presence of a language in the linguistic experiences of group members in their individual networks of linguistic contacts. The relative frequency of minority-language experiences in contacts with family, relatives, friends and neighbours, in cultural institutions and events, in political organizations and institutions, at work and in economic institutions, and in the physical environment (e.g., on the signs put up by government and by commercial institutions) is strongly influenced by the group's EV at the macrosocial level. These linguistic experiences determine the development of psychological factors which are strongly related to the language behaviour of minority-group members.

Language-related *psychological factors* constitute the third level of analysis. Cognitive-academic and communicative language competencies in the minority- and majority-group languages, linguistic community- and language-related beliefs and beliefs concerning oneself with respect to language and linguistic communities (Allard and Landry, 1994), and ethnolinguistic identity, represent the factors which determine group ascription and the psychological disposition determining language use and production in intergroup contexts.

In the first part of this chapter, we present descriptive data and information on the actual vitality of the Acadian community and the French language in New Brunswick. In the second, we discuss present trends and potential events which may affect their future vitality. The chapter concludes with the consideration of some of the means envisaged to ensure and increase their vitality.

PRESENT VITALITY OF THE ACADIAN COMMUNITY AND OF THE FRENCH LANGUAGE IN NEW BRUNSWICK

Objective EV of the Acadian community [4]

Demographic capital

Roughly 58 per cent of New Brunswick's 250,175 francophones reside in the north, 35 per cent reside in the southeast, and 7 per cent live in the centre and southwest of the province. Their strong concentration in four counties, their relatively high proportion in three others, the geographical contiguity of these seven counties, and the fact that three share a border with Quebec and that four have been relatively isolated from contacts with English-speaking majorities (they have the sparsely populated centre of the province to the west and the Atlantic Ocean or the Northumberland Strait to the east) – all these have played an important role in the maintenance of the vitality of the Acadian community in these regions, and in the province as a whole. These data show why population means concerning New Brunswick Acadians and the French language must be interpreted with caution, and why researchers often analyse variables as a function of the regional demographic concentration of the Acadian population.

Had it not been for its once very high fertility rate – which was among the highest ever registered for an ethnolinguistic group (Lapierre and Roy, 1983) – and a birth rate from 9 per cent to 15 per cent higher than that of women of English ethnic origin in New Brunswick between 1921 and 1961 (Roy, 1980), the present demographic vitality of the Acadian community, in terms of absolute and relative numbers, and territorial concentration, would no doubt be much weaker than it is at present. While 16 per cent of the 1871 population was of French ethnic origin (Lapierre and Roy, 1983), nearly 46 per cent of the population is now at least in part of French origin (Statistics Canada, 1992).[5] Since 1976, however, the francophone fertility rate cannot ensure the renewal of the population (Dallaire and Lachapelle, 1990). It is slightly lower than that of anglophones for 1981–1986 (Roy, 1995), and therefore contributes to a decrease in the relative demographic vitality of the francophone community.

The rate of exogamy among francophones was 12 per cent in 1986 (Roy, 1995), and linguistic continuity – i.e., the proportion of the French-as-mother-tongue population which habitually speaks French at home – is affected by exogamy. While 97 per cent of the school-aged children of francophone endogamous couples maintain French as their mother tongue, only 27 per cent of the children of exogamous couples do so (CNPF, 1994). The rate of assimilation[6] among New Brunswick francophones in 1991 was close to 9 per cent (Cyr, Duval and Leclerc, 1996). Assimilation was negative in the northwest (–1 per cent), very weak in the northeast (2 per cent), weak in the southeast (7 per cent), and very high (46 per cent) in the remainder of the province, confirming that the more francophones are in a majority position and concentrated within a given territory, the lower the assimilation rate (Roy, 1995).

Political capital

The concentration of the francophone population in certain counties has made it possible, since the institution of single-member constituencies in

1974, for the community to elect from 30 per cent to 35 per cent of the fifty-eight Legislative Assembly members. Also, in federal counties, francophones have been able to elect four of New Brunswick's ten representatives to the House of Commons.

The debate on official languages in Canada, and the efforts of group leaders and elected representatives, have led to the adoption of several significant pieces of linguistic legislation. The Official Languages Act of 1969 made New Brunswick the only officially bilingual province. In 1976, Section 12 of the Act was proclaimed, establishing the right to education in the mother tongue (Bastarache and Boudreau Ouellet, 1995). The recognition of the rights of francophones took another important step forward when, in 1981, the Act Recognizing the Equality of the Two Official Linguistic Communities in New Brunswick was passed. In the same year, the Schools Act was amended to implement an education system abolishing bilingual classes and schools, in which the anglophone and francophone communities have exclusive management of their respective public education systems. Parents are guaranteed the freedom to choose their child's language of instruction, provided, among other reasons, that he/she has a 'sufficient knowledge' of the language of instruction. The Official Languages Act (1969), the Canadian Charter of Rights and Freedoms (1982), the Official Languages Act (1988), and enshrinement in the Canadian constitution of the principle of the equality of status of the official linguistic communities in New Brunswick (in 1993), have all contributed significantly to the efforts of New Brunswick's Acadian community. Because the Charter seeks to abolish discrimination on any basis, including language, and because it guarantees the right to instruction for official language minorities, Bastarache and Boudreau Ouellet (1995, p. 397) consider that it 'contributed most to the advancement of linguistic and cultural rights in Canada'.

The presence of francophones in the provincial civil service, in Fredericton, has increased from 11 per cent (1978) to 21 per cent (1990). In the same period, their representation in the entire province increased by 6 per cent, to 33 per cent, a figure which is close to their population proportion. Francophones are very well represented, for example, in education, health and welfare, but they are severely underrepresented in economic development, natural resources and primary industries, transportation and communications, and general services (Cyr *et al.,* 1996). Finally, because the francophone minority and the French language have official status, New Brunswick has participated, with Canada and Quebec, in international meetings of francophone countries. As a result, the political status of the francophone minority and French have improved.

The relatively small, but determined, proportion of the population which is opposed to the official recognition of the French language in New Brunswick has been represented primarily by the Confederation of Regions Party, which stands for English unilingualism.

Associations in the political domain.[7] The Société nationale de l'Acadie, a federation which now groups many organizations and associations of Acadian life in the three Maritime provinces, was particularly active on the New Brunswick political scene from 1955 into the 1970s. The Société des Acadiens et des Acadiennes du Nouveau-Brunswick, created in 1973, has played a very important role in political debates and consciousness-raising efforts concerning the Acadian community's status, culture and language. It now has 20,000 members and sixteen councils in five regions of the province. At the municipal government level, the Association des municipalités du Nouveau-Brunswick groups thirty-two of New Brunswick's forty-eight francophone municipalities.

Cultural capital

Education. New Brunswick's francophones have made their most significant gains in the field of education. After decades of struggle for education in French – leading to the legislation described in the previous section – francophones now control one-third of the school districts. In 1994–95, 45,298 primary and secondary students in all regions of New Brunswick received their education in French (Department of Education, 1995). Since 1974, the Department of Education has had a dual structure in order to better ensure equality of language treatment.

The Université de Moncton was created in 1963, at a time when Louis J. Robichaud, the only Acadian to become premier by election, was in power. With campuses in Edmundston, Moncton and Shippagan, it is one of New Brunswick's four universities and the largest French university (i.e., not bilingual) outside Quebec. Its research and development centres, chairs and institutes are active in the sciences and technologies, education, applied linguistics, law, regional development, cooperative studies, Acadian studies, international commercialization, and entrepreneurship. Its art gallery, which has an important collection of works by Acadian artists, provides documentation describing their work and presents exhibitions by Acadian and other artists. French community colleges in Bathurst, Campbellton, Dieppe and Edmundston offer programmes in a variety of trades and technologies. Francophones also administer schools of nursing in Bathurst, Edmundston and Moncton; these are now being integrated into the Université de Moncton.

Arts. The Université de Moncton and the classical colleges which preceded it, the National Film Board of Canada and Radio-Canada have been important catalysts in the cultural development of many New Brunswick francophone artists (Laurette, 1995). Acadian writers, a majority of whom are New Brunswickers, produce novels, poetry, theatre, essays and children's literature (Boudreau and Maillet, 1995). Their work has warranted the preparation of a history of Acadian literature (Maillet, 1983). These authors, the most renowned being Antonine Maillet who won the coveted Prix Goncourt for French literature in 1979, have been published in France and in Quebec, but the majority of their works have been issued by New Brunswick publishers such as Éditions d'Acadie, Éditions Marévie and Éditions Perce-Neige. Many poets and writers of short works publish in *Éloizes*, the publication of the Association des écrivains acadiens founded in 1978.

Acadian theatre has 'succeeded in acquiring a specific flavour and the means for an authentic cultural institution, given the resources at its disposal and the population it intended to serve' (Chiasson, 1995, p. 722). Several of the professional theatre companies created since 1960 ceased to operate after a few years, but two companies, Le Théâtre populaire d'Acadie and L'Escaouette, have been on the theatrical scene for some two decades.

Acadians have a reputation as skilled musicians. Several of them have succeeded on the national and international scenes, in the interpretation of classical, popular and folk music and song, and choir singing (Cormier, 1995). Acadian visual artists have also been productive, as have others involved in filmmaking, particularly documentary films (Laurette, 1995). Acadian artists in various fields participate in the annual Festival Acadien in Caraquet. Noteworthy examples of cultural events in which Acadian artists participate alongside artists from other countries are the Festival international du cinéma francophone en Acadie (in Moncton) and the Festival international de musique baroque de Lamèque.

Boudreau and Maillet (1995) consider that there has been a transition from a poetry on Acadia to a poetry of Acadia. This transition seems to be ongoing in each of the arts. From a nearly exclusive focus on Acadian history (especially the deportation and the events surrounding it) and folklore, the arts are progressively evolving into arts of Acadia.

Religion. A very large majority of the Acadian population is of the Catholic faith. Parishes are organized on a linguistic basis and services are offered in French throughout the province. Up to the 1960s, religious communities of priests and nuns played a particularly important role in the development of

hospitals and secondary and post-secondary education institutions
(L. Thériault, 1995).

Mass media. Francophones have had access to the French press since
1867. Its history is a turbulent one (Beaulieu, 1995), with newspapers preceding
and following *L'Évangéline*, which holds the record for longevity (1887–1982).
The daily *L'Acadie nouvelle*, established in Caraquet in 1984, presently strives
to serve francophones throughout New Brunswick. In addition, there are six
weekly regional French newspapers, and the magazine *Le Ven d'Est* has
been published bimonthly since 1985.

Radio-Canada, the French counterpart of the CBC Radio network, has
studios in Moncton. In addition, there are three private French radio stations
and eight French community radio stations, one of which is at the Université de
Moncton. A French Radio-Canada television station and production studio are
also present in Moncton. Since the 1980s, eight relay stations have made Radio-
Canada television available in New Brunswick. French TV signals originating
in Quebec are received in northern New Brunswick, and cable TV makes the
programming of an international French TV network (TV5) and of French TV
networks from Quebec and Ontario available to most New Brunswick
francophones.

The rapid development of the Internet, and the domination of English on
the network, have made it difficult for the Acadian community to keep apace.
The challenge is not limited to Acadians, since other governments are investing
in the development of technology aimed at ensuring the presence of French on
the network (Roy, 1996). The creation in 1996 of an international centre for the
development of the Internet in French at the Centre Universitaire Saint Louis
Maillet of the Université de Moncton is one part of this strategy.

Sports and recreation. Francophones manage the institutions and organizations for sports and leisure activities in regions where they are a majority or a
very strong minority. In regions where they are a small minority, the presence of
francophone community centres makes it possible for Acadians to organize and
participate in these activities. The Institut de leadership, created in 1972, trained
many francophone volunteer leaders in the fields of physical activity and recreation. It now directs its efforts towards services and professional resources in
information, research, and development in sports and recreation.

Associations in the cultural domain. The Conseil provincial des sociétés
culturelles, created in 1972, groups sixteen francophone cultural associations,
and an estimated 500 volunteers and 12,000 members. It promotes and co-
ordinates cultural production and activity, and acts as a pressure group on

behalf of the artistic community. In the field of education, the Association des enseignants et des enseignantes francophones du Nouveau-Brunswick, created in 1969, groups 2,850 teachers. It and its predecessors have contributed to the development of French-language education services in New Brunswick. The Comité de parents du Nouveau-Brunswick, with its 4,000 members, seeks to integrate the points of view of francophone parents in its collaborative efforts with teachers and administrators. Finally, in sports, the Société des Jeux de l'Acadie has organized, since 1979, the Jeux de l'Acadie, in which some 4,500 junior high school students participate annually. The Jeux represent the most widely attended annual public event in Acadia (O'Carroll, 1995). Their organization helps municipalities and regions in the development of modern, accessible and diversified infrastructures.

Economic capital

The economic situation in New Brunswick is difficult, particularly for the francophone population. Desjardins (1994) found that the per capita income in each county is below the Canadian average, but francophone income is 75 per cent of the national average, while that of anglophones is higher, at 84 per cent. Census Canada defines lowest-income regions as those in which the average income is below 70 per cent of the Canadian average. According to this criterion, all four of the counties in which francophones are a majority are lowest-income regions, compared to six of the eleven counties where anglophones predominate. The fact that most francophones reside in regions with a great dependence on seasonal employment is largely responsible for this situation.

The level of francophone manpower activity (61 per cent) is slightly lower than that of anglophones (64 per cent), and their unemployment rate is 19 per cent (anglophones, 14 per cent). Interestingly, the higher francophone unemployment rate is due to residence in economically disadvantaged counties, and not to ethnicity (Desjardins, 1994). The occupational level of anglophones is higher than that of francophones: the percentage of the former in management and liberal professions is slightly higher than that for the latter, and approximately 68 per cent of francophones are in white collar occupations, compared to 78 per cent of anglophones.

Cyr *et al.* (1996) compared the educational levels of francophones in regions where they are the majority to those of anglophones in anglophone-majority regions. In 1961, 27 per cent of the anglophones had completed from nine to twelve years of schooling, compared to 9 per cent of the francophones. By 1991, however, approximately 36 per cent of each group had completed such schooling.

While francophones have made gains in post-secondary education nearly parallelling those of anglophones between 1961 and 1991, they are still lagging far behind, with 41 per cent having attended a post-secondary institution, compared to 50 per cent for anglophones. Also, more francophones (24 per cent) than anglophones (14 per cent) have completed fewer than nine years of schooling. It seems clear, however, that had it not been for the important gains made in education legislation on linguistic matters, and the development of French-language public and post-secondary institutions, the educational level of francophones would be much worse.

Acadians have met with some success in large business ventures (e.g., Assumption Mutual Life Insurance Company and the Credit Union movement), but these cannot be compared with the successes of the Irving and McCain empires. The businesses controlled by Acadians are usually small, and provide goods and services locally. Recently, however, many Acadians have been making their mark as entrepreneurs (Beaudin and Leclerc, 1995).

Associations in the economic domain. The Conseil économique du Nouveau-Brunswick was created in 1979 to give an 'economic voice to Acadians'. It groups more than 1,000 Acadian business people and entrepreneurs. Acting as spokesperson and pressure group for the Acadian business community, the CENB is respected by government, the provincial and national business communities, and by the Acadian population. Francophone associations are also very active in the cooperative movement, in fishing and in agriculture.

This overview of the present vitality of New Brunswick's Acadian community shows that its demographic growth and distribution, the rising level of its education, the leadership and entrepreneurial skills of many Acadians, and the development and availability of communication systems in the province, are factors which have contributed to important gains reflected in the development of Acadian institutions and in the participation of Acadians in municipal and provincial institutions. Their presence in the latter varies greatly, however, depending on the sector of activity. Gains have been few in many areas, as we will see below.

The vitality of French as reflected in language networks and behaviour

French vitality is reflected in the extent to which the language is present in the contact networks of New Brunswick francophones. French language use is linearly related to the demographic capital of their communities (Landry and Allard, 1994a, 1994b). Francophones from northern New Brunswick, a strong majority, use French only slightly less than do Quebec francophones (from a region where they represent nearly 100 per cent of the population), while francophones from southeast New Brunswick, a strong minority, use French much less than the Quebec group (Landry and Allard, 1994a). These tendencies prevail in all domains of language use. There are, however, differences in French language use among domains.

Throughout New Brunswick, French use is highest, and much higher than that of English, in the social domain – i.e., in the home, with the immediate family and among relatives and close neighbours. A significant generation effect has been found with family language use (Landry and Allard, 1994b). While a very large majority of francophone adults use French with their parents, a slightly smaller majority use French with brothers and sisters, and a still smaller majority use French with their children. Also, the effects of exogamy on the use of French with relatives should be noted, since only four out of five adults use French with relatives.

The use of French in the political/governmental and economic domains is also high, although slightly less than in the social domain. In the southwest, where francophones are a very small and sparsely distributed minority, it is in the economic domain that the use of French is lowest. A majority of francophones do business with institutions which post French or bilingual signs, but the use of French on signs is far from reflecting the demographic presence of francophones in the province (Landry, 1994; Landry and Allard, 1994b). The cultural domain provides for both very high and very low uses of French. It is at school and in their family that young francophones most use French (Landry, 1994), but it is as consumers of cultural products that both young and adult francophones least use French (Godin and Renaud, 1994; Landry and Allard, 1994b). English-language mass media have penetrated francophone households and communities, and more English than French TV programmes, audiocassettes, records, videos and movies are chosen. However, French newspapers, books, magazines and radio programmes are more popular than their English equivalents. Finally, a very large majority of francophones attend religious services in French.

Language competencies, ethnolinguistic beliefs, and ethnolinguistic identity

French language competencies

The French cognitive-academic competencies of Grade 12 francophone students, as measured by 'closure' tests, are significantly but weakly related to the French vitality of the region in which the students reside (Landry and Allard,

1994a). Thus, student competencies in regions with strong vitality are almost equivalent to those of a unilingual French group from Quebec; those from lower French vitality regions are only slightly weaker. This is believed to be due to the presence of French public schools and education throughout the province (Landry and Allard, 1994a).

In an international study designed to evaluate the French writing skills of Grade 9 students (Groupe DIEPE, 1995), New Brunswick's francophones fared less well than students from France, Belgium and Quebec. Also, in a recent national study of French reading and writing skills (CMEC, 1994), they did as well as their Ontario and Manitoba counterparts, but more poorly than Quebec students. The comparatively poor showing of New Brunswick's francophone students could, in part, be due to the non-equivalence of the samples (MENB, 1996).

Student and adult self-evaluations of French-language competencies are related to the French vitality of their regions (Boudreau and Dubois, 1992; Godin and Renaud, 1994; Landry and Allard, 1994a, 1994b). While a very large majority of respondents from francophone majority regions evaluate their French language skills as very good, significantly smaller proportions of respondents do so in francophone minority regions. Finally, a majority of New Brunswick's francophones evaluate their English skills as being good or very good, and consider themselves fluently bilingual. Many others are passive bilinguals.

Ethnolinguistic beliefs

Francophone student and adult perceptions of the *present vitality* of the francophone and anglophone communities of New Brunswick are generally closely related to objective indices of the vitality of the francophone and anglophone communities in the regions where they reside (Allard and Landry, 1992; Landry and Allard, 1994b). The knowledge of the gains made by Acadians probably influences their beliefs concerning the *future vitality* of their community. An important majority of francophone adults believe that, in twenty years time, French will be as strong or stronger than it is now (Landry and Allard, 1994b). Francophone student perceptions of the future vitality of French are generally slightly less optimistic. On average, students from all regions believe that it will be similar to or slightly weaker than its present vitality (Allard and Landry, 1992). Interestingly, the same study reported that two groups of anglophone students from southeast New Brunswick (where francophone demographic vitality is moderately low) believed that the future vitality of French in the region would be higher, and that the future vitality of English would remain higher than that of French, and stable.

Landry and Allard (1994b) found that a large majority of adults have a strong preference for the use of French in the social, economic and politico-governmental domains. Indeed, a strong preference for the use of English in these domains, and for education primarily in English for their children, is expressed by fewer than one in twenty francophones. In the cultural domain, however, with respect to the language of TV programmes, only 34 per cent of the adults in the sample prefer French, while 19 per cent prefer English and 50 per cent prefer French and English equally. Also, 51 per cent of francophones would prefer that their children be educated in both languages equally, and 60 per cent would prefer that French and English be equally present on commercial signs. The latter results may be expressions of a certain social naïveté on the part of many francophones. We will return to this point later.

Ethnolinguistic identity

With respect to their *ethnolinguistic identity*, a large majority of New Brunswick's francophone adults consider themselves to be completely or mostly francophone. However, the degree to which they consider themselves francophone is strongly related to their proportion in the region in which they reside (Landry and Allard, 1994a, 1994b). Landry and Allard (1994a) found that the francophone identity of Acadian students in northeast and northwest New Brunswick, where francophones represent more than 90 per cent of the population, is only slightly weaker than that of a unilingual francophone group from Quebec, while that of students in the southeast, where francophones represent one-third of the population, is considerably weaker than that of the Quebec students. This research attests to the presence and effects of a powerful social determinism. Francophone demographic vitality largely determines linguistic experiences in French, and their combined effects determine the French linguistic competencies, ethnolinguistic vitality beliefs, and ethnolinguistic identity of members of the Acadian community in New Brunswick (Landry and Allard, 1990).

FUTURE VITALITY OF THE ACADIAN COMMUNITY AND OF FRENCH IN NEW BRUNSWICK

Due to its sustained efforts, its significant demographic capital, and related events and circumstances in the Canadian context, the Acadian community has realized important accomplishments which help it to maintain itself as a distinct and active collectivity. Outside observers and New Brunswick francophones themselves often perceive these as capable of ensuring future dynamism and vitality.[8] Three accomplishments in particular are frequently mentioned to justify this evaluation.

In the political domain, the official recognition of the francophone community of New Brunswick – i.e., the legal recognition of its right to be active on the provincial scene and to develop itself as a distinct and equal linguistic community – has provided it (and the majority group) with an increased sense of legitimacy. In the social domain, the development of institutional structures (community centres) which facilitate and promote the maintenance of permanent networks of contacts with the French language and culture among minority-group members, in regions where the minority is weak and sparsely distributed, is a second important achievement. By consolidating ethnolinguistic minority spaces – spaces of residence and activity – in a relatively circumscribed physical environment, the centres contribute to collective political, economic and cultural activity, and promote a sense of group belongingness (Gilbert, 1996). A third accomplishment, in the cultural domain, is the Acadian community's relative autonomy in the control of educational institutions which are responsible for the transmission of its language and culture. The provincial provision of a dual public education structure is perhaps the clearest illustration of this autonomy.

However, given the many factors which can affect the vitality of an ethnolinguistic minority and its language, most Acadian leaders and analysts do not believe that these accomplishments guarantee that the community will succeed in maintaining its present distinctiveness and dynamism in the future. While extrapolations based on the gains described in the first section of this chapter provide the basis for some optimism concerning future vitality, a number of trends and events threatens or could considerably weaken this vitality. A few of these are examined below, and some of their implications for the future are explored.

Demolinguistic trends

Data concerning certain aspects of the demographic vitality of the Acadian community are indicative of a gradual weakening (see section on demographic vitality, above). Exogamy is increasing, contributing to higher levels of assimilation and acculturation, and the francophone community's fertility and birth rates are not sufficiently high to contribute positively to its demographic capital, relative to that of the anglophone majority. If the present trends persist, the linguistic continuity of the francophone minority is threatened (Castonguay, 1995).

Francophone psychological disempowerment

Different forms of psychological disempowerment are often observed in ethnolinguistic minorities (Cummins, 1989). In spite of the progress made in several domains by the Acadian community, manifestations of this disempowerment are still present in the behaviour of many of its members, especially in regions where francophone vitality is low.

Linguistic insecurity

In the diglossic situation in southeast New Brunswick, many francophones use a language variety called '*chiac*', a blend of French and English (Péronnet, 1995). Most experience disparaging remarks concerning their vernacular, and many experience significant hardships in learning 'standard' French in school. Also, particularly in the southeast and northeast regions of New Brunswick, old French words and accents persist, and Acadians are often led to believe that these are incorrect, generally by persons ignorant of linguistics, who compare their skills and accents to the 'French norm' which is taught in the schools and is present in the media. These experiences lead to relatively negative perceptions of French language skills, and to linguistic insecurity, the tendency to evaluate one's language or mastery thereof overly negatively when comparing oneself to others. The proportion of students who are linguistically insecure in the francophone minority region is much larger than that in the francophone majority region (Boudreau and Dubois, 1992).

The consequences of linguistic insecurity are felt, at the level of the individual, as a lowering of self-esteem, since the language one speaks is often intimately related to one's self-opinion (Boudreau and Dubois, 1992). Linguistic insecurity leads to less productivity in French, and to a progressive withdrawal from French self-expression and participation in important aspects of the francophone community's activities. Furthermore, when francophone students who are insecure in French increase their mastery of English, many come to believe (often erroneously) that their mastery of English is superior to that of French (Landry, 1979) and, consequently, feel more confident using English than French. They are predisposed to converge to English, not only with anglophones but also with francophones having the same linguistic insecurity, thereby accelerating the processes of linguistic assimilation and acculturation. As well, they are reluctant to initiate conversations in French. For example, many tourists in southeast New Brunswick, including Quebecers, are surprised to learn that one-third of the population in the region is francophone, because practically everyone talks to them in English.

Social naïveté

A majority of minority-group members recognize the importance of bilingualism. It is hardly surprising, therefore, that 51 per cent of New Brunswick's francophone adults state that they would prefer that their children be educated in both languages equally (Landry and Allard, 1994b). In many minority contexts, this preference reflects a certain 'social naïveté' (Landry and Allard, 1993). First, in these contexts, parents are not generally conscious that the vitality of the dominant group is such that the majority group's language can be learned to an important degree with little or no formal schooling. Also, they do not know that cognitive-academic proficiency in the first language, developed through schooling in that language, is transferred to the second language to an important degree. Second, many parents view the school as if it were in a social 'vacuum'. It is as if they were unaware that schools are embedded in a wider social context in which the majority group's language and culture are omnipresent, thereby negating the possibility of true equality in the factors which influence cultural and linguistic development. They do not see, therefore, that the 50/50 formula in bilingual classes and schools usually contributes to the linguistic and cultural assimilation of minority students.

Another example of social naïveté is found in the economic domain. A majority of francophone adults (60 per cent) would prefer that both French and English be used equally on *commercial signs* (Landry and Allard, 1994b). This is true even in the regions where French vitality is very high. This preference for both languages on commercial signs may express a desire for the just and equitable treatment of both languages and linguistic groups. But it also reflects a lack of consciousness of the importance of this visual aspect of their environment for the perception of French vitality in a region and for the development of a sense of belonging to a francophone community (Landry and Bourhis, 1997). Furthermore, it may be a manifestation of a 'bilingual' identity, a subject to which we now turn.

Subtractive bilingual identity

Ethnolinguistic identity is considered to be that aspect of the minority group member's cognitive-affective disposition which is most resistant to assimilation and acculturation. Minority-group members will gradually lose their competencies in their mother tongue, not feel that they belong to the ethnolinguistic minority, and yet maintain parts of their ethnolinguistic identity (Edwards, 1985). Many, however, will become insecure and ambivalent about the value of their own identity due to their interactions with the dominant group (Cummins,

1989). As a result of being bilingual, and, perhaps, because of an insecure and ambivalent identity, from one to four out of ten francophone adults (depending on the French vitality in the region) consider themselves 'equally Francophone and Anglophone' (Landry and Allard, 1994b). These considerations may help to explain why a major source of preoccupation for many Acadian leaders is the high percentage of group members who, being bilingual, consider that theirs is a bilingual, rather than a francophone, identity (M. Doucet, 1995).

In sum, the linguistic experiences of many francophones lead to French psychological disempowerment, which manifests itself in linguistic insecurity and social naïveté where language is concerned, in the development of an ambivalent and insecure subtractive identity, and in the tendency to assimilate into the English-language community and culture.

Socio-economic, socio-political, and socio-cultural events

Due to developments in communications and transportation, the Acadian community is rapidly moving from a 'closed' to an 'open' society, from isolation to participation in modern society (Péronnet, 1995). In addition, most Acadians reside in *economically disadvantaged regions* which are dependent on primary-sector industries such as forestry, mining, fishing and agriculture. The combined effects of these factors are such that many Acadians are moving from traditionally Acadian rural areas to cities where the proportion of anglophones is much larger than that of francophones. The implications for eventual assimilation are clear, and lead some analysts to state that the disadvantageous regional economy of the Acadian regions constitutes the primary threat to Acadian vitality (Allain, McKee-Allain and Thériault, 1995).

The gradual *decentralization of the Canadian federation*, spurred by efforts to reduce the federal debt and to eliminate areas of conflict contributing to the ongoing constitutional crisis, has led to cutbacks in the funding of several programmes which are particularly important for the relatively young institutions of the Acadian minority. The federal government's transfer payments to the provinces are being reduced, as are equalization payments which transfer monies from the richer to the poorer provinces. In the future, New Brunswick will have less money for health services, higher education, and for its official languages programmes. At the federal level, cutbacks in the Société Radio-Canada and the Office National du Film du Canada, while difficult and even seen as a threat to national identity by many anglophone majority leaders, are particularly threatening for the francophone minority since they play an important role in its maintenance and visibility. Finally, the federal government is also reducing, often drastically, the amounts of funding for cultural associations and institutions which help to maintain networks of contacts in the minority group's language and culture.

The possibility of a *political union of the Maritime provinces* has often been discussed (Cyr *et al.*, 1996; P. Doucet, 1995). Although it is not envisaged in the immediate future, most Acadian leaders consider that such a union would pose an important threat to the francophone minority of New Brunswick. Cyr *et al.* (1996) found that a strong majority of francophones are opposed to such a union, and that this majority becomes even stronger when francophones are informed that their proportion in the population would drop from 32 per cent in New Brunswick to 14 per cent in the new Maritime union.[9] This weakening of Acadian demographic capital would lead to significantly weaker political capital. The Acadian community would be much less capable of exerting pressure on the different levels of government, and its associations would have a proportionately smaller voice in matters of public interest and opinion.

The *separation of Quebec* could have important consequences for Acadians, since the percentage of francophones in Canada would fall from 25 per cent to 4 per cent of the population. Some analysts are optimistic, believing that a Canada without Quebec would provide its francophone minority with the institutions and services that Quebec provides its anglophone minority. But most are pessimistic, considering that policies of bilingualism would be short-lived in a Canada in which only a small percentage of the population would be francophone (P. Doucet, 1995). For some, the worst-case scenario would be the separation of Quebec, followed by the union of the Maritime provinces.

Finally, in the sociocultural domain, the effects of the 'geoeconomic-marketplace-driven' *globalization and massification of culture* (Mattelart, 1996) are being felt throughout Canada. In francophone New Brunswick, for example, the very strong presence of Anglo-American television, cinema and music is such that it is legitimate that the Acadian community be preoccupied by the consequences of this *cultural and linguistic hegemony* (Roussy, 1996) for its cultural identity.

Taken as a whole, the preceding trends and events show that the Acadian community of New Brunswick should be wary of being lulled into a false sense of security by its recent gains and present status. If it is to survive as a distinct and dynamic collectivity, it must vigilantly attend not only to the issues that have preoccupied it in the past but also to possible future events.

CONCLUSION

We have briefly described and analyzed the present vitality of the Acadian population of New Brunswick and of their language, French, from a social psychological perspective.[10] We have seen that, in spite of important gains in certain domains, their future vitality is threatened by a number of demolinguistic, economic, political and cultural factors. This explains why different measures are proposed to create conditions which would increase the probability that the Acadian community will maintain itself as a distinct and dynamic entity. These measures can be seen as being directed at the macrosocial, microsocial and psychological levels of the model described in the introduction.

Bastarache and Boudreau Ouellet consider that New Brunswick is not yet genuinely bilingual and bicultural, and that the true empowerment of the Acadian people has yet to be attained. They state: 'Equality will only be attained by the introduction of a genuine policy of bilingualism in the public service and by the imposition of obligations on municipalities and all public services, whether private or government-controlled' (1995, p. 412). This policy would therefore implement linguistic duality in order to ensure minimal francophone institutional completeness (see New Brunswick, 1982, 1986) at the macrosocial level. Landry and Allard (1994b), Péronnet (1995), and Phlipponneau (1991) also see the need for institutional change, and recommend the creation of an official body which would be responsible for language planning efforts. Péronnet (1995) considers that the failure to do so 'can give rise to defeatist attitudes and a feeling of powerlessness as a result of a linguistic free market in which the minority stands no chance; or the linguistic power can be usurped by well-intentioned but incompetent individuals or groups' (p. 480).

J. Y. Thériault (1995, 1996) stresses the importance of cooperative development and the enhancement and strengthening of networks of contacts at all levels of the Acadian community, to reinforce a 'civil society' in which entities of governance derived from regional solidarities and concertation are particularly well adapted to change. In his estimation, it is through regionalization, and the management of territory, resources, health services and welfare, that Acadian society and identity would experience empowerment and avoid becoming folklore.

At the microsocial and psychological levels, Landry and Allard (1994b) propose that educational efforts be aimed at increasing citizens' social consciousness of the factors which contribute to the eventual disappearance of linguistic and cultural minorities. We consider that a better comprehension of the role played by macrosocial, microsocial and psychological factors in language maintenance and loss, and of the collective consequences of individual acts, can empower the minority-group individual who would choose to participate in the development of the francophone collectivity.

The maintenance and development of linguistic minorities is highly complex, due to the interplay between the logics of politics and economics, on the one hand, and social and individual factors, on the other. Strategies incorporating the principal strengths of the measures noted above will therefore be needed to attain the desired goal: a dynamic and distinct Acadian collectivity. Furthermore, if the Acadian community is to reach this goal in a context dominated by the hegemony of the English language and Anglo-American culture, it will have to join its efforts to those of Quebec and other francophones in North America, and work in concert with the international francophone community. It will also need the understanding and support of that large segment of the anglophone community which is sympathetic to its needs, and of federal, provincial and municipal governments which have the political will to implement the systematic language planning needed to transpose into practice the formally recognized equality of the anglophone and francophone communities and of the English and French languages in New Brunswick.

In the end, the future remains inscrutable. In the ongoing worldwide tensions between globalization and diversity of languages and cultures, the identification and implementation of the conditions which will allow minorities to flourish in a living testament to the richness of diversity remain a challenge for human ingenuity and research.

Notes

1 Total of single and multiple responses in the 1991 census: for New Brunswick, 32.7 per cent single and 1.9 per cent multiple. Percentages in the remainder of the chapter are rounded to the nearest unit.

2 In this chapter, we use the terms 'Acadians' and 'francophones' interchangeably to refer to the French-speaking population of New Brunswick. The term 'Acadians' now refers not only to the descendants of the former colonists, mainly French, who settled the original Acadia, but by extension to all French-speaking persons and all persons of French origin who live in New Brunswick. In other words, 'Acadians' is used to designate the French-speaking minorities of New Brunswick, Nova Scotia and Prince Edward Island, while the similar-sounding 'Cadiens' or 'Cajuns' is used to designate the Louisiana descendants of Acadians who were deported to that region.

3 See Daigle (1995) for a brief history of Acadie before the deportation, and L. Thériault (1995) for a historical synthesis of the period between the Treaty of Paris in 1763 and 1990.

4 A detailed presentation of the demographic, economic, cultural and political capital of the Acadian community of New Brunswick is beyond the scope of this chapter. See the following chapters in Daigle (1995) for more facts and analyses on demographic (Roy) and geographic (Arseneault and Lamarche) capital; on political capital (Doucet; Bastarache and Boudreau Ouellet); on economic capital (Desjardins, Deslierres and LeBlanc; Beaudin and Leclerc); and for cultural capital, see Thériault on ecclesiastical structures, Beaulieu on media, LeBlanc, Godin and Renaud on education, O'Carroll on sports, LeBlanc and LeBlanc on material culture, Chiasson, Cormier, Deschênes and Labelle on folklore, Boudreau and Maillet on literature, Chiasson on theatre, Laurette on art, and Cormier on music.

5 33 per cent single origin and 13 per cent multiple origin.

6 Rate of assimilation can vary slightly depending on the calculation method used.

7 Associations play an important role in Acadian community life and reflect its vitality. See Allain (1996), for an overview.

8 The success and media coverage of an event like the 1994 *Congrès mondial acadien* (1996) no doubt contribute to this perception. An estimated 65,000 Acadians from North America and Europe attended this ten-day event concentrated in southeast New Brunswick, during which 2,000 persons participated in a three-day colloquium – *L'Acadie en 2004* – on the economy, communications, education, and culture and heritage (Allain, 1996).

9 Cyr *et al.* used single response data. The percentages are 35 per cent and 17 per cent respectively when multiple responses are also considered.

10 See Allain, McKee-Allain and Thériault (1995) for a sociohistorical analysis of Acadian society, and Péronnet (1995) for an analysis of French in New Brunswick from the point of view of linguistics.

References

Allain, G. (1996). Fragmentation ou vitalité? Les nouveaux réseaux associatifs dans l'Acadie du Nouveau-Brunswick. In B. Cazabon (ed.), *Pour un espace de recherche au Canada Français: Discours, objets et méthodes* (pp. 93–125). Ottawa: Presses de l'Université d'Ottawa.

Allain, G., McKee-Allain, I. and Thériault, J. Y. (1995). Acadian society: Interpretations and conjunctures. In J. Daigle (ed.), *Acadia of the Maritimes* (pp. 329–370). Moncton: Chaire d'études acadiennes, Université de Moncton.

Allard, R. and Landry, R. (1992). Ethnolinguistic vitality beliefs and language maintenance and loss. In W. Fase, K. Jaspaert and S. Kroon (eds.), *Maintenance and Loss of Minority Languages* (pp. 171–195). Amsterdam: Benjamins.

(1994). Subjective ethnolinguistic identity: a comparison of two measures. *International Journal of the Sociology of Language, 108,* 117–144.

Allardt, E. (1984). What constitutes a language minority? *Journal of Multilingual and Multicultural Development, 5,* 195–205.

Bastarache, M. and Boudreau Ouellet, A. (1995). The linguistic and cultural rights of Acadians from 1713 to the present. In J. Daigle (ed.), *Acadia of the Maritimes* (pp. 371–414). Moncton: Chaire d'études acadiennes, Université de Moncton.

Beaudin, M. and Leclerc, A. (1995). The contemporary Acadian economy. In J. Daigle (ed.), *Acadia of the Maritimes* (pp. 243–286). Moncton: Chaire d'études acadiennes, Université de Moncton.

Beaulieu, G. (1995). Media in Acadia. In J. Daigle (ed.), *Acadia of the Maritimes* (pp. 485–522). Moncton: Chaire d'études acadiennes, Université de Moncton.

Boudreau, A. and Dubois, L. (1992). Insécurité linguistique et diglossie: étude comparative de deux régions de l'Acadie du Nouveau-Brunswick. *Revue de l'Université de Moncton, 25*(1–2), 3–22.

Boudreau, R. and Maillet, M. (1995). Acadian literature. In J. Daigle (ed.), *Acadia of the Maritimes* (pp. 679–719). Moncton: Chaire d'études acadiennes, Université de Moncton.

Castonguay, C. (1995). Évolution de l'anglicisation des francophones au Nouveau-Brunswick, 1971–1991. Unpublished paper.

Chiasson, Z. (1995). Acadian theatre: a cultural institution. In J. Daigle (ed.), *Acadia of the Maritimes* (pp. 721–756). Moncton: Chaire d'études acadiennes, Université de Moncton.

CMEC (1994). *Lecture et écriture, Programme d'indicateurs de rendement scolaire (PIRS), rapport sur l'évaluation de la lecture et de l'écriture.* Conseil des Ministres de l'éducation du Canada.

CNPF (1994). Là où le nombre le justifie . . . Saint Boniface, MA: Commission nationale des parents francophones.

Congrès mondial acadien: L'Acadie en 2004: Actes des conférences et des tables rondes. (1996). Moncton: Éditions d'Acadie.

Cormier, R. E. (1995). Music and the Acadians. In J. Daigle (ed.), *Acadia of the Maritimes* (pp. 807–838). Moncton: Chaire d'études acadiennes, Université de Moncton.

Cummins, J. (1989). *Empowering Minority Students.* Sacramento: California Association for Bilingual Education.

Cyr, H., Duval, D. and Leclerc, A. (1996). *L'Acadie à l'heure des choix.* Moncton: Éditions d'Acadie.

Daigle, J. (ed.). (1995). *Acadia of the Maritimes.* Moncton: Chaire d'études acadiennes, Université de Moncton.

Dallaire, L. M. and Lachapelle, R. (1990). *Profil démolinguistique – Nouveau-Brunswick.* Ottawa: Secrétariat d'État.

Department of Education (1995). *Annual report for the school year ending June 30, 1995.* Fredericton: Province of New Brunswick.

Desjardins, P.-M. (1994). Profil socioéconomique des deux communautés linguistiques du Nouveau-Brunswick. *Égalité, 36,* 97–106.

Doucet, M. (1995). *Le discours confisqué.* Moncton: Éditions d'Acadie.

Doucet, P. (1995). Politics and the Acadians. In J. Daigle (ed.), *Acadia of the Maritimes* (pp. 287-327). Moncton: Chaire d'études acadiennes, Université de Moncton.

Edwards, J. (1985). *Language, Society and Identity.* Oxford: Blackwell.

Gilbert, A. (1996). L'espace francophone: regard sur les pratiques linguistiques dans différents milieux. In B. Cazabon (ed.), *Pour un espace de recherche au Canada Français: discours, objets et méthodes* (pp. 53-73). Ottawa: Les Presses de l'Université d'Ottawa.

Giles, H., Bourhis, R. Y. and Taylor, D. M. (1977). Toward a theory of language in ethnic group relations. In H. Giles (ed.), *Language, Ethnicity and Intergroup Relations* (pp. 307-348). New York: Academic Press.

Godin, A. and Renaud, A. (1994). *Attitudes et habitudes linguistiques des jeunes du Nouveau-Brunswick.* Moncton: Centre universitaire de Moncton.

Groupe DIEPE (1995). *Savoir écrire au secondaire: Étude comparative auprès de quatre populations francophones d'Europe et d'Amérique.* Brussels: Éditions De Boeck.

Landry, R. (1979). Caractéristiques linguistiques des gradués d'une polyvalente francophone dans un milieu minoritaire. *Revue de l'Association canadienne d'éducation de langue française, 8*(2), 8-15.

(1994). Diagnostic sur la vitalité de la communauté acadienne du Nouveau-Brunswick. *Égalité, 36,* 11-39.

Landry, R. and Allard, R. (1990). Contact des langues et développement bilingue: Un modèle macroscopique. *Revue canadienne des langues vivantes/Canadian Modern Language Review, 46,* 527-553.

(1991). Can schools promote additive bilingualism in minority group children? In L. Malave and G. Duquette (eds.), *Language, Culture and Cognition* (pp. 198-231). Clevedon: Multilingual Matters.

(1993). Beyond socially naive bilingual education: the effects of schooling and ethnolinguistic vitality of the community on additive and subtractive bilingualism. *Annual Conference Journal* (National Association of Bilingual Education 1990-1991), 1-30.

(1994a). The Acadians of New Brunswick: demolinguistic realities and the vitality of the French language. *International Journal of the Sociology of Language, 105/106,* 181-215.

(1994b). *A Sociolinguistic Profile of New Brunswick Francophones.* Moncton: Centre de recherche et de développement en éducation, Université de Moncton.

Landry, R. and Bourhis, R. Y. (1997). Linguistic landscape and ethnolinguistic vitality: an empirical study. *Journal of Language and Social Psychology, 16,* 23-49.

Lapierre, J.-W. and Roy, M. (1983). *Les Acadiens.* Paris: Presses universitaires de France.

Laurette, P. C. (1995). Aspects of an Acadian art history. In J. Daigle (ed.), *Acadia of the Maritimes* (pp. 757-805). Moncton: Chaire d'études acadiennes, Université de Moncton.

McLaughlin, Y. A. (1986). Le Nouveau-Brunswick: province diffuse. *Égalité, 18,* 27-52.

Maillet, M. (1983). *Histoire de la littérature acadienne.* Moncton: Éditions d'Acadie.

Mattelart, A. (1996). Vers la mondialisation de la culture? In *Universalia 1996* (pp. 106–111). Paris: Encyclopaedia Universalis France.

MENB (1996). *L'enseignement du français au Nouveau-Brunswick: rapport du comité d'étude du rendement scolaire en français.* Fredericton: Ministère de l'Éducation du Nouveau-Brunswick.

New Brunswick (1982). *Towards the Equality of the Official Languages of New Brunswick.* Fredericton: Consultative Committee on Official Languages.

New Brunswick (1986). *Report of the Advisory Committee on the Official Languages of New Brunswick.* Fredericton: Official Languages Branch.

O'Carroll, D. (1995). Sports in Acadia. In J. Daigle (ed.), *Acadia of the Maritimes* (pp. 563–576). Moncton: Chaire d'études acadiennes, Université de Moncton.

Péronnet, L. (1995). The situation of the French language in Acadia: a linguistic perspective. In J. Daigle (ed.), *Acadia of the Maritimes* (pp. 451–484). Moncton: Chaire d'études acadiennes, Université de Moncton.

Phlipponneau, C. (ed.). (1991). *Vers un aménagement linguistique de l'Acadie du Nouveau-Brunswick.* Moncton: Centre de recherche en linguistique appliquée, Université de Moncton.

Prujiner, A., Deshaies, D., Hamers, J. F., Blanc, M., Clément, R. and Landry, R. (1984). *Variation du comportement langagier lorsque deux langues sont en contact.* Quebec: Centre international de recherches sur le bilinguisme.

Roussy, M. (1996). L'influence des médias sur l'identité culturelle acadienne et l'importance de l'éducation aux médias. In *Le Congrès mondial acadien: L'Acadie en 2004* (pp. 143–155). Moncton: Éditions d'Acadie.

Roy, J.-L. (1996). La rentabilité de la promotion de la langue et de la culture. In *Le Congrès mondial Acadien: L'Acadie en 2004* (pp. 516–528). Moncton: Éditions d'Acadie.

Roy, M. K. (1980). Peuplement et croissance démographique en Acadie. In J. Daigle (ed.), *Les Acadiens des Maritimes* (pp. 135–207). Moncton: Centre d'études acadiennes.

(1995). Demography and demolinguistics in Acadia, 1871–1991. In J. Daigle (ed.), *Acadia of the Maritimes* (pp. 135–200). Moncton: Chaire d'études acadiennes, Université de Moncton.

Statistics Canada (1992). Census of Canada. Ottawa: Ministry of Industry, Science and Technology.

Thériault, J. Y. (1995). *L'identité à l'épreuve de la modernité.* Moncton: Éditions d'Acadie.

(1996). Penser l'Acadie comme société civile. *Ven d'est* (July–August), 28–32.

Thériault, L. (1995). Acadia from 1763 to 1990: An historical synthesis. In J. Daigle (ed.), *Acadia of the Maritimes* (pp. 45–88). Moncton: Chaire d'études acadiennes, Université de Moncton.

225

11 French outside New Brunswick and Quebec

Raymond Mougeon

INTRODUCTION

In this chapter I will examine various measures of the vitality of the francophone minorities living outside Quebec and New Brunswick. These will include information on the availability of French-medium schooling and other kinds of institutional support for French, and statistics on the French mother-tongue population – e.g., retention of French at home, use of French in other domains of society, bilingualism in English, birth rate, rate of linguistic reproduction, etc. This examination will lead to an assessment of the chances of short- and longer-term survival of these francophone communities.

BRIEF HISTORY

The presence of about 750, 000 French-speaking Canadians outside New Brunswick and Quebec can be traced back to two distinct sources. East of New Brunswick, in the provinces of Nova Scotia and Prince Edward Island, the great majority of francophones are of Acadian ancestry. In the province of Newfoundland, francophones who reside on the island are mostly of Acadian ancestry,[1] while those in Labrador are chiefly of *Québécois* ancestry or are Quebec-born. Before being deported by Britain in 1755, Acadians had expanded beyond their original colony in Port-Royal, Nova Scotia (a settlement dating from 1605) to various regions of the Atlantic provinces (e.g., eastern New Brunswick, Prince Edward Island and Cape Breton). A few decades after deportation, a significant number of Acadians were allowed to come back to the Atlantic provinces, where they joined the few who had escaped deportation, and settled in several regions of these provinces. Nearly all of today's Acadian population located east of New Brunswick is the result of this process of resettlement. West of Quebec, the presence of francophone communities is primarily the result of immigration originating mostly from Quebec, that started as early as the end of the seventeenth century.[2] These migratory waves can be ascribed to three factors:

226

a) development of the fur trade (in the seventeenth and eighteenth centuries); b) overpopulation in several rural areas of Quebec (emigration due to this factor started in the first half of the nineteenth century); c) lack of employment opportunities in certain sectors of Quebec industry.

Ontario was the first province where Quebecers came to settle, arriving at the turn of the 18th century. In Manitoba, the first settlers from Quebec arrived around 1720, in Saskatchewan around 1760, in Alberta about 1780 and in British Columbia around 1800. Francophones started to arrive in the Northwest Territories and in the Yukon towards the turn of the twentieth century. In historical terms, then, the arrival of francophones, east of New Brunswick and west of Quebec, clearly predates the arrival of the immigrants from continental Europe and even from Britain. Indeed, in the early stages of the history of Manitoba, Saskatchewan and Alberta, the presence of French-speaking *Métis* (people of French-Canadian and Indian ancestry) was so substantial that the Manitoba Act of 1870 and the Northwest Territories Act of 1891 included sections which accorded an official status to the French language in the legislative assemblies, in the courts of justice and (in Manitoba) in the educational domain. Francophone emigration from Quebec to Ontario and to the western provinces has continued up to the present with varying strength. Therefore, the *Québécois* roots of francophones west of Quebec go back to a more or less remote period of Canadian history.

During the eighteenth century and the first half of the nineteenth century, in the area of English Canada under study, francophones were generally able to establish more or less self-contained communities with the help of the Catholic church. In such communities, they were mostly involved in a limited number of primary-sector economic activities (e.g., agriculture, fishing), they had their own parish schools and churches which were run by members of the French Canadian clergy and, hence, they were in a strong position to reproduce the traditional linguistic and cultural heritages of the Acadians and of the *Québécois*. After this period, however, they lost much of their cutural and economic autonomy – for several main reasons. With the establishment of the Canadian confederation in 1867, education became a provincial responsibility and, during the second half of the nineteenth century and the early part of the twentieth century, all the provinces located east and west of Quebec (including New Brunswick) passed educational acts which enshrined the principles of centralized education. These acts banned the use of French as a medium of instruction in the systems of public schools and/or abolished the provision of financial support to Catholic schools.[3] Immigrants who did not speak French (initially, mostly anglophones) arrived in increasing numbers, both east and west of Quebec, and developed sectors of the economy that became increasingly important for the survival of francophones (e.g., commerce and industry). Because they were under anglophone control, these sectors were an additional source of exposure to the Canadian English language and culture. The influx of growing numbers of non-French-speaking immigrants also meant that, in all of the provinces east of New Brunswick and west of Quebec, francophones became very small minorities (see below). This probably made it easier for provinces such as Manitoba, Saskatchewan and Alberta to pass legislation which put an end to the special or official status formerly accorded to French by their own Legislative Assemblies or by the Northwest Territories Act – or simply to cease to abide by the old legislation. Two other factors contributed to the erosion of the economic, linguistic and cultural autonomy of French Canadians: the growth of the public sector (e.g., government and health) – and hence of key institutions in which French is not used; and expansion of the mass media, another domain which is largely dominated by English.

Another important stage in the history of the French-Canadian minorities needs to be mentioned. Up to the beginning of Quebec's 'Quiet Revolution' in the early 1960s, these minorities, and especially their leaders, had strong ties with each other and most crucially with their *Québécois* counterparts. French Quebecers and francophones outside Quebec would refer to themselves as French Canadians (*Canadiens français*). This unity proved important during the darkest times. For instance, when Ontario passed its infamous regulation banning the use of French in all of its public schools, in 1912, Franco-Ontarians were able to organize a strong movement of resistance thanks to the help of various Quebec-based religious, cultural and political organizations. During the 1960s and 1970s, however, francophones in Quebec developed a strong sense of national distinctive identity. They no longer referred to themselves as French Canadians but as *Québécois*. They also became less and less concerned about the fate of Canada's francophone minorities and took a series of major steps to (re)gain control of the economy of their province and to ensure the continued survival of French in Quebec. In consequence, the different francophone minorities developed their own distinctive identities and started to refer to themselves by distinctive names (e.g., *Franco-Ontariens, Franco-Manitobains, Fransasquois*). They also realized that their survival depends less and less on what the federal state can or will do to advance their cause and is increasingly influenced by decisions made by their respective provincial governments. Consequently, over the last twenty-five years, much of their political struggle to (re)gain linguistic rights has been waged primarily without the help of Quebec and has been oriented to their provincial governments. As the twentieth century draws to a close, the French-Canadian community has entered what seems to be an irrevocable stage of fragmentation as well as one of increased estrangement between Quebec and the French Canadian minorities.[4]

THE FRENCH CANADIAN MINORITIES TODAY

Institutional support for French

While much of the history of the French-Canadian minorities has been characterized by a significant erosion of their economic, cultural and linguistic autonomy – brought about in part by a series of discriminatory or assimilationist measures taken by various provincial governments – there has been a partial reversal of such measures in relation to French-medium education and to the use of French in public-sector institutions over the last twenty-five years or so. I will deal first with education.

In the late sixties, two provinces took steps which allowed the use of French as a medium of instruction in the public schools – Manitoba, which allowed francophones to be schooled in French for half of the school day from 1967, and for the entire day from 1970; and Ontario, which allowed Franco-Ontarians to be schooled entirely in French in its public schools from 1968. Prior to this, Ontario had tolerated the use of French as a medium of instruction in its Catholic schools. More recently, when Canada repatriated its constitution in 1982, it adopted a new Charter of Rights and Freedoms; this includes two sections on the linguistic rights of Canadians (one on the official languages of Canada and another on the educational rights of Canada's official minorities – francophones outside Quebec and anglophones in Quebec). The Charter section on educational rights states quite clearly that Canadians who live outside Quebec and who claim French as a mother tongue have the right to send their children to French-medium 'educational facilities provided out of public funds', provided that there is a sufficient number of children to warrant the establishment of such facilities.[5] During the 1980–81 negotiations which led to the drafting of the Charter, and after its adoption, all of the provinces west of Manitoba and east of New Brunswick, and the Northwest Territories and the Yukon, took steps to offer French-medium schooling to their francophone minorities.[6] It should be noted, however, that in many instances these measures were taken after a series of court actions launched by the francophone minorities and backed financially by the federal government which has committed itself, in its Official Languages Acts (see below), to providing significant sums of money to help the anglophone provinces to establish French-medium schools.

Several studies (Churchill, Frenette and Quazi, 1985; Martel, 1994; Tymm and Churchill, 1987) show that there is growing support for French-medium schools among the francophone minorities. For instance, in Ontario, the great majority of children of French mother tongue are enrolled in elementary French-medium schools. The implementation of the right to French-medium schooling in anglophone Canada seems already to have had several positive outcomes. Before the creation of elementary and secondary French-medium schools, French Canadians were lagging considerably behind English Canadians in average level of schooling and, notably, in literacy. Studies carried out in the provinces where French-medium public schools were established in the 1960s (e.g., Ontario) suggest that this gap may narrow because of these schools. For instance, Churchill, Frenette and Quazi (1985) point to the fact that before the establishment of French-medium public schools, Franco-Ontarians had school drop-out rates which were much higher than those of Anglo-Ontarians; in contrast, during the 1970s, Franco-Ontarian drop-out rates have decreased significantly. In a related vein, Porter, Porter and Blishen (1982), in their study of educational inequalities in the Ontario schools, found that Franco-Ontarian students enrolled in French-medium schools have much more positive academic self-concept and higher post-secondary aspirations than counterparts enrolled in English-medium schools. It is also important to point out that French-Canadian students enrolled in minority French-medium schools have been found to have much higher rates of French achievement compared to French-Canadian students who are primarily or entirely schooled in English (see, for instance, Hébert's 1976 study of the school achievement of Franco-Manitoban students).

If considerable progress in the area of French-medium elementary and secondary education has been made during the last twenty-five years, there is still much room for improvement at the post-secondary level, even in those provinces which took early steps to establish French-medium education facilities. For instance, Ontario has yet to establish a full-fledged French-medium university comparable to the English-medium universities of Quebec, and has only very recently started to establish French-medium community colleges on a scale comparable to that of Quebec's English-medium 'CÉGEPS' (Collèges d'enseigne-ment général et professionnel). East of New Brunswick and west of Ontario, the availability of French-medium post-secondary schools is even more restricted than in Ontario. It is reasonable to assume that progress made on this front will also have positive impact on the educational levels of the francophone minorities, and that this in turn may bring about an increase in the proportion of francophones in the occupational categories where they have been underrepresented (e.g., administration, natural sciences and engineering, medicine and health). Progress here would also narrow the differential in average income between francophones and anglophones which still exists in most of the majority anglophone provinces (see Bernard, 1991b).[7]

Let us now turn to the use of French in public-sector institutions. The federal parliament passed two Official Languages Acts, one in 1969 and another in 1988, which commit it: (a) to provide services in French or in English in the institutions which fall within its jurisdiction (ministries, agencies, national public broadcasting companies) in designated areas; (b) to increase the proportional representation of francophone civil servants outside Quebec and anglophone civil servants in Quebec; (c) to offer (more) opportunities to francophone civil servants outside Quebec to use French at work. As noted earlier, the Canadian Charter of Rights and Freedoms also includes a section which declares that French and English are the two official languages of Canada and which confirms that Canadians have the right to receive services in the official language of their choice.

In a recent evaluation of Canada's official languages policies, Fortier (1994), former Commissioner of Official Languages, noted that the objective of proportional representation of francophones in the federal government has been met, but that significant progress still needs to be made in the attainment of the first and third goals. As a user of federal government services in one of the areas that were designated for the implementation of the 1988 Official Languages Act – namely, Toronto – I agree with the Commissioner's assessment, especially regarding the third objective. Still, the implementation of the Official Languages Acts has had a number of positive effects on exposure to French among Canada's French-speaking minorities. Most of the written information produced by federal government institutions for the general public (ads, brochures, forms, signs, etc.) is now available in French; the French CBC radio and television stations are now readily available in most regions of the anglophone provinces where French Canadians are located; and recently the Canadian Radio-Television and Telecommunications Commission passed a regulation which has improved the availability outside Quebec of the French-language programmes offered by the international consortium of French television companies (TV5), and of the new continuous news television channel run by the French CBC. It should be borne in mind, however, that these French media are vastly out-numbered by a large array of English ones (all the more so now that cable television has become more widely available) which offer a much wider spectrum of programmes (including programmes that are reflective of the local communities).

As concerns the use of French in the institutions which fall under the jurisdiction of the provincial governments, it can be pointed out that only two provinces (Ontario and Manitoba) and the Yukon and Northwest Territories have taken steps somewhat analogous to the federal Official Languages Acts. The 1986 French Languages Services Act passed by the Ontario government deserves a special mention. Although its implementation entails only limited provision of oral French services and is unlikely to have much of an impact on the use of French as language of work, it has had a noticeable impact on the availability of official information written in French (e.g., forms, ministry or crown agency publications, signs, etc.) and of spoken French media. Since 1988, Franco-Ontarians have had access, via cable television, to a full-fledged educational television channel (TFO) supported by provincial funds. Beyond its primary impact, this channel also provides significant assistance to Ontario's network of French-medium elementary and secondary schools.

In contrast to Ontario and Manitoba, the other provinces have either abstained from taking special measures to promote the use of French in the institutions which fall within their jurisdiction or, like Alberta and Saskatchewan, have actually moved to restrict the language rights of their francophone minorities. These restrictive measures were taken when the two provinces were reminded, by rulings of the Supreme Court of Canada, of their obligation to abide by the rules of parliamentary, legislative and judiciary bilingualism formulated in Section 110 of the 1891 Northwest Territories Act.

Except for the 1975 federal regulations which make it mandatory to produce bilingual packages, labels and user manuals for products sold in Canada, language-centred government interventions in the private sector have been minimal. In theory, the regulations on bilingual packaging are important for exposure to French in English Canada. However, the quality of the French version of the bilingual text is often poor and sometimes grossly inaccurate, a strong disincentive to its use by francophones in anglophone Canada (particularly since almost all of them are able to read the English versions; see below). Since there is a lack of precise information on the use of French as a language of work in private-sector institutions in English Canada, and on the services which they offer in French, I cannot report on these matters.[8]

Demographic strength of francophones

According to the last census (1991) there were 732,920 individuals, east of New Brunswick and west of Quebec, who claimed French as a mother tongue. Table 11.1 shows that these individuals make up 3.8 per cent of the total Canadian population and that their proportional representation in each province, and in the Yukon and the Northwest Territories, is uniformly small (5 per cent or less). Canadians who claim non-official languages as mother tongues outnumber those who claim French in all but two of the provinces under study (Prince Edward Island and Nova Scotia) and in the Yukon and the Northwest Territories. West of Quebec, the numerical superiority of non-official language speakers over francophones is quite evident. It is true that the former include many different language groups, but some of these groups are actually comparable or superior in size to francophones – e.g., the speakers of Ukrainian or of German in Manitoba and Alberta, or the speakers of Chinese, of German and of Punjabi in British Columbia. West of Quebec, then, the francophone minorities, in spite of their official status, increasingly run the risk of being seen as marginal (at least in demographic terms) by those in power; they may have to fight even harder to gain linguistic rights or even to retain those already won. Table 11.1 also shows that the numerical preponderance of the English mother-tongue groups is quite evident in all of the provinces under study and in the Yukon – but not in the

Table 11.1 Population claiming French, English and non official languages as mother tongues (1991)

Province	French mother-tongue claimants		English mother-tongue claimants		Non-official language mother-tongue claimants	
	Number	%	Number	%	Number	%
Newfoundland	2,860	0.5	555,925	98.5	5,150	1.0
Prince Edward Island	5,750	4.4	120,765	94.3	1,585	1.3
Nova Scotia	37,525	4.2	831,575	93.3	21,850	2.5
Ontario	503,340	5.0	7,443,540	74.6	2,030,170	20.4
Manitoba	50,775	4.7	793,325	73.5	235,295	21.8
Saskatchewan	21,790	2.2	812,595	83.2	141,650	14.6
Alberta	56,735	2.2	2,045,905	81.2	416,545	16.6
British Columbia	51,585	1.5	2,562,245	78.9	633,675	19.6
Yukon	905	3.2	24,550	88.8	2,200	8.0
Northwest Territories	1,455	2.5	31,700	55.2	24,280	42.3
Total	733,920	3.8	15,222,125	78.2	3,512,395	18.0

Source: Statistics Canada, 1991 census, *Mother Tongue*: 20 per cent sample data.

Table 11.2 Population claiming French as a single mother tongue or as one of two or three other mother tongues (1986 and 1991)

Province	Only French		French and English		French and a non-official language		French, English and a non-official language	
	1986	1991	1986	1991	1986	1991	1986	1991
Newfoundland	2,085	2,400	1,065	790	–	20	60	20
Prince Edward Island	5,045	5,415	1,215	850	5	–	45	15
Nova Scotia	30,835	34,005	7,895	5120	65	120	150	170
Ontario	422,770	464,040	96,910	70,860	3,700	5,695	1,520	6,705
Manitoba	40,050	46,925	9,925	7,330	185	445	820	595
Saskatchewan	21,205	19,695	4,660	4,085	210	270	425	250
Alberta	47,480	51,000	12,940	11,505	630	1,025	1,635	1,130
British Columbia	38,605	45,265	11,495	10,785	785	1,115	290	1,515
Yukon	600	815	80	125	5	5	–	–
Northwest Territories	1,265	1,380	255	135	15	20	40	10
Total	609,940	671,040	146,440	111,585	5,600	8,720	4,925	10,410

Source: Statistics Canada, 1991 census, Knowledge of Official Languages: 100 per cent sample data; 1986 census: 20 per cent sample data.

234

Northwest Territories, where the speakers of non-official languages (almost all aboriginal languages) represent over 40 per cent of the total population.

In 1986 and in 1991, Statistics Canada allowed census respondents to claim more than one mother tongue; previous censuses permitted only one. Consequently, the global mother-tongue statistics presented in table 11.1 hide interesting information about single versus multiple mother-tongue claiming.[9] In table 11.2 we can examine French mother-tongue population and its break-down into single, dual and multiple responses. We note that, in the area of English Canada under study, this population includes a sizable core of single mother-tongue claimants, a smaller but non-negligible group of respondents who claim both French and English as mother tongues and two marginal groups of respondents (those who claim French and a non-official language and those who claim French, English and a non-official language). Table 11.2 also shows that there were fewer respondents who claimed French and English as mother tongues in 1991 than in 1986 and, conversely, more respondents who claimed French as a single mother tongue in 1991 than in 1986. Saskatchewan is the only exception. This latter result is in fact a sign that the linguistic assimilation of francophones has accelerated in that province (this trend will be confirmed below). The decline in the number of respondents who claimed both French and English as mother tongues in 1991 is not due to a sudden shift in patterns of first-language learning, but rather to changes in the definition of mother tongue used by Statistics Canada and in the format of the long census questionnaire distributed to 20 per cent of the Canadian population in 1991. The new long questionnaire regrouped all the questions on language under a single rubric, with the result that respondents were more accurate in their answer to the mother-tongue question and reported several mother tongues less often. In 1986, mother tongue was defined as the first language learned in childhood and still understood but, in 1991, it was defined more narrowly as the first language learned at home in childhood and still understood. This more narrow definition may also have reduced the number of respondents who claimed both French and English, since those respondents who learned French at home and English outside it, in their childhood, could claim only French as their mother tongue in 1991.

Knowledge of French and English among francophones

The Canadian census provides data on the respondent's knowledge of the country's two official languages. Such knowledge is defined as the ability to conduct a conversation in those languages. As crude as this self-report measure may be (i.e., it does not allow us to ascertain levels of proficiency), it does allow us to assess the size of three basic components of the French mother-tongue population: (a) those who can only converse in French (i.e., monolingual or quasi-monolingual individuals); (b) those who can converse in both French and English (i.e., individuals who are at least functionally bilingual); (c) those who can only converse in English (i.e., individuals who have lost active competence in French, or who never acquired such competence – but who, none the less, are included in the French mother-tongue population, since mother tongue is defined as the first language which is still understood). Note also that there are census respondents who acquired French in early childhood (i.e., as their true mother tongue) and who lost passive competence in this language. Because Statistics Canada ties the concept of mother tongue to retention of passive language competence, such individuals are forced to claim English or a non-official language as their mother tongue. Lachapelle (1992) estimates that, if these individuals were included in the French mother-tongue population, the rate of loss of French-language competence outside Quebec would be about 2.5 per cent higher on average.

In table 11.3 we can see that, among the respondents who claim French as a single mother tongue, there are many who can converse in both French and English and few whose skills are in only French *or* English. It can also be seen that there is not much geographical variation in rates of bilingualism and loss of spoken French competence. The rates of French monolingualism, however, evidence a higher level of geographical variation. The highest rates are found in Ontario and Newfoundland and the lowest (almost ten times lower) are observable in British Columbia and Saskatchewan. Note also that, in general, the rates of loss of spoken French competence are higher than the rates of French monolingualism (the difference is particularly evident in the case of British Columbia and Saskatchewan). The only two exceptions to this pattern are (again) Ontario and Newfoundland. It should also be borne in mind that French monolingualism is overwhelmingly concentrated among the youngest French mother-tongue individuals (see Dallaire and Lachapelle, 1990) and that among adolescents and adults one can observe rates of bilingualism which are even higher than the provincial rates presented in table 11.3. The general picture which emerges, then, for those respondents who claim French as a single mother tongue is one of very widespread bilingualism, and only marginal loss of spoken French competence.

Among respondents who report having learned French along with English at home in their early childhood, the proportion who report being unable to communicate in English is nil or minute; however, the proportion of those who

Table 11.3 Distribution of French mother-tongue population by knowledge of official languages (1991: percentages)

	Mother tongue claimed					
	French only			French and English		
	Conversational skills claimed			Conversational skills claimed		
Province	French only	French and English	English only	French only	French and English	English only
Newfoundland	8.3	85.0	6.6	–	83.3	16.6
Prince Edward Island	4.7	88.5	6.7	–	56.2	43.7
Nova Scotia	4.0	91.6	4.3	0.3	75.3	24.3
Ontario	10.1	86.6	3.2	1.1	81.8	17.0
Manitoba	3.7	90.3	5.9	–	74.8	25.1
Saskatchewan	1.8	89.4	8.7	–	75.4	24.5
Alberta	3.1	89.2	7.6	0.5	69.2	30.2
British Columbia	1.5	88.0	10.4	0.8	71.6	27.5
Yukon	2.8	92.5	4.6	–	75.0	25.0
Northwest Territories	4.7	89.4	5.8	–	76.9	22.9
Total	7.9	87.6	4.4	0.8	76.0	23.1

Source: Statistics Canada, 1991 census, *Knowledge of Official Languages*: 20 per cent sample data.

can converse only in English is not negligible (23.1 per cent on average) and consequently there are proportionally fewer bilinguals among this category of respondents. Inability to converse in French may be ascribed to either loss of spoken French competence later in life or to incomplete learning of French from the outset. Overall, the rates of bilingualism do not vary much along the geographical dimension; however, the rates of loss of spoken French competence, or incomplete learning of French, do so to a greater extent. Once again, the lowest rates are found in Ontario and Newfoundland and the highest rates are found in the western provinces. The exceptionally high rate found for Prince Edward Island may be ascribed in part to random fluctuation due to the very small size of the group of respondents who claim both French and English as mother tongues in that province.

To sum up, the statistics on knowledge of French and English among the two groups of French mother-tongue claimants indicate that – in the area of

English Canada under study – there are many pressures and opportunities to learn English outside the home – since the great majority of single mother-tongue claimants report being able to converse in both French and English, and a small proportion of them even report the loss of spoken French competence (i.e., a radical form of subtractive bilingualism). When French is learned alongside English in early childhood, pressure and opportunities to learn English outside the home take a heavier toll on the attainment or retention of spoken French competence, and subtractive bilingualism becomes a much greater possibility. This lends support to the idea that the individuals who report having learned both French and English at home occupy a more peripheral position in the francophone community.

As noted, the way that Statistics Canada defines knowledge of the official languages (ability to converse in them) makes it impossible to distinguish between levels of bilingualism. However, sociolinguistic surveys carried out in specific francophone communities in English Canada (Beniak and Mougeon, 1985; Landry and Allard, 1987; Mougeon and Beniak, 1991) – where the respondents were asked more detailed questions about their linguistic competence – have shown that French mother-tongue bilinguals include at least three sub-groups: (a) French-dominant bilinguals (better speaking skills in French than in English); (b) balanced bilinguals (equal competence in spoken French and spoken English); (c) English-dominant bilinguals (better speaking skills in English than in French). It is therefore reasonable to assume that, in English Canada, the group of bilingual French mother-tongue claimants revealed by the census is also made up of sub-groups who display unequal competence in spoken French. Should Statistics Canada decide to refine its definition of knowledge of official languages, such a hypothesis could be verified and – more crucially – one could arrive at a more accurate measurement of attainment and retention of French-language skills among French Canadians.

Use of French in different domains of society

In this section, I will examine data on the extent to which, in the area of English Canada under study, francophones use French or the majority language – in several domains of society (e.g., in the immediate neighbourhood, at work, in church, at school), or when communicating with different interlocutors (e.g., parents, siblings, children, friends, etc.). These data not only provide us with additional explanations for the very high levels of bilingualism found in the francophone minority communities, but they also allow us to better assess the vitality of these communities. One survey (CROP, 1982) provided detailed data here; however, it had a relatively small respondent sample and so its findings must be taken with some caution.

For the work domain, it was found that although the majority of the respondents reported using English often, or all of the time, 34 per cent of them claimed to use French as often or more often than English. It was also found that proportionally more respondents from the Atlantic provinces than from the western provinces reported using French at work. The respondents from British Columbia hardly ever reported using French in this domain. We have thus an indication that, although English dominates the work world in the eight provinces under study, francophones can, to some extent, find jobs where they can use French.

Of the respondents, 45 per cent reported using French as often or more often than English with neighbours, and there was geographical variation here. Over 70 per cent of the respondents from Prince Edward Island and Nova Scotia reported using French as often or more often than English, only 9 per cent of the respondents from British Columbia. These findings indicate that although francophones in the provinces under study almost always reside in regions where they are clearly outnumbered by anglophones (see Dallaire and Lachapelle, 1990), they can live in localities or neighbourhoods where they represent a substantial proportion of the local population.[10]

Of the respondents, 22 per cent reported using French as often or more often than English in shops. Use of French in this domain was also reported more often by respondents from the Atlantic provinces than by those from the west. The fact that fewer respondents reported using French as often or more often than English while shopping than while at work or when conversing with neighbours suggests that the availability and quality of products may be more important a factor in determining the choice of a particular store than the language abilities of the store personnel. It may also reflect the fact that proportionally fewer French Canadians than English Canadians have jobs or own businesses in the commercial sector.

The CROP survey also asked two questions about language use in two institutions over which francophones can exercise total or significant control – namely, the *Caisses populaires* (Credit Unions which were specifically established to provide banking services to the local French-Canadian population) and the local Catholic church. The proportions of respondents who reported using French as often or more often than English in these two institutions were, respectively, 65 per cent and 71 per cent. Furthermore, there was considerably less geographical variation here. These findings underscore the importance of the existence of separate or community-controlled institutions for the maintenance of French in anglophone Canada.

The recently created French-medium schools are also, of course, institutions which are controlled by francophones. Unfortunately the CROP survey does not provide data on school language use. We have to turn to a nation-wide survey of students enrolled in a sample of secondary and post-secondary French-medium schools (Bernard, 1991a) to find such data which, unfortunately, are not fully comparable to those furnished by the CROP survey (because Bernard breaks his statistics down by regional levels of francophone concentration and not by province). None the less, it is interesting to point out that a majority of the respondents from areas of weak or relatively weak francophone concentration (most of the francophones from the eight provinces under study reside in such areas) report having been taught only or primarily in French at the elementary and secondary levels. A great majority of the respondents also report using French as often or more often than English in school-related activities (i.e., home work and school-book reading). They further report that, in the schools that they have attended, students used French most of the time when communicating with their teachers, but only half of the time when communicating with other students outside the classroom. All in all, then, these findings indicate that the French-medium schools are a major source of exposure to French and of opportunities to use it. The finding that French is used significantly less often in peer-group communication is partially understandable because French-medium schools include students who are dominant in English. It is natural that such students would rather communicate in this language in a situation where they feel less constrained to use French. However, these same French-medium schools also include students who are either dominant in French or who are equally proficient in both English and French. Research by Mougeon and Beniak (1991) and by Heller (1994), in Franco-Ontarian schools located in majority anglophone settings, has shown that this latter group of students is also prone to make frequent use of English in peer-group communication. This suggests that, in English Canada, French-medium schools include students who communicate in English with their peers for reasons that are more related to the high level of sociosymbolic prestige assigned to this language in their community than to less than perfect mastery of oral French.

If we turn to exposure to French via the media, we note that the CROP survey revealed that theatrical plays and television programmes are the main sources. Over 40 per cent of the respondents reported that they go to see French plays as often or more often than English plays, and 30 per cent reported watching

French television as often or more often than English television. The proportions of respondents who reported listening to French radio programmes, reading French newspapers and magazines and going to see French movies as often or more often than English ones were, respectively, 20 per cent, 18 per cent and 5 per cent. Findings from the Bernard survey confirm these patterns – the only difference is that the proportions of respondents who report using the French media as often or more often than the English ones tend to be somewhat lower than in the CROP survey. The findings on theatrical plays are interesting inasmuch as they indicate once again that institutions over which francophones can exercise significant control are associated with higher levels of use of French or exposure to it. The finding that French television programmes are somewhat more popular than French radio ones may be attributed to the fact that radio stations tend to provide a more narrow range of programmes than do television channels. The finding on movies is not surprising, given that this sector of the media is overwhelmingly controlled and dominated by the American film industry. Overall, then, francophones in English Canada do not make frequent use of the French media. The fact that the latter are much less developed and varied than their English counterparts largely accounts for this general trend.

The most important domain for the survival of French in English Canada is probably the home. It is at home that parents pass French on to their children and where they sustain the language maintenance efforts of the French-medium schools by continuing to speak French to their children as they become older.

The Canadian census provides data on language use at home. As with the mother-tongue question, that on home language was modified in 1986 to allow census respondents to report the use of more than one language at home. The data allow us to calculate a rate of French-language retention or loss at home among the French mother-tongue population (recall that mother tongue is defined as the first language learned at home in early childhood). Since loss of French at home involves adoption of another language, some researchers refer to it as a rate of linguistic mobility (e.g., Dallaire and Lachapelle, 1990). Instead of calculating rates of French-language retention for the entire French mother-tongue population, I have (following Castonguay, 1994) focused on the thirty-four–forty-five-year-old respondents. This age cohort is particularly interesting since, as Castonguay points out, it includes respondents at a stage in life where they may have chosen to stop using their mother tongue at home (e.g., as a result of linguistic exogamy, child rearing, etc.). As with my examination of rates of monolingualism and bilingualism, I will deal here only with the two main sub-groups of French mother-tongue respondents – namely, those who report

Table 11.4 French mother-tongue population by home language (35–44-year-old respondents; percentages)

Province	Mother tongue	Language use at home			
		French	English	French and English	Other languages[1]
Newfoundland	French	29.9	68.2	1.8	–
	French and English	–	66.6	–	33.4
Prince Edward Island	French	42.4	55.3	2.2	–
	French and English	–	100	–	–
Nova Scotia	French	46.8	51.3	1.8	–
	French and English	5.3	68.4	21	5.3
Ontario	French	52.1	43.5	3.8	0.5
	French and English	11.6	69.4	18.1	0.8
Manitoba	French	34.8	61.9	3.2	–
	French and English	–	90.1	9.8	–
Saskatchewan	French	17.1	80.1	2.7	–
	French and English	–	67.4	32.6	–
Alberta	French	22.7	73.9	2.9	0.4
	French and English	3.0	86.0	10.9	–
British Columbia	French	19.0	77.5	3.0	0.4
	French and English	1.3	79.5	16.3	2.8
Yukon	French	36.9	58.7	4.3	–
	French and English	–	100	–	–
Northwest Territories	French	38.4	58.4	3.1	–
	French and English	–	71.4	28.5	–

[1] Other languages = French and a non-official language; French, English and a non-official language; English and a non-official language; a non-official language.
Source: Statistics Canada, 1991 census, *Language Retention and Transfer*: 20 per cent sample data.

French as a single mother tongue and those who report both English and French as mother tongues.

Table 11.4 shows that in all but one of the provinces under study (Ontario) and in the Territories, more than half of the respondents who claim French as a single mother tongue have shifted to English as their language of communication at home, either radically (English only) or relatively (English and French). The former kind of shift is much more frequent than the latter. The pattern of geographical variation in rates of English-language shift at home is reminiscent of the patterns found in other societal domains. Note, however, that the rates of shift found for the most western provinces (Saskatchewan, Alberta and British

Columbia) are very high, over 80 per cent. The rates of shift to English found for those respondents who claim both French and English as mother tongues exhibit considerably less geographical variation, but only because they are uniformly high. We saw earlier that simultaneous acquisition of French and English in early childhood was associated with higher rates of loss of French-language competence; the same association obtains with rates of English-language shift at home in the Territories and in all but two of the eight provinces under study (Newfoundland and Saskatchewan).

Generally, then, in the age group under study, the French mother-tongue population evidences a surprisingly low rate of French retention at home (except in Ontario). It is surprising because we saw earlier that, in other domains (e.g., the church, the school, the *caisses populaires*), francophones exhibit relatively high levels of French-language use – hence we would have expected that, in the private domain of the home, French-language use would have been just as high if not higher. A major explanation for this unexpected finding lies in the phenomenon of linguistic exogamy. We know from previous research by Castonguay (1979) that French Canadians who marry outside the francophone community shift massively to English at home; in contrast, where both partners are of French mother tongue, French is generally retained at home. Statistics Canada provides data (1991) on the mother tongue of Canadians who live in a husband and wife relationship and who have children; I was thus able to calculate rates of linguistic exogamy for this component of the thirty-five–forty-four-year-old French mother-tongue population in the provinces and territories under study. The rates are as follows: Newfoundland (77 per cent), Prince Edward Island (53 per cent), Nova Scotia (52 per cent), Ontario (45 per cent), Manitoba (53 per cent), Saskatchewan (71 per cent), Alberta (66 per cent), British Columbia (75 per cent),Yukon (60 per cent) and the Northwest Territories (56 per cent). As can be seen, these rates of linguistic exogamy are very much in line with the rates of shift to English at home displayed in table 11.4, an indication that exogamy continues to play a major role.

The high levels of language shift at home displayed by the thirty-five–forty-four-year-old French mother-tongue population should not make us lose sight of the fact that English language shift at home is not a complete measure of individual linguistic assimilation. Individuals who have shifted to English at home can none the less use French in other domains (e.g., at work, at school, in church, in the neighbourhood, etc.) and remain competent in the language. We should remember, too, that there is only limited loss of oral French proficiency among the French mother-tongue population overall. Still, when a francophone parent married to an anglophone parent shifts to English at home, or when two bilingual francophone parents do likewise, there is a real chance that this will translate into an erosion of French among the subsequent generation. The best evidence that such an erosion is taking place would be information on the mother tongue of the children of francophone parents who shift to English at home. Since Statistics Canada does not provide such detailed cross-tabulations in its publications, we have to rely on other evidence, which will be examined in the next section.

Erosion of the French mother-tongue population

In order to understand the effect that shift to English at home has on the French mother-tongue population, we will: (a) look at the evolution of francophone rates of linguistic reproduction over the last forty years or so; (b) examine data on the mother tongue of the children of French mother-tongue parents.

Castonguay (1994) and other demolinguists use a measure of linguistic reproduction which is based on a comparison of the number of francophones who are between twenty-five and thirty-four years of age with those who are nine years old or younger.[11] This is the measure which was used to calculate the rates of linguistic reproduction which appear in table 11.5 below. Rates which are higher than 1 mean that linguistic reproduction is high enough to ensure group survival; rates lower than 1 mean the contrary. The merit of this measure

Table 11.5 Rates of linguistic reproduction of French mother-tongue respondents in 1961, 1971, 1986 and 1991 and of English-mother tongue respondents in 1991

	French mother tongue				English mother tongue
Province	1961	1971	1986	1991	1991
Newfoundland	0.47	0.91	0.49	0.35	0.83
Prince Edward Island	1.76	1.45	0.51	0.36	0.97
Nova Scotia	1.19	1.01	0.44	0.35	0.79
Ontario	1.34	1.08	0.51	0.36	0.85
Manitoba	1.42	1.13	0.55	0.49	0.96
Saskatchewan	1.17	0.97	0.37	0.36	1.03
Alberta	1.02	0.84	0.34	0.30	0.89
British Columbia	0.41	0.49	0.25	0.22	0.86
Yukon and Northwest Territories	0.46	0.56	0.30	0.34	1.01

Source: The 1961, 1971 and 1986 rates are taken from Castonguay (1994). I have added the rates for 1991. All rates were calculated with the 100 per cent data base.

is that it offers a contemporary picture of linguistic reproduction for each of the census years under consideration. Evidently, this measure of group reproduction should not be confused with the measure of natural reproduction which is the ratio of children per parents or mother in a given group, and which is simply referred to as birth rate in this study.

Table 11.5 shows that, with the exception of Newfoundland – we should remember that the francophone population of this province includes Quebec-born residents – francophone rates of linguistic reproduction have been declining steadily over the last three decades, from levels that were high enough to ensure community survival to levels which are considerably below the survival threshold. A partial explanation for this decrease lies in the evolution of the birth rates of the two linguistic groups. About fifty years ago, the birth rates of francophones were somewhat higher than those of anglophones in the area of English Canada under study. Over the last couple of decades, however, the birth rates of francophones have fallen markedly, to the extent that they are now on a par with those of anglophones (i.e., only fractionally higher or lower; see Dallaire and Lachapelle, 1990). However, if we compare the 1991 francophone and anglophone rates of linguistic reproduction, we see that the latter are about three times higher. Since francophone birth rates are currently on a par with those of anglophones, this suggests that failure to transmit French to young children is also an important cause in the decline of linguistic reproduction levels.

Let us now consider the evidence provided by the statistics on the mother tongue of children of French mother-tongue parents. Statistics Canada provides a cross-tabulation of 1991 census data which allows us to calculate rates of mother-tongue transmission, and to distinguish marriages where both partners are of French mother tongue from linguistically exogamous marriages (francophones married to anglophones).

The data in table 11.6 reveal that the decrease in francophone linguistic reproduction established earlier is to a large extent related to linguistic exogamy. We can see that in all but one of the provinces under study (Ontario) and in the Territories, the rates of transmission of English by linguistically-mixed couples are higher than 80 per cent and that, in contrast, the rates found for the non-mixed couples are considerably lower. Note, however, that in the provinces west of Manitoba and in the Northwest Territories, non-mixed couples also exhibit a non-negligible trend towards transmission of English. The data in table 11.6 also show that the rates of transmission of English by linguistically-mixed couples are somewhat lower when the mother, rather than the father, is francophone (see Castonguay, 1979, for a similar finding in relation to home-language

Table 11.6 Rates of English-language transmission to children by French mother-tongue parents as a function of marriage type and sex of the French mother-tongue parents (percentages).

| | | Mixed marriages | | |
Province	All	French mother-tongue father	French mother-tongue mother	Non mixed marriages
Newfoundland	91.4	94.1	88.0	11.1
Prince Edward Island	91.0	95	87.3	11.7
Nova Scotia	88.9	92.3	85.7	15.1
Ontario	79.8	88.1	70.7	6.4
Manitoba	87.0	90.8	81.5	16.2
Saskatchewan	92.9	95.9	88.9	37.0
Alberta	90.7	94.3	85.3	25.5
British Columbia	89.2	95.7	86.5	29
Yukon	85.7	96.4	73.6	6.2
Northwest Territories	85.0	91.8	78.3	23.3

Source: Statistics Canada, 1991 census, Mother Tongue: 20 per cent sample data.

use). It can also be pointed out that the current rates of transmission of English by linguistically-mixed couples displayed in table 11.6 are quite similar (only fractionally lower) to the rates of English-language shift at home of linguistically-mixed couples, found by Castonguay (1979) in the eight provinces under study. This means that there is a strong link among linguistic exogamy, English language shift at home and transmission of English to young children. However strong the association among the three phenomena is, the role of linguistic exogamy in shift to English and transmission of English can be more aptly characterized as mediating or catalytic than causative, since, as we have just seen, shift to English also takes place in linguistically-homogeneous marriages. In fact, the more one goes back in time, the more English-language shift at home took place primarily within non-mixed couples. Furthermore, it would be wrong to view the decision to switch to English at home, and to transmit English, by linguistically exogamous francophones as the sole result of the need to accommodate unilingual anglophone partners (the proportion of bilinguals among anglophones in English Canada is quite low). It seems reasonable to also assume that there are linguistically exogamous francophones (and linguistically endogamous ones) who base their decision to shift and to pass English on to their children on an assessment of the instrumental value of English and French

246

(at the local or provincial level), of their own socioeconomic position, of their own skills in English and in French, and so on.

We must, finally, discuss the implications of the statistics on linguistic reproduction for the survival of Canada's francophone minorities. If we consider (together) the rates of linguistic reproduction of the twenty-five–thirty-four-year-old francophones, the rates of transmission of English by francophone parents and the rates of linguistic exogamy, we can predict that in three provinces (Saskatchewan, Alberta and British Columbia) the number of French mother-tongue individuals in the youngest age cohorts (i.e., the replacement generation) will soon be very small indeed. Hence, the survival of francophone communities in these provinces will be very much threatened (unless, of course, francophone immigration provides new blood). We have seen that, in English Canada, francophone parents increasingly avail themselves of the right to send their children to French-medium schools – the survival of Canada's francophone minorities is no longer solely dependent on the efforts of parents at home. However, it should be borne in mind that most students who attend French-medium schools in minority francophone communities, and who are not raised in French at home, are dominant in English – i.e., they do not attain first-language fluency in French by the end of secondary school (see Mougeon and Beniak, 1991, 1994).[12] Consequently, in provinces such as Newfoundland, Saskatchewan and British Columbia, if the francophone minorities rely primarily or solely on the French-medium schools to ensure linguistic maintenance, the replacement generations will include individuals who will probably not go on to transmit French to their own children. While it is conceivable that some of these students may later elect to enrol their children in French-medium schools and thus prolong the existence of their community, it is clear that the process of natural linguistic reproduction (i.e., the reproduction of native speakers of Canadian French) will have come to an end.

In the other provinces under study, and in the Territories, French appears to have a better chance of surviving in the short term. English-language shift among the French mother-tongue population is not as advanced, francophone rates of linguistic reproduction are somewhat higher and rates of linguistic exogamy are significantly lower. Of all the francophone minorities who live in these latter regions, Franco-Ontarians appear to have the best chances of survival, both in the short term and the longer term. Franco-Ontarians make up only 5 per cent of Ontario's population, but they number over half a million individuals. They have the lowest rate of linguistic exogamy, the lowest rate of English-language transmission to children by linguistically-mixed and non-mixed couples and, finally, they enjoy the greatest degree of institutional support for French.

CONCLUSION

In a study devoted to language policy for endangered languages, Fishman (1987) points out that linguistic minorities should, above all, concentrate their efforts on buttressing the position of their community's language in what he calls the primary determinants of language transmission (home, neighbourhood, elementary school, work sphere and religious domain). In the area of English Canada under study, the francophone minorities tend to reside in areas where they can communicate in French with their neighbours, they exhibit a high level of French-language maintenance in their churches and, to some extent, they are able to find jobs where they can use French. We have also seen that they have won the right to French-medium schooling (both at the elementary and secondary levels) and that they increasingly support such schools. In the private domain of the home, however, French-language retention is not high and French mother-tongue parents tend not to pass French on to their children. In fact, the generation of francophones currently placing their children in French-medium schools shows high levels of shift to English at home. I have pointed out that most children who attend French-medium schools and who are not raised in French at home do not achieve first-language proficiency in French, and that when they grow older they are unlikely to transmit French to their own children. If the growing support for French-medium schools is the expression of a real interest in the survival of francophone linguistic and cultural heritage, then the minorities need to go one step further, and attempt to reverse the process of English-language shift at home. Obviously, this is easier said than done, since this shift has been going on for decades and is deeply rooted in several powerful socio-political factors (e.g., urbanization, superior utilitarian value of English, negative views of local French and francophones among anglophones, etc.). If the reversal of the shift to English does not start to take place soon, however, then there is a strong chance that – given the current context of government-budget restriction (both at the federal and provincial levels) – the French-medium schools and other forms of government-funded institutional support for French will be curtailed or abolished (as they have been abolished in the past).

If Quebec were to separate from the rest of Canada, this too could have an impact on institutional support for French in anglophone Canada. On the one hand, the backlash against francophones that Quebec secession might cause could also result in the curtailment of institutional support for French. On the other hand, if Quebec remained economically associated with Canada, it is conceivable that anglophone provinces which have strong commercial ties with Quebec (e.g., Ontario) would be willing to strike reciprocal agreements guaranteeing institutional support for the anglophone and francophone minorities. It remains, however, that reversal of shift to English at home is probably the best weapon against a possible roll back of institutional support for French in English Canada and is ultimately the key factor in the survival of French.

Notes
I would like to thank Terry Nadasdi and Charles Castonguay for their useful comments on a preliminary draft of this article and the latter author for his expert guidance on some of the statistics used in this study.

1 There are a few villages which were settled primarily by French people from France in the second half of the 18th and the first half of the 19th centuries (e.g., Cape Saint George on the Port-au-Port Peninsula, southwestern Newfoundland).

2 In the twentieth century some Acadians from New Brunswick and the other Atlantic provinces emigrated to the provinces west of Quebec, notably to Ontario and Alberta. In Saskatchewan there are also localities which were settled by French people from France (e.g., Saint-Brieux, northeast of Saskatoon in Saskatchewan)

3 This last measure was not taken in Ontario, where the provision of Catholic education was guaranteed by the 1867 British North America Act.

4 Thus, every now and then, one can read or hear statements by political leaders or authors from Quebec to the effect that the French Canadian minorities are a lost cause, and statements by political leaders from the French Canadian minorities which deplore the fact that the various governments in Quebec have been pursuing a policy of increased autonomy which may trigger anglophone backlash against the minorities.

5 In 1984, Ontario removed the 'where numbers warrant it' clause from its Education Act and committed itself to offer French-medium schooling to all Franco-Ontarians who wish to avail themselves of the right to such schooling for their children.

6 One such action made it clear that French-medium schooling for the francophone minorities is not to be confused with the French immersion programmes or schools of Canada's anglophone community.

7 Note that west of Quebec it is the average income of francophone men which is lower than that of anglophones. In Ontario and in the western provinces, francophone women are slightly ahead of anglophone women in average income.

8 In contrast, the Quebec government, following the implementation of the French Language Charter, has gathered considerable information on the use of French in provincial private-sector institutions.

9 To arrive at the global statistics presented in table 11.1, the number of dual or triple answers to the mother tongue question were divided by two or three. The statistics

presented in table 11.2 were not so adjusted. This explains why the total figures of table 11.2 are higher than those of table 11.1.

10 One can point out (for instance) that, at the locality level in Ontario, the rate of francophone concentration can be as high as 85 per cent and that, in localities where Franco-Ontarians are outnumbered by anglophones overall, the former may none-theless reside in neighbourhoods where they are strongly concentrated (e.g., in the cities of Ottawa and Welland).

11 The number of twenty-five–thirty-four-year-old respondents is augmented by 2 per cent to compensate for early childhood mortality.

12 It may be also mentioned that the French of these students is removed from the variety of local Canadian French spoken by the older generations (see Mougeon and Beniak, 1991). This is understandable since these students have primarily, or entirely, learned French at school and have confined their use of the language to that setting.

References

Beniak, É. and Mougeon, R. (1985). *Contact des langues et changement linguistique: étude sociolinguistique du français parlé à Welland.* Quebec City: International Centre for Research on Bilingualism.

Bernard, R. (1991a). *Un avenir incertain: comportement linguistique et conscience culturelle des jeunes Canadiens français.* Vol. III. Ottawa: Fédération des jeunes Canadiens français.

(1991b). *Le choc des nombres: dossier statistique sur la francophonie canadienne.* Vol. II. Ottawa: Fédération des jeunes Canadiens français.

Castonguay, C. (1979). Exogamie et anglicisation chez les minorités canadiennes françaises. *Canadian Review of Sociology and Anthropology, 16,* 39–52.

(1994). Évolution récente de l'assimilation linguistique au Canada. In C. Poirier (ed.), *Langue, espace, société: les variétés du français en Amérique du Nord* (pp. 277–312). Quebec City: Les Presses de l'Université Laval.

Churchill, S., Frenette, N. and Quazi, S. (1985). *Éducation et besoins des Franco-Ontariens: le diagnostic d'un système d'éducation, Vol. 1: Problèmes de l'ensemble du système, l'élémentaire et le secondaire.* Toronto: Conseil de l'éducation franco-ontarienne.

CROP. (1982). *Étude des communautés francophones hors Québec, des communautés anglophones au Québec, des francophones au Québec et des anglophones hors Québec.* Ottawa: Secretary of State.

Dallaire, L. and Lachapelle, R. (1990). *Demolinguistic Profiles of the Official Language Minority Communities.* Vols. 1–10. Ottawa: Secretary of State, Promotion of Official Languages Branch.

Fishman, J. (1987). Language spread and language policy for endangered languages. In P. Lowenberg (ed.), *Language Spread and Language Policy: Issues, Implications, and Case Studies* (pp. 1–15). Washington: Georgetown University Press.

Fortier, D. (1994). Official language policies in Canada: a quiet revolution. *International Journal of the Sociology of Language, 105/106,* 69–98.

Hébert, R. (1976). *Rendement académique et langue d'enseignement chez les élèves franco-manitobains.* Rapport final. Saint-Boniface: Centre de recherches du Collège universitaire de Saint-Boniface.

Heller, M. (1994). *Crosswords: Language, Education and Ethnicity in French Ontario.* Berlin: Walter de Gruyter.

Lachapelle. R. (1992). Utilisation des données de recensement dans la mise en œuvre des lois linguistiques. In *Actes du Colloque sur les critères de reconnaissance des organismes municipaux et scolaires et des établissements de santé et des services sociaux* (pp. 5–48). Quebec City: Office de la langue française.

Landry, R. and Allard, R. (1987). Étude du développement bilingue chez les Acadiens des provinces maritimes. In R. Théberge and J. Lafontant (eds.), *Demain, la francophonie en milieu minoritaire* (pp. 63–111). Saint-Boniface: Centre de recherches du Collège universitaire de Saint-Boniface.

Martel, A. (1994). Évolution des services et des droits éducatifs des minorités de langue française du Canada. In C. Poirier (ed.), *Langue, espace, société: les variétés du français en Amérique du Nord* (pp. 239–76). Quebec City: Les Presses de l'Université Laval.

Mougeon, R. and Beniak, É. (1991). *The Linguistic Consequences of Language Contact and Restriction: The Case of French in Ontario, Canada.* Oxford: Oxford University Press.

(1994). Bilingualism, language shift and institutional support for French: the case of the Franco-Ontarians. *International Journal of the Sociology of Language, 105/106,* 99–126.

Porter, J., Porter, M. and Blishen, B. (1982). *Stations and Callings: Making it through the School System.* Toronto: Methuen.

Tymm, W. and Churchill. S. (1987). *Évaluation du programme des langues officielles dans l'enseignement.* Final report. Ottawa: Secretary of State, Program Evaluation Branch.

12 English: Canadian varieties

J. K. Chambers

The sociology of Canadian English (CE), though far from simple, is readily comprehensible. This is perhaps surprising, given the vast territory of Canada, the linguistic complexity of a nation with two official languages, and the diverse ethnicity of the anglophone population. But these complex conditions have mitigating adjuncts. In land mass, Canada occupies more space than any other nation save Russia, but the population of about 27,300,000 (in the 1991 census, according to Statistics Canada, 1992, 1993, the source of all current statistics in this chapter) is relatively compact, largely concentrated in cities or towns, mainly in a long, narrow band within 200 kilometers of the Canada–US border. Of the official languages, English predominates with about 63 per cent speaking English and another 13 per cent admitting to neither official language but who are largely speakers of English as a second language (ESL); outside Quebec, the francophone heartland, about 95 per cent speak English (including ESL). The ethnic diversity of the anglophone population is almost entirely the result of immigrations in this century, but the earlier immigrations – the ones that supplied the formative anglophone influences linguistically and in numerous other ways, as we will see below – were ethnically homogeneous; only now is ethnic diversity beginning to affect our native accents.

STANDARD AND NON-STANDARD IN CANADIAN ENGLISH

My purpose in this chapter is to describe the main historical, social and linguistic events that gave CE its varieties. Of those varieties, the only one I will discuss in any detail is the standard accent – that is, urban, middle-class English as spoken by people who have been urban, middle-class, anglophone Canadians for two generations or more. Even this narrowly defined sub-group admits an exception: the standard accent of St John's, Newfoundland, for reasons we will see below, cannot be included. Otherwise, the standard accent spans the country. It is, as standard accents must be, non-regional. In this book, the accents of

252

St John's and of the numerous other districts, enclaves and outports that differ (slightly or greatly) from the standard one will be dealt with in the geographically-based chapters. Here, I can only describe the general conditions or circumstances that led to their differentness.

To some readers, it may appear that the definition of standard CE in the terms used above is narrow. In one sense it is, but perhaps not in the sense a non-Canadian might anticipate. It is the qualification that people must belong to the second (or later) generation of urban, middle-class anglophones that is most restricting, because the proportion of non-anglophone immigrants in the population is fairly large, and most of them enter the country in the working class. Happily, Canada remains a mobile society – until recently, it was highly mobile – and the offspring of immigrant workers (and, for that matter, non-immigrant workers) have ready access to education, training and employment that can raise them into the middle class. If they so rise, and if in turn their offspring retain the same status, then it is that generation – the worker's middle-class grandchildren – whose speech, by definition, will be standard CE.

The other qualifications – being anglophone and urban for two or more generations – are hardly restricting, because the country is overwhelmingly anglophone and urban. It is also overwhelmingly middle-class. The intersection of Canadians who are urban and anglophone and middle-class makes a majority, though the intersection of Canadians who have been all these things for two or more generations may not.

In all sociopolitical aspects – mobility, preponderance of the middle class, highly active immigration, ethnic diversity of immigrants, and other aspects not relevant here, such as the regionalization of many political initiatives – Canada is a typically New World society, more comparable to other New World societies like the United States and Australia than to any Old World society. Linguistically, colonies and former colonies are famously conservative; they have less regional variety than the mother country and undergo fewer innovations as time goes by. In this respect, Canada represents an extreme case. It is, if anything, more conservative linguistically than the United States and Australia. Canada has nothing comparable to, for instance, the distinctive American dialect regions known as Northern and Southern, or to the American transitional region known as Midland. Instead, standard CE is almost indistinguishable from one end of the country to the other, from Fredericton and Halifax on the Atlantic coast to Vancouver and Victoria on the Pacific coast – a distance of more than 5,000 kilometres. Nor is this an artifact of the way I have defined standard CE, for the accents of second-generation middle-class Americans from, say, Albany,

253

New York, in the Northern dialect region of the United States are easily distinguishable from their counterparts in, say, Richmond, Virginia, in the Southern dialect region. In Canada, the accents of second-generation middle-class anglophones from Halifax or Ottawa or Winnipeg or Edmonton are indistinguishable, even though all those cities are further apart than the American ones. There are no regional standard accents in Canada as there are in the US.

Like Canada, Australia is known for the widespread homogeneity of its urban middle-class speech from Cairns to Sydney and Perth (for example, Bernard, 1981), but, even compared to Australia, Canada is linguistically conservative. Australia's dialect homogeneity covers a vast area, but the distances between its cities are less than the Canadian ones, of course. Moreover, unlike Canada, sociolinguists in Australia have now described another accent that exists alongside General Australian as an urban, sometimes middle-class accent. It is called Broad Australian (see Horvath, 1991), and it too has a claim on standardness because it is not regional, though it is easily distinguished from the accent called General. There is nothing comparable to this in Canadian dialectology – no distinctive second accent alongside standard CE, no such thing as 'Broad Canadian'.

In this respect, then, CE makes a unique pattern even compared to its closest congeners. Among linguistic conservatives, it appears to be the most conservative. Standard CE is heard in cities and towns from sea to sea with virtually no variation. That is not to say that CE lacks variation, only that standard CE does. Canadians who are not (at least) second-generation, middle-class city-dwellers have varied accents. Because of them, our cities resound with numerous accents and dialects, many of them second-language accents, as we will see below. Many rural areas form enclaves of non-standard accents of a very different kind. Those accents are markers of indigenousness, passed on from generation to generation. Accelerating urbanization since mid-century has taken away many speakers but the enclaves themselves are probably just as numerous as they ever were.

Canada thus presents a linguistic situation in which the isoglosses of traditional dialectology do not have any semblance of meaning. It is a situation that is firmly rooted in the history and sociology of the land.

OLD WORLD RIVALRIES IN A NEW WORLD

The English language came to be spoken in Canada because of the English aptitude for warfare. Prior to the era of imperialist exploration, in the late Middle Ages, the English people themselves narrowly escaped becoming colonials dominated by the Normans, and in extricating themselves they inadvertently developed the political and military strengths that would eventually lead to the spread of their language to Canada and, indeed, globally. Protracted wars against Normandy in particular and France in general, especially the Hundred Years' War (1337–1453), led to the development of military prowess and brought about a readiness for aggression. Defending the surrounding seas required the English to develop navigational skills and sea-faring know-how. As a result, when the era of New World exploration dawned following Columbus's discoveries in 1492, the English were well equipped to compete with their European rivals.

In Canada, as in Australia, New Zealand, South Africa, and the United States, British explorers discovered vast land masses sparsely populated by native hunters or subsistence farmers. Exactly the same discoveries were made by the Spanish in Argentina, the Portuguese in Brazil, the Belgians in the Congo, the French in Vietnam, and the Dutch in Indonesia. In all instances, the European imperialists subdued the native peoples either by conquest or treaty. In North America, the native peoples often became allies of their British overlords, joining them in battles against their European rivals, especially the French. For more than two centuries, European foreign policies were dominated by these imperialist struggles. Although the historical record shows the English as world-beaters, fending off the Dutch in South Africa, the Spanish in the southern United States, and the French in Canada, in all these countries conflicts still arise among groups divided along linguistic lines. The descendants are now united not by fealty to the mother countries but by their loyalty to their distinctive regional cultures.

THE ENGLISH LANGUAGE IN CANADA

Newfoundland, the tenth province, was the first part of present-day Canada discovered by English explorers. It had a very different settlement pattern and colonial history from mainland Canada, and consequently it is the most linguistically distinctive region of English-speaking Canada.

Newfoundland was claimed by the English in 1497, just five years after Columbus. This early arrival of English adventurers is the result of proximity: Newfoundland is almost a whole time zone closer to Britain than any other part of Canada. In the sixteenth century, its surrounding waters teemed with codfish, and fishermen from Portugal as well as England rushed to harvest them. The Portuguese and English lived together quite amicably in outports where they established processing plants (Story, 1975). Permanent settlers arrived soon after, mostly from southwestern England, especially from the seafaring regions of Devon, Dorset, Somerset and Hampshire. Then, in the eighteenth century, Irish immigrants began arriving in such great numbers as to dominate many of the populous areas, including the capital, St John's.

Newfoundland joined the Canadian confederation in 1949, after years of autonomy. In the sound of its speech and in its vocabulary, there are many features that distinguish it from mainland Canada. Recent sociolinguistic studies show, however, that the successive post-confederation generations, especially the urban middle-class, are adopting some mainland features. As time passes, the differentness of Newfoundland English will undoubtedly diminish to some extent.

Further south, in the Atlantic region of the present Maritime provinces, the French arrived before the English. They laid claim to the territory in 1534 and established colonies there starting in 1604, in what they called Acadia. A few years later, starting in 1627, the French also established colonies inland on the St Lawrence River in the vicinity of present-day Quebec City and Montreal. By 1760, the colony had about 10,000 settlers.

In the eighteenth century, France's imperial claims in Canada were lost. After suffering defeats to England in two wars, the French were forced to cede both colonies. In 1716, the Treaty of Utrecht resolved Queen Anne's War, and one of its terms made Acadia a British possession. In 1763, England's victory on the Plains of Abraham in Quebec ended the French and Indian War, and in the Treaty of Paris France was forced to surrender its hold on the inland colony. As a direct consequence of these military campaigns, then, the trickle of francophone immigrants from France to Canada, which had never been abundant, came to an end. Belatedly and at first slowly, Canada began receiving anglophone settlers.

THE ROOTS OF CE HOMOGENEITY

In 1867, almost a century after the French and Indian War, five provinces joined in the Canadian Confederation. Nova Scotia, New Brunswick and Prince Edward Island were the original Acadia, Quebec was originally France's inland colony, and Ontario was a large, almost primeval region further inland, with a relatively new population from the two earliest immigrations discussed below. Further expansion into the vast western territory known as Rupert's Land came soon after: Manitoba (1870), Saskatchewan (1905), Alberta (1905) and British Columbia (1871) followed the development of the transcontinental rail link. The subarctic regions, including the northernmost regions of present-day Ontario and Quebec, as well as the Yukon and the Northwest Territories, were incorporated as territories, not provinces, in 1875. As already noted, Newfoundland, including sub-arctic Labrador, joined as the tenth province in 1949.

The centuries of bitter rivalry between imperialist France and England were acted out on Canadian soil when the British deported thousands of Acadians in 1758 because they mistrusted their loyalties in the French and Indian War. The event lives in infamy in Canadian history, but, happily, it was not taken as a precedent after the British took possession of Quebec. On the contrary, the British governors seem to have taken no coercive measures to undermine the francophone presence in Quebec. They were determined, however, to establish and sustain an anglophone majority in the relatively unsettled regions of the west. Their initiatives in doing so inadvertently established the homogeneity of standard CE throughout the land.

The first government-sponsored settlers in the western provinces were white Protestants from southern Ontario. Their demographic profile was not accidental. In 1870, when the Canadian governors first attempted to carry out a land survey of the Red River Valley – the region around present-day Winnipeg, then (as now) the most populous part of Manitoba – they were opposed by the people who were already there. The strongest opposition came from the Métis, French-speaking Catholics of mixed *Québécois* and Algonquian ancestry who comprised about half the population of 12,000. When their protests were ignored, the Métis seized Fort Garry and used its arsenal and ramparts to hold off the Canadian troops, but their rebellion was soon quelled and their leader, Louis Riel, fled the country. He returned in 1885 to lead a second rebellion against Canadian expansion in Saskatchewan. This time, when the rebels were defeated by Canadian troops at Batoche, the Métis capital, Riel was captured. He was imprisoned in Regina, tried for treason, and hanged.

One political initiative undertaken in response to the rebellions was that the governors of Canada made generous land grants to the infantry volunteers and to other Ontarians in order to ensure that the first significant wave of settlers in the prairies would be sympathetic to their plans for expansion. In doing so, they transplanted not only the central Canadian ethos but also, inevitably, the Ontario accent. That accent, in turn, had its roots in the first of four large-scale immigrations that form the basis of the anglophone population of Canada.

THE PEOPLING OF ANGLOPHONE AND FRANCOPHONE CANADA

The four significant waves of immigration took place over slightly less than two centuries. Each wave had linguistic implications – that is, the immigrants influenced the way in which English is spoken in Canada to some extent. In the sections that follow, I discuss the immigrations in turn, with their linguistic implications.

Immigration is only one of the possible strategies by which a nation can expand its population base. In the twentieth century, it has been so dominant as to virtually eclipse the other strategies, which include annexation and positive birthrate. Annexation tends to be unstable, often perilously so, as the dissolutions of multinational conglomerates from the Roman Empire to the Soviet Union show. Positive birth rates have been unfashionable since at least mid-century, when 'zero population growth' became an international rallying cry. The principle of zero growth or, put positively, stable (or negative) birth rates has been promulgated by social scientists for at least 150 years, perhaps most influentially by the economist Thomas Malthus (1776–1834).

Canada, like other New World countries, adopted immigration naturally, as a critically underpopulated nation with an abundance of uncultivated land, unmined natural resources, and, latterly, underdeveloped industry. Indeed, these factors proved so attractive to prospective immigrants that immigration policies had to be made increasingly selective in this century, not only in Canada but also in the United States and Australia. Since mid-century, even some Old World nations such as England and the Netherlands, without the advantages of underpopulation or available land, are robust immigration targets, mainly for former colonials with historical claims to citizenship in the mother country.

The sociocultural contrasts between societies with significant and continuous immigration and those with stable populations, that is, without significant influxes from outside, are sharp. Belief systems in immigrant societies tend to be diffuse because of the importation of diverse creeds, rites, and customs. Ethnicities are more diverse and racial mixing more common. Language is more varied and unstable across generations, with second-language varieties as well as native varieties, different mother tongues in the same household, and loanwords, code-switching and interlanguage. Patriotism is likely to be more diffuse (less focussed) and less fervent.

These contrasts have cultural resonances far beyond the enumerable aspects, and they underlie some of the most fundamental differences between anglophone Canada and francophone Canada. Immigration is a sociopolitical factor in English-speaking Canada almost exclusively. In Quebec, only the city of Montreal receives immigrants at a rate comparable to the major anglophone cities. Elsewhere in Quebec immigration is negligible.

Significantly, this contrast has distinguished the francophone and anglophone regions from the beginning of Canadian history. After 1763, the end of the French and Indian War, Quebec received no further colonists from France.

The population growth from about 10,000 citizens in 1760 to about seven million today includes an influx of about 20,000 anglophones by the end of the eighteenth century, mostly refugees from the American Revolution as described in the next section, but otherwise the growth is almost entirely due to Quebec's birthrate (Lachapelle and Henripin, 1982). Throughout the nineteenth century and the first half of this century, Quebec's birthrate was around 65 per 1,000, one of the highest in the world. It is now around 13 per 1,000, one of the lowest in Canada. Because Quebec's population is decreasing proportionately in Canada, in 1988 the provincial government began paying a cash bonus to mothers with three or more children (Joy, 1992).

THE LOYALIST BASE

The first of the four major immigrations in Canadian history began in 1776 and reached its peak in 1793, when thousands of refugees from the Thirteen Colonies entered Canada. These were the people known in Canadian history as Loyalists, erstwhile citizens of the newly-formed republic of the United States who chose to maintain their allegiance to Britain, and who fled participation in the American Revolution. (For further details on this and the second immigration, see Chambers, 1991.)

There were two main paths of immigration for the Loyalists. One was from the coastal New England States – especially Connecticut and Massachusetts, where the first skirmishes of the Revolution took place in 1776, but also Maine and Rhode Island – into the Canadian province of Nova Scotia. Many of these refugees, perhaps most, bided their time in Halifax or Lunenburg, the main seaports of the province, until they could arrange their passage to England. Some others stayed in Nova Scotia or in nearby New Brunswick and Prince Edward Island, finding work on the land or in towns. Still others took advantage of government offers of generous land grants further inland, along the banks of the St Lawrence River and the north shore of Lake Ontario, and made the trek into the regions of Lower and Upper Canada.

These refugees from New England brought with them a distinctive home dialect. New England speech was then, as it is now, r-less and also has several readily identifiable vowel sounds. Wherever the New England refugees became the founding population of a community, the local speech came to sound like New England English. But this happened only in a very small, highly localized region. The town of Lunenburg itself and some rural areas in Lunenburg County and the Annapolis Valley were marked linguistically as descendants of the New

England dialect region. In this century, with accelerated mobility and urbanization, the distinctive sound of that New England ancestry has receded in these regions but it could still be heard in a few rural enclaves into the 1960s.

Perhaps surprisingly, no trace of the New England accent persevered or survived in the inland regions, although the number of New Englanders who moved inland from Nova Scotia was significant. By the time these Loyalists reached their destinations in the Eastern Townships of Quebec and the Kingston-Belleville-Port Hope region of Ontario, they were greeted by other Loyalists – refugees who had taken the second route into Canada. And though they too were native Americans, they brought with them a very different accent in their English.

These other Loyalists set out principally from the states of Pennsylvania, New Jersey, New York, and Vermont, and they moved by inland routes to entry points along the St Lawrence or on the Niagara River or the Detroit River in the Great Lakes basin. There, they were met by Canadian government officials and sent, with a modest allotment of provisions and tools, to homesteads in the richly forested parklands. In every district where they landed, they formed the first settled population. Native peoples – the Iroquois (Hurons, Tobacco, Oneidas and others) and Algonquians (mainly Delawares, Odawas, Ojibwas) – circulated through the regions harvesting roots or grains and hunting game, and white or mixed-blood trappers (*coureurs de bois*) cut across the regions chasing pelts and hides. But the Loyalists were the first people to fence in parcels of land, clear them of roots and rocks, and raise houses and outbuildings on them. Where their numbers were concentrated, some of them quit farming to provide goods and services for the others: mills for lumber and mills for flour, blacksmithing, slaughterhouses, tanning, spinning and weaving, rooms and meals for travellers, spelling and arithmetic lessons, Sunday sermons. Towns grew up as central places for distributing goods and services, with churches, schools, markets, and stores.

These people became the founding population of inland Canada. Socially, they brought with them the manners and mores of the midland American states where they originated. Linguistically, they brought with them the sounds and syntax of those same middle states on the Atlantic coast. As true pioneers, they had to set standards and develop routines for all their activities, such as land-clearing, crop selection, house construction, religious observance, and educational practices. They set the pattern for country roads and town streets, established norms of communal cooperation (midwifery, health care, sewing bees, barn raising) and set the moral tone of the community.

The founding population of any place exerts many subtle and largely unintentional dictates on those who succeed them. One of the subtlest – and one seldom considered because it is beneath consciousness – is linguistic. The people who come after the founding population, the second or third generation of settlers, may come from far and wide, but their children will speak, under ordinary circumstances, just like the children whose parents arrived before them. So it came to pass in inland Canada – Quebec and especially Ontario, destined to become the economic and political wheelhorse of the nation in the next century – that the sound of the speech was directly descended from midland American.

Because of the Loyalist base of CE, it is a common experience of young Canadians today, whether their ancestry be Scottish, German, or Bangladeshi, to be mistaken for Americans when they go travelling across the globe. To foreigners, unless they have a good ear for small differences, they sound American.

THE BRITISH AND IRISH ARRIVALS AFTER 1812

The second significant wave began around 1815 and reached its peak around 1850. Thousands of immigrants from England, Scotland, and latterly Ireland (because of the Potato Famine of 1845-7) arrived in Canada as a result of systematic, large-scale recruitment by the British governors of the colony. The influx was intended to counteract pro-American sentiments among the settlers.

A generation or so after the Americans won their independence, they began looking covetously at their northern border. In June 1812, the United States declared war on Britain and launched a series of raids on the Canadian borders. The event is known as the War of 1812 but it actually lasted until 1814, when the Treaty of Ghent ended the conflict. The American invasions took place at the very sites where the Loyalists had entered the country. At the time, the British were embroiled in the Napoleonic Wars in Europe and could spare very few troops for defending their North American colony, but the outnumbered defenders eventually beat back the American insurgents. The Canadian victories aroused the first significant show of national pride, and today virtually all the battle sites are marked by monuments.

British intelligence later discovered that the Americans relied on finding widespread sympathy for their cause in Canada. They had expected their invading armies to be swelled by anti-English sympathizers as they marched through the colony. Though the Canadians proved their loyalty, the governors felt uneasy about the broad base of American ancestry in Canada, and they set about diluting it by recruiting British settlers with promises of transport and generous gifts of land.

Between 1830 and 1860, thousands of British emigrants settled in Canada, especially along the north shores of the two Great Lakes, Ontario and Erie, but also inland in regions where the Loyalist presence was sparse, in the river valleys of the Ottawa (Pembroke, Ottawa, Hull), the Otonabee (Peterborough), the Grand (Brantford, Guelph), and the Thames (Chatham, London). In the later years, they were joined by hundreds of Irish immigrants.

Their numbers more than doubled the population of Upper Canada, the second- and third-generation descendants of the Loyalists. Economically, the immigrants broadened the consumer base and brought new initiatives. Politically, they brought debating skills and imperialist powerlust; it is an astounding fact that three of our first five prime ministers were British-born – Macdonald (in office 1867–73 and 1878–91) and Mackenzie (1873–78) were Scots natives, and Bowell (1894–96) English. But linguistically, the long-term influence of the British immigrants was highly restricted. Most of the immigrants settled, naturally, in the towns and villages founded by the Loyalists, and, predictably, their Canadian-born children grew up speaking not like their parents but like their schoolmates and playmates. The essential Loyalist character of CE persisted.

Naturally, CE came to develop its own distinctive features, and the most distinctive one may ultimately be traceable to the broad representation of Scots people in Canada from the earliest times. Many astute listeners distinguish Canadians from other North Americans by the pronunciations of words like *house, couch,* and *about.* Canadians pronounce the diphthong in these words in a singular way, so that outsiders sometimes claim that we are saying, for example, *aboot the hoose* for 'about the house'. Their perception is not phonetically accurate, but what they are noticing is the higher vowel at the onset of the diphthong – phonetically, the vowel is mid, back and unrounded (Chambers, 1989; Joos, 1942). The distinctive diphthong is known among linguists everywhere as Canadian Raising (Chambers, 1973), and it occurs before voiceless consonants but not elsewhere: thus *house* has a different diphthong from *houses* and *how.*

Exactly how this feature originated in Canadian English is uncertain. One certainty is that a similar diphthong occurs very generally in Scots English, not only in words like *south* and *house* but also in words like *aloud* and *foul* (where it never occurs in Canadian speech). Dialect records of elderly, conservative Canadians made in the 1950s reveal some instances of the Scots diphthong in their speech (Thomas, 1991), suggesting that it was commonly heard around the turn of the century. One plausible explanation (from Trudgill, 1984) is that Canadian Raising came about by adapting the Scots vowel into the Canadian sound system.

BRITISH AND IRISH INFLUENCE ON CE

In two accidental senses, the British and Irish accents and dialects of the mid-nineteenth-century influx made a direct and indisputable impression on Canadian speech. First, in relatively isolated regions where the immigrants became the founding population, their speech formed the basis of the local accent. To this day, one can discern the Scots roots of rural speech in Cape Breton, Pictou and Antigonish counties in Nova Scotia, the Ottawa Valley, Peterborough county, the West Lorne district on the north shore of Lake Erie, and other places. Of course, since Newfoundland joined the Confederation, Canada has come to encompass a large and influential enclave where the speech descends from Irish ancestors.

The second impression was made at the opposite pole, so to speak. Though the English immigrants could not impose their speech sounds on their offspring, they often did succeed in imposing norms of propriety and correctness on them, and on the community in general. Many English immigrants frankly promulgated their linguistic superiority to the benighted natives. Thus Susanna Moodie – whose snide and snobbish account of her immigrant experience, *Roughing It in the Bush* (1852), amused the Victorians she left behind in England – described the first Canadian dialect she ever heard, that of the immigration recruiter, by saying he 'had a shocking delivery, a drawling vulgar voice; and he spoke with such a twang that I could not bear to look at him or listen to him. He made such grammatical blunders that my sides ached laughing at him.'

Some English immigrants took it upon themselves to try and change linguistic practices that differed from their own. In almost all cases, the offensive practices were based on American rather than British models. The first schoolteachers in inland Canada were Loyalists or their descendants, and they used the pedagogical tools they were familiar with. Noah Webster's spelling-book, for instance, was almost universally used in Ontario schools (Canniff, 1869). It included such spellings as *color, neighbor, center, meter*, and *connection* instead of *colour, neighbour, centre, metre*, and *connexion*, and it included such pronunciations as *secret*ARY, *ren*AI*ssance, lootenant* (for *lieutenant*), and *zee*, instead of *sec*ret*'ry, renaiss*ANCE, *leftenant*, and *zed*.

One result of the belated intervention on language standards by the English immigrants is the Canadian double standard in many matters of spelling and pronunciation. Wherever British and American practices differ from one another, Canadians usually tolerate both. For instance, many Canadians freely vary their pronunciation of *either* without noticing any discrepancy or raising any controversy, and different regions sometimes maintain different norms, as when, for instance, Ontarians prefer the spellings *colour* and *neighbour* but

Albertans prefer *color* and *neighbor* (Ireland, 1979). These double standards are the linguistic legacy of the first two immigrations in our history.

Another legacy of the mid-nineteenth-century immigration, much less obvious but no less real, was attitudinal. Canadians came to regard British standards as superior, whether or not they were the ones we ourselves practised. This attitude insinuated itself into the Canadian ethos politically as well as linguistically. At many points in our history, being patriotically Canadian has defined itself as being anti-American, either mildly or vitriolically, and in decades past – though probably not since the 1950s – it often also entailed being pro-British. In the first half of this century, many genteel Canadians affected British speech and manners. Canadian-born military officers, diplomats, professors, CBC newscasters, actors, and other members of the self-styled cultural elite made themselves 'Anglo-Canadian'. The poet Irving Layton memorably satirized a professor at Queen's University, a Kingston native who attended Oxford for three years, by saying, 'Now his accent/makes even Englishmen/wince, and feel/unspeakably colonial' (Scott and Smith, 1967, p. 75).

Nowadays, the Anglo-Canadian gentlefolk have become relics, along with the Union Jack, the British Commonwealth, and 'God Save the Queen'. These were the trappings of the Anglo-Saxon hegemony that dominated Canada in the formative decades. That hegemony has been overwhelmed by the ethnically diverse immigrations of this century, and as a result its trappings have become increasingly irrelevant.

CANADIAN ETHNIC DIVERSITY

Though historians speak of two major immigrations in this century, it is almost as useful to think of them as one continuous immigration with a hiatus for the two world wars, when movement was dangerous, and the great depression, when movement was foolhardy.

The third wave began in the 1890s and reached a peak around 1910. It brought in thousands of immigrants from Scotland and Ireland but also many from more diverse European homelands such as Germany, Italy, Scandinavia, and Ukraine, recruited as farmers for the vast wheatlands of the newly-opened Prairie provinces and as workers for the industrializing central cities in Ontario and Montreal. Even when the immigrants came from non-English-speaking countries, most of them became speakers of English (rather than French) as a second language (Joy, 1972; for current evidence, see table 12.1 below).

The fourth wave began in 1946 and reached a peak around 1960, when a highly diverse immigrant population arrived, first, as a result of the post-war

Table 12.1 Retention of immigrant languages at home or transfer to an official language at home by native speakers of immigrant languages in Canada in 1991, by age (based on Statistics Canada, 1993, table 2, pp. 46–47).

Age	Home Language					
	English		French		Immigrant Language	
0–4 (156, 180)	14.48%	(22,615)	1.08%	(1,705)	84.43%	(131,860)
5–9 (147, 885)	27.37	(40,490)	1.87	(2,770)	70.74	(104,625)
10–14 (160,550)	35.67	(57,270)	2.49	(4,000)	61.83	(99,280)
15–19 (185,445)	39.21	(72,710)	2.41	(4,485)	58.37	(108,250)
20–24 (238,540)	42.39	(101,140)	2.08	(4,985)	55.51	(132,415)
25–29 (303,215)	44.81	(135,875)	2.43	(7,380)	52.75	(159,960)
30–34 (331,520)	46.06	(152,700)	2.52	(8,370)	51.4	(170,450)
35–39 (317,155)	46.74	(148,230)	2.49	(7,900)	50.77	(161,025)
40–44 (317,985)	49.16	(156,325)	2.54	(8,090)	48.29	(153,570)
45–49 (256,735)	51.18	(131,400)	2.27	(5,840)	46.54	(119,495)
50–54 (257,405)	51.04	(131,390)	1.82	(4,705)	47.12	(121,310)
55–59 (254,590)	50.86	(129,490)	1.41	(3,605)	47.72	(121,495)
60+ (792,915)	48.8	(387,145)	1.20	(9,550)	49.97	(396,220)
All ages (3,720,120)	44.80%	(1,666,780)	1.97%	(73,385)	53.22%	(1,979,955)

diaspora in Europe – with thousands of Italians, Portuguese, Dutch, Belgians, Greeks, Ukrainians, Poles, Finns and Yugoslavians, among others – and later, even more diversely, from Hungary, Czechoslovakia, Korea, China, Vietnam and the United States, as a result of political unrest.

In the last twenty-five years Canada has received another significant wave of diverse immigrants, often as political refugees from such countries as Pakistan, Chile, Brazil, Cambodia, Somalia and El Salvador, but also from English-speaking countries in the Caribbean and from Hong Kong.

Under ordinary circumstances, the immigrants do their best to conform to the linguistic norms they find in their new surroundings. Their children, of course, grow up speaking just like native Canadians of their age and social stratum, though they are usually bilingual, speaking their parents' language as well as CE. Their children's children – the second-generation Canadians – are often indistinguishable linguistically (and in every other way) from people whose Canadian ancestry is several generations older than their own.

This was certainly the typical pattern in the first half of this century. In the second half, however, the rapid, one-generation accommodation appears to be only one possible pattern taken by immigrants. Under the weight of numbers, immigrant communities in our large cities are relatively stable, having existed for longer than the current generation has lived in them, and they are often self-sustaining. Linguistically, in our cities ESL varieties are almost as commonly heard as standard CE, and the linguistic norms to which the immigrants' offspring unconsciously conform may not be as well-defined as they used to be.

Several years ago I recorded what I took to be an astonishing indicator of our linguistic diversity: based on 1961 census figures, more than one person in six in Ontario, with a population then of about 7.7 million, spoke an immigrant language natively (Chambers, 1979). A generation later, the census figures show that that proportion has increased in Ontario and now holds across the country: in 1991, almost one in three people (32 per cent) in Toronto – population about three million – speak an immigrant language natively, as do 27 per cent in Vancouver, 21 per cent in Winnipeg, and 17 per cent in Montreal (Statistics Canada, 1992).

The impact of this large and constant population is greater than it might otherwise be because Canadian government policies support multiculturalism and, with it, multilingualism in numerous ways. Canadians take some pride in contrasting the 'melting-pot' metaphor used in the United States with our own metaphor of the cultural mosaic (coined by the sociologist Porter in 1965). Anglophone Canada is a linguistic mosaic.

A powerful indicator of both the presence and the persistence of ESL varieties in CE is shown in table 12.1, based on 1991 census figures. The census bureau, in a unique and ingenious response to our multilingual reality, asked respondents to distinguish between their 'mother tongue', the language they spoke first, and their 'home language', the language they use daily with their immediate families in domestic situations. In table 12.1, I have analysed the clear cases. The subjects are all those who claimed a 'non-official' mother tongue, that is, people with mother tongues other than English or French. I omitted those who claimed more than one mother tongue (509,225 out of more than four million) as possibly unclear cases, thus eliminating people who misunderstood 'mother tongue' to mean any language in which they had some fluency as well as those who legitimately spoke two or more languages from birth. This also excludes most of the non-immigrants who speak non-official languages, mainly native peoples, who are likely to be true bilinguals if they retain their ancestral language. The leftmost column in table 12.1 enumerates the Canadians whose mother tongue is an immigrant language by age, and the other columns show how they are distributed in terms of their home languages: either as speakers of English, French, or their mother tongue. Switching their home language to

English or French is a clear marker of acculturation, and retaining their mother tongue a reasonably clear marker of the persistence of ESL (or FSL) varieties. Table 12.1 provides a striking, multifaceted statistical snapshot of the linguistic situation in Canada. For one thing, it dramatically illustrates the negligible effect of immigration on Quebec: fewer than 2 per cent of immigrants adopt French as their home language. Acculturation almost exclusively involves accommodation to English, or resistance to it. For another thing, it shows that the immigrant languages persist as the home language for slightly more than half the immigrants. This retention rate is extremely high, and its pattern is elucidated by the age-grading in the table.

To see the age-grading facts more clearly, the language retention data in table 12.1 are plotted graphically in figure 12.1. The percentage of Canadians whose immigrant mother tongue is also their home language makes a gentle decline through childhood and adolescence. As expected, the pre-school years (0–4), when parents are the main linguistic models, have the highest retention rates, and the influence of peers brings about sharp reductions in the school years, most dramatically in the elementary school years (5–14) and then more gradually in the high school years (15–19). In early adulthood (20–24) the decline slows further and from that point (25 onwards) the line is relatively flat. In cultures in which rapid assimilation of immigrants is the norm, as in the US and probably most other nations, we would expect to see further sharp declines in mother-tongue retention in early adulthood, under the influence of contacts beyond the local community – in colleges, universities, offices and factories – removal from the parental home and the ultimate formation of independent familial ties. Instead, we see stable retention of the immigrant language in the home by about 50 per cent of the population. This is a natural response to a cultural climate that encourages multilingualism by, for instance, posting multilingual notices in hospitals, government bureaus and other public buildings, erecting street signs in the language of the neighbourhood, and subsidizing immigrant-language classes for children. As Pringle (1983) puts it, 'The linguistic aspect of the Canadian mosaic owes something to the fact that the pressure on newcomers to "adjust" has always been less forceful in Canada than in the United States' (pp. 116–17).

This persistence of immigrant languages, with the concomitant persistence of Canadian ESL varieties rather than native CE varieties, has been commonplace since mid-century. In the most densely populated parts of anglophone Canada, people encounter ESL speakers regularly, perhaps daily, and they have done so for two generations or more.

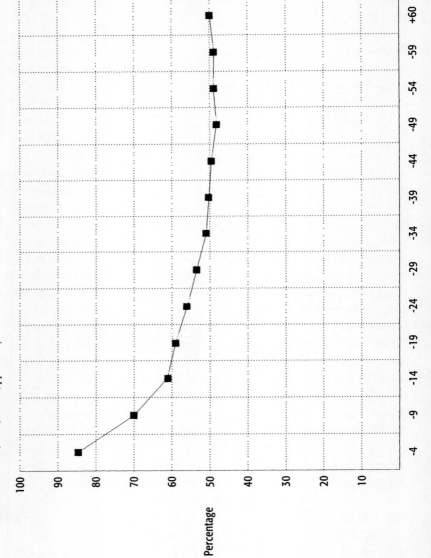

Figure 12.1 Retention of immigrant languages as the home language in Canada in 1991 by age groups (based on Statistics Canada, 1993, table 2, pp. 46–47)

VARIABILITY AND FOCUS IN CE

The attitudes that promote and sustain the Canadian linguistic mosaic probably underlie two results, hitherto unexplained, that have arisen persistently in my sociolinguistic research on CE in the last seventeen years.

First, CE admits more pronunciation and vocabulary variants than other English varieties. Though I first reported this some years ago, it has become glaringly obvious recently in my dialect survey of the Golden Horseshoe (Chambers, 1994), which includes eighty Americans across the Niagara River from the 935 Canadians in the sample. For instance, the Americans invariably pronounce *either* as ['ijðɚ] but the Canadians sometimes say ['ijðɚ], sometimes ['ajðɚ] and sometimes both. In the most extreme example, the subjects were asked what they called the schoolboy prank in which boys hoist another boy up by the back of his underpants; of those who had a word for it, the Americans unanimously called it a *wedgie*, but the Canadians offered dozens of different words, including *wedgie* and various derivatives (37 per cent), *gotchie* and its derivatives (39 per cent), *rooney* (11 per cent), and *snuggy* and its derivatives (5 per cent). Zeller (1993) called this 'linguistic asymmetry' in her survey of dialects on a geographic continuum from Toronto to Milwaukee. She found, for instance, that almost all Americans used *washcloth* (94 per cent) but Canadians used both *washcloth* (50 per cent) and *facecloth* (62 per cent); that all Americans (100 per cent) called post-secondary institutions *college* but Canadians called them *university* (95 per cent) or *college* (44 per cent). The evidence of CE speakers using several variants where Americans use few or none (but not vice-versa) is abundant.

Second, standard CE appears to be a less focussed variety than it was a few decades ago. This conclusion emerged unbidden and unsuspected from two different studies of two variables. The first study involved Canadian Raising. Developmental studies begun in the 1970s (summarized in Chambers, 1989) showed that young Canadians are altering the traditional CE pattern by fronting the vowel in words like *how, houses* and *house* and failing to raise the vowel in *house*. Phonetically, for young Canadians the vowels in *houses* and *house* can be identical (as they never are for their parents) and, furthermore, sound the same as they do in most American accents. Another study involved the use of the word *chesterfield* with what was once the uniquely Canadian meaning, as the generic term for all kinds of long, stuffed seats for two or more people. Since the 1970s, surveys show that young Canadians are much more likely to use the word *couch*, the word that is also used in the northeastern United States, though their parents and grandparents used *chesterfield* (Chambers, 1995).

So two of the most telling Canadianisms are disappearing from CE. My best efforts at establishing a chronology for these two features in CE (Chambers, 1989, 1995) indicate that they have a parallel history. Both became established by the 1920s, and both were in decline by the 1970s. That fifty-year period marks what might be called the peak years of CE as an autonomous dialect, though it does not, of course, mark its start and end points. At the current rate of decline, both Canadian Raising and generic *chesterfield* will persist in CE for some decades into the next century, albeit as markers of old-fashioned and eventually quaint speech. Similarly, both no doubt had growing currency before their use was recorded, pushing their effective origins back toward the beginning of this century. But from about 1920 to 1970, the peak years, they were indisputable markers of standard CE, remarked upon far and wide, known to everyone who ventured into other dialect areas, and mimicked – often badly in the case of Canadian Raising – by anyone who wanted to sound Canadian.

These peak years were also, as I have pointed out elsewhere (1995), the years of rabid Canadian nationalism, fuelled by the international achievements of Canadian troops in World War I and sustained by protectionist trade relations and subsidized local initiatives in commerce and industry. They encompass all the iconic events historians point to as emblems of nationalism: world trade markets in the industrializing 1920s, supra-regional alliances in World War II, the Grey Cup football championship as a week-long national celebration start-ing in 1948, the unfurling of the new national flag in 1965. The autonomy of standard CE appears to have arisen naturally and subconsciously as the medium for this heady nationalistic thrust.

THE FUTURE OF CE

Now that autonomy appears to be declining, and what shall we make of it? Old-style nationalists will inevitably see it as further evidence of disinteg-ration, along with the loss of commercial control in an unprotected economy ('free trade'), the rise of regional politics not only in Quebec but in the prairies and among aboriginal peoples (decentralization), and the internationalization of publishing, performance arts and sport (loss of 'cultural sovereignty'). From another viewpoint, what we are experiencing is not so much disintegration as reformation, and it is not just Canadian but international. Multinational eco-nomies, decentralized governments, and supranational culture heroes are already well entrenched. They appear to be not the wave of the future but of the present.

As a result of the cosmopolitan immigrations in this century, the great majority of Canadians no longer trace their ancestry to either Loyalist or British ancestors. Integrating the diverse peoples forces changes in the social fabric. (They are probably not much different from the ones that came about with the integration of the Scots and English in the 1850s though much greater in number.) Some of those changes are linguistic. Two of the more consequential ones are already becoming clear. First, the persistence of ESL varieties in our cities for almost a century and especially for the last fifty years will break down the homogeneity of CE if some features of those ESL varieties persist in the native varieties of immigrants' children and grandchildren. Though no one has yet studied such persistent features, they clearly exist: because of them, listeners can often identify speakers as having, say, Yiddish ancestry or an Italian background, even though those speakers are themselves native Canadians far removed from their immigrant roots. As the rate of immigration slows in the next century, some of the diversity currently heard as interlanguage will be heard instead as urban CE accents. Second, the continuous immigration for two centuries has introduced countless variants in our speech, and those variants, as we noted earlier, exist hardily, very often in the speech of the same individual. The profusion of variants is not solely the result of this century's immigrations, although much of it is. To take a simple example, in our cosmopolitan cities, many people know and use as many as three different words for meat grilled on a skewer – *brochette* from French, *souvlaki* from Greek, and *shishkebab* from Turkish. Some of the variants we use first came into CE a century and a half ago, as we have seen, when the British immigrants overlaid their usage on the North American words and pronunciations they found when they arrived here. Somehow, against all linguistic odds, both variants survived in many cases, apparently because people preferred to add the other person's word to their vocabularies rather than argue about which one was better. Undoubtedly it was that tolerance that formed the linguistic bedrock of our current rampant variability in CE. In any case, in Canada the way people say things – ['ijðɚ] or ['ajðɚ], tom[ej]to or tom[a]to, *chesterfield* or *couch, wedgie* or *gotchie* or *rooney* – occasionally draws a comment but seldom causes an argument.

Let us hope that that linguistic tolerance is deeply imprinted in our cultural heritage. We will need it sorely in the diversification of CE that lies ahead.

References

Bernard, J. R. (1981). Australian pronunciation. In *The Macquarie Dictionary.* Sydney: Macquarie Library.

Canniff, W. (1869). *The Settlement of Upper Canada.* Toronto: Dudley & Burns.

Chambers, J. K. (1973). Canadian raising. *Canadian Journal of Linguistics, 18,* 113–135.

(1979). Introduction. In *The Languages of Canada* (pp. 1-11). Montreal: Didier.

(1989). Canadian raising: Blocking, fronting, etc. *American Speech, 64,* 75-88.

(1992). Canada. In J. Cheshire (ed.), *English Around the World: Sociolinguistic Perspectives* (pp. 89-107). Cambridge: Cambridge University Press.

(1993). 'Lawless and vulgar innovations': Victorian views of Canadian English. In S. Clarke (ed.), *Focus on Canada* (pp. 1-26). Amsterdam: Benjamins.

(1994). An introduction to dialect topography. *English World-Wide, 15,* 35-53.

(1995). The Canada-U. S. border as a vanishing isogloss: The case of *chesterfield. Journal of English Linguistics, 23,* 155-166.

Horvath, B. M. (1991). Finding a place in Sydney: Migrants and language change. In S. Romaine (ed.), *Language in Australia* (pp. 304-317). Cambridge: Cambridge University Press.

Ireland, R. (1979). Canadian spelling: an empirical and historical survey of selected words. Toronto: York University, PhD Thesis.

Joos, M. (1942). A phonological dilemma in Canadian English. *Language, 18,* 141-144.

Joy, R. (1972). *Languages in Conflict: The Canadian Experience.* Toronto: McClelland & Stewart.

(1992). *Canada's Official Languages: The Progress of Bilingualism.* Toronto: University of Toronto Press.

Lachapelle, R. and Henripin, J. (1982). *The Demolinguistic Situation in Canada: Past Trends and Future Prospects.* Montreal: Institute for Research on Public Policy.

Porter, J. (1965). *The Vertical Mosaic: An Analysis of Power and Social Class in Canada.* Toronto: University of Toronto Press.

Pringle, I. (1983). The concept of dialect and the study of Canadian English. *Queen's Quarterly, 90,* 100-121.

Scott, F. R. and Smith, A. J. M. (eds.) (1967). *The Blasted Pine.* Toronto: Macmillan.

Statistics Canada. (1992). *Mother Tongue/Langue Maternelle.* Ottawa: Minister of Industry, Science and Technology.

(1993). *Language Retention and Transfer.* Ottawa: Minister of Industry, Science and Technology.

Story, G. (1975). Newfoundland dialect: an historical view. In J. K. Chambers (ed.), *Canadian English: Origins and Structures* (pp. 19-24). Toronto: Methuen.

Thomas, E. R. (1991). The origin of Canadian raising in Ontario. *Canadian Journal of Linguistics, 36,* 147-170.

Trudgill, P. (1984). New-dialect formation and the analysis of colonial dialects: the case of Canadian raising. In H. Warkentyne (ed.), *Papers from the Fifth International Conference on Methods in Dialectology* (pp. 35-46). Victoria, BC: University of Victoria.

Zeller, C. (1993). Linguistic symmetries, asymmetries, and border effects within a Canadian/American sample. In S. Clarke (ed.), *Focus on Canada* (pp. 179-199). Amsterdam: Benjamins.

13 **English Quebec**

Gary Caldwell

INTRODUCTION

English Quebec is the product of very particular historical circumstances and, as we must begin somewhere, let us start with the British conquest of 1759, itself a sequel of the geopolitics of Europe of the time. To make a long story short, we now know, thanks to Philip Lawson's recent work (1989) – although Gustave Lanctôt and A. L. Burt maintained as much over a century ago – that the British military and civil administrators, most of whom were Anglo-Irish or Scottish, became of the mind that French Quebec society was worth saving, and that the error of Ireland (the 'Protestant Ascendancy') was to be avoided. The concretization of this consensus was the Quebec Act of 1774, the motivations behind which have been, until the work of Lawson, attributed almost wholly to short-term strategic considerations – of buying 'Canadian' resistance to the rebelling 'Americans'.

As the Parliament of Great Britain had contributed to saving Quebec from 'Anglicization', so French Quebecers helped to save Canada from Americanization. From their efforts, infused with the determination to save their society of the 60,000 'new subjects' of 1774, and the determination of the 60,000 Loyalists who came north shortly afterwards (in 1783) to remain under British institutions, was born the Canadian political project: a conspiracy to conserve societies distinct from America. This project took definitive form in the Confederation of 1867, spurred again by the geopolitical threat represented by the Union victory in the American Civil War and its imposing military establishment – the largest in the world at the time – which resuscitated the colony of Quebec as a province, while providing for English Quebecers within the province.

Another essential dimension of the English historical experience in Quebec, in addition to its relationship to French Quebec, was Protestantism. Despite the very important Irish-Catholic presence early in the first half of the nineteenth century (a presence which later contracted), English Quebec was profoundly

Protestant in religion; and in culture, inasmuch as the British Protestant tradition produced a distinct cultural type. Although the role of the church, or rather the churches, was not as important institutionally as was that of the Roman Catholic Church in French Quebec, religion's influence was – I hazard to advance – as great. One need only to compare the role of Protestantism in the 'Imperialist' movement of the last quarter of the nineteenth century to the role of Catholicism in Henri Bourassa's thought to be struck by the parallel (Lacombe, 1993).

And of course, English Quebec had a particular role in the economy of Quebec. Although at the time of Confederation the majority of English Quebecers were farmers, there crystallized in Montreal a commercial bourgeoisie that was largely Scottish in origin. This bourgeoisie, which extended its activities to finance and industry as capital accumulated, became so socially prominent that it overshadowed the rest of the indigenous English leadership throughout Quebec.

The aristocratic pretensions of this Montreal elite which became more British than the British, and its preoccupation with its connections in England and its financial empire which spanned Canada, probably stunted the emergence of a more indigenous English cultural tradition. Had it not been so prominent, local elites in Quebec City, Trois Rivières, the Eastern Townships and the Gaspé areas might have had more of an impact than they did. By the time of the demise of this Montreal bourgeoisie – the interwar period – other cultural influences were making themselves felt in English Quebec, notably the influence of English-Canadian nationalism and the Jewish milieu of Montreal.

This brief synopsis of some of the salient historical features of English Quebec serves to remind us that being English in Quebec meant more than speaking the English language; it also meant participating in a culture. And it is of course culture – shared experiences, shared values and a shared vision of the world – that creates community. Obviously, the culture in question has changed and evolved since the nineteenth century; but when one speaks of a community one speaks of a reality that is none the less culturally defined.

A CULTURAL DELIMITATION

What then is the contemporary socio-cultural reality which is commonly designated by the term 'anglophone Quebec'? The most appropriate answer is probably that the social reality behind the language indicator has been evolving and, consequently, the only meaningful approach to the question is historical, particularly when one considers that the social identity, 'anglophone', in Quebec has only recently come into existence.

For present purposes we can take 1931 as our baseline, as it is from this year that we have sufficiently detailed census data to observe the evolution of the English-speaking population of Quebec. Before World War II, having English as one's mother tongue and being of British (English, Scottish, Irish or Welsh) ethnic origin were almost coterminous: in fact 95 per cent of the English mother-tongue population of Quebec was of British ethnic origin in 1931.

However, this cultural reality is no longer. Half a century later, British ethnic origin and English mother tongue are no longer synonymous in Quebec, far from it. At the time of the 1986 census there were only 280,000[1] English mother-tongue Quebecers who declared themselves as being of English or British ethnic origin – which means that no more than half of the overall 670,000[2] English mother-tongue population of Quebec considered itself to be of British origin.[3]

The factors contributing to this change – transformation would be a more appropriate term – were several: large scale non-British, non-French immigration which later assimilated to the English-language milieu; anglicization of the Yiddish-speaking Jewish community; the assimilation of some French-Canadians to English; the continuing out-migration of the more anglicized elements of the English-speaking population as well as, more recently, those unable or unwilling to learn French; and last but not least, substantial American immigration. With respect to this last factor, it is instructive to note that in 1986 there were more American-born immigrants (34,750) in Quebec than there were British-born immigrants (31,900).

If, then, the English-speaking population of Quebec can no longer be characterized in terms of British cultural traditions, what *does* characterize it, culturally? Who are, in a cultural sense, the non-'francophones' ('francophone' being operationalized, culturally, as Quebec-born and of French mother tongue) in Quebec? They include everyone not born in Quebec to French-speaking parents – French-Canadians born elsewhere in Canada, Haitians, French from France, francophone Americans and Sephardic Jews, all English mother-tongue Quebecers born in Quebec, most North American Indians and almost all Inuit in Quebec and, of necessity, *all* others born elsewhere in the world. This definition of who is and who is not a Quebec 'francophone' may appear restrictive to some; however, an 'Acadian' born in New Brunswick but living in Quebec would be among the first to insist that there is an important cultural difference between being a francophone from New Brunswick and being a '*Québécois*'!

But who, amongst these non-'francophones', are the 'anglophones' of Quebec? One thing we can be sure of is that not all of the non-'francophones', many of whom *are* in fact francophones in the strict linguistic sense, are 'anglophones'. Two limiting criteria apply: if one was born outside Canada and does not possess English as one's mother-tongue, one is not a Quebec 'anglophone'. The next question is whether we can go further and consider as sufficient each of the two criteria, non-foreign birth and English mother tongue, taken separately. Is, for instance, an American-born resident whose mother tongue is English a Quebec 'anglophone'? Undoubtedly the popular perception, at least of journalists, academics and non-Canadian observers would be 'yes'. However, the American living in contemporary Quebec is not a Quebec 'anglophone' because, not having been socialized to the English/French dynamic in Canada, chances are that he or she has become either a francophile or a francophobe.

I would then eliminate from our 'anglophone' cultural category all those born outside of Canada. As for the second of our residual criteria, English mother tongue, it is necessary on the assumption that one cannot participate fully in a culture without having been socialized to it, the most important part of socialization taking place in the first five years of life. Because it is, by definition, the language first learned, mother tongue is a reasonably valid and reliable indicator of early socialization. Hence we are left with two necessary (as opposed to sufficient) criteria of inclusion in the 'anglophone' category and can delimit English Quebec as being composed of those born in Canada and having as their mother tongue English.

Having now delineated what I consider to be the English population of Quebec (those of English mother tongue and Canadian birth), what do the census data on self-declared ethnic origin of one's ancestors tell us about the cultural traditions involved?

Among the half-million English in Quebec there are at least four major ethnic cultural traditions – English, Scottish, American and Jewish – and three major religious traditions, Protestant, Catholic and Jewish. Of these seven cultural and religious traditions, the two Jewish are almost entirely one and the same. In the 1986 census, 81,000 Quebecers indicated Jewish as their ethnic origin; of these at least fifty thousand are Canadian-born and of English mother tongue. They constitute approximately one-tenth of English Quebec (Anctil and Caldwell, 1983).

As for the British cultural tradition in Quebec, I have already noted those 280,000 Quebecers who gave an English mother-tongue (single) response and who *also* gave a British (Scottish, English, Irish, Welsh and some 'colonial') ethnic-origin (single) response in 1986. If one were to assume that they were all Canadian-born, they represent only one-half of English Quebec. This half certainly includes many Americans who, in Canada, probably give 'English' as ethnic origin.

Other than those of a Jewish or British cultural tradition, we are left with four-tenths of English Quebec composed of people who are, variously, children of western, eastern and southern European immigrants, Caribbean immigrants from former British colonies and Quebecers of Asiatic origin, notably Chinese. Western and eastern Europeans quickly learned English, producing second-generation Canadian-born ethnic Germans, Hungarians, Poles and Ukrainians who are of English mother tongue, and hence English Quebecers. The established Greek and Chinese communities (Helly, 1987) in Quebec are largely English-speaking, and both have been established long enough to have produced substantial English mother-tongue offspring. As for the Italian ethnic population – the largest after the French and British ethnic-origin groups in Quebec – a substantial part of it, particularly those born in the 1960s and 1970s, is of English mother tongue.

Finally, a definite American cultural influence must be noted. Historically this began with Loyalists fleeing the American revolution, and not-so-loyal American immigrants who moved across the border to take up unoccupied land. This was especially the case in the Eastern Townships of Quebec. More recently, the American cultural tradition received a fresh infusion with the arrival of draft-dodgers who came to Canada to avoid the Vietnam War. Indeed, as mentioned earlier, there were more American immigrants living in Quebec in 1986 than there were immigrants born in the United Kingdom, an interesting commentary on the evaporation of traditional British immigration to Quebec.

Hence we have an English Quebec, half of which is of British cultural tradition, one-tenth Jewish, and four-tenths of various European, Asiatic and central Caribbean and American cultural origins.

In terms of religious traditions, the so-called British cultural tradition segment is probably only half Protestant, the consequence of assimilation by intermarriage with Catholics, the presence of a remaining Irish group and American Catholic immigration. All of this means that the so-called WASP (white Anglo-Saxon Protestant) presence in Quebec probably does not exceed 100,000 souls, despite the existence of an English-speaking Protestant denominational school system. These remaining WASPs constitute then, at most, *one-fifth of English Quebec or 1.5 per cent of the total Quebec population.*

Gary Caldwell

Returning, in conclusion, to the delimitation of contemporary English Quebec, in 1986 the total population of Quebec was some 6,732,000. Of these, 574,000 were of English mother tongue and born in Canada. *This then is our English population of Quebec*, representing 86 per cent of the overall English mother-tongue population of 670,000,[4] the other 14 per cent being those born outside of Canada. Of these 574,000 English Quebecers, four-fifths were born in Quebec. To recapitulate, when we speak of English Quebec we are talking of a population of *over half a million* in 1986 (down slightly to 563,000 in 1991) constituting from 8 per cent to 9 per cent of the overall Quebec population.

A DECLINING BUT STABLER POPULATION

What we have called English Quebec is experiencing serious decline, although it is more stable than the overall English mother-tongue population, the size of which is greatly dependent on the level of retention of English mother-tongue immigrants. Hence, the English in Quebec, of whom 80 per cent live in the Montreal area, form a community which is, with reason, fearful for its long-term prospects. It is a population that is aged, more than 11 per cent being sixty-five or older (compared to 8.3 per cent among the French). At the same time, the under twenty-five age group is *also* greater in the English population (40.8 per cent, compared to 38.6 per cent in the French). From the 1960s, there has been a marked decline in fertility in the French population, while English fertility is rising, largely because of changes in social structure (see below).

In the decline of the English-Quebec population there are other demographic forces at work which have been as determining as fertility, or more so: they are migration and assimilation. Historically, at least since Confederation in 1867, there has been a steady stream of out-migration of English Quebecers to destinations elsewhere in Canada and, to a lesser extent, the United States. Indeed, at the turn of the century when the west was being settled, some English townships lost as much as half of their population (Bellavance, 1982). Since World War II, English Quebecers have been ten times more disposed to leave Quebec than French Quebecers (Termote and Gauvreau, 1988).

In fact, between 1966 and 1976 the out-migration rate – measured in terms of mother tongue – to the rest of Canada was thirteen to fourteen times as high for the English as for the French. During the rather exceptional five-year period from 1976 to 1981, which began with the election of the Parti Québécois, the rate was nineteen times as high (Termote and Gauvreau, 1988). Recent out-migration of English mother-tongue Quebecers is much higher for the well educated and the young. During the same 1976 to 1981 five-year period more than *one-quarter* (more than *one-third*, among those aged twenty-five to thirty-four) of all English mother-tongue Quebecers with a university degree left Quebec for another province. Approximately 100,000 and 130,000 English mother-tongue Quebecers, respectively, left Quebec for another province in each of the two five-year periods, 1966 to 1971 and 1976 to 1981 (Baillargeon, 1986).

From 1981 until 1991, out-migration of English Quebecers to elsewhere in Canada slackened considerably, the outflow having fallen from 132,000 during the period 1976 to 1981, to 71,000 and 52,700 in the periods 1981–1986 and 1986–1991, respectively. It remains to be seen what the 1991 to 1996 outflow will have been, the outcome of the 1995 referendum having undoubtedly influenced departures in the seven months in this period between the referendum and the 1996 partial census. A more marked and sustained decline is noticeable in terms of international emigration (Baillargeon, 1986), the outflow having fallen from 70,000 between 1966 and 1971 to 22,000 between 1976 and 1981.

If, however, the out-bound movement of English Quebecers has moderated, the inflow appears to be declining even more rapidly, particularly since 1976: English mother-tongue interprovincial in-migration has fallen from approximately 45,000 per five-year period to 25,000 to 30,000. In terms of international immigration an even more drastic decline is evident: the numbers of English mother-tongue immigrants having arrived in Quebec between 1966 and 1971 and still present in 1971 was 45,000, almost 10,000 a year; whereas, between 1981 and 1986, only 12,000 English mother-tongue immigrants, in total, entered Quebec. Given that a significant number of these recent immigrants would have left by 1986, the level of international immigration into English Quebec (the Quebec-born children of these immigrants would be English Quebecers) has declined to one-fifth of what it was only fifteen years ago.

To sum up with respect to migration: had the loss resulting from inter-provincial migration that prevailed during the decade 1971 to 1981 – a net loss to the population of 3 per cent annually – continued, the situation would be quite desperate, especially given declining international immigration and low English fertility. However, migratory movements, in and out, have become much less important and English fertility shows signs of improvement. The consequences of this are a more stable population – although one still destined to further numerical decline – but a population with fewer 'organic' links with the rest of Canada. In future it is unlikely that one-fifth of English Quebecers will have been born elsewhere in Canada, and fewer will have family networks elsewhere in Canada. Moreover, those born elsewhere in Canada or outside of Canada are among those most likely to leave (Baillargeon, 1986; Caldwell, 1992). Unfortunately, the more educationally qualified are also more likely to leave (Baillargeon, 1986; de Vries, 1985).

The other non-fertility factor that greatly determines the demography of English Quebec is language assimilation. The results of 'language assimilation' in Canada are tallied in terms of 'language shifts': a shift is established by comparing language most used at home ('home language') with mother tongue, information available in the Canadian census since 1971.

The aspect of language shift which has attracted the most attention in Quebec is the outcome of the integration of immigrants whose mother tongue is neither French nor English, the question being whether they shift to English or to French. As the literature on the subject is enormous, I will not attempt here even to distill it. Suffice it to say that one of the purposes of Quebec's language legislation has been to reduce the assimilation of immigrants and francophone Quebecers to English. Immigration has ceased to be as important for English Quebec as a source of demographic recruitment as it once was: more and more immigrants are francophile and there are fewer and fewer immigrants.

The other type of language shift that has a bearing on the English population is that between the English and French populations of Quebec. Although, given our definition of English and French, this shift does not immediately affect the two populations, it does affect their progeny; consequently there is an impact on the next generation. The rate of language shift to French in the English mother-tongue population was, and appears to remain, constant, at a level from four to five times the rate of shift to English in the French population. None the less, given the greater relative size (ten times) of the French mother-tongue population, these rates of shift continue to represent a *net* and growing gain (24,000, 34,000, and 37,000 as of 1971, 1981 and 1986, respectively) to the English population (Castonguay, 1988).

A CONTRACTING MIDDLE CLASS AND LARGE FAMILY NETWORKS IN A SOCIALLY BI-MODAL POPULATION

Over the last quarter century there have been some very substantial changes, as reflected by its social composition, in the human capital of English Quebec. The greater part of these changes is the consequence of selective out-migration. In the twenty-year period 1966 to 1986, 520,000 English mother-tongue Quebecers left Quebec, which – if one adds the 53,000 that left between 1986 and 1991 for other provinces, and an as yet unestimated international emigration in the same period – all adds up to a total of 600,000 in twenty-five years (less than a generation) or the equivalent in numbers of the entire English mother-tongue population presently in Quebec.

Out-migration, as is usually the case, was selective, young people and the most educated and those who had already migrated being the most likely to move. This undoubtedly contributed to one of the most important changes in the social composition of English Quebec, which was the 'hollowing-out' of the middle class, the mid-middle class composed of small business men and women, store owners, contractors, salespersons and junior management people. One consequence of this was to reduce the average income disparity between English and French Quebecers.

As of 1981, English mother-tongue Quebecers were still over-represented in managerial and sales occupations in Quebec – a fact not unrelated to their higher concentration in the Montreal area – but the disparity in average incomes between English and French Quebecers was declining. If one considers average wages and salaries of unilingual French speakers in 1971 as a reference point, earnings of unilingual anglophones were 59 per cent higher in 1970 but only 22 per cent higher in 1980. In the case of bilinguals, in 1970 anglophones enjoyed earnings 23 per cent higher than those of bilingual francophones, a difference that had disappeared by 1980 (Vaillancourt, 1988). Other studies, notably those of Béland (1987) have shown that social mobility is now equal in both language groups.

Between 1980 and 1990 there was an overall occupational restructuring of the Quebec economy, reflected in an increase of white-collar jobs and a decline in blue-collar jobs. However, the evolving occupational distributions reveal that the English and French mother-tongue working populations did not participate to the same extent in this change. Although the proportion of English workers who are professionals or semi-professionals increased more than in the French working population (17 per cent as opposed to 15 per cent), the increase in the proportion of managerial, administrative and other white-collar jobs was much less than in the French population. In the managerial and administrative category the French increase was almost twice the English increase (92 per cent as opposed to 50 per cent); the proportion of French workers in other white-collar jobs increased by 25 per cent, while the proportion of English Quebecers in such jobs actually declined marginally (–1 per cent)!

We have, in the relative lagging of the English workforce in the proportion of white-collar jobs other than professional or semi-professional, a manifestation of this 'hollowing-out' of the middle class, a phenomenon even more marked outside of the Montreal metropolitan area. In fact, the English population of

Quebec appears to be becoming bi-modal in terms of occupational status and income: a small well-educated professional upper sector holding well-paying secure jobs and a rather socially isolated and less mobile, poorly educated and occupationally insecure lower one.

This bi-modalization of the English population subsequent to the hollowing-out of the middle class has had consequences other than the relative reduction of average English incomes. A middle class plays a very important role in terms of sustaining community associations and activities: middle-class members have the cultural, financial and psychological resources to fill such roles as scout leader, hockey coach or Sunday-school teacher. These roles are being left unfilled in English Quebec and the resilience of English civil society has suffered accordingly. Yet, the erosion of English civil society is only one factor contributing to the isolation of the lower sector. There is also their effective linguistic minority status which compounds their social isolation, this last intensified by the rarity of middle-class children in their schools. Social class and linguistic isolation also render the lower sector particularly vulnerable to mobilization by the neo-liberal 'rights' rhetoric.

EDUCATION AND THE TECHNOCRACY

Given the institutional fragmentation of English churches, a low level of participation in the provincial state and the distance of the federal state (staffed, in Quebec, almost exclusively by French Quebecers) and the rarity of English dominance in municipal government in recent times, the separate English educational facilities have become – over the last half century – the pivotal institution of English civil society. School provided a common socialization experience and a common focus for community activities for all, with the exception of English Catholics in the Montreal and Quebec City areas. Outside of Montreal, English Catholic children have, since the 1970s, commonly participated in English Protestant schools under 'inter-board' agreements. In Montreal and Quebec City, where English Catholics are the most numerous – almost half of the English population – they go to English-language schools administered by the French-Catholic boards, an arrangement which contributes further to their social isolation.

For reasons having to do with a low fertility existing since the 1930s, the heavy out-migration of young adults in the late 1960s and the 1970s, the obligation of immigrants to send their children to French-language schools and, last but not least, the almost universal practice whereby the English elite send their children to French elementary schools, the English school system has been contracting drastically. Enrolment has decreased by 57 per cent in the last twenty years (Ministère de l'Éducation, 1992) from a 1972 level of one-quarter million students in public and private English elementary and secondary schools. Between 1976 and 1986 the decline was particularly abrupt, enrolment being one-third lower in 1981 than it was five years earlier. All regions, without exception, have thus seen their enrolments halved over two decades!

However, this very drastic contraction is about to be followed, according to Ministry of Education predictions, by a levelling-off, even an increase, in the period 1990 to 1995. If this materializes, we would have a confirmation of our assessment that the English population in about to become much stabler, not only in terms of its composition but also in terms of numbers – after having experienced, none the less, a very disconcerting shakedown.

The English elite's practice of sending their children to French elementary schools, so that they will be able to function well in French, has been noted. Now in Montreal, over a fifth of all children eligible to attend English schools are in fact in French elementary schools. Elsewhere, outside of the major concentration of the English population, parents often send their children to a French school because it is the neighbourhood school. The unheralded consequence of this has been an immense cultural deprivation for the English school population: these absent young middle-class people, as well as their parents, were the cultural leaven of the English schools.

In the English educational system – and the word 'system' is a little strong, since it is rather a constellation of institutions with varying statuses – there are of course community colleges (CEGEPs) and universities. The English-language community colleges (five public and two private) were created in conformity with the CEGEP model, whereby they are defined as regional public institutions. In fact the CEGEPs of Quebec have become state colleges, carefully controlled by the Ministry of Education working in close collaboration with local administrators. The English colleges being thus part of the provincial technocracy are not, with the exception perhaps of Heritage in Hull, rooted in local or regional Anglo-Quebec communities. In fact, the college administrators – as opposed to their boards – are, as long as they remain deferential toward Quebec authorities, free to indulge in bureaucratic empires.

NEW CONTACTS WITH THE FRENCH: FRENCH SCHOOLS, BILINGUALISM AND INTERMARRIAGE

In 1971, 37 per cent of the English mother-tongue population declared itself to be bilingual, a proportion that had risen to 53 per cent in 1981 (Termote and Gauvreau, 1988). It appears to have remained at that level, the 1986 census figures showing a proportion of 54 per cent (single mother-tongue responses: Dallaire and Lachapelle, 1990). Incidentally, this increase from 37 per cent to 54 per cent does not necessarily mean that a further 17 per cent of English Quebecers learned French. What it reflects is that while English youngsters were indeed learning French, either at home or in French-language schools, more non-bilinguals than bilinguals left Quebec in the twenty intervening years; or, that more had one French parent. Still, half of contemporary English Quebec now considers itself bilingual.

With regard to the learning of the French language, French immersion classes in Protestant school boards are undoubtedly a factor. Over half of all students in English schools experience immersion education (Quebec, 1992). A further 20 per cent are actually in French elementary schools, which ensures access to the French cultural code, by no means the case with immersion language training.

An indicator of social interaction that is perhaps the most revealing is inter-marriage. Bilingualism facilitates intermarriage, and of course intermarriage often (but not necessarily) produces bilingual children. As it happens, the degree of intermarriage (or exogamy) in English Quebec is growing rapidly. At the time of the 1971 census, twenty years ago, the exogamy rates of English mother-tongue Quebecers were 17 per cent and 18 per cent for men and women, respectively; thus, endogamy rates were 82 per cent and 83 per cent. By 1986, fifteen years later, the endogamy rates for the same population were 70 per cent and 71 per cent (Dallaire and Lachapelle, 1990). Undoubtedly, the out-migration that took place in the intervening period was selective in this regard, there having been – in all probability – an over-representation of English endogamous mar-riages among out-migrants. Incidentally, the overwhelming majority of English exogamous marriages in Quebec is with French Quebecers, as opposed to marriage with those of other mother tongues.

Increasing bilingualism and intermarriage are, I suggest, factors that are not only interdependent, but compound one another; they are also a consequence of the minoritization of the English population. The proof of this is that the rates are higher in the regions where the ratio of English to French is much lower. Hence more bilingualism, more intermarriage and further minoritization of the English population all interact in a dynamic which leads to further bilingualism and more intermarriage.

THE CULTURE ISSUE

English Quebec, until very recently, shared the complacency of dominant societies with regard to their culture. The positive face of their complacency was, historically, a willingness to contribute generously to the arts. All of the major arts institutions in Montreal were literally created by the Anglo-Protestant elite of Montreal. During a century, from the middle of the nineteenth to the middle of the twentieth, this elite took upon itself to encourage and patronize the 'arts' in Montreal. Moreover this cultural (in the restricted sense of the term) vocation was not limited to the English-language milieu: it was, for example, the last representatives of this elite who were responsible for the rehabilitation of '*Vieux-Montréal*'. However, as population size declines, school populations contract and French becomes the language of public discourse in Quebec, this complacency has been replaced by a real fear that English culture in Quebec has become problematic. Upon the heels of this realization has come a concern to take action to ensure cultural survival.

A striking institutional manifestation of the concern with cultural survival is the Chambers Report (Quebec, Ministère de l'Éducation, 1992). In the very first paragraph, concern is expressed about the need for the definition of 'cultural values', as well as with 'cultural, social and economic identity'. In the second paragraph the report talks of the distinct character of (English Quebec) aspirations, traditions and potential. And in the third paragraph it is affirmed that one of the missions of English education is to see that students achieve a knowledge of their English-language 'cultural heritages [*sic*]'. The educational system is seen as having a responsibility to transmit, in addition to the English language, values and culture. It is affirmed that 'English education retains the character of its separate traditions: an English-Scottish-Protestant core of beliefs, cultures and leadership to which were added Jewish and other non-Catholic elements, and an Irish-Italian-Catholic core which until recently remained distinct' (p. 3).

Indeed, this conscience-taking leads directly to the need for clarity or definition of the culture at stake: 'The English-speaking community has a well developed set of institutions. It needs to define its own cultural and educational goals as well as the degree of independence and self-determination it wishes to pursue in its education system' (p. 5). And indeed English educational facilities are seen as being able to contribute, if there is strategic planning, to the survival of the community. Witness the following 'strategic' – both in content and intention – premise: 'If English education is to survive in Quebec and make its proper contribution to Quebec education and society, it must develop a system of strategic planning. There needs to be coordination and cooperation among all the elements of the English-language education system and the broader community that it serves' (p. 14).

285

English-Quebec culture is indeed a culture under siege: largely ignored by a Quebec State preoccupied by French culture (Arpin, 1991) and doubtful of the existence of English-Canadian culture, let alone English-Quebec culture; belittled by official Ottawa which, when it is not mesmerized by Quebec French culture, tends to see English-Quebec culture as a dependent colony of the English-Canadian cultural establishment; but, above all, besieged by American popular culture.

This massive American influence is growing. Young English Quebecers are increasing their cultural dependence on television – a cultural medium which is overwhelmingly American. Quite recently this has begun making inroads among the young *French* of Montreal, dislodging the previously pre-eminent French programming: in 1978 over 70 per cent of those attending French-language schools watched primarily French television, whereas the percentage was under 60 per cent in 1990 (Locher, 1992). Even the newly acquired role of Quebec-produced (as most French television programming is produced in Quebec) television as a new cultural reference for French Quebec appears to be under siege, at least in the case of the minds of young pople. None the less, French Quebec has succeeded in creating a new cultural reference for the French-speaking population in general, and it has been done via television.

A question that has occurred to several is: would it not be possible for English Quebec, with an English-language viewing audience of over half a million, to create new cultural references with television, as French Quebec has done? Certainly the material base in terms of equipment, talent and a potential audience is there. But the issue is perhaps whether the members of this English-speaking audience share enough that is particular to them, on the basis of which they could be interested in local Montreal-produced television.

Turning to the contemporary 'arts' cultural scene, there is one milieu that has shown signs of a certain ferment. Montreal has attracted native English Quebecers, a host of English Canadians and English speakers from elsewhere in the world to an arts scene that revolves around theatre, literature and publishing. Those who participate in these English arts activities in Montreal have demonstrated a creativity and vitality that belies the general depression prevailing in the English population. Most of this activity takes place outside of mainstream institutions and is rather marginal financially. Yet it has generated enough excitement and achieved enough to sustain, spiritually, an artistic community.

A factor exercising a brake on the vitality of the Anglo-Quebec arts scene is the cultural isolation of the English-Quebec Catholic population from the rest of

English-Quebec cultural activity. This social distance, no doubt a consequence of the fact that English Catholics and Protestants did not go to the same schools, remains intriguing. There is also, as remarked above, the increasing socio-cultural isolation of the 'lower mode' of the English population, as manifested particularly in a retreat to the domestic sphere. Contributing also to the fragmentation of cultural resources is the American cultural alignment of the Jewish intelligentsia: for example, Jewish social scientists participate in American professional associations and are largely absent from the parallel Canadian ones. Finally, as noted, English-Quebec cultural activities have been somewhat overlooked by provincial arts bureaucrats – but this is perhaps a blessing in disguise.

FROM ENGLISH-CANADIAN NATIONALISM TO NEO-LIBERALISM

English Quebecers were, until the 1960s, adherents to what may fairly be called English-Canadian nationalism. This nationalism was the product of three-quarters of a century of collective groping by English Canadians to find their own way, politically, culturally, and intellectually. It took forms as varied as the creation of a separate Canadian command in the British forces that fought in World War I, the Statute of Westminster in 1931 that gave Canada control of its foreign policy, the emergence of Canadian art forms such as that of the celebrated Group of Seven, the creation of Canadian international industrial enterprises such as Massey-Harris and 'national' transportation systems such as the Canadian National and Canadian Pacific railway networks.

Out of these earlier achievments grew more mature efforts such as a separate Canadian Army during World War II, Canadian aircraft manufacture and Canadian national institutions such as the Canadian Broadcasting Corporation and the National Film Board. Almost all of these achievements were English-Canadian and they drew, to a large extent, upon British inspiration and expertise. English-Canadian, as opposed to a more contemporary supposedly pan-Canadian, nationalism can be characterized as being Anglo-Saxon, Protestant and British in inspiration – traits which were not incompatible with a determined commitment to Canadian dignity and autonomy and a Canadian way of doing things. Indeed, the Canadian way was seen as being more democratic and more egalitarian than the English way. Participation of a contingent of Canadian volunteers in the republican cause in the Spanish Civil War is an instance of this, as is the Canadian decision in mid-century not to accord or recognize British aristocratic titles or honours. However, fundamental elements of British culture were retained: parliamentary government, the monarchy and

Protestantism remained an integral part of the political and intellectual culture of educated English Canadians until the 1950s.

Since then a revolution has occurred in English Canadian political culture, a revolution because of the speed with which it took place and the total displacement it effected. Price (1980) has shown that 1963 was the last year in which, in letters to the editors of the *Montreal Star* and *The Gazette,* references to the British monarchy were prevalent. It was the same year that Prime Minister Diefenbaker presented his Bill of Rights to the Canadia.. Parliament.

It was in the middle 1960s that Canada embarked on the neo-liberal revolution of its political culture. The civil rights movement in the United States captured the imagination of a 'cultural generation' while, at the same time, a generation of social science university professors infatuated with historical materialism (Marxism) relegated British history to the moral dustbin of 'imperialism'. By the 1970s 'God Save the Queen', the Red Ensign and the 'Royal' in Canadian Navy and Air Force had been expurgated from Canadian public ritual, and the public domain purged of all traces of 'archaic' British symbolism.

In the early 1980s, notably with the repatriation of the British North America Act, the entrenchment of a charter of rights and freedoms – all of this against the symbolic background of the new Canadian flag – consecrated the accession of Canadians to the doctrine of neo-liberalism: rights replaced justice, and a written constitution the unwritten constitution. Lawyers fighting for rights before judges became the new social champions and deputies representing their constituents in parliaments lost their lustre. Before long, American legal precedents began replacing British and Canadian ones, and courts became the ultimate arbitrators of constitutional issues. Canadians had liberated themselves from their past, and part of this past was that of being a hyphenated Canadian, English or French. Now Canadians were to be part of one nation (rather than a country) of individuals possessing individual rights: there would be no discrimination based on religion, race or national origin; everyone would be an equal citizen with the same rights. This neo-liberalism, and the civic religion it engenders, is now the political culture of Canada, and the elites of English Quebec, particularly the Montreal leadership, have embraced it. In the regions of Quebec where there are still English-Quebec communities – the Gaspé, the Eastern Townships, the Ottawa Valley and the Quebec City area – the old political culture has not been so effectively supplanted. There are still Protestant schools in the Eastern Townships in which one finds the Red Ensign displayed, portraits of the Queen and citations from Lord Nelson.

At the moment, however, the new neo-liberal culture holds sway in
Montreal and it has largely mobilized the Jewish community, which does
not have the same historical consciousness as those who were socialized to
English-Canadian nationalism. Mordecai Richler's *Oh Canada! Oh Quebec!*
(1992) is revealing in this respect: it never occurred to him that appealing to the
American public over the heads of Canadians (the thesis of the book was first
published in the *New Yorker*) was, given Canadian history, somehow disloyal.
In the regions, although the old culture has solid but aging roots, the thinning-
out of the middle class, those able to explicitly state their position, has left the
population – particularly the economically insecure and socially isolated 'lower
mode' – very vulnerable to the 'rights' rhetoric of the new political culture.

CONCLUSION

What is likely to become of English Quebec? One might well smile at
the futility and the pretentiousness of such a question, smile because such things
as the futures of cultural sub-groups are so complex that the likelihood of fore-
telling outcomes is minimal. None the less, the question is of more than academic interest for Quebecers and Canadians, and hence worth considering, on
the off chance that this might be of some use to some of the actors involved in
the outcome. Or, to cite an adage of rural Protestant culture: better to have
tried and failed than to have done nothing at all.

One thing that seems reasonably certain – barring separation – is that in the
present, and for the immediate future, the population base of English Quebec is
stabilizing. Furthermore, this stabilization will be more substantial in the rural
non-metropolitan areas than in the Montreal region where, admittedly, over
four-fifths of the English-Quebec population lives. Moreover, there will be less
turnover within the population; and again, this will also be truer for the rural
than for the urban population. In fact, the islands of rural English Quebec are
on the threshold of being able to reproduce themselves while at the same time
becoming more indigenous or locally based. This is the good news.

The bad news is that there are very real and consequential pressures bearing
on this stabilized and more fertile population, pressures which render its long-
term future quite problematic. One of these is increasing minoritization. As a
group becomes an increasingly small proportion of the overall population while
remaining fragmented territorially, assimilation pressures – notably via the
social mechanisms of bilingualism and intermarriage – increase.

Obviously this is what has happened to French-Canadians outside of
Quebec, where assimilation has taken place at a rate of about 50 per cent in

the current generation. At something over 5 per cent, the English-Quebec assimilation loss rate seems middling in comparison; yet it has been increasing and will increase further, particularly outside of Montreal.

Further pressure arises from increasing social isolation, which produces cultural and linguistic barriers making the dominant local economy and public institutions less accessible and, in the process, reducing economic and social mobility. As well as isolation from the local French society, those in the lower mode of the truncated English Quebec class structure suffer isolation from the mainstream of their own society.

Such pressures do not lead to confidence in the future of the community; members lose faith in the ability of the community to project itself into the future (the 'future reach' of Alfred Schultz: Rose, 1985). Such incipient doubt, or simply the non-existence of confidence in the community's capacity to be there in the next generation, leads – in modern industrial society – to out-migration, or to encouraging one's children to leave.

Loss of confidence leaves the community vulnerable, in the present socio-political context, to the corrosive effect of the neo-liberal message which is spilling over from Ontario and western Canada and being relayed by the Montreal leadership. The rights rhetoric (Morton, 1993) of the neo-liberal political culture provides an easy rationale for the 'victimization' perception associated with the 'whining' posture of English-Quebec self-representation (Legault, 1992) – understandable in a community that has lost faith in its future and is cut off from its past.

Notes
This chapter is an abridged rendering of a book entitled *La question du Québec anglais*, Institut Québécois de Recherche sur la Culture, Québec, 1994, Presses de l'Université Laval. Sources not given in this text can be found in the full French text.

1 Single responses only, a total of 280, 295 respondents in the categories English, Irish, Scottish, Welsh, etc. who were also English mother-tongue single-response respondents.

2 Single responses plus one half of double 'English + French' responses.

3 One must also allow for the fact that since the introduction of self-enumeration in 1971 there has been a definite tendency for assimilated persons of non-British/non-French ethnic origins to give 'English' as their ethnic origin (Castonguay, 1977). Furthermore, in 1986 the origin question referred not only to *ancestral* ethnic origin but also to *present* ethnic origin, widening further the comprehensiveness of the category 'English'.

4 Paillé (1989), with a more generous interpretation of multiple responses, comes up with an English mother-tongue population of 696,000 in 1986.

References

Anctil, P. and Caldwell, G. (1983). *Juifs et réalités juives au Québec*. Quebec: Institut québécois de recherche sur la culture.

Arpin, R. (1991). *Une politique de la culture et des arts* (2nd edn). Quebec: Gouvernement du Québec.

Baillargeon, M. (1986). L'évolution et les caractéristiques linguistiques des échanges migratoires interprovinciaux et internationaux du Québec depuis 1971. In *L'état du français au Québec. Bilan et perspective* (tome 1). Quebec: Conseil de la langue française.

Béland, F. (1987). A comparison of the mobility structures of francophones and anglo-phones in Quebec: 1954, 1964, 1974. *Canadian Review of Sociology and Anthropology, 24*(2), 232–251.

Bellavance, M. (1982). *A Village in Transition: Compton, Québec 1880–1920*. Ottawa: Parks Canada.

Caldwell, G. (1992). *The Whereabouts of Young English Townshippers: Out-migration 1981–1991*. Sherbrooke: The Townshippers' Association.

Castonguay, C. (1977). La mobilité ethnique au Canada. *Recherches Sociographiques, 18*(3), 431–451.

———. (1988). Virage démographique et Québec français. *Cahiers québécois de démographie, 17*(1), 49–61.

Dallaire, L. and Lachapelle, R. (1990). *Demolinguistic profiles of minority-language communities. Demolinguistic profiles, Quebec*. Ottawa: Secretary of State.

De Vries, J. (1985). Interprovincial Migrants and Their Language Characteristics, 1976–1982. (Research Paper No. 18). Ottawa: Statistics Canada.

Gauthier, H. (1988). *Les migrations au Québec: aspects régionaux*. Quebec: Les Publications du Québec.

Helly, D. (1987). *Les Chinois à Montréal 1877–1951*. Quebec: Institut québécois de recherche sur la culture.

Lacombe, S. (1993). Race et liberté: l'individualisme politique au Canada, 1896–1920. Doctoral thesis. Paris: Université de Paris V.

Lawson, P. (1989). *The Imperial Challenge: Quebec and Britain in the Age of the American Revolution*. Montreal and Kingston: McGill-Queen's University Press.

Legault, J. (1992). *L'Anglo Québec: L'invention d'une minorité*. Montreal: Boréal Express.

Locher, U. (1992). La force d'attraction du français et les attitudes et les comportements des jeunes. Communication prepared for the Conseil de la langue française.

Morton, F. L. (1993). The politics of rights. *The Literary Review of Canada, 2*(5).

Paillé, M. (1989). *Nouvelles tendances démolinguistiques dans l'Île de Montréal: 1981–1996*. Notes et documents no. 71. Quebec: Conseil de la langue française.

Price, K. (1980). The Social Construction of Ethnicity. Doctoral thesis, Toronto, York University.

Québec (Ministère de l'Éducation) (1992). Task Force on English-Speaking Education ('Chambers Report'). Quebec.

Richler, M. (1992). *Oh Canada! Oh Quebec! Requiem for a Divided Country.* Toronto: Penguin Books.

Rose, C. (1985). The concept of reach and the Anglophone minority in Quebec. *Canadian Ethnic Studies, 17*(3), 1–15.

Termote, M. and Gauvreau, D. (1988). *La situation démolinguistique au Québec, évolution passée et prospective.* Dossier no. 30. Quebec: Conseil de la langue française.

Vaillancourt, F. (1988). *Langue et disparité de statut économique au Québec, 1970–1980.* Quebec: Conseil de la langue française.

14 The teaching of international languages

Jim Cummins

When Canada launched a new era of social policy with its 1971 proclamation of multiculturalism within a bilingual framework of two official languages (English and French), it did not take long for the inherent ambiguities and tensions to erupt into public debate. In particular, Quebec was unhappy with the multicultural policy, which was interpreted by some as a federal plot to reduce the status of Quebec culture to one among the many others that comprised what federal politicians were fond of calling the 'Canadian mosaic'. It was also unclear what status languages other than English and French would hold. Ethnocultural communities, particularly in the prairie provinces, argued strongly that a multicultural policy that did not include financial and institutional support for multiple language promotion was vacuous. The status of aboriginal languages was also unclear; while not 'official' languages, they clearly had a different status from those of more recently-immigrated groups, particularly since many aboriginal varieties were seriously endangered.

This chapter focuses on the evolution of public policy during the past twenty-five years in relation to what have come to be termed 'international' or 'heritage' languages – namely, those used in Canada other than French, English and aboriginal languages. The term 'heritage language' is commonly used although, in 1994, the Ontario government replaced it with 'international language', on the grounds that 'heritage' connotes learning about past traditions rather than acquiring language skills that have significance for children's overall educational and personal development. I will use both these terms in the present chapter, with 'heritage' preferred for early initiatives and 'international' for those that have taken place more recently. A variety of other terms has also been used to refer to international languages: for example, 'ethnic', 'minority', 'ancestral', 'third', 'modern' and 'non-official' have all been used at different times and in different provinces. The term commonly used in Quebec is '*langues d'origine*', although the term '*langues patrimoniales*' was introduced in 1993 when the federal government funded the Centre de Langues Patrimoniales.

During the past quarter-century, immigration to Canada has increased substantially in response to falling birthrates and an aging population. This has resulted in a dramatic increase in ethnic and linguistic diversity in Canada's cities which, in turn, has given rise to intense debate among virtually all sectors of society – policy-makers, educators and the general public – about appropriate ways of educating students whose mother tongue is other than English or French. A major issue has been the extent to which the public school system should play a role both in supporting the continued development of children's mother tongues and in encouraging communities to maintain or revitalize heritage languages. Since the mid 1970s, partly in response to the federal multiculturalism policy, ethnocultural communities have strongly pressed the case for the teaching of their languages within the public school system. However, these demands have outraged those who see heritage languages as having no place within the Canadian mainstream. I will first outline the demographic and political context within which the debate about heritage-language teaching is taking place and then review the major issues of contention in this debate.

THE DEMOGRAPHIC AND POLICY CONTEXT

Approximately one-third of the Canadian population is of an ethnic origin other than Anglo/Celtic, French or Aboriginal. I will use the term 'ethnocultural' to refer to this sector of the population. This proportion is increasing as immigration continues to remain at elevated levels. To illustrate, immigrants to Canada numbered 84,302 in 1985 but increased steadily during the late 1980s to a high of more than 250,000 in the early 1990s. Current levels have dropped somewhat but remain above 200,000 annually.

Within the schools of major urban centres, linguistic and cultural diversity has increased substantially in recent years. For example, in Toronto and Vancouver, close to half the school population comes from a non-English-speaking background. In Quebec, the large immigrant populations in many Montreal schools are seen by some politicians and media commentators as a serious threat to the cultural integrity of the province (Cummins and Danesi, 1990). Ethnocultural communities have tended not to be supportive of aspirations for Quebec independence, which has increased the ambivalence or even hostility with which they are regarded by some francophone Quebecers.

Federal policy with respect to heritage-language teaching takes place within the context of Canada's national policy of multiculturalism, proclaimed by then Prime Minister Trudeau in October 1971. One outcome of this policy was the commissioning of a study of non-official languages (O'Bryan *et al.*,

1976), which found substantial support among ethnocultural communities across the country for heritage-language teaching within the public school system. A parallel study on ethnic attitudes (Berry *et al.*, 1977) found some lukewarm support for the policy of multiculturalism among anglophone and francophone Canadians, but significant opposition to the use of public monies to support the teaching of heritage languages. Despite the ambivalence of many anglophones and francophones, the federal government initiated the Cultural Enrichment Program in 1977. This provided some very modest support directly to ethnocultural communities for the teaching of heritage languages (approximately 10 per cent of the operating costs of supplementary schools, usually conducted on Saturday mornings). This support was eliminated in 1990 (as part of a more general fiscal belt-tightening). Since that time, the federal government has provided more indirect support for heritage-language instruction through funding of innovative language teaching and curriculum development projects organized by community groups and through its financial support for the Centre de Langues Patrimoniales at the Université de Montréal.

PROVINCIALLY-SUPPORTED PROGRAMMES
Because education is under provincial jurisdiction, the federal government cannot provide support directly to school systems for the teaching of heritage languages. Most provincial governments, however, operate programmes designed to encourage the teaching of heritage languages and a limited number of languages are taught within the public school system for secondary school credit.

The most extensive provincial programme is Ontario's Heritage Languages Program, initiated in 1977, which has recently been renamed the International Languages Program; this provides funding to school systems for two-and-one-half hours per week of heritage-language instruction. School systems are mandated to implement a programme in response to a request from community groups who can supply a minimum of twenty-five students interested in studying a particular language. Currently, more than sixty languages are taught to about 120,000 students outside the regular five-hour school day. This allows for three basic options, namely, on weekends, after the regular school day, or integrated into a school day extended by half-an-hour. This last option has been highly controversial within the Toronto Board of Education, occasioning a teacher work-to-rule for several months during the early 1980s. Although the controversy receded from the mid-1980s through the mid-1990s, the status of the programme remains fragile in light of massive financial cutbacks to the

Ontario education system in 1996/97 (estimated at close to $1 billion in cuts out of a total budget of $14 billion).

In Quebec, the Programme d'Enseignement des Langues d'Origine (PELO) was also introduced in 1977. This was established on generally similar lines to the Ontario programme, but on a considerably smaller scale. In 1993/94, 13 languages were taught to 6,144 students. The Quebec government initially took responsibility for the development of programmes of study, and curriculum guides were developed at the elementary level for Greek, Italian, Portuguese and Spanish. Subsequently, the ministry delegated the responsibility to school boards who wished to offer courses in other languages. While it is possible for school boards to offer the language within the regular school day, this happens only rarely, with most courses being offered for thirty minutes daily during the lunch break or before or after school. In addition to supporting the PELO, the Quebec government also provided financial support to community groups that offered heritage-language classes outside the public school system, but that support was eliminated in 1992.

The Quebec provincial government subsidizes full-time private ethnic schools for about 80 per cent of their operating costs, subject to certain conditions. Most of these schools are trilingual to a greater or lesser extent, with French, English and the heritage language used as mediums of instruction in varying degrees at different grade levels. The bulk of these schools use Hebrew as an instructional medium but private schools are also operated by Greek and Armenian communities.

In the prairie provinces of Manitoba, Saskatchewan and Alberta, provincial governments have been generally very supportive of heritage-language teaching, partly because of the high proportion of the population of these provinces that is of ethnocultural background, and because, unlike Ontario, there has been relatively little controversy surrounding the teaching of heritage languages. In these three provinces, bilingual programmes involving 50 per cent of the instruction through a heritage language are in operation, although the numbers of students involved are small. The two most common languages taught in these bilingual programmes are Ukrainian and German, although in Edmonton programmes involving Hebrew, Yiddish, Chinese (Mandarin), Arabic and Polish are also in operation. A variety of heritage languages is also taught as subjects within the school systems and by community groups with some financial support from the provincial governments. In an era of financial cutbacks, however, this support is fragile. For example, in 1996 the Alberta government eliminated its $250,000 annual funding for the International Heritage Language School programme, a move that affected more than 10,000 students studying more than forty languages in the province.

In British Columbia, the provincial government has been supportive of the teaching of economically-significant Pacific Rim languages in public schools, and several innovative programmes in languages such as Japanese and Mandarin Chinese exist at both elementary and secondary levels. Although no major provincial funding is provided for international-languages instruction, the Education Act in British Columbia does not restrict school districts from offering bilingual or core-subject heritage-language programmes, as is the case in Ontario. The Ministry of Education also offers credit to students who are taking approved heritage-language courses at the secondary level either in community-run or regular school programmes. In the late 1980s, prior to the termination of federal government support for community-run programmes, close to 15,000 students were enrolled in 140 supplementary schools teaching twenty-six languages. One Russian-English bilingual programme was started in 1983 and continues to operate in Castlegar.

In the Atlantic provinces (New Brunswick, Newfoundland, Nova Scotia and Prince Edward Island) in the late 1980s, there were approximately 1,500 students enrolled in supplementary language programmes that received funds from the federal government. No financial assistance is provided by the provincial governments and no classes are taught within the regular school programme. Arabic is the most commonly taught heritage language in the Atlantic provinces. Although Scottish Gaelic is close to extinction in Nova Scotia, there have been attempts (e.g., in the Iona district of Cape Breton) to institute preschool playgroups in the language modelled after successful Gaelic-language ones in Scotland and Ireland.

International-languages programmes implemented across the country are not remedial or compensatory in nature, unlike most bilingual programmes for minority-language students in the United States and some European countries. Their major goal is to promote proficiency in the international language. In terms of the three orientations to language planning distinguished by Ruiz (1988), remedial programmes clearly fall into the *language-as-problem* category (the problem being minority students' low academic achievement), whereas the Canadian international-language programmes share aspects of what Ruiz calls the *language-as-right* and *language-as-resource* orientations. Ethnocultural communities have argued that government support for international-language teaching is a right, in view of federal and provincial multicultural policies, and they have also suggested that heritage languages represent both an individual and a national resource that entails considerable economic and diplomatic benefits for the country as a whole. These arguments tend to be more persuasive to governments and the general public in an era of economic plenty than in the current context of severe fiscal restraint.

RESEARCH FINDINGS

Canadian research on international language teaching and learning has been both sporadic and fragmentary (see Cummins and Danesi, 1990, for a comprehensive review). Some of the major outcomes of survey research, evaluation studies, and more general correlational studies will be noted here.

Survey research

A survey of school boards carried out by the Canadian Education Association (1991) indicated that 'satisfaction with the heritage language programs runs high in almost every school board surveyed' (pp. 47-48). Among the advantages cited by teachers, parents and students were the following:

positive attitude and pride in one's self and one's background;
better integration of the child into school and society;
increased acceptance and tolerance of other peoples and cultures;
increased cognitive and affective development;
facility in learning other languages;
increased job opportunities;
stronger links between parent and school;
ability to meet community needs.

Disadvantages cited by boards of education were far fewer than advantages. According to the CEA's report, most boards mentioned primarily administrative difficulties connected to scheduling, classroom space, class size, etc., as well as shortages of appropriate teaching materials in the target language.

The positive orientation to heritage-languages programmes depicted in this survey should be treated cautiously in view of the fact that at times of political controversy in relation to the teaching of heritage languages (e.g., 1983/84 in Metropolitan Toronto – see Cummins and Danesi, 1990) a substantial number of regular programme teachers have expressed strong negative attitudes about the educational wisdom of teaching heritage languages.

Evaluation research

Two examples will serve to illustrate the evaluation research conducted on bilingual and trilingual programmes involving heritage languages in Canada. The first is the evaluation of the Ukrainian–English bilingual programme conducted by the Edmonton Public School Board during the 1970s and the second is the evaluation of the Hebrew–French–English trilingual programmes in the Montreal area conducted by Genesee, Tucker and Lambert (1978a, 1978b).

In September 1973, the Edmonton Public School Board (EPSB) introduced an English–Ukrainian bilingual programme at the kindergarten level. All of the instructional time in kindergarten was in Ukrainian, after which it was divided equally between English and Ukrainian. Mathematics, English language arts, and science were taught in English; social studies, physical education, Ukrainian language arts, art and music were taught in Ukrainian. More than three-quarters of the students came from homes in which one or both parents could speak Ukrainian and only about 10 per cent of the students had no Ukrainian ancestry. However, only about 15 per cent were fluent in Ukrainian on entry to school. Unlike typical students in French immersion programmes, the bilingual students were representative of the EPSB system in terms of both ability level and parental socioeconomic status. For example, their Grade 1 score (averaged over five years from 1974 to 1978) on the *Metropolitan Readiness Test* was only one point above the EPSB mean, and less than 50 per cent of the parents had post-secondary education (Edmonton Public Schools, 1980). In the first year of the evaluation, control students were chosen – from regular unilingual English programme classes across the EPSB system – whose parents had the same socioeconomic level and knowledge of Ukrainian as the programme parents. In subsequent years control students were randomly chosen from the same schools as students in the bilingual programme. The selection was stratified on the basis of gender, school and ability level. No consistent pattern of differences emerged in comparisons of English and mathematics skills between programme and control students in the early grades. However, at the Grade 5 level (the last year of the evaluation), the first cohort of bilingual programme students performed significantly better than control students in mathematics and on both decoding and comprehension subtests of the standardized reading test that was administered.

The evaluation carried out by the EPSB also examined whether the programme was equally appropriate for students of different ability levels. This was done by dividing students into high, medium and low ability levels and testing for programme-by-ability interaction effects in a two-way analysis of variance design. No evidence of interaction effects was found, indicating that low-ability students had no more difficulty in the bilingual programme than they would have had in the regular programme. A study by Cummins and Mulcahy (1978) was carried out with Grade 1 and 3 students in order to investigate bilingual children's metalinguistic development. It revealed that students who were relatively fluent in Ukrainian, because their parents used it consistently at home, were significantly better able to detect ambiguities in English sentence structure than either equivalent unilingual English-speaking children not in the programme or children in the programme who came from predominantly English-speaking homes.

The EPSB evaluation also reported that students' Ukrainian skills developed in accord with programme expectations and that they also expanded their appreciation for and knowledge about Ukrainian culture. In addition, a large majority of the parents and programme personnel were pleased with the programme, felt the students were happy, and wished the programme to be continued to higher grade levels.

Similarly positive outcomes are reported by Genesee, Tucker and Lambert (1978a, 1978b) for the Hebrew–French–English trilingual programmes in Montreal. Because the programme variations are complex, only the general pattern of findings is reported here. The basic design involved comparing groups of students who participated in two slightly different 'early double immersion' (EDI) programmes (i.e., Hebrew–French–English trilingual programmes) with students who attended a more traditional Hebrew day school (most initial instruction through the medium of English and Hebrew, but with increasing amounts of French-medium instruction in the intermediate grades of elementary school). The Hebrew time allocation and curriculum were similar in all three schools. In one of the EDI schools, English language arts was introduced in Grade 3, and in Grade 4 in the other school. The academic performance of students in these schools was also compared with that of students in regular French immersion and core French-as-a-second-language programmes. It was found that, at the Grade 4 and 5 levels, both EDI groups achieved as well in English as all other groups, despite considerably less time spent in English-medium instruction than the traditional Hebrew day school or core French-as-a-second-language groups. No group differences were evident in mathematics, despite the fact that the EDI groups had received all initial mathematics instruction in French, whereas the traditional Hebrew day school students received all such instruction in English. The EDI students scored almost as well as the regular French immersion students on measures of French proficiency. On measures of Hebrew, the EDI students tended to score higher than students in the regular Hebrew day school despite the similarity of programme and time allocation.

Genesee and Lambert (1980) conclude that programmes of bi- and trilingualism are feasible and effective ways of enriching students' elementary education insofar as '[t]he Hebrew day schools were able (1) to achieve the goals of regular school programs with regard to native language development and academic achievement, (2) to maintain important religious, cultural and linguistic traditions, and (3) at the same time, to develop the children's competence in a language of local importance' (p. 25). The authors acknowledge that the students in the trilingual programmes were highly capable and motivated youngsters, but point out that the existing evidence (e.g., Cziko, 1975) pertaining to the suitability of single French immersion programmes for students who are less economically and intellectually advantaged suggests that these students would also benefit academically and linguistically from programmes of double immersion.

All of the other evaluations of various kinds of heritage-language bilingual programmes support the conclusion drawn by Cummins and Danesi (1990): 'Virtually all the evaluations reviewed, whether of enrichment or transition programs, show clearly that time spent with the minority language as the medium of instruction results in no academic loss to students' progress in the majority language' (p. 133). This conclusion is also consistent with the outcomes of bilingual education research elsewhere (Cummins, 1996).

Correlational research

A considerable number of international studies suggest that subtle metalinguistic and cognitive advantages may result from continued development of two languages and the attainment of literacy in both (e.g., Cummins, 1996; Mohanty, 1994; Ricciardelli, 1992). In the Canadian context, Swain and Lapkin (1991) examined the influence of heritage-language proficiency on the learning of additional languages. The study involved more than 300 Grade 8 students in the Metropolitan Toronto Separate School Board French–English Bilingual Program, which starts at the Grade 5 level and entails 50 per cent of the time through each language. Students also have the opportunity to study a heritage language outside regular school hours. Swain and Lapkin compared four groups of students on various measures of French proficiency: those who had no knowledge of a heritage language; those with some knowledge of, but no literacy skills in, the heritage language; those with heritage-language literacy skills but who mentioned no active use of heritage-language literacy; and finally, those who understood and used the heritage language in the written mode. The first group had parents with higher educational and occupational status than those of the other three groups, who did not differ in this regard.

Highly significant differences in favour of those students with heritage-language literacy skills were found on both written and oral measures of French. There was also a trend for students from romance-language backgrounds to perform better in oral aspects of French but the differences between romance- and non-romance-language background students were not highly significant. The authors conclude that there is transfer of knowledge and learning processes across languages, and that development of first-language literacy entails concrete benefits for students' acquisition of subsequent languages.

CONCLUSION

There is extensive teaching of international languages across Canada, although programmes take different forms in different provinces. In most cases the language is taught as a subject, either in community-operated supplementary schools or in provincially funded programmes operated by boards of education. There are relatively few examples of full bilingual programmes involving international languages, which contrasts with the widespread implementation of French immersion programmes across the country.

By the same token, much less research has been undertaken on international-language issues than is the case for the teaching of official languages. However, the research that has been undertaken supports the educational merits of teaching international languages, particularly in the context of bilingual and/or trilingual programmes. No adverse effects on academic attainment in English (or French) have been noted. When the international language is taught only as a subject (as opposed to its use as a medium of instruction), anecdotal accounts suggest that language proficiency outcomes are modest for students who have limited proficiency in the language to begin with. However, this issue has not been systematically investigated in the Canadian context.

There is still considerable opposition among educators, policy-makers and the general public to the use of 'taxpayers' money' for the teaching of international languages. This opposition was vehement in some parts of the country throughout the late 1970s and 1980s. The case for the opposition is succinctly put in a submission to the Toronto Board of Education (cited in Johnson, 1982): 'Many people of diverse backgrounds fear balkanization of school communities, loss of time for core curriculum subjects, undue pressure on children, disruption in school programming and staffing, inadequate preparation for eventual employment, and indeed, a dramatic shift of direction in Canadian society.' This latter point appears to be at the heart of the debate. At issue are very different perspectives on the nature of Canadian society and how it should respond to demographic changes that are radically increasing the extent of linguistic and cultural diversity. While the dominant anglophone and francophone groups are generally strongly in favour of learning the other official language, they see few benefits to promoting international languages for themselves, for Canadian society as a whole, or for children from ethnocultural backgrounds. They feel that the educational focus for such children should be on acquiring English (or French) and becoming Canadian rather than on erecting linguistic and cultural barriers between them and their Canadian peers.

In short, whereas advocates of international-language teaching stress the value of bilingual and multilingual skills for the individual and society as a whole, opponents see these languages as socially divisive, excessively costly, and educationally retrograde in view of minority children's need to succeed academically in the school language. These issues are likely to remain controversial, particularly as school systems throughout Canada experience long-term financial cutbacks affecting programmes that many people view as having higher priority than teaching international languages to the children of immigrants. Neither the potential utility of these languages in an era of increased global interdependence nor research supporting the educational merits of bilingual or trilingual proficiency are likely to be persuasive to Canadians increasingly concerned to identify the essence of Canadian identity at a time of widespread disillusionment with the 1971 vision of 'multiculturalism within a bilingual framework'.

References

Berry, J. W., Kalin, R. and Taylor, D. M. (1977). *Multiculturalism and Ethnic Attitudes in Canada.* Ottawa: Supply and Services Canada.

Canadian Education Association. (1991). *Heritage Language Programs in Canadian School Boards.* Toronto: Canadian Education Association.

Cummins, J. (1996). *Negotiating Identities: Education for Empowerment in a Diverse Society.* Ontario, CA: California Association for Bilingual Education.

Cummins, J. and Danesi, M. (1990). *Heritage Languages: The Development and Denial of Canada's Linguistic Resources* Toronto: Our Schools, Our Selves/Garamond.

Cummins, J. and Mulcahy, R. (1978). Orientation to language in Ukrainian–English bilingual children. *Child Development, 49,* 1239–1242.

Cziko, G. (1975). The effects of different French immersion programs on the language and academic skills of children from various socioeconomic backgrounds. MA thesis, Department of Psychology, McGill University.

Edmonton Public Schools. (1980). *Summary of the Evaluations of the Bilingual English-Ukrainian and Bilingual English-French Program.* Edmonton: Edmonton Public School Board.

Genesee, F. and Lambert, W. E. (1980). Trilingual education for the majority group child. Unpublished research report, McGill University.

Genesee, F., Tucker, G. R. and Lambert, W. E. (1978a). An experiment in trilingual education: Report 3. *Canadian Modern Language Review, 34,* 621-643.

(1978b). An experiment in trilingual education: Report 4. *Language Learning, 28,* 343-365.

Johnson, W. (1982). Creating a nation of tongues. *Globe and Mail,* 26 June.

Mohanty, A. K. (1994). *Bilingualism in a Multilingual Society: Psychological and Pedagogical Implications.* Mysore: Central Institute of Indian Languages.

O'Bryan, K. G., Reitz, J. and Kuplowska, O. (1976). *Non-official Languages: A Study in Canadian Multiculturalism.* Ottawa: Supply and Services Canada.

Ricciardelli, L. (1992). Bilingualism and cognitive development in relation to threshold theory. *Journal of Psycholinguistic Research, 21,* 301-316.

Ruiz, R. (1988). Orientations in language planning. In S. L. McKay and S. C. Wong (eds.), *Language Diversity: Problem or Resource?* (pp. 3-25). New York: Newbury House.

Swain, M. and Lapkin, S. (1991). Heritage language children in an English–French bilingual program. *Canadian Modern Language Review, 47,* 635-641.

15 **French immersion in Canada**

Fred Genesee

French–English bilingualism has been a prominent feature of Canadian life, and French immersion has played a prominent role in Canada's response to the exigencies of bilingualism. This chapter reviews some historical antecedents of French immersion, current programmatic and pedagogical aspects of it, and the educational and social impact that immersion education has had.

A BRIEF SOCIOPOLITICAL HISTORY OF ENGLISH–FRENCH RELATIONS

To understand the origins and development of immersion, it is useful to start with a brief historical review of its sociopolitical antecedents, especially in Quebec where it originated (see Bourhis, 1984, for more complete coverage). Like many parts of the New World, Canada was settled and governed by European nations during its early development. The first colonization of Canada was undertaken by the French, beginning with Jacques Cartier's landing in 1534. French control gave way to British control in 1763, when the British defeated the French at the Battle of the Plains of Abraham near Quebec City (Cook, Saywell and Ricker, 1977). French-Canadian culture was deeply rooted in North America at the time of the British conquest. Thus, it resisted the assimilationist efforts of British legislation and immigration policy which would have eroded the vitality of a less entrenched ethnolinguistic group.

The British North America Act of 1867 legally constituted the Canadian confederation, which at the time consisted of Ontario, Quebec, New Brunswick and Nova Scotia. Analogous to the American Declaration of Independence, the BNA Act affirmed Canada's linguistic duality only in Quebec, where the use of French and English was required in the Parliament and courts of the province. It was not until 1969, with the passage of the Official Languages Act, that *both* languages were granted official status nation-wide. According to Canadian bilingualism policy, federal government services are to be made available in both French and English throughout the country, where numbers warrant. This policy does not apply to services provided by Canada's ten provincial governments or by the three territorial governments in northern Canada. At the provincial level, only one province, New Brunswick, also recognizes French and English as official languages. The remaining nine provinces are monolingual, with eight recognizing English and one, Quebec, recognizing French as the official language.

The official-language policies of the provincial governments tend to reflect their respective constituencies. Thus, the one officially bilingual province, New Brunswick, has a sizeable percentage of both French-speaking (34 per cent) and English-speaking residents (66 per cent); Quebec, which recognizes French as the only official language, is inhabited predominantly by French-speaking residents (85 per cent); and the remaining eight provinces, which all recognize English as the official provincial language, have predominantly English-speaking residents. Despite the lack of official status for *both* English and French in most provinces, certain government services are now available in both languages in many provinces. There is an increasing move in this direction, particularly evident in regions outside Quebec with a relatively large representation of speakers of French – for example, along the border between the provinces of Ontario and Quebec, in northern Ontario, and in regions of Manitoba and Alberta.

Notwithstanding regional differences in the prevalence of English and French, in general both languages are important features of Canadian life. Consequently, competence in English *and* French is an important asset in Canadian political, cultural and economic affairs, and bilingual competence is often associated with tangible and/or intangible rewards. The reward value associated with this bilingualism is enhanced by the international status and utility of each language. Notwithstanding the historical importance of the French and English cultures in the early development of the country, the federal government recognizes neither as official. Canada has adopted an official policy of multiculturalism which recognizes the legitimacy and value of all cultures represented among its citizenry. While generally accepted in most English-speaking parts of the country, this policy is controversial in the province of Quebec, which sees multiculturalism as a threat to the survival of French culture in North America.

Despite its historical importance during the early colonization and subsequent development of Canada, despite its contemporary status as an official national language, despite its demographic significance as the native language of approximately 25 per cent of the Canadian population and despite even its international status as a major world language, French has until recently been the disadvantaged partner in Canadian confederation. This has been true to a large extent even in Quebec, where (as noted above) the vast majority of the population speak French as a native language; indeed, many Quebecers speak only French. Evidence of the inferior status of French has been evident in at least three areas: legislation, patterns of language use and language attitudes. The following review will focus on Quebec because extensive documentation on language relations in this province exist and serve to highlight national patterns.

Legislation and the French language

As has already been noted, French is recognized as an official language by only two of Canada's ten provinces (Quebec and New Brunswick) and by none of the territorial governments. While the eight 'English provinces' do not now recognize French as an official provincial language, they do not forbid its use. The legislative picture was not always so tolerant. The use of French, particularly in public schools, has been forbidden by law in certain provinces at certain periods during the years since confederation. For example, in 1890 the government of Manitoba revoked an earlier law requiring the use of French in the provincial parliament and permitting its use in public schools. As a result of this repeal, francophone students caught using French in Manitoba schools could be punished. The 1890 law has since been repealed, and political efforts have been made to restore French to its original status. According to the new Canadian Charter of Rights and Freedoms (1982), public education is to be made available in all provinces in both official languages, where numbers warrant.

Patterns of language use

Widespread daily use of French, except in communication with official federal government agencies, is limited to the provinces of Quebec and New Brunswick, and to other specific regions with sizable French-speaking communities (see above). Even in these areas, however, English often predominated over French as the *lingua franca*. This was particularly true in public settings and in business and commerce. This situation has changed substantially in Quebec as a result of expanded and intensified programmes of French-language instruction in English schools in the province; it is now estimated that there is a larger percentage of English–French bilinguals of anglophone background than of francophone background, although there are no definitive statistics to back this up. Provincial laws which mandate the use of French in businesses of a certain size and in all public notices and announcements have also contributed substantially to the expanded use of French.

Language attitudes

Perhaps no other single piece of evidence attests more to the disadvantaged or inferior status that the French language had relative to English than the results of a study carried out by Lambert, Hodgson, Gardner and Fillenbaum (1960). In what has become a classic study in the social psychology of language, Lambert and his colleagues asked groups of English and French Canadians in Montreal to listen to and give their impressions of people speaking either French or English. Unknown to the listeners, they were actually hearing the same perfectly bilingual individuals on separate occasions, sometimes speaking French and sometimes English. Analyses of the listeners' reactions to the speakers indicated that they were much more favourable towards the English 'guises' than towards the French ones. In other words, the same speakers were perceived significantly differently when heard using each of their two languages – it is as if they were two different people. Furthermore, it was found that not only did English Canadians express more favourable impressions of the English guises than of the French guises – evidence of in-group favouritism – but so did French Canadians. That the French Canadian subjects perceived the speakers more favourably when they spoke in English meant a denigration of members of their own ethnolinguistic group.

Genesee and Holobow (1989) examined to what extent and how attitudes towards Quebec French had changed some twenty-five years after Lambert's pioneering study. They found that, in comparison with Lambert's French-Canadian respondents, *their* French-Canadian respondents expressed more positive attitudes towards French speakers on traits associated with in-group solidarity (e.g., likeable, warm), indicating a shift towards increased solidarity and in-group favouritism. Interestingly, however, there was little change in either the French- or English-Canadian respondents' attitudes towards French and English along *status* dimensions (e.g., intelligent, dependable) – in other words, both groups still associated English with more prestige and power than French.

FRENCH IMMERSION:
A COMMUNITY EXPERIMENT IN SOCIAL CHANGE

Discontent over these linguistic and cultural inequities had been developing for some time, particularly in Quebec. Early attempts by the French-speaking community to arrive at a more equitable relationship with the English community through negotiation had been largely unsuccessful. Repeatedly faced with an apparent lack of responsiveness on the part of the English community to their concerns, French-speaking Quebecers began to make vocal and public demands for change. This culminated in the early 1960s with concerted political, social and, in some cases, militant action. There were, for example, mass demonstrations against public institutions that would or could not communicate with French-speaking Quebecers in French. The social unrest manifested during this period has come to be called the Quiet Revolution.

During the last twenty years, some Quebec politicians have called for separation from the rest of Canada, and a political party having the goal of establishing Quebec as a separate country has won three elections in Quebec. One of the most important pieces of legislation which this government passed was Quebec's Bill 101, which became law in 1976, declaring French the only official language of the province. This law aims to ensure the linguistic rights of the French-speaking majority of Quebec. Current provincial law also requires that non-English-speaking immigrant students attend French-medium schools; all public signs must be in French; and businesses of a certain size must be able to demonstrate the ability to conduct business in French.

At the same time that the French community in Quebec was expressing dissatisfaction with inequities in the language situation, English-speaking Quebecers were also becoming concerned about English–French relations and about their children's abilities to function effectively in a French-speaking community. More specifically, there was an emerging awareness in the English community, precipitated by the events just described, that French was becoming more important as a language of communication in most spheres of life in Quebec and, concomitantly, that English alone would no longer assure social and economic success in the province. (The coexistence of French and English Canadians has been characterized by Canadian novelist Hugh MacLennan (1945) as *two solitudes*, an apt metaphor in this and many other communities inhabited by people of different linguistic and cultural backgrounds.) Faced with the evolving importance of French as the main working language of Quebec, and with increasing dissatisfaction with the linguistic barriers that separated the English and French communities, a concerned group of English-speaking parents in the small suburban community of St Lambert, outside of Montreal, began to meet informally in the early 1960s to discuss strategies for change (Lambert and Tucker, 1972).

They felt that their incompetence in French contributed to the two solitudes whose existence, in turn, effectively prevented them from learning the language from their francophone neighbours. They felt, too, that their inability to communicate in French was also attributable to inadequate methods of second-language instruction in English schools. At that time, French was taught for relatively short periods each day (twenty to thirty minutes) by teachers who were usually native English speakers with competence in French-as-a-second language that varied from excellent to poor. There was an emphasis on teaching vocabulary and grammar rules and on using pattern practice drills based on then popular audiolingual techniques. This approach was common to many second-language programmes throughout North America at that time, except that second-language instruction in Quebec began in elementary school and continued systematically until the end of secondary school. This is still true, and it has become customary to varying degrees in the other Canadian provinces. Despite this additional exposure to French, however, English-speaking students graduated from English schools with insufficient proficiency in French to function effectively in a francophone community.

In their search for better methods of second-language instruction for their children, the St Lambert parent group recommended the creation of an experimental form of second-language instruction which became the prototype for the development of immersion programmes nation-wide. The first immersion class was opened in September 1965. The primary goals of the St Lambert programme and most contemporary Canadian programmes are:

1. To provide the participating students with functional competence in both written and spoken aspects of French.
2. To promote and maintain normal levels of English-language development.
3. To ensure achievement in academic subjects commensurate with the students' ability and grade level.
4. To instill in students an understanding and appreciation of French Canadians, their language and culture, without detracting in any way from the students' identity with and appreciation for English-Canadian culture.

Thus, it was in the educational system, and in French immersion in particular, that the St Lambert parents sought a response to important sociolinguistic changes that were taking place around them. Moreover, it was through educational innovation that they sought to bring about social change in their own communities. Improved French-second-language learning was not intended to be the sole goal of immersion. Rather, it was intended to be an intermediate goal leading to improved relationships between English and French Quebecers and, thus, ultimately to a breaking down of the two solitudes that prevailed. Many parents across the country have since come to share this view. Parents have also supported immersion enthusiastically because of the economic and sociocultural benefits their children gain through the knowledge of two major world languages. The community involvement that characterized the creation of the St Lambert programme has been repeated many times in other communities around the country.

THE CURRENT SITUATION IN IMMERSION

Since the St Lambert programme was opened, immersion has expanded dramatically. Between 1977 and 1994, the number of schools in Canada offering French immersion increased from 237 to 2,099 and the number of students enrolled increased from 37,835 to 305,149 (Commissioner of Official Languages, 1994). A number of alternative forms of immersion are currently available (see Genesee, 1987, for a complete summary). Differentiations are often made between *early, delayed* and *late* immersion. Programmes also differ with respect to the amount of instruction provided in French (*total* versus *partial*) and/or the number of years during which French is used as a major medium of instruction. Immersion is also now available, incidentally, in a variety of languages other than French (see below).

Early immersion

Early immersion begins in kindergarten or grade one (when the students are about five years of age). In early *total* immersion programmes, only French is used as the medium of instruction during the primary grades. In some schools, instruction in English is begun in Grade 2; in others it is delayed until Grade 4, or even later. English is initially used to teach English language arts and, in successively higher grades, it is used as a medium of instruction for different academic subjects. At no time are the same subjects taught through both English *and* French. The use of English varies from as little as 20 per cent of total instructional time to 40 per cent, depending on the school district. As much as possible, different teachers are used for teaching in English and French. Immersion teachers are usually native speakers of French or, at least, have native-like proficiency, and they virtually never use English in class with their students; this is done in order to encourage the students to think that their teachers are monolinguals and, thus, to use French as much as possible. In order to maintain and further develop the students' French skills, early immersion during the elementary grades is followed in some schools by a maintenance programme which extends to the end of secondary school. During the secondary grades, the students are offered selected courses in French by subject specialists.

These may be content-based, such as history or geography, or language-based, such as literature or drama.

In early *partial* immersion programmes, approximately half the instruction in all elementary grades is presented in French, the other half in English. Different subjects are taught through each language from the beginning; language arts are generally taught in both languages. In secondary school, optional language-based or content-based courses are provided in French. The number and types of such subjects available to students depend on the school.

Early double immersion

In at least one documented case, native English-speaking Canadian children are taught through two second languages – Hebrew and French (Genesee and Lambert, 1983). French was chosen by this Montreal community as one of the second languages because of its daily social, cultural and economic importance. Hebrew was chosen because it is an important religious and cultural component of the community's Jewish heritage. In one double immersion school, English is not used as a medium of instruction until Grade 4, at which time English language arts are taught. In the primary grades, French is used to teach the conventional academic curriculum, comprised of mathematics, science and social studies, as well as language arts. Hebrew is used to teach language, history, and religious and cultural studies. In another double immersion school, English, French and Hebrew are used for instructional purposes from the beginning. The teachers in these schools are native or native-like speakers. In most other respects, these programmes are the same as immersion programmes of the single language variety.

Delayed immersion

In delayed immersion, the use of French as a medium of instruction is delayed until the middle elementary grades, usually Grade 4 (when the students are about nine or ten years of age). At this time, either all instruction – with the exception of English language arts – or about half of it is presented in French. In subsequent grades, a form of partial immersion (varying with respect to how much each language is used) is provided. Students entering these programmes have generally had some prior instruction in French.

Late immersion

Late immersion usually begins in the first year of secondary school, when students are about twelve years of age (Genesee, 1981a, 1987). The

312

students have had some prior French instruction; the amount varies depending on the school district. Such prior exposure is necessary if the students are to make a successful transition to schooling in their second language. All subjects, except English language arts, are taught in French by native or native-like speakers of the language; this may last for one year or two years. The curriculum during this time is essentially the same as that in a regular English language programme, the difference being that it is taught in French. In the higher grades, selected courses – such as history, geography and mathematics – are taught in French. In Quebec, these courses are the same as those prescribed by Le Ministère de l'Education du Québec for francophone students in the province, attesting to the students' ability to follow the same advanced courses as native French speakers. As in early immersion alternatives, late immersion students are required to address all classroom comments in French and, of course, all of their reading and written assignments in their French classes are done in French as well.

Heritage and indigenous language immersion

As mentioned previously, immersion education is now available in a variety of languages other than French, under the general heading of heritage or indigenous language programmes. *Indigenous language immersion* includes languages that are native to North America, such as Mohawk (Lambert, Genesee, Holobow and McGilly, 1984). These programmes are offered in communities where the language is at risk of extinction because it is no longer being learned as a maternal variety. *Heritage language immersion* includes languages that are part of the cultural background of the parents of the participating children, but that are not indigenous to Canada – for example, Hebrew, Ukrainian or Chinese. Like French immersion, heritage and indigenous language immersion programmes are populated by students whose first language is English. They are also similar to other immersion programmes with respect to most other programmatic features, including the timing and sequencing of languages, and so on. Whereas a goal of French immersion is to promote proficiency in Canada's two official languages, indigenous and heritage language immersion programmes seek to ensure the survival of languages and cultures that are of some significance to the children and their communities. These programmes reflect Canada's commitment to multiculturalism.

PEDAGOGICAL OUTCOMES OF IMMERSION

Several large-scale longitudinal evaluations have been conducted to measure the effectiveness of immersion (see, among others, Genesee, 1987;

313

Lambert and Tucker, 1972; Swain and Lapkin, 1982). The three primary concerns of much of this research are: (a) the impact of schooling in immersion on the students' first-language development; (b) the effect of academic instruction through the medium of a second language on academic achievement; (c) the linguistic competence and functional proficiency of the students in their second language. The results from these evaluations are extensive and provide a detailed and reliable indication of the linguistic and academic outcomes of immersion. Since a comprehensive review of these findings is not possible here, the following sections focus on the most salient results from studies of early and late immersion (see Genesee, 1987, for a comprehensive summary of the research).

Early immersion

English-language development. Typically, early total immersion students show a lag in their development of English literacy skills during those grades where no instruction in English is given; they demonstrate no lags in English speaking and listening skills during this time. After one year of formal English language arts instruction, students achieve parity in all skills in comparison with control students who have received all academic instruction through the medium of English. One exception to this pattern is spelling, in which immersion students often continue to lag for another year. Subsequent testing in higher grades reveals that immersion students perform as well as control students in all aspects of English that have been assessed, including spelling (see also Lambert and Tucker, 1972; Swain and Lapkin, 1982). That immersion students catch up to students educated entirely in English, within one year, suggests that the skills they acquire in conjunction with the second language can be and are transferred to their first language. The quick catch up in first-language reading may also be due to the students' extensive exposure to written forms of English outside school. Comparisons among above-average, average and below-average students, as defined by performance on IQ tests, indicate that below-average immersion students score at the same level as their below-average counterparts in English-medium schools; as expected, both groups score lower than average students who, in turn, score lower than above-average students (Genesee, 1976). In sum, there has been no evidence of long-term deficits in the English language development of early total immersion students.

Academic achievement. Immersion students score at the same level as control students on standardized tests of mathematics and science administered in English, even if the immersion students have received all maths and science

314

instruction through their second language. It has also been found that the academic achievement of below-average immersion students is comparable to that of below-average control students, albeit lower than that of average and above-average students. In other words, below-average students are not handicapped in their academic development as a result of the immersion experience.

Second-language proficiency. The second-language proficiency of immersion students is vastly superior to that of English control students who have had conventional second-language instruction; this has been found to be true for all aspects of second-language acquisition. French immersion students often score at the same level as native French-speaking students on tests that assess listening and reading comprehension. The performance of immersion students on tests that assess productive language skills (that is, speaking and writing) is generally very impressive (see Hammerly, 1992, for an opposing view). Immersion students are able to understand and make themselves understood in all academic contexts, and they demonstrate an uninhibited and creative use of their second language for communication that is seldom achieved by students in more conventional second-language programmes. At the same time, their usage is less than native-like: (a) there is often transfer from English lexicon and syntax; (b) they often have restricted vocabulary and simplified grammar; (c) their usage is non-idiomatic (see Harley, 1992).

It has been found that the acquisition of second-language literacy skills is associated with the students' overall ability, so that above-average students generally score higher on tests of reading and writing in the second language than do average or below-average students (Genesee, 1976). In contrast, the acquisition of interpersonal communication skills (that is, listening comprehension and speaking) has not been found to correlate with overall ability – below-average students are often rated as highly as above-average students on these skills during a face-to-face oral interview (Genesee, 1976). It would appear from these results that students representing a wide range of academic ability levels may be able to acquire comparable levels of interpersonal communication skills in a second language in immersion contexts. These findings are consistent with those of other researchers who have demonstrated that general intellectual ability is not the only or the most important determinant of second-language achievement (Gardner and Lambert, 1972).

Late immersion

English language development. There has been no evidence that the English language skills of late immersion students suffer. Nor has there been evidence that below-average students are handicapped in their English language development as a result of the immersion experience – their language skills have been shown to develop as well as those of below-average students in English-medium programmes.

Academic achievement. The academic achievement of late immersion students is not impeded by the use of a second language for academic instruction. Moreover, evaluations in Montreal have shown that this is the case for below-average students as well as for average and above-average students. These findings have been demonstrated using standardized achievement tests, as well as examinations prepared by local educational authorities (Genesee, 1977a; Genesee and Chaplin, 1976). The latter results are of particular interest because they demonstrate the students' ability to use their second language in conjunction with advanced-level academic subjects, such as geography, chemistry and history.

Second-language proficiency. The results of second-language testing in late immersion follow the same basic pattern as those from early immersion: immersion students achieve native-like or near native-like levels of functional proficiency in listening and reading comprehension in the second language, and advanced levels of functional proficiency – but less than native-like competence – in second-language production skills (writing and speaking). As in early immersion, acquisition of literacy skills in the second language has been found to be positively correlated with overall ability. However, in contrast to early immersion results, acquisition of interpersonal communication skills in late immersion has also been found to be positively correlated with overall ability. Whether the latter findings are due to student-selection factors or an actual difference in the language-learning style of adolescents is not clear. In any case, they attest to the differential effectiveness of late immersion depending on the ability of the individual student; such differential effects are not found in early immersion.

Taken together, these findings indicate that immersion programmes are suitable for students with diverse characteristics, provided they are members of a majority-language group, such as English Canadians. Similar patterns of results have been found for *English-speaking* students from minority ethnic backgrounds – for example, Mohawk students (Lambert *et al.*, 1984). Proponents of second-language immersion programmes for majority English-speaking children have generally doubted their applicability for children from minority-language backgrounds who do not enjoy the same linguistic and social support that English speakers in North America do. English immersion programmes for French-speaking Canadians have not been recommended because this form of education is thought to pose a threat to French in Canada. Indeed, French-speaking children in Quebec are not eligible to attend English-medium schools prior to junior college, despite the fairly widespread existence of such schools, and instruction in English-as-a-second-language prior to Grade 4 is not encouraged by government legislation. Such legislation is predicated on the belief that too much English too soon could undermine the vitality of French.

Outstanding pedagogical issues

There are a number of unanswered questions concerning the pedagogy of immersion and its suitability for all students; some of these issues are the focus of current research activity (Lapkin, Swain and Shapson, 1992). Concerns about the quality of immersion students' second-language competence have led to questions about how best to integrate language and content instruction in ways that will maximize language learning without sacrificing the communicative approach that is the hallmark of immersion (see Day and Shapson, 1991; Lyster, 1994; Swain, 1988, for studies on this issue). At present, we do not know how immersion teachers model appropriate language when teaching new content and/or whether some methods of using language while teaching content are more effective than others for promoting second-language development (Swain and Carroll, 1987). Nor do we know whether there are ways of integrating language and content instruction that are particularly effective at certain ages or stages of language development. Extending our understanding of these critical instructional issues will better permit Canadian educators (and, indeed, educators working in immersion settings around the world) to develop an effective pedagogy of immersion. At present, this is lacking.

While research to date has examined certain learner characteristics that put children at risk in school, there are other factors that have not been examined systematically in immersion contexts – for example, chronic hearing and visual impairments and speech disorders. Consequently, some educators are unsure of the suitability of immersion for all students (Wiss, 1989). There is a lack of generally accepted and validated procedures for identifying the special needs of students in immersion, since it can be difficult at times to distinguish between students experiencing short-term academic difficulty associated with incomplete mastery of the second language from students with underlying developmental delays who are likely to experience chronic academic problems (Wiss, 1987). In addition, there is lack of agreement on the most appropriate and effective treatment of students experiencing difficulty in immersion – some educators recommend transferring such students to all-English programmes in the belief that their problems can be remedied by English-only instruction, while others seek to meet their needs within immersion, believing that such students will have comparable difficulties whatever the language of instruction (see Bruck, 1985). There is some evidence for the latter belief (see Genesee, 1992), but, as noted earlier, not all at-risk factors have been thoroughly examined.

THE EDUCATIONAL AND SOCIAL IMPACT OF IMMERSION

The impact of immersion on the educational system in Canada has been enormous. As noted earlier, more than 300,000 elementary and secondary school students were enrolled in some form of immersion programme in 1994. Overall, this represents about 6 per cent of the total Canadian school population; enrolments in some provinces are much higher – in Manitoba, New Brunswick and Quebec, for example, 10 per cent, 17 per cent and 34 per cent, respectively, of the provincial school population is in immersion (Commissioner of Official Languages, 1994). Enrolments continue to increase, although less dramatically than in the past, despite early concerns that immersion would turn out to be a fad and despite unresolved political conflicts surrounding Quebec's role in Canada and the attendant lowering of people's motivation to learn French that this might have.

The educational impact of immersion is also evident in the establishment of a number of important professional associations. For example, Canadian Parents for French (CPF), a national volunteer association, was established to promote French immersion and to improve the quality of instruction in French-as-a-second-language. CPF has played a major role in collecting and disseminating information about French-language instruction and in advocating more and improved programmes of French instruction for English-speaking Canadian children. University departments of education across the country have developed special preparation courses for immersion teachers, and a professional teachers' association (Association Canadienne des Professeurs d'Immersion) was created in 1977 to provide ongoing professional development services; its current membership is 1,500. Thus, immersion has clearly become a prominent part of the educational landscape in Canada.

The wider social impact of immersion is more difficult and complex to discern. Returning to the early concerns of the founding members of the St Lambert parents group which inaugurated immersion in 1965, the social impact of immersion can be examined from a number of perspectives: (a) the participating students' perceptions of themselves, English Canadians, and French

Canadians; (b) their attitudes towards French Canadians and French–English relations; (c) their attitudes towards and actual use of French. Most of the research on these issues was conducted in Montreal during the 1970s and 1980s and, thus, may currently lack validity because of the passage of time, and because of changes in the Canadian sociopolitical climate.

Immersion students' ethnolinguistic perceptions

Cziko, Lambert and Gutter (1980) and Genesee (1977b) have examined the ethnic identity of early immersion students, in comparison to English control students, in two separate studies using multidimensional scaling techniques. The students were asked to indicate how similar, or dissimilar, a number of ethnic and personal concepts (including the self) were to one another. Both studies revealed that the social perceptions of the immersion students were similar to those of English-speaking students in all-English programmes in two important respects. First, both groups of students identified two major ethnolinguistic clusters, one associated with 'English Canadians', the other with 'French Canadians'. Second, both the immersion and non-immersion students perceived themselves to be associated with the English-Canadian cluster, indicating that both identified primarily with English Canadians. At the same time, the immersion students differed from the non-immersion students in that the former saw the English-Canadian and French-Canadian clusters to be more similar and, of particular interest, they also tended to view themselves as more similar to French Canadians than did the non-immersion students. It would appear from these findings that participation in immersion may have caused the immersion students to perceive less social distance between themselves and French Canadians. Perhaps this is because, as bilinguals, they share a salient characteristic of French Canadians; or perhaps it follows from their increased experiences with French Canadians in the immersion programme. At the same time, immersion did not appear to have had any adverse effects on the immersion students' identification with English Canadians.

In a related vein, Swain (1980) examined immersion students' views on being Canadian and on sociopolitical relations between English and French Canadians. Swain's findings were based on analyses of compositions written by Grades 5 and 6 early total immersion students in response to the prompt '*Why I like (or do not like) being Canadian*'. Swain's analyses revealed that the immersion students reported a much greater number of reasons for liking being Canadian than did the non-immersion students, and that more immersion than non-immersion students were likely to comment on the rich and varied cultural and linguistic composition of Canada and the possibility of using other languages in Canada. In a similar study, Blake, Lambert, Sidoti and Wolfe (undated) asked groups of English-speaking students in immersion and regular English programmes to write essays in which they proposed solutions to problems faced by English and French Canadians. The bilingual immersion students were much more likely than the unilingual non-immersion students to suggest solutions involving greater intergroup contact between English and French Canadians, through schooling or exchange programmes.

Immersion students' attitudes towards French and French Canadians

Studies of immersion students' ethnic attitudes have yielded more complex results. In their pioneering longitudinal study of the St Lambert immersion programme, Lambert and Tucker (1972) assessed the attitudes of students towards themselves, English Canadians, and French Canadians. Their results revealed that in the primary elementary grades the immersion students saw themselves and English Canadians in a more favourable light than did students in all-English schools. Similarly, the attitudes of the immersion students towards French Canadians were more positive. When the attitude profiles of the same students were examined in the senior elementary grades, relatively few significant differences were found between the two groups. Genesee, Morin and Allister (1974) found similar patterns of attitudes among late immersion students – that is, more positive attitudes towards French Canadians among Grade 7 late immersion students, but no differences among Grade 11 students. Genesee (1987) has suggested that this shift may reflect the lack of ongoing contact between English and French Canadian students and, thus, the lack of a real substantive basis for maintaining positive attitudes.

Immersion students' use of French outside school

Genesee (1978, 1981b) has conducted a number of surveys in Quebec on the language habits of immersion students outside school since, after all, it was the recognition of the growing importance of French as a medium of communication in Quebec that motivated the establishment of immersion in the first place. Immersion as well as non-immersion students (and their parents) were asked to indicate in specially prepared diaries what they had done during the preceding day or weekend, with whom, and in which language. Diary entries were made for several days in a row and covered activities from early morning to bed time. The students and parents were also asked to answer a number of questions about their feelings about learning and using French.

The immersion students reported that they felt more comfortable and confident when speaking French with francophones than did English-speaking students who had not attended immersion. They also indicated that they were more likely to respond in French when spoken to in French and that they were less likely to avoid situations where French would be spoken. In fact, their diary entries revealed that they used French significantly more often than did non-immersion students – with friends, sales clerks and other service providers. At the same time, there was little indication from their diaries that they were more likely to actively seek out situations where French was used (for example, by watching French television, listening to French radio, or reading French magazines). Furthermore, the actual frequency and duration of usage of French in these ways was negligible when compared to their use of English in the same ways. The same response patterns were obtained from the parents of immersion students. Additional evidence based on immersion students' evaluative reactions to simulated encounters between English- and French-speaking Canadians in public settings also attests to limitations in their tolerance towards the use of French at the expense of English in situations where English would normally be expected (Genesee and Bourhis, 1982).

In sum, there have been some positive social outcomes of immersion in Canada, as attested by immersion students' views and attitudes of themselves, English Canadians and French Canadians, and by their actual use of French. There is also, however, evidence of limitations on the types and extent of social outcomes arising from immersion.

SUMMARY AND DISCUSSION

Systematic research over the last thirty years has consistently shown French immersion programmes (as well as heritage and indigenous language immersion programmes) to be feasible and effective forms of education for English-speaking Canadian students. More specifically, it has been found that students in elementary and secondary level immersion programmes demonstrate the same levels of English development and academic achievement as comparable students in all-English schools. At the same time, they acquire levels of functional proficiency in French that, although not entirely native-like in certain respects, are far superior to those of students in other types of second-language programmes in Canada. These results have been documented in English-dominant, French-dominant and bilingual regions of the country and, thus, are robust and reliable. Even students with learner characteristics that often limit their academic performance have been shown to benefit from immersion. Comparisons among immersion alternatives indicate that the effectiveness of particular variants depends on a combination of factors, including exposure time to the second language, the age of the learners and pedagogical methods.

French immersion has had substantial effects on the educational system in Canada and significant but qualified broader social effects. That French immersion did not result in the unqualified social effects that might have been hoped for at its inauguration should not be surprising when viewed within the broader sociocultural context in which it unfolded (Clément, 1995). The socially focused research just reviewed was conducted during a period of intense political change in Quebec – among other events, French was declared the only official language in Quebec, which had previously granted English official status; children of immigrant parents were obliged to attend French-medium and not English-medium schools, leading to a substantial decline in the population of English schools; it became illegal to use English on public signs (with some exceptions) throughout the province, in contravention of historic rights to freedom of public speech in Quebec and Canada; and a referendum was held in Quebec in 1978 which invited Quebecers to seek separation from Canada as a means of protecting the French language and culture in North America. It is not difficult to imagine the depressing effects such events might have had on the participants in immersion programmes and on intergroup relations in general.

With respect to immersion itself, the Quebec government has not recognized immersion as a distinct educational programme in the English school system; indeed, there were no official statistics regarding enrolment in immersion programmes in Quebec in 1977, some twelve years after their inauguration. Nor are graduates of immersion given special credit or recognition by Le Ministère de l'Education du Québec. On the occasion of his retirement in 1989, Wallace Lambert, regarded as the father of immersion, was interviewed in Montreal by a reporter from the largest French newspaper in Quebec. Five minutes into the interview, the reporter asked: 'C'est quoi l'immersion? [*What's immersion?*]'. What was regarded by the English-speaking community as a major initiative to bridge the two solitudes apparently went virtually unnoticed in the French-speaking community of Quebec.

Clearly, an interpretation of the social impact of French immersion must take into account the broader sociocultural context of which it is a part. The empirical effects of contextual factors are evident in the reactions of individual second-language learners and in the second-language learning environments created by immersion. Genesee, Rogers and Holobow (1983) found that

English-speaking students' perceptions that their French-speaking compatriots supported their learning French were a significant predictor of their second-language learning. The effects of perceived outgroup support were independent of the learners' own motivations. In an extensive ethnographic study of an early immersion school, Cleghorn and Genesee (1984) found that there were informal divisions and implicit conflicts between English- and French-speaking teachers that could be traced to intergroup conflicts and tensions in the community at large. Thus, despite its best intentions and expressed aim to model and promote a new social order based on bilingual competence, the school appeared to be perpetuating the two solitudes that it sought to reconcile. Thus, while French immersion has been an important part of sociolinguistic change in Canada, it is only one part of a complex constellation of social, economic, cultural and political factors that mediate that change.

References

Blake, L., Lambert, W. E., Sidoti, N. and Wolfe, D. (undated). Students' views of inter-group tensions in Quebec. Unpublished report, Psychology Department, McGill University, Montreal.

Bourhis, R. (1984). *Conflict and Language Planning in Quebec.* Clevedon, Avon: Multilingual Matters.

Bruck, M. (1985). Predictors of transfer out of early French immersion programs. *Canadian Modern Language Review, 6,* 39–61.

Cleghorn, A. and Genesee, F. (1984). Languages in contact: An ethnographic study of interaction in an immersion school. *TESOL Quarterly, 18,* 595–625.

Clément, R. (1995). The acquisition of French as a second language in Canada: towards a research agenda. In J. W. Berry and J. Laponce (eds.), *Ethnicity and Culture in Canada: The Research Landscape* (pp. 410–434). Toronto: University of Toronto Press.

Commissioner of Official Languages (1994). *Annual Report.* Ottawa: General Services and Public Works.

Cook, R., Saywell, J. and Ricker, J. (1977). *Canada: A Modern Study.* Toronto: Clark, Irwin.

Cziko, G., Lambert, W. E. and Gutter, J. (1980). The impact of immersion in a foreign language on pupils' social attitudes. *Working Papers on Bilingualism, 19,* 13–28.

Day, E. and Shapson, S. (1991). Integrating formal and functional approaches to language teaching in French immersion: an experimental study. *Language Learning, 41,* 25–58.

Gardner, R. C. and Lambert, W. E. (1972). *Attitudes and Motivation in Second Language Learning.* Rowley, MA: Newbury House.

Genesee, F. (1976). The role of intelligence in second language learning. *Language Learning, 26,* 267–280.

(1977a). *Departmental leaving examination results: June 1977*. Report submitted to The Protestant School Board of Greater Montreal.

(1977b). *French immersion students' perceptions of themselves and others: An ethnolinguistic perspective*. Report submitted to The Protestant School Board of Greater Montreal.

(1978). Second language learning and language attitudes. *Working Papers on Bilingualism, 16,* 19–42.

(1981a). A comparison of early and late second language learning. *Canadian Modern Language Review, 13,* 115–128.

(1981b). Bilingualism and biliteracy: a study of cross-cultural contact in a bilingual community. In J. Edwards (ed.), *The Social Psychology of Reading* (pp. 147–172). Silver Spring, MD: Institute of Modern Languages.

(1987). *Learning Through Two Languages: Studies of Immersion and Bilingual Education*. Rowley, MA: Newbury House.

(1992). Second/foreign language immersion and at-risk English-speaking children. *Foreign Language Annals, 25,* 199–213.

Genesee, F. and Bourhis, R. (1982). The social psychological consequences of code switching in cross-cultural communication. *Journal of Language and Social Psychology, 1,* 1–27.

Genesee, F. and Chaplin, S. (1976). *Evaluation of the 1974–75 grade 11 French immersion class*. Report submitted to The Protestant School Board of Greater Montreal.

Genesee, F. and Holobow, N. E. (1989). Change and stability in intergroup perceptions. *Journal of Language and Social Psychology, 8,* 17–38.

Genesee, F. and Lambert, W. E. (1983). Trilingual education for majority language children. *Child Development, 54,* 105–114.

Genesee, F., Morin, S. and Allister, T. (1974). *Evaluation of the 1973–74 grade 7 French immersion class*. Report submitted to The Protestant School Board of Greater Montreal.

Genesee, F., Rogers, P. and Holobow, N. (1983). The social psychology of second language learning: another point of view. *Language Learning, 33,* 209–224.

Hammerly, H. (1992). French immersion (Does it work?). In S. Rehorick and V. Edwards (eds.), *French Immersion: Process, Product and Perspectives* (pp. 301–313). Welland, ON: Canadian Modern Language Review.

Harley, B. (1992). Patterns of second language development in French immersion. *French Language Studies, 2,* 159–183.

Lambert, W. E., Genesee, F., Holobow, N. E. and McGilly, C. (1984). An evaluation of a partial Mohawk immersion program in the Kahnawake Schools. Unpublished research report, Psychology Department, McGill University, Montreal.

Lambert, W. E., Hodgson, R., Gardner, R. C. and Fillenbaum, S. (1960). Evaluational reactions to spoken languages. *Journal of Abnormal and Social Psychology, 60,* 44–51.

Lambert, W. E. and Tucker, G. R. (1972). *Bilingual Education of Children: The St Lambert Experiment.* Rowley, MA: Newbury House.

Lapkin, S., Swain, M., and Shapson, S. (1992). French immersion research agenda for the 1990s. In S. Rehorick and V. Edwards (eds.), *French Immersion: Process, Product and Perspectives* (pp. 392–428). Welland, ON: Canadian Modern Language Review.

Lyster, R. (1994). The effect of functional-analytic teaching on aspects of French immersion students' sociolinguistic competence. *Applied Linguistics, 15,* 263–287.

MacLennan, H. (1945). *Two Solitudes.* Toronto: Macmillan.

Swain, M. (1980). French immersion programs in Canada. *Multiculturalism, 4,* 3–6.

(1988). Manipulating and complementing content teaching to maximize second language learning. *TESL Canada Journal, 6,* 68–83.

Swain, M. and Carroll, S. (1987). The immersion observation study. In B. Harley, P. Allen, J. Cummins and M. Swain (eds.), *The Development of Bilingual Proficiency: Final Report, Volume II* (pp. 190–341). Toronto: Modern Language Centre, OISE.

Swain, M. and Lapkin, S. (1982). *Evaluating Bilingual Education: A Canadian Case Study.* Clevedon, Avon: Multilingual Matters.

Wiss, C. (1987). Issues in the assessment of learning problems in children from French immersion programs. *Canadian Modern Language Review, 43,* 302–313.

(1989). Early French immersion programs may not be suitable for every child. *Canadian Modern Language Review, 45,* 189–202.

Map 2 Newfoundland and Labrador

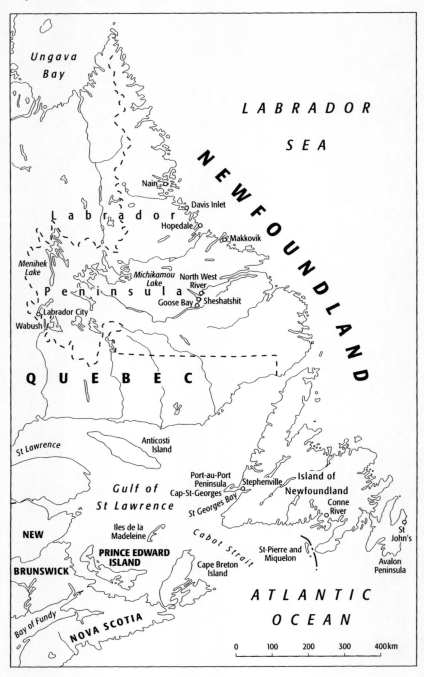

16 Language in Newfoundland

Sandra Clarke

INTRODUCTION

In 1949 the island of Newfoundland, along with its continental portion, Labrador, became the tenth province of the Canadian confederation, of which it constitutes the largest of the four Atlantic provinces. From a linguistic perspective, present-day Newfoundland/Labrador is the most homogeneous area of the country. The overwhelming majority of Newfoundlanders – some 98 per cent, or 559,620 of a total population of 568,475 – claim English as their sole mother tongue (Statistics Canada, 1991). The number of aboriginal-language speakers in the province is very small; although languages representing both the Algonquian and Eskimo-Aleut families are still found in Labrador, these must today be classified as endangered. As to European languages, Newfoundland/Labrador has a rich linguistic history, since it was one of the earliest areas of the New World to be discovered: beginning in approximately AD 1,000, visitors to its shores have included speakers of Norse, Basque, Spanish, Portuguese, French, Irish Gaelic and Scots Gaelic. Most of these languages, however, have totally disappeared, leaving no trace of their passage other than toponymic evidence.

Twentieth-century immigration has played an important role in much of urban Canada, where it has created considerable linguistic diversity. In Newfoundland, however, where in-migration peaked in the first half of the nineteenth century, its effects have been minimal. According to the 1991 census, over 92 per cent of residents of Newfoundland were born within the province; fewer than 2 per cent were born outside Canada, the majority of these being from the United States or Britain (Statistics Canada, 1991).

In this overwhelmingly English-speaking setting, it is perhaps not surprising that the province appears to have paid little attention to the situation of its linguistic minorities. Before this important issue is addressed, however, an outline is presented of the languages of Newfoundland and Labrador, both European and aboriginal.

LANGUAGES OF NEWFOUNDLAND AND LABRADOR:
A HISTORICAL OVERVIEW

European languages

By the mid nineteenth century, small enclaves of the predominantly English-speaking island of Newfoundland had been occupied by settlers who spoke French, Irish Gaelic and Scots Gaelic. Today, however, only French still possesses fluent speakers and, in the face of the overwhelming influence of English, even the future of Newfoundland French is by no means assured.

English. The history of continuous English settlement in Newfoundland is one of the lengthiest in the New World, dating back to the beginning of the seventeenth century. By far the greatest number of English immigrants to Newfoundland came from the West Country of England, in particular the counties of Dorset and Devon, with Poole serving as a major embarkation point.

As Newfoundland remained relatively isolated up to the Second World War, the varieties of English spoken both on the island and in Labrador are remarkably conservative, and display many non-standard phonological, grammatical and lexical features which also characterize their source dialects, whether southwest British or southeast Irish. Some of these are outlined in Paddock (1982), Kirwin (1993) and Clarke (in press). In the face of the increasing incursion of standard mainland Canadian English, however, many such features are tending to disappear among younger speakers (see, for example Clarke, 1991), a process reinforced by the generally negative stereotyping of non-standard Newfoundland speakers on the part of mainland Canadians.

French. According to the 1991 census, approximately 18,500 residents of the province, or just over 3 per cent of the population, claimed to speak both French and English (Statistics Canada, 1991). This is slightly higher than the 2.6 per cent rate of bilingualism – the lowest in Canada and well under the overall Canadian average of 16.2 per cent – recorded in the 1986 census (Statistics Canada, 1986). In 1991, only 1,235 residents of the province reported French as their language of use in the home, although 2,405 claimed it as a mother tongue (Statistics Canada, 1991).

Three distinct groups of French-language origin are currently found in the province; all but the third comprise recent, and to some degree transient, residents. The first consists of approximately 1,000 francophones located in and near the capital city, St John's. This group is primarily *Québécois*, but also contains French speakers from Europe and St-Pierre/Miquelon; many work for the federal government, as well as the school and university system. The second group, also primarily of *Québécois* origin, is located in the Labrador City/ Wabush area of western Labrador, where the earliest francophones arrived in the late 1950s to work in the developing iron ore industry. In 1971, over 2,000 people, or approximately 11 per cent of the population of western Labrador, were francophone. By 1986 however, after a downturn in the mining industry, the French-speaking population had decreased by approximately two-thirds (Charbonneau and Barrette, 1994).

The third group is located in the southwestern part of the island of Newfoundland, in the area of the Port-au-Port peninsula and St George's Bay. The first French speakers settled this area at the end of the eighteenth century. These were Acadians from Cape Breton and the Magdalen Islands, along with a small number of fishermen directly from France, particularly Brittany and Normandy (see Butler, 1995, for further details). By 1850, the population of this area was 80 per cent French.

The twentieth century proved a period of major cultural and linguistic assimilation for the French speakers of Newfoundland's west coast, which was reinforced – at least until 1970 – by the lack of minority-language rights. While the church had attempted to provide French-speaking priests throughout the nineteenth century, this ceased after 1928. Whatever schooling was available was provided exclusively in English, and punishment was meted out to students using French at school (see Butler, 1994). The decline of French language and culture accelerated after 1940 with the construction of an American air force base near Stephenville, the largest of the francophone west-coast communities; the employment opportunities offered by the base drew a large number of English-speaking Newfoundlanders to the area. Newfoundland's confederation with Canada in 1949 did nothing to curb the assimilation process. Indeed, as Waddell and Doran (1993, p. 223) point out, it 'increased the ethnic marginality of the people and their dependence on a larger economic order'. From an educational perspective, the introduction of an obligatory provincial curriculum meant that the local variety of French was further undermined, in that standard European French – at least in so far as it had been mastered by English-speaking Newfoundland teachers – was the only variety legitimized by the French-as-second-language programmes offered by the school system (see King, 1988). By the mid-1970s, no resident of Stephenville under the age of fifty spoke French as a mother tongue. The assimilating effects of the majority culture, while not quite as great, were also readily apparent in the several small French villages on the Port-au-Port peninsula (Cap-St-Georges, la Grand'Terre, l'Anse-à Canards/Maisons d'Hiver) which, until the middle of the present century, had been almost exclusively francophone. The 1986 census reports that only 720 people, or just over 10 per cent of the population of the entire peninsula, claimed French as a mother tongue; this represents a decline of 12.2 per cent over fifteen years (Waddell and Doran, 1993).

By the beginning of the 1970s there had none the less emerged – along with the availability of federal government support for French minority groups and the recommendation that the Port-au-Port peninsula become a federal bilingual district – a growing sense of francophone identity among Newfoundlanders of French origin. With the financial support of the Office of the Secretary of State for Canada, several francophone associations were founded, the first of these (les Terre-Neuviens français) in 1971; these have assumed an important role in fostering linguistic and cultural identity (see Charbonneau and Barrette, 1994). In 1974, French-language television was introduced from Montreal, and in the following year a bilingual school was established in the village of Cap-St-Georges. More recent developments, in at least some of the Port-au-Port communities, have included bilingual postal services and a French-language community television channel. The provincial government has also made some effort to provide French-language medical and legal services to its French-speaking residents, particularly in Labrador City/Wabush. Such developments are still in their infancy, however, and talks are ongoing between the francophone associations and the provincial government to augment French-language use through the establishment of an Office of Francophone Affairs.

Irish Gaelic. The Irish have had a long history in Newfoundland. They first came to the island as transient workers in the fishery, starting in about 1675, when ships from southwest England began calling regularly into ports in the southeast of Ireland on their journeys to Newfoundland. The vast majority of permanent Irish settlers, however, were not to emigrate until the first three or four decades of the nineteenth century; these originated almost entirely in an extremely concentrated area within thirty miles of the southeastern Irish port of Waterford (Mannion, 1977). In Newfoundland, Irish settlement is likewise concentrated in the southern part of the Avalon peninsula, south of the capital city of St John's. Various small Irish pockets are, however, to be found elsewhere on the coastline, which otherwise was settled primarily by emigrants from the southwest of England.

Precise details on language use among early Irish fishery workers and migrants are impossible to ascertain. Yet it is clear (see Foster, 1979; Kirwin, 1993) that some of this group spoke Irish Gaelic and little if any English. As Kirwin points out, there are none the less few actual accounts of Irish being spoken in Newfoundland, or of Irish being passed on within families from generation to generation. The language did linger on in certain rural areas, however, until the early years of the twentieth century.

Scots Gaelic. From approximately 1844, a relatively small number of Scottish families from Cape Breton, drawn in search of agricultural land, settled in the southwestern corner of the island of Newfoundland, south of St George's Bay. They brought with them their Scots Gaelic tongue which, some 150 years later, is still not extinct in the area – in spite of the numerical superiority of English-speaking settlers, and the total lack of institutional or educational support for the minority-language group. It is, however, safe to say that there remain no fluent speakers of the language, and that Scots Gaelic appears to be largely confined to particular intragroup situations, such as those involving traditional tales and songs, where it plays a largely symbolic cultural role (see Bennett Knight, 1972; Foster, 1982).

Aboriginal languages

Two of the province's four aboriginal languages (Beothuk and Mi'kmaq) are no longer spoken. The remaining two (Montagnais-Naskapi or Innu-aimun, and Inuktitut) continue to serve as the first languages of small indigenous populations in Labrador. Mi'kmaq and Montagnais-Naskapi are members of the Algonquian language group, the latter being fairly closely related to the Cree dialects spoken from James Bay to Alberta; Inuktitut (or, as it is known in Labrador, Inuttut) belongs to the Eskimo-Aleut family of languages. The writing systems of all indigenous languages of the province utilize the Roman alphabet, and not the syllabic system employed for both Inuktitut and Cree in the Eastern Arctic and James Bay areas.

According to the 1991 census, 5,340 residents of the province claimed only aboriginal descent, with a further 7,770 claiming aboriginal as well as other origin (Tanner, Kennedy, McCorquodale and Inglis, 1994).

Beothuk. The last known speaker of Beothuk died in 1829. The small Beothuk group, which inhabited the island at the time of arrival of the first Europeans, became, after European contact, the victim of hostilities, disease and starvation. Its language survives today only in the form of three short vocabularies, separately elicited from three young Beothuk females by English speakers with no particular linguistic training, and riddled with errors as a result of many recopyings. The result is that although there are sufficient similarities to lead some linguists to the conclusion that Beothuk was an Algonquian language (see Hewson, 1978), this conclusion will in all likelihood remain uncertain.

Mi'kmaq. The Newfoundland Mi'kmaq are today concentrated in a single community on the south coast of the island, Conne River, where approximately 650 people live as the Mawpukek Band. The Mi'kmaq were recognized as status Indians in 1984 under Canada's Indian Act – a designation not achieved by some 1,500 people of mixed Mi'kmaq/French/English origin who live elsewhere on the island. While the ancestors of the Newfoundland Mi'kmaq migrated to the island from Nova Scotia, it is unclear whether their arrival antedated that of Europeans; this point is of some contention with respect to the issue of land claims. The twentieth century has proven for the Mi'kmaq a period of particularly rapid assimilation, involving loss of the traditional hunting and trapping lifestyle, as well as considerable intermarriage with non-aboriginals; even as early as 1921, some one-third of male heads of households had spouses who knew little if any Mi'kmaq. These factors have led to the actual demise of the Mi'kmaq language in Newfoundland, the last fluent speaker having died in 1979.

Innu-aimun (Montagnais-Naskapi). In the anthropological and linguistic literature prior to the past decade or so, the Labrador Innu have been identified as either Montagnais or Naskapi. The former are traditional forest dwellers, closely related to those Innu who today live on Quebec's Lower North Shore, as far west as Sept-Iles. The latter, also known as Mushuau Innu, or 'Barren Ground People', have traditionally hunted in the largely treeless tundra to the north. Since the late 1950s, the Montagnais group, with traditional ties to the Hudson's Bay post at North West River, some twenty-five miles from the town of Goose Bay, has established permanent residence in this community – or, more accurately, directly across the river from it in the Indian settlement of Sheshatshit ('at the big outlet'), which has a current population of approximately 1,000. The Naskapi group of some 500 or so resides today in the coastal community of Davis Inlet (Utshimassit: 'at the store clerk's place'); this band has close historical links with the Naskapi now located in Schefferville, Quebec. Although forced to settle in these Labrador communities in order to obtain government services, the Innu have not totally abandoned their traditional nomadic lifestyle, and a number of families spend several months each year in the country. In both communities, employment opportunities are few; the Innu live in conditions of fairly abject poverty, in homes that, for example, often lack running water.

According to the 1991 census, 1,100 residents of the province claimed Montagnais-Naskapi as their home language (Statistics Canada, 1991). In both Sheshatshit and Davis Inlet, in fact, the vast majority of Innu families use the language at home, and the young still speak it as a first language, although the range of grammatical forms which they command is more restricted than that of their parents' and grandparents' generations. Outside the home, however, the situation is different: until very recently, English was the language in which all basic services were provided, and was necessary for interaction with teachers, medical personnel, or the police and court system. This situation is now in the process of change; for example, the Innu are gaining more control over education (see below), and native police officers have recently been appointed. Sporadically, funding administered by the local band councils has been used for the publication of an Innu-language newsletter and, in Sheshatshit at least, to support a local Innu-language radio station.

Linguistically, the Innu varieties of Sheshatshit and Davis Inlet, while mutually comprehensible with some degree of difficulty, differ considerably with respect to lexicon, phonology and grammatical structure. Within both communities there is also considerable linguistic variation, the result of settlement by several different traditional hunting groups. Labrador Innu-aimun has been described in a number of fairly recent linguistic studies, listed in MacKenzie (1991); a short description of the language, along with a brief historical overview, is provided by MacKenzie (1982).

Inuktitut (Inuttut). The province's Inuit are concentrated primarily in the three coastal Labrador communities of Nain, Hopedale and Makkovik. These were established as Christian missions – as early as 1771 in the case of Nain – by the Moravians, a German Protestant sect which had from 1733 founded such missions among the Greenland Inuit. Until the middle of the present century, when the Labrador Inuit finally abandoned their traditional nomadic lifestyle, they occupied these Moravian settlements largely on a seasonal basis. Though Moravian influence waned after the early twentieth century, its linguistic effects can still be seen in a small group of lexical borrowings from German into Labrador Inuttut, including the word for 'potato', as well as the names for days of the week and months of the year (see Jeddore, 1979; Peacock, 1974).

Today, Nain is the most northerly settlement in Labrador and, with a population of 1,069 in 1991, is also its largest primarily aboriginal community. Hopedale and Makkovik, with current populations of less than 500, have a higher proportion of non-Inuit inhabitants. In all of these communities, the Inuttut language is in serious decline. According to 1991 census figures, just under 500 residents of the province claimed Inuktitut as their sole mother tongue (Statistics Canada, 1991). Almost 300 of these live in Nain, where most are in the older age group (Mazurkewich, 1995). Intermarriage over a number of generations with the small European population in Labrador has played some role in this, resulting in a 'Settler' group of mixed ancestry. The use of English as the medium of instruction in twentieth-century Labrador has also been a primary contributor to language attrition (see below), as of course has the general prestige associated with English society and culture that has precipitated language shift among aboriginal groups in much of North America. As Mazurkewich (1995) points out, Inuit children in the community of Nain rarely use Inuttut in their everyday interactions; English is being increasingly used even in the home domain. Even in households where Inuttut *is* the primary language of communication, children are generally able to function in English by the time they enter school (Mazurkewich, 1991). Use of the local language is none the less reinforced by the availability of Inuktitut-language radio and television from outside Labrador, including a CBC station from Iqaluit, as well as a local radio station broadcasting in Inuttut. In addition, ready access to health, medical and other services is made possible for Inuttut speakers via programmes providing translation and other support.

Linguistically, Labrador Inuttut is most similar to the dialects of northern Quebec and Baffin Island. Descriptions of this variety may be found in Smith (1977, 1978).

MINORITY-LANGUAGE PRESERVATION IN NEWFOUNDLAND AND LABRADOR

Minority-language maintenance is closely linked to the utility and viability of such languages in public as well as private domains. Yet when it comes to the linguistic rights of its minority groups, the province of Newfoundland and Labrador has no official policy. The only minority whose linguistic rights are governed by legislation are the Newfoundland French, and the legislation in question is federal rather than provincial: Article 23 of Canada's Charter of Rights and Freedoms guarantees French-language education for children of Canadian citizens whose mother tongue is French, at least where numbers are sufficient to warrant this.

The following section briefly examines the present situation of French-language education in the province. This is followed by an outline of two unique sets of circumstances which have had an impact on minority-language maintenance in Newfoundland and Labrador: the existence, firstly, of a church-controlled education system, and, secondly, of special governance arrangements which affect the province's aboriginal groups.

French-language education

According to 1986 census figures, 1,555 residents of the province between the ages of five and nineteen were entitled to French-language instruction under the provisions of Article 23; one-third of these lived on the Port-au-Port peninsula (Vienneau, 1990). Yet by no means all eligible Newfoundland francophones have enrolled their children in French-language schools, of which there are at present five in the province: two on the Port-au-Port peninsula, two in Labrador, and one in St John's. According to a recent newspaper report, the current total registration of these schools is only 325 (St John's *Evening Telegram*, 1 February 1996). One outstanding issue is school governance, which does not appear to have been addressed in the revised Schools Act still to be brought to the provincial legislature. Indeed, after unsuccessful attempts to negotiate this issue, the Newfoundland and Labrador Federation of Francophone Parents took the government to court early in 1996.

Non-francophone Newfoundland students in several urban centres have the option of French-language education via French immersion programmes. The 1994 report of the Commissioner of Official Languages states that these had a 1994/95 enrolment of 4,515, or just under 3 per cent of the province's 155,920 school students. A total of forty schools offers this option, in some thirteen different school districts, generally in the form of early rather than late immersion programmes.

The role of the churches

For over 150 years, the churches have had official control of the Newfoundland and Labrador school system, and although the responsibilities of government in matters of administration and curriculum have increased considerably during the past fifty years, the system still remains a denominational one (though this is about to change). Church control of education has had both positive and negative effects on minority-language preservation. On the positive side, it has in some cases produced literacy in the aboriginal language among groups who otherwise would not have achieved this. The Labrador Inuit, for example, were schooled exclusively in Inuttut by the Moravian missionaries, and by the mid nineteenth century displayed a considerably higher rate of literacy than that to be found among the non-aboriginal population of Newfoundland and Labrador (see Jeddore, 1979). On the negative side, while the churches did not operate a full-fledged residential school system for aboriginals in Newfoundland and Labrador (as they did in western Canada), their effect was often no less assimilatory. For example, although Mi'kmaq was taught in the Conne River school until 1910, after 1911 the Roman Catholic church began to actively discourage the maintenance of Mi'kmaq culture and language; in 1924 a priest succeeded in abolishing the office of chief and forcing the incumbent out of the province over such issues as the use of Mi'kmaq in church and school (Tanner *et al.*, 1994). The negative effects of the churches were not limited to aboriginal languages: even in areas of extensive Irish settlement in southeastern Newfoundland, there is no nineteenth-century record of education ever having been conducted in Irish Gaelic by the priests and nuns imported directly from Ireland (Foster, 1979). These facts do not imply, however, that an exclusively government-controlled education system would have made better provision for its linguistic minorities; the post-1949 educational experience of the Labrador minority groups, indeed, might suggest the contrary.

Aboriginal-language education

Unlike their counterparts in other provinces of the country, the aboriginal peoples of Newfoundland and Labrador do not come under the direct jurisdiction of a distinct federally run administrative system (that is, apart from the Mi'kmaq group, who were registered under the Indian Act in 1984). Instead, they receive most government services through joint federal–provincial funding agreements formally administered by the provincial government to all residents of those communities in which aboriginal people constitute a sizeable portion of the population (Tanner *et al.*, 1994). One important consequence of this is that the aboriginal peoples of Newfoundland/Labrador have no direct control over the allocation of funds which affect all economic and social aspects of their lives, including their cultural and linguistic heritage; indeed, there does not even exist at the provincial government level a department for aboriginal affairs, or even a 'formal interdepartmental committee to coordinate all government policy-making related to aboriginal people' (Tanner *et al.*, 1994, p. 76).

The effects of the lack of native input and control are nowhere more obvious than in the area of education. After Newfoundland and Labrador joined Canada in 1949, schooling became compulsory to age fifteen, and the provincial government assumed a greater degree of responsibility for the education of its indigenous population. One unfortunate outcome was that education was provided solely in the majority language, typically involving English-speaking teachers from outside the community who were often unfamiliar with its language and culture. By the 1970s, the degree of linguistic and cultural shift was apparent to at least some of the province's native population, who were increasingly recognizing the importance of aboriginal language education in language maintenance. Today, all aboriginal communities in the province have in some way or other incorporated the native language into the school curriculum. At the very least, it is taught as a core subject, as in the Mi'kmaq community of Conne River; here, a native speaker of Mi'kmaq is brought over from Cape Breton, Nova Scotia for short periods several times per year. Several communities, including Nain and Sheshatshit, have succeeded in implementing programmes in which the aboriginal language is used as the medium of instruction in the early grades, with a switch to English-language instruction in Grade 3. Only in Conne River, however – where, somewhat ironically, it is too late to restore the Mi'kmaq language – does an aboriginal group have full control over the school system.

The introduction of aboriginal languages into the education system has not been without its share of problems, not the least of which are, as elsewhere in Canada (see Clarke and MacKenzie, 1980a, 1980b), the lack of trained teachers and of educational materials in the indigenous languages. Since the 1970s, aboriginal teacher aides have functioned in Labrador schools, and in 1978 a diploma programme for their training was formally established within the Education faculty of Memorial University. In 1989, this was broadened to a degree-granting programme in native and northern education, which produced its first graduate in 1993. As to indigenous language teaching materials, production has been impeded by the lack of standardized orthographies. The Inuit have been faced with the problem of updating the old Moravian script, which does not provide a phonemic representation of modern Labrador Inuttut. And although an ortho-graphic standard has largely been agreed upon by Montagnais speakers in Quebec, the same is not true of the Innu communities of Labrador, where there is still considerable individual variation in spelling (see MacKenzie, 1991).

CONCLUSION

At the close of the twentieth century, Newfoundland and Labrador is an overwhelmingly English-speaking province in which minority languages, whether of aboriginal or European origin, are seriously threatened. Given the small numbers of speakers of these languages, as well as their almost total lack of legal protection, it is difficult to see how the ongoing process of rapid assimilation in the direction of majority language and culture can be reversed.

Note

I would very much like to thank Alana Johns, John Joy, Marguerite MacKenzie, Irene Mazurkewich, John Noel and Adrian Tanner for the information that they provided on various aspects of minority-language use in Newfoundland. Without them this article would not have been possible. In addition, a certain amount factual information, the source of which is unacknowledged owing to space constraints, derives from the five-volume *Encyclopedia of Newfoundland and Labrador.*

References

Bennett Knight, M. (1972). Scottish Gaelic, English and French: some aspects of the macaronic tradition of the Codroy Valley, Newfoundland. *Regional Language Studies... Newfoundland, 4,* 25–30. (Memorial University of Newfoundland, Department of English Language and Literature).

Butler, G. R. (1994). L'Acadie et la France se rencontrent: le peuplement franco-acadien de la baie St-Georges, Terre-Neuve. *Newfoundland Studies, 10,* 180–207.

(1995). *Histoire et traditions orales des franco-acadiens de Terre Neuve.* Quebec: Septrention.

Charbonneau, P. M. and Barrette, L. (1994). *Against the Odds: A History of the Francophones of Newfoundland and Labrador* (trans. M. Luke). St John's, Nfld.: Harry Cuff Publications.

Clarke, S. (1991). Phonological variation and recent language change in St. John's English. In J. Cheshire (ed.), *English Around the World: Sociolinguistic Perspectives* (pp. 108–122). Cambridge: Cambridge University Press.

(in press). The role of Irish English in the formation of New World Englishes: the case from Newfoundland. In J. Kallen (ed.), *Focus on Ireland.* Amsterdam and Philadelphia: Benjamins.

Clarke, S. & MacKenzie, M. (1980a). Education in the mother tongue: tokenism versus cultural autonomy in Canadian Indian schools. *Canadian Journal of Anthropology, 1,* 205–217.

(1980b). Indian teacher-training programs: an overview and evaluation. In William Cowan (ed.), *Papers of the Eleventh Algonquian Conference* (pp. 19–32). Ottawa: Carleton University.

Commissioner of Official Languages. (1978–1994). *Annual Reports.* Ottawa: Ministry of Supply and Services.

Encyclopedia of Newfoundland and Labrador, Vols. 1–5. (1981–1994). St John's, Nfld: Harry Cuff Publications.

Foster, F. G. (1979). Irish in Avalon: an investigation of the Gaelic language in eastern Newfoundland. *Newfoundland Quarterly, 74,* 17–22.

(1982). Gaeldom and Tír (N)úr – 'the New-found Land': sociological patterning of Scottish Gaelic in western Newfoundland. In H. Paddock (ed.), *Languages in Newfoundland and Labrador* (2nd version, pp. 14–41). St John's, Nfld: Memorial University of Newfoundland, Department of Linguistics.

Hewson, J. (1978). *The Beothuk Vocabularies.* St John's, Nfld: Technical Papers of the Newfoundland Museum, no. 2.

Jeddore, R. P. (1979). The decline and development of the Inuttut language in Labrador. In B. Basse and K. Jenses (eds.), *Eskimo Languages* (pp. 83–91). Aarhus: Arkona Publishers.

King, R. (1988). Le français terre-neuvien: aperçu général. In R. Mougeon and E. Beniak (eds.), *Le français canadien parlé hors Québec. Aperçu sociolinguistique* (pp. 227–244). Quebec: Les Presses de l'Université Laval.

Kirwin, W. J. (1993). The planting of Anglo-Irish in Newfoundland. In S. Clarke (ed.), *Focus on Canada* (pp. 65–84). Amsterdam and Philadelphia: John Benjamins.

MacKenzie, M. (1982). The language of the Montagnais and Naskapi in Labrador. In H. Paddock (ed.), *Languages in Newfoundland and Labrador* (2nd version, pp. 233–278). St John's, Nfld: Memorial University of Newfoundland, Department of Linguistics.

(1991). A survey of research on Montagnais and Naskapi (Innu-aimun) in Labrador. *Journal of the Atlantic Provinces Linguistic Association/Revue de l'Association de linguistique des provinces atlantiques, 13,* 47–56.

Mannion, J. J. (1977). Introduction. In J. J. Mannion (ed.), *The Peopling of Newfoundland* (pp. 1–13). Memorial University of Newfoundland: Institute of Social and Economic Research.

Mazurkewich, I. (1991). Language maintenance in Labrador: trying to hold the line. *Journal of the Atlantic Provinces Linguistic Association/Revue de l'Association de linguistique des provinces atlantiques, 13,* 57–69.

(1995). The attrition of Inuttut as a first language. Paper presented at the Symposium on Language Loss and Public Policy, University of New Mexico, Albuquerque, June–July 1995.

Paddock, H. (1982). Newfoundland dialects of English. In H. Paddock (ed.), *Languages in Newfoundland and Labrador* (2nd version, pp. 71–89). St John's, Nfld: Memorial University of Newfoundland, Department of Linguistics.

Peacock, F. W. (1974). Languages in contact in Labrador. *Regional Language Studies... Newfoundland, 5,* 1–3. (Memorial University of Newfoundland, Department of English Language and Literature).

Smith, L. R. (1977). *Some Grammatical Aspects of Labrador Inuttut (Eskimo): A Survey of the Inflectional Paradigms of Nouns and Verbs.* (Canadian Ethnology Service Paper 37, Mercury Series). Ottawa: National Museum of Man.

(1978). *A Survey of the Derivational Postbases of Labrador Inuttut (Eskimo).* (Canadian Ethnology Service Paper 45, Mercury Series). Ottawa: National Museum of Man.

Statistics Canada. (1986, 1991). *Census of Canada.* (Table LA86801; Catalogues 93–313 & 95–302). Ottawa: Ministry of Supply and Services.

Tanner, A., Kennedy, J. C., McCorquodale, S. and Inglis, G. (1994). *Aboriginal Peoples and Governance in Newfoundland and Labrador.* St John's, Nfld: Report prepared for the Governance Project, Royal Commission on Aboriginal Peoples.

Vienneau, J. G. (1990). *French Educational Needs Assessment for the Port-au-Port Peninsula.* St John's, Nfld: Report submitted to the Newfoundland and Labrador Department of Education.

Waddell, E. and Doran, C. (1993). The Newfoundland French: an endangered minority? In D. R. Louder and E. Waddell (eds.), *French America. Mobility, Identity, and Minority Experience Across the Continent* (pp. 212–228). Baton Rouge and London: Louisiana State University Press. [Orig. published in 1983 as *Du continent perdu à l'archipel retrouvé: le Québec et l'Amérique française.* Quebec: les Presses de l'Université Laval].

Map 3 Prince Edward Island

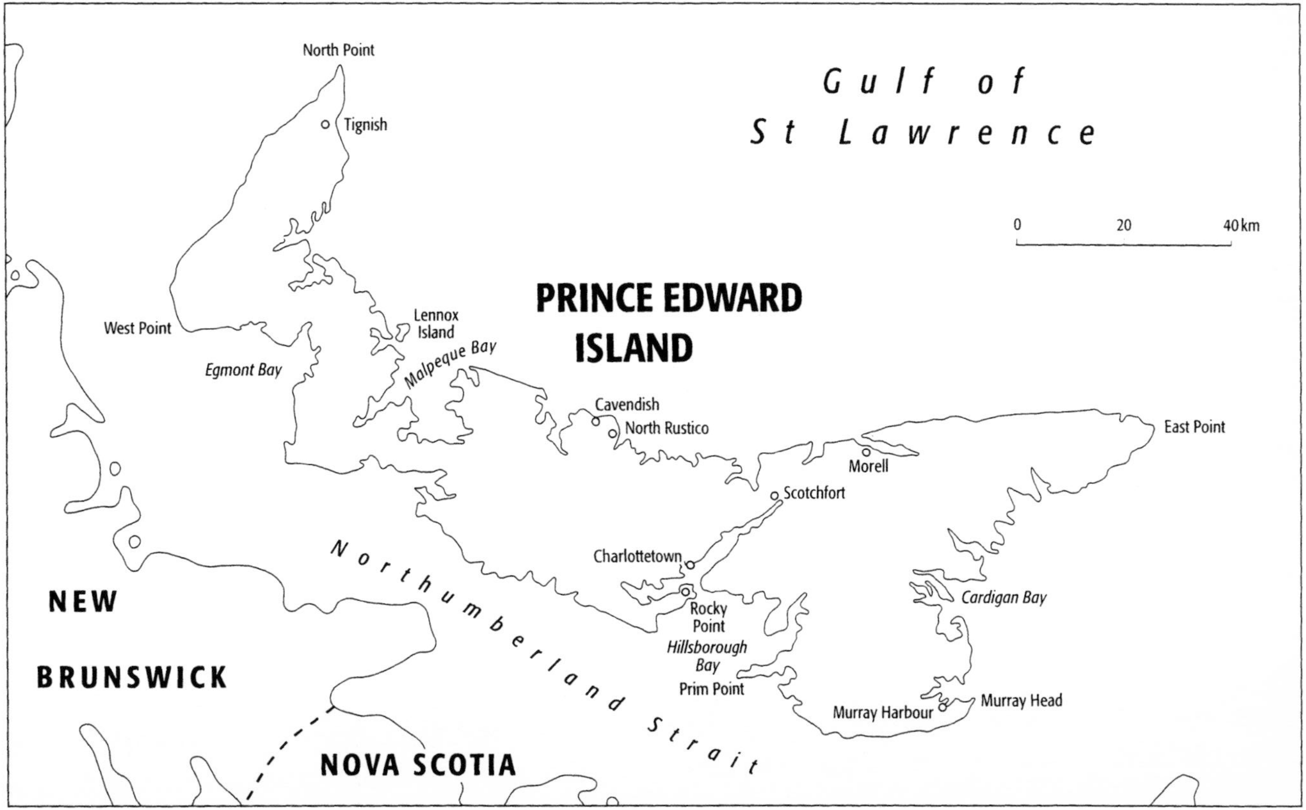

Gulf of St Lawrence

PRINCE EDWARD ISLAND

North Point
Tignish
West Point
Egmont Bay
Lennox Island
Malpeque Bay
Cavendish
North Rustico
Charlottetown
Rocky Point
Hillsborough Bay
Prim Point
Scotchfort
Morell
Cardigan Bay
Murray Harbour
Murray Head
East Point

Northumberland Strait

NEW BRUNSWICK

NOVA SCOTIA

0   20   40 km

17 Language in Prince Edward Island

T. K. Pratt

If Quebec leaves Canada, the province of Prince Edward Island will probably become unilingually English within a short time. This contention is based both on table 17.1 and on my conviction that Quebec's departure would spell the end of the admirable efforts in this province, by francophones and anglophones alike, to foster French. No other languages are in a position to survive at all. English is so dominant on Prince Edward Island that its state of health is not very interesting.[1] More interesting are French and Micmac, the latter because provincial and federal government policies have brought it, the province's one aboriginal tongue, to the point of extinction. Accordingly, this chapter will be devoted to these two languages only.[2]

FRENCH

The history of Island French could be described as a series of waves, each peak somewhat lower than the one before. To substantiate this claim in what follows, I draw upon the work of Arsenault (1989), Baldwin (1985) and King (1996). In 1713, the Treaty of Utrecht gave 'the Acadian peninsula' of Nova Scotia to England, while France retained the rest of what would become the Maritime provinces. Shortly afterwards, the French began building the fortress of Louisbourg in Cape Breton, to protect the approaches to their principal colony, Quebec. The troops and ships of Louisbourg needed provisions; to help supply them, 250 French settlers were landed in 1720 on the island they called Ile Saint Jean (i.e., Prince Edward Island), claimed by Cartier for France almost two centuries earlier. The settlers built Port LaJoie, opposite the present capital of Charlottetown, and outposts on the North Shore. They were joined by a trickle of Nova Scotia's Acadians, who were reluctant to leave the cleared homeland where they had farmed for a century, and where they had become a people distinct in culture and dialect from both Quebec and France. Nevertheless the trickle became a steady stream after the British built a rival to Louisbourg at Halifax in 1749,

Table 17.1 Percentages of speakers on Prince Edward Island

	Mother tongue		Home language		Ability to converse	
	1981	*1991*	*1981*	*1991*	*1981*	*1991*
English	94.1	94.3	96.5	97.3	99.8	99.7
French	4.8	4.5	3.1	2.4	8.2	10.3
Other	1.1	1.2	0.4	0.3	na	1.4

Source: Adapted from Harrison and Marmen (1994)

and the stream a flood when Britain expelled its Acadian subjects for refusing to take an unconditional oath of allegiance in anticipation of the coming new war with France. By 1756, at the beginning of the Seven Years War, there were some 5,000 speakers of French in Ile Saint Jean, most of them Acadian refugees. This was the first and highest peak of their language on this island.

The fall of Louisbourg in 1758 was followed by the famous deportation of the Acadians from the whole Maritimes region, except for a few individuals who escaped into the forest. In 1764, Samuel Holland, surveying for its new masters the re-named Saint John's Island (later, Prince Edward Island, for a son of George III), reported finding thirty French-speaking families scraping out a miserable existence. But little by little the dispersed Acadians began their celebrated return. By 1800, the main Acadian families whose names – Arsenault, Doucette, Gallant, Gaudet – are familiar on Prince Edward Island today were established, first on the North Shore, then in western Prince County. Their numbers in 1843 stood again at 5,000, but now within a total population of about 50,000.

Despite the triumph of this second wave, Island French was not so firmly established as before. It is true that in the first half of the nineteenth century there was little assimilation to English in the Acadians' isolated communities. But the land lottery of 1767, which had given to favourites of George III the sixty-seven townships, or lots, into which Samuel Holland had divided the entire Island, completely overlooked the Acadians, despite the amnesty that had allowed their return. Too poor to pay the rents demanded by the absentee landlords, and too uneducated to make their case with the land agents, the Acadians could only remain on land that 'official' settlers did not want. Frequently they had to shift from farms they had themselves cleared, as new tenants arrived; many turned from farming to fishing. The steady encroachment of English settlements 'would prove to be an important predictor of degree and rate of assimilation to English' (King, 1996, p. 4).

Like the French Canadians in Quebec, Acadians now began to link the survival of their language with that of their faith. Yet there were seldom enough priests, and those sent might well be English-speaking Irish, whose presence would undercut their parishioners' language. 'Wherever French is still intact', wrote a visitor in 1924, 'there is a zealous Acadian priest who, with the support of his obedient parishioners, is upholding the respect for the ancestral language' (Arsenault, 1989, p. 184).

Of even greater importance was education. When, after 1825, Island legislators began to vote a little money for schools, they naturally established the requirement that the teachers be fluent in English. In 1860, the government required that teachers be licensed by Charlottetown's Normal School, where the training was only in English. As Arsenault puts it, '[i]t was a paradoxical state of affairs: before setting out to teach in French, Acadian candidates had to demonstrate their proficiency in English . . . The long-term effect . . . was the anglicization of Acadian schools' (1989, p. 117). The School Act of 1877 ruled that all public PEI schools be non-confessional, which eliminated many texts in French with a religious bias, along with the responsibility of the local priest to ensure that the local teacher could speak the language. The Island's French schools did not even secure a francophone Inspector until 1892.

Despite all these drawbacks during the nineteenth century, Prince Edward Island French rose again, through a general renaissance of Acadian culture in the century's later years, which was aided by the fact that French was now a national language of the new country of Canada. In the words of an early Island leader, 'the Acadian people will find the strength and resources to gain respect for our rights which have been ignored for too long, and to preserve the integrity of our national character and the language we love and that our mothers taught us' (trans. in Arsenault, 1989, p. 155). The language's new surge included the first French newspaper (*L'Impartial*, 1893–1915), private schools, convent schools, and participation in national Acadian conventions. In the political sphere, Island francophones gained influence for the first time, through membership in the provincial legislature, the House of Commons and the Senate, and even through a premier, Aubin-Edmond Arsenault, 1917–1919. The justly named 'Evangéline' region in western PEI has sent a francophone to the Island legislature ever since.

The key issue for the leaders was again education. They created the Acadian Teachers' Association in 1893, the first such in the Maritime provinces, explicitly aimed at bettering the teaching of French. The Association in turn founded the Saint Thomas Aquinas Society, 1919, which rapidly became what it remains today, the main pressure group for Island francophones. Its immediate aim was to raise scholarship money for French-speaking students interested in a professional career, so that the doctors, lawyers, priests, teachers and civil servants of the community need no longer be from outside. The long-range goal was the preservation of Acadian life, and especially French, on a very English Island.

But how to promote French when English was clearly the best path to advancement, and how to break out of isolation and yet avoid assimilation? In 1937, Professor J.-Henri Blanchard, a founder of the Saint Thomas Aquinas Society, summarized the weak promotion of French in Acadian schools thus:

> The French curriculum in the sixty-two schools in Acadian localities is limited
> to instruction in reading, grammar, dictation and a bit of composition. A few
> rare schools teach the history of Canada in French. In some schools French is
> used for arithmetic and geography, but as a general rule these subjects are taught
> in English. In most schools even beginners are introduced to the different subjects
> by means of the English language. (trans. in Arsenault, 1989, p. 176)

Arsenault (p. 176) calls these observations 'valid for almost the entire 1890 to 1945 period'. He also notes the continuing shortage of francophone teachers, many of whom, in any case, were ill-equipped to teach the language as such, since their teacher-training still had to be in English.

As for assimilation, the Canadian census tells a clear tale: in 1921, 17 per cent of the province's approximately 12,000 Acadians no longer had French as a mother tongue. In 1941 the figure was 28 per cent, and in 1951, 42 per cent (Arsenault, 1989). According to King, in communities outside the Evangéline region, 'assimilation to English was already pronounced by the 1880's' (1996, p. 6). Even at the first national convention of Acadians on the Island, in 1884, mainland delegates were astonished to discover the extent of the anglicization, down to casual conversations, the programme, and the dinner tickets. In short, even as it began, the third hopeful wave of Prince Edward Island French was breaking.

The end of the Second World War brought the beginning of a fourth and still present surge. The post-war boom sparked a renewed interest in education across the Island. The provincial government began to renovate and then consolidate its schools, especially after the massive federal-provincial Development Plan of 1969, the aim of which was to build an economy diversified beyond the primary industries, which in turn would produce jobs for those Islanders with enough education to take them. In the same year, the new Trudeau government in Ottawa passed the Official Languages Act, which meant that a certain number of federal civil servants on the Island would have to be bilingual.

The provincial government came at last to recognize that French education required special attention. In 1960, Ecole Régionale Evangéline high school was built, with its administration and programme almost entirely in French. Prompted by the 1982 Canadian Charter of Rights and Freedoms, and by rulings from the Supreme Courts of both the province and the nation, the Department of Education in 1991 handed over full management of the school's board to francophones. Now there are three school boards on PEI: two anglophone, which divide the Island between them, and one francophone, with responsibility for first-language French across the province, wherever – in the language of the Charter – 'numbers warrant'. In 1992, this Board was responsible for 610 students (Commissioner of Official Languages, 1989, 1993; Gallant and Carbon, 1989; LeBlanc, 1990). Another federal-provincial arrangement saw the transfer of the Department of Veterans Affairs from Ottawa to Charlottetown, along with the construction in 1992 of a French-language school in the capital for the children of DVA employees (Anon., 1988; Commissioner of Official Languages, 1993, 1995).

French immersion on PEI currently enjoys the highest participation rate in the country, outside the special provinces (in this regard) of Quebec and New Brunswick: 14.1 per cent of those eligible, according to the 1991 Census. The comparable figures in neighbouring Newfoundland and Nova Scotia are 3.4 per cent and 3.3 per cent, respectively (Harrison and Marmen, 1994). One innovation is a 'middle immersion' programme in North Rustico that begins in Grade 4, to accommodate the high concentration of Acadians in the area whose mother tongue is now English (Commissioner of Official Languages, 1995; Lowther, 1996). Graduates of this programme can then move on to a francophone high school.

Prince Edward Island is also considerably ahead of its neighbours with respect to health services in French, although 'it still has a considerable distance to go', according to Sloan (1994). The province has provided bilingual signage, reception services, nurses and technical training in its two main hospitals. Promotion of tourism is also now partially bilingual. In addition, the government runs a programme of French-language training for its civil servants, and a French-language provincial services centre in the Evangéline region (Gallant and Carbon, 1989). Other local organizations have taken the cue: the Confederation Centre of the Arts now mounts a French show in its Summer Festival; Island Telephone has more bilingual operators; and the Canada Winter Games of 1992 did its best to provide services in both official languages for visiting athletes (Commissioner of Official Languages, 1989, 1991; Laforest, 1991). Almost always, such initiatives are partly funded by Ottawa.

346

The percentage of the Island's population reported in the 1991 Census as able to speak French – 10.3 per cent – is higher than that in any province outside Quebec other than New Brunswick and Ontario, which have the advantage of bordering on Quebec. Similarly, English–French bilingualism was measured at 10.1 per cent, far outstripping Newfoundland's 3.3 per cent and Nova Scotia's 8.6 per cent. It is, in fact, second in the country outside Quebec and the officially bilingual New Brunswick, just behind 11.4 per cent in Ontario (Harrison and Marmen, 1994).

Acadians themselves have again rebounded, founding cultural clubs, youth camps and a museum; sending teacher-trainees to the French-speaking Magdalen Islands, and later to the new Education faculty of the nearby Université de Moncton; and providing an Evangéline campus for a Nova Scotian community college (Arsenault, 1989; Commissioner of Official Languages, 1991–1995). In the view of the Commissioner of Official Languages in 1994, '[t]he 5,280 Francophones of Prince Edward Island (4.0 per cent of the population) form a community whose vitality exceeds its demographic weight' (1995, p. 96). The Saint Thomas Aquinas Society celebrated its seventy-fifth anniversary in that year. Marking the occasion in a local newspaper, *La Voix Acadienne* (itself an award-winning emblem of the new era), the President of the Society wrote, 'I am confident about the future ... since Acadians have never been as well equipped not only to face the challenges we must face, but also to profit from them' (trans. in Commissioner of Official Languages, 1995, p. 96).

Unfortunately, this optimism may be wishful only. After all, before the Second World War there were still forty-five schools on Prince Edward Island with a majority of Acadian pupils, and in which French was the normal first language (King, 1996) – whereas now there are only two (or one, if we rule out the non-Acadian Charlottetown school). In every Acadian district outside Evangéline, school consolidation has meant a consolidation into English (Arsenault, 1989). An obvious example is the Tignish area, where twelve Acadian schools have entirely disappeared, and assimilation – albeit to an interestingly French-coloured English – is profound (Gallant and Carbon, 1989; King, 1996). French immersion programmes downplay the Acadian dialect, and the command of French by their Acadian graduates remains significantly weak compared with that of their truly francophone counterparts (Arsenault, 1989; King, 1996). Nor has the province ever provided enough immersion classes to meet the demand. Only a few days before this writing, the Charlottetown *Guardian* carried a story of parents sleeping overnight at a school in a formerly francophone community, in order to be in line to enrol their children the next

morning, because the Department had reduced the number of classes
(Wightman, 1996). Such late-winter, sometimes open-air, vigils have been
the tradition in Prince Edward Island since immersion began.

It is not hard to find other recent examples of official neglect of French on
PEI. The University of Prince Edward Island, most significantly its Education
Faculty, has few courses delivered in French. Francophone tourists find it
difficult to get good service in their language on the ferries and in Cavendish
National Park (Commissioner of Official Languages, 1994). There is no French
outlet of the CBC. Echoing an old complaint, a presentation by the Saint Thomas
Aquinas Society to the Roman Catholic Bishop of Charlottetown in 1965 stated
that Acadian parishioners 'are unable to listen to a prayer or a sermon in French
in their own churches and yet Acadian priests are sent to serve in English
parishes' (Arsenault, 1989, p. 237).

The policy of official bilingualism, at both the provincial and the federal level
in PEI, has been only a mixed success. There was at first some enthusiasm for
the French classes offered to anglophone civil servants, but in latter years it has
waned, both because of the scant need for actual practice on the job (given that
88 per cent of Island francophones are bilingual, as compared with 5 per cent
of anglophones [Dallaire and Lachapelle, 1990]), and because of the continued
political uncertainty surrounding Quebec. A 1994 survey of the Island's 'bilingual'
federal offices – some 17.5 per cent of the 2,405 total, chiefly in the Department
of Veterans Affairs – found that French was actually available in those offices
only 80 per cent of the time (Commissioner of Official Languages, 1995).

Then there is the backlash. In 1987, a report for the Commissioner of
Official Languages maintained that '[t]here appears to be no reason to fear an
Anglophone backlash to the prospect of more French-language services' in
Prince Edward Island (Anon., 1987, p. 18). But in 1990, imitating the famous
action of the Ontario town of Sault Ste Marie earlier in the year, a meeting of
twenty people in Murray Harbour voted this village of 400 officially 'English
only'. The numbers were small, perhaps absurdly so, but the story made national
headlines as the first such resolution in Atlantic Canada. The action was, of course,
condemned in many letters and calls to local media. But almost as many voices
rose in the village's defence, citing as justification Quebec's discriminatory language laws, the ineffectuality of official bilingualism and, above all, the fact that
access to jobs in an economically depressed region should not be made more
difficult through enforced bilingualism. The defenders protested that they were
not anti-Acadian, simply pro-employment. But a position that included letters
like the following could only distress the francophone community:

> The city of Charlottetown should retaliate [like Murray Harbour, against Quebec]
> by declaring English only, but we have not the guts as we are now dictated to a
> [*sic*] small minority of Francophones, we do what they want ... One place most
> notable here in PEI is Parks Canada, they employ tour guides at Province House
> and every guide must be bilingual. One would think they would require less than
> half bilingual ... We are now considering building a $7 million French school here
> in Charlottetown and we can't afford to repair and upgrade our present schools.
> (Disgusted and discriminated Anglophone, 1990)

Finally, even without the negative factors noted above, the fourth wave of
Prince Edward Island French has been in steady decline, simply from voluntary
assimilation into English. In 1951, the population reporting French as a mother
tongue was 8,477, or 8.6 per cent of the total (Harrison and Marmen, 1994).
Subsequently, the figures are these: 1961 (7,958, or 7.6 per cent); 1971 (7,360, or
6.6 per cent); 1981 (5,835, or 4.8 per cent); 1991 (5,750, or 4.5 per cent). Persons
reporting French as the language most often spoken at home declined from
3.9 per cent in 1971 (the first year the question was asked), to 3.1 per cent in
1981 and 2.4 per cent in 1991, only half of the mother-tongue population. Castonguay (this volume) points out that, through a combination of anglicization
and insufficient fertility, the francophone reproduction rate for the province is
only 0.37. In other words, by his calculations, which are supported by those
of Dallaire and Lachapelle (1990), francophones on Prince Edward Island are
currently disappearing at the rate of 63 per cent per generation.

Arsenault sums up the forces contributing to the massive anglicization:

> French was taught on a limited basis in many schools, even if Acadians were in the
> majority. There was a shortage of qualified francophone teachers. Several Acadian
> parishes had anglophone priests for a long time. With the arrival of television, much
> more English was introduced into the home. Urbanization caused an increase in
> the number of marriages between francophones and anglophones. In order to find
> work, more and more Acadians had to move to Summerside and Charlottetown
> where the English-speaking environment made it difficult for families to preserve
> French, particularly since there were no French schools for their children.
> ... [T]he Acadian dialect ... was often ridiculed. It is not surprising, therefore,
> that many people associated their inferior socio-economic status with their Acadian
> origin and the French language. Thus they purposefully chose assimilation for them-
> selves and their children as a means for social advancement. (1989, pp. 249–50)

MICMAC

In contrast to the wave pattern of Acadian French, the Micmac language
could be described as moving through modern PEI history in an ever-decreasing

circle. There are no figures available for the number of Micmac speakers who, before European contact, typically inhabited or visited the island they called Abegweit ('cradled on the waves'); recent estimates for the total number of speakers throughout the Maritimes at this time vary from 3,000 to 200,000. The French left the aboriginal language on the Island undisturbed in any direct way, even during their first period of settlement, 1720–1758. However, French fur traders began the distortion of the hunting and gathering economy, French priests initiated the breakdown of traditional spirituality and identity, and the French contact in general introduced European diseases that killed perhaps nine-tenths of all natives who contracted them. By the end of the period of colonial warfare, there were about 300 Micmacs permanently fixed on the Island, and reliant on Europeans for their survival (Baldwin, 1985; Crossley, 1994; Maloney, 1973; McKenna, 1993).

In that warfare, the Micmac had the misfortune to ally themselves with the losing side, and consequently were treated harshly by the victorious British. In addition, the land lottery of 1767 took no more notice of the aboriginal people than it did of the Acadians. Thus, in contrast to the situation in other provinces, there was no crown land for assignment to Indian reserves. Although the Micmac continued for a time to roam, hunt and gather, they were more and more constricted by the arriving British and Acadian settlers. Ironically, one of their most favoured encampments, Lennox Island, had been left out of the lottery by mistake. When the oversight was discovered, these 1,320 acres were assigned to one of the lots retroactively. It was the first of several chances that the colonial government deliberately missed to apportion some land to its native subjects. But as an observer of 1829 remarked, speaking unwittingly for the whole of this clash of cultures and languages, '[The Micmac] form no obstacle to the progress of the settlers, before the effects of whose industry, they are perceptibly dwindling away' (Crossley, 1994, p. 11; see also Baldwin, 1985; McKenna, 1993). An Indian Commissioner appointed by the government in 1856 made some attempt at preserving the language through the writing of a grammar, but he got no encouragement and his work was never published (Crossley, 1994).

Some stability for the Micmac people, though not for their language, was achieved when Prince Edward Island joined Confederation in 1873. Lennox Island had in fact become a reserve in 1870, through its purchase by a charitable society in London; by 1917, after many political convolutions, three other small and separated pieces of land – in Morell (183 acres), Scotchfort (143 acres) and Rocky Point (7 acres) – had been similarly assigned as reserves (Baldwin, 1985;

Crossley, 1994; McKenna, 1993). Indian affairs were now the responsibility of the federal government and, for about a century after Confederation, the province used this fact to wash its hands of any concern for them.[3] Aiding in this neglect was, and is, the widespread conviction that Island settlers were themselves victims, first of the absentee landlords who drew or inherited the land-lots, and later of the economic conditions dictated by Confederation (Crossley, 1994).

An Indian elementary school was founded on Lennox Island in the late nineteenth century, but federal education policy insisted on the use of English at all times (Anon., 1993). By 1916, 82 per cent of Island Micmacs were fluent English speakers (Battiste, 1986). It appears that Micmac was still the most common home language until the end of World War II (McKenna, 1990), but a new policy, continuing into the 1950s, of sending native Island schoolchildren to the Shubenacadie residential school in Nova Scotia, was wreaking disastrous effects on the language. The rigid rules of this school included not only exclusive English, but also the forbidding of visits, letters, and even presents from parents. Some children lived at this school for several years before returning home (Battiste, 1986; Saxon, 1992). Inevitably, it was not the despised Micmac language that they passed on to their own children. In 1961, the Director of Indian Affairs 'noted triumphantly that ... Lennox Island is one of the few reserves in the Maritimes where children coming to school for the first time are all able to speak English' (McKenna, 1993, p. 18).

The Development Plan of 1969 had little impact on Island natives except for the building of a causeway to Lennox Island (Baldwin, 1985), which strengthened their access to markets, but further weakened their language. In 1981, a new elementary school was built there; it now gives three hours a week of instruction in Micmac as a foreign tongue. Many of the materials are translations from English (Edmonds, 1983; Edmonds, 1993; Ryder, 1995). Even this minimal instruction comes to an end after Grade 6, when the children are bussed to non-native schools. The lack of support for the language is not aided by rival writing systems (Battiste, 1986), or by animosity among the four organizations who are the political advocates for aboriginal affairs (Crossley, 1994). In 1992, the Director of Education for Lennox Island estimated that 2 per cent of the 1,880 people who claimed some aboriginal origin in the 1991 Census retained some speaking knowledge of their ancestral tongue (Saxon, 1992). But according to Edmonds (1993, p. 200): 'Today, one would be hard-pressed to find someone on Prince Edward Island who speaks fluent Mi'kmaq, or who can write in it.' For various reasons, the true totals of aboriginal people and of Micmac speakers on Prince Edward Island have not been officially tabulated, and I decline to probe further. But there is no question that the language is on its deathbed here.

Notes

1 For a description of Prince Edward Island English, including its internal divisions, see my *Dictionary of Prince Edward Island English*, and particularly the appended essay, 'The dictionary in profile'.
2 There are some sixty different nations represented on Prince Edward Island (Baldwin, 1985), but their speakers have assimilated to English in the same manner as elsewhere, or perhaps even faster because fresh immigration is very low (Harrison and Marmen, 1994).
3 Natives on Prince Edward Island have remained almost invisible to the provincial government right through the present era. The decline of the Micmac language has certainly played a role in this complacent ignorance: 'it seems likely that most Islanders look at the aboriginal community and, seeing few obvious differences in language, religion, or employment between themselves and the aboriginal people, conclude that no significant differences exist' (Crossley, 1994, pp. 43, 87).

References

Anon. (1987). The garden of the gulf. *Language and Society, 21*, 18–19.

(1988). Acadian affairs in Prince Edward Island. *Language and Society, 22*, 21.

(1993). Program of studies for Indian schools. *Abegweit Review, 7(2)*, 128–30.

Arsenault, G. (1989). *The Island Acadians: 1720–1980.* (Trans. Ross, S.) Charlottetown: Ragweed.

Baldwin, D. (1985). *Abegweit: Land of the Red Soil.* Charlottetown: Ragweed.

Battiste, M. (1986). Micmac literacy and cognitive assimilation. In J. Barman, Y. Hébert and D. McCaskill (eds.), *Indian Education in Canada, I* (pp. 23–44). Vancouver: University of British Columbia Press.

Commissioner of Official Languages. (1989–1995). *Annual Reports.* Ottawa: Supply and Services Canada.

Crossley, J. (1994). Relations between the province and aboriginal peoples of Prince Edward Island. Submission to *Royal Commission on Aboriginal Peoples, Canadian Governments and Aboriginal Peoples Project.* Charlottetown: University of Prince Edward Island.

Dallaire, L. M. and Lachapelle, R. (1990). *Demolinguistic Profile: Prince Edward Island.* Ottawa: Secretary of State.

Disgusted and discriminated Anglophone. (1990). Letter. *The Guardian* (Charlottetown), 5 April.

Edmonds, E. L. (1993). The Mi'kmaq of Prince Edward Island. *Abegweit Review, 7(2)*, 199–204.

Edmonds, K. (1983). The Micmac Indians of Lennox Island, Prince Edward Island. *Canadian Journal of Native Education, 10(3)*, 5–15.

Gallant, R. and Carbon, J. (1989) The Island Acadians: courage and perseverance. *Language and Society, 26*, 20–21.

Harrison, B. and Marmen, L. (1994). *Languages in Canada*. Ottawa: Statistics Canada/Prentice Hall.

King, R. (1996). The lexical basis of syntactic borrowing: Variation and change in Prince Edward Island French. Unpublished manuscript.

Laforest, J. (1991). Gold medal or paper? Canada Winter Games in Prince Edward Island. *Language and Society, 35*, 35.

LeBlanc, J. (1990). Minority language education after the Supreme Court decision. *Language and Society, 32*, 31.

Lowther, L. (1996, Feb. 19). Letter to the author.

McKenna, M. O. (1990). *Micmac by Choice: Elsie Sark – an Island Legend*. Halifax: Formac.

   (1993). Indian–white relations on Prince Edward Island, 1492–1992: a clash of cultures. *Abegweit Review, 7(2)*, 7–23.

Maloney, J. H. (1973). And in the beginning... In F. W. P. Bolger (ed.), *Canada's Smallest Province: A History of PEI* (pp. 1–10). Charlottetown: The Prince Edward Island 1973 Centennial Commission.

Pratt, T. K. (1988). *Dictionary of Prince Edward Island English*. Toronto: University of Toronto Press.

Ryder, R. (1995). Levi takes children back to roots. *The Guardian* (Charlottetown), 26 September.

Saxon, T. (1992). Trying to save the Micmac language. *The Islander* (Charlottetown), 8 February.

Sloan, T. (1994). A variable picture [in health care]. *Language and Society, 46*, 35.

Wightman, R. (1996). Parents spend night for French Immersion. *The Guardian* (Charlottetown), 21 February.

Map 4 Nova Scotia

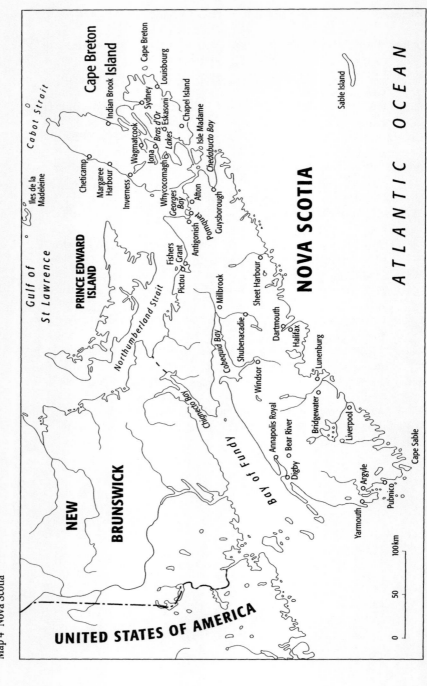

18 Language in Nova Scotia

Ronald Cosper

INTRODUCTION

Nova Scotia is one of the predominantly English-speaking Maritime provinces that joined Canada at the time of Confederation. British culture and language have had a dominant presence since the eighteenth century. Initial British settlement in Halifax and the western parts of the province was augmented by an influx of 'Loyalist' settlers from the 'New England states' fleeing the republicanism of the American Revolution. Prior to English settlement in Nova Scotia, the province was known as Acadia, a possession of France that had had a history of 150 years of French rule and colonization. The French presence remained strong, especially in Cape Breton, where the Fortress of Louisbourg, a bastion of French power, was eventually conquered by the British in 1758. Despite its loss, and the dislocations of the Acadian expulsion in 1755, French remained a minority language.

Before the arrival of Europeans, Nova Scotia was inhabited by Algonquian-speaking people known as Micmacs. (The spelling currently favoured by some, Mi'kmaq or Mi'gmaw, reflects an effort to come closer to Micmac phonology, in which the apostrophe represents a long vowel. In most Algonquian languages, voicing is not a distinctive feature of stop consonants.) Despite some apparent population loss earlier, the aboriginal population of the province has rebounded, and the Micmac language continues to be used, particularly on reserves in eastern Nova Scotia. It is interesting that native languages continue to be spoken more in eastern Canada than in the west. This seems to be in part a function of the greater linguistic diversity of the west; the more recent spread and relative uniformity of Algonquian languages over most of eastern Canada have meant these languages, especially Cree, remain useful.

Relatively early in the European history of Nova Scotia, as a result of the Highland clearances, substantial numbers of settlers arrived from Scotland, going especially to Cape Breton and eastern Nova Scotia. They brought Gaelic with them, and this remained the language of their homes in Nova Scotia for several generations. The use of Gaelic is nominally encouraged by the government, along with other aspects of Scottish culture, in part for purposes of promoting tourism. Today, Gaelic is spoken in a few homes in Cape Breton, especially by older residents, and some Nova Scotians have learned it as a second language.

In the eighteenth and nineteenth centuries, German and Dutch immigrants took up farming in several of the agricultural regions of the province, and at one time West Germanic languages (in addition to English) were widely spoken. Most of the earlier immigrants no longer use these languages, but more recently arrived settlers continue to speak Dutch and German.

Although the Maritimes have attracted nothing like the numbers of immigrants who have come to Upper Canada in recent decades, most Maritime-bound migrants have come to Nova Scotia. Earlier in the twentieth century, many eastern European immigrants came to Cape Breton, attracted by prospects of work in mines and factories. South Europeans and Asians, along with some Latin Americans and Africans, have come to urban areas, especially Halifax. All of these peoples brought their languages with them, and many continue to use them at home and within ethnic contexts. Another major group is the Blacks, or Afro-Canadians; many of these came as Loyalist settlers from the United States, and others subsequently came from the West Indies or Africa. Many Afro-Canadians are native speakers of English or English Creole dialects, although some Haitians, speaking French Creole, have also settled (see, generally, Campbell, 1978; Cosper, 1984; Jabbra and Cosper, 1989).

MICMAC

The earliest known language in Nova Scotia is Micmac; it has probably been here for more than 1,000 years. The Eastern Algonquian languages are fairly similar, however, so it is likely that the language arrived here from the Great Lakes area within the past 2,000 years or so. Earlier, Proto-Algonquian was probably spoken in the western part of its present-day range (Lake Superior to Lake Winnipeg).

In 1772 Haliburton estimated that the aboriginal population of Nova Scotia was 865, although this figure seems fairly low. An economy based on hunting, fishing and gathering does not permit high population densities, but it is likely that contact with Europeans had already reduced native populations in Nova Scotia, as elsewhere. A century later the population classified as 'Micmac' amounted to 3,459, but this includes persons in all three Maritime provinces, as well as Quebec. It is uncertain how complete this figure was, or whether persons of aboriginal ancestry living off the reserves were included. The 1921 Census, the first to include questions on language use, enumerated 2,048 persons of 'Indian racial origin', largely in eastern Nova Scotia, although with small populations in every county of the province. This population was increasing at the time, having been 1,629 in 1901. In 1921, nearly all aboriginal people over age 10 spoke both Micmac and English, with only 5 per cent monolingual in English and 3 per cent speaking only Micmac. Three per cent of aboriginal people could also speak French. Females were three times as likely to be monolingual in Micmac as males.

In 1941 the Micmac language reportedly had 1,988 mother-tongue speakers. As in the past, 99 per cent of Micmac speakers resided in rural areas. Their age distribution was similar to that of the general Nova Scotia population, except that higher than average fertility meant that more children spoke the language. In 1961, 2,335 persons in the province spoke Indian or 'Eskimo' languages, with over half residing in Cape Breton County. By 1981, the number of persons reporting an 'Amerindian language' as a mother tongue had increased to 2,675 and, of these, 84 per cent used it as their home language. Of persons with an Amerindian mother tongue, 93 per cent reported they could also speak English, however. Of persons having an aboriginal mother tongue, 88 per cent still resided in rural areas. Eight per cent of women and 7 per cent of men were monolingual speakers of Micmac.

In 1991 7,530 persons indicated they were of aboriginal origin, and 3,725 of these (49 per cent) said Micmac was their mother tongue. A few more, a total of 3,845, said they 'know' the Micmac language, and 2,985 persons used Micmac at home. The aboriginal population of Nova Scotia has thus expanded numerically, as has the number of speakers of Micmac. However, the percentage of persons of Micmac ethnic origin speaking the language has declined. In fact, it is only on the larger reserves in eastern Nova Scotia that the language continues to be spoken and learned by the young. Most residents (85 per cent) of Eskasoni Reserve in Cape Breton County report that their mother tongue is Micmac, as do 88 per cent of those living in Whycocomagh (Inverness County), and 81 per cent of those in Wagmatcook in Victoria County. On Eskasoni and Whycocomagh most residents say they currently also know Micmac and use it as a home language. By contrast, only 26 per cent of people in Millbrook and 13 per cent of those in Indian Brook (both located in central Nova Scotia) still report Micmac as mother tongue. Only 7 per cent of Millbrook residents use Micmac at home, 4 per cent in Indian Brook. There are also fair numbers of Micmac speakers in Membertou

(Cape Breton County), Chapel Island (Richmond County), Fishers Grant (Pictou County), and Pomquet and Afton (Antigonish County). As well, there are numbers of persons of Micmac ethnicity elsewhere in the province (Queens County north of Liverpool, Bridgewater town, Bear River in Digby County, Yarmouth, the South Mountain area of Kings County, Lunenburg and Sheet Harbour), although few of these are able to speak the language any longer. There are 425 persons of aboriginal ancestry living in the capital city of Halifax, although only 20 of these say they know the language, and none presently use it as the language of their home. In Dartmouth, there are 230 aboriginal people, and 75 say they know the language. At one time there was an independent reserve in Dartmouth, now surrounded by urban growth.

FRENCH

France was the first European country to colonize Nova Scotia, and settlements were established in the early seventeenth century at Port Royal (present-day Annapolis) and subsequently on Isle Royale (Cape Breton Island) and other locations on the mainland. Precise demographic data are sparsely available from this period, but by 1749 the French population of the Acadian Peninsula (mainland Nova Scotia) was approximately 13,000, most of whom lived in the northern part, from Annapolis Royal to Windsor, with some also on Cobequid and Chignecto Bays. The French population of Isle Royale was estimated to be 1,000 at this time, but this was subsequent to the capture of Louisbourg by the English in 1745. The expulsion of the Acadians in 1755 reduced the mainland population to 1,200. The retaking of Louisbourg by the British in 1758 further reduced the Acadian population to 700. After this time the French-speaking population gradually increased, due to the partial return of Acadians, and their ordinary rate of natural increase. By 1771 the francophone population of all Nova Scotia was 2,780; by the census of 1871, it had reached 32,833.

In 1921, the total population of 'French racial origin' (traced on the paternal side) was 56,619. If the Acadian population had continued reproducing at a rate of 1.025 per year, their population growth over this fifty-year period should have been on the order of 344 per cent. Either the rate of growth had slowed considerably (to under 1 per cent per year), or Acadians had left the province or been underenumerated in the census. In 1921 most Nova Scotians of French origin reported French to be their mother tongue; only 4.4 per cent said their mother tongue was not French (in most cases English). It is possible that some persons of French ancestry were already not counted as such, because of assimilation. Only 13 per cent of those of French racial origin were monolingual in French.

Acadian females were more likely to be monolingual than were the males. In 1931, 39,018 persons reported French to be their mother tongue, a significant decrease from 1921. By 1941, this figure had increased again to 41,340. The number stating that French was the only official language they could speak was 6,800, or 16.4 per cent of those with French as mother tongue. It is likely that linguistic assimilation had proceeded further by 1941. More persons of French mother tongue lived in rural Nova Scotia than did those of English mother tongue (73 per cent versus 52 per cent), and most unilingual francophones in that year lived in rural areas. The age distribution of speakers of French appears to show evidence of language decline by 1941; proportionally more French speakers than English speakers were elderly. Females were also more likely to be unilingual francophones than were males.

In 1961, the number of people with French as their mother tongue was down only slightly overall – to 39,568. There were also 5,938 French unilinguals, although these were generally small children. The requirements of school and work served as a major impetus to learn English; by age twenty-five unilingual females began to outnumber unilingual males, although unilinguals are a small minority for both genders. French continued to show a higher proportion of elderly users than English, although many children were obviously still learning French, especially in the rural areas. Acadian speakers were only slightly more likely to farm than were those of English mother tongue. However, French speakers were far more likely to be classified as 'rural non-farm' than the English population, reflecting the residence of Acadians in smaller towns and villages, compared to the more urban habitats of anglophones. By 1961, the major Acadian areas of Nova Scotia were Yarmouth, Digby, Richmond and Inverness Counties. Many francophones also joined the migration of rural Nova Scotians into Halifax (for the Acadians generally, see Roy, 1982).

According to the census of 1981, there had been a slight decrease overall in the number of persons of French mother tongue, to 35,695. Of these, the majority (or 62.8 per cent) still used French as their principal home language, while 5 per cent said they were then unable to speak French, and another 5 per cent stated that they were unilingual francophones. Urban francophones were far less likely to use French at home (36.3 per cent) than were rural francophones (75.4 per cent). Nearly all urban persons with French as a mother tongue were also able to speak English, whereas 6.4 per cent of rural francophones were monolingual. The population of French mother tongue remained predominantly rural (67.7 per cent), in comparison to the anglophone population, which was only 44.2 per cent rural.

Table 18.1 Mother tongue by age, Nova Scotia, 1991

Age	English	French	Non-official languages
0–4	58,265	1,285	955
5–9	59,570	1,125	785
10–14	59,595	1,165	890
15–19	64,510	1,435	1,165
20–24	63,075	2,490	1,500
25–29	71,505	3,390	1,790
30–34	73,510	3,555	1,755
35–39	67,230	3,015	1,690
40–44	62,310	3,160	1,980
45–49	48,140	2,705	1,810
50–54	37,780	2,055	1,690
55–59	35,580	1,995	1,260
60–64	33,175	2,075	970
65+	95,870	7,165	2,800
Total	830,115	36,615	21,040

Source: Canada (1993), table 2.

Table 18.2 Use of mother tongue as home language, by age, 1991 (percentage)

Age	Language		
	English	French	Non-official
0–4	99.9	92.2	85.3
5–9	99.8	90.7	79.6
10–14	99.9	81.5	71.3
15–19	99.9	73.9	63.1
20–24	99.9	67.7	66.3
25–29	99.8	55.6	52.5
30–34	99.8	53.6	49.6
35–39	99.9	48.4	41.4
40–44	99.9	49.1	42.4
45–49	99.8	48.8	38.1
50–54	99.9	51.1	41.4
55–59	99.9	48.6	38.9
60–64	99.9	52.5	33.0
65+	99.9	58.8	33.4
Total	99.9	58.3	48.8

Source: Canada (1993), table 2.

By 1991, there were 55,305 people of French (single) ethnic origin, 34,010 listing French as sole mother tongue and another 5,415 listing French as one of their multiple mother tongues. Numerically, French seemed to have held its own in Nova Scotia over the decade, although 831 fewer people (21,585) used French as a home language. Fully 78,045 Nova Scotians now say they are able to converse in French, of whom 39,420 are persons of English mother tongue and 1,310 with other non-official mother tongues. French is far more likely to be used as a home language in rural than in urban areas, whereas more English-speaking people live in urban areas. This reflects in part the residential patterns of Acadians, who are far more likely than British-background people to live in rural areas (58.1 per cent as compared to 46.2 per cent, respectively). As one would expect in a predominantly anglophone province, most (96.0 per cent) persons of French mother tongue also learn English, while only 4.7 per cent of native anglophones also learn French. French does continue to be used at home by over half (58.3 per cent) of native francophones.

The 1991 census appears to show some evidence of language loss among French-speaking people, however. The percentage of the population who learned French as their first language has declined from 6.5 per cent for persons age sixty-five and over to 2.1 per cent for persons under age five. This decline is in part explicable by the growth of the anglophone population through immigration, however. Data in table 18.1 indicate that there are many more children of English mother tongue than old people, as one would expect in a population experiencing normal fertility and mortality rates. For persons of French mother tongue, however, the opposite is true: the number of francophone old people far exceeds the number of children, which is suggestive of a decline in the passing on of French, at least as a mother tongue, to subsequent generations. This discrepancy is somewhat reduced when we take into account persons who consider their home language to be *both* English and French. This calculation increases the use of French as a home language among children 0–4 to 1,465, a figure which is nevertheless much less than the 2,571 expected if French were retained as well as English. The data from table 18.1 on people whose mother tongue was a non-official language are hard to interpret, but some of the numbers among middle-aged people probably derive from more recent immigration.

In table 18.2, the percentage of Nova Scotians using their mother tongue as a home language is calculated by age for English, French and 'non-official' languages, the only categories available in the census. This table shows that, as expected, nearly all persons of anglophone mother tongue continue to use English as their home language. The only surprising finding here is the nearly exceptionless regularity of the rule. This indicates that virtually all persons using French as a home language have learned the language as a mother tongue, and that the *use* of French is confined to the Acadian ethnic group. (Actually, the census data indicate that only 735 (less than 1 in 1,000) persons of English mother tongue 'transfer' to French as a home language.) We should caution, however, that this method of measuring language retention is valid in a long-term perspective only in those cases where the home is the sole place of acquiring a language. In the case of an official language, like French, for which there are immersion schools, training courses for government workers, mass media, political and occupational uses, and so on, people can come to be speakers through means other than home transmission. Nevertheless, the number of persons with French as a mother tongue continues to gradually decline in Nova Scotia.

French is now maintained as a daily language by a significant number of people in very restricted and localized parts of the province. In Digby County, 34 per cent of the population has French as a mother tongue, especially in Clare Municipality, which has 6,365 French speakers. In Richmond County, Cape Breton, 32.3 per cent speak French, mostly in Subdivision C (Isle Madame) and on the adjacent portion of Subdivision A. In Yarmouth County 25.7 per cent are of French mother tongue, most notably in Argyle Municipal District, which is 57.1 per cent francophone. A portion of Inverness County – on the west coast, north of Margaree Harbour and centring on Cheticamp – is also heavily French; 2,970 people there have French as their mother tongue, which accounts for 46 per cent of Subdivision A, altogether.

To examine in more detail an area where French seems to be thriving: in the municipality of Clare 6,010 people of 9,654 say they are only of French ancestry, while another 2,240 say they are at least partly of French descent; 6,365 give French as their mother tongue and, altogether, 7,445 say they 'know' both French and English; another 330 are unilingual speakers of French. In sum, 80.5 per cent of the people of Clare say they are able to speak French. This is probably not an exaggeration, because 6,635 report that French is the only language of their home, and 6,840 make at least some use of French at home. It is in these very restricted communities that the French language continues to be used to this extent. It is only in Clare, the Cheticamp area and Argyle where most or all people of French ethnicity continue to learn French and use it in the home. On Isle Madame, even though most people are of French ethnicity and say they know French in addition to English, the majority of households (59.9 per cent) make use of English, rather than French. In the rural area adjoining Yarmouth, where over half of the population is of French or part-French ancestry, only

13 per cent are bilingual in French and English, and there are no more French monoglots. In Yarmouth town, itself, where also more than half the population is at least part-French, only 14.5 per cent profess a knowledge of French, and a trace (2.4 per cent) use it as their sole home language.

In the cities of Nova Scotia, a different picture emerges. A sizable number of people of French background reside in Halifax. Of these 5,975 people of single French origin, 3,235 have French as a mother tongue, and another 770 say they have both English and French as mother tongues. Yet only 1,180 use French as their main home language. Fully 13,730 in Halifax indicate they are bilingual in English and French; many of these have learned French through formal education, travel or other non-traditional means.

ENGLISH

English is the mother tongue of the overwhelming majority of Nova Scotians and has been the dominant language since the eighteenth century. In 1710, the British captured Port Royal, and the rest of the mainland was ceded to Britain by treaty in 1713. The French remained the majority, however, until later in the century. Governor Cornwallis brought 2,544 persons to Nova Scotia from England in 1749, and in 1755 the banishment of the Acadians began. The 'British' population was estimated at 8,104 in 1762 and 17,000 in 1772. Later in the decade some British settlers left, but were more than replaced by the arrival of 20,000 Loyalist refugees from the American Revolution. By 1784 the British population of Nova Scotia was approximately 32,000, or about 73 per cent of the total. In the year 1861, according to the first census that enumerated the population of Nova Scotia, the overall population had grown to 330,857, although no linguistic data are available for that year. The census of 1921 indicated that the mother tongue of 88.4 per cent of non-aboriginal Nova Scotians was English. Most of these people gave their ethnic origins as 'British', but a large minority were of other West Germanic linguistic background. In 1931 the percentage of English had dropped slightly to 85.1 per cent but, by 1941, it had climbed back to 88.9 per cent. Most francophone Nova Scotians were already bilingual by 1941, so the percentage able to converse in English was actually 97.8. English was more uniformly the standard in the urban areas than the rural, since most of the linguistic minorities in Nova Scotia were traditionally made up of surviving rural remnants rather than by new immigrants.

In 1961, 92.3 per cent gave English as their mother tongue, and 99.0 were able to converse in English. In 1981, the proportion of people giving English as their mother tongue had risen again to 93.6 per cent, despite some increase in immigration from abroad during this period. The urban use of English continued to be greater than the rural. Specifically, it was the towns of 10,000 to 30,000 population that had the highest percentages of English speakers. Of farmers, 98.3 per cent were of English mother tongue, while the rural non-farm population was only 93.8 per cent English. In 1991, again about 93 per cent of the population gave English as their mother tongue. The areas that are most heavily English are the southern coast of the mainland, from Shelburne to Guysborough counties, with the exception of Halifax, as well as the central and northern counties of Colchester, Cumberland and Pictou, and the 'valley' counties of Annapolis and Hants. It is these counties that have few Micmac, French or Gaelic communities. Halifax is excepted because of its population of in-migrants from Nova Scotia and abroad.

GAELIC

Scottish Gaelic is a Celtic language quite similar to Irish, and its presence is one of the more unusual features of the Nova Scotia linguistic scene (see Edwards, 1991). Immigration from Scotland began in the eighteenth century and included Gaelic-speaking Highlanders as well as lowlanders speaking a dialect of English (Lallans). The census of 1921 gives a figure of 148,000 persons in Nova Scotia of Scottish ancestry, a large proportion of whom were certainly of Highland stock. This census provides no hint of the number speaking the language, however. By the census of 1941 the number of Nova Scotians giving Gaelic as their mother tongue had fallen to 12,065. Nevertheless, Gaelic was the third most widely spoken language after English and French, and it is perhaps an indication of its marginality that it was ignored in previous census reports. The census classifications, of course, reflect the priorities of central Canada, rather than those of smaller provinces. Of Gaelic speakers, 79 per cent lived in rural areas, compared with only 52 per cent of the English-speaking population at the time. In this way Gaels were similar to Acadians (73 per cent rural) and Micmacs (99 per cent rural). The 1941 census also has data on age by mother tongue and province. Gaelic speakers were old; 60.4 per cent were at least forty-five years old, as compared with just 23.8 per cent of persons whose mother tongue was English. Only 5.0 per cent of Gaelic speakers were under ten years old, compared with 20.4 per cent of anglophones. Gaelic speakers were also slightly more likely to be male than the general population.

By 1961, the number of people giving Gaelic as their mother tongue had declined further to 3,702. Those still reporting rural residence constituted 68 per cent, compared with only 46 per cent of the general population. Moreover, 40 per cent of rural Gaels still farmed, as compared to only 17 per cent of the wider population. In 1961, 76 per cent of Gaelic speakers lived in just two areas of Cape Breton Island: Cape Breton County and Inverness County. By 1981, there were only 1,270 persons giving a 'Celtic' language as their mother tongue, and just 5 (a rounded figure) of these were unable to speak English as well. Just 14 per cent, or 175 persons, used 'Celtic' as their home language. In 1981, 61 per cent of Celtic speakers still lived in rural areas, and 74 per cent of those using a Celtic language as the normal home language lived in rural areas.

CONTINENTAL WEST GERMANIC

Migration from present-day Netherlands and Germany to Nova Scotia began in the eighteenth century, originally because of a deliberate British policy to recruit agricultural settlers to counter the French colonists. In 1921, persons of Dutch racial origin numbered 11,506, and German, 27,046. These were numerically the most important ethnic affiliations after British and French in the Nova Scotia population. It must be remembered, however, that in this post-war period there was considerable anti-German sentiment among Canadians, while attitudes were generally favourable towards the Dutch. It is perhaps reflective of this attitudinal contrast that the reported German ethnic identity of the population declined steadily in the censuses of 1901 to 1921, from 41,020 to 38,844 to 27,046. During the same period, those calling themselves 'Dutch' increased from 2,941 to 4,179 to 11,506. The greatest decrease in those calling themselves 'German' occurred in the first post-war census, that of 1921. The combined ethnicities of German and Dutch remained relatively constant, except for a decrease from 43,023 before the war to 38,552 after the war. It is likely, therefore, that the distinction between 'Dutch' and 'German' in the census of Nova Scotia is less an indicator of provenance than it is a measure of war-induced xenophobia. Certainly, many Germans began referring to themselves as 'Dutch' (viz. *'deutsch'*) during the time of hostilities in Europe, and others – for example, those of mixed parentage – undoubtedly chose to overlook the German side of the family. By 1921, however, most people of continental West Germanic origin were already using English. For the population aged 10 and over, only 743 said their mother tongue was German and another 249, Dutch. Actually, it is Flemish that was retained most in the province; 359 persons spoke Flemish, or 54.7 per cent of those of 'Belgian' origin. The Belgians are also interesting in that 36.6 per cent were trilingual, speaking Flemish, French and English; French was nearly as common a language as English among this group. Nearly all persons originating in the Netherlands or Germany who could speak their own language were also bilingual in English.

The census of 1931 and 1941 showed another Germanic presence on the scene; by this time the largest Germanic language was Yiddish, the language of more recently arrived European Jews, spoken by 1,603 persons in 1931 and 1,103 in 1941. In comparison with the other Germanic languages, the speakers of which were predominantly rural, nearly all of the Yiddish speakers lived in the cities of Nova Scotia. In 1941, the German-speaking population was over-represented in older people, and had few young speakers, as is typical of assimilating populations. The Yiddish-speaking population was more over-represented in persons in their middle adult years, which is more typical of new immigrant groups (see Medjuck, 1986).

By 1961 the number of persons speaking continental Germanic languages had increased again, presumably due to additional post-Second World War immigration. There were 4,452 persons speaking German, Dutch or Yiddish then. More children of Germanic mother tongue were also recorded in that year, indicating that young adult migrants' children were raised with Germanic mother tongues. An unusually high proportion of the Dutch speakers were farmers; 41.7 per cent were classified in the rural farm population. Only 5.0 per cent of German speakers lived on farms, a figure even lower than that of the English-speaking Nova Scotians. Fully 89.5 per cent of Yiddish speakers lived in cities, mostly Halifax and Sydney. The German speakers were more dispersed, living in the farming counties of Colchester and Cumberland in northern Nova Scotia, where German cultural activities persist today, and in the 'valley' counties of Kings and Annapolis. The Dutch speakers tended to live more in north-eastern Nova Scotia, including Pictou and Antigonish Counties, as well as Cape Breton and in other farming regions of the province.

According to the 1981 census, there were still many persons whose mother tongues were either German or Dutch, 3,800 altogether, although Yiddish speakers did not have a separate category in that year (only five still used it as a home language). As before, most Dutch lived in rural areas, while most German speakers were in urban regions of the province. Some of these speakers of Germanic languages (11 per cent) were trilingual in that they knew English and French, in addition to their mother tongue. In the most recent census (1991), the number of continental West Germanic speakers had increased slightly to 4,010. German speakers lived disproportionately in Hants County, while Dutch people were especially likely to be found in Antigonish, Kings and Colchester Counties.

ARABIC

People began coming to Nova Scotia from the Levant in the nineteenth century, many to work as merchants or pedlars. The 1921 census classified 1,140 as 'Syrians', of whom approximately 78 per cent spoke their native mother tongue, presumably Arabic in most cases. It seems likely that much of this immigration occurred after 1901, since the census lists 'Turks' (i.e., subjects of the Ottoman Empire, which included most of the Near and Middle East) as increasing from 0 in 1901, to 535 in 1911, to 1,161 in 1921. Proportionately, most Arabic speakers lived in Cape Breton and in Lunenberg Counties, although substantial numbers lived in Halifax and in Yarmouth County as well. Most 'Syrians' were bilingual in English, and 6 per cent could speak French as well. The number of Arabic speakers was little changed in 1931, being 847. By 1941, however, this number had declined to 534, most of whom lived in urban areas. It is interesting that in 1941, Arabic, English and Gaelic were the only mother tongues over-represented in Nova Scotia in comparison to the population of Canada as a whole. Arabic was already declining by 1941, however; the age distribution of speakers revealed lower proportions of children knowing Arabic than was the case for English or French. By 1961, the number of Arabic speakers had further declined to 398. However, subsequent immigration of Levantines (especially from Lebanon) to Nova Scotia brought the total number of persons giving Arabic as their home language back up to 710. Most of these lived in Halifax, but 100 lived in rural areas, half as farmers. By the year 1991, Arabic continued to be revitalized with 1,480 persons claiming it as their mother tongue. Arabic is still spoken in Halifax and Lunenburg Counties, as well as in Hants County. It has ceased to be numerically important in Cape Breton, however (see Jabbra and Jabbra, 1984).

SLAVIC

In 1911, 535 people of Polish racial origin lived in Nova Scotia, and ten years later there were 980. In addition, in 1921, 520 persons said they were of Russian origin, 389 were Ukrainian, 229 Czech, and 107 Serbo-Croatian. These people showed little evidence of linguistic assimilation, in that over 90 per cent had a Slavic language as mother tongue. Nevertheless, the majority of Slavic people indicated that they could speak English as well as their own ethnic language. The Ukrainians were least assimilated in this sense; 28 per cent could speak no English. In 1931, there were 3,233 persons of Slavic mother tongue, and 2,880 by 1941. By far the largest group was the Poles, of whom 1,473 were of Polish mother tongue. Next most numerous were the Ukrainians, who stood at 628 in 1941. Most Slavic immigrants lived in Sydney and Halifax. The size of the Polish and Ukrainian communities in Nova Scotia led to greater cohesiveness and retention of their language; at least children from these groups were still learning their ethnic languages. The numerically smaller languages of Russian, Slovak and Serbo-Croatian, by contrast, were largely spoken by middle-aged people.

In 1961, there were still about a thousand people speaking each of the major Slavic languages, Ukrainian and Polish. In both of these groups, most speakers were middle-aged, but quite a number of small children continued to learn the languages. School-age children, on the other hand, were the least likely to be recorded as having a Slavic language as a mother tongue. Although they may have learned their ethnic tongue as a first language, some undoubtedly stopped using it when exposed to the environment of English-speaking peers and school mates. Poles and Ukrainians were able to maintain their languages despite living in urban communities, in part because of the contact with Europe fostered by continuing immigration to Canada. Moreover, the majority of Poles and Ukrainians lived in Cape Breton County, where proximity fostered greater ethnic identity. By 1981, a marked linguistic change had taken place in these Slavic communities. The number of mother-tongue speakers had declined to less than 700 for each, and most of these were using English as a home language. Poles were somewhat less assimilated than Ukrainians, largely because of some continuing immigration from Poland. Over the next ten years, more Poles arrived in Nova Scotia, raising the number of mother-tongue speakers again to over 1,000, while those speaking Ukrainian had continued to decline to 305. The number 'having knowledge' of Polish was actually considerably greater than the number reporting it as a mother tongue, which reflects in some cases the results of Polish language instruction given to the children of immigrants.

CHINESE

Chinese immigration to Canada began in the nineteenth century, but few came to Nova Scotia until World War I. By 1921 there were 315 persons of Chinese origin residing in the province. Nearly all early Chinese immigrants were male; the journey was long and expensive, and only Chinese men were allowed into Canada to work as labourers. In 1921 the Chinese population of Nova Scotia was 98 per cent male and 97 per cent over age ten. Nearly all of these immigrants spoke Chinese, though many could speak English as well, undoubtedly pidgin English in many cases. By 1941, there were still 325 persons in Nova Scotia whose mother tongue was Chinese, although 17 per cent had been born in Canada, and by then the Chinese population included thirty-four females. Nearly all lived in urban areas, and there were still relatively few children.

In 1961, 427 persons spoke Chinese, 36.5 per cent of whom were female. This population was highly urban, with 81.5 per cent living in Halifax and Sydney. By 1981, the Chinese-speaking population had increased to 1,120, with a more normal gender distribution. A third of these people were using English as a home language, but 190 knew no English or French. In 1991, continuing immigration raised to 1,575 the number of persons using Chinese as their mother tongue; of these 875 spoke the language at home. Of people of Chinese ethnic origin, 90 per cent in 1991 still said they knew Chinese.

GREEK

Greek is another language spoken by twentieth-century immigrants to Nova Scotia. In 1911 there were 114 people of Greek origin, and 150 recorded in the census of 1921. Of people of Greek racial origin, 89 per cent reported that Greek was their mother tongue. As is typical of most populations of international migrants, the Greek population in 1921 was heavily male (69 per cent). In 1941 there were still only 160 persons of Greek mother tongue in Nova Scotia, nearly all of whom resided in urban areas. The Greek-speaking population in 1941 was still 68 per cent male and predominantly adult. By 1961 the number of persons of Greek mother tongue had increased to approximately 500. The 1981 census recorded another doubling of the population of hellenophones, to 1,185, making Greek one of the more widely spoken languages in the province. Most Greeks continued to use the language at home (approximately 71 per cent), although over 90 per cent also spoke English. The 1981 census recorded no Greeks at all living in rural areas. In fact, most live in Halifax, where there is a strong community centred on the Greek-language Orthodox church.

CONCLUSIONS

English is the first language of the overwhelming majority of Nova Scotians, although other languages are spoken as well, particularly in fairly isolated rural segments and among recent urban immigrants. Micmac continues to be spoken and learned as a mother tongue on the more eastern reserves of the province, and Acadian French is also learned as a mother tongue in several rural towns at the eastern and western ends of the province. Gaelic continues to be used as a home language by a few families, spoken by farming people in Cape Breton. Dutch and German are still spoken by some, Dutch again tending to be more a language of farm people. Arabic is a twentieth-century language, recently revitalized by additional immigration. Polish today continues to be used by a minority in the province. There are also communities of Greeks and Chinese, especially in Halifax.

Language retention appears to be favoured in Nova Scotia by several factors, including rural residence, exclusive occupancy of a territory by a linguistic minority, continuing immigration from a country of origin and contact with the homeland, the presence of a focus for the ethnic community (such as a church), cultural divergence from the English majority, non-xenophobic attitudes on the part of the majority, and regional political dominance. Government policies also have an effect on language retention, especially in the case of French, where immersion programmes have enjoyed some success; this is also true of Gaelic on a much smaller scale. Earlier policies tended to be assimilationist – for example, in the case of the Micmacs. The (Roman Catholic) Church also played a role in the teaching of English (and, earlier, French) to aboriginal Nova Scotians. Ethnic organizations themselves tend to favour and work towards preservation of the language, though with varying degrees of commitment and success. The perceived utility of a language is also an important influence on second-language learning, notably for French. In this case, the widespread use of French in Canada, together with its literary tradition and perceived international status and prestige, are undoubtedly influential.

Although there is steady conversion from other languages to English – due to continuing urbanization and the demands of education, work and participation in civil society – the future prospects of French in the province are relatively good. Micmac may survive, providing sustained efforts are made at this critical juncture. The existence of other languages probably depends largely on the extent of immigration of new speakers.

References

(*Note*: Canadian census material has been used extensively in this chapter; the only specific reference, however, is to the source cited in tables 1 and 2.)

Campbell, D. F. (ed.) (1978). *Banked Fires: The Ethnics of Nova Scotia*. Port Credit, Ontario: Scribbler's Press.
Canada (1993). *Language Retention and Transfer, 1991, Dimensions*. Catalogue No. 94–319. Ottawa: Statistics Canada.
Cosper, R. (1984). *Ethnicity and Occupation in Atlantic Canada: The Social and Economic Implications of Cultural Diversity*. Halifax, Nova Scotia: International Education Centre, Saint Mary's University.

Edwards, J. (1991). Gaelic in Nova Scotia. In C. Williams (ed.), *Linguistic Minorities, Society and Territory* (pp. 269-297). Clevedon, Avon: Multilingual Matters.

Jabbra, N. W. & Cosper, R. (1989). Ethnicity in Atlantic Canada: a survey. *Canadian Ethnic Studies, 20(3)*, 6-27.

Jabbra, N. W. & Jabbra, J. (1984). *Voyagers to a Rocky Shore: The Lebanese and Syrians of Nova Scotia*. Halifax, Nova Scotia: Dalhousie University, Institute of Public Affairs.

Medjuck, S. (1986). *Jews of Atlantic Canada*. St John's, Newfoundland: Breakwater Books.

Roy, M. (1982). Settlement and population growth. In J. Daigle (ed.), *The Acadians of the Maritimes: Thematic Studies* (pp. 125-196). Moncton, Nouveau-Brunswick: Centre d'études acadiennes, Université de Moncton.

Map 5 New Brunswick

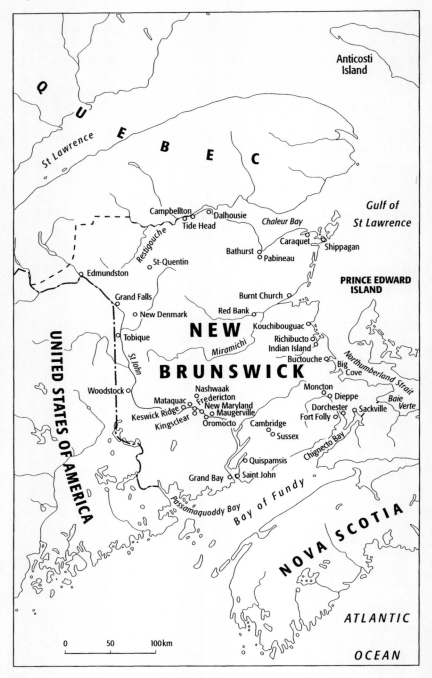

19 Language in New Brunswick

Robert M. Leavitt

INTRODUCTION

As Canada's only officially bilingual province, New Brunswick retains – in demographic, geographical, linguistic and cultural terms – the duality of the Acadian and Loyalist groups who were the first European immigrants to settle in the Maritime region. About two-thirds of the population is English-speaking; the remainder speak French as a first language. The French-speaking population is concentrated along the northern and eastern sides of the province, from Grand Falls to the Quebec border, along the north shore, and south towards Nova Scotia along the Gulf of St Lawrence coast. The English-speaking population lives mainly in the area bounded by Maine and the Bay of Fundy, extending eastward to Sussex and Sackville and north to the Miramichi watershed. In each of these two areas there are also communities where the 'other' language predominates. Linguistically, the province maintains separate school systems for the two groups, although every school district enrols children from both groups. Each district also offers instruction in English or French as a second language, either through the popular French immersion programmes or in classes where the language is taught as a subject. Similarly, at the post-secondary level, the Université de Moncton attracts primarily francophone students, while the student population at the University of New Brunswick and Mount Allison and St Thomas Universities is mainly anglophone; the same may be said of the many community colleges in the province. Culturally, New Brunswickers also enjoy a variety of English and French newspapers, theatre productions, music, and radio and television stations.

New Brunswick has another linguistic duality, perhaps less well known. Speakers of the two indigenous languages of the province, Maliseet and Micmac, also live in distinct areas, where they maintain their linguistic and cultural heritage. Both languages are taught in school and community settings, and very recently both may be heard in local radio and television broadcasts. It is evident

373

– and not only in the indigenous place names which are used officially – that the
Maliseet and Micmac cultures have had a lasting influence on those which the
Acadians and Loyalists brought to the region beginning in the 1500s. Fiddleheads,
salmon and shellfish are familiar parts of every New Brunswicker's diet; canoes
and toboggans carry people and gear in all parts of the province; and both native
and non-native people still move their households from their permanent places
of residence to seasonal camps where they hunt and fish or simply enjoy the
fresh- or salt-water environment. Beyond these obvious influences, it is important to note that, despite the profound effects of colonialism over the past 500
years, native educators, political leaders, artists and teachers are significant participants in provincial affairs today. New Brunswick has four mother tongues,
each with a long history; although their current proportional representation
in the province may not reflect their relative importance, the four languages
– Maliseet, Micmac, English, French – have a continuing influence on the way
all New Brunswickers live.

New Brunswick's official policy on multiculturalism 'recognizes the
great value of cultural diversity set in the context of the province's official bilingual status'. It 'strives for a unity which does not deny or eradicate diversity, but
which recognizes and transcends it'. The policy is also 'guided by principles of 1)
equality, 2) appreciation, 3) preservation of cultural heritages, and 4) participation . . . in . . . democratic processes' (Province of New Brunswick, 1986). While the
policy does not make specific reference to heritage or indigenous languages, its
intent is clearly to create a climate which fosters the use and maintenance of
these languages, not only because they are means of communication and cultural transmission but also because they are integral to the unique identity
of those who speak them.

HERITAGE LANGUAGES IN NEW BRUNSWICK

Of course, the indigenous and official languages are not the only ones
heard in New Brunswick communities. Speakers of European and Asian languages also live permanently in the province (see table 19.1), and there are small
numbers of speakers of African languages. As in the other provinces, the earliest
immigrants came to New Brunswick for the economic opportunities available
here; later, the province became a destination for refugees, and for students and
other visitors, some of whom took up permanent residence. Most of these have
been a minority in their community. In exceptional cases settlements were
founded by a group of immigrants who shared a common culture – for example,
at New Denmark, or the early Gaelic-speaking settlements (Woznow, 1995). In

Table 19.1 1991 Census: Speakers of indigenous and
heritage languages in New Brunswick (languages with
more than 300 speakers, and other languages shown in
table 2)

Maliseet	355
Micmac	1,685
Arabic	465
Chinese[1]	1,170
Danish	490
Dutch	1,050
German	3,075
Greek	380
Hindi	335
Italian	985
Polish	305
Romanian	50
Serbo-Croatian[1]	50
Spanish	2,025
Tagalog	120
Vietnamese	250

[1] There is no separate information in the data for Cantonese
or Mandarin (cf. table 2). The total for Serbo-Croatian
combines figures given for 'Croatian' (30), 'Serbian' (10)
and 'Serbo-Croatian' (10).
Source: Statistics Canada (1992).

such settings a heritage language might survive for generations, and community members could maintain their identity without needing to learn English or French – or without having the opportunity to do so. (The same factors allowed the indigenous languages of the province to remain strong until the middle of this century.) Recently, however, ease of communication and movement has made it possible for immigrant groups to maintain contacts with families abroad and to visit their countries of origin or have visitors come to Canada. It is not only possible but also practical to keep a heritage language alive and teach it to children – and other Canadians will be interested in taking lessons in Chinese or Spanish as well.

Although immigrants to New Brunswick bring with them a variety of languages, many move on to larger centres outside Atlantic Canada and thus have little lasting impact on the linguistic makeup of the province (Blair, 1995). Those who stay may form 'cultural communities' of substantial size in a particular

Table 19.2 Languages of recent immigrants: Mother tongue of permanent residents
destined to New Brunswick, 1990–1995 (languages with more than 20 speakers in at
least one year, and others shown in table 1)

	1990	1991	1992	1993	1994	1995[1]
Arabic	75	23	32	31	19	29
Chinese[1]	123	119	156	88	110	77
Danish	–	1	6	3	1	–
Dutch	5	5	–	2	2	5
German	29	26	35	29	32	33
Greek	–	–	7	5	–	–
Hindi	9	10	1	–	2	10
Italian[1]	–	–	–	–	–	–
Polish	35	1	7	7	6	0
Romanian	10	16	23	9	6	10
Serbo-Croatian	1	0	1	13	69	90
Spanish	85	108	43	56	17	14
Tagalog	5	4	14	16	23	5
Vietnamese	40	62	38	45	39	11

[1] 1995 figures are for January to September only. The totals for Chinese include figures for
'Cantonese', 'Chinese' and 'Mandarin' in each year. Presumably there were no Italian-speaking
immigrants in the years 1990–1995; a dash (–) in any column indicates that the language is not
listed for that year.
Source: Citizenship and Immigration Canada (1995).

settlement or region, or they may remain as distinctive but relatively isolated
family groups.

German immigrants have arrived in the province in a relatively steady
stream for many generations (Woznow, 1995), and this pattern continues, as is
evident in table 19.2. Others have arrived at particular periods of time, when war
or other disasters have driven them from their homeland. They may live here
for a while but then move on, as have many Central American or East European
families in recent years, Hungarians and Czechoslovakians in the 1950s and
1960s, and Southeast Asians in the 1970s and 1980s. The pattern is an old one:
the first immigrant settlers in New Brunswick were Acadian refugees, and later
Loyalists, also fleeing poverty, persecution and war.

The population of immigrants differs regionally in the province, according
to their route of arrival or the particular attraction of an area. Saint John was
the port of entry for Loyalists arriving by ship from New England, who settled in
the river valley running inland from the city. Newly arriving francophones have
tended to settle in southeastern New Brunswick, near the Université de Moncton
and the other cultural centres of the area (Woznow, 1995). Fredericton is a centre

of activity for the province's Lebanese immigrants, who maintain an active cultural programme there. Many New Brunswickers of Greek origin live in Saint John, where there is a Greek Orthodox church, which is also a centre for language instruction.

The experiences of three of the province's heritage-language groups, the Lebanese, the Chinese and the Dutch, are typical of those of many recent immigrant groups.

Lebanese settlement in New Brunswick dates back at least to 1890, when the first recorded family arrived in Saint John, followed soon by relatives, who settled in Fredericton (Jabbra and Jabbra, 1987). These cities have remained the principal centres of immigration, with most newcomers settling in Fredericton. The Lebanese have Arabic, in several dialects, as their mother tongue, and about half of the immigrants in recent years speak French as a second language (Citizenship and Immigration Canada, 1995).

As is the case in many immigrant families, Arabic is understood but not spoken by second-generation Lebanese, and virtually disappears from use by the time that third-generation children are growing up, despite efforts to keep the language alive through classes. One problem is that the language classes are based on formal, written Arabic, which differs from the spoken dialects. The Lebanese situation is unusual, however, in that a public forum has been established in which the heritage language thrives.

The majority of the Lebanese community in New Brunswick are Christians. Meeting in 1983, they decided to establish a Maronite church in Fredericton. Since then, St Charbel's has been the focal point for the community and a centre for the maintenance of Lebanese culture and traditions. Mass is celebrated in English or Arabic, with some sections of the service in Aramaic. The current priest, Reverend Elie Chedid, who is originally from Beirut, also heads a Lebanese school, with weekly Arabic classes held in the church. In 1995, some forty-five elementary and 'older' students were in attendance, helping to restore and maintain the language in the community. For the Lebanese the language remains a central part of their culture and community. Other, smaller groups in Fredericton, mainly from Islamic origins, also speak Arabic.

The first wave of Chinese immigrants also came to New Brunswick in the 1890s, from southern China, and settled in the three principal centres, Saint John, Moncton and Fredericton. The 1921 census reported 113 Chinese residents in these cities. Most were attracted by the promising work opportunities of the time (Seto and Shyu, undated). Later immigrants also settled on the north shore, in the upper St John River valley and in the Miramichi.

Like the Lebanese, the Chinese community became concerned with 'the loss of cultural traditions and language among children and grandchildren' (Shyu, Lin and Tai, 1988, p. 39). In the mid-1970s they formed the Chinese Cultural Association and opened a school in Fredericton, with assistance from the Secretary of State. This school continues to operate, with instruction in oral and written Mandarin and Cantonese. About sixty children attend the weekly classes, together with a small group of adults. These classes have been more important for Mandarin-speaking families, whose younger generations are losing the language, than for Cantonese speakers, whose language is continually renewed by the many students and immigrants arriving from Hong Kong and other Cantonese-speaking regions of China.

After the fall of Saigon, in 1975, there was a dramatic increase in the Asian population in New Brunswick, with refugees arriving from Vietnam, Laos and Cambodia. The first ethnic Chinese family from the region came to Fredericton under federal government sponsorship. This opened the door (Shyu, Lin and Tai, 1988), and other families followed after an appeal from Premier Richard Hatfield asking New Brunswickers to sponsor refugees. By 1980 there were about 130 Southeast Asians living in Fredericton, most with little or no knowledge of English. The government, with assistance from the provincial Multicultural Association, began to offer English classes, many at the local YMCA-YWCA, and these are still available to newcomers today.

According to a recent study, 74 per cent of people of Dutch ancestry living in New Brunswick retain knowledge of their first language, as compared with 59 per cent Canada-wide; this may be because those in New Brunswick live primarily in rural areas (van den Hoonaard, 1991). Centres of Dutch settlement include Keswick Ridge, Maugerville and Sussex, as well as the areas around Moncton and Saint John. In Fredericton, with more than 150 Dutch households, Dutch is also frequently heard. In practical terms, however, only about one-third of Dutch New Brunswickers use the language in everyday conversation; the words of one woman, however, indicate some of the potential for maintaining Dutch in Canada:

> So when our children picked up a few words, they couldn't really speak it. Our oldest daughter took a Dutch course at college. So actually she can really understand it ... And then [our] oldest boy, he worked with a Dutch emigrant for many years.... and he's gone to Holland, and once he's there he has no big problem. You know they laugh at his accent but he can make himself understood. (van den Hoonaard, 1991, p. 47)

INDIGENOUS LANGUAGES

The indigenous languages of New Brunswick are Maliseet-Passamaquoddy and Micmac, eastern members of the Algonquian language family. Maliseet and Passamaquoddy are the New Brunswick and Maine branches, respectively, of a single language, differing slightly only in 'accent' and usage, much like Canadian and American English. Micmac is closely related to Maliseet but the two languages are not mutually intelligible. Although the Micmacs are among the earliest indigenous people to have had contact with Europeans, five centuries ago, their language still flourishes.

Indigenous placenames – Mactaquac, Nashwaak, Quispamsis, Kouchibouguac, Restigouche – are all most non-native New Brunswickers know of the languages that were spoken here when the first Europeans arrived. These placenames are a record of what the original inhabitants of the land found significant, as are those in English and French which name or describe a geographical feature: Grand Bay, Baie Verte, Tide Head. No indigenous placename refers to a person, as does Fredericton or St-Quentin; and none, so far as we know, is borrowed from another placename – as is New Denmark – although it has been suggested that Restigouche, in Micmac *Listuguj* or *Ulastuguj*, derives from a diminutive form of the name for the St John River, in Maliseet Wolastoq 'beautiful river' or 'good river' – in reference to the ease with which it may be travelled and the abundance of resources its waters provide.

Today there are more indigenous names used for rivers, towns, and other places in New Brunswick than in any of the other Atlantic provinces. Their abundance shows not only that the early settlers depended upon Maliseet and Micmac guides when they travelled, which was true everywhere, but also that, perhaps because they were later in extending permanent settlements into the province, they found many indigenous placenames already well established. Thus the placenames used today reveal some of the social and political history of the province. Over the centuries, most of the Maliseet or Micmac names were replaced with names of foreign origin, until the majority were European. Loyalist settlers named towns and cities after places in the British Isles (Cambridge) or the United States (New Maryland), or after members of the royal family. Acadians used French placenames and, commonly, the names of saints. In many cases, however, the original placenames survived, though they were borrowed into English or French as loan-words, with the corresponding changes in pronunciation. Maliseet *Meqtoqek* (pronounced MEHKW-t'-gweg) became Mactaquac in English; Micmac *Lsipugtug* ('l-zee-BOOK-toog) became Richibuctou in French.

The original versions of these names are still in use among Maliseet and Micmac speakers.

Maliseet is indigenous to the St John and St Croix River valleys. It is no longer spoken at St-Basile (Edmundston), but there are speakers in each of the other New Brunswick Maliseet communities – Tobique, Woodstock, Kingsclear, St Mary's and Oromocto. Speakers are almost without exception forty years of age or older; few if any children today speak Maliseet as a first language. The situation in the Passamaquoddy communities of neighbouring Maine is similar. Among the people themselves, the speakers considered truly 'fluent' are usually those in their late fifties and older. The most recent census identified 355 Maliseet-speakers in New Brunswick, with some 40 living elsewhere in Canada (Statistics Canada, 1992). These figures, like those for Micmac, should be regarded as conservative, since response to the census is often low in First Nations communities.

Micmac is spoken from the Gaspé peninsula of Quebec to Cape Breton Island, with speakers in northern and eastern New Brunswick, from Eel River Bar (near Dalhousie) to Pabineau, Red Bank, Eel Ground, Burnt Church, Big Cove, Indian Island, Buctouche and Fort Folly (near Dorchester). There are also Micmac communities in Prince Edward Island, throughout Nova Scotia and in Newfoundland. In certain communities, some children still speak Micmac as a first language; in others the youngest speakers are adults. Micmac is thus a language whose survival is in the balance. Today it is in 'better condition' than Maliseet, but the trend towards disuse continues. Recent census data record a total of 6,870 speakers in Canada, with 1,685 living in New Brunswick (Statistics Canada, 1992).

Many Europeans learned Micmac even before the time of permanent European settlements. Traders along the North Atlantic coast in the sixteenth and seventeenth centuries spoke a pidgin using Micmac and Basque (Bakker, 1991), and a few Basque loan words persist in Micmac today, including, for example, *eleke'wit* (pronounced eh-leh-GEH-weed) 'king' and *atlai* (AH-d'lai) 'shirt' (Bakker, 1989). The Maliseet word for 'king' is *kincemoss* (geen-CHEH-m'ss), a later borrowing of 'King James', from English. Europeans borrowed words from both languages to expand their own vocabularies – toboggan, sachem, wigwam, tomahawk and many others. The Micmacs and Maliseets borrowed in turn, at first from French – Micmac *te'sipow* (DEH-zee-bohw) 'horse' from *des chevaux*, or Maliseet *lahkap* (LAH-kahb) 'cellar' from *la cave* – and later from English – Micmac *tma'tos* (d'-MAH-dohz) 'tomato' or Maliseet *leptanet* (lep-TAH-ned) 'lieutenant'.

Until the middle years of this century the indigenous languages remained vital, productive and widely spoken. Storytellers born in the 1930s maintain the eloquence of the oral tradition today. The census data of 1981 indicate that at that time, in eastern Canada overall, indigenous language maintenance was lowest among those between thirty-five and forty-four years of age (Burnaby and Beaujot, 1986) – i.e., those who were young children during and just after World War II.

Several factors contributed to the gradual decline in the use of Micmac and Maliseet. Changes in the education system – especially the establishment of the residential schools and later the integration of native students into provincial schools – put children in environments where they did not speak their mother tongue or, in the worst cases, were severely punished for doing so. Teachers, moreover, routinely encouraged parents to speak to their children in English so that they might do better in school. With the new mobility that accompanied World War II came increased intermarriage and lopsided cultural interchange – sports leagues, television, higher education – between native and non-native communities. English began slowly to displace Micmac and Maliseet as the language of the home and community.

What is being lost? The indigenous languages of New Brunswick embody a 'way of knowing' markedly different from that of English or French. They express a world-view which establishes physical and social environments in relative terms and not as absolutes, independent of the effects of human perception and participation (Leavitt, 1995). For example, Micmac and Maliseet speakers normally locate objects and events in relation to themselves and the people they are speaking with – Maliseet *elomaskutek* (el-mah-sкoo-deg) 'where a field extends away' or *weckuwaskutek* (wech-koo-wah-sкoo-deg) 'where a field extends toward here'. Interestingly, there is no noun for 'field' in the languages; instead, the notion of 'field' is expressed in verbs like these. Because the environment is constructed in this way, it is unnatural to speak of it as something separate from humankind; people are an integral part of the world they live in.

Micmac and Maliseet exemplify a way of speaking and thinking which is intrinsically egalitarian, and a social order in which leaders are those whose wisdom and experience command respect rather than those whose authority gives power. The languages reveal a way of life in which personal identity is dynamic, determined according to changing relations with the natural world (as indicated in the previous paragraph) and with family and community. For example, in Maliseet and Micmac, the reciprocal forms of transitive verbs – those with meanings such as 'we see one another' or 'they hear one another' – are

381

grammatically intransitive and are much like the plural forms of ordinary intransitive verbs. This seems to imply that plurality and reciprocity are closely connected concepts; and in fact the Maliseet and Micmac cultures reflect a concern with sharing and giving to one another as a fundamental social value. An examination of the grammatical persons in these languages (I, you, etc.), reveals two other features of interest: a single pronoun has the meaning 'he or she'; and two pronouns have the meaning 'we' – 'another and I' as distinct from 'you and I'. In these and other ways, the languages reflect cultures which are non-sexist, and in which care is taken to include the listener explicitly in what is said.

For the Maliseets and Micmacs, survival of the ancestral languages is an important factor in the maintenance of their distinctive identities and cultural integrity. In response to the threat that the languages may disappear, they have initiated a variety of programmes for teaching Maliseet or Micmac, most notably through school and community-based classes, and 'language nests', where speakers and non-speakers from several generations gather regularly to share stories, songs, and oral history in an informal setting. These efforts to revitalize the indigenous languages rely upon a spirit of collaboration between teachers and learners, each of whom wishes to keep alive the oldest traditions of the region.

It is perhaps reflective of the intentions of New Brunswick with regard to language policy that, in connection with the Equal Employment Opportunity Program and the Department of Advanced Education and Labour, the government has formed a 'language bank', listing more than 80 people in the public service with expertise in twenty-five languages other than English and French (Caldwell, 1995). One purpose of the language bank is to make official visitors to the province feel welcome; another is to assist any government department in communicating with those who do not speak English or French. In addition, the Department of Education employs an Aboriginal Education Consultant, currently a Maliseet speaker, whose responsibilities include the development of Maliseet and Micmac language curriculum and materials for programmes in the provincial schools. These recent developments augur well for the many languages which are spoken in New Brunswick.

Note

The author wishes to acknowledge the able assistance of Eve Nash in the research for this chapter.

References

Bakker, P. (1989). Two Basque loanwords in Micmac. *International Journal of Linguistics, 55,* 258–261.

(1991). La lengua de las tribus costeras es medio vasca: Un pidgin vasco y amerindio utilizado por europeos y nativos americanos en Norteamérica, h. 1540 – h. 1640. *International Journal of Basque Linguistics and Philology, 25,* 439–467.

Blair, J. (1995). Personal communication. [Blair is Immigration Program Specialist, Canada Immigration Centre, Fredericton, NB.]

Burnaby, B. and Beaujot, R. (1986). *The Use of Aboriginal Languages in Canada: An Analysis of 1981 Census Data.* Ottawa: Department of the Secretary of State.

Caldwell, R. (1995). The government language bank: a good idea. *Perspectives* (Winter), 10.

Citizenship and Immigration Canada (1995). Permanent residents destined to New Brunswick by official language ability by mother tongue [data compiled at the Fredericton, NB, office of CIC].

Jabbra, J. G. and Jabbra, N. W. (1987). *People of the Maritimes – Lebanese.* Tantallon, NS: Four East Publications.

Leavitt, R. M. (1995). *Maliseet and Micmac: First Nations of the Maritimes.* Fredericton: New Ireland Press.

Province of New Brunswick (1986). *Policy on Multiculturalism.* Fredericton: Department of Labour.

Seto, W. and Shyu, L. N. (undated). *The Chinese Experience in New Brunswick: A Historical Perspective.* Fredericton: The Chinese Cultural Association of New Brunswick.

Shyu, L., Lin, K. C. and Tai, G. (eds.) (1988). *Embarking on a New Milestone: 1977–1987.* Fredericton: The Chinese Cultural Association of New Brunswick.

Statistics Canada (1992). *Knowledge of Languages.* Ottawa: Industry, Science and Technology Canada (1991 Census).

van den Hoonaard, W.C. (1991). *Silent Ethnicity: The Dutch of New Brunswick.* Fredericton: New Ireland Press.

Woznow, B. (1995). Personal communication. [Woznow is Multiculturalism and Immigration Officer, Office of Advocacy Services, New Brunswick Department of Advanced Education and Labour.]

Map 6 Quebec

BAFFIN ISLAND

Coats
Island

Mansel
Island

Hudson Strait

LABRADOR

SEA

NEWFOUNDLAND

HUDSON BAY

Ungava
Bay

Belcher
Islands

L a b r a d o r

Clearwater
Lake

Lac
Bienville

Schefferville

James
°
Bay

P e n i n s u l a

Saguenay-Lac St. Jean
region

Q U E B E C

Lake
Mistassini

Sept-Iles

Anticosti
Island

Island of
Newfoundland

St Lawrence

Gaspé

Gulf of
St Lawrence

Betsiamites
Lake
St John

Restigouche

Iles de la
Madeleine

Maniwaki

Mauricie
region

Quebec
City

PRINCE EDWARD
ISLAND

Cape
Breton
Island

Ottawa

Trois Rivières

Beauce
region

NEW

Ile des
Allumettes

Joliette

Montreal

BRUNSWICK

Hull

Island of Montreal

Bay of Fundy

ONTARIO

NOVA SCOTIA

Lake Ontario

UNITED STATES

OF AMERICA

A T L A N T I C

O C E A N

0   50   100   150 km

20 Language in Quebec: aboriginal and heritage varieties

Josiane F. Hamers and Kirsten M. Hummel

Although Quebec is the only officially unilingual francophone province in Canada – with a francophone majority and an anglophone minority – there are, as in the other provinces, language communities whose members speak neither French nor English as their mother tongue. As elsewhere in Canada, an important distinction is made between aboriginal and allophone (persons not of French-, English- or aboriginal-language origin) communities.

The First Nations, descendants of communities established in North America about 10,000 years before the arrival of Europeans in the sixteenth century, include Amerindian and Inuit societies. The allophone communities arrived after the French and English ones were well established, from the nineteenth century onwards, and were traditionally from European origins other than French or Anglo-Celtic. Since the 1960s, non-European allophone communities have been growing rapidly. Compared to the rest of Canada, the percentage of speakers of a language other than French or English is relatively small in Quebec (6.8 per cent versus 14.9 per cent). In 1986, there were approximately 650,000 allophone Quebecers of neither French nor English origin, 73,590 Amerindians and 7,355 Inuit.

As a predominantly French-speaking entity, Quebec constitutes a distinct society in English-speaking North America. Language planning by successive provincial governments has transformed the society from an English-dominant to a French-dominant one. Quebec's implementation of language policies is unique (Hamers and Hummel, 1994) and, as a result, the linguistic adaptation of the native and allophone communities has followed a distinct path. Although in Quebec, as in other provinces, aboriginal languages are endangered and poorly protected, statistics demonstrate that they are better maintained, and more taught, than in the rest of Canada (Laporte, 1992). In 1982, the First Nations of Quebec demanded that the provincial government recognize their rights, including their status as distinct nations with a right to their own culture and language, and the right to control education (Trudel, 1992).

HISTORICAL BACKGROUND

The ethnolinguistic mosaic of the present-day province of Quebec is
the result of: (a) French and British colonial expansion and conflicts in the Americas during the sixteenth, seventeenth, and eighteenth centuries; (b) contacts
between the aboriginal communities and the colonial powers; (c) immigration
trends in the nineteenth and twentieth centuries. In 1534, when Jacques Cartier
took possession of the St Lawrence Valley in the name of the king of France,
present-day Quebec was occupied by three important ethnolinguistic groups:
the Eskimo-Thulians in Northern Quebec and Labrador; the Algonquians in the
northern forest of the Canadian Shield and in the Appalachian forests; and the
Iroquoians in the St Lawrence Valley. The total population living in Quebec
then has been estimated at about 20,000 (Dorais, 1992).

During the seventeenth century the French established a number of settlements in the St Lawrence Valley, including Quebec City in 1608, and Ville Marie
– later to become Montreal – in 1642. By 1673, there were about 7,000 French
settlers in the St Lawrence Valley. The eighteenth century witnessed the disappearance of the French colonial empire in North America; in 1763, with the
Treaty of Paris, all of New France, with the exception of the islands of St Pierre
and Miquelon, was lost to the British Empire. As a direct consequence, the province of Quebec was created. The Quebec Act (1774) entitled French Canadians
to keep their language and religion and to develop as an autonomous group
inside the North American colony. By 1867, the British North America Act
created the Dominion of Canada, in which Quebec constituted one of the four
provinces. The Act did not explicitly legislate on language matters, but it did
contain two sections relevant to language policies: parliamentary and
legislative matters were to be conducted bilingually (Article 113); and
education would be the responsibility of provincial governments (Article 93),
who could thus exercise the choice of language (Hamers and Hummel, 1994).
Until the mid-twentieth century francophones survived as a rural, Catholic
community, growing demographically by a high birthrate – known as '*the
revenge of the cradle*'.

With the eighteenth-century conquest, a growing Anglo-Celtic population settled in Quebec City, in the Montreal area and, to a lesser extent, in the
Eastern Townships and the Gaspé Peninsula. Anglo-Celtic immigrants joined
the Loyalists fleeing the United States after 1776, and the Irish immigrants who
came after the potato famine of 1847. Until the Second World War, immigrants
from the British Isles outnumbered the others. At the turn of the century they
were joined by Europeans from other countries: Jews fleeing the pogroms in

eastern Europe and eastern and southern Europeans, mainly Italians, seeking better economic conditions.

During the early years of the colony, contacts between Europeans and native people were mainly economic and religious. Important population movements took place in the seventeenth century. Following European expansion on the lower St Lawrence north shore, the Inuit retreated north of Hamilton Inlet; the Iroquoians left the lower St Lawrence Valley and settled closer to Montreal; Micmacs and Malecites from New England settled in the Gaspé Peninsula. Indian nations were weakened by warfare; in 1650, for example, the Senecas and the Mohawks destroyed the Huron Nation. Not only did Amerindians not grow in numbers, but they were decimated by epidemics introduced by the Europeans – in the 1730s, half of the Huron population died from smallpox. Between 1600 and 1850, the Quebec Amerindian population was reduced to almost one-third of its original size. Only in the 1960s did it again reach the demographic levels of the sixteenth century (Dorais, 1992). The dwindling of the native population, in addition to the increase in the number of francophones and anglophones, led to a progressive minorization of the aboriginal communities.

According to French Catholic missionaries, Christianization was more successful if native people lived in special villages, close to European settlements. From 1650 onwards, such settlements were established near Quebec City and Montreal, often on the land of present-day reserves such as Wendake, near Quebec City, and Kahnawake, Akwasasne, and Kanesatake near Montreal. As a result, the southern communities rapidly acculturated to the French (and later to the English) culture, while the more isolated communities in the north survived longer in their traditional ways.

When the Europeans arrived, they were treated as equals by the Indians, who exchanged goods with them, had diplomatic relations and made political alliances. The French considered them as conquered nations subject to royal authority, while the Amerindians continued to view themselves as independent nations. After the conquest and the end of the American War of Independence, the minorization of native people accelerated. The British North America Act considered native people and the lands allotted to them as the exclusive responsibility of the federal government. In 1875, the Indian Act conferred the status of minor on Indians: they were deprived of their economic autonomy, their legal capacity and their political independence. The Act introduced the distinction between Indians with and without status (Vincent, 1992). The paternalistic ideology expressed in this Act – modified in 1880, 1886, 1906 and 1927 – prevailed in the first half of the twentieth century. In 1951, the poor living conditions in native communities prompted the federal government to review the *Indian Act* (Savard and Proulx, 1982) and provide some social welfare programmes. It was only in 1960 that native people obtained the right to vote in federal elections and were considered Canadian citizens. In Quebec they had to wait until 1969 to obtain the right to vote at the provincial level.

THE NATIVE PEOPLE OF QUEBEC

Today the aboriginal population forms less than 1 per cent of the total population of Quebec. The languages of the present-day native communities in Quebec reflect their ethnolinguistic origin and belong to three linguistic families: the Eskimo-Aleutian, the Iroquian, and the Algonquian. Nine aboriginal languages are still spoken in Quebec: Inuktitut (Eskimo-Aleutian) in Nunavik (Arctic Quebec); seven Algonquian languages (Abenaki, Algonquin, Attikamek, Cree, Montagnais, Micmac and Naskapi); and one Iroquoian language, Mohawk. Wendat, an Iroquoian language spoken by the Hurons, died out in the beginning of the twentieth century. Estimates indicate that the most widely spoken aboriginal languages are Cree, Montagnais and Inuktitut, all used by more than 5,000 people (Dorais, 1992). According to 1991 census figures, 27,000 persons in Quebec declared an aboriginal language as their mother tongue (Gouvernement du Québec, 1994).

The Canadian Charter of Rights and Freedoms (Article 35(2)) recognizes and confirms the existing rights of native peoples. The administration of aboriginal languages and cultures is under the responsibility of the Canadian Department of Indian and Northern Affairs, the Heritage Office (Service du Patrimoine) in the Ministère de la Culture et des Communications in Quebec, and, in part, by the Ministère de l'Éducation and the Secrétariat aux Affaires Autochtones (SAA) in Quebec. Several laws govern the status of some of the native languages. In Quebec, the status of Cree and Naskapi is governed by the Canadian Constitution Act of 1982, the Law on the Cree and Naskapi of Quebec, the Education Act for Cree, Inuit and Naskapi Native Persons (which established the Cree School Board), the James Bay and Northern Quebec Agreement, and statutes of Cree organizations that provide for language use in meetings. Inuktitut is governed by the Constitution Act of 1982, the Education Act for Cree, Inuit and Naskapi Native Persons (which established the Kativik School Board), the James Bay and Northern Quebec Agreement, statutes of Inuit organizations that provide for language use in meetings, and the 1987 resolution of the Quebec National Assembly on the administration of New-Quebec. For the other native languages used in Quebec (Abenaki, Algonquin, Attikamek, Micmac, Mohawk, and Montagnais) only the Constitution Act of 1982 defines their status (Collis, 1992).

During the 1980s the Quebec government took a number of steps towards recognizing the status of aboriginal languages. The Quebec Charter of Human Rights and Freedoms recognizes that ethnic minorities have 'the right to maintain and promote their own cultural life with the other members of their group'. In 1983, the Quebec Council of Ministers adopted fifteen principles that were to guide relations with aboriginal peoples of Quebec, some of which explicitly recognize their right to manage institutions corresponding to their needs in the linguistic and cultural domains. In 1985, the Quebec National Assembly adopted a 'Motion for the recognition of aboriginal rights in Quebec' which made the 1983 principles official. In 1989, the Secrétariat des Affaires Autochtones produced a working document on 'Safeguarding and promoting aboriginal languages in Quebec' which constituted Quebec's first clear political declaration in the domain of aboriginal languages. Nevertheless, this declaration remains very general and fails to specify the precise means by which native languages will be protected and encouraged – nor does it specify the financial means which are to be used, or propose a calendar for achieving its objectives (Trudel, 1992). At present, the only independent native authority with the theoretical right to decide on linguistic matters is that of the Inuit in Nunavik (Collis, 1992).

NATIVE LANGUAGE USE IN QUEBEC

As a general tendency, the aboriginal languages that have been best preserved are those whose communities are the most geographically isolated (Dorais, 1992). In Quebec these include Inuktitut, Naskapi, Cree, Montagnais and Attikamek, languages which continue to be widely used in their respective communities. According to Dorais, Cree is the aboriginal language with the most speakers in Quebec, with close to 11,000 (including Attikamek speakers), followed by the Montagnais-Naskapi group, and the Inuit, with approximately 5,000 speakers each. In more geographically accessible communities, however, even Montagnais and Algonquin are in difficulty. Languages which are in abrupt decline include Abenaki, Mohawk and Micmac (Dorais, 1992). Inuktitut benefits from the development of a considerable body of written material, greater than that for any other aboriginal language in Quebec. In particular, the Kativik School Board has published a large number of school texts and readers in Inuktitut (Drapeau, 1992).

For most native groups, the aboriginal language is often the variety used in municipal administration (band councils), and it is always used in such situations by the Naskapi and the Inuit. The provincial Ministère de la Santé et des Services Sociaux publishes six pamphlets in aboriginal languages and provincial health services can be received in aboriginal languages through the use of interpreters, unlike most other provincial and federal services (Collis, 1992). The spoken (but not the written) use of aboriginal languages is allowed in the court system; however, judges do not pronounce legal decisions in aboriginal languages. According to Collis (1992), the only aboriginal language into which laws have been officially translated, and in which municipal laws are written, is Naskapi.

The Ministère de la Culture et des Communications funds several native community radio stations; some of which broadcast only partially in aboriginal languages (southern Quebec), while others operate almost entirely in aboriginal languages (northern Quebec) (Trudel, 1992). A few hours of television broadcasting are produced weekly in Inuktitut and Cree.

Certain native groups have opted for French as their second language (Montagnais, Attikamek, Huron and Abenaki), while for others it has been English (Cree, Mohawk, Micmac, Naskapi, Inuit). The Algonquin tend to opt for English, although French is widely spoken on some reserves. In recent years, greater numbers of natives are able to speak both French and English. Some Cree and Inuit are now being schooled in French rather than English (Dorais, 1992). Dorais points out that aboriginal languages are gradually losing ground to official languages: from 1961 to 1971, the percentage of aboriginal people with a native language as first language decreased from 76 per cent to 58 per cent. However, there are indications that the decrease is slowing, perhaps due to more schooling in aboriginal languages – from 1971 to 1986 there was a further decrease of only 8 per cent (although Dorais points out that this figure may in fact be an underestimate; the nonparticipation of the Mohawk in the 1986 census may have distorted figures). The Inuit have the highest level of native-language preservation (92.5 per cent according to the SAA, 1988), while only 48 per cent of Amerindians speak an aboriginal language as their mother tongue (Dorais, 1992).

EDUCATION IN NATIVE COMMUNITIES

Although in the early years Christianization was introduced through aboriginal languages, European education – which aimed at the 'civilization of the savage' – was conducted exclusively in French and later in English. As early as 1639, a religious order, the Ursulines, established a French school for Indian girls in Quebec, in order to transform them into good Catholics assimilated to the French. In 1875, native education came under federal control and for over a century the federal government adopted assimilation policies. These financed missionaries and religious orders, Catholic and Anglican, to provide education for the Indians and the Inuit, in French and in English. Reserve and residential schools were created, and the federal ideology prevailed: native pupils had to abandon their culture and language and assimilate to the dominant culture. The quality of education was poor; besides elementary literacy, only unskilled or semi-skilled training was given (Trudel, 1992). Throughout this period and at least into the 1950s, aboriginal languages were banished from classrooms.

This first educational policy was a failure. In 1951, almost half of native children had received no formal schooling; of the other half, only one-third had completed their third year and only one-tenth had completed their sixth year of elementary school (Trudel, 1992). A revision of the Indian Act in 1951 entitled the federal government to sign agreements with provincial governments and school boards to provide education for native children aged six to seventeen. Federal schools were opened and boarding schools exclusively for native pupils were entrusted to religious orders which pursued cultural assimilation. Despite the assimilation policy, the number of Indians and Inuit attending school increased, as did the number of years of schooling. Education was in English or French; native cultures and languages were completely banished. A federal White Paper on Indian Policy (Gouvernement du Canada, 1969) suggested that the responsibility of education be transferred to the provinces. Shocked by its paternalistic content, the Canadian Brotherhood of Indians replied in 1972 with a powerful declaration, including claims for Indian control of education, better training of native teachers, and more time devoted to the teaching of native cultures and languages (Trudel, 1992). From 1973 onwards, greater autonomy of native communities was conceded by both the federal and the provincial governments. In Quebec, a number of organizations were created which entitled native communities to attain greater control over educational matters, although overall control remains largely in the hands of non-natives (Trudel, 1992).

In matters of language of education, Bill 101 (see below) is binding for all minorities except Anglo-Quebecers, Amerindians and the Inuit. The Bill recognizes that aboriginal peoples of Quebec have the right to maintain and develop their culture and language of origin. The use of Amerindian languages and of Inuktitut is permitted in schools attended by Amerindians and the Inuit. Native communities may also maintain their traditional official language (French or English). The use of aboriginal languages in education varies from one community to the other. The greater autonomy gained by native communities has led to a number of experimental educational programmes. For example, in

Betsiamites, a Montagnais reserve on the north shore of the St Lawrence, education is provided in the mother tongue until the end of Grade 3 (Drapeau, 1984). In a growing number of communities, education includes mother-tongue teaching. In 1979, the Ministère de l'Éducation created a programme providing for native educational research, teacher training and school materials. The University of Quebec in Chicoutimi has a technolinguistic programme in Montagnais, while McGill University has an Inuit teacher-training programme (Trudel, 1992).

Despite the improvement in native education in the last four decades, much remains to be achieved. In 1989–1990, only 847 native children received some schooling through their mother tongue. In 1993–1994, 1,834 native children (out of 9,212) received some schooling through their mother tongue. Virtually no mother-tongue education is provided after Grade 3. At least three ethnolinguistic groups provide mother-tongue education: the Inuit, to 720 pupils (total: 3,417; 1,745 attend French and 952 English schools); the Cree, to 762 pupils (total: 3,007; 1,156 attend French and 1,089 English schools); and the Attikamek-Montagnais, to 351 pupils (total: 2,464; 2,095 attend French and 18 English schools). Naskapi, Algonquin and Micmac communities do not have mother-tongue education, although aboriginal languages are taught in schools in some native communities (Gouvernement du Québec, 1995).

The number of native children attending school through their mother tongue in the early years has been increasing over the last decade. (So has the number of degrees obtained by native people, although no reliable statistics are available.) Evaluations of the programmes are still scarce; however, when an evaluation is done, as in the Kativik School Board in Nunavik, results are promising (Stairs, 1985). The communities have taken on responsibility for education, and aim at the maintenance of culture and language. Since the 1980s, both the federal and provincial governments recognize the right of the First Nations to control their own cultural identity and, hence, to develop their own approach in matters of education. However, as pointed out by Trudel (1992), many native groups are unable fully to exercise control over educational policy development and implementation in their communities, because of the complexity of the provincial educational system.

THE ALLOPHONE COMMUNITIES IN QUEBEC

As of 1991 census figures, Quebec's population comprised 6,810,300 persons, of whom 82 per cent were French native speakers, 9 per cent English native speakers, less than 1 per cent native speakers of aboriginal languages, and 8 per cent allophones.   Among the allophone population, the largest group is that of native Italian speakers (133,210), followed by Spanish (51,735), Arabic (46,165), Greek (46,110), Portuguese (33,890), Chinese (30,755) and Haitian Creole (25,180) (Gouvernement du Québec, 1994). Slightly more than two-thirds of the allophone group is composed of these seven groups. In terms of language families, 41 per cent of allophones speak Romance languages. The other language families are much more diversified.

Immigrants constitute 9 per cent of the population of Quebec and non-permanent residents constitute less than 1 per cent of the population. While the proportion of immigrants slightly increased between the 1986 and 1991 censuses (from 8.2 per cent to 8.7 per cent of the population), this percentage is much lower than in some other provinces. For instance, immigrants constitute 23.7 per cent of the population of Ontario, 23 per cent of the population of British Columbia, and 15 per cent of the population of Alberta (Gouvernement du Québec, 1993). In 1991, the immigrant population included 104,990 persons for whom French is the only native language (18 per cent), 79,920 English native speakers (14 per cent), and 384,750 (65 per cent) others (Gouvernement du Québec, 1994).

The size of the different language groups varies with immigration period. Among the population arriving before the early 1970s, one finds individuals whose native language is of European origin, such as French, English, Italian, Greek, German and Portuguese. Among the population arriving from the mid-1970s on, one observes an increase in the numbers of Spanish, Arabic, Chinese, Creole and Vietnamese speakers. A number of groups arrived many years ago and, today, receive relatively few new members through immigration. These include speakers of Baltic languages (of whom 96 per cent arrived before 1971), Ukrainian, Italian, Yiddish, Hungarian, Dutch, German and Greek. On the other hand, other groups have arrived mainly during the ten years preceding the last census – including, for instance, native speakers of Spanish, Arabic, Chinese, Creole, Vietnamese, Romanian and Khmer (Gouvernement du Québec, 1994). Although official figures are not currently available, groups arriving since the 1991 census include large numbers of Serbo-Croatian speakers, primarily of Bosnian origin.

LANGUAGE USE IN ALLOPHONE COMMUNITIES

Of the entire Quebec population, 93 per cent declared in 1991 that they were able to carry on a conversation in French, and 41 per cent could do the same in English. Nearly a third (31 per cent) of native French speakers declared being able to converse in English, while 58 per cent of English speakers said they could converse in French. Among the allophone population, 22 per cent declared being able to carry on a conversation in French only, 46 per cent could in French or English, 21 per cent in English only, and 11 per cent in neither French or English. Thus, 68 per cent of allophones said they were able to converse in French and 67 per cent in English (Gouvernement du Québec, 1994).

In 1991, 82 per cent of Quebec's overall population declared that they usually speak French at home, 10 per cent usually speak English, and 5 per cent another language. Some 98 per cent of francophones use their native language as the only language spoken at home, 88 per cent of anglophones use only English at home, and 57 per cent of allophones use another language at home. Recent immigrants are more likely to use a language other than French or English in the home: 72 per cent of allophones who arrived during the years 1986–1991, compared to 56 per cent among those who arrived before 1971. The loss of the native language in favour of French or English as the language most often used at home increases with the length of stay of immigrants – ranging from 17 per cent shift among groups arriving between 1986 and 1991 to 37 per cent for groups arriving before 1971 (Gouvernement du Québec, 1994). Still, language maintenance and transmission rates of heritage languages tend to be higher in Quebec than in the rest of Canada (Pendakur, 1990). Quebec is the only province where a language shift occurs more towards French than towards English.

LANGUAGE LEGISLATION

In the last twenty years, the Quebec government has passed legislation aimed at strengthening the status of French in Quebec. Bill 22, also known as the Official Language Act – passed in 1974 – established French as the sole official language of Quebec. While previously Quebecers were free to send their children to the schools of their choice, Bill 22 restricted access to the English public school system to children with a sufficient knowledge of English, as determined by language tests. Following the 1976 election which brought the Parti Québécois to power, the 1977 Charter of the French Language (Bill 101) protected the status of French in the workplace, and further restricted access to public school instruction in English. The law established that immigrants to Quebec, including those of English-speaking origin, would have to send their children to French schools. The right of Quebec's native people to school their children in the language of their choice remained protected.

Language legislation seems to have had a major impact on the use of French in the home by allophone groups. A dramatic change in the choice of French or English at home is associated with period of immigration. For allophones who arrived before 1971, 71 per cent opted for English, while over two-thirds of immigrants arriving since 1976 (i.e., following Bill 101) have opted for French as the language of the household (Gouvernement du Québec, 1994).

EDUCATION IN ALLOPHONE COMMUNITIES

As just noted, Bill 101 means that all immigrant children in Quebec must enrol in the French school system; all children must attend French schools, with the exception of the children of Anglo-Quebecers who have, themselves, attended an English school in Quebec, Canadians arriving from other provinces, Amerindians and the Inuit. In 1993–1994, of 1,147,190 children in elementary and high schools, 956,593 came from a French mother-tongue home, 94,433 had English as their mother tongue, 9,212 an aboriginal language and 86,952 were allophones. Among the latter there are several ethnolinguistic communities with more than 5,000 school children; these communities include the Hispanic, mainly from Latin America (12,730), Italian (12,198), Arabic (9,904), Haitian Creole (6,642), Chinese (6,212), Greek (5,730) and Portuguese (5,539) (Gouvernement du Québec, 1995).

Before 1974 (Bill 22), the choice of language of education was possible; traditionally most immigrant communities preferred the English schools because of the social dominance of the English language (Laferrière, 1985a). For cultural communities whose members arrived before the language legislation was passed, it was still possible to send their children to English schools. The Italian community (about 200,000 members) is the largest and the oldest cultural minority in Quebec. In 1993–1994, 68.8 per cent of Italophone children attended English schools. In the Jewish community, another long-established group, 88 per cent of the children are in English schools. However, a number of children of these two communities are in French immersion programmes. Greek and Portuguese school children attend English schools to a lesser extent (23.5 per cent and 24.5 per cent, respectively). Children from more recently established communities, mainly from Asia, receive some English education: 22.7 per cent of the Chinese children and 50 per cent of the Indo-Pakistani (Urdu, Punjabi, Gujerati and Hindi speakers) are in English-language schools. On the other hand, virtually all Indochinese (Vietnamese, Cambodian and Laotian) children attend French schools (more than 99 per cent). This is also true for children from Arabic, Creole (mostly Haitian), Hispanic (over 95 per cent) and African communities (99 per cent) (Gouvernement du Québec, 1995).

Recognition of the cultural diversity of Quebec includes some public funding of private ethnic schools (e.g., Jewish schools). Also, along with Quebec language legislation a number of social policies were introduced in order to integrate immigrants into the French majority. Special classes, *classes d'accueil*, were set up in order to teach the French language to newly arrived immigrant children. The *classes d'accueil* extend from kindergarten through high school, and were attended by 7,346 children in 1993–1994 (Gouvernement du Quebec, 1995).

In 1978, the PELO (Projet d'enseignement en langue d'origine) was initiated by the Ministère de l'Éducation in a number of Quebec public schools. The implementation of this programme, which consists of teaching allophone children their language of origin, gave rise to several problems. For instance, due to lack of demand at the secondary-school level, the programme had to shift its emphasis to primary school. Additionally, the programme met with some opposition from parents, who feared their children would be deprived of important school subjects and would be ostracized by being put into special language classes (Laferrière, 1985a, 1985b). Currently, within the PELO programme, heritage-language courses are offered at the primary-school level and are largely scheduled before or after regular school courses, or during the noon hour; 6,000 students take part in this programme and twelve languages are taught. All courses are offered in the Montreal area, except for an Algonquin programme offered in Abitibi.

Although immigrant children do integrate well into the Quebec public school system, community leaders think there is still discrimination towards visible minorities. One study (Laferrière, Lefebvre, Ruimy-Van Dromme and Van Dromme, 1985) reported that ethnic community leaders would favour private bilingual (French/English) schools if they were free to choose. For many years, such leaders have expressed dissatisfaction with the organization of Quebec schools along religious lines, and they consider public schools to be of weak academic standing (Laferrière *et al.*, 1985).

CONCLUSION

Although the situation of native and heritage languages in Quebec is in many respects similar to that in the rest of Canada, the level of language maintenance of both native and heritage languages is slightly higher. However, in Quebec, as elsewhere, there is concern that the use of aboriginal languages is gradually declining under official-language pressure. There are some indications that this decrease may be slowing, perhaps since native communities have been able to play a greater role in native education, and programs in mother-tongue education are being developed. Similarly, heritage-language programmes supported by the provincial government have been considered inadequate by some members of allophone communities. Legislation requiring that immigrants enrol their children in the French-language school system remains controversial. Such legislation appears to have had a considerable impact on language shift patterns; contrary to the situation prevailing twenty years ago in Quebec, current language shifts among the allophone population occur significantly more towards French than towards English. Finally, the current political uncertainties (most importantly, the unresolved issue of Quebec separation) are likely to accentuate the desire on the part of native and allophone communities to play a major role in any decisions that might have repercussions on the status of their mother tongues.

Note
We would like to thank Darla Sloan for her help in obtaining relevant documentation.

References
Collis, D. R. F. (1992). Le statut des langues autochtones et leurs domaines d'utilisation au Québec. In J. Maurais (ed.), *Les langues autochtones du Québec* (pp. 115-148). Quebec: Les Publications du Québec.

Dorais, L. J. (1992). Les langues autochtones d'hier à aujourd'hui. In J. Maurais (ed.), *Les langues autochtones du Québec* (pp. 61-113). Quebec: Les Publications du Québec.

Drapeau, L. (1984). Une expérience originale d'implantation du Montagnais comme langue d'enseignement à Betsiamites. *Recherches Amérindiennes au Québec, 14 (4),* 57-61.

— (1992). Bilan de l'instrumentalisation et de la modernisation dans les langues autochtones dans la perspective de l'aménagement du corpus. In J. Maurais (ed.), *Les langues autochtones du Québec* (pp. 183-231). Quebec: Les Publications du Québec.

Gouvernement du Canada (1969). Énoncé du Gouvernement du Canada en matière de politique. Ottawa: Imprimeur de la Reine (Livre Blanc).

Gouvernement du Québec (1993). Population immigrée recensée au Québec en 1991: caractéristiques générales. Quebec: Ministère des Communautés Culturelles et de l'Immigration.

— (1994). Population du Québec selon les langues maternelles, 1991. Quebec: Ministère des Affaires Internationales, de l'Immigration et des Communautés Culturelles.

— (1995). Statistiques de l'éducation: Enseignement primaire, secondaire, collégial, et universitaire. Quebec: Ministère de l'Éducation.

Hamers, J. F. & Hummel, K.M. (1994). The francophones of Quebec: language policies and language use. *International Journal of the Sociology of Language, 105/106,* 127-152.

Laferrière, M. (1985a). L'éducation des enfants des groupes minoritaires au Québec. *Canadian and International Education, 14 (1),* 29–48.

(1985b). Language and cultural programs for ethnic minorities in Quebec: a critical view. *Canadian and International Education, 14 (1),* 49–58.

Laferrière, M., Lefebvre, L. M., Ruimy-Van Dromme, H. and Van Dromme, L. (1985). L'école et l'intégration des communautés ethno-culturelles au Québec: une étude des perceptions des leaders ethniques. *Canadian and International Education, 14 (1),* 93–107.

Laporte, P. E. (1992). Avant-propos. In J. Maurais (ed.), *Les langues autochtones du Québec* (pp. v–vii). Quebec: Les Publications du Québec.

Maurais, J. (ed.) (1992). *Les langues autochtones du Québec.* Quebec: Les Publications du Québec.

Pendakur, R. (1990). *Speaking in Tongues: Heritage Language Maintenance and Transfer in Canada.* Ottawa: Department of Multiculturalism and Citizenship.

Savard, R. and Proulx, J. R. (1982). *Canada. Dernière épopée, les autochtones.* Montreal: L'Hexagone.

Secrétariat aux Affaires Autochtones (SAA) (1988). *Les autochtones du Québec.* Quebec: Les Publications du Québec.

Stairs, A. (1985). La viabilité des langues autochtones et le rôle de l'écrit: L'expérience de l'Inuktitut au Nouveau-Québec. *Recherches amérindiennes au Québec, 15-3,* 93–95.

Trudel, F. (1992). La politique des gouvernements du Canada et du Québec en matière autochtone. In J. Maurais (ed.), *Les langues autochtones du Québec* (pp. 151–182). Quebec: Les Publications du Québec.

Vincent, S. (1992). La révélation d'une force politique: les autochtones. In G. Daigle and G. Rocher (eds.), *Le Québec en jeu* (pp. 749–790). Montreal: Les Presses de l'Université de Montréal.

Map 7 Ontario

21 Language in Ontario

Ruth King

INTRODUCTION

Ontario is Canada's second largest province, with a land mass of some 916,733 square kilometres. Its population is the largest and most urbanized of any Canadian province or territory (10,084,855 according to the 1991 federal census, with 81.8 per cent classified as urban).[1] Ontario is the country's industrial base: it has always been the leading manufacturing province and it includes Canada's largest city (and business and financial centre), Toronto, and the national capital, Ottawa. These demographics help explain the province's present-day multicultural, multilingual makeup, outlined below.

While 84 per cent of Ontarians report speaking English as their home language, this figure masks considerable linguistic diversity. While Ontario's francophone population is a small minority, 300,000 people report French as their home language and almost 500,000 identify French as their mother tongue; indeed, Ontario is home to by far the largest (and the healthiest) francophone population in Canada outside of Quebec. Equally noteworthy is the fact that, since World War II, well over half the immigrants coming to Canada have settled in Ontario and, of these, the majority settle in the metropolitan Toronto area. The 1950s saw heavy immigration from the United Kingdom and continental Europe and, more recently, there have been significant levels of immigration from India and Southeast Asia, the Caribbean and Latin America. At present, native speakers of Italian, Chinese,[2] Portuguese, German and Polish exceed 100,000 and many more languages have significant numbers of speakers, particularly in Ontario's Golden Horseshoe (i.e., the industrial region stretching from Oshawa past Toronto to Hamilton and St Catharines). In metropolitan Toronto, one in three residents speaks an immigrant language natively. In addition, over 100,000 Ontario residents report an aboriginal identity and, of those, 16.6 per cent report speaking an aboriginal language, with either Cree or Objibwa – both members of the Algonquian language family – spoken by the vast majority (Aboriginal People's Survey, 1991). In this chapter I shall review the (linguistic) settlement history of the province, outline the present status of the languages of Ontario, and point to current issues in language education and language planning.

HISTORICAL AND GEOGRAPHICAL OVERVIEW

Large-scale settlement of Upper Canada (now the province of Ontario) began in the early 1780s (the presence of aboriginal peoples, of course, dates to prehistoric times). The first major group of immigrants was the United Empire Loyalists, American anti-revolutionaries who left the United States in the wake of the American Revolution. At around the same time, scattered French settlements developed, especially in the area near Detroit. By about 1840 waves of immigration from the British Isles began, driven in part by fears of American republicanism, as well as by economic conditions in the home country; this brought many Scots and Irish settlers in particular, with settlement peaking between 1851 and 1861. More localized, and representing smaller numbers, was nineteenth-century immigration from Quebec, due to a lack of available land caused by a combination of poor farming methods and high childbirth rates. The first settlers of Upper Canada were mostly farmers, but urbanization dates from the mid nineteenth century. By the time of World War I, Ontario was predominantly urban and has remained so. Subsequent waves of immigration at the turn of the century brought more British settlers, and Germans, Dutch and Belgians as well.

The period following World War II saw the arrival of large numbers of immigrants from continental Europe, in particular, from Italy, Germany, the Netherlands, Poland and Greece. As noted above, the postwar period has changed Ontario's linguistic landscape significantly. In some cases, immigration waves have been caused by post-World War II political crises – e.g., the late 1950s saw substantial Hungarian immigration, the 1970s the beginnings of Vietnamese immigration and the 1990s Somalian immigration. The takeover of Hong Kong by China has caused the numbers of Chinese speakers in Ontario to rise dramatically, as in other areas of Canada (particularly British Columbia). It is also important to keep in mind that Ontario – and especially metropolitan Toronto – has long attracted residents of Canada's poorer (anglophone) provinces searching for jobs and a better life, at least in economic terms.

The geographical distribution of Ontario residents by language is most easily outlined by reporting concentrations of speakers from language backgrounds other than English, since English – as the dominant and only official language – is in widespread use throughout the province. Algonquian languages are spoken throughout northern and most of southern Ontario, while Iroquoian languages are spoken in the southwest. As we shall see below, determining the actual number of speakers of aboriginal languages is difficult. Francophones constitute strong majorities in southeastern Ontario, in a largely agricultural area near the Quebec border (Mougeon and Beniak, 1991). This includes the Ottawa metropolitan region, where more than one-quarter of the 600,000 respondents in the 1991 census claimed French as their mother tongue. In this case, the high concentration of francophones is linked to more than proximity to Quebec: Ottawa is the seat of the officially-bilingual federal government, a major employer. Other communities with sizeable francophone populations are located in central and northern Ontario, in regions where mining and forestry are prominent, and in scattered communities in central and eastern Ontario. In southern Ontario, francophone populations constitute weak minorities in towns such as Welland and Windsor.

Ontario's immigrant population (well over 2 million) is overwhelmingly (more than 90 per cent) urban and has tended to locate in the southern part of the province, in particular in its industrial areas. The successive waves of immigration outlined in broad terms above have resulted in a degree of multiculturalism and multilingualism unparalleled elsewhere in Canada. Broadening the perspective from non-native speakers of English born outside the country to the total population who speak a language other than English or French as their mother tongue, the 1991 census 'top ten' is as follows: Italian (282,990), Chinese (205,170), German (147,760), Portuguese (132,710), Polish (107,720), Spanish (75,880), Dutch (66,865), Greek (60,435), Ukrainian (49,630) and Tagalog (42,890).

VARIATION IN ONTARIO ENGLISH

Chambers (this volume) reports an amazing degree of homogeneity in Standard Canadian English, a homogeneity which he argues is unparalleled in the English-speaking world. There is, however, clear variation in Ontario English at the level of the vernacular, some long-standing and some more recent in origin. While regional variation in francophone Canada is well-documented, the same cannot be said of regional variation in anglophone Canada, with the exception of research conducted in Newfoundland. Thus it is possible to point to the existence of variation in Ontario English but, as we shall see below, for the most part this variation has not been studied systematically by linguists.

Regional variation may be traced to early settlement patterns. For instance, Irish settlement of the Ottawa valley (a rural area located along the Ottawa

River, a major tributary of the St Lawrence) from the early 1800s to the 1870s produced a distinctive Ottawa Valley 'brogue' marked by Hiberno-English features, at least at the level of phonology (Pringle and Padolsky, 1983). Chambers (1991) notes the existence of a Scots–Irish enclave in the area of Peterborough County, northeast of Toronto, which informal observation indicates has retained its linguistic roots, at least among isolated speakers. Linguistic diversity due to the influence of other languages also remains unstudied. For instance, we know little of the effects (retention of 'non-English' speech features, for example) of language contact on the English of Waterloo County, home to the descendants of both German immigrants and Pennsylvania Dutch, or on the English of the Niagara Falls area, also the site of Pennsylvania Dutch settlement (see Chambers, 1991, for further discussion).

Chambers has discussed the relationship between Canadian English and its American counterpart and notes that – particularly in the case of younger speakers – Ontarians, like other Canadians, have American as well as traditional Canadian variants in vocabulary and pronunciation as part of their linguistic repertoire (Chambers, 1989; Zeller, 1993). However, recent work on the vowel systems of younger southern Ontarians (see Clarke *et al.*, 1995) points to strikingly different pronunciations of a number of vowels from those of residents of northeastern United States cities, Americans whose speech patterns have been so well documented (e.g., Labov, 1991). By way of example, in the northeastern United States, /æ/ is raised (*bad* is typically pronounced [bɛəd] or [bɪəd]) while, in Ontario, English /æ/ is never raised and is actually retracted in particular environments (*laughed* is often pronounced [laft] or [lɑft]). While the work of Clarke and her colleagues is based on a limited number of speakers, it confirms the impressions of sociolinguists based in southern Ontario. Further exploration of linguistic divergence on the Canada/United States border is of major interest to those studying the paths of linguistic change and/or interested in the current sociosymbolic status of linguistic features.

The English of the descendants of speakers of non-official languages should also be the subject of more linguistic study. In metropolitan Toronto, the average person may remark on the Italian-accented English of people of Italian descent who do not speak Italian fluently (or at all).[3] My own impressions are that some phonological features which characterize this 'Italian' accent (e.g., dentalization of alveolars, release (and sometimes aspiration) of word-final voiceless stops) are not limited to the Italian-Canadian community but probably extend to the speech of other ethnic groups, such as the descendants of Greek immigrants. Vitale and Ortepi (1994) provide empirical support for the existence

of such features in the speech of young, English-speaking residents of Woodbridge, a largely Italian community on the outskirts of metropolitan Toronto.
Further documentation is needed, as is research into the longevity of such
'foreign' elements and their (potential) influence on the speech of other
ethnic groups, including English-Canadians.

VARIATION IN ONTARIO FRENCH

Ontario French can be characterized structurally as a variety of Quebec
French – not surprising, given the francophone settlement of this province by
Quebecers. The primary focus of research here has been on the linguistic effects
of language contact. Poplack (1988), reporting on a major study of the French
spoken in the neighbouring cities of Ottawa (on the Ontario side of the border)
and Hull (on the Quebec side) shows that the degree of use of English borrowings (e.g., nouns such as *groceries* and *check*; morphologically-incorporated
verbs such as *entertainer* and *patroller*) is related to both neighbourhood
(Ottawa residents from both working-class and middle-class neighbourhoods
used more English borrowings than did their Hull counterparts) and class
(working-class speakers used more English borrowings than did middle-class
speakers). Similarly, Poplack observed differences in code-switching behaviour
– i.e., in the use of sequences from both English and French within the same
utterances: while both Ottawa and Hull residents tended to flag linguistically
their switches from French to English, the Ottawa residents' codeswitches were
interpreted as more often having the function of providing *le mot juste*, while
those of Hull residents more typically involved metalinguistic commentary.
While the entire repertoire of bilingual phenomena is shared by Hull and
Ottawa residents, the latter were found to be more innovative in the
incorporation of English elements.

The work of Mougeon, Beniak and a number of their colleagues has
dealt with the French of smaller Ontario communities, from those in which
French is the majority language (like Hawkesbury), to those in which it has near-
equal status with English (like Cornwall), to those in which it is a weak minority
language (e.g., North Bay and Pembroke). Mougeon and Beniak (1991) link
variation in the French of francophone children and adolescents in these
communities to the degree of restriction in the domains and frequency of interaction in French and to community structure: those speakers who were less
restricted in their use of French *and* who lived in communities where French
was spoken by a majority of residents were less influenced by English. Mougeon

and Beniak's work deals primarily with social factors promoting lexical and morphological influence; Nadasdi (1995) finds similar results at the level of syntax.

LANGUAGE MAINTENANCE, ATTRITION AND LOSS

Aboriginal languages

The proportion of the Ontario aboriginal population who speak an aboriginal language as their mother tongue has declined dramatically over the past four decades. In 1951, the total population of aboriginal ethnic origin was 37,388; of these, 66.4 per cent claimed an aboriginal mother tongue. The corresponding figures for 1961, 1971 and 1981 were 48,074 (55.7 per cent), 63,175 (44.6 per cent), and 104,215 (16.0 per cent), respectively (see Burnaby and Beaujot, 1986). The latest (1991) census gives 71,005 as the total aboriginal population and, of those, 6.5 per cent are reported to speak an aboriginal language as their mother tongue. These data must be interpreted with caution since statistics on aboriginal populations are incomplete in many areas due to census non-response. In fact, estimates indicate that as many as one-third of Ontario's aboriginal population did not participate. When we turn instead to data from the somewhat more reliable 1991 *Aboriginal People's Survey*, also produced by Statistics Canada, the following picture emerges: 74,410 adults fifteen years of age and older and 40,485 children from five to fourteen years of age report an aboriginal identity, bringing the total to 114,895. Of those, 16.6 per cent speak an aboriginal language: 15,845 adults (21.3 per cent) and 3,230 children (7.9 per cent). About 14.5 per cent speak an aboriginal language at home: 13,660 adults (18.4 per cent) and 3,000 children (7.4 per cent). An additional 12,080 adults (16.2 per cent) and 2,870 children (7.0 per cent) do not speak, but understand, an aboriginal language. The picture is somewhat brighter than that reported in the main 1991 census, and a detailed survey with high rates of participation across language groups might yield somewhat better numbers. However, language attrition and loss are still apparent if we consider, along with the 1991 survey results, those of community-level studies conducted by linguists (e.g., Burnaby, 1981).

Ojibwa and Cree are two of only three aboriginal languages (the third is Inuktitut) considered to have an excellent chance of survival in this country. The 1991 *Aboriginal People's Survey* shows that Ojibwa and Cree are the major aboriginal languages still spoken in Ontario: 10,340 Ojibwa speakers aged fifteen plus, and 2,120 between the ages of five and fourteen; 3,755 Cree speakers aged fifteen plus, and 760 between the ages of five and fourteen. Ontario's Ojibwa-speaking population constitutes 46.1 per cent of the total for the country as a whole, and its Cree-speaking population constitutes 6.3 per cent.

These survey results mask a certain amount of diversity, since the health of the particular language depends on which dialect is in question. In Ontario, Oji-cree, usually referred to as 'Severn Valley Ojibwa' by linguists, is the healthiest of the Ojibwa dialects, while 'classical' Ojibwa is fairly safe and Nishnaabemwin is in serious decline (John Stanley, personal communication). To make matters more complex, the issue of language versus dialect is a matter of some debate. For instance, Oji-cree is treated as a separate language under Ontario's Aboriginal Language Standardization Project (see below), because it is written exclusively in a syllabic system and because its speakers feel strongly that they belong to a distinct language community (Stanley, 1995).

Another problem we encounter with data on aboriginal peoples is that large-scale surveys deal best with large numbers. For instance, the 1991 federal census reports that 500* (the asterisk indicates a figure to be used with caution) adults speak 'Iroquoian languages', but *what* Iroquoian languages are involved is not reported since the number of their speakers is small. The Iroquoian language family includes Cayuga, Mohawk, Oneida, Onondaga, Seneca and Tuscarora. Stanley (1995) estimates that Mohawk may have as many as 5,000 speakers in Ontario, but acknowledges that few people under fifty speak the language natively. An article in Toronto's *Globe and Mail* (Platiel, 1996) reported that Helen Salter, presumed to be the last person in Canada to speak Tuscarora fluently, died in December 1995. In the same article, Amos Key, director of the Woodlands Cultural Centre at the Six Nations Reserve in Brantford, gave the following breakdown of Iroquoian language speakers left on that reserve: 127 Cayuga speakers, 80 Mohawk, 36 Onondaga and one Seneca; he noted, as well, 245 Oneida speakers living on another reserve near London. Stanley (1995) estimates that in all of Ontario there appear to be no more than 100 Oneida speakers, 40 Onondaga , and 5 Seneca. While the Algonquian language family includes Algonquin, Delaware and Potawatomi, in addition to Cree and Ojibwa, only speakers of the last two figure in the 1991 census or aboriginal survey data. Stanley (1995) notes that, while a few Algonquin speakers remain in Maniwaki, Quebec, there is none left in Golden Lake, Ontario. He estimates that only five Ontario Delaware speakers remain, and that Potawatomi is no longer spoken in the province. The precarious position of aboriginal languages other than Cree and Ojibwa clearly cannot be underestimated.

Immigrant languages

Immigrants may use their native language for many purposes – for instance, as an expression of in-group solidarity or as a strategy for resisting unequal power relations – or they may simply use it because it is the one in which they are most proficient. For newcomers to Canada, the immigrant language may be the language of work, in businesses organized along ethnic lines. However, as Chambers (this volume) notes: '*under ordinary circumstances* ... immigrants do their best to conform to the linguistic norms of their new surroundings' (my italics). With the next generation, and certainly by the one following that, the number of (fluent) speakers of the immigrant language will have declined dramatically. This is not say that subgroups within the community may not exhibit linguistic behaviour which differs from the larger community – for instance, in her study of the decline of Ukrainian-language use in Toronto, Chamak-Horbatsch (1987) notes that one second-generation subgroup were actively involved in preserving the language and had maintained it as the home variety.

A comparison of data for the major immigrant languages in Ontario is given in table 21.1. Knowledge of a particular language is defined by Statistics Canada as the ability to carry on a conversation in that language. In the case of languages taught in the province's educational institutions, such as Spanish and German, second-language students and native-speaker immigrants would be classed together. In order to get as accurate a picture as possible of language decline, the percentage of speakers who speak their mother tongue as their

Table 21.1 Major immigrant languages spoken in Ontario

Language	Respondents claiming knowledge of language	Respondents claiming language as mother tongue	Respondents claiming language as home language	Retention of mother tongue as home language (%)
Italian	435,975	282,990	152,830	54.0
German	262,525	147,760	40,960	27.7
Chinese	259,595	205,170	187,680	91.5
Portuguese	177,065	132,710	98,735	74.4
Spanish	161,880	75,880	61,710	81.3
Polish	146,540	107,720	68,875	63.9
Greek	88,240	60,435	39,695	65.6
Ukrainian	71,120	49,630	19,185	38.7
Tagalog	67,880	42,890	24,730	57.7
Punjabi	64,105	38,530	36,880	95.7

home language is given in the rightmost column of the table. Most clear from this table is the decline in the languages of the period of immigration immediately following World War II. If we consider the case of Italian, the most common immigrant language, we see a clear difference between mother-tongue and home-language figures, and a sharp difference when we compare these figures with the knowledge-of-language figure. German and Ukrainian are spoken at home by a minority of those who claim the languages as their mother tongue. Chinese, on the other hand, appears much healthier, not surprising since many of its speakers are more recent immigrants, from Hong Kong and from a number of southeast Asian countries. Other languages which have large numbers of recent immigrants, such as Spanish, also appear healthy.

LANGUAGE AND EDUCATION

Some of the most pressing concerns for language and education in Ontario involve the non-native speaker of English. There are a multitude of English-as-a-Second-Language (ESL) programmes, some aimed at the adult learner in the workplace, others at those who do not work outside the home, and still others at students enrolled in the province's educational institutions. The teaching of international languages (the new designation for what had been called 'heritage' languages) has been a matter of some controversy and is subject to different modes of delivery. Finally, work on preserving the province's native languages ranges from immersion programmes aimed at children to adult literacy programmes, a variety of initiatives aimed at curbing the growing influence of English and the concomitant loss of aboriginal languages. Educational policy and programmes in each of these language areas is outlined below.

English as a second language

Provision of ESL instruction involves government at all levels – federal, provincial and municipal – along with the involvement of unions and community groups. Federally-sponsored programmes include Canadian Job Strategies, aimed at immigrants destined for the paid labour force, and Language Instruction for Newcomers to Canada, aimed particularly at immigrant women who do not work outside the home (Burnaby, 1992). At the provincial level, three branches of the Ministry of Education (Colleges and Universities, Education and the Ontario Training and Adjustment Board) and the Ministry of Citizenship are involved.

While school boards are the major providers of adult language training, and much training is conducted in the traditional classroom setting, types of adult

ESL training range from one-on-one tutoring in basic literacy, to classes in the workplace, to distance education courses. Goals vary from basic literacy to communicative competence. In urban centres one finds private ESL providers along with government-sponsored programmes. As for primary and secondary education, it is important to note that ESL students have rapidly become the mainstream population in the province's urban centres: both the schools themselves and the Faculties of Education which train teachers must deal with a new reality.

The view from ESL practitioners is that, while the provincial Ministry of Education promotes mainstreaming – in this case the integration of ESL students into the regular classroom (every teacher effectively becomes an ESL teacher) – it has failed to give direction in the development of policy concerning the roles of the ESL specialist and the non-specialist, or to provide appropriate models to allow school boards to meet the needs of the ESL student. Among the recommendations of a 1994 report of the Ontario chapter of Teaching English as a Second Language (TESL), are (a) 'Ontario schools should develop language policies that specify the roles of all teachers in supporting ESL students' acquisition of academic content' and (b) 'Faculties of Education should prepare prospective teachers for the urban school population that exists today rather than the school population that existed 25 years ago' (p. 6). A pressing need, then, is for clear direction from the Ministry of Education and for appropriate linkages with Faculties of Education, school boards and school personnel.

International languages

The teaching of what were (until 1994) officially referred to as 'heritage' languages began in Ontario's schools in 1977. Currently, more than sixty languages are taught to more than 120,000 students, the bulk of whom live in southern Ontario (Cummins, 1994). Since 1988, government legislation has ensured that such programmes are provided when community groups can supply a minimum of twenty-five students who wish to study a particular language. Typically, international-language teaching takes place outside the regular school day, at the end of the school day or on weekends. The option of extending the school day to integrate international-language teaching into the curriculum has occasionally been implemented but has sparked a great deal of controversy (Cummins and Danesi, 1990). In general, while the relevant pedagogical literature shows that international-language instruction does not hinder students' progress in English and has positive affective results in terms of students' appreciation of their linguistic heritage, reactions to international-language teaching reflect attitudes towards multiculturalism in the society at large: for some, it is seen as a waste of taxpayers' money, for others a valorization of ethnic diversity.

Aboriginal languages

A number of initiatives has been undertaken in the face of the decline in speakers of aboriginal languages. The Ministry of Education established a native-language teacher's certificate programme in 1985. The certificate qualifies its holders to teach their language of specialization in elementary and secondary schools. The Algonquian component of the programme – Cree, Delaware and Ojibwa – is taught at Lakehead University, in Thunder Bay, while the Iroquoian component – Cayuga, Oneida and Mohawk – is taught at Brock University in St Catharines. In 1994–95 (the most recent year for which statistics are available), twenty-five non-reserve schools offered one or more aboriginal languages as a regular school subject, with a total of more than 2,000 children enrolled, while seventy-four reserve schools taught an aboriginal language (one school taught two aboriginal languages, and another three), with more than 9,000 children enrolled. The Ontario Training and Adjustment Board, a branch of the Ministry of Education, has been involved since 1993 in the Aboriginal Language Standardization Project. The project aims 'to ensure the revitalisation of Ontario's Aboriginal languages' and 'to respond to the needs of Aboriginal peoples in Ontario in ensuring the survival and functional use of their language' (Stanley, 1995, p. 1). The linguistic activities supported by the project include the development of standard orthographies for the languages in question, production of dictionaries and grammars, and establishment of literacy programmes with appropriate teaching materials. Other new initiatives include a Native-as-a-Second-Language programme which has been optional since 1987 (in 1994–95, twenty-eight schools were involved). As of September 1995, school boards are required to offer NSL instruction in an aboriginal language during the regular school day if parents of fifteen or more students request such instruction and a qualified NSL teacher is available.

CONCLUSIONS

In this chapter we have seen that the language situation in present-day Ontario is a complex one. A discussion of English in Ontario involves a discussion of vernaculars of various sorts – vernacular English in the traditional sense of the term, vernacular in terms of the new Englishes spoken by recent immigrants and their descendants. The current situation is also one in which the province's educators must assume, particularly in urban industrial areas, that the 'mainstream student' speaks English as a second language or standard English as a second dialect. While linguistic exogamy and increased urbanization have had negative effects on the health of French in the province, the sheer number of Franco-Ontarians, over half a million individuals, gives the language a better chance of survival than in any other Canadian province outside of Quebec. The situation of aboriginal languages must be viewed seriously, given the small numbers of speakers involved, particularly for the Iroquoian languages.

A major area of concern for those involved in language issues in Ontario is the election of a neoconservative provincial government in June 1995 on a platform of deficit reduction, which some would argue is to be achieved regardless of cost to the social fabric. While it is too early to determine the effects of budget cuts on language, it is clear that the status quo for government funding of language-oriented programmes will not be maintained and that, at the very least, restructuring of existing programmes should be expected. A right-wing agenda also has an indirect effect on language issues; for instance, cuts to subsidized daycare make it more difficult for many women to take advantage of ESL classes. However, whatever measures are undertaken by the present government and whatever their effects on language policies and programmes, Ontario will clearly remain a multicultural, multilingual province.

Notes

I wish to thank Barbara Burnaby, Jim Cummins, Nick Elson, Greg Guy, Michael L. Kay and John Stanley for discussing some of the issues raised in this chapter with me. Thanks go as well to Jack Chambers, Sandra Clarke and Raymond Mougeon for showing me early drafts of their own chapters.

1 Unless otherwise indicated, all statistics are taken from the 1991 Canadian census.
2 Census data present certain problems for those interested in the sociology of language. For instance, Chinese is used as a cover term and distinctions are not made among speakers of its many varieties (varieties of Chinese are often categorized by linguists as separate languages, following the criterion of mutual intelligibility). Immigration statistics enable us to infer to some extent the proportion of, say, Cantonese versus Mandarin speakers, but it is difficult, if not impossible, to determine the proportion of speakers of Chinese varieties less well-known in the west (e.g., Hakka, Hsiang, etc) or to make finer distinctions (e.g., among dialects of Cantonese). A further problem in census reporting is that a speaker of a minority language may well report as the mother tongue or home language one s/he can reasonably assume to be a familiar one – e.g., a Malayalam speaker from southern India may report Hindi as his/her mother tongue, an Ilocano speaker from the Philippines may report Tagalog (Pilipino), etc.

3 Linguistic research on the Italian community in Ontario has centred on the influence of English upon Italian, specifically on the incorporation of English loanwords into Italian. See, for example, Clivio (1976) and Danesi (1985).

References

Aboriginal Peoples Survey. (1991). *Language, Tradition, Health, Lifestyle and Social Issues.* Ottawa: Statistics Canada.

Burnaby, B. (1981). Language shift in Northern Ontario. In W. Cowan (ed.), *Papers of the Twelfth Algonquian Conference* (pp. 114-120). Ottawa: Carleton University.

(1992). Official language training for adult immigrants in Canada: features and issues. In B. Burnaby and A. Cumming (eds.), *Socio-political Aspects of ESL* (pp. 3-34). Toronto: OISE Press.

Burnaby, B. and Beaujot, R. (1986). *The Use of Aboriginal Languages in Canada: An Analysis of 1981 Census Data.* Ottawa: Ministry of Supply and Services.

Chamak-Horbatsch, R. (1987). Language use in a Ukrainian home: a Toronto sample. *International Journal of the Sociology of Language, 63,* 99-118.

Chambers, J. K. (1989). Canadian raising: blocking, fronting, etc. *American Speech, 64,* 75-88.

(1991). Canada. In J. Cheshire (ed.), *English around the World: Sociolinguistic Perspectives* (pp. 89-107). Cambridge: Cambridge University Press.

Clarke, S., Elms, F. and Youssef, A. (1995). The third dialect of English: some Canadian evidence. *Language Variation and Change, 7,* 209-228.

Clivio, G. (1976). The assimilation of English loan-words in Italo-Canadian. In P. A. Reich (ed.), *The Second LACUS Forum* (pp. 584-9). Columbia, SA: Hornbeam Press.

Cummins, J. (1994). Heritage language learning and teaching. In J. W. Berry and J. A. Laponce (eds.), *Ethnicity and Culture in Canada: The Research Landscape* (pp. 435-456). Toronto: University of Toronto Press.

Cummins, J. and Danesi, M. (1990). *Heritage Languages: The Development and Denial of Canada's Linguistic Resources.* Toronto: Our Schools/Our Selves Education Foundation and Garamond Press.

Danesi, M. (1985). *Loanwords and Phonological Assimilation.* Ville LaSalle, PQ: Didier.

Labov, W. (1991). The three dialects of English. In P. Eckert (ed.), *New Ways of Analyzing Sound Change* (pp. 1-44). New York: Academic Press.

Mougeon, R. and Beniak, E. (1991). *Linguistic Consequences of Language Contact and Restriction: The Case of French in Ontario, Canada.* Oxford: Oxford University Press.

Nadasdi, T. (1995). Variation morphosyntaxique et langue minoritaire: le cas du français ontarien. Unpublished PhD thesis, University of Toronto.

Platiel, R. (1996). Vanishing languages imperil native culture. *The Globe and Mail,* 1 March, A1, A8.

Poplack, S. (1988). Language status and language accommodation along a linguistic border. In P. H. Lowenberg (ed.), *Language Spread and Language Policy: Issues, Implications and Case Studies* (pp. 90–118). Washington, DC: Georgetown University Press.

Pringle, I. and Padolsky, E. (1983). The linguistic survey of the Ottawa valley. *American Speech, 58,* 325–44.

Stanley, J. (1995). *Aboriginal Language Standardization Project: Progress Report.* Toronto: Ontario Training and Adjustment Board.

TESL Ontario Conference. (1994). *Report of the Symposium on Integration Issues.* Toronto: TESL Ontario.

Vitale, C. and Ortepi, L. (1994). *And It All Happened in Woodbridge.* North York, Ontario: Unpublished York University ms.

Zeller, C. (1993). Linguistic symmetries, asymmetries, and border effects within a Canadian/American sample. In S. Clarke (ed.), *Focus on Canada* (pp. 179–99). Amsterdam: Benjamins.

Map 8 Manitoba

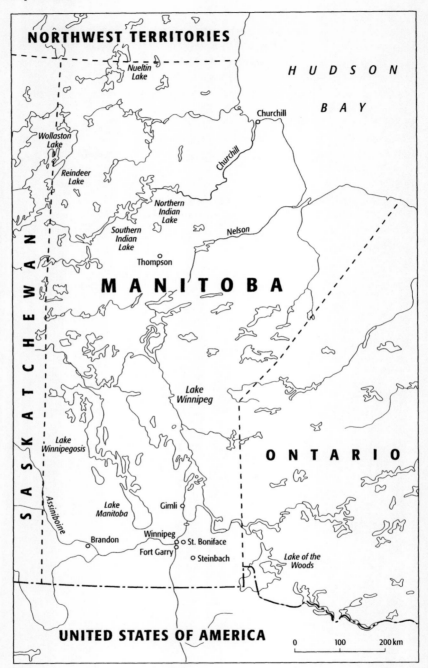

22 Language in Manitoba

Leo Driedger

Manitoba is unique in that it was the first province to join the confederation of Canada after 1867. In 1870, only three years later, Manitoba became the fifth keystone province, the gateway to the northwest. 'Keystone', because it comprised only a small territory around the heart of Fort Garry at the conjunction of the Red and Assiniboine rivers, which later expanded many times to its present size. It was the 'gateway' to the northwest, because fifteen years later, when the railway came to Winnipeg in 1885, it became the link for eastern entrepreneurs who warehoused their products at Fort Garry (Winnipeg, 1874), and distributed these manufactured goods westward to the prairies and beyond.

LANGUAGE POLICIES

For hundreds of years the aboriginals had the flat lowlands, where Winnipeg is now located, as a camping ground, using the Assiniboine river as a waterway from the west, and the Red river as a route from the south and the north. So it is not surprising that both the French Northwest Fur Trading Company, working out of Montreal from the east, and the British Hudson's Bay Company coming down from the north, began to build trading posts at the forks. Thus, Fort Garry also became the first natural meeting place of the aboriginals, the French and the British. The French La Verendrye expeditions first established fur-trading communities in southern Manitoba in the 1730s and 1740s, and the British actually began a settlement in 1812 with the Selkirk settlers. The administration of the Red River settlement after 1835 was supervised by the Hudson's Bay Company, and the community was called the Council of Assiniboia, with representatives from the Métis, French and English communities. They published their laws in both French and English (Friesen, 1996).

French Métis leader Louis Riel, supported by both French- and English-speaking representatives of the Assiniboia community, drew up a list of 'rights' which formed the basis of Manitoba's entrance into confederation (Jaenen, 1984). The Manitoba Act passed in the Canadian House of Commons in 1870, and established in Section 23 that French and English would be the languages in Manitoba's official record and journals in the legislative debates and courts; it also specified that the Acts of the legislature be printed and published in both languages (Bourhis, 1994). The Act was also passed in the British parliament in 1871 (Friesen, 1996). The first appointed lieutenant governors were bilingual, and the province was governed in the two languages. Sessions, statutes and records were printed in French and English, when both groups comprised about 5,000 residents each (Jaenen, 1984).

However, the original electoral laws which created twelve 'French' and twelve 'English' constituencies were soon under pressure. Many English newcomers arrived, particularly from Ontario, so that English residents swamped French settlers. By 1874 the equal number of ridings had changed to twice as many English ones. By 1876 the Upper House in the legislature, which was designed to protect French concerns, was abolished and in 1879 Premier John Norquay and the English-speaking MLAs (Members of the Legislative Assembly) moved to abolish all French rights in the province, which the Lieutenant Governor refused to sign.

Ten years later, in 1889, the new liberal Premier Greenway abolished the dual Roman Catholic and Protestant school system and replaced it with a single non-denominational school system; also abolished was the official use of French in legislative documents and courts. Both were devastating blows to the French-speaking Catholic community. French Catholics chose to fight the school rather than the legislative language law, and won a compromise which permitted religious instruction at the end of the school day (Bourhis, 1994). The compromise also guaranteed bilingualism (English and another language) in the schools, which lasted twenty years (Friesen, 1996).

What early planners did not foresee was that: (1) few French immigrants would come to replenish the early French settlers; (2) the English Ontarians would come to the Fort Garry area in large numbers; (3) other, mainly German and Icelandic, settlers would also come to southern Manitoba in significant numbers (Jaenen, 1984). In 1916 Premier T. C. Norris abolished the bilingual school guarantee which, again, was a blow to the French, Mennonites, Poles and Ukrainians who were teaching their ethnic languages (Clark, 1968). Large numbers of conservative Mennonites left for Mexico in the 1920s because of this 1916 decision. In 1976, a Franco-Manitoban, Georges Forest, challenged the legality of an English-only parking ticket, and won a Supreme Court of Canada judgment declaring the 1890 language act unconstitutional and restoring the official use of French in Manitoba (Friesen, 1996; see also below).

DEMOGRAPHIC HISTORY

While the French- and English-speaking communities in 1890 had roughly 5,000 residents each, the influx of new English-speaking settlers soon changed the demographic character of the small province and upset the French/English balance (Jaenen, 1984). By 1875, 7,000 Mennonites, several thousand Icelanders, and a stream of migrants from Ontario arrived to add to the heterogeneity of the mix. By 1881 there were 9,688 French (16 per cent), 37,155 English (60 per cent) and 8,427 German (14 per cent) residents (other groups comprised 10 per cent). By 1901, the French (16,021) had dropped to 6.3 per cent of the Manitoba population, with the English comprising 64 per cent, the Germans 9 per cent, aboriginals 6 per cent, Scandinavians 3 per cent and Ukrainians 2 per cent (Jaenen, 1984). These demographic changes led to marked attitudinal changes towards the French language, as well as demands for change and for the redistribution of legislative seats. The compact between the two founding European groups was challenged and, as early as 1874, the two old French and English parishes had to give up two seats each to new settlements – creating three categories with eight seats each.

Provincial comparisons

By 1991, 73.5 per cent of the more than one million residents of Manitoba reported English as their mother tongue, 4.7 per cent reported French and 21.8 per cent reported another language (table 22.1). Over the last 120 years English has become dominant and the French mother tongue now ranks fourth (after German and Ukrainian) (deVries, 1994).

Use of languages is also illustrated in table 22.1, under home language (HL). English language use at home in 1991 is up to 87.7 per cent, while home language use of French is down to 2.3 per cent, and use of other languages is down to 9.9 per cent. The higher percentage for the use of English at home (as opposed to English as original mother tongue) also obtains in each of the other provinces and territories. The difference, however, is especially great west of Ontario. Use of French as a home language is lower than percentages for French as original mother tongue in all provinces except Quebec, where it is 1.0 per cent higher. Differences between French mother-tongue percentages and use of French at home are highest in the west (they mirror the differences for English). Use of other languages at home (9.9 per cent) in Manitoba, compared to mother tongue (21.8 per cent), is less than half as high, another gap evident in all regions.

Table 22.1 Mother tongues and use of language at home by regions, 1991 (percentages)

	English		French		Other	
	MT	HL	MT	HL	MT	HL
Newfoundland	98.6	99.2	0.5	0.2	0.9	0.5
Prince Edward Island	94.3	97.3	4.5	2.4	1.2	0.3
Nova Scotia	93.3	96.3	4.2	2.5	2.5	1.2
New Brunswick	64.6	68.2	34.0	31.2	1.4	0.7
Quebec	9.2	11.2	82.0	83.0	8.8	5.8
Ontario	74.6	85.2	5.0	3.2	20.3	11.6
Manitoba	73.5	87.7	4.7	2.3	21.8	9.9
Saskatchewan	83.3	94.4	2.2	0.7	14.5	4.9
Alberta	81.2	91.5	2.3	0.8	16.5	7.7
British Columbia	78.9	89.5	1.6	0.4	19.5	9.9
Yukon	88.7	96.7	3.3	1.4	8.0	1.9
Northwest Territories	55.2	66.8	2.5	1.2	42.3	32.0
Canada	60.4	68.8	24.3	23.3	15.3	8.4

MT – mother tongue
HL – home language
Sources: Statistics Canada, 1993a, 1993b.

Continuity, bilingualism, immersion

To summarize the consistency between learning a mother tongue, and the actual use of that language at home, we present scores based on a language continuity index in table 22.2. We see that English language use at home is higher than English mother tongue (equal use would be 100) in all of the regions of Canada, with Manitoba scoring at about the national average, at 112. The scores for French and other languages are under 100, except for Quebec, where the use of French is somewhat higher than French mother tongue. French (with a score of 49) and other language (46) continuity in Manitoba is well below the Canadian average. The French national continuity average (96) is almost twice the French language continuity in Manitoba (49). Language continuity of other languages (46) in Manitoba is somewhat lower than the national average (55), and is very similar to the Manitoba French score. From a position of equity in 1870, French continuity had dropped drastically by 1991.

English–French bilingualism in Manitoba grew from 7.9 to 9.2 per cent between 1981 and 1991, highest in the west, and fifth highest in the nation. Participation in French immersion in Manitoba increased five times (to 10.2 per cent)

Table 22.2 Language continuity, bilingualism and French immersion by regions

	Language continuity (scores)[1] 1991			English–French bilingualism (%)		Enrolment in French immersion (%)	
	English	French	Other	1981	1991	1980–81	1990–91
Newfoundland	101	45	61	2.3	3.3	0.3	3.4
Prince Edward Island	103	53	25	8.1	10.1	4.9	14.1
Nova Scotia	103	60	49	7.4	8.6	0.3	3.3
New Brunswick	106	92	48	26.5	29.5	5.4	18.9
Quebec	122	101	66	32.4	35.4	–	–
Ontario	115	63	57	10.8	11.4	2.7	7.3
Manitoba	112	49	46	7.9	9.2	2.2	10.3
Saskatchewan	113	33	34	4.6	5.2	0.8	5.4
Alberta	113	36	47	6.4	6.6	3.2	5.6
British Columbia	114	28	51	5.7	6.4	0.9	5.4
Yukon	109	44	23	7.9	9.3	0.7	7.1
Northwest Territories	121	47	76	6.0	6.1	0.3	2.9
Canada	113	96	55	15.3	16.3	2.1	6.8

[1] Numbers under language continuity are scores indicating equality, 'gain' or 'loss'.
Sources: Harrison and Marmen, 1994; Statistics Canada, 1993a, 1993b.

between 1981 and 1991, one of the largest increases of any region. The historical French presence seems to have encouraged learning French by immersion, and this effort seems to have increased bilingualism substantially in one decade alone. The rise of French immersion and bilingualism in Manitoba in the 1990s is an encouraging sign after a long history of setbacks.

Survival of non-official languages

Up to now we have mainly followed the official charter languages, but non-official languages are the first mother tongues of more than one-fifth of Manitobans; we need to examine this linguistic heterogeneity more closely. Of the 1,079,390 residents in Manitoba in 1991, 97.4 per cent were categorized by the census as reporting a single mother tongue only (some 28,585, or 2.6 per cent, gave 'multiple' responses).

Of the 203,940 single respondents in Manitoba who reported non-official mother tongue (19.4 per cent), roughly one-third (6.9 per cent) reported Germanic tongues, mostly German (63,140 or 6.0 per cent). Roughly one-fifth (48,385

Table 22.3 Comparisons of official and non-official mother tongues, language use, and language continuity, Manitoba, 1991 (for those reporting a single mother tongue)

Languages	Mother Tongue		Home Language		Language Continuity
	N	%	N	%	
Official languages	846,865	80.6	958,770	90.9	111
English	799,935	76.1	935,225	88.7	112
French	46,930	4.5	23,545	2.2	49
Non-official languages[1]	203,940	19.4	96,420	9.1	46
Germanic	73,420	6.9	23,880	2.3	33
German	63,140		22,790		36
Dutch	4,420		680		15
Scandinavian	3,275		130		3
Other	2,585		280		
Slavic	48,385	4.6	13,655	1.3	28
Ukrainian	32,805		6,895		21
Polish	10,865		5,045		48
Other	4,715		1,715		
Romance	16,005	1.5	9,400	0.9	59
Portuguese	6,670		4,025		60
Italian	4,885		1,960		40
Spanish	3,915		3,150		80
Other	535		265		
Aboriginal	30,820	2.9	21,775	2.0	71
Cree	21,195		16,385		77
Ojibway	7,955		4,500		57
Other	1,670		890		
Asian	25,540	2.4	22,400	2.1	88
Tagalog (Pilipino)	10,015		8,500		85
Chinese	8,285		7,380		89
Indo-Iranian	5,065		4,155		82
Vietnamese	2,175		2,365		109
Other	9,770	1.0	5,310	0.5	
Total single	1,050,805	100.0	1,055,190	100.0	

[1] not all non-official languages are listed here.
Sources: Statistics Canada, 1993a, 1993b.

or 4.6 per cent) reported Slavic mother tongues, mostly Ukrainian (32,805 or 3.0 per cent). The 16,005 who reported Romance mother tongues, mainly Portuguese, Italian and Spanish, represented only 1.5 per cent of Manitobans. There were 30,820 respondents (2.9 per cent) who reported aboriginal mother tongues, mostly Cree (21,195) and Ojibway (7,955). Manitobans with Asian mother tongues included Tagalog (Pilipino) (0.9 per cent), Chinese (0.8 per cent), Indo-Iranian (0.5 per cent) and Vietnamese (0.2 per cent) speakers.

Use of these non-official mother tongues at home varies considerably in Manitoba. Overall, home use is much lower than original mother-tongue levels. While for anglophones the language continuity score is well above 100 (meaning more used English at home), for all others it is much lower. The older Germanic and Slavic Europeans, who arrived roughly 100 years ago, show language continuity scores ranging from 3 to 48, lower than the French (49). Those who learned Romance mother tongues arrived much later, so many are first and second generation, and these scores are somewhat higher (40-80) than the French. Aboriginal continuity scores are higher still (57-77), because many speakers are geographically isolated in the north. Most Asians came very recently – many are first generation – and they have the highest continuity scores of all (82-109), well above those of the French, but not as high as the English (112). Thus we see that English-language continuity in Manitoba is dominant, French continuity is similar to that of non-official language users overall, aboriginal continuity is high because of isolation, and Asian continuity is high because of recency of immigration.

RECENT CRISES AND EDUCATION

While Manitoba began as an officially bilingual province in 1870, the French community was illegally stripped of both its legislative and French-schools rights until the 1980s. While the English- and French-speaking populations were roughly of equal size when Manitoba became a province, the French declined to a small minority of 16 per cent within five years; this resulted in loss of seats and political power. The 1890 act which made English the official language in Manitoba was challenged twice (in 1892 and 1909) and ruled unconstitutional, but Manitoba governments ignored the rulings.

When Pierre Trudeau declared Canada a bilingual and multicultural country in 1971, this federal formula again provided an impetus for Franco-Manitobans to assert their legal linguistic and educational rights. Georges Forest, a St Boniface insurance agent, took his case to the Supreme Court, which in 1979 declared the 1890 act invalid (Youngs, 1985). The English-only parking ticket Forest used as the basis for his challenge forced the Conservative government to begin the arduous task of translating 4,500 Manitoba unilingual statutes. When the NDP government of Howard Pawley came into power in 1981, it presented legislation negotiated with the *Société Franco-Manitobaine* to translate about 10 per cent of these unilingual statutes. The Tories, now in opposition, strongly opposed the legislation; they left the legislature, the division bells rang for 263 hours, and finally the legislative package died (Youngs, 1985). Again, the legal and court directives had been politically defeated. While rallies both in support of and opposed to the new legislation occurred, it was clear that a majority of Manitobans did not support the NDP attempt to reverse past injustices. In 1985 the Supreme Court again unanimously ruled that the 4,500 English-only statutes were invalid until they were translated into both official languages. In 1985 both Premier Pawley (1985) and Conservative opposition leader Gary Filmon (1985) gave their positions on the matter.

In the meantime, the Commissioner of Official Languages processed seventy-eight complaints in 1993 and forty-eight in 1994 in Manitoba. French-language services were found to be available 76 per cent of the time, the highest west of Quebec (Goldbloom, 1995). With 47,800 francophones in Manitoba, there were 665 bilingual positions but only 380 francophone public servants in the province. In 1994 Canada and the Franco-Manitoban community agreed that the federal government would provide about $10.7 million over five years, to promote the French language and francophone projects. Winnipeg has adopted a plan for the implementation of French-language services, which also includes the bilingualization of 13,000 road signs in the Riel district of the city.

On 1 July 1994, the francophone community officially received a Franco-Manitoban School Division, seventy-eight long years after they lost control in 1916 (Goldbloom, 1995). The new school division includes twenty schools with some 4,200 students in the division, and a little over 1,000 other students outside the DSFM. The Manitoba and federal governments have also signed an agreement on school management whereby Manitoba would receive core funds of $15 million for DSFM and French immersion. While French immersion enrolment in 1977-78 was 1,667 in 13 schools, by 1994-95 there were 19,863 students in 104 schools (Bienvenue, 1986). There seems to be a flicker of hope for francophones more recently, after long dark difficult times for more than 100 years.

References

Bienvenue, R. M. (1986). Participation in an educational innovation: enrollment in French immersion programs. *Canadian Journal of Sociology, 11*, 363–377.

Bourhis, R. Y. (1994). Introduction and overview of language events in Canada. *International Journal of the Sociology of Language, 105–106*, 5–36.

Clark, L. (1968). *The Manitoba School Question: Majority Rule or Minority Rights?* Toronto: Copp Clark.

deVries, J. (1994). Canada's Official Language communities: an overview of the current demolinguistic situation. *International Journal of the Sociology of Language, 105–106*, 37–68.

Filmon, G. (1985). The Opposition view: the other side of the question. *Language and Society, 16,* 13–15.

Friesen, G. (1996). Bilingualism in Manitoba: the historical context. In G. Friesen (ed.), *River Road* (pp. 72–94). Winnipeg: University of Manitoba Press.

Goldbloom, V. C. (1995). *Annual Report, 1994.* Ottawa: Minister of Supply & Services.

Harrison, B. and Marmen, L. (1994). *Languages in Canada: Focus on Canada.* Ottawa: Statistics Canada.

Jaenen, C. J. (1984). The history of French in Manitoba: local initiative or external imposition? *Language and Society, 13,* 3–16.

Pawley, H. (1985). The Government perspective: on with the job. *Language and Society, 16,* 9–12.

Statistics Canada (1993a). *Mother Tongue: The Nation* (Catalogue 93–313). Ottawa: Statistics Canada.

(1993b). *Home Language and Mother Tongue* (Catalogue 93–317). Ottawa: Statistics Canada.

Youngs, F. (1985). Linguistic wrongs and rights: a political football. *Language and Society, 16,* 3–8.

Map 9 Saskatchewan

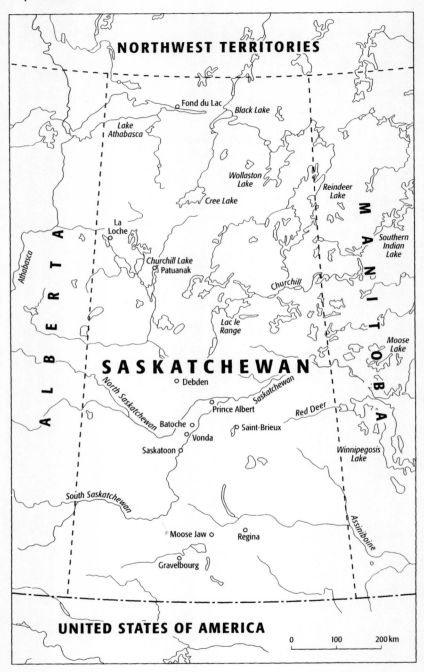

NORTHWEST TERRITORIES

Fond du Lac

Black Lake

Lake
Athabasca

Wollaston
Lake

Reindeer
Lake

Cree Lake

M
A
N
I
T
O
B
A

Southern
Indian
Lake

La
Loche

Churchill Lake
Patuanak

Churchill

Athabasca

A
L
B
E
R
T
A

Lac le
Range

Moose
Lake

SASKATCHEWAN

Debden

North Saskatchewan

Saskatchewan

Batoche

Prince Albert

Red Deer

Saint-Brieux

Vonda

Saskatoon

Winnipegosis
Lake

South Saskatchewan

Assiniboine

Moose Jaw

Regina

Gravelbourg

UNITED STATES OF AMERICA

0   100   200 km

23 Language in Saskatchewan: Anglo-hegemony maintained

Wilfrid Denis

INTRODUCTION

Saskatchewan's history and demography have dictated to a large extent that English should dominate and non-anglophones should assimilate to English. Different policies in earlier times could have created a different social reality, but history cannot be re-written. Saskatchewan's language policies appear quite varied over time; yet, for non-English groups, these policies – as in most of English Canada – share the common outcome of maintaining the dominance of English, in spite of protracted resistance by other language groups. Gramsci's (1971) concept of ideological hegemony (the manner by which a dominant class imposes its culture, ideology and world view on subordinate groups) provides a useful lens through which to analyse language policy and can be applied to Anglo-domination in English Canada. A full account of the mechanisms of Anglo-domination and minority-group responses would extend beyond the limits of this chapter, especially since the experiences of domination and resistance are different for aboriginal, French and immigrant groups. For all three, education is the major policy domain, but French has also been important in other areas. Minority-group struggles to maintain their language, identity and culture will remain in the background here as I focus on mechanisms of domination.

The study of a policy area must consider the combined impact of apparently unrelated laws which together form a particular legislative regime. At times these include policies and legislation beyond the particular jurisdiction of interest. Each regime circumscribes collective and individual action and imposes on social groups a distinct climate. For Saskatchewan, the British North America Act provides a convenient starting point, although ideally its socio-historical context should be considered as well (Denis, 1990). Policies range from the Northwest Territories' ordinances to beyond the recent Canadian Charter of Rights and are grouped here into four different language regimes. The analysis identifies the mechanisms which initially established Anglo-hegemony and then maintained it, even under regimes favourable to minority languages.

ESTABLISHING ANGLO-HEGEMONY: 1875–1930

The period 1875 to 1930 opens with a linguistic regime that is largely undefined. In 1867, the BNA Act (Article 133) made French and English official languages for the federal and Quebec governments. These fairly narrow provisions allowed provinces to legislate on language in their own jurisdiction (Tremblay and Bastarache, 1989). Following the precedents of the BNA Act and the Manitoba Act, an ordinance of the Northwest Territories in 1877 recognized French and English as the official languages in the Territorial Council, its courts, and its official documents. This legal recognition was congruent with the demographic and commercial importance of francophones, particularly the Métis, as well as with the common and almost preponderant use of French as the language of business in Manitoba and the Territories (Purich, 1988; Sheppard, 1971). In addition, the BNA Act (Article 93) placed education, including the language of instruction in schools, under provincial jurisdiction. The Northwest Territories Act of 1875 also provided for the establishment of schools, but without specifying any language of instruction. Language communities could operate their institutions in their own language, although weak immigration at the time made such choices relevant primarily for French and English. French was the language of instruction in some of the first territorial schools in the 1870's. These ordinances clearly acknowledged the legitimacy of French in education, the courts and government, and established its legal status. Weak as these ordinances were, they constitute the legislative high point for languages other than English in the Territories and for most of Saskatchewan's history.

Religious divisions between Catholics and Protestants across Canada were intimately tied to language; they often surfaced in territorial ordinances. Between 1886 and 1892, Catholic educational rights were eroded as Catholics lost departmental control of their schools, textbooks, programmes, teaching methods and teacher certification. Such losses also applied to language because of the link between Catholicism and French.

In 1892, the Territorial Assembly adopted an amendment to end the publication of its proceedings in French which had been done since 1878 (Sheppard, 1971). This was justified on the grounds of 'economy, convenience and necessity', since 'the Journals were rarely needed by any person who was unable to read them in English' (*Regina Leader Post*, 26 January 1892, in Denis and Li, 1988,

p. 354). The proposition was never proclaimed as law and would become the basis for the Mercure case in 1980 (see below). Some argued that French was, therefore, still an official language of Saskatchewan (Rottiers, 1977; Sheppard, 1971), a claim rejected by the Territorial and later the Saskatchewan government. In fact the unproclaimed proposition was interpreted broadly as eliminating provincial French rights entirely and, in practice, French lost 'even the grudging deference accorded to it prior to 1892' (Sheppard, 1971, p. 86). French remained without any recognized status in Saskatchewan's legislature or courts – despite its technical legal basis – until the Mercure case.

In 1901, a clause in the school ordinance specified English as the only language of instruction, except that school districts could allow a primary course in French and 'competent persons [could] give instruction in any language other than English' as long as this did not interfere with the regular teacher. Boards could also collect money from the parents concerned to pay these special language instructors. As well, other modifications to the ordinance confirmed the removal of the dual confessional education system, similar to Quebec's, and similar to Manitoba's system from 1871 to 1890. Instead, Catholics and Protestants could establish separate schools only in those districts where they constituted the minority; otherwise, the majority group had to establish a public school. In 1905, federal legislation created the provinces of Alberta and Saskatchewan, given the significant increase of their respective populations. Prime Minister Laurier attempted unsuccessfully to reinstate in that legislation the dual confessional system of 1875. The resignation in protest of Clifford Sifton, federal Minister of the Interior, ensured that the 1901 system was left in place (Courcelles, 1969).

By this time, many anglophones perceived rising immigration as a threat to the predominance of English and British institutions, and a climate of intolerance spread throughout western Canada. With the First World War and the Russian Revolution, nativist fears led to the prison-camp internment of over 8,000 immigrants, mostly Germans and Ukrainians. In Saskatchewan, intolerance produced increasingly oppressive changes, primarily in education. According to Barber (1978, p. 293) 'the English speaking Protestant majority attempted to assert the dominance of its ideals for the nation', leading eventually to 'a hostile demand for immediate and total conformity'. By 1918, anglophone xenophobia – originating in numerous Protestant groups, but also the Rural Municipalities Association, the School Trustees' Association and the Saskatchewan Grain Growers' Association – finally forced Premier Martin to amend the 1901 School Act and to restrict the language of instruction to English only (Lupul, 1982). The only exception was a primary grade of French, and French as a subject for one hour a day in other grades (Huel, 1970). As well, a daily half hour of religious instruction could be in French.

Other restrictive legislation included the Compulsory School Attendance Act (1917), which forced Mennonites and others to build public schools and to enrol their children. To these parents, the exclusive use of English, and the emphasis on British culture and institutions, were major threats to their language and values (Denis, 1993). And, for Mennonites, this was contrary to an agreement that they obtained from the federal government in 1873, known as 'The Privilegium', which guaranteed certain religious rights. Non-compliance with the Act led to harsh fines and jail sentences – about $26,000 in fines in 1920–21 alone, some 5,493 school prosecutions between 1918 and 1925, and imposition of fines into the 1930s (Ens, 1994; Epp, 1982). Intolerance continued unabated into the 1920s in even more extreme forms, like the Ku Klux Klan which contributed to the election of the Conservatives in 1929 (Calderwood, 1968; Kyba, 1964; Macleod, 1968). Almost immediately, the Attorney General ruled that religious instruction had to be in English. In 1930, the School Act was changed to prohibit religious symbols in public schools or religious garb by teachers; school meetings now had to be in English, and trustees had to read and write in English. A year later, the French primary grade was removed although, ironically, French as a subject remained. Again, penalties and enforcement were harsh. They included the decertification of teachers, heavy fines, disqualification of trustees and loss of provincial education grants. Inventories of religious symbols and garb in schools were taken before and after implementation of the amendments (Denis and Li, 1988). Indeed, school inspectors still harassed Catholic communities into the 1950s, and some were denied education grants (Huel, 1977, 1980).

Two other pieces of legislation are part of this first regime. First, the Indian Act (1876) had a profound impact on aboriginal languages. Although silent on language itself, it relegated all 'Indian' matters to the federal Department of Indian Affairs; under its authority, educational arrangements consistent with the prevailing ideology of assimilation and Anglo-conformity were imposed. The history and the long-term effects of residential schools are just beginning to attract public attention (Titley, 1986). Since this Act made 'Indian' matters a federal responsibility and since there was little recognition of the Métis throughout this period, the provincial legislators and departments for the most part ignored these groups until the 1960s. The other legislation is the Immigration Act (1896,

1910), whose selection criteria favoured British immigrants over those of other countries and ensured an over-representation of the former early in this century. The Act also impressed upon immigrants that British institutions prevailed in their country of adoption.

Minority groups resisted the restrictive legislation in many ways. In response to exclusion from the regular school in 1918, many reverted to out-of-school language classes or established convents and private schools. Thus, the Ukrainians sought to provide teachers, materials and instruction in Ukrainian language, history, tradition and culture (Swyripa, 1982). The Mennonites also opened private or bible schools (Epp, 1982) and more than 1,000 left Saskatchewan in the 1920s for Mexico and Paraguay, to escape the intolerance (Ens, 1994; Epp, 1982). Beginning in 1926, French Canadians set up their own curriculum with textbooks, school inspectors and annual exams to provide for the daily hour of French instruction allowed by law (Denis and Li, 1988).

Minority response also took many other forms but it is clear that the legislative regime made it difficult for virtually all non-anglophone groups to develop institutional structures favouring their languages. As table 23.1 indicates, those of British origin still accounted for 47.5 per cent of Saskatchewan's population in 1931. The third column reveals that for all groups except the British, there is a loss between 'origin' and 'mother tongue'. Calculated as an index of language continuity (LC per cent), the last column for 1931 shows a high rate of continuity for the Chinese, aboriginal and Ukrainian communities but, for the Dutch group, losses were already quite severe. Most minorities were experiencing a decline in language continuity years before it appears in census data. The British rate of 118 per cent reflects the assimilation of many minority groups towards English as a mother tongue. The last major change in the first legislative regime occurred in 1931, which marks the lowest point for minority-language rights in Saskatchewan after years of systematic erosion. The major mechanisms which established Anglo-hegemony include public pressure and control of the media, restrictive legislation and control of institutions – especially schools, with controls on the qualification of teachers, textbooks and programmes, dress codes, language of operation and so on. Coercive measures, including heavy fines, jail, decertification and loss of grants, emerged from political institutions dominated by Anglophone politicians who generally shared a common conception of Canada as a British nation, and who were to dominate during the next period as well (Smith, 1968).

Table 23.1 Ethnic origin, mother tongue (MT) and language continuity (LC) for various groups in Saskatchewan, 1931, 1961, 1991

	1931				1961				1991				
	Origin		Language		Origin		Language		Origin		Language		
Group	N	%	MT	LC%	N	%	MT	LC%	N	%	MT	LC1[2]	LC2[2]
Aboriginal	15,268	1.7	14,627[1]	96	55,645	6.0	25,932	47	96,580	9.9	21,030	22	32
British	437,836	47.5	516,842	118	373,482	40.4	638,156	171	470,710	48.2	818,110	174	509
Chinese	3,501	0.4	3,458	99	3,660	0.4	3,073	84	9,340	1.0	7,240	78	96
Dutch	24,695	2.7	9,493	38	29,325	3.2	8,054	28	44,805	4.6	2,505	6	22
French	50,700	5.5	39,799	78	59,824	6.5	36,163	60	119,610	12.3	22,725	19	76
German	129,232	14.0	98,720	76	158,209	17.1	89,650	57	297,200	30.4	42,255	14	35
Hungarian	13,363	1.4	10,668	80	16,059	1.7	8,030	50	22,650	2.3	3,520	16	44
Polish	25,961	2.8	16,612	64	28,951	3.1	10,585	37	55,575	5.7	4,295	8	37
Scandinavian	72,324	7.8	48,875	68	67,553	7.3	19,511	29	87,755	9.0	3,835	4	16
Ukrainian	63,400	6.9	59,354	94	78,851	8.5	67,087	85	131,105	13.4	27,615	21	49
Province	921,785	100.0	–	–	925,181	100.0	–	–	976,035	100.0	–	–	–

[1] Aboriginal mother-tongue data extrapolated from Table 56 (1931 Census) for population 10 years and older.

[2] LC1 Language continuity for total response (single and multiple responses); LC2 is for single response only.

Sources: 1931 Census of Canada, Vol. III tables 16, 56 and 61; 1961 Census of Canada, 92–545 (origins) table 37; 1961 Census of Canada, 92–549 (official language and mother tongue) table 66; 1991 Census of Canada, 93–315 (ethnic origin) table 2A pp. 78–93; 1991 Census of Canada, 92–549 (official language and mother tongue) table 66.

HEGEMONY THROUGH INSTITUTIONAL CONSTRAINTS:
1931–1964

No language legislation was adopted in Saskatchewan between 1931 and 1964. Throughout this period, hegemony was maintained by existing institutional structures and, with minor exceptions, modifications to these strengthened the domination. The Liberals maintained the previous Conservative repressive legislation from 1934 to 1944. The Cooperative Commonwealth Federation (CCF), elected in 1944, relaxed the enforcement of this legislation, which attenuated feelings of antagonism and persecution. Complaints to the Department of Education regarding Catholic religious garb continued, although less frequently, into the 1960s (Huel, 1980). The actual legislation stayed in effect until a major re-drafting of the School Act in 1978.

In 1944, the Larger School Unit Act centralized school administration away from small local school boards. For non-anglophones this loss of operational autonomy and control – and the centralization of many schools themselves – ensured *de facto* domination of English as the common language both in the school yard and in the classroom. Contradictions between old policies and the need for change surfaced in the Department of Education in the early 1960s. While still having an advisory committee on 'English and Citizenship' – as though the two were synonymous – it also established a committee to develop and improve curriculum materials for Northern Indian and Métis groups (Saskatchewan Department of Education, 1959–60, 1962–63). Ukrainian, German and Russian were reintroduced at the high school level during the 1950s, and were accredited along with Latin in the early 1960s. In 1961, a high school credit was finally granted for the French course developed by the French community and offered since 1926 (Saskatchewan Department of Education, 1961–62). However, tensions between francophone organizations and the government still attracted considerable media attention (Denis, 1993).

By the early 1960s, problems often arose at the level of school units. Francophone parents challenged them in court or withheld students from school; the units retaliated with intimidating tactics against parents and teachers. In 1965 a major confrontation over teaching religion in French in an elementary school in Saskatoon led to francophone parents withdrawing their children in protest and establishing Saskatchewan's first totally French immersion school. The confrontation resulted in the Tait Commission, which investigated the question of language use and instruction in the School Act. The Commission agreed with the parents that contradictions in the Act were detrimental to the use of French, and thus recommended favourable amendments (Denis and Li, 1988).

If favourable changes have positive effects on minority-language transmission, these effects will appear much later in census statistics. As table 23.1 indicates, the 1961 census data reflect the conditions established under the first legislative regime, and carried forward for most of the second. The only two groups that have retained a fairly high rate of language continuity from origin to mother tongue are the Chinese (84.0 per cent) and the Ukrainians (85.1 per cent). Those of Dutch, Polish and Scandinavian origin are all undergoing major losses whereas the only group with any gains is the British group, where a language continuity of 170 per cent reflects the assimilation to the English language of non-anglophones.

This period closes with a mixture of serious confrontations and growing openness by authorities. The institutional regime established in the earlier decades continued to restrict languages other than English in the whole education system, as well as in other public institutions. Faced with only a few credit courses and out-of-school classes (Royal Commission, 1970), minority groups could only turn to their communities, churches, a few newspapers, volunteer organizations and families to maintain their language.

HEGEMONY THROUGH CO-OPTATION: 1965–1990

The climate began to change in the mid-1960s, both nationally and in Saskatchewan. The Royal Commission on Bilingualism and Biculturalism was drawing attention to linguistic issues which refused to fade away, despite decades of overtly assimilationist policies. Some of the first signs of change were the appointing of a Supervisor of French Instruction in the Department of Education (in 1966), and implementing the Tait Commission's recommendations in the School Act. A first amendment in 1967 reversed the 1930 legislation and allowed the use of French not just as a subject but as the language of instruction for one hour a day. The following year, the Department accepted full financial and administrative responsibility for the French programme and a second amendment allowed the government to 'designate' schools in which French could be used beyond one hour a day. All other languages were extended the privilege of language of instruction (in 1974) and a distinction between French as a first and a second language was recognized. A new section in the Act allowed for attendance at designated schools; although important in principle, such a clause remains without effect if no means of transportation are provided as well.

Under the impetus of federal funding for bilingual programmes across the country, Saskatchewan Education created the Official Minority Language Office in 1980 to oversee the teaching of all French programmes. This office facilitated the teaching of French to francophones, but most of its resources and energies in the first decade were spent developing and supervising programmes of French-as-a-second-language for non-francophones, especially via French immersion.

In spite of these positive departmental changes, school boards often resisted implementation, which led to numerous confrontations. Implementation problems occurred in Debden in 1971–72, and transportation problems in Saskatoon in 1979–80. Francophone parents in Prince Albert and Vonda finally brought their grievances to court in 1980. An appeal of the Vonda case was rejected by the Supreme Court, which then confirmed to Saskatchewan francophones that French education – and, by extension, that of all other minority languages as well – was entirely at the discretion of the Minister of Education (Denis and Li, 1988). Other controversies led the government, in 1976, to institute a second commission on language opportunities in school. On this commission's recommendations, the designation of schools was extended to languages other than French in 1978. The only Ukrainian bilingual school ever to be established, and which offers 50 per cent of instruction in the Ukrainian language, opened in 1979–80; by the time Grade 12 was reached, school enrolments stabilized at around 200 students (see table 23.2).

As for aboriginal education, the first native unit board trustee took office in 1974. That year, six pilot projects to teach native languages to native children were expanded to seventeen projects (Saskatchewan Department of Education, 1973–4). A Native Education Consultant was appointed in 1975–76 and, by 1980, an Urban Native Teacher (SUNTEP) programme, a Native Curriculum Development Committee and an urban Native Survival School had been established. By 1984–86, Native Studies courses were accredited for high school; an Indian and Métis Education Section in the Department of Education, a Development Program for School Boards, a Five Year Action Plan and an Indian and Métis Awareness Inservice Program were all in place. Native organizations were becoming more vocal in specifying problems and needs in education, and more native schools were established under band control. Jurisdictional problems between the Department of Indian Affairs, the Saskatchewan Department of Education and band schools hinders a comprehensive view of these developments, or an assessment of their impact on First Nations' languages.

Again, provincial language issues were affected by national policies, such as the Official Languages Act in 1969 (Pal, 1993; Tremblay and Bastarache, 1989) and the multicultural policy of 1971, which became the Multiculturalism Act in 1988 (Pal, 1993). Other major events include the 1976 election of the Parti Québécois in that province and the subsequent referendum on 20 May 1980.

Finally the 'kitchen accord' of November 1981 between certain federal and provincial leaders excluded Quebec and established the climate of federal–provincial relations for the next decades, in spite of repatriating the Constitution and creating the Charter of Rights in 1982 (Russell, 1993).

These events and policies had many ramifications for minority-language groups (Pal, 1993), and two aspects in particular deserve our attention. First, under the Official Languages Act, the Secretary of State provided funds to francophone groups for community development, and to the Saskatchewan Department of Education for bilingual education. About 75 per cent of the latter was for teaching French to anglophones, while the other 25 per cent supported francophone education. Similarly, funds for multiculturalism were provided to some ethnic groups for heritage-language instruction from 1978 to 1990 (Lee, 1996). Funds were also made available for non-treaty aboriginal groups. Secondly, the Secretary of State instituted the national Court Challenges Program in 1978, with about $2 million annually to help prepare and present constitutional rights cases in court. Official-language minorities in Quebec and English Canada benefited tremendously from this programme.

In the early 1980s, attempts by Saskatchewan francophones to negotiate greater access to French instruction and greater control over their children's education were met with a government rejection. Their only recourse, as in virtually every English province, was to challenge educational legislation in court under Section 23 of the new Charter of Rights and Freedoms (Bastarache, 1989). The Court Challenge Program supported this case, which went to trial in 1987. On 15 February 1988, Judge Wimmer rendered his decision, which supported the parents' claim that their Charter rights as an official-language minority gave them the right to manage and control their own schools. Similar cases in other provinces created a new jurisprudence around Section 23 of the Charter. However it was only when the Mahé case from Alberta was eventually heard by the Supreme Court that a definitive judgment was made on 15 March 1990. Although Saskatchewan's Education Act was declared unconstitutional in 1988, the government did not act, in the hope that the Supreme Court ruling would reduce the scope of provincial obligations.

In the late 1970s and early 1980s, many reassessed linguistic rights in arenas other than education. In Saskatchewan in 1980, Father Mercure used a speeding ticket to revive in court the argument that Article 110 of the Northwest Territories Act was still in force and that, consequently, court documents should have been available in both French and English. Much like the Forest case in Manitoba, this case underwent a number of appeals, including to the Supreme

Court, which judged it to be sufficiently important to hear its final appeal even though Mercure had died in the meantime. The Court's decision, finally rendered on February 25, 1988, agreed with Mercure and could have required that all provincial laws since 1905 be translated into French, and that English and French be allowed in both provincial courts and legislature. However, the Court also ruled that these rights were part of the internal constitutions of Alberta and Saskatchewan, and not of the Constitution of Canada, and could therefore be changed unilaterally by the provinces (Tremblay and Bastarache, 1989).

Within weeks of the Supreme Court decision, the Conservative government adopted Bill 02 to reverse the decision and to abolish all linguistic rights in Article 110. Certain privileges were retained, such as the translation of some laws into French at the discretion of the government. As a further blow to the province's francophone community, Collège Mathieu, the only French high school in the province, burned to the ground on 14 May 1988. The extinction of language rights in the context of negotiation of the Meech Lake Accord embarrassed the federal government considerably. Intervening directly, it signed a ten-year framework agreement with the province to fund educational programmes for francophones, translate certain laws, establish a provincial government office to coordinate francophone affairs, build a language institute in Regina and rebuild Collège Mathieu (Saskatchewan Department of Education, 1988–89).

Thus the period 1965–90 closed with a Supreme Court decision that required amending the Education Act to give francophones management and control of their schools. Federal funding of language groups improved the teaching conditions for non-official languages. Provincial legislation made immersion schools possible in any language, and significant changes were occurring in First Nation education. But, simultaneously, the Secretary of State eliminated funding of heritage-language programmes and the provincial government, which had been taking years to implement a court decision on French management of schools, wiped out the newly re-established francophone linguistic rights in only a few weeks. 1990 marks the end of another language regime.

HEGEMONY THROUGH ATTRITION: 1991–2000

The next decades will be crucial to Saskatchewan's linguistic physiognomy; indeed, since 1990, important changes have already taken place, some of which appear in education statistics as in table 23.2. Following the Supreme Court ruling on education rights, the province amended the Education Act in 1992. Eight francophone school boards, each managing one school, were elected in June 1994 and assumed control as of 1 January 1995. Start-up funds from the

Table 23.2 Language education statistics for Saskatchewan, 1980–1994

Year	Province total N¹	Heritage languages				French		Ukrainian		Aboriginal N¹	German (Grades 10–12 only) N¹	Japanese N¹
		Taught in School N¹	Taught out of school			First lang.³ N¹	Immersion⁴ N¹	Core K-12 N¹	Bilingual N¹			
			Lang. taught N¹	Organizations² N¹	$							
1980-81	204,261	3,817	13	42	–	–	2,566	2,306	28	–	–	–
1981-82	199,447	3,622	14	46	–	–	3,127	2,250	58	–	–	–
1982-83	198,781	3,451	15	46	–	–	3,952	1,958	60	–	–	–
1983-84	198,552	3,198	20	50	–	–	4,740	1,766	73	–	–	–
1984-85	199,227	3,225	18	55	–	–	5,862	1,679	85	–	–	–
1985-86	199,909	3,057	21	58	–	–	7,212	1,576	101	–	–	–
1986-87	200,212	2,770	22	65	–	–	8,784	1,231	126	–	–	–
1987-88	201,143	2,298	22	71	–	944	9,868	993	131	–	–	–
1988-89	200,158	2,110	25	82	–	1,189	10,977	821	145	–	–	–
1989-90	198,025	1,969	25	81	–	1,238	11,353	699	159	184	419	22
1990-91	195,566	1,540	25	92	–	1,400	11,854	572	166	304	385	4
1991-92	195,936	1,693	28	101	89,950	1,491	12,306	516	188	397	372	11
1992-93	210,428	–	27	106	91,360	1,145	12,882	538	187	316	390	222
1993-94	210,333	–	25	102	87,800	1,106	12,762	499	191	720	365	187
1994-95	197,566	–	27	101	89,170	1,001	11,026	451	217	788	319	225

[1] number refers to student enrolment unless otherwise specified; blanks mean data is unavailable.
[2] refers to the number of community organizations involved in offering out-of-school language classes.
[3] statistics for eight schools which obtained management and control in 1994.
[4] does not include students in French-as-first language schools.

Sources: Saskatchewan Education Annual Report, various years, and unpublished department data.

436

federal government will be available until 1998; if such funding is insufficient, the province is unlikely to provide supplementàry support – so this newly instituted system which, constitutionally, the province is obliged to provide could be jeopardized. Enrolment in these eight schools rose to a peak of 1,400 students in 1991–92 but has since declined by almost one third to about 1,000 students (see table 23.2). It is too early to tell whether management and control by francophones will have a positive impact on enrolments. French is also taught as a second language to non-francophones in a variety of formats, of which immersion has been very popular over the years, due in part to federal funding. As table 23.2 indicates, French immersion increased every year until a peak enrolment of 12,882 in 1992–93, but has been followed by a significant drop since.

As to other languages, Ukrainian has been offered as a core programme (forty minutes, three times a week in elementary school, and a total of 100 hours per semester in high school) since the 1970s. The decline in enrolments in this programme, from 2,306 in 1980–81 to 451 in 1994–95, has been offset only slightly by the increased enrolments in the only Ukrainian bilingual school in the province. Enrolment in other in-school language courses such as German, Latin and Russian, established in the 1960s or earlier, is declining significantly from a high of 3,817 in 1980–81 to a low of 1,693 in 1991–92, the last year for which data were available. With the adoption of the federal multicultural policy in 1971, non-official languages became identified as 'heritage languages'. Federal funding from the Secretary of State was available up to 1990 for programmes of 'heritage language instruction'. However, this funding was tied to the old format of after-school and Saturday classes, used since 1918. Many ethnic groups organized language delivery around this format. When federal funds were cut in 1990, the province moved its own fairly nominal funding for such programmes from the Department of Culture and Youth to Education, and provided additional funds. As table 23.2 indicates, the number of students taught in out-of-school classes increased from 1,546 in 1980 to a peak enrolment of 3,114 in 1991–92. Since then enrolments declined to about 2,800 students. The number of languages taught out-of-school has doubled to 27 but the number of community groups involved in class delivery has increased from 41 to over 100. Government grants average about $30 per student per year, hardly enough to cover basic supplies, let alone salaries or space. The figures in table 23.2 provide no indication of the tremendous commitment of volunteer labour, energy and community resources – including an overwhelming contribution by women – to maintain these classes in operation (Lee, 1996). Only Spanish, Japanese and aboriginal languages are making gains (see also Saskatchewan Indicators, 1995).

Thus, under present conditions, heritage languages are declining seriously in credit classes and the underfunded out-of-school programme is barely stable, like French and Ukrainian immersion. Increases in Spanish and Japanese enrolments are driven by job considerations and do not reflect native-speaker increases; Saskatchewan's Spanish mother-tongue population was 1,800 and the Japanese was 175, in 1991. These are offered, then, as 'languages of consumption' rather than as heritage languages. The situation of aboriginal languages is different, partly because of significant increases in students. The Department of Education has committed important resources to native programmes and curriculum development, and a growing number of schools is under the direct control of the First Nations.

First Nation languages and French as a first language provide clear examples of the nexus of factors required for non-dominant languages to survive. Beyond a vibrant community, these include a pool of native speakers, the development of curriculum and teaching materials, selection and training of qualified teachers, teaching resources (including library and audio-visual material), a significant degree of institutional management and control, adequate teaching facilities, and integration into the regular school programme as a language of instruction and not simply as a subject. Finally, the language must be contextualized in the group's identity, culture and experience. Only then does it become a living vehicle to transmit that identity and culture from one generation to the next. Without these conditions a language tends towards the other extreme – a second language devoid of identity and culture, a language of consumption and job prospects rather than a language of participation and collective expression.

Declining enrolments for in-school courses and totally inadequate resources and conditions for out-of-school language instruction jeopardize the future of heritage languages in Saskatchewan. For most of the languages, these conditions are replacing the more favourable climate and language regimes of the last decades and will ensure that attrition completes the task that oppression began in the 1920's. Already, the 1991 census data (see table 23.1) reveal the cumulative negative impact of unfavourable regimes. The positive effects of the last regime will not manifest themselves in census data for another decade. But the scale of losses does not bode well at all, especially if institutional support for minority languages is undermined by major cutbacks or other institutional re-arrangements. The 1991 census data are not entirely comparable to those of previous years because, for the first time, Statistics Canada allowed persons to choose multiple ethnic origins. Thus the 'Language Continuity 1' column provides data on all those who share some common ethnic origin. This column represents the worst-case scenario, where virtually all groups except the Chinese have losses above 78 per cent. The column 'Language Continuity 2' consists of single responses, that is, persons who identify only one ethnic origin. Language retention is higher for these smaller groups who are less affected by exogamy. However, even with this best-case scenario, losses are very high for most groups. Only the Chinese (95.9 per cent) and the French (75.6 per cent) have a high or reasonable rate of continuity. Again, only the British group, with a language continuity rate somewhere between 174 and 509 per cent, is making any gains through the assimilation of members of other groups.

CONCLUSION

Languages respond to changes in environment; they flourish or die more as the outcome of power struggles, of relations of oppression and resistance among groups in specific socio-historical contexts, than through any intrinsic quality or weakness. Language regimes usually materialize from unrelated government policies which combine to support one language to the detriment of all others; the long-term effects of such regimes usually outlast the actual policies. In Saskatchewan, four different regimes have been identified, regimes which vary significantly from one another in appearance, but which share a common orientation. From 1875 to 1930, clearly repressive and restrictive language legislation imposed English on all minority groups and established Anglo-hegemony through coercion. The period 1931–64 is one of legislative silence in which anglo-hegemony was maintained through existing institutional arrangements. The third regime, of 1965–90, is one of favourable government funding and policies which, nevertheless, assured hegemony by assuming and supporting Anglo-domination. In the current regime of 1990 and beyond, market forces are presented as a substitute to government funding and policy. Claims of a public debt crisis are forcing virtually all governments into debt control which justifies funding cuts to 'non-essential' areas such as language. Cutbacks and institutional restructuring are likely to restrict access to resources and to continue reducing minority languages to purely symbolic forms with very little meaning in everyday life. The only exceptions will be aboriginal languages and French, where constitutional obligations may force some government support. A few languages such as Japanese and Spanish, may benefit from market imperatives but will not involve the transmission of group identity or heritage.

Other factors beyond language policies may have lasting repercussions on minority languages in Saskatchewan. These include the possibility of Quebec's independence and a possible anti-francophone backlash in English Canada, the coming to power of contemporary nativist political parties (such as the Reform Party) with their anti-minority orientation, and the cultural impact of multinational corporations and media. Globalization will further standardize English as the medium for international communication and extend Anglo-hegemony world wide, primarily through American technology, films and videos, video games, magazines, school material and computer software. With modern technology and communications systems, the disappearance of non-dominant languages will undoubtedly escalate, especially in the absence of compensating government support.

References

Barber, M. (1978). Canadianization through the schools before World War I: the attitudes and aims of the English speaking majority. In M. L. Kovacs (ed.), *Ethnic Canadians: Culture and Education* (pp. 281–294). Regina: Canadian Plains Research Centre.

Bastarache, M. (1989). Education rights of provincial official language minorities (Section 23). In G. Beaudoin and E. Ratushny (eds.), *The Canadian Charter of Rights and Freedoms* (pp. 687–705). Toronto: Carswell.

Calderwood, W. (1968). The rise and fall of the Ku Klux Klan in Saskatchewan. Unpublished M.A. thesis, University of Regina, Regina.

Courcelles, L. (1969). Problèmes scolaires dans l'Ouest. In Wade, M. (Ed.), *Regionalism in the Canadian Community* (pp. 83–99). Toronto: University of Toronto Press.

Denis, W. and Li, P. (1988). The politics of language loss: a Francophone case from Western Canada. *Journal of Education Policy*, 3, 351–370.

Denis, W. (1990). The politics of language. In P. Li (ed.), *Race and Ethnic Relations in Canada* (pp. 148–185). Toronto: Oxford University Press.

(1993). Ethnicité et conflits scolaires en Saskatchewan de 1905–1980. In L. Cardinal (ed.), *Une langue qui pense* (pp. 77–100). Ottawa: Les Presses de l'Université d'Ottawa.

Ens, A. (1994). *Subjects or Citizens? The Mennonite Experience in Canada, 1870–1925.* Ottawa: University of Ottawa Press.

Epp, F. (1982). *Mennonites in Canada, 1920–1940.* Toronto: Macmillan.

Gramsci, A. (1971). *Selections from Prison Notebooks.* New York: International Publishers.

Huel, R. (1970). The French Canadians and the language question, 1918. *Saskatchewan History*, 23, 1–15.

(1977). The Anderson Amendments and the secularization of Saskatchewan public schools. *Study Sessions, Canadian Catholic Historical Association*, 44, 61–76.

(1980). The Anderson Amendments: a half century later. *Study Sessions, Canadian Catholic Historical Association*, 47, 5–21.

Kyba, J. B. (1964). *The Saskatchewan General Elections of 1929.* Saskatoon : University of Saskatchewan, unpublished M. A. Thesis.

Lee, J. (1996). Constructing the Nation Through Multiculturalism, Language and Gender: An Extended Case Study of State Regulation and Community Resistance. Saskatoon: University of Saskatchewan, unpublished PhD Thesis.

Lupul, M. (ed.). (1982). *A Heritage in Transition: Essays in the History of Ukrainians in Canada.* Toronto: McClelland & Stewart.

Macleod, K. (1968). Politics, schools and the French language, 1881–1931. In N. Ward and D. Spafford (eds.), *Politics in Saskatchewan* (pp. 124–150). Don Mills: Longman.

Pal, L. (1993). *Interests of State.* Montreal: McGill-Queen's University Press.

Purich, D. (1988). *The Métis.* Toronto: James Lorimer.

Rottiers, R. (1977). *Soixante-cinq années de luttes ... esquisse historique de l'oeuvre de l'ACFC.* Regina: Author.

Royal Commission on Bilingualism and Biculturalism. (1970). *Report, Book IV: The Cultural Contribution of the Other Ethnic Groups.* Ottawa: The Queen's Printer.

Russell, P. (1993). *Constitutional Odyssey.* Toronto: University of Toronto Press.

Saskatchewan Department of Education. (1950–1992). *Annual Reports.*

Saskatchewan Education Indicators (1995). *K-12 Update.* Regina: Saskatchewan Education Training & Employment.

Sheppard, C. A. (1971). *The Law of Languages in Canada.* Ottawa: Information Canada.

Smith, D. (1968). The membership of the Saskatchewan legislative assembly: 1905–1966. In N. Ward and D. Spafford (eds.), *Politics in Saskatchewan* (pp. 178–206). Don Mills: Longman.

Swyripa, F. (1982). The Ukrainians and private education. In M. Lupul (ed.), *A Heritage in Transition: Essays in the History of Ukrainians in Canada* (pp. 244–262). Toronto: McClelland & Stewart.

Tremblay, A. and Bastarache, M. (1989). Language rights (Sections 16–22). In G. Beaudoin and E. Ratushny (eds.), *The Canadian Charter of Rights and Freedoms* (pp. 653–685). Toronto: Carswell.

Titley, B. (1986). Indian industrial schools in western Canada. In N. Sheehan, J. Wilson and D. Jones (eds.), *The West: Essays in Canadian Educational History* (pp. 133–153). Calgary: Detselig.

Map 10 Alberta

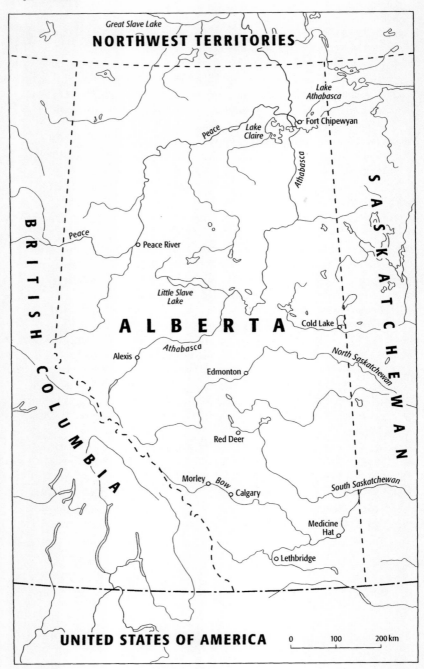

442

24 Language in Alberta: unilingualism in practice

James Frideres

INTRODUCTION

Coureurs de bois, natives and missionaries constituted the initial Albertan population and most non-English European minority languages lacked prestige as settlers came to Alberta. Moreover, pressure was exerted on the immigrant settlers to abandon their culture and linguistic heritage. While early settlers existed in heterogeneous linguistic, religious and ethnic communities, they enjoyed the freedom to use their mother tongue in their home and with friends and neighbours. Nevertheless, doing business with surrounding farmers and businessmen required the use of the *lingua franca* of the area – English. As Prokop (1990) points out, the economic success of 'King Wheat' necessitated a greater openness to the world and to the anglophone culture. The identification with, and support of, the political system also played an important role in the anglicization of immigrants.

During the first three decades of the twentieth century, the francophone presence was substantially weakened as other western European immigrants arrived. As Alberta became more urban and industrialized, it further linked itself to the anglo world. Still, the role of French in Alberta has a unique and important role in the language debate now taking place. Any attempt to treat the French as a special group in Alberta has long been resisted by provincial authorities, supported by its residents. Members of 'other' groups have supported the dominant language group's (English) argument that French should not hold a favoured position in the language hierarchy of Alberta and have felt that teaching French only promoted linguistic or ethnic chauvinism (Aunger, 1993b). As a result, there are problems in resolving the differences between constitutional provisions about language rights and the actual implementation of these rights. For example, it would seem that it is legal to speak French in the Legislative Assembly, yet it is not accepted. In addition, although the federal government has proclaimed a policy of bilingualism, it applies only to federal affairs; provincial governments are not obliged to implement such a policy.

HISTORY

From the late nineteenth century until mid twentieth, the dominant ideological perspective in Canada was imperialism (Ewanyshyn, 1994). Canada was to play a supporting role in British domination, and was to ensure that all its new citizens settling in the west (including native people) were proficient in English (Laferrière, 1984). The educational system was considered the prime agent and the Alberta government took significant steps to ensure that the children of immigrants would be exposed to schooling aimed at rapid assimilation. As Hornofluk (1995) notes, provincial authorities quickly came to realize that the public school was the most powerful mechanism for assimilating foreigners, and it instituted a massive campaign to encourage ethnic communities to establish public schools. At the same time, the province took various steps to ensure that it controlled the structure and content of education (Prokop, 1990a).

The Northwest Territories' constitutional provisions of 1877 established the use of French or English in the Legislative Assembly and in the courts – the first bilingual statement in the west. Given the large number of French in the area, this provision made sense. However, when the province was given the right to decide the language of the Assembly in 1892, it quickly opted to carry out its proceedings in English only.[1] With Alberta's entry into Confederation in 1905, the *Alberta Act* continued the official status of English and French in the legislative assembly and the courts even though the working realities of the province meant that all business was carried on in English (Lazaruk, 1992). There were provisions made for the use of languages other than English in some institutional settings during the early twentieth century but they were often not exercised because they were laden with state controls or placed undue burdens on the local residents. For example, a 1901 ordinance allowed for the hiring of a person to teach a course in any language, but parents had to cover all the costs.

As Julien (1995) argues, Alberta has not been favourably disposed to having any 'official' languages other than English since 1905. The linguistic make-up of the province throughout the first half of this century involves a preponderance of English speakers, a very small francophone minority and a large minority of speakers of other languages and English. This pattern has remained and today there is an even greater proportion of English-only speakers (90.1 per cent), a small group of French-only speakers (1 per cent) and a growing number of 'other'- only language speakers (6.9 per cent).

By 1915, the Alberta Legislature had passed a motion outlawing bilingualism in any form in the school system. And, for all practical purposes, French was outlawed in the Legislature and the judicial system (Sokolowski and Oishi, 1993). By 1919, bilingual public schools had been eliminated. Strict control over private non-English schools was exercised through a complex process of certification, hiring practices and school inspections. Regions with high numbers of French and Ruthenians were of particular interest to school boards, and schools were closed if they did not offer proper and efficient (read English) instruction (Jaenen, 1970; Prokop, 1990b). This policy of English unilingualism remained the dominant ideology in Alberta until the 1960s. Many ethno-cultural groups had attempted, but failed, to gather support for the offering and legitimizing of 'ethnic' languages at school.

During the 1960s, all language groups in Alberta benefited from the larger struggle for human rights across the nation. The adoption of the Canadian Bill of Rights in 1960 and the radical liberalization of federal immigration regulations in 1962 marked the beginnings of a new phase in Canada's approach to cultural diversity (Nesbitt and Young, 1995). The creation of the Bilingualism and Biculturalism Commission in the early 1960s provided both a reaffirmation of French as a 'charter' language and the necessary legitimization francophones needed to move forward in their quest for a bilingual Canada. The Royal Commission recommended that bilingual and unilingual French schools be created in all of the provinces (Russell, Knopff and Morton, 1990). The subsequent passing of the Official Languages Act in 1969 made Canada an officially bilingual country, and this formalized the legal use of French or English in parliament, in federal agencies and in the federal courts. At the same time, the Commission also acknowledged the social and economic contributions of other ethnic groups to the creation and vitality of Canadian society (Schneiderman, 1991). This legitimacy allowed these unofficial groups to continue their demands for rights – including language rights – they had previously thought unattainable, and established the groundwork for the creation of a multicultural policy in 1971.

However, more than 100 years after the implementation of the Northwest Territories Act, the Alberta Legislature adopted Resolution 27, which declared English to be the working language of the Assembly. Then, one year later, under the new provincial Languages Act of 1988, Albertans lost the right to have bills, statutes, records or journals of the Assembly printed in any language other than English. This occurred because of a 'language challenge' in which a member rose in the Legislature and began to speak in French. He was ruled out of order and required to speak English in the Assembly; he appealed the decision and a committee was created to resolve the issue. The central point was whether or not French could be spoken as guaranteed under Section 110 of the original

Northwest Territories Act, or if this had been repealed by subsequent Acts passed in the Northwest Territories and Alberta. While the committee did not answer the question, Resolution 27 was passed. This means that only English will be spoken in the Assembly unless a member gives the Speaker prior notice.

In 1988, the Supreme Court of Canada (in the *Mercure* case) upheld the validity of speaking French in Saskatchewan. Since both Saskatchewan and Alberta emerged out of the same Northwest Territories, francophone Albertans had the same rights by implication (Aunger, 1989). This case also relates to the use of French in the courts and suggests that the accused, the judge and court officials have the right to use either French or English, and that an interpreter must be available for those who are unable to understand one of the official languages. In 1994 the Supreme Court (R. vs. Tran) clearly defined the meaning of the right to interpreter assistance under Section 14 of the Charter, and noted that any violation of this section would result in the quashing of any conviction and lead to a new trial. Alberta has resisted implementing this decision even though the ruling would not seem to cause great harm or to be fiscally irresponsible.

In summary, the province of Alberta has taken a strong and vigorous approach to maintaining a unilingual policy. While there has been a softening of this approach over the past decade, the province has continued to argue for and maintain a dominant English thrust. The province argues that English is the second most commonly used language in the world with some 500 million speakers (French has 100 million). External events, such as the passing of the Multiculturalism Act and the heavy influx of immigrants from non-traditional sources, have forced the government to make some provisions for languages other than English and French.

LANGUAGE IN SOCIAL AND DEMOGRAPHIC PERSPECTIVE

Alberta's initial settlement occurred in the late nineteenth and early twentieth centuries with western European agricultural immigrants. Later immigrants were much better educated and settled in the urban centres. However, because Alberta remained tied to agricultural and oil/gas extraction activities, few immigrants found the province attractive. By the late 1970s and the early 1980s, the annual number of international immigrants approached 20,000 and most did not originate in the traditional European source countries. As the 1980s progressed, and Alberta experienced a severe recession, the numbers decreased, reaching a low of 9,000 in 1985. Today, it is estimated that well over 20,000 immigrants enter Alberta per year; over half are from Asia (52.9 per cent), with substantial numbers coming from Europe (25.8 per cent). The remainder are

Table 24.1 Mother tongue of Albertans for selected groups, 1921–1991 (percentage)

Language	1991[1]	1961	1941	1921[2]
English	83.4	72.2	62.9	69.8
French	2.1	3.2	4.0	4.7
Aboriginal	1.0	1.2	2.4	–
German	2.9	7.3	7.9	6.8
Italian	1.0	1.0	<1.0	<1.0
Polish	<1.0	1.3	2.4	<1.0
Chinese	2.1	<1.0	<1.0	1.0
Dutch	1.0	1.9	1.0	<1.0
Ukrainian	1.5	6.3	9.4	<1.0
Scandinavian[3]	<1.0	1.0	5.1	6.7
Japanese	<1.0	<1.0	0.0	0.0
Russian	<1.0	<1.0	1.1	1.7
Hungarian	<1.0	1.0	1.1	1.7
Other	7.0	1.0	4.8	5.7

1 Single only responses
2 Mother tongue of population ten years and older, exclusive of Aboriginals
3 Includes Norwegian, Swedish, Danish
Source: Census of Canada.

from Central and South America (9.3 per cent), Africa (5.5 per cent), the USA (4.3 per cent) and Australia and the South Pacific (2.1 per cent) (Nath, 1991).

The ethnic distribution of Alberta since the turn of the century reveals that, with the exception of native peoples, few demographic changes occurred until the 1970s. Since then there has been an influx of many different ethnic groups (all settling in the major urban centres) which has produced the current multi-cultural profile. For example, Asians made up 6.8 per cent of the 'ethnic' population of Alberta by 1991 – prior to this time they constituted less than 1 per cent of the population. There has also been a dramatic decrease in the percentage of 'ethnics' from traditional European sources.

The language profile of Albertans has of course shifted with these ethnic changes. Table 24.1 shows that the influence of English has become pervasive over time, with dramatic decreases in 'traditional languages' like German, Scandinavian and Ukrainian. However, in the recent past there has been an increase in new mother tongues (e.g., Chinese, Indo-Iranian and Vietnamese). Census data (not shown in table 24.1) reveal that six languages (Spanish, Portuguese, Arabic, Tagalog, Vietnamese and Punjabi) were virtually absent until the 1971 census. Today, each makes up between three quarters and one percent of Albertans speaking a non-official mother tongue. On the other hand, we find that languages such as Slovak, Romanian and Yiddish have almost disappeared; each had a sizeable number of speakers at the turn of the century. In spite of the diverse ethnic and linguistic population, most individuals today (over 83 per cent) have English as their only mother tongue.

The census question asked about language use at home only assesses language patterns in one domain; it does not ascertain language use in other social contexts (e.g., work, school). Nevertheless, it would be reasonable to assume that the home is the domain in which the original language will be used the most, and the last domain in which it would be used before the individual shifts his/her language use. As such, deVries (1990) suggests that the use of an ethnic language at home may be taken as indicating at least *some* degree of ethnic language maintenance; conversely, the lack of an ethnic language at home indicates that a language shift is occurring. Some 92 per cent of all Albertans now speak English at home. However, many of these individuals are bilingual and thus may also speak another home language besides English. Still, among older immigrant groups, such as Ukrainians, Germans and Italians, home 'ethnic' language use has declined substantially over the years. For example, fewer than 10 per cent of Germans and Ukrainians speak their language at home.

French (and other romance languages), aboriginal and Indo-Iranian varieties are also spoken at home but the data show that fewer than 1 per cent of Alberta residents exclusively speak these languages there. A comparison of mother-tongue and home-language use shows that 99.5 per cent of those with English mother tongue speak English in the home, while only 31 per cent of those with French mother tongue speak French at home. Among those individuals who have neither official language (as mother tongue), 41.7 per cent speak a non-official language at home while 51.9 per cent speak English. For example, Portuguese, South Asians and Chinese have a home-language use rate between 50 and 67 per cent.

While the province is cautiously supportive of multiculturalism, it wants it placed within the context of English (Aunger, 1989). Resistance to bilingualism (of any sort) has been long-standing and Simeon and Blake (1980) have concluded that, while other regions in the country were becoming more conciliatory towards the use of French, Albertans were becoming more resistant. Overall, the data in table 24.1 show a high level of English usage and demonstrate that language shift for the older immigrant groups has nearly been completed. Nevertheless, the influx of non-English-speaking immigrants, as well as the globalization of the economy, have had an impact on both official policy and the programmes supported by provincial authorities.

448

LANGUAGE IN THE EDUCATIONAL CONTEXT

Up until the first half of this century, native languages and cultures were suppressed. However, since education for natives was considered a federal responsibility, provincial authorities did not concern themselves when native educational services were contracted out to various religious organizations. In a residential school structure, the teaching and speaking of native languages were forbidden and native cultures verged on extinction. By the 1970s, however, provinces were encouraged to provide educational services for status Indians through the establishment of 'integrated' schools. While the venue changed, the legitimacy of native language and culture by educational authorities did not. Nevertheless, by the late 1970s, native people had convinced the federal government to develop a policy of native control of education. As a result, native education today can range from federally supported but locally controlled schools on the reserves, to provincially supported schools with varying degrees of local control over curricula and the hiring of teachers. In 1985, the Language Services Branch of Alberta Education formed the Native Language Ad Hoc Committee to develop guidelines for native language programmes. Two criteria guided their actions. First, they involved the native community in developing the programme and, second, they made sure that the programmes met the needs of the local community. The Native Education Project of Alberta Education is also involved in developing native language programmes.

Notwithstanding the many issues that emerged from the Native Education programme, much of the concern about languages in schools has focused on French.[2] Since the 1870s, bitter political battles over French in the classroom have occurred (Prokop, 1990b). At the time the province was created, there was a large French-speaking population whose influence in the social and economic structure was considerable. However, by the early twentieth century, the proportion of French speakers in Alberta had decreased considerably, and French mother-tongue claimants have since remained stable at between 2.4 and 2.8 per cent. Nevertheless, this group has been an educational 'flashpoint'. The impact of Quebec's concern with language has also influenced provincial authorities in Alberta. The end result has been a continuous debate between francophones and the province regarding their rights and limitations.

Alberta's main goal was to assimilate early settlers to the ideals of Canadian and British nationalism (Hornofluk, 1995), and various strategies were employed to encourage parents to send their children to school. For example, foreign-language instruction was introduced in certain areas of the province. Once in school, however, the students were exposed to a curriculum which minimized language (other than English) and focused on English history, geography and literature. The hidden agenda of assimilation was more powerful than the token gestures of language courses (Harasymiw, 1994).³ Provincial officials were quick to remind immigrants that English was the language of the country and was to be the language of the schools (Jaenen, 1970).

The educational system of Alberta maintained, for nearly half a century, that French was not a language the province wanted to support. It would not be until the 1950s that some softening occurred, and the province agreed that one hour of French could be taught per day. By 1955 there were about 6,000 students enrolled in French in 240 classrooms, although most of them were in northern Alberta. In 1968 and 1970 there were additional amendments to the Alberta School Act which extended French into the first year of high school and allowed for the establishment of local advisory boards. Boards could, by resolution, also instruct a school board to authorize the use of any language as the medium of instruction.⁴

Until 1982, no guarantees existed for French-language schooling (Aunger, 1995). Formal bilingual education was never provided for in legislation and, from 1903 onward, instruction in languages other than English was restricted to the last hour of the school day. It would not be until the mid-1960s that any substantial change to this ideology was introduced, when it was seen that the policy of assimilation had not been successful, and the rejection of second languages in the school system was reversed (Hornofluk, 1995). The famous UNESCO statement of 1953, which claimed that the best medium of instruction is the child's mother tongue, was influential (Harris, 1995). The next decade brought about a new acceptance of ethno-cultural groups' attempts to preserve their unique identities. The movement to establish bilingual schools was spearheaded by the Franco-Albertan communities, whose efforts were supported by the newly established Bilingual and Bicultural Commission. While its views were not binding, this Commission recommended that the official-language minority be guaranteed its own schools in districts where it constituted at least ten percent of the population, or in urban areas where the numbers warranted (Aunger, 1995). Moreover, the adoption of the Official Languages Act in 1969 influenced both provincial-government and individual attitudes.⁵

In 1964, the Alberta School Act was changed so that French could be the language of instructon from Grades 1 to 3 (Julien, 1995). By 1968, seeing the Official Languages Act on the horizon, the province further liberalized its policy and allowed French to be taught from kindergarten to Grade 12. Further amendments to the Alberta School Act were made in 1971. First, 'other' languages were allowed as mediums of instruction and a pilot project with Ukrainian was approved (Sokolowski, 1991). The second change allowed for instruction in languages other than English or French for up to half the day.

Julien (1995) argues that the popularity of French immersion schools in the 1970s was influential in the wider use of French in Alberta. Moreover, it could now be the language of instruction for half the school day. By 1976, with the passing of the French Language Regulation, all restrictions on the use of French at school were removed, with the exception that English had to be taught as a subject. The Language Services Branch was established in 1978 and became responsible for providing services to the second-language students (e.g., immersion programmes). During the decade 1974–84, Sokolowski (1991) argues, Alberta actually became the leader in heritage-language education in Canada. There was widespread acceptance of the 'two-language interaction' explanation of minority-group children's educational performance (Cummins, 1978). This explanation basically held that the poor performance of minority children arose because the first language was not maintained in the school system long enough for the student to become proficient in his/her minority language, before adding on the majority language (Harris, 1995).

By the 1980s, francophones in Alberta were rejecting the model outlined by the provincial government and demanding separate school facilities for their students. Up until this time, many people felt that immersion was an acceptable strategy for learning French. In fact, most francophone educators and the Association canadienne-française d'Alberta supported it and, by 1982, there were nearly 13,000 students enrolled in French immersion programmes. However, community leaders and visionary educators began to demand further changes. They argued that while immersion programmes allowed anglophone students to learn French, they did not sufficiently fulfil the rights of francophone parents and were, in fact, 'assimilation factories'. They insisted that French-language rights were entrenched in Section 23 of the Charter of Rights and Freedoms. There was considerable resistance to this argument by school boards and politicians, and attempts by the community to create French schools were further delayed.

Communities began to organize in an attempt to lobby for their cause. For example, in 1982, Edmonton francophones formed the Association de Julie-et-Georges Bugnet. This body condemned the immersion school and advocated the creation of separate schools and school boards for francophone students (Aunger, 1993a). Although the association was able to create a francophone school, it was short lived and closed after only a few months of operation.

451

More important was the court action the association launched, which argued that the Alberta government had denied their rights to establish a school, pursuant to the Charter. The province agreed to recognize minority schools as distinct from immersion schools and adopted a new School Act in 1988. This new Act did not provide, however, for the management of these schools by a French-speaking minority.

The Language Education Policy for Alberta was passed in 1988. Within the legal framework of the School Act, this policy provides a guide for future discretionary action; it also provides Albertans with an opportunity to learn languages other than English and French, even though second-language study is not a mandatory component of school programming in Alberta, as it is in most other regions of Canada. The new policy officially acknowledged francophone rights, and also formalized a language hierarchy for the province (Hébert, 1989). English is the most important language and all efforts are to be made to ensure that students whose first language is not English will receive the necessary classes to make them proficient. There is a programme of 'rapid mainstreaming' which allows non-English-speaking individuals to receive language training. There are, at the same time, promises to provide heritage and aboriginal language programmes.

In 1990, the Supreme Court ruled that the Act was legally incompatible with the Charter and held that francophones had the right to their own schools and to some degree of control over their operation. At the same time, the court ruled that sufficient numbers of students were necessary before provinces could be compelled to enact the rights granted under Section 23 of the Charter. It instructed the Alberta government to make its language laws compatible with the Charter and the government agreed to introduce legislation to bring its School Act into line (Le Blanc, 1995). However, it was two years before Alberta introduced legislation to conform to the Court's decision; it created seven francophone education regions, as well as establishing French-language school boards in 1994.[6] Until 1995, the school board was the cornerstone of the administration of educational programmes. However, recent legislative changes have changed this structure and new authority structures are emerging.

At the same time, a parents' group pushed for a separate francophone public school system in Edmonton; their arguments were similar to those presented by francophones elsewhere in the province. Intense lobbying by a variety of French organizations occurred when it was learned that the annual rate of assimilation in education was 63 per cent, and that the number of individuals speaking French at home had dramatically decreased.[7] Figures showed that there had been a substantial loss of French speakers between 1981 and 1991 (20,000 to 30,000).

Unlike other provinces, Alberta established a working group on French-language education to devise a strategy for implementing a new policy. Their mandate was to make recommendations to the provincial government regarding the establishment of francophone school boards, and to bring the School Act in line with the Charter. Before the final report, the group recommended that francophone school boards be created (Munro, 1991). In the final report itself, several recommendations were made. However, the Minister of Education refused to bring these before the Legislative Assembly, arguing that other Albertans should have some imput before a bill was drafted. In light of the government's delay, school boards across the province refused to take action on the establishment of francophone schools. Nevertheless, by 1992, Alberta agreed to accept, in principle, the concept of francophone school boards. With the exception of taxation, these school boards have the same powers as existing school boards.

In summary, while French is now entrenched within the school system, three important changes date from the implementation of the 1988 policy. First, school boards for the provision of French instruction are now in place. Second, the French-language programme can now be used exclusively for francophone students. A third change is that any school wishing to deliver instruction in French no longer has to submit its proposal to the Minister of Education for approval.

LANGUAGE PROGRAMMES AND USE TODAY

Even though the federal government has delegated authority for education to the provinces, it still plays a role. Its impact can be seen in the legislation that governs official languages, minority education rights and the creation of a multicultural Canada. There continues to be federal funding of minority-language education and second-language instruction programmes, although funding for out-of-school international-language programmes has ceased.[8] Out-of-school programming is covered by the Alberta Department of Citizenship, Policy and Programs. Various federal government departments, such as Heritage Canada, also support specific requests for innovative projects. Moreover, private philanthropic organizations support some language programmes.

Today there are five basic types of language instruction taking place in the Alberta educational system. The first is the French language programme. Here the entire school operates in French and all subjects are taught in French.

The board takes into consideration the interests of the French community. The second type is French immersion: French is the sole medium of instruction in Grades 1–3 and comprises 80 per cent of the instruction in Grades 4–12; students of any cultural or linguistic background may enrol. Schools may be within the public or separate system. A third type of instruction is partial immersion, or a bilingual programme. Languages other than English are used in the classroom up to 50 per cent of the time. At present, there are only six provincially-approved bilingual language programmes: Ukrainian (1974), Hebrew (1975), German (1978), Arabic and Chinese (1982), and Polish (1984). These programmes are optional alternatives to the regular programmes in which English is the language of instruction; they follow the regular Alberta curriculum. Enrolment in bilingual programmes has shown moderate increases over the past few years. In the 1994–95 year, enrolments were as follows: Arabic (435), Mandarin (855), Hebrew (291), Polish (320), German (537) and Ukrainian (1,309). The fourth type of instruction is the 'second language programme' in which a language is the *subject* (not the medium) of instruction. Generally, heritage and/or international-language programmes are offered under this heading, optional second-language courses that are offered for up to forty minutes per day. However, they can also be offered as partial immersion programmes. At present, German and Ukrainian are offered at the junior high school level while German, Ukrainian, Italian, Latin, Japanese and Spanish are offered at senior high schools. Each programme is provincially sanctioned and follows provincial curricula.[9] Finally, there is a fifth type of language instruction – the 'cultural schools programme' – which involves private instruction outside of provincially approved schools and outside of school hours (e.g., special arrangements exist for Hutterite Colonies).

Currently, the Alberta school system offers courses in seventeen different languages. Table 24.2 provides a general picture of enrolment trends over the past five years. Over one-third of all Alberta high school students enrol in a second-language course, about 85 per cent of them in French. However, students do not continue with their second-language studies; depending upon the specific language, between 40 per cent and 85 per cent attrition rates occur between Grades 10 and 12.

THE FUTURE OF SECOND LANGUAGES IN ALBERTA

Table 24.2 indicates considerable interest in languages at the elementary and secondary school levels. In addition, post-secondary institutions have become more active in the teaching of international languages, and there has been a steady increase in enrolment figures for language classes over the past

Table 24.2 Language courses and enrolments in Alberta high schools, 1989–1995

Language	1989–90	1990–91	1991–92	1992–93	1993–94
Arabic		3		3	7
Blackfoot	27	74	87	122	153
Chinese	111	214	304	386	568
Cree	86	133	256	282	153
French	32,386	32,670	38,490	40,134	36,637
German	2,420	2,533	2,769	2,844	3,010
Greek	22	43	37	56	91
Hebrew	12	10	9	19	29
Hungarian		9	4		2
Italian	313	346	423	491	489
Japanese	100	300	423	517	513
Latin	162	142	188	167	226
Polish	28	42	63	53	95
Portuguese	372	458	673	1,168	1,471
Swedish	8	8	13	13	13
Ukrainian	252	263	273	302	355

Source: Personal correspondence, J. Sokolowski, Alberta Department of Education, Edmonton, Alberta.

two decades. The language of choice has changed from Latin and French, to languages of the early western European immigrants, to more global languages. For example we find that, in the past decade, enrolments in Spanish, Chinese and Japanese have shown the greatest increase.

Armed with community and student support, many cultural and linguistic groups have now begun actively to lobby for bilingual programmes. They have found support for their concerns in the federal Act for the Preservation and Enhancement of Multiculturalism in Canada. Section 3 of the Act aims to preserve and enhance the use of languages other than French and English, while strengthening the status and use of the official languages (Landry, 1993). Section 23 of the Charter also lends support to bilingual education, and Section 22 safeguards the rights and privileges of non-official languages in Canada.

At the same time, anti-language forces have pointed to the high cost of running language programmes with small enrolments, and question the efficiency and effectiveness of such programmes. Some provincial politicians have asked the government to more formally specify the role of English – more restrictive provisions with regard to international languages would make English the official language of government, and they feel that the government has an obligation to preserve and enhance the role of English. There has been some discussion of even more restrictive measures, such as stopping bilingual education, particularly French. The practical consequences would mean that budgets for schools providing bilingual education would be cut. At a more symbolic level, government would be sending a message that current immigrants are unwilling to participate in the larger community, and have to be coerced into learning English. There might also be increased resentment and hostility towards speakers of foreign languages, which might lead to 'English-only' workplace rules.

CURRENT ISSUES FOR ALBERTA

Current trends in Europe and elsewhere indicate that most countries are increasing the emphasis on language training. This is particularly true for non-traditional languages such as Japanese and Mandarin, now considered economically critical. There is a belief that, if countries are to be competitive in the global economy, they must have a facility in languages extending beyond those of their traditional trading partners. The province of Alberta has recently become a cautious supporter of international-language training in the schools. The new line of thinking reflects the efforts of the lobbying activities of the business sector in their quest for creating new markets. In short, support for international-language programmes is based upon their economic significance for the province. In order to develop new markets, Alberta will need to link with nontraditional trading partners, many of which will not have English as the *lingua franca*. For example, while Albertans stand to benefit under the NAFTA Agreement, very few have the language skills necessary to carry out business in a Spanish milieu.

The 1988 language education policy made school boards responsible for initiating new language programmes. However, it is clear that in times of constraint and cutback, they will be unable to augment their language programmes. As Ewanyshyn (1994) notes, this policy provides a framework, and some direction for schools, but it does not direct funds. On the one hand, bilingual education is supported in provincial legislation and policy. However, at the same time, bilingual programmes are considered alternative ones and not part of basic education. As such, they receive equal treatment with French-as-a-second-language, French immersion and native-language programmes.

Finally, many of the language programmes are closely associated with specific ethno-cultural groups and the policy of multiculturalism, not with economic or other policies. Thus, as multiculturalism has come under attack, so have the language programmes. Moreover, the language policy of Alberta does not mention federal and provincial legislation which provides for diverse language instruction.

It neglects to identify the government's responsibility to promote a favourable public climate for language learning. Furthermore, it discriminates among English, French, ESL and other language programmes by providing substantially different types of government support, depending upon the language taught. Finally, the government of Alberta does not recognize that once diverse language instruction is accepted, and becomes a provincial programme where numbers warrant, funding and services must be provided equitably and sufficiently to ensure that all students, regardless of the programme, have a high quality of education. Local school boards now use the 1988 policy to distinguish between official and 'other' language programmes; they support them differently because the province funds them differently. In addition, as schools are forced to take cutbacks, low funded programmes are cut first.

Notes

1 However, it would seem that there was not an official proclamation of this decision and thus French continues to have a legal status. This position was upheld in the Alberta Court of Queens Bench in 1982.

2 It would seem that there has not been any serious concern about aboriginal languages becoming part of the overall provincial linguistic mosaic, no doubt due to the prevailing negative stereotypes of native people.

3 In 1913, the Truancy Act and Compulsory Attendance Act was amended so that trustees could not close their schools without the approval of the minister of education. This was important because the Ukrainian schools usually closed during the thirty-one days of the year that coincided with Ukrainian religious holidays. The new Act stopped this practice and only allowed for closure during Christmas.

4 A distinction is made between the use of a second language as a 'subject of instruction' and as a 'language of instruction'.

5 The province has supported the principle of French-language minority schools for some time (e.g., it supported the Charter); however, it has resisted the actual establishment of these schools in the province.

6 In 1984, there were two francophone schools in Alberta. By 1992, over 12 schools were operating, with a student enrolment of 2062, up from 367 in 1984.

7 This figure represents the percentage of students who drop out of a French language program in primary and secondary school.

8 Funding for in-school international-language programmes does not exist.

9 There are also locally developed heritage and international-language courses which do not have provincial curricula. These courses are designed to meet the needs of the community and are available at both the junior and senior high school level. At present the programmes are: Arabic, Hebrew, Japanese, Hungarian, Mandarin, Polish and Swedish. At one time or another, courses in Lithuanian, Spanish and Russian have also been offered.

James Frideres

References

Aunger, E. (1995). Segmental autonomy and dispersed minorities: French-language school boards in Canada. Paper given at the Conference on the Governance of Dispersed Ethnic Groups, University of Ottawa, June.

(1993a). La legislation Albertaine en matiere de language. Paper presented at L'Association des juristes d'expression française de l'Alberta, Edmonton. October.

(1993b). The decline of a French-speaking enclave: a case study of social contact and language shift in Alberta. *Canadian Ethnic Studies, 25*(2), 65–83.

(1989). Language and law in the province of Alberta. In P. Pupier and J. Woehrling (eds.), *Language and Law* (pp. 232–265). Montreal: Wilson & Lafleur.

Cummins, J. (1978). Educational implications of mother tongue maintenance in minority language children. *Canadian Modern Language Review, 34,* 395–416.

deVries, J. (1990). Ethnic language maintenance and shift. In S. Halli, F. Trovato and L. Driedger (eds.), *Ethnic Demography* (pp. 163–178). Ottawa: Carleton University Press.

Ewanyshyn, E. (1994). Implementation of a heritage language program: critical issues in Ukrainian bilingual education. *Alberta Modern Language Journal, 31*(3), 8–16.

Harasymiw, E. V. (1994). Alberta's language education policy: vision in the rearview mirror. *Alberta Modern Language Journal, 30*(3), 4–24.

Harris, S. (1995). Evolution of bilingual education theory in northern territory aboriginal schools. *International Journal of the Sociology of Language, 113,* 7–22.

Hébert, Y. (1989). A language education policy for Alberta. *Multicultural Education Council Newsletter, 11* (3), 1–5.

Hornofluk, C. (1995). Ukrainian education in Alberta – a historical overview. *Multicultural Education Journal, 13* (1), 21–27.

Jaenen, C. (1970). Ruthenian schools in western Canada. In D. Jones, N. Sheehan and R. Stamp (eds.), *Shaping the Schools of the Canadian West* (pp. 39–58). Calgary: Detselig.

Julien, R. (1995). The evolution of Francophone schools: the case of Alberta (1962–1993). *Canadian Modern Language Review, 49* (4), 717–733.

Laferrière, M. (1984). Languages, ideologies, and multicultural education in Canada. In R. Samuda, J. Berry and M. Laferrière (eds.), *Multiculturalism in Canada* (pp. 171–183). Toronto: Allyn and Bacon.

Landry, R. (1993). Déterminisme et détermination: vers une pedagogie de l'excellence en milieu minoritaire. *Canadian Modern Language Review, 49,* 887–925.

Lazaruk, W. (1992). Heritage and intergenerational language education in Alberta. *Alberta Modern Language Journal, 29* (1), 11–16.

Le Blanc, J.-C. (1995). Guidelines for the implementation of Part VII of the Official Languages Act. *Canadian Centre for Linguistic Rights, 2* (2), 14–17.

Martel, A. (1991). *Official Language Minority Education Rights in Canada: From Instruction to Management.* Ottawa: Office of the Commissioner of Official Languages.

458

Munro, K. (1991). French language and educational rights in Alberta: an historical perspective. In D. Schneiderman (ed.), *Language and the State* (pp. 251-264). Quebec: Yvon Blais.

Nath, S. (1991). *Calgary's Demographic and Social Trends.* Calgary: Statistical Services Division.

Nesbitt, B. and Young, J. (1995). Canada's policy of multiculturalism. *Mezinarodni Politika* (Czech Republic), 14-24.

Prokop, M. (1990a). *The German Language in Alberta.* Edmonton: University of Alberta Press.

Prokop, M. (1990b). A historical view of legislation governing second languages in Alberta schools. *Alberta Modern Language Journal, 27*(1), 16-25.

Russell, P., Knopff, R. and Morton, T. (1990). *Federalism and the Charter.* Ottawa: Carleton University Press.

Schneiderman, D. (1991). *Language and the State.* Quebec: Yvon Blais.

Simeon, R. and Blake, D. (1980). Provincial political cultures in Canada. In D. Elkins and R. Simeon (eds.), *Small Worlds: Provinces and Parties in Canadian Political Life* (pp. 77-105). Toronto: Methuen.

Sokolowski, J. (1991). Bilingual education in Alberta: past, present and future. *Alberta Modern Language Journal, 28* (1), 17-25.

Sokolowski, J. and Oishi, M. (1993). Native language and culture programs in Alberta provincial schools: a brief overview. *Alberta Modern Language Journal, 30* (2), 39-42.

Map 11 British Columbia

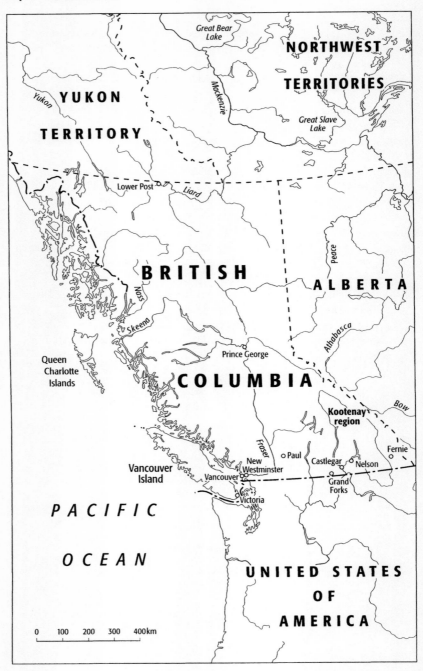

25 Language in British Columbia

Gunter Schaarschmidt

The ideal format for a linguistic profile of British Columbia would no doubt have been along the lines of Beltramo's (1981) profile of Montana in the USA. However, due to time and space limitations, the present outline can only touch upon the three major groups in British Columbia (henceforth BC) – First Nations languages, the founding languages and heritage languages.

FIRST NATIONS LANGUAGES

Beringia – the Bering Strait land bridge – allowed Paleo-Siberians, or Paleo-Indians, to migrate across a 1,000-mile stretch of tundra from Asia to North America roughly 50,000 years ago (see Champagne, 1994). It is assumed 'that stable communities have existed along the northwest Pacific for about 10,000 years – roughly since the civilization of the Egyptians' (Kramer, 1994, p. 14). At present, there are seven distinct aboriginal language families located in BC: Tsimshian, Athapaskan (part of the Na-Dene phylum), Haida, Salishan, Wakashan, Tlingit and Kutenai (for the northwest coast, see Sturtevant, 1990; for interior BC, see Hawthorn *et al.*, 1960).

Table 25.1 shows the number of speakers of First Nations languages in BC as opposed to the relevant population size (the data are based on Grimes, 1988).

According to the 1981 Census of Canada, 3 per cent of BC's population identified themselves as native people (the Canadian average is 2 per cent). In Canada, as a whole, six out of ten native people reported English as the first language they learned as children, while only three in ten claimed a native language as their mother tongue. These data are borne out by the statistics given in table 25.1 – less than 25 per cent of BC's native population actually speak a First Nations language. Yet, it seems that there is hope in the numbers reported in the 1991 census: the percentage of persons identifying themselves as native people has gone up to 5 per cent (Canada total, 3.7 per cent), and the number of

Table 25.1 First Nations languages of British Columbia

Language family	No. of speakers	Population	Area (if beyond BC)
Athapaskan			
Beaver	500	600	Alberta
Carrier (Central)	1,500	2,100	
Carrier (Southern)	500		
Chilcotin	1,200	1,800	
Kaska	500	700	Yukon
Sekani	150	600	
Tahltan	100	750	
Haida	295	2,000	US
Kutenai	100		US
Salishan			
Bella Coola	150	700	
Comox	400	800	
Halkomelem	500	6,700	
Lillooet	500	2,800	
Okanagan	500	3,000	US
Pentlatch	extinct	40	
Straits Salish	50	3,000	US
Sechelt	15	550	
Shuswap	500	3,000	
Squamish	20	1,300	
Thompson	350	3,000	
Tlingit	135	9,500	US
Tsimshian			
Nass-Gitksan	2,500	5,000	
Tsimshian	1,435	4,000	US
Wakashan			
Heiltsuk	450	1,200	
Kwakiutl	1,000	3,300	
Nootka	500	3,500	

speakers seems to have risen as well for certain languages or language groups. For example, 2,605 people identified themselves as speakers of Wakashan (as opposed to the total of 1,950 reported in table 25.1), while Kutenai seems to persist, with a slight increase to 135 speakers. But the other groups all seem to have suffered a numerical decline, with Haida down to 135 speakers and Salishan to 2,370. All in all, the 1991 census reported 192,765 First Nations speakers in Canada, of whom 7.1 per cent reside in BC. If the group of BC First Nations speakers was not as diverse as it is, that figure could be compared with the total of 196,895 speakers of a heritage language, viz. Polish, of whom also

7.1 per cent reside in BC. As things stand, however, to use Kinkade's terminology (1991), none of the First Nations languages in BC is 'viable' – i.e., with a large enough base of speakers at all ages to ensure long-term survival. A few, such as Chilcotin and Carrier (Athapaskan) are fortunate enough to be located in relatively isolated areas of BC, and as long as this situation continues there is little reason for the more than 1,000 speakers of each language to switch to English. Nass-Gitksan (Tsimshian) owes its relatively large language maintenance rate to a strong language awareness in a well-organized community. However, the entire Salishan language family, most of Wakashan, and the isolates Haida and Kutenai are on the list of endangered languages, even though educational revival programmes exist for some of these languages or some bands within them. The increasing importance of native-studies programmes within educational institutions will no doubt also aid in the development of language programmes for children and adults. More importantly, perhaps, the possibility of creating a national First Nations University would be one of the best means of ensuring the survival of at least larger First Nations languages, especially Cree (for the concept of a First Nations University, see Hampton and Wolfson, 1994). How such a global approach to aboriginal education might aid the First Nations language groups in BC is difficult to foresee. It is no doubt correct that, of all the First Nations languages of Canada, 'Cree surely comes closest to occupying the position of a national language' (Kaye, 1979, p. 22). But the fact remains that Cree is not spoken in BC. Would First Nations speakers of BC be prepared to accept Cree as a First Nations common language in Canada, or would they prefer to continue on the road towards English? The current debate on this issue is inconclusive but it is worth noting that the Native Education Centre (NEC) in Vancouver does not offer First Nations languages as part of its day programmes (Cree and Gitksan were taught at night school at one time) even though students seem to feel that at least one First Nations language should be taught (Haig-Brown, 1995).

FOUNDING LANGUAGES

English
While the large majority of British Columbians have English as their first language, their total weight in the province is steadily declining. In the early 1990s one in every five British Columbians spoke a language other than English (in the 1986 census, 81 per cent gave English as their first language; in 1991, 79.4 per cent).

French

Of the two founding languages of Canada, French has become a minority variety in BC. Although they never formed any concentrated settlements in any particular area or town district, the French-Canadian *voyageurs* (pioneers and explorers recruited mainly from the St Lawrence Valley) made up 60 per cent of the non-native coastal population in 1838; in 1986, only 1.3 per cent of the province's population was French-speaking (Greene *et al.*, 1991). At least, there has not been a decrease in French-speaking British Columbians: the 1991 census reports 45,265 persons with French as their first language out of the total BC population of 3,282,065.

Interest by the English-Canadian population in French has been considerable, judging from the number of schools offering immersion courses and the number of students enrolled in such courses. After the decision in 1970 by the Secretary of State of Canada to fund education programmes for French minorities in the various provinces, BC launched French immersion programmes in fifty-six schools among the seventy-five provincial school boards, with a total enrolment of 4,800. It is worth noting that Vancouver Island 'has the highest proportion of Immersion Schools in all English Canada' (Greene *et al.*, 1991, p. 173). Students can begin the immersion programme at the kindergarten level or in Grade 1.

HERITAGE LANGUAGES

With the exception of Chinese and Russian, BC does not have large-scale concentrated settlements of immigrant communities. There seems to have been a bit of a spillover from Alberta, with Ukrainian communities (probably migrant) in the Peace River district and in the mining area of Fernie, close to the Alberta border (Young, 1931). Chinese settlement is both of distant and very recent date, and most of it is concentrated in the Vancouver area, with a sizeable community in Victoria as well. Between 1986 and 1991, the size of the Chinese-speaking population rose from 2.9 per cent of the province's population to 4.3 per cent. The next-largest heritage language in BC, German, has, by comparison, gone down from 3.4 per cent of the province's population in 1986 to 2.5 per cent (the total number of German-speaking British Columbians stayed the same in that five-year period).

The concentrated Russian community is in the interior of BC, in the East Kootenay area, around the towns of Castlegar, Nelson and Grand Forks. This is the area the Doukhobor Russians selected as their home after a large number of them left Saskatchewan during the second decade of this century. Originally, the

Doukhobors emigrated to Canada in the late 1890s from an area known as Transcaucasia (for details, see Woodcock and Avakumovic, 1977; and, more recently, Tarasoff, 1982).

From a linguistic point of view, the term 'Doukhobor Russian' becomes applicable only for the period after 1801 – i.e., the time when, by an ukase of Tsar Alexander I, the first concentrated settlement of Doukhobors was created in an area near the river Molochnaya (actually 'Milk River', but generally referred to as 'Milky Waters'). Before that time, even though the founders of the Doukhobor movement came from an area close to Milky Waters and had created a fairly substantial amount of oral literature, the community was spread all over the Russian Empire (Tarasoff, 1982). After they were brought together in Milky Waters, the Doukhobors began to form a homogeneous speech community based on the southern Russian dialect. It may be assumed that their moves to the Caucasus and to Canada did not significantly alter the dialect that had been formed in the span of little more than a generation (1801–1845) in Milky Waters, except perhaps by adding loanwords from non-Russian inhabitants of Transcaucasia and, later, from Ukrainian co-settlers in Canada. The Doukhobor dialect at the end of the nineteenth century must therefore have been very close to the dialects spoken to the present day in what is Ukraine's Zaporizhzhya province, with the city of Molochansk and the river Molochnaya that flows into the Sea of Azov.

Doukhobor Russian is a minority language in Canada but, as a form of Russian (see Xruslov, 1994), it is also part of one of the major languages of the world. It is therefore in a much better position, as regards the rate of maintenance, than are language isolates – e.g., some of Canada's First Nations languages, or Sorbian in Germany. Yet, the possibility of the Doukhobors switching massively to English as the only means of communication is very real; in addition, however, the threat of assimilation by Standard Russian should not be underestimated.

The specific dialect of Russian that the Doukhobors have been using and modifying to their own needs for almost 200 years (counting from their settlement in Milky Waters) has never been described comprehensively. The last fieldwork results date back a generation and there appears to exist no single study aimed at tracing the historical development of the dialect (for a possible research strategy, see Schaarschmidt, 1995).

The term 'Doukhobor' (in Russian either *duxobor*, plural *duxobory*, or *duxoborec*, plural *duxoborcy*; in English, 'spirit wrestler[s]'), as seen from a Canadian point of view, denotes an ethno-religious group where the ethnic part of the hyphenation refers to the group's Russian origin. In Russia, the term 'Doukhobor' denotes a geographic-religious group where 'geographic' is understood in the sense of 'Southerner' (cf. Leo Tolstoy's reference to a group of Doukhobor women as *južanki* 'Southerners [feminine]' in Popov, 1948). Neither in Canada nor in Russia does the term 'Doukhobor' denote a linguistic group separate from Standard Russian. Thus, in using the term 'Doukhobor Russian' (or, perhaps more cautiously, 'Doukhobor dialect'; see Harshenin, 1961), reference is made to the Canadian version of the South Russian dialect used by the Doukhobors.

Currently, there are about 13,000 persons of Doukhobor descent living in BC. Following the migration to Canada, Russian language use was vigorous as the Doukhobors resisted the use of English. After all, they had come to Canada 'to preserve the cultural identity of which their language is an intimate part' (Harshenin, 1964, p. 39). Thus, they borrowed from English only what was absolutely essential to their work environment – i.e., terms relating to the railroad, the sawmills, gadgets, units of measure, money (see the list compiled by Harshenin, 1967). However, since the 1920s, and especially after 1945, there have been some significant losses: the 1991 census lists 9,095 Russian speakers in BC; that figure probably includes some 2,500 Russians (assuming that the Russian speakers from the cities of Vancouver [2,465] and Victoria [180] comprise only a few Doukhobors) from the former Soviet Union, meaning that of the 13,000 Doukhobors in BC, fewer than 60 per cent still speak the language. Nonetheless, this is still quite a respectable figure and guarantees vigorous language use for more than one or two generations to come. In September 1983, Russian immersion instruction was introduced at the kindergarten level in Castlegar at a rate of 100 per cent, with follow-up immersion instruction (50 per cent) provided in Grades 1–3, beginning in September 1987.

CONCLUSION

In what often seems to the rest of Canada to be an 'English' province *par excellence* – BC – there actually exists a mosaic of language groups. Thus, the majority of Canada's First Nations language families are found in BC. It can be seen, however, that this diversity of First Nations languages creates the need for a common language (somewhat similar to the need for Chinook Jargon at the beginning of this century; see Thomas, 1970). At the moment it is doubtful that this common language will be one of the northwestern First Nations languages. There is still the possibility that Cree might be adopted to serve this function; more likely, however, the common language will continue to be English: it is already used by at least 60 per cent of First Nations people as a first language.

466

British Columbians' continued interest in learning French, especially in popular immersion programmes in early schooling, must be considered a success story in a context where official bilingualism is being eroded, and where there is the possibility of Quebec separating. This picture may change, and has possibly already changed, with the increasing trend towards offering Chinese and, to some extent, Japanese as school subjects. It is not impossible to envisage a time when these languages may become prestige languages at the expense of French. Whatever may happen to the linguistic profile of BC in the next sixty years – two generations – Doukhobor Russian will still be spoken in the area where it is actively used today – i.e., the East Kootenays – perhaps not at the present rate of 60 per cent, but more likely at the rate at which First Nations languages are spoken today (i.e., 30 per cent or less).

References

Beltramo, A. F. (1981). Profile of a state: Montana. In C. Ferguson and S. B. Heath (eds.), *Language in the USA* (pp. 339–380). Cambridge: Cambridge University Press.

Champagne, D. (ed.) (1994). *Chronology of Native North American History: From Pre-Columbian Times to the Present.* Detroit: Gale Research.

Greene, J., Lapprand, M., Moreau, G. and Ricard, G. (1991). *French Presence in Victoria B.C.: 1843–1991.* Sidney, BC: L'Association historique francophone de Victoria.

Grimes, B. F. (ed.) (1988). *Ethnologue. Languages of the World.* Eleventh Edition. Dallas: Summer Institute of Linguistics.

Haig-Brown, C. (1995). *Taking Control: Power and Contradiction in First Nations Adult Education.* Vancouver, BC: UBC Press.

Hampton, E. and Wolfson, S. (1994). Education for self-determination. In J. H. Hylton (ed.), *Aboriginal Self-Government in Canada: Current Trends and Issues* (pp. 90–107). Saskatoon: Purich.

Harshenin, A. P. (1961). The phonemes of the Doukhobor dialect. *Canadian Slavonic Papers, 5,* 62–71.

(1964). English loanwords in the Doukhobor dialect: 1. *Canadian Slavonic Papers, 6,* 38–43.

(1967). English loanwords in the Doukhobor dialect: 2. *Canadian Slavonic Papers, 9,* 216–30.

Hawthorn, H. B., Belshaw, C. S. and Jamieson, S. M. (1960). *The Indians of British Columbia: A Study of Contemporary Social Adjustment.* Toronto: University of Toronto Press.

Kaye, J. (1979). The Algonquian languages of Canada. In J. K. Chambers (ed.), *The Languages of Canada* (pp. 20–53). Montreal: Didier.

Kinkade, D. M. (1991). The decline of native languages in Canada. In R. H. Robins and E. M. Uhlenbeck (eds.), *Endangered Languages* (pp. 157–176). Oxford/New York: Berg.

Kramer, P. (1994). *Native Sites in Western Canada.* Canmore, Alberta: Altitude Publishing.

Popov, I. I. (1948). Lev Nikolaevič Tolstoj i duxoborcy. In P. N. Malov [Peter N. Maloff], *Duxoborcy, ix istorija, žizn' i bor'ba. K 50-letiju prebyvanija duxoborcev v Kanade. Vol. 1* (pp. 578–579). Thrums, B. C.: Peter N. Maloff.

Schaarschmidt, G. (1995). Aspects of the history of Doukhobor Russian. *Canadian Ethnic Studies, 27,* 197–205.

Statistics Canada (Census of Canada). (1981). *Canada's Native People.* Ottawa: Minister of Supply and Services.

(1986). *Language.* Ottawa: Minister of Supply and Services.

(1991). *Language.* Ottawa: Minister of Supply and Services.

Sturtevant, W. C. (ed.) (1990). *Handbook of North American Indians.* Vol. 7: *Northwest Coast.* Washington, DC: Smithsonian Institute.

Tarasoff, K. J. (1982). *Plakun Trava – The Doukhobors.* Grand Forks, BC: Mir Publication Society.

Thomas, E. H. (1970). *Chinook: A History and Dictionary of the Northwest Coast Trade Jargon.* Portland: Binfords and Mort.

Woodcock, G. and Avakumovic, I. (1977). *The Doukhobors.* Toronto: McClelland and Stewart.

Xruslov, G. V. (1994). *Jazykovye prava etničeskix men'šinstv v sfere obrazovanija.* Moscow: Institut nacional'nyx problem obrazovanija.

Young, C. H. (1931). *Ukrainian Canadians.* Toronto: Nelson.

Map 12 Yukon and Northwest Territories

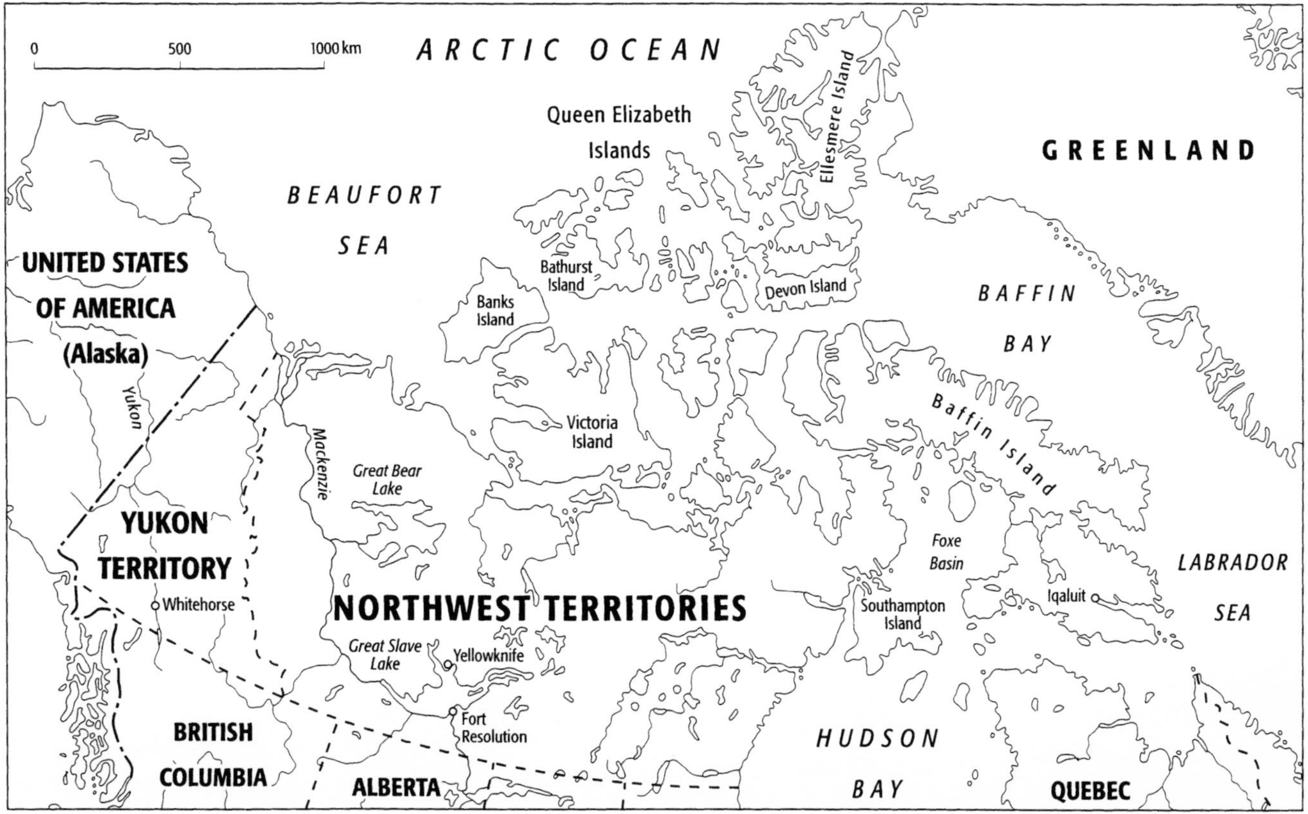

26 Language in the Northwest Territories and the Yukon Territory

Betty Harnum

INTRODUCTION

The northern part of Canada still holds a special mystique for many people. It is often thought of as a frozen frontier awaiting development, inhabited by only a few hardy individuals who suffer at the unkind hands of the elements, eking out a meagre living. In fact, there are many developments in this region that are envied by people in other parts of Canada and the world. At the same time, some major issues still need to be addressed. This chapter identifies both accomplishments and challenges related to the languages of the north.

It is perhaps because the north has only recently begun to develop the type of institutions that Europeans and southern Canadians have known for generations that there is greater opportunity for innovation. In addition, Canadians have, fairly recently, achieved a new awareness about the linguistic and cultural diversity of this country, and about the contributions made by aboriginal people. Further, because the Northwest Territories (NWT) will be divided into Nunavut and a separate western territory in 1999, and because aboriginal people in the north are beginning to settle their claims and establish their own forms of self-government, northern residents find themselves facing the enormous responsibility of recreating every aspect of society. Some people welcome this opportunity to work towards cooperation and harmony, but others are troubled by the level of uncertainty that accompanies such major change.

LINGUISTIC CHARACTERISTICS OF EACH TERRITORY

The NWT is the only political region in Canada in which aboriginal peoples are a majority – approximately 63 per cent of the population. In 1999, when Nunavut is created, the Inuit will represent about 90 per cent of the population in this new eastern arctic territory, while aboriginal people in the western arctic territory will become a minority. In the Yukon, aboriginal peoples account for about 20 per cent of the population. Because aboriginal peoples in the north represent such high percentages of the population, they can often exert greater

470

influence than in other provinces where they comprise a smaller proportion of the population, despite larger numbers.

Some people are still unilingual in one of the many aboriginal languages spoken in these two territories; in the 1991 census, approximately 5,000 NWT residents claimed that they did not speak or understand either English or French. In the NWT, the Athapaskan-Eyak and Eskimo-Aleut language families predominate, but there are some speakers of Cree, which is an Algonquian language. In the Yukon, most aboriginal languages belong to the Athapaskan language family, but there are also speakers of Tlingit, an isolate which is somewhat related to Athapaskan. In addition, French is the first language of a small percentage of northern residents, and a second language for many more, including many aboriginal people who attended mission schools. English, however, has become the first language of the majority in both territories, a trend which is of great concern to all the linguistic minorities.

According to Foster's (1982) data, there are fifty-three aboriginal languages spoken in Canada. Eight of the languages he identified are spoken in the Yukon (but he does not mention Upper Tanana), and seven are spoken in the NWT. Other estimates, which identify some dialects as separate languages, suggest that there may be ten aboriginal languages in the Yukon and nine in the NWT. These groups could be divided again, into 'sub-dialects', according to minor speech differences. In fact, in some of these languages, there are no equivalent terms to represent the speech communities the English names suggest, such as North and South Slavey. In classifying languages and dialects, many criteria must be considered – linguistic, political, geographic, familial, and so on.

The Athapaskan (Dene) languages found in the NWT are Chipewyan, Dogrib, Gwich'in, North Slavey and South Slavey, the Eskimo (Inuit) languages are Inuktitut, Inuinnaqtun and Inuvialuktun, and the Algonquian language is Northern Plains Cree. Athapaskan languages – Gwich'in, Han, Kaska, Tahltan, Northern Tutchone, Southern Tutchone, Tagish, Upper Tanana, Mountain Slavey – are spoken in the Yukon, as is the Tlingit isolate.

In addition to these languages, the Métis Nation of the NWT has also identified about 150 people who speak Michif – a language which combines French and one or more aboriginal languages. The name 'Michif' is actually the word 'Métis', as pronounced by speakers of this language. Michif-Cree and Michif-Saulteaux have been well documented elsewhere but, in the NWT, research and documentation are just beginning, so it is not possible to provide further information at this time. There may perhaps be speakers of Michif in the Yukon as well, but I am not aware of them.

HISTORY

The history of the two territories is similar in that the indigenous peoples who have inhabited these lands for thousands of years have been greatly affected by the influx of non-native people associated with exploration, the fur trade, the churches, non-renewable resource development, the construction of transportation routes and national defence facilities, the establishment of different forms of government, and so on. The difference, however, is that this is much more recent in the Yukon, where sustained contact has occurred for only about the last 150 years (Coates, 1991). In the NWT, contact with the Inuit began in the 1500s, or earlier, while the Chipewyans encountered Europeans in the Hudson Bay area in the early 1700s, being probably the first Athapaskans to do so on what would later be claimed as Canadian soil (McMillan, 1988).

These early contacts resulted in devastating epidemics of smallpox, influenza, measles, whooping cough, scarlet fever, tuberculosis and other diseases, significantly reducing the number of speakers of many indigenous languages. Some accounts estimate that up to 90 per cent of certain nations died (McMillan, 1988). As alliances and trade between the newcomers and aboriginal nations increased, new rivalries were set in motion and linguistic groups spread beyond their former borders, initiating lasting impacts on other aboriginal groups.

In the area north and east of Great Slave Lake, the distinction between the Yellowknives (so called because of their copper knives) and other surrounding nations disappeared progressively between 1870 and 1900 (Fumoleau, 1973). Although their language was thought to be a dialect of Chipewyan (McMillan, 1988), and is now generally considered to be extinct, some Dogrib-speaking residents of Dettah and Ndilo, near Yellowknife, identify themselves as descendants and are now calling themselves the Yellowknives Dene. Similarly, the intermediary role of the Tlingit in the coastal trade brought the influence of their language and culture to some Yukon nations.

Although the newcomers to the north created conditions that were not always conducive to linguistic survival, they also forged new linguistic ties among groups that had previously not affected each other. The emergence of the Métis, born of aboriginal and non-aboriginal parents – especially French, English and Scottish – marked the creation of not only a new and uniquely 'Canadian' population, but also of a new language (Michif: see above). The Métis and their language were instrumental in facilitating, among other things, major economic growth during the nineteenth and early twentieth centuries.

Unaware of the existing relationships between northern peoples, or choosing to ignore them, the newcomers gradually established forms of government and legislation based on their own traditions. With the 1670 charter granted to the 'Governor' and Company of Adventurers of England, trading into Hudson Bay, and with the Royal Proclamation of 1763, when France surrendered its 'holdings' in this country to Great Britain, a new hierarchy was set in motion. The British North America Act of 1867, the Manitoba Act of 1870 (which included the present NWT), the NWT Act of 1875, the Indian Act of 1876, the *Yukon Act* of 1898 and various other statutes imposed legal concepts – such as land ownership, status and federal-provincial-territorial relations – upon peoples who did not understand how or why such actions were taken. After so many years of contact, many people now assume that such ideas are well understood by aboriginal peoples, but when languages derive from such different cultures, rarely are exact translations found. Words such as *rights, country, province, boundary* and *law* still create problems. The *Crown*, for example, is sometimes translated as 'the old lady with the hat' and *police* as 'those who speak the truth'. The same difficulties arise when trying to find suitable translations in languages like English or French for words and concepts in aboriginal languages. However, because most of the translating and interpreting that is done today channels information from the Euro-Canadian cultures to aboriginal peoples, this is often seen as a problem with the aboriginal languages, rather than vice versa.

Beginning in 1781, the British Crown signed treaties with native nations across the vast territory which was to become Canada. Treaties 8 and 11 were signed in 1899 and 1921 in the Mackenzie River (Deh Cho) district, but neither the Inuit nor the First Nations of the Yukon signed treaties (except that a small part of the Yukon was covered by Treaty 11). The federal government had a 'best left as Indians' policy towards the Yukon until the mid-1900s, in contrast to the policy of establishing treaties elsewhere (Coates, 1991).

Trying to establish the meaning of treaties has become a daily exercise in this country. How were these agreements made, between individuals who did not speak the same language nor share the same cultural frame of reference? Some of the interpreters who mediated the exchanges reportedly used the word 'money' for 'treaty', which would explain why there are such divergent understandings of what transpired at that time. Further, the newcomers did not recognize existing religious, educational, social, legal or political structures, and set about establishing their own institutions. Nor did they respect age-old linguistic traditions, and they began to insist, for the most part, that everyone learn English or French. But not all native peoples protested. In the prairies, for example, when developments in the mid to late 1800's became a threat to the new Canadian national initiatives, the Métis, under Louis Riel, fought not only for the recognition of their rights to the land and for adequate services from government, but also for the recognition of French as an official language.

Today, many northerners recall how their aboriginal language was literally beaten out of them while they were forced to attend schools far from their families, often not allowed to return home for many years. Others lost their language while isolated for long periods of time in hospitals, trying to recover from the newcomers' diseases. Significant numbers of aboriginal people died in southern institutions and, because of language barriers, the families were never contacted and still do not know where their relatives are buried. Many of those who did return were no longer able to communicate effectively with others in their community, and elders, who were traditionally the most respected advisors, began to lose their link with the younger generations.

Gradually, the traditional seasonal travel associated with a hunting and gathering lifestyle was replaced by the sedentary requirements of wage labour, and by the establishment of trading posts, schools, health facilities and permanent housing. Native peoples were slowly being convinced that their way of life was not as valuable as that of the new settlers, and they began to adopt new cultures and languages. Some, though not convinced, had no choice. Yet in the face of such adversity, some families maintained their language, at least in the home.

The Canadian government administered both territories from the south for a long time, but gradually local structures have emerged which take into account the unique conditions of these northern regions. Because of new agreements, some elements of traditional society and government are now being revived. Language revitalization efforts are evident in most, if not all, aboriginal communities but, in some cases, only a handful of speakers remain, so the challenge is enormous. Speakers of these languages must also struggle to convince others, sometimes their own people, of the value of preserving different languages and cultures, since they have been denigrated for so long.

RECENT DEVELOPMENTS

Currently, the NWT is governed by a distinctive consensus-type legislature, where members do not represent political parties. This type of government has repeatedly come under attack by those who espouse the value of political partisanship but, to date, the NWT has resisted. Aboriginal members form the majority in this legislature, and it is more in keeping with their traditions not to have the adversarial forum created by a party system. In addition, the NWT legislature is the only one in Canada where some members are unilingual in an aboriginal language and interpretation is available in eight languages.

On the other hand, the Yukon has adopted political parties, but does not have any significant representation of aboriginal peoples in its legislature. A lack of participation in this forum does not mean that First Nations are not active politically, but rather that they have opted to pursue their goals through other channels. In fact, the Yukon First Nations finalized their agreement with the federal government in 1994, setting the stage for self-government in the Yukon. The numerous claims recently settled in the NWT will have the same result.

One of the most important recent developments to affect northern languages was the repatriation of the Canadian Constitution and the creation of the Charter of Rights and Freedoms in 1982. The federal government thereby acknowledged that Indians, Inuit and Métis are the aboriginal peoples of Canada, they affirmed existing aboriginal and treaty rights (which arguably include aboriginal language rights) and they established the primacy of French and English. Soon afterwards, the federal government insisted that the Yukon and NWT governments implement the Official Languages Act of Canada. Naturally, this caused a stir among many northern politicians, who have been moving for many years towards more autonomy, and provincial status, and who are concerned about the desperate state of aboriginal languages. Both territories responded in a similar way. They agreed to adopt their own language legislation rather than becoming subject to the federal act. It was, then, this insistence of the federal government that French and English be given official status that led to specific legislation and funding agreements for the aboriginal languages in these jurisdictions.

The Northwest Territories

In the NWT, the government adopted the NWT Official Languages Act in 1984, recognizing not only English and French, but also seven aboriginal languages – Chipewyan, Dogrib, North Slavey, South Slavey, Gwich'in, Inuktitut and Cree. In 1990, when the Act was amended, North and South Slavey were merged under the name 'Slavey' – the definition section clarifies that this includes both North and South Slavey and also that Inuvialuktun and Inuinnaqtun are included in Inuktitut. This remains the only statute in Canada that gives official status to aboriginal languages. (See *Report of the Task Force on Aboriginal Languages*, 1986.)

The act focuses on the use of official languages in communications between the public and territorial government institutions, and their use in the courts and the legislature. The provisions for French and English are different from those for aboriginal languages. French and English must be used, for example, in adopting, printing and publishing all acts of the legislature. This is not required for aboriginal languages, although it is explicitly permitted by one section. This is reasonable since such a requirement would occupy almost all aboriginal translators for a long time, and would result in the production of an immense volume of material that very few individuals would or, in some cases, could read.

By some, this different treatment is thought to undermine the 'equality of status' that the Act prescribes, but it has become increasingly evident that this equality does not mean the *same* treatment for all linguistic groups. Indeed, at this point, treating all linguistic groups in the same manner would simply perpetuate existing imbalances. Even the Canadian Constitution states that special treatment is warranted where required to correct a traditional disadvantage of an identifiable group. Since aboriginal peoples are a clearly identifiable group, and since they have suffered linguistic disadvantage for many years, remedial steps are justified and urgently required. Equality must be understood as an ongoing process, as it is very rarely a reality.

With the funding received by the NWT government for official-language matters, a flurry of activity has occurred. The production of teaching materials in aboriginal languages has increased, and two detailed guides now exist to explain to teachers the principles and values of the Dene and Inuit. A similar guide to Métis culture has not yet been produced, however. Many more aboriginal teachers are completing the teacher-training programme, while interpreters and translators of all the official languages have received several years of specialized training, especially in the legal and medical fields. Literacy rates and the use of recently standardized writing systems are increasing. However, some controversy about orthographies still exists – an older roman writing system competes with the revised one in some Inuit communities (Harper, 1992), and an older syllabic system is supported by some Dene people over the new roman one. (See *Report of the Dene Standardization Project*, 1989.) Oral history projects abound, though much work still remains to be done while the most fluent speakers of northern languages, the elders, are still with us. Place-name research has revived the use of traditional aboriginal names. Communities have received grants to record traditional knowledge, and produce dictionaries and films. Radio and television programmes, such as those on the new Television Northern Canada channel, have brought all of the northern cultures and languages into the home on a daily basis. Unfortunately, many of these recent activities, jointly funded by the federal and territorial governments, are already beginning to suffer from major funding cuts.

476

To indicate its commitment, the NWT legislature created, in 1990, the office of the Languages Commissioner, to deal with complaints about any NWT act or regulation relating to the status or use of official languages. Since the appointment of this Commissioner in February, 1992, detailed annual reports have been tabled in the legislature, and are required each year. The government also established a unit in the Premier's office to oversee planning and implementation of the Official Languages Act and to negotiate funding agreements. They released their first *Annual Report on Official Languages*, for the year 1994–95.

Another important development in the NWT was the adoption, in 1986, of an amendment to the Jury Act, which allows unilingual aboriginal-language speakers to be on juries. This has opened the door for elders to participate in the justice system since, prior to this, a person had to speak English or French to be on a jury – as is still the case elsewhere in Canada. As a result, many northerners participated in intensive legal interpreter training, but this programme has been devastated by severe funding cuts, despite the fact that the *Tran* decision in the Supreme Court of Canada in 1994 established high standards for court interpretation.

With regard to education, the NWT adopted a new act in June 1995. After five years of consultation, the bill proposed major changes, but also caused some confusion, especially for groups who did not have a translation to work from in the final stages. The clauses affecting language rights provoked a spirited debate, and were actually deferred until the end of the session in an effort to resolve some of the serious concerns about them. In the end, some people were concerned that the act respects neither aboriginal and treaty rights nor minority language education rights as granted by the Charter. (It is interesting to note that, in Nunavut, both francophones and anglophones will be minorities.)

Some members of the Assembly worry that the increase in local control under the new act will undermine aboriginal-language programmes. For example, the community education councils previously had the authority to determine the language of instruction from kindergarten to Grade 2 – no conditions attached. From Grades 3 to 12, they could determine the language of instruction in consultation with the minister. Under the new act, the newly named district education authority can only choose the language of instruction, from kindergarten to Grade 12, if they can demonstrate that there are enough materials, enough trained teachers available, and a significant demand (which is undefined). The minister's approval is then required. No corresponding obligation is created for the minister to ensure that adequate resources are allocated to teacher training and materials development (in contrast to the Yukon Education Act discussed below).

In addition, children who are in the majority previously had the right to be taught their first language (most often, an aboriginal language), at least as a subject, in the first three years – if it was not the language of instruction. Now, any official language can be taught, regardless of the first language of even the majority of the students. Since there is no provision for guaranteed representation of linguistic minorities on education authorities and since, in some communities, these groups have not participated to any great extent in such bodies in the past, the possibility exists for the loss of whatever foothold aboriginal languages *did* have in the schools. Good will on the part of linguistic majorities, and a greater understanding of the needs of minorities, will be the necessary ingredients in any future plan. Supporters of these provisions argue that local control and the development of alternative systems, which can be negotiated with the minister, are adequate provisions.

The Yukon

In 1988, the Yukon adopted its Languages Act, avoiding the use of the word 'official', but giving recognition to English, French and the Yukon aboriginal languages, which are not named. Certain rights are guaranteed in the debates and proceedings of the legislature, but the provisions regarding aboriginal languages centre more upon preservation, development and enhancement activities rather than services.

One major focus has been on establishing a management framework and support system for activities undertaken pursuant to the act and funding agreements with the federal government. Within the Yukon government, Aboriginal Language Services is responsible for this task, but their strong community-based approach to language planning has set the directions wherever possible. Some language services have been made available through community representatives, who not only provide interpretation when required, but also try to promote the revitalization and use of aboriginal languages in everyday life. Interpreter training is also on the rise. Gatherings which bring together speakers of the same language have been attended by increasing numbers. At the first such meeting in 1994, aboriginal languages were used very little but, at the most recent one, they were used half of the time.

In 1990, the Yukon adopted a new Education Act. Its provisions for French minority-language education rights are similar to those of the NWT, and there is a separate section on Yukon First Nations. It clearly states that any land claim or self-government agreement will prevail in the event of a conflict between provisions. Local Indian Education Authorities and First Nations can request aboriginal language programmes, and the minister must authorize such a programme, after considering the number of students to be enrolled, the availability of resources and personnel, the feasibility of such a programme, and its effect on students who receive their instruction in English. The minister is obligated to provide for the development of aboriginal-language materials, to train and employ aboriginal teachers and ensure appropriate recognition, and to establish policies, guidelines and timetables in consultation with Local Indian Education Authorities, school boards and councils. The minister must also meet annually with the Central Indian Education Authority, to be established by the Council for Yukon Indians, and consult with them on any matter affecting aboriginal education and language of instruction.

This would appear to be a powerful regime through which aboriginal people can ensure the appropriate use of their languages. However, with the election of a new government, things have not progressed as rapidly as might have been expected. For example, the Central Indian Education Authority has yet to be established, and the Council for Yukon Indians – now the Council for Yukon First Nations – has undergone its own struggles, so that some First Nations are no longer members. Aside from this, the Yukon Native Language Centre, which has jurisdiction over school language programmes, continues to conduct research, produce teaching materials and offer teacher training and literacy development in aboriginal languages. Currently, all rural schools but one have a native language programme of some kind. Tagish is the only aboriginal language which is not taught. The junior high schools have cultural, rather than language programmes, but the language classes resume in high school.

THE CURRENT LINGUISTIC PICTURE

A sensible first step was taken by the Yukon government when it received funding from the federal government in 1988 for language initiatives. It established detailed baseline data for each language. The resulting report, *A Profile of Aboriginal Languages in the Yukon* (1991), based on an extensive survey among 5,300 aboriginal people, identifies 28 per cent as belonging to the Southern Tutchone group, 21 per cent to Northern Tutchone, 18.4 per cent Kaska, 17.5 per cent Tlingit, 7.3 per cent Gwich'in, 7.0 per cent Han and 0.7 per cent Upper Tanana. Only three speakers of Tagish were found (but, a few years ago, it was believed that only one speaker remained). Since small numbers of Tahltan and Mountain Slavey people are dispersed throughout the territory, and were not identified prior to the survey, they were not included.

The report shows that serious language loss has occurred in only 150 years of contact. Only about one-third of the Yukon First Nations' population speaks their language well or fairly well, and these are mostly in the age group fifty-one and over. With 25 per cent of the Yukon aboriginal population under age sixteen, and another 44 per cent aged sixteen to thirty-five, incremental language loss seems inevitable. A large number of those interviewed are poor speakers, understand but do not speak their language, or do not speak or understand their language at all. Two of the strongest factors identified as contributing to the retention of aboriginal languages are use of the language at home and participation in traditional activities. Greater language loss usually correlates with more formal education, but one exception is found among the Gwich'in speakers.

In the NWT, although the data gathered are not as detailed, it is apparent that the same general picture exists. Inuktitut is the strongest language, although some of its dialects have few speakers. Gwich'in is suffering the greatest loss, while Dogrib is the Dene language that is best maintained. In the Canadian Census of 1991, about 40 per cent of the population reported one of the aboriginal languages or French as their mother tongue, but only 30 per cent reported using this as the main language at home. The use of English as a home language increased from the previous census, while the number of homes in which two languages were equally used diminished. Again, older people speak their language better than younger people, and with 40 per cent of the aboriginal population under fifteen years of age, and another 36 per cent under thirty-five, there is cause for concern about the survival of even the most widely spoken aboriginal language.

In both territories, many people have indicated that they want to learn or relearn their language, but not all of them are doing so. School language programmes are often available for children, but they range from instruction totally in a native language for the first three years – such as in some Inuit communities – to being non-existent – such as for Tagish in the Yukon. Generally, they take the form of several twenty to sixty minute periods a week, which is hardly adequate given the state of the languages involved. In addition, there is a need for language-learning opportunities in the middle age group so that parents can support the language development of their children. Few programmes target those who are the victims of past repressive policies of governments, churches and residential schools.

It should be noted, however, that not all past practices had negative linguistic impact. Writing systems, dictionaries, grammars, prayer books, hymn books, and collections of stories in aboriginal languages are testimony to the dedication and sensitivity of some officials. Further, some non-native people have learned aboriginal languages, though these figures are extremely low, probably because learning opportunities are scarce.

THE FUTURE

In the Yukon, the legislative scheme appears to be based mainly on responding to demonstrated need, especially for government services. Revitalization activities are the focus, since so few people have been identified as speakers of aboriginal languages. The Yukon Education Act seems to provide stronger protection for aboriginal languages in the schools than does the NWT Education Act. Generally though, the NWT scheme is based more on rights and obligations, and addresses the need for services in all the official languages, since many people are already known to be unilingual or to prefer using a language other than English to communicate with government.

Substantial funding from the federal government for language initiatives in the two territories has resulted in some existing activities being enhanced, and new activities undertaken. The future of such agreements is in jeopardy, however, because the federal government continues to take drastic measures to ease the national debt. Some cuts to the original amounts have already been applied. In addition, the debate about the effectiveness of school language programmes rages on. Supporters of the new education acts feel that they will help to turn the tide by providing the necessary guarantees on which new strategies can be based. But a legal foundation does not, of itself, ensure that change occurs. A great deal of responsibility still rests on the shoulders of those who will actively participate in implementation. Again, the two territories have chosen a somewhat different approach in their legislative frameworks, and only future developments will reveal which strategies are successful.

In 1995, when Statistics Canada consulted with northern residents, it was suggested that the census questions regarding languages be redrafted to provide clearer measures of language use, loss and trends. It is hoped that the next census will elicit the type of detailed data required for effective language planning or that more informative local studies can be undertaken.

CONCLUSION

Today, most people agree that aboriginal languages can best be maintained through the cooperative efforts of many individuals – speakers, learners, clergy, educators, linguists, political leaders, legislators, administrators, the media and others.

It is imperative that those who identify with each linguistic group play the major role in the planning process. Planning must also be realistic and based on the actual human resources available. No amount of funding can replace the commitment of capable individuals willing to participate in the process. Some groups, like the Kaska in the Yukon, want to see 90 per cent of their people achieve bilingualism by the year 2000. Other groups, such as the Tlingit, want their youth to at least gain a basic familiarity with their language, to increase self-esteem and cultural identity. In the NWT, one goal is to significantly increase the number of aboriginal teachers in the schools by the year 2000. Each of these goals requires a different type of planning as well as continuous evaluation.

Aboriginal peoples across Canada are taking steps to establish their own self-government structures. With the creation of Nunavut in 1999, the new eastern territory will have a large majority of Inuit. Meanwhile, in the west, where Dene, Métis and Inuvialuit have negotiated several regional claims, aboriginal peoples will become a minority. Each group will undoubtedly take a different approach to implementing the varied clauses in their agreements that deal with language and culture. As the shape of northern government changes dramatically in the near future, preserving northern languages will continue to be a special challenge.

References

A Profile of Aboriginal Languages in the Yukon (1991). Whitehorse: Government of the Yukon.

Aboriginal Peoples Post Censal Survey (1991). Ottawa: Statistics Canada.

Annual Report of the Languages Commissioner of the NWT (1993, 1994, 1995). Yellowknife: Office of the Languages Commissioner.

Annual Report on Official Languages, 1994–1995 (1996). Yellowknife: Government of the NWT.

Coates, K. S. (1991). *Best Left as Indians – Native–White Relations in the Yukon Territory, 1840–1973.* Montreal: McGill-Queen's University Press.

Foster, M. K. (1982). Canada's indigenous languages: present and future. *Language and Society, 7,* 7–16.

Fumoleau, R. (1973). *As Long as This Land Shall Last – A History of Treaty 8 and Treaty 11, 1870–1939.* Toronto: McClelland & Stewart.

Harper, K. (1992). *Current Status of Writing Systems for Inuktitut, Inuinnaqtun and Inuvialuktun.* Yellowknife: Government of the NWT.

McMillan, A. D. (1988). *Native Peoples and Cultures of Canada.* Vancouver/Toronto: Douglas & McIntyre.

Report of the Dene Standardization Project (1989). Yellowknife: Government of the NWT.

Report of the Task Force on Aboriginal Languages (1986). Yellowknife: Legislative Assembly of the NWT.

Index of names

Index of language families, languages, dialects

Index of subjects

Note: this index omits many thematic entries for which the relevant material is either widely scattered throughout the book, or can be easily found via chapter titles and headings.